DEBORAH :
OF COALBRO(
1754-181ʊ

C000270524

Front Cover: From watercolour by Mary Grierson, with the Iron Bridge of Coalbrookdale featured on the mug holding the flowers, and a picture of Sunniside *lower right-hand corner (with the deer in the park).*

Back Cover. Meeting Houses: Top: Rathangan, Co. Kildare, Ireland; Centre: Roaring Creek, Pennsylvania, USA; Bottom: Bewdley, Worcestershire, England.

In memory of Dr Arthur Raistrick and Dr G. Frederick Williams, who together founded, with the whole-hearted support of Allied Iron Founders, the first museum in Coalbrookdale, out of which the Ironbridge Gorge Museum Trust was able to develop the present museum, now a World Heritage Site.

Without their devoted and imaginative work the Ironbridge Gorge Museum would not have become a reality, nor would the original furnace have been saved for posterity.

Deborah Darby
of Coalbrookdale
1754-1810

Her visits to America, Ireland, Scotland, Wales, England and the Channel Isles

by
Rachel Labouchere

William Sessions Limited
York, England

Rachel Katharine Labouchere, the author of *Abiah Darby (1716-1794) of Coalbrookdale*, published 1988, is a direct descendant of Abraham Darby I (see genealogy page xvii).

She has now written the story of Abiah Darby's daughter-in-law, Deborah, taken from Deborah's own diary, a beautifully hand-written account in Lady Labouchere's own possession.

Many of the houses mentioned in the story still exist in the Dale today, and two of them, Dale House and Rosehill have been finely restored. The latter is open to the public, and Dale House will also be ready to welcome visitors shortly.

Rachel Labouchere although not a member of the Society of Friends shares much of their understanding of the Quaker faith and has shown a deep insight into the way of life portrayed by Deborah Darby and her mother-in-law, Abiah. Because of these connections with the Darby family, she inherited many of the family's possessions, which can now be seen in various parts of the Ironbridge Gorge Museum, a World Heritage Site which lies in the gorge of the River Severn in Shropshire.

ISBN 1 85072 100 9

Printed in 10 on 11 point Plantin Typeface
by William Sessions Limited
The Ebor Press
York, England

Contents

List of Illustrations

*   By permission of the Library Committee of London Yearly Meeting of the Religious Society of Friends.

**   Courtesy of the Ironbridge Gorge Museum Trust.

†   Courtesy Friends Historical Library, Swarthmore College, USA.

††   William Sessions Archives.

‡   Courtesy Swanbrook Library, Dublin.

Quaker Glossary

RELIGIOUS SOCIETY OF FRIENDS (QUAKERS) is the official name of the society. 'Quaker' originally a term of derision, is now generally accepted. Thus the terms 'a Quaker' and 'a Friend' are interchangeable. The word 'meeting' can mean one of two things: either a collection of people who meet with each other, or in Quaker parlance it is used as a noun for a Meeting for Worship or for Quaker business affairs.

P.M.	Preparative Meeting, the business meeting of a Friends' Meeting, or Particular Meeting; a Meeting forming part of a Monthly Meeting.
M.M.	Monthly Meeting, the business meeting of a group of Meetings in an area, as set up in 1666 by George Fox.
Q.M.	Quarterly Meeting, the business meeting of a group of Monthly Meetings, originally organised on a county basis before 1666 by George Fox; replaced in 1966 by General Meetings on a similar regional basis.
Meeting for Sufferings	The Executive Committee of London Yearly Meeting now held monthly on a Saturday; originally set up to take action over the distress caused by persecution.
Morning Meeting (1673-1901)	A weekly Meeting of men ministers in London charged with the oversight of ministers labouring in and around London; also with the supervising of Quaker publications, and the granting or withholding of certificates for ministers travelling in Friends' service. In 1697 Women Friends were asked to send a representative to the Men's Morning Meeting.

ix

General Meeting	Established in 1656 and replaced in 1678 by Yearly Meeting, which has met regularly ever since.
London Y.M.	Yearly Meeting, the annual national assembly of Friends lasting several days, with representatives from the Yearly Meetings for Wales, Scotland and the national Half-Yearly Meeting for Ireland, and accredited visitors from overseas.
Wales Y.M.	A Yearly Meeting for Wales was established in 1668 with three Quarterly Meetings.
Bristol Y.M.	Besides the Yearly Meeting in London, there was established in 1695 a Yearly Meeting in Bristol to which certain QMs sent representatives and whose queries they answered. It was an occasion when Friends travelling in the ministry could meet together and when Meetings for Worship open to the public were held. The Bristol Yearly Meeting's importance diminished as the Circular Yearly Meeting of the Western Counties grew in importance. It might be added that both London Yearly Meeting and Bristol Yearly Meeting were sometimes referred to as 'annual' meetings.
Circular Meeting	The Circular Yearly Meeting of the Western Counties was started in 1720 at the suggestion of Bristol Yearly Meeting. It usually lasted three days, in which time there would probably be two Select† Meetings (for ministers, elders and perhaps other Friends) and four Public Meetings. There were many non-Friends attending including those 'called the "quality", the gentry and several national priests'; and also 'high professors of religion' and a 'mixed multitude of all sorts and notions'. Overflow meetings often had to be held and ministers 'preached to great multitudes', up to 4,000 being mentioned for one meeting.

Ireland Y.M. and Province Meeting	Friends in Ireland were, until 1797, organised in a three-tier structure: (a) the monthly meeting; (b) the province meeting; (c) the national meeting. The national meeting was a half Yearly Meeting, always held in Dublin. The Province Meetings were in many cases barely distinguishable from Monthly Meetings. There was no Province Meeting for Connaught. In 1797 the half Yearly Meeting became the Yearly Meeting of Friends in Ireland (Commonly called Dublin Yearly Meeting), the Province Meetings were renamed Quarterly Meetings, and a body known as the Yearly Meeting's committee was established to deal with business in the interim between Yearly Meetings.
Women's Meeting	Friends recognised women from the outset as both temporal and spiritual helpers and established Women's Meetings for this purpose. From the beginning Women Friends were influential leaders of the Quaker movement, notably Margaret Fell (widow of Judge Fell of Swarthmoor Hall and later wife of George Fox). Women's Meetings were held separately until 1896, concerns being brought in person from Women's to Men's Meetings and vice versa.
Elders	Friends appointed to have special concern for the pastoral care of members.
Minister	In 1723 Yearly Meeting decided Friends must produce a certificate from their Monthly/Quarterly Meeting before being recorded as a minister – a Friend whose speaking in Meeting for Worship was recorded by his Monthly Meeting as acceptable: a practice discontinued in 1924. Travelling ministers were voluntary unpaid Friends.
Meeting of ministers and elders	In operation 1727-1876.

Select Meeting†	From 1876 Select Meetings were held on ministry and oversight, composed of ministers and elders and sometimes overseers.
Business meetings	All business meetings, held in the spirit of worship, deal corporately with both spiritual and practical aspects of Christian discipleship. There is never a vote, but instead a patient endeavour to find consensus.
Ministry	Out of the expectant silence of Quaker worship vocal ministry can be given by any one of the worshippers, under the leadings of the holy spirit. It was early recognised that the gift of vocal ministry was given in greater measure to some than to others, and these (men and women) came to be known as **publick Friends** (i.e. Friends who might preach the gospel and give a public testimony to their faith). In the early 18th century a more systematic form of recognition by monthly meetings was seen to be desirable and the Friends so recognised were known as 'acknowledged' or 'recorded' ministers. The practice of recording was abolished by decision of London Yearly Meeting 1924.
Public [k] Meeting	A Meeting for Worship held in a public hall or place to which anyone who cared to attend was invited – most likely non-Quakers.
First Day	Sunday, the first day of the week. Friends declined to use the names of pagan gods for the names of the days and months. Thus 'First Day', 'Second Day' to 'Seventh Day' and 'First Month', 'Second Month' to 'Twelfth Month'.
Discipline	Religious teaching, or the regulation of life by religious teaching, or a body of such regulations: thus 'The Books of Discipline'.

Meetings for Discipline	Meetings for the business of the Society (not now current).
Truth	Spiritual reality or the gospel in the experience of Friends: hence the phrase 'Friends of the Truth as it is in Jesus', or just 'Friends of the Truth'.
Weighty Friend	Those whose ministry in Meeting and whose advice and conduct were such as to make their words and council carry weight (now only used in its historical connotation).
Concern and Liberation for religious service	A concern was a compulsive course of action taken under deep religious conviction, which in early days often entailed visits to Meetings in order to visit and minister in other areas of Britain or frequently abroad. From an early date it became the practice that an individual's concern should seek the unity of Monthly Meeting, and if endorsed, a certificate of liberation would be presented as evidence. For service outside Great Britain the endorsed concern would often go forward to Q.M., Meeting for Sufferings and eventually Y.M. On return from these visits, the certificate would be handed back.
Favoured Engaged An opportunity	The exercise of ministering in Meeting, or at table, or whenever the Spirit moved (an expression not now current).
Marrying Out	Until the mid 19th century Friends insisted on marriage only being entered into with another member of the Society. If one partner of the marriage was not in membership, the Friend concerned was deemed to have 'Married Out', and was disowned* by the Society of Friends. In hindsight this caused great spiritual loss to Quakerism.

Disownment*	Among disownable offences were: non-attendance at Meeting for Worship, drinking to excess, commercial dishonesty, bankruptcy, paying tithes, joining the army, marriage by a priest or being present at such an occasion.
Reinstatement	Disownment did not prohibit attendance at Meeting and for those who did so eventually reinstatement was possible.
Visits to Families and Meetings in Deborah's time	Quarterly Meetings were encouraged to consider the appointment of a few concerned Friends to attend, in Christian love, the various Meetings within their limits, extending this service sometimes to the families of Friends so as to promote the growth of their members in the Truth and their active service for Christ. These visits were found to be a means of strengthening the bond of Christian fellowship and often brought the visitors to a more intimate knowledge of their fellow members and afforded opportunities for mutual counsel, encouragement and help.

COALBROOKDALE HOUSES

Dale House, centre; *Rosehill*, front right below *Teakettle Row*; *Sunniside*, top right. *All looking over Upper Furnace Pool.*

The clematis vitalba *(Travellers' Joy or Old Man's Beard) which frames the picture, festoons the trees throughout the Severn Gorge.*

DRAWN BY RACHEL LABOUCHERE

The DARBYS
of COALBROOKDALE

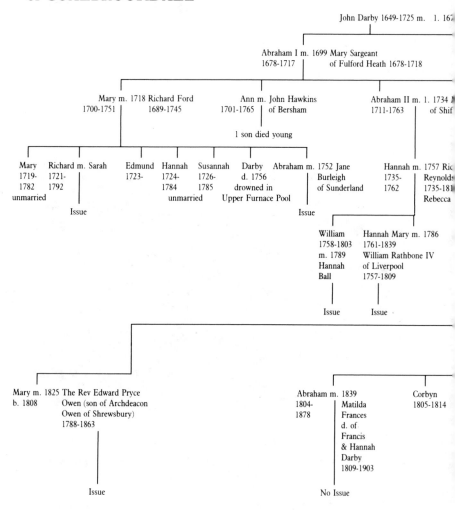

John Darby 1649-1725 m. 1. 16?

Abraham I m. 1699 Mary Sargeant
1678-1717 of Fulford Heath 1678-1718

Mary m. 1718 Richard Ford
1700-1751 1689-1745

Ann m. John Hawkins
1701-1765 of Bersham

Abraham II m. 1. 1734 ?
1711-1763 of Shif

1 son died young

Mary 1719-1782 unmarried

Richard m. Sarah 1721-1792
Issue

Edmund 1723-

Hannah 1724-1784 unmarried

Susannah 1726-1785

Darby d. 1756 drowned in Upper Furnace Pool

Abraham m. 1752 Jane Burleigh of Sunderland
Issue

Hannah m. 1757 Ric 1735-1762 Reynolds 1735-181 Rebecca

William 1758-1803 m. 1789 Hannah Ball

Hannah 1761-1839

Mary m. 1786 William Rathbone IV of Liverpool 1757-1809

Issue

Issue

Mary m. 1825 The Rev Edward Pryce b. 1808 Owen (son of Archdeacon Owen of Shrewsbury) 1788-1863

Issue

Abraham m. 1839 1804-1878 Matilda Frances d. of Francis & Hannah Darby 1809-1903

Corbyn 1805-1814

No Issue

xvi

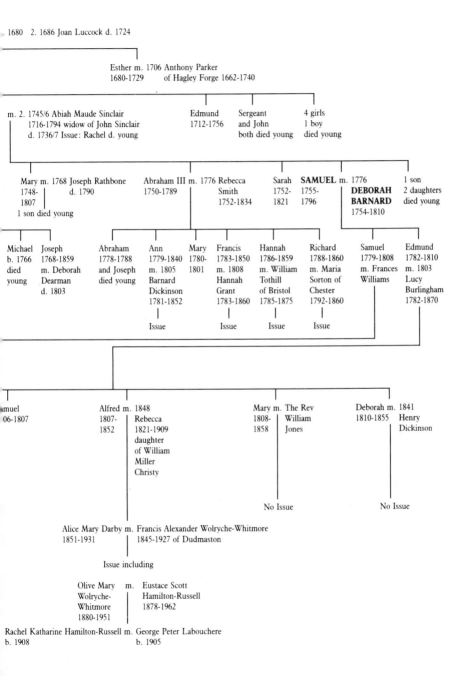

The BARNARDS
of UPPERTHORPE

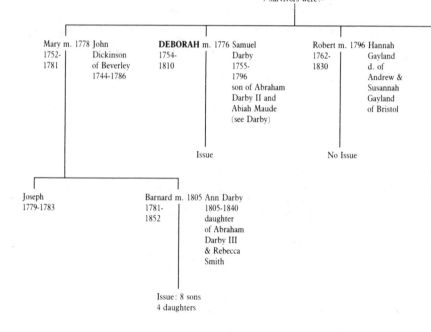

JOHN BARNARD (1732-1789)
Tanner of Upperthorpe near Sheffield
Son of **JOHN BARNARD** and **DEBORAH FISHER**
married 1751 HANNAH
daughter of **JOHN** and **DEBORAH WILSON** of Kendal
Issue: 6 sons and 8 daughters (2 sons and
5 daughters died as children) the
7 survivors were:–

Mary m. 1778 John
1752- Dickinson
1781 of Beverley
 1744-1786

DEBORAH m. 1776 Samuel
1754- Darby
1810 1755-
 1796
 son of Abraham
 Darby II and
 Abiah Maude
 (see Darby)

Issue

Robert m. 1796 Hannah
1762- Gayland
1830 d. of
 Andrew &
 Susannah
 Gayland
 of Bristol

No Issue

Joseph
1779-1783

Barnard m. 1805 Ann Darby
1781- 1805-1840
1852 daughter
 of Abraham
 Darby III
 & Rebecca
 Smith

Issue: 8 sons
4 daughters

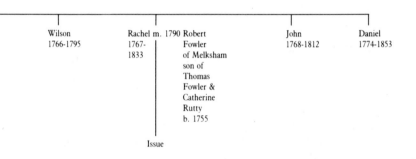

Wilson
1766-1795

Rachel m. 1790 Robert
1767-   Fowler
1833   of Melksham
                 son of
                 Thomas
                 Fowler &
                 Catherine
                 Rutty
                 b. 1755

John
1768-1812

Daniel
1774-1853

Issue

Acknowledgements

FIRST OF ALL I OWE MY MOST grateful thanks to Hugh Barbour, who has helped me with his knowledgeable counsel in bringing forward the contribution of both Abiah and Deborah Darby to friendship across the Atlantic. His invaluable advice on the world in which Deborah travelled in the years 1793/96 gives illumination to this book.

To Clayton Faraday also my very warm thanks are due for his scholarly help over this same period of Deborah's journey.

Edwin Bronner has always given me encouragement, and has now added his excellent advice on the American journey. Also greatly appreciated is the gift of Ann Taylor Bronner, for her father's book on the *Life of William Savery*, which has greatly helped me to understand not only that well-known Friend, but also Deborah.

Many thanks are due to Elizabeth Potter Brown of Haverford College Library's Quaker Collection; Mary Ellen Chijioke, Curator, and Albert Fowler of Friends' Historical Library of Swarthmore College. I am also grateful for the kind assistance of the following: Dr J. William Frost; Westchester County Library; Elizabeth Moger (Keeper of Records, Havilands Record Room of New York Yearly Meeting); the historian of Guilford College, North Carolina, and my gratitude goes to Elizabeth H. Cadbury for a letter from Ann Warder in her possession.

Deborah also travelled for many miles in Ireland on several occasions, and many thanks are due to Gerald Hodgett for permission to quote from his article in the Journal of the Friends Historical Society Vol. 54, No. 5 on the Shackletons of Ballitore in Ireland; Maurice Wigham and Julian Watton of Waterford, Robert Jacob of Dublin and to Mary Shackleton of the Swanbrook Library, Dublin, for their valuable assistance on the Irish chapters and map of 1794.

I also owe deep gratitude to Edward H. Milligan, who over many years has helped me to research the Darby family, and above all for his kindness in writing the Foreword for this book, for undertaking much of the checking of the accuracy of dates and information in the List of Personalities as well as allowing me to use extracts from the excellent

xx

Quaker Glossary 'My Ancestors were Quakers', which he and Malcolm J. Thomas produced in 1983.

Grateful thanks are also due to Malcolm Thomas and his staff of Friends' House Library, London and to Russell Mortimer and Pearson Thistlethwaite for their kind advice on maps, places and people.

I would also like to say how indebted I am for all the help I have received from Margot Sessions, without whom this account of a Friend such as Deborah Darby would not have been possible to produce.

I also wish to thank Mr Barnes, Archivist for the Guildhall Library, the Corporation of London, for information, and also Miss Ruth Bagley, Archivist of Shropshire County Record Office and Mr John Powell, Librarian of the Ironbridge Gorge Museum Library, for their kind help during the preparation of this book. My thanks go too to the London Library.

I would like to add my grateful thanks to Mrs Della Sard and Mrs Vera Hares for their valuable assistance in typing the manuscript, and hope I will be forgiven if I have omitted acknowledgements to any of the many people who have given such willing help in the writing of this book.

Foreword
by Edward H. Milligan

DEBORAH DARBY DIED, AT THE AGE of 56, on 14th February 1810. Just over a month later Hannah Dudley, daughter of one of Deborah's contemporaries, died in her 26th year. An account of the young woman's last illness recalls that 'She several times mentioned dear Deborah Darby (of whose death we did not inform her, though it occurred during her illness), saying she had dreamt of her, and often remembered her and her companion's sweet visits to our family when last in Ireland'.

The companion was, of course, Rebecca Young of Shrewsbury, later Rebecca Byrd of Marnhull in Dorset, who outlived Deborah by nearly a quarter of a century. They were but two of the many ministering Friends – British, Irish and American – of the later 18th and early 19th century whose travels, on both sides of the Atlantic, did so much not only to bind together the meetings in the Quaker world but to proclaim to others the Quaker message.

It was another ministering Friend, Henry Hull of New York, who visited Coalbrookdale a few months after Deborah's death:

> As I sat in the meeting here, I sensibly felt the loss which the church has sustained by her removal, having known her in America, and shed tears of endearing sympathy for her in the sufferings she underwent, and which were inseparable from travelling in a wilderness land. But she bore them all cheerfully, setting an example of devotedness, not common among those in affluent circumstances; and though wanting for nothing which the riches of the world could command, she freely surrendered all her domestic comforts, and gave up to spend and be spent for the Gospel's sake, both in her own country and in foreign lands.

While from the rise of Quakerism Friends had practised a form of worship where, out of silent expectant waiting, the ministry of the word might be given to any of the worshippers, women as much as men, it was early recognised that some had the gift of vocal ministry in larger measure than others. It was also early apparent that there were those who 'rambled up and down the country in their own wills' and so in order to control this the practice developed whereby Monthly Meetings, the area meetings for church affairs, would record in their minutes when they had unity with the ministry of one or other of their members. Such Friends became known as recorded ministers and, if they felt a call to travel in the ministry beyond their own area, they would seek the unity of the Monthly Meeting and, if this were obtained, would be 'liberated' for their travel 'under concern'.

Thus it came about that Deborah Darby found a congenial companion in Rebecca Young, a member of her own Monthly Meeting. But there were others – Mercy Ransom, or Sarah Stephenson, or Mary Jefferys. And the journeys of Friends travelling in the ministry criss-crossed so that they tended to be an inner community even within the close-knit Quaker world of the 18th and early 19th centuries.

Travelling ministers visited not only the large Meetings but also the tiny and isolated. Their ministry brought fresh life to small and sometimes silent Meetings; through their appointed Meetings they brought the Quaker message to the outside world; they were the bringers of news of Friends in distant places; they exercised pastoral gifts – and on occasion (*pace* David Sands) they interfered quite unwarrantably in meetings for church affairs (we may feel confident that Deborah was never at fault in this last respect). John Pemberton, Thomas Scattergood and Samuel Emlen of Philadelphia were as familiar to Quakers in remote meetings in Britain, as Rachel Wilson, Deborah Darby and Samuel Fothergill were in the backwoods of America.

When ministering Friends moved from Meeting to Meeting it was the responsibility of local Friends to provide a guide. The journeys would often need such expert help – and on occasion there was danger beside. George Miller of Edinburgh was once guide to Deborah Darby and Rebecca Young as they rode across a long dreary district of moorland in the south of Scotland. It was a wet day and he wore the accustomed long riding gaiters and a martial-looking cloak, half-covering horse as well as rider. He had been delayed behind the women who, pushing ahead, were suddenly stopped by highwaymen. But soon George Miller's figure came in sight, his horse galloping toward them at full speed while the highwaymen, doubtless mistaking him for a dragoon, took to their heels in flight.

What do we know of Deborah's vocal ministry? James Jenkins, a London Quaker stockbroker, writing his *Records and recollections*, on learning of her death, commented:

> Her voice was sweet and harmonious. When in the exercise of her gift she generally expressed herself in short sentences, every one of which had a tuneful termination. She was a woman of fine person; in her air and aspect dignity was mingled with sweetness, for I have heard from those who knew her much better than myself, that in the disposition of her mind conscious elevation of sentiment was softened by mild and other aimiable affections.

We may give the more weight to this commendation when we recognise that James Jenkins could be critical enough, as when he wrote of Catherine Phillips, a ministering Friend a generation older than Deborah, that 'she was constitutionally of a high and dominating disposition – fond of power, and the exercise of undelegated authority'. When, in the journals of other travelling ministers she is always 'dear Deborah Darby', the adjective is not lightly given. Perhaps Patience Brayton of Rhode Island spoke for those who came in touch with Deborah when, visiting Coalbrookdale in 1785, she described her as 'a sweet spirited woman, to whom my heart was nearly united'.

Deborah became a member of Coalbrookdale Meeting when she and Samuel moved to Sunniside in 1779. It was a constituent Meeting of Shropshire Monthly Meeting, the area Meeting for church affairs. Perhaps curiously, but geographically sensibly, Shropshire Monthly Meeting was part of North Wales Quarterly Meeting (which confusingly covered mid and not north Wales) and of the Yearly Meeting for Wales. That Yearly Meeting was, throughout the 18th century, not only an occasion for transacting the necessary business but also an opportunity for what 20th century Friends tend to call outreach, for Friends with a gift in the ministry would be at specially-appointed Meetings for Worship to which 'the world's people' would flock in large numbers.

Another occasion for outreach was the Circular Yearly Meeting for the Western Counties, which had no administrative functions but was held normally, for some three days, as at Evesham in 1771 when there were two public meetings on Sunday, two on Monday and a parting meeting on Tuesday, all in a large booth 80 yards long and 70 broad put up for the purpose in a field near the town at a cost of £56 (then a very considerable sum). The booth, however, substantial as it was, 'was several times found insufficient to hold the people who flocked thither, and the overflow used to follow such ministers as left the booth, and repaired to the Town Hall and Friends Meeting House'. This required substantial local organisation and finance. The Circular Yearly Meeting, which lasted until 1786, was held in different towns each year in counties ranging from Warwickshire to Cornwall.

It will be evident from this that 18th century Quakerism was not, as is too often unthinkingly reiterated, a period of inactivity. If it is true that the latter part of the century was dominated by quietism then it is the more important to understand what quietism is and what it is not. In an age of reason the quietists stressed the need to go beyond reason (William Blake, of course, did no less). It may be that in their insistence on the insufficiency of reason they tended at times to belittle the human intellect. They did not, however, belittle activity: they warned against *creaturely* activity as lacking the depth which the religious life demanded. They approved the image of the Aeolian harp which, being nothing in itself, was nevertheless the means of producing music when the winds played through it. Similarly, they urged, the human soul, emptied of self-will and 'the runnings of the creature', was potentially an instrument through which the winds of God could play. The tireless journeyings of Deborah Darby and many another ministering Friend, the immense energies in organising the Circular Yearly Meetings and other occasions which were 'felt to be in right ordering' demonstrate that the winds of God could be mighty indeed.

Quaker Meetings for Worship in the latter part of the 20th century seldom last above an hour. Those in Deborah's days were customarily at least twice as long. Neither clock nor hour glass determined their duration: the elders knew by an instinct developed in long experience when the Meeting was ended. Many Meetings, even very large ones, were held wholly in silence. The Dublin doctor John Rutty noted in 1770 his attendance at the twenty-second successive silent Meeting (save one) in that city. Meetings might be largely silent but when ministering Friends were moved to speak it was often at length. 'It was a brave meeting we had at Tivetshall' wrote Sarah Lynes Grubb, a ministering Friend a generation younger than Deborah, 'I do not think I was on my feet less than two hours.' This might be unusual but an hour was not uncommon, though it must not be thought that all ministering Friends spoke at such length. There was, for example, 'the meek, the loving, the every way good, old Bessy Brook' who 'sometimes preached to us four times in the course of two hours for, being feeble, said but little at a time'.

Deborah was born in 1754, the year before the Lisbon earthquake shattered the 'tout est bien' assumptions characteristic of so much thinking of the first half of the century. Wesley responded to the earthquake in a powerfully evangelical pamphlet and by the time of Deborah's death the evangelical movement had become a force in national life and was beginning to find expression in Quaker writings and ministry. It may be that, as evangelical thought permeated the Quaker world, Deborah's theology was seen as belonging to a bygone age. Can this be why she did not even find a place in the tenth part of *Piety promoted*, which appeared in the year of her death? Certainly she was seen as conservative in dress, never adopting the Quaker bonnet which had by her later years become almost universal. James Jenkins comments upon this: 'Although getting out of fashion with even our plainest women friends, she retained the beavor-hat, so generally worn by Quaker females in the days of my youth'.

Not only was she not included in *Piety promoted* but no 'Life and gospel labours' appeared in the years following her death. If we ask ourselves why, we may puzzle for an answer. We may note that the equally well-travelled Rachel Wilson was similarly neglected. We must resist the temptation to attribute this neglect to the fact that they were women for, to go no further, the *Memoirs of the Life of Catherine Phillips* appeared in 1797, while the undoubtedly eminent Samuel Fothergill, who died in 1772, had no published memoir until 1843. The pattern of Quaker publishing between (say) 1780 and 1820 merits careful study.

We must be profoundly grateful to Rachel Labouchere for now enabling us to enter into Deborah's 'Life and gospel labours'. Rachel Labouchere has lived with Abiah Darby and with Deborah for many many years, lovingly poring over and reflecting upon their journals. We cannot even begin to assess the amount of work that lies behind this volume. In 1926 Norman Penney, the first librarian of the Society of Friends in Britain, wrote that 'A biography of this woman [Abiah Darby] is much to be desired; there is abundance of data' and the following year he announced that he was preparing a memoir. He may well have been defeated by the sheer abundance of the data. Rachel Labouchere has not been defeated. It has been a labour of love but no less a labour for all that. Let us rejoice and give thanks on the completion now of Deborah's life, the second of these Darby biographies.

January 1993

Introduction

I<small>T WAS THE DESTINY AND PRIVILEGE</small> of Deborah Darby that she would have an important influence on the lives of two remarkable people, one on each side of the Atlantic; in England, Elizabeth Fry, and in North America, Stephen Grellet.

In 1795 young Stephen Grellet, recently arrived in New York with his brother Joseph, both emigrés from the French Revolution, heard Deborah Darby speak at a Friends' Meeting in Newtown, Long Island, and although not able to understand fully what she said, her meaning flowed into his heart and meeting her again later at the home of Colonel Corsa at dinner, she spoke directly to him.

In 1798 when Elizabeth Gurney, who was to become Elizabeth Fry, came as a young girl of 18 to visit her cousin, Priscilla Hannah Gurney, living at that time in Dale House, the home of Richard and Rebecca Reynolds in Coalbrookdale, she several times met Deborah Darby who influenced her very strongly, encouraging her along the path she had found of devotion and service, revealed to her a few months before by the American Friend, William Savery.

The fact that Deborah had known William Savery well, had worked side by side with him in America, and also travelled back together with him in the same ship in 1796, may have made more possible a deeper understanding of Elizabeth Gurney's frame of mind and they would also have been able to talk of this mutual Friend together, which confirmed Elizabeth in her feelings for what he had said to her and the truth of the Revelation that was flooding her heart.

The diaries which both women wrote of these summer days speak of their accord and understanding. In *The Life of William Savery*,[1] the Friend who had had such a profound effect upon Elizabeth Gurney, it is remarked that:

> At times we are inclined to ask, what results are achieved from such devoted and selfless service as William Savery rendered? Why are such results not crystallised into some form that will last, more substantial than the fleeting fragrance of a human life spent? Perhaps we must hark back to the first principles of which he preached, to

realise that society to avoid decay, must be based upon personality rather than crystallised 'Things', and that the benediction of his influence for Christ, upon Elizabeth Gurney, was a part of the true apostolic succession, in which William Savery planted and that devout Mother in Israel, Deborah Darby, watered, until the personality of Elizabeth Gurney blossomed and ripened into fruition to the bringing forth of spiritual sons and daughters of God in generations since.

Sunniside – From an early photograph, pre 1856 when the house was pulled down.

This book about Deborah Darby has been written in the first place because of her influence upon the young Betsy Gurney, afterwards the famous Elizabeth Fry, and Stephen Grellet the French emigré, who with his brother Joseph arrived in the United States during Deborah's ministerial journey there. Both became influential and remarkable people.

The narrative is also intended to show the close links from 1735 into the 19th century between American Quakers and Coalbrookdale, as every year Friends from the different States came to visit the families of the Darbys and the Reynolds in the Severn Gorge. Here they attended the Dale and New Dale Meetings in the area famous for being the site of the Industrial Revolution in the Iron Industry.

Spelling of names and places in Deborah's Diary sometimes differ from current spelling, which has been mainly followed in this edition.

PART ONE

Deborah at Upperthorpe

DEBORAH, WHO WAS BORN ON 25th August 1754, was the second daughter of a tanner, John Barnard of Upperthorpe, a small place to the north-east of Sheffield in the Wappentake of Strafford and Tickhill.[2]

Upperthorpe had undoubtedly a good supply of running water in a stream from the hills above, and so was most suitable for the tanning trade which could be very profitable, but required capital, as the processes were protracted and needed many hours of work. The Barnards were neighbours of the Aldams, who were prominent Tanners and well known members of the Society of Friends of Hartshead Meeting in Sheffield.

Sheffield, in the West Riding of Yorkshire, had been built on three hills, and the confluence of the Rivers Don and Sheaf was within the walls. The former was navigable from a few miles outside the town through to the port of Hull on the east coast, whence the large quantities of manufactured goods were exported all over the world, including the Americas and West Indies. Hartshead Meeting, to which the Barnards belonged, was a large one. The first mention of their names in Balby Monthly Meeting records is that of John's parents, John and Deborah (Fisher) whose childrens' births start with Robert, born 1718. The Meeting House and Burial Ground were situated to the south-east of Sheffield, on the opposite side of the town to Upperthorpe, so to reach them the main streets had to be traversed.

The Membership of the Quaker Meeting at Hartshead was chiefly made up of several families whose names were well known for their industry and commerce, and who were linked by relationship, particularly across the northern counties. They received in their homes large numbers of visiting Friends from all parts of the British Isles as well as those from North America, and the names of Hoyland, Aldam, Fairbank and others recur in accounts and correspondence.

At the time of Deborah's birth, Sheffield was a place of much activity, particularly in the manufacture of cutlery which had been made there as early as the 14th century. An impetus to the trade had been given by the

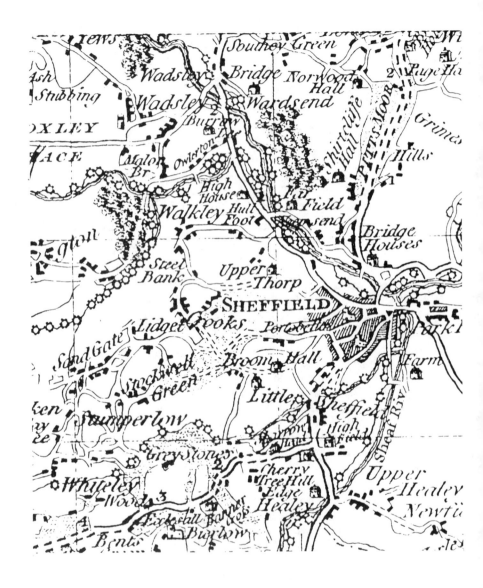

1787 map by John Tuke, Land Surveyor, son of William and Elizabeth Tuke, showing position of Upper Thorpe, north of Sheffield, in the County of York.
REPRODUCED BY PERMISSION FROM THE COPY IN YORK MINSTER LIBRARY

discovery of the crucible process by Benjamin Huntsman in 1740, and about the same time Thomas Boulsover found out how to fuse silver to copper ingots and so roll the silver plate, by which process Sheffield became known throughout the world.

The public affairs of the town were conducted under the direction of seven of the principal inhabitants, who were called Regents or Collectors; four of them from the Established Church and three from other denominations. Non-conformity had been a strong element in the north for some generations, accounting for the large number of Friends in the counties of that part of the country. The fact that the Barnards and some of the Wilsons, were both in the same trade of Tannery was perhaps the reason that John Barnard and his future wife, Hannah Wilson, became acquainted, besides the usual likely connections between Friends.

Deborah's mother, Hannah, was the daughter of John and Deborah Wilson of Kendal; the latter was also a Wilson by birth, being the daughter of Thomas Wilson of Kendal, who had given a property in Stramongate to provide the first Friends Meeting House in 1686. This building, with extensions, lasted into the early 19th century as the main Friends Meeting House there. Deborah's maternal grandmother, after whom she had been called, had been a friend of Abiah Darby's and had paid visits to her in Coalbrookdale. The Wilsons were, for the most part, engaged in the woollen and leather trades, as Kendal had been a centre for both for several centuries, being surrounded by the many sheep farms in the hilly countryside of the neighbourhood. The chief families of Kendal lived in large stone houses along the main streets of the town, and Hannah's home was in Stramongate where the Meeting House also stood. As travelling was both time-consuming and laborious, Friends took the opportunities of Monthly and Quarterly Meetings to conduct business at the same time as their attendance. In the Wilson family, Hannah's sister Rachel, married to a kinsman, Isaac Wilson, had made the journey as a minister to North America in 1768, and so her niece Deborah, would have had first-hand knowledge of this exciting and challenging adventure, which Rachel described with skill.

Both Deborah and Mary, her eldest sister, were well educated and had probably been taught at first with other Friends' children living in the immediate neighbourhood, as was frequently the case. There is no reference extant to this period of Deborah's life, and it is only possible to assume that the sisters were taught together. Quaker families, where there were sufficient financial circumstances to allow it, sent their children away, when they were older, to one of the small Quaker boarding schools which had been set up in different parts of the country, but there is no evidence that this had happened in the case of either Deborah or her older sister Mary.

Such Quaker children were taught to read the Bible and the main Quaker religious works, and they always, from a young age, attended Meeting. Also on visits to the large houses where much hospitality was given, they would have heard the instructive words of visiting ministers, for the community, as a whole, was never static and so they had, when old enough to understand the conversations of their elders, early knowledge of the outside world and other places, and were probably more aware than most children of their age about their own country and possibly of some distant lands beyond the seas, where people of their own faith were living.

Because their mother, Hannah, belonged to such a large family as the Wilsons of Kendal, it meant that when they visited there they had many relatives to see. They also went to Settle in the Yorkshire Dales, both places being not too far distant from Sheffield, to stay with Hannah's sister Sarah and her husband, John Birkbeck, who lived there with their family of five sons and two daughters, several of whom were to become personal friends and business associates of the Darbys later in life. The Birkbecks had developed a wool trade, and their home being not too far from Upperthorpe was, in fine weather, fairly easily reached on horseback over the beautiful hilly countryside.

Settle was in an area of limestone rocks and crags, and from Castleberg 300 feet above the town, a pattern of many narrow streets and small courtyards would be seen. In the main square were the large stone houses of the wealthier citizens one of which was the home of the Birkbecks.

In an ink plan,[3] drawn by Dr Coakley Lettsom as a young man doing his apothecary's training there, and which he had given later to Joseph Rathbone,[4] the Birkbeck house was drawn in and named.

All children rode from childhood, if it was at all possible to arrange mounts, as it was essential to be able to do so to go about the country. Pillion was often practised for the younger children with a grown-up, and this was also used as a method of travel sometimes for women. They were, therefore, all accustomed to long hours in the saddle from youth, so later Deborah's immense journeys in England and North America came naturally to her, and could be sustained in all weathers. Upperthorpe was sited on the edge of the Peak District, so they were used to travelling across moorland; indeed it is pleasant to think of these children, in the months of fine weather, making excursions into this area of hills and moors with the swiftly running streams, where the sights and sounds of the birds and wild creatures were around them, and the changing weather afforded spectacular effects of colour and light and shade.

Deborah's purpose in life, even when young, was to bring the help and knowledge of the Grace of God to her fellow men as she had early experienced a deep 'tendering' which she knew to be of great value. She and her sister, Mary, were of like mind and perhaps today might be described as believing in a spiritual composition of the universe. They, therefore, felt compelled, even before they were fully grown up, to aid those around them to find their path towards the radiance of the Truth. Mary expressed herself also in poetry, published later in several editions by a Quaker firm. The sisters were, however, to have very few years of companionship as both married young and thereafter lived in different parts of the country.

The first authentic glimpse of Deborah and Mary comes in an account given in the journal of a young American Friend Deborah Morris, who was travelling with her step-Aunt, Sarah Morris of Philadelphia, a Quaker minister, in the summer of 1772. They sailed from Chester, Pennsylvania, on the 3rd March in the *Pennsylvanian Packet*, Commander Peter Osborne, and landed at Dover on 10th April. This was the same year that John Woolman came on his last journey, arriving somewhat later with Samuel Emlen Junior and John Bristow, (the latter described as a 'constant Friend and Minister'), and others in the *Mary and Elizabeth*, James Sparke being the Master. They had also sailed from Chester, but a little later on 1st May, arriving in London on 6th June, in time for Yearly Meeting which they all attended. These voyages appeared to be shorter than normal, so the westerly winds must have been favourable that year ensuring a quick passage.

Deborah Morris' record is a valuable one as it is written in a clear and lively style, and gives an accurate account of their travelling and of John Woolman's last journey, for sadly he was to catch the smallpox while in York for Quarterly Meeting, which began on 15th September, and despite being nursed devotedly by Friends, died there on 7th October 1772. During the summer the Morrises had frequently been at Meetings together with him, but they did not appear often to be lodged under the same roof. Wherever he went John Woolman was apt to cause a stir and also some curiosity because of his dress, and people were inclined to come not only to hear him but from a wish to see him, but they were almost invariably caught up and impressed by the sweetness of inspiration of his discourse.

He had many scruples about wearing certain products which were made by slave labour, and so he chose to dress only in materials that had not been bleached or dyed by slaves and so did not hide any dirt. Consequently his apparel was all white, and so unusual. His advent at Meetings was sought after and descriptions were given in Friends' accounts of his Ministry. Sarah Morris had also appeared on this journey as they went northwards, and it was said of her that she was 'a surprising woman for her years; she was about 70, widowed, with a strong natural capacity, her doctrine sound, delivery quite unaffected and she speaks with great propriety'.[5]

It was high summer when the Morrises approached Sheffield, and they eventually reached the town after visiting a very old and venerable Friend named John Haslam, of Woodhouse Meeting, on 31st July. Deborah

Morris described this as a smallish 'house' where there were 'few Friends but full of some sort. . . . . Aunt had a pretty instructive time and J. Woolman close work'. There had, she learned, been 12 'public Friends' belonging to the Meeting, that is Friends with an acknowledged gift in the local Ministry, but there was now only their aged host, John Haslam. After they had all dined with him, the Morrises went on to the Barnards at Upperthorpe, and it appeared that John Woolman went directly to Sheffield to stay with William Fairbank, who had married Mary, daughter of Joseph Foster and Jane Birkbeck. Deborah Morris remarked that their host, John Barnard, at Upperthorpe had married 'Rachel Wilson's sister Hannah', and that their house was five miles away from where they had been at Woodhouse. She also said the Barnards were 'a pretty family of two daughters, Polly (Mary) and Debby, solid lasses'.

On 1st August they had a 'sweet sitting in the family' and the next day they went to a Meeting in Sheffield, one mile away; it was a 'large town and a pretty large house . . . More Friends than many other places, but I thought was chiefly filled with other[s]. Aunt [Sarah Morris] had a large open time here, John Woolman also dined at John Barlow[']s],[6] who has two pretty daughters. All three went to Meeting which was much crowded and many went away and stood out of doors. John [Woolman] was very large and lively but too deep for the greatest part. Aunt much favoured in prayer and after her John stood up again and spoke more affectingly to the youth. Wherever we go there is such thronging there is not time but when in bed for retirement.'

They continued to see many Friends at the Barnards and some 'coming on the afternoon of the 3rd to visit them when they had a remarkable sitting. Some of the youth I hope will ever remember it'.

On the 4th of August they 'spent this morning in agreeable and edifying conversation, and after dinner took leave of this agreeable family to go to the part called High Flatts, 20 miles. The Friend of the house, John Barnard, his daughters Mary and Debby, and Debby Birkbeck with John Aldam and Joseph Hedley, Isaac Radcliffe went with us. Were kindly received by Joshua Marsden and his wife . . . who made our short stay very agreeable.

'On 5th August went to their Meeting which was large for a country Meeting. Here we met J. Woolman who had a fine time, my Aunt also, though short. Dined at Edward Dickinson[']s] close by the Meeting House and after dinner John [Woolman] and Aunt had a reasonable and uniting time with the young folk and a few others. A solemn parting time indeed.' He then went on to Huddersfield and the Morrises to Hollingthorpe. At the Meeting at High Flatts the adults were impressed by John Woolman's message to the young people. Mary Barnard noticed him particularly and was also evidently 'deeply affected'.

After John Woolman's sad death some weeks later in October, Mary composed poetry 'to the memory of the late Samuel Fothergill, William Hunt and John Woolman, eminent Ministers amongst the people called Quakers'. The latter two had attended Yearly Meeting in London that year and she wished to record this fact as well as their different qualities. Mary's poetry, written soon after the last of the three, John Woolman, died on 7th October, was 'dated 25th of 10th month 1772' and described as being by 'M. Barnard a young woman of Upperthorpe near Sheffield'. She says of John Woolman: 'and thou, oh Woolman, venerable seer, art highly worthy of this plaintive lay', and she continued for 17 lines in praise of his character and life's work.[7]

NOTES

[1] *Life of William Savery of Philadelphia, 1750-1804*, by Francis R. Taylor, A.M., LL.B., The MacMillan Company, New York, 1925.
[2] See Tuke Map 1787, p. 2.
[3] Now in the Ironbridge Gorge Museum.
[4] Joseph Rathbone became the husband of Samuel Darby's sister Mary.
[5] Letter written by Tabitha Hoyland to Sarah Tuke. In the Bevan-Naish Collection at Woodbrooke.
[6] John Barlow of Sheffield. See *John Woolman* by Henry Cadbury, Friends Historical Society, 1971.
[7] Annual Monitor No. 3 for 1815. It was not only printed separately as a broadsheet, but reprinted and became a poem for entering into Commonplace Books.

Deborah and Samuel

THE FIRST AUTHENTIC GLIMPSE OF DEBORAH, after the John Woolman visit to Sheffield and High Flatts, was in a letter from Mary Knowles, (wife of the well known London physician, Dr Thomas Knowles) to her cousin Susannah Appleby of Durham, who had come to live at Sunniside in Coalbrookdale as a companion to Sarah Darby. Susannah was a young woman, through whom eventually because of her careful preservation of correspondence, some valuable information of this period has been preserved.

In an early letter dated 19th January 1776, Mary gives news of the budding romance between Deborah and Samuel Darby. Their acquaintance may have come about through Wilson Birkbeck, Deborah's first cousin, who was working with Samuel in London as clerk and assistant. Mary, writing to Susannah Appleby tells of the acquaintance and romance in these words 'after having had an enquiry about Samuel from a young relative of the Barnards called Peggy Trout, not herself a Friend but very serious and sensible, and who showed Mary silhouettes of her cousins, Mary and Deborah, which indicated very comely faces indeed'. She asked 'if Debby was likely to settle in town and to what kind of gentleman?' Evidently Mary Knowles knew already of the match being talked of between Samuel Darby and Deborah and wrote 'I said that if the match talked of took place it was likely to prove a very happy one for her – that the young man was wealthy and handsome, sensible and religious, dutiful to his parent, affectionate to his relations, kind and liberal to mankind in general. Have I said too much? – too much I confess for him to see, so take care of that – but not too much according to my skill of discriminating character. Peggy Trout rejoiced in this description and thinks her dear cousin deserves it all'.

The match was going to be a union of love and affection, but how fortunate for Deborah cannot be evaluated. Later she was to suffer from Samuel's mental breakdowns and because of them she had to give up her own home and live at Sunniside though this did make her free to leave him and her children in the care of loving relations while she undertook her long ministerial journeys.

This golden moment, however, appeared to indicate a satisfactory and happy future for them both and the match was encouraged by both families. They were an attractive pair as Deborah was very nice looking and had charming and gentle ways, with a soft musical voice always a delight to her hearers. Samuel was of good character and possessed a considerable income, with an important place in the family firm which was of good repute. He was only 21 years of age and was to marry five years younger than his elder brother Abraham did when 26. 1776 was a particularly momentous year for them both as in that year Abraham became engaged to Rebecca Smith of Doncaster and also began to build the cast iron bridge over the River Severn which was to become famous from the time of completion.

1755

Samuel Darby was born on 16th January 1755 in the new house called Sunniside,[1] which his parents, Abraham Darby II and Abiah (Maude), had built five years before. It was situated high on the north bank of the River Severn above and to the west of Coalbrookdale, and was a plain red brick Georgian house with stone quoins and chimney stacks at either end of the slated roof. Set in a small park there were cottages to the west behind the main house, and also an area of garden against the walls. A dwelling full of light from the many windows, pleasant to live in and with plenty of space for the family and their many visitors, who came either travelling in the Quaker faith, or on business to be shown the latest innovations in the manufacture of iron.

It was an unusual scene around them in Coalbrookdale, as fields and woodlands closed in on the industrial heart of the iron manufacture, whence the smoke and steam rose into the sky, night and day, and at times, according to the weather and the light, caused spectacular effects. Below in the river, within the Severn Gorge, as many as 100 boats of different types could be seen at any one time, as this was part of the main waterway between Wales and the great port of Bristol, many miles to the south.

The homes of the Darby family and their immediate relations were built near to one another and close to the Company Works. From here their surveillance of activities took place, not only with their skill in management, but with their knowledge of the handling of iron during its processes of smelting and manufacture, and their ability to take part personally with the work force, in carrying these through.

Samuel's mother, Abiah, had had a difficult time at his birth and did not recover fully for some time, although she was able to feed her baby. The arrival of this child coincided with a period of much activity in the Coalbrookdale Company, for his father, Abraham Darby II, had finally succeeded in smelting iron with coke as a fuel suitable for the forges. His father before him, Abraham Darby I, had hoped, after his initial success in

1755

The Darby Houses in Coalbrookdale, 1758. (1) Dale House (restored 1993); (2) Rosehill (restored 1989); (3) Sunniside (demolished 1856); (4) Teakettle Row (still in existence); (5) Furnace Pool (still in existence).

1709, to have been able to achieve this, but he had not succeeded in his short life time. Samuel's father, first because of his youth, and then in the years when he and Richard Ford, his brother-in-law, were fully engaged in building a pattern of trade for the Company, had not together been able to continue the essential series of trials. It was only, therefore, after Richard's death in 1745 when Abraham Darby II was in sole charge of the Company, that he was able to find enough time to continue these necessary experiments with sufficient vigour to obtain success. This had begun to happen from about 1749 onwards, when Abraham had decided that additional furnaces were essential. He, therefore, leased from Roger Slaney of Hatton Grange some land at Horsehay a few miles distant, where there was a sufficient water supply, and also, at the same time, took the lease of mines at Ketley and entered into a further lease of mines that belonged to Lord Gower's estate at Dawley. In this Horsehay venture he enlisted the financial help of Thomas Goldney III, the main shareholder in the Coalbrookdale Company. Abraham however, from the resources of the Company, was prepared to undertake most of the mining operations. The water supply for the furnace pool at Horsehay gave them some anxiety but this difficulty was finally overcome, but not before Abraham and Abiah had had to take out a mortgage on their new house, Sunniside, for £1,000. Also later, when the furnace proved successful, more coal was required so another area was leased on the edge of Wellington and Dawley, and developed into the New Dale Holding, a name which was to become well known later to Friends, as a Meeting House was to be opened there in 1768.

Their earliest guests at Sunniside that year of 1755 were Isaac Thompson and his wife Rachel, Abiah's youngest sister, on their way home from London to Newcastle-upon-Tyne. They had long been intending to come and had been encouraged continually to do so by Abraham's daughter by his first wife, Hannah, in her delightful letters to her step-Aunt Rachel after she had stayed with them in the North. Isaac was the proprietor and editor of the *Newcastle Gazette*, which often reached Sunniside ahead of family letters so that the Darbys, since Abraham's marriage to Abiah, were therefore always informed of events in the northern part of the country.

Isaac was also Chief Agent for the Coalbrookdale Company for that area and would wish to discuss new processes with his brother-in-law at this particular time. He was an intelligent and well informed man, had published a number of books and was interested in philosophy, on which subject he had given some lectures. Also, in his youth, he had written a small book[2] of verse in which he mentioned his friend Peregrine Tysack; they had both been known to the Maude sisters in their circle of young Friends who came to Sunderland.

The Thompsons were the first of Abiah's family to see her new child, arriving in mid-February in the Company's boat from Worcester, whence

1755

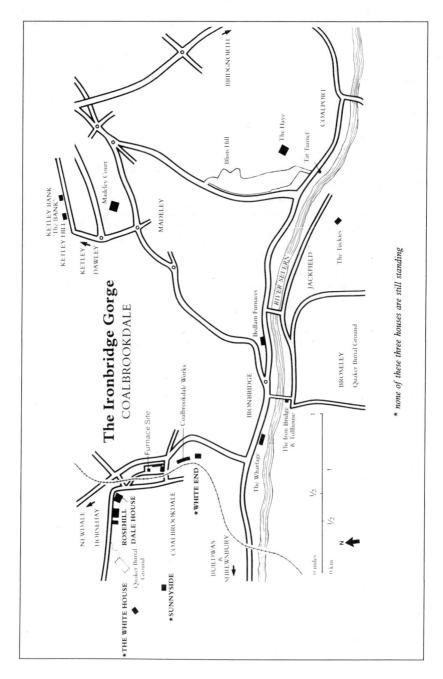

The Ironbridge Gorge
COALBROOKDALE

* none of these three houses are still standing

KETLEY BANK
'The BANK'

KETLEY HILL

KETLEY

DAWLEY

Madeley Court

MADELEY

Bliss Hill

The Hayc

COALPORT

Tar Tunnel

RIVER SEVERN

The Tuckies

JACKFIELD

Bedlam Furnaces

BROSELEY

Quaker Burial Ground

Furnace Site

Coalbrookdale Works

IRONBRIDGE

The Iron Bridge
& Tollhouse

The Wharfage

NEWDALE

HORSEHAY

ROSEHILL DALE HOUSE

Quaker Burial
Ground

* THE WHITE HOUSE

* SUNNYSIDE

COALBROOKDALE

* WHITE END

BUILDWAS
&
SHREWSBURY

N

0 miles   ½   1

0 km   ½   1

Abraham and Hannah had gone down to fetch them. Provided the height of the water on the River Severn was suitable at the time and likely to be so, it was often the easiest way to travel by boat in winter as the roads could be in a very bad state indeed. The Thompsons stayed some days, then travelled north by the coach from Lichfield.

The furnace at Horsehay, fired throughout the winter, came into blast successfully on 5th May 1755. The Coalbrookdale Company then gave a feast for the workforce and their families to celebrate; indeed this success was to usher in a period of great activity, when the East Shropshire Coalfield was to become, for a time, the area of greatest production of iron then known. Visitors soon came from the neighbourhood and further afield to see the new furnaces that summer. Thomas Goldney III arrived from Bristol on 2nd June to see for himself this success and to discuss the future with Abraham. Sampson Lloyd II came from Birmingham on 14th July: his family had been closely connected with the Darbys for several generations, both as Friends and in business. Both men stayed at Sunniside and could, therefore, also discuss together with Abraham how the increased production, in a wider field, could affect both the port of Bristol and the Midlands. They left together on 16th July, Abraham seeing them off by coach.

1756

The beginning of the year of 1756 was very cold and stormy: little Samuel became ill, 'with difficulty in breathing and a bad hoarseness'. As he was only one year old this condition was alarming. The other children evidently had a tendency to the same condition, but a home-made cure appeared to relieve him, despite his extreme youth.

There was another important development in the works as a railroad was finished by the end of January, and a first 'waggon of pigs' came down from Horsehay to the wharves on the River Severn. It was however to prove also a year of family tragedies as Abraham Ford, Samuel's first cousin, still a young man, was drowned in the Upper Furnace Pool, and some months later, in the early summer, Abraham's only brother, Edmund, died after a bad riding accident.

Thomas Goldney came again to sign the new Coalbrookdale Company lease on 16th April, and at the same time he and Abraham agreed to build a second furnace at Horsehay. Thomas Goldney stayed until 29th April and then decided to send his own representative to the works to keep him even more closely informed: his choice fell on young Richard Reynolds from Bristol, the son of the older Richard Reynold of the firm Daniels & Reynolds, Iron Merchants. He had recently completed his apprenticeship with William Fry, a grocer of Bristol, and was to become a Freeman of that city the following year as his father had been before him.

Richard Reynolds arrived in Coalbrookdale in the month of August, providing for Abraham's daughter Hannah a very welcome distraction and a delightful companion. He was a very intelligent and attractive young man and very energetic. He and Hannah Darby soon fell in love and he found her not only charming in person, but he much admired the quality of her mind and, above all, her kindness of heart. He was to remain in Coalbrookdale for the rest of the century and was destined to influence the course of events of the people of the Severn Gorge and beyond for several generations.

Abiah gave birth to her son William, on the 5th of December, and expressed thankfulness to have been able to pass through this ordeal.

1757

The weather was cold and frosty in January 1757, and travelling was dangerous; so the guests who had arrived at Sunniside had to stay on for sometime longer than they intended.

Hannah Darby's marriage to Richard Reynolds took place at Shrewsbury Meeting on the 20th May 1757, and a wedding party was held afterwards at Sunniside. The young couple went to live at a house called Ketley Bank, not far from the new area of Horsehay which Richard was managing, having a third share with Thomas Goldney and Abraham Darby II in the furnace and mines of that area belonging to the Coalbrookdale Company.

The house was a pleasant brick building with sash windows, and Hannah's diary gives an account of their day-to-day life of simple events, punctuated by short visits to her 'Dicky', as she called Richard, at his work, and of course there was much coming and going to Coalbrookdale and Sunniside. Eleven years later in 1768, when a Meeting House was constructed called New Dale, Richard Reynolds gave a great deal of hospitality, but this did not happen during Hannah's short life time.

There was again family sorrow this year as Abiah and her small son, William, were both ill with a 'swelling' in July and the baby did not recover, dying on 11th of the month.

Abraham purchased, during 1757, part of the Haye Farm, opposite Coalport further down the river and this was later to become the second home, after marriage, of his eldest son, Abraham Darby III, from 1780 until he died in 1789. This was an old and pleasant house, part of an ancient building; standing on a hill with splendid views in all directions, it had good farmland on all sides.

That year of 1757 there was continued distress in the neighbourhood and clothes were distributed. Abiah gave out a hundred garments just before she left in September for a visit to the north, Abraham having decided he wished to see the New Road which crossed from Carlisle in the west to Newcastle in the east. They took the two eldest children with them,

Mary aged nine and Abraham seven, and were met and conducted on their way by Isaac Thompson with whom they eventually stayed while in Newcastle.

Before returning home they also spent a few days with Mark and Hannah Burleigh in Sunderland, Hannah being Abiah's eldest sister. They attended Quarterly Meeting in Durham and reached Coalbrookdale in October. This was the first time the two elder children had been taken on such a long journey and it was therefore very full of interest for them.

1758

In 1758 the smallpox was very prevalent in the area and the Darbys became afraid for their children. Abiah was again pregnant and not far from her time, but they decided all four children should be 'put under preparation for the smallpox innoculation'. Abraham was anxious for this to be done and Abiah knew the illness had been fatal in all the families connected with them. The practice of innoculation, however, was still dreaded, though it had become more universal and better known than in the first few years after Lady Mary Wortley Montagu brought the idea and practice from Turkey in 1718. So the children were innoculated on 14th April at Buildwas, between 'four and five in the afternoon', and the eruption came out a week later. Mercifully they recovered well, although the strain and anxiety much disturbed Abiah, whose baby Jane was born on 9th June. She had a difficult time with this child, their last, who only lived until the autumn, dying in October. Abiah was much saddened and made no further entries in her Journal after the death of Jane until the following summer.

1759

The young Darbys, in childhood, were called by nicknames – Mally, Aby, Sally and Sammy; the first two faded in use, but Sarah and Samuel were sometimes referred to in this manner later in life. They were taught in a similar way to the Barnards when very young with the children of other Friends living nearby. Abiah herself instructed them in religion, in the reading of the Bible and Quaker works of importance. She had also written a small book for them herself entitled *Useful Instruction for Children*, which was to be published in several editions for the children of the Society of Friends generally.

The contents were easy to follow in the form of questions and answers, and lively enough to hold the attention of the young and to aid them to remember what they were being taught. The first question was 'Who created thee and all Mankind?' and the answer went straight to the heart of the matter, placing human existence clearly before the child in the answer 'God the Almighty, Father Creator of Heaven and Earth and all things that are therein'. She followed the Old and New Testaments in the same manner, in a clear and lively way, keeping up momentum and interest and holding the thread of the long unfolding story, so that her childish listener could follow her, engaging their interest and imagination, and hoping therefore that they would be instructed and inspired for life.

It was certain that by the time the young Darbys were sent to boarding school they had received enough suitable tuition, both religious and secular, to profit to the full. Abraham and Abiah chose James Fell's school at Worcester, not too far away, so that the journey could be undertaken by river or road in a day. Quaker schools were usually conducted by a husband and wife, so that there was the advantage of a family environment for the pupils and, in the case of the Fells, there was also mention of their daughters, Molly and Peggy, who stayed at Sunniside for a few days in August 1763. The children's health and welfare in a family setting was the better ensured generally by these arrangements. The Darbys knew several families of Friends at Worcester – Fords, Bevingtons, Lowes and Thomas Beesley, all mentioned in Abiah's Journal and letters. The Darbys attended Meeting there quite frequently, so enabling them to visit the children simultaneously several times a year.

Worcester could be approached from land or water. It presented a fine silhouette dominated by the Cathedral with houses of all periods radiating from the Close and forming the main streets. The structure of the Cathedral was witness to the long history of the place, where the tomb of King John lay before the high altar.

There was a long water front, always busy with shipping moving up and down stream, for much trade was carried by the River Severn. There was also commercial activity on the roads, involving waggons and pack horses, which had been increased by the more frequent coaches and other wheeled vehicles as the century advanced, but there were always very many travelling on horseback. The city was closely surrounded by farmlands and the changing seasons brought many interesting aspects to travellers as they came and went to this county town set on the edge of an important fruit growing area of the country.

Mary and Abraham Darby were sent to school as soon as they were considered old enough, and there is evidence of what they were taught in Abraham's exercise books which have been preserved. They were instructed in the usual subjects of that period, with emphasis upon a good knowledge of foreign currencies, weights and measures in addition to those of the British Isles, which would be useful to them in their trades and industries. They also had instruction in book-keeping as well as mathematics, and both Abraham and Samuel found their education in these respects adequate later on in their iron founding business. The sisters, Mary and Sarah, undoubtedly also benefitted when both became partners in the

Coalbrookdale Company, involving ownership of shares and their transfer on the deaths of the men of the family.

Most boys at the school went on into apprenticeships; the Darbys naturally into the iron trade, and others into divers of the other metal manufacturers, as well as the woollen and tanning industries. Grocery was sometimes chosen, often allied to ironmongery, and of this calling a number later grew into the well known makers of food products, such as the Frys of Bristol. Other boys trained as apothecaries, or at Edinburgh and Leiden Universities as doctors and amongst these of the 18th century were a few who initiated the development of more sophisticated medicines and treatments.

An expansion in financial arrangements for industry became essential as the century advanced, and several of the Quaker families in different parts of the country founded joint-stock banks, among whom were the Lloyds of Birmingham, Barclays & Freames of London, Gurneys of Norwich and the Goldneys of Bristol; families all well-known to the Darbys and several in close touch with them for generations.

1760/61

Samuel, as a small boy, would have become aware of the visits of some Friends and others visiting the Company who stayed at Sunniside. Abiah was frequently away from home on her ministerial journeys, usually for short periods, but now and then for as long as for several months. One or two Friends came frequently, one of them a life-long friend of Samuel's father, Samuel Fothergill, a Tea Merchant, who with his wife, Susannah, lived at Warrington, so when staying at Sunniside he may have brought gifts of different kinds of the delicious tea leaf from China and India, as the drinking of tea was so often mentioned in the family Journals and letters of the period; a little later this would have been drunk from one of the bowls or cups of china from Caughley and Coalport, made in the neighbourhood. Samuel was a brother of the well-known Dr John Fothergill, connecting the Darbys with a wider circle interested in education and horticulture as well as medicine.

The Darby children were accustomed to being taken occasionally into the Company workshops and seeing the molten metal poured from the roaring furnaces, an awesome sight and one never to be forgotten once seen in youth. Around them also were the familiar agricultural rotation of crops. There were many horses kept on the Darby farms, bred for work in the Company. They were powerful animals with huge hooves and hairy fetlocks, and the thundering noise they made when galloping free over grassland, was awe-inspiring for a child.

Also an occasional ride, with an adult, on their broad backs was an event that both thrilled and frightened them in youth.

1761

There were the usual number of visitors that summer, Joseph White from Pennsylvania was with them for a few days, coming with Ralph Mulliner. William Maude, Abiah's favourite nephew, was also with them that year from Sunderland, carrying out work for his uncle on the pumps in the mines of the Coalbrookdale Company. Samuel was still at home, but Sarah had joined her sister and brother at James Fell's school, and Samuel no doubt missed her a great deal as on no-one else in his life did he depend upon to the same extent in childhood or indeed when he grew to be a man.

1762

In the year of 1762 James Fell, the children's schoolmaster, came to stay for a few days, but the length of the visit is not disclosed. The weather became very bad and although Abiah wished the children could come home for the holiday, they were unable to travel because of heavy falls of snow, and so did not reach Sunniside until 17th February. The roads were in some places impassable and the storms so severe that there were several deaths in the Severn Gorge.

In May a great tragedy befell the family as Hannah, wife of Richard Reynolds, contracted the measles and died after a brief illness, a terrible loss for her husband, for her young children and for her father, Abraham, as he had brought her up since she was aged five, her own mother having died in 1740. Hannah was buried at Broseley and in her step-mother Abiah's Journal the account of these very sad days was given in full.

In September Abiah went to see the three children at Worcester and continued on a long journey with Agnes Horton. At Bristol they stayed with Thomas Goldney at Clifton and saw the many improvements and additions he had made to the gardens. He had constructed his famous shell grotto with the shells brought back by the Goldney ships from the Indies. This ultimately proved to be one of the finest examples of an intricate work in gardens of the 18th century, and the Coalbrookdale Company had been commissioned to make special tiles for the flooring.

Thomas Goldney had, on occasions, given the young Darbys some shells during his visits to Sunniside and several fine pairs were in the possession of Abraham Darby III when he died at The Haye in 1789, these appearing in the Sale Catalogue shortly after his death. Sarah also had a small collection of shells which she kept all her life, and she and Samuel, no doubt, had been able in the larger suitably shaped ones, to listen 'to the sound of the sea', a delight of childhood down the generations. Thomas Goldney was also interested in the introduction now taking place of new kinds of trees and plants from overseas, and occasionally brought to the Darbys a specimen or two of these thought suitable for the climate of the Severn Gorge.

Abiah and Agnes, after leaving Bristol, travelled to London attending Meetings at a number of places on the way. When in the capital, Agnes fell ill and was unable to continue, and Abiah had to find another companion in Susannah Rowe, to complete her mission to the eastern counties.

1763

Thus Abiah spent most of the last months of 1762 away from home on this arduous journey of about 1,000 miles, returning on 23rd January 1763 to find Abraham in poor health, his asthma very much worse and he much weaker. He had sent for his lawyer in February and drawn up a new will with most careful provision for the future of his family. In spite of his care though this was to create difficulties in the future. He lived for some weeks, showing much fortitude and patience. His condition was testified to by William Maude, Abiah's nephew, who had come initially to complete some work in the mines, but he found his uncle too weak to be able to attend to business of any kind. Abraham died, to Abiah's great sorrow, on 31st March and was buried as he had directed in the piece of ground on the steep hillside below Sunniside, which he had designated as a Friends' Burial Ground and left as a gift to Coalbrookdale Meeting. (Abiah then arranged to have a brick wall built around this area.)

She was able to say at his funeral 'The Lord giveth and the Lord taketh away, Blessed be the Name of the Lord'.

She now faced the task of bringing up the children alone, and of preparing the boys for their eventual places in the business. In this she was to be assisted by Richard Reynolds, who had undertaken overall direction of the Company and was to move on 29th August into Dale House.

They spent that summer at Sunniside in their sorrow, with the flowers blossoming outside in the garden, fields and woods. They were very sad at heart and with their quill pens in their hands, Abiah with her daughter Mary strove to convey their deeper feelings at their loss, in the more difficult literary form of verse as this was considered a greater tribute than prose for a much loved personality.

Thomas Beesley and Thomas Goldney III were two of the executors who helped Abiah to face the future in a practical manner. Abraham, in his will, had stipulated what should happen, and the portions for her and the four children were clearly defined.

Mary, Abraham and Sarah were away at school and Abiah now decided to send Samuel also: he was then eight years old and would benefit from the companionship of others of his own age. Sarah, had joined her older sister and brother at Worcester a year or two before. Mary now came home to be with her mother and was evidently a most sympathetic and loving companion, mature for her years. She was always a good listener and the

Ketley Bank, known as the Bank.
Drawn by Rachel Labouchere from an old photograph.

The White House. Rebecca Darby and her six children lived here after the death of her husband, Abraham Darby III (1750-1789). She moved out in 1808 to Sunniside to share her family home with Sarah and Deborah Darby, her two sisters-in-law, leaving the White House to her eldest son, Francis, on his marriage to Hannah Grant. It was here that Francis received Stephen Grellet for tea on a winter afternoon in 1834.
Drawn by Rachel Labouchere from an old sketch.

family, throughout her life, were to come to her in any distress and always received a kind and very understanding hearing.

Ministers and others continued to visit Abiah who, like Abraham, was always glad 'of the company of sensible Friends', but she was very heavy of heart and found herself 'very low in mind'. William Maude had had to go home to Sunderland in April and Thomas Goldney who as an executor had come to help her, left on 2nd June taking young Samuel down to Worcester to school on his way home to Bristol.

At the end of June, Samuel Fothergill and young Sampson Lloyd II visited them and Abiah was able to talk about Abraham to Samuel Fothergill. Hugh Thomas and Thomas Fisher of Philadelphia came on 4th August, staying until the 15th. The latter was of a very important Quaker family and Abiah found that his grandmother was a Maude of Yorkshire and she believed of her own family. The Fishers dealt in cotton goods and traded with John Cash of Coventry who found them very prompt indeed with their payments. Very soon after Deborah's arrival in America, 30 years later, she was to meet Thomas Fisher and his family frequently during her visit.

Richard Reynolds had taken over the direction of the Coalbrookdale works on 6th June. He was already finding difficulty in attending to all the extra work as well as endeavouring to spend enough time with his very young children, William and Hannah Mary. He was also very lonely indeed as he and Hannah had been a most devoted couple, so he decided he would marry again, choosing Rebecca Gulson, daughter of William Gulson of Coventry, a friend of Hannah's whom he knew well. She was a kind and intelligent young woman and an understanding stepmother to Hannah's children. The marriage took place on 1st December at Coventry: Abiah attended, pleased that Richard should find happiness in life again, as he was a young man with heavy responsibilities.

1764

The winter of 1764 was very wet with the River Severn in continuous flood, affecting all the low ground. This caused much distress among the poorer citizens and contributions were sought for their relief. Abiah visited James Fell's school on 3rd February, finding also that the Worcestershire countryside had been inundated in many places. She spoke to all the children at the school as she always did before returning home.

Thomas Goodwin, an American Quaker Friend, a brother of John Goodwin who lived in Wales and whose father and mother had settled in North America, came to stay among others in February. Hannah Thomas,[3] (who married Thomas Rose), had been closely associated with the Darby family. She was the only daughter of John and Grace Thomas who had come up with Samuel's grandfather from Bristol at the beginning of the 18th century. She was a very fine needlewoman – her chief accomplishment –

and she now and again accompanied Abiah to some Meetings as she was at the time 'under religious exercise'. She would also tell the younger members of the family of the past, and her accounts give a picture of what had taken place long ago in Bristol and Coalbrookdale, which evidently so much interested Sarah that later she arranged for Hannah to write these down for posterity.

Robert Williams, 'a solid Friend' came from North America in July, to where he had earlier emigrated from South Wales. Samuel went in the chaise with his mother to Shrewsbury on the last day of July, his brother Abraham and Robert Horton riding beside them and they all went on to Welshpool, an experience for Samuel then aged nine. He and Abraham were on holiday until 10th August when Abiah took them back to school at Worcester, speaking again to all the pupils there as was her custom.

1765/66

Abiah was very active in 1765, making several short journeys to the more distant Meetings. She suffered a deep and unexpected sorrow in May as her favourite nephew, William Maude died suddenly. He had upheld her at the time of her Abraham's last illness and death, and she had found him a young man of considerable qualities leading a deeply religious life, which she admired.

Sarah and Samuel came home for a short holiday in June and she herself took them back to Worcester on 14th July. The same pattern of holidays from school took place in the following year of 1766 after a very cold winter.

1767

Early in the year a shortage of food caused much distress; Abiah and her household fed as many as a hundred people at the door of Sunniside in one day and did all they could to alleviate suffering, but it was a very disturbing time. The situation affected whole areas, so the children would probably have been aware of what was happening, even as far off as Worcester, where they were at school, for Friends always tried to give assistance where needed in situations such as this.

1768

Abraham, at the age of 18, undertook the direction of the Coalbrookdale Company with his brother-in-law, Richard Reynolds, who, with his young family then moved back from Dale House to his own house of Ketley Bank. Abraham continued to live at Sunniside with his mother who still provided the hospitality necessary for visiting Friends and that year as many as 12 all came at one time on their way to Wales Yearly Meeting. There were also always guests coming to visit the Company, to see the new developments made by Abraham.

That summer Mary Darby became engaged to Joseph Rathbone of Liverpool who was a partner, with his cousin William Fawcett, in the Coalbrookdale foundry established in that great port; he had therefore been coming and going to Coalbrookdale for some years. The wedding took place on 19th July and there was a large gathering afterwards at Sunniside. Samuel Fothergill came from Warrington which was part of the same area Meeting for church affairs, Hardshaw Monthly Meeting, as Liverpool to which Joseph belonged. The Isaac Thompsons were with them from the north, and after the marriage the young couple travelled across country in their company. Later, young Samuel, aged 14, during his summer holidays went to stay with his sister and Joseph in their new home which was probably a Rathbone family house in Thurloe Street, Liverpool. The visit would have been one of excitement for him, for the activity of a large port and busy city was full of new interests and strange sights.

1769

Thomas Goldney had died at the end of the year of 1768, but the news did not reach Sunniside until early 1769. He had been a central figure in their lives and had given them personal support as well as providing the main finance for the Company.

His estate was inherited by his brother Gabriel and his sister Ann, and the interest of the Goldney family in Coalbrookdale now began to decline until finally some years later both Abraham Darby III and Richard Reynolds bought up the respective Goldney shares in Coalbrookdale, Horsehay and Ketley.

Abraham and Sarah went to Wales Yearly Meeting at Cowbridge and the Rathbones came to Sunniside with the Irish Friend, Thomas Greer, and later Abraham went to London for Yearly Meeting.

Samuel had been at school from 1763, only returning for holidays or occasionally for some special family event. He spent the last of his school-days on his own as Sarah had returned home, probably about the time when Mary married Joseph Rathbone of Liverpool in 1768. These close relatives were to play a large part in Samuel's life very soon afterwards.

Abiah's Journal ended in the year of 1768, so the family history has to be pieced together from letters and minutes of Meetings until Deborah's Journal began 10 years later. Abraham Darby III was an active member at Meetings as were also Richard and Rebecca Reynolds. New Dale Meeting opened in 1769 and the Reynolds from then on gave hospitality to visiting Friends attending there, continuing to do so as long as they lived at Ketley Bank.

1770

It was decided now that Samuel should leave school at the normal age of 15 and become an apprentice in the Coalbrookdale Company, but that he should serve his time in the branch at Liverpool with his brother-in-law, Joseph Rathbone. Accordingly, a document was drawn up, written by Abiah, giving the terms of his apprenticeship. This new situation would give him more experience of life in new and active surroundings, and put him in touch with a family of many interests. He would take part with other young people in work and recreation, in a wide and intelligent circle, centred in the very busy life of this great port where the Rathbone family were prominent shipowners and exporters.

The Rathbones' Meeting belonged to Hardshaw Monthly Meeting, and Samuel regularly attended First Day Meeting with them although his certificate of removal from Coalbrookdale was not received much before he was about to leave in 1775. He lodged with his sister Mary and her husband Joseph, and she no doubt saw to his welfare and that he was properly cared for in practical ways.

From time to time Samuel came home for short visits, but they are unrecorded. Sarah, who was then living at home and had taken Mary's place as companion to her mother Abiah, now made some of the ministerial journeys with her and took an active part in Meetings. She was an intelligent person and fast developing into a strong and self-reliant character, and Samuel would always continue to lean on her for support. She went from time to time to Liverpool during these years to stay with the Rathbones and be with her younger brother.

1772

Samuel's brother, Abraham, kept a private ledger of expenses which was to include a few years later all the costs of the Iron Bridge. In this book in January, there was an entry for payment of £20 to Samuel aged 17 years and away from home, and this was followed up by other similar payments to him from time to time.

Samuel Fothergill died that summer on 15th June. He was a great loss to Abiah and her family as he and Thomas Goldney, who had died in 1768, had been their chief advisers and friends since the death of Abraham Darby II, and both had always been frequent visitors to Sunniside.

Towards the end of the year Abraham paid a visit to the Company's London concern in which in three years' time Samuel was to be involved after he had completed his apprenticeship.

1773

Abiah and Abraham began to be anxious over the conduct of the trustees under the provision of Abraham Darby II's will, and so consulted lawyers who concurred with them that certain matters to do with the mines had not been correctly carried out over the years. Thankfully they realised that in

1776 these trusteeships would end with Samuel's coming of age, when the childrens' portions would all be released into their own hands.

1774

Abiah, writing to her niece, Rachel Maude, after a long visit to the north and to Scotland in 1774, found herself, on reaching home, somewhat short of time as she was 'making some new shirts [or helping rather] for my dear son Samuel before he returns to Liverpool'. He had evidently been home on vacation to see her after her journey and she found his clothes in need of replenishment; nearly every garment had always been made for them all at home or in the immediate neighbourhood .

Samuel Joins London Office
1775

This year Samuel's apprenticeship was completed and he was destined to go to London to conduct the Company's business begun by his father and located on the bank of the Thames. There was a foundry at Southwark in Stoney Lane to the east of London Bridge between Bridge Stairs and Pickle Herring Stairs, which ran north from Tooley Street to the Thames. A list of rents for the following year showed that Abraham and Samuel Darby paid £100, the largest sum in that street. There was also an office and warehouse together with a dwelling house in George Yard, which was to be Samuel's home, north of the river, at No. 26 Upper Thames Street in Greenhithe Ward to the west of Broken Wharf, where the eastern portion known as Timber Yard opened at one end onto the wharves of the River Thames.

Some of these premises were sold off in May 1775 for the sum of £65 and this must have helped to pay for the office furniture, including a desk for £8.9s.0d from a firm called Pitt & Co., also later for the repairs of the Great Boat used on the Thames costing £2.19s.10d. Abraham was in London for a part of the year 1775 as a Bill was passing through Parliament allowing for the construction of a bridge over the River Severn, which ultimately culminated in the construction by him of the famous cast iron bridge during the next few years. He must also have used some of this time in the capital in arranging for Samuel to take over the management of the Company's interests in London and to plan for his future.

1776

When Samuel came to live in George Yard in the winter of 1775/6 Sarah came too to be with him and do his housekeeping. In January 1776 Samuel became 21, to the great relief of all the family as this brought about the end of the Trust created by the will of his father, Abraham Darby II, whose children would now be in full possession of their own shares by April.

Wedding Certificate of Samuel Darby and Deborah Barnard, 8 August 1776. Note signatures of near relatives in right hand column. (See page 27).

PART TRANSCRIPTION OF WEDDING CERTIFICATE AND RELATIONS SIGNATURES

Samuel Darby of London in the County of Middlesex, Ironmaster, Son of Abraham Darby of Coalbrook Dale in the County of Salops, Ironmaster, deceased, and Abiah his wife; and Deborah Barnard, daughter of John Barnard of Upperthorpe near Sheffield — — having declared their intention of taking each other in marriage before several Meetings of the people called Quakers in the counties of Middlesex and York aforesaid — —

after due enquiry and deliberate consideration thereof by the said Meetings — — having consent of parents and relations concerned, these are to certify all whom it may concern that for the accomplishment of this marriage this 2nd day of the eighth month called August in the year one thousand seven hundred and seventy six, they the said Samuel Darby and Deborah Barnard appeared in a Publick Meeting of the aforesaid people — — in Sheffield and — — Samuel Darby taking — — Deborah Barnard by the hand did openly and solemnly declare "Friends, in the name of the Lord and before this assembly — — I take this my Friend, Deborah Darby, to be my wife, promising through divine assistance to be unto her a loving and faithful husband until it shall please the Lord by death to seperate us."

And the said Deborah Barnard declared "I take this my Friend Samuel Darby — — to be my husband, promising through divine assistance to be unto him a loving and faithful wife, until it shall please the Lord by death to separate us."

Abiah Darby	Deborah Birckbeck
John Barnard	Ann Burgess
Hannah Barnard	Eliz. Barnard
Abraham Darby	Jane Maude
Mary Rathbone	Joseph Birkbeck
Sarah Darby	H. M. Reynolds
Mary Barnard	Wilson Birckbeck
Joseph Rathbone	Deborah Birckbeck, Jr.
Rebecca Darby	Ann Smith
Robert Barnard	John Wilson, Jr.
Warren Maude	Wm. Smith
Rachel Thompson	Wilson Barnard
Sarah Maude	

Abiah, in a letter to Rachel Maude, her niece, in Sunderland dated 13th January, told of how they had all had influenza at both Sunniside and London, and how Sarah had had the infection three times. The brother and sister attended Gracechurch Street Meeting in the capital where Samuel was to become a member.

Abraham had for some time been negotiating with others over the building of the new bridge which now had received Parliamentary approval, though it was not until 1777 that the final decision was made by the partners in the promotion that the structure was to be made of cast iron and that Abraham was to be given the contract. Abraham now had the intention of marrying Rebecca Smith of Doncaster, who was the niece by marriage of Richard Reynolds, as her mother, Ruth Gulson, was a sister of his second wife, Rebecca. Their wedding took place at Warmsworth in Yorkshire on 3rd May. The signatures of the family and the many Friends who signed their wedding certificate, showed that the numbers there were considerable.

Samuel, although five years younger, decided to marry that same year and his and Deborah's wedding took place at Hartshead Meeting at Sheffield on 8th August: again many members of the Darby family travelled north to attend. The wedding evidently was also a big one for the Meeting had a large membership. Abiah wished to say rather more than she was able to on this occasion as Esther Tuke, who attended from York, took up a good deal of time and so disappointed her, which happening disturbed Abiah sufficiently to record the fact in her Journal with regret.

The young couple came back with Abiah and the Darby family to Sunniside and stayed a week before going on to London. Samuel would have shown his bride as much of the surroundings as he could in the time available and would have introduced her to the people of their circle who had helped him in his youth. Her winning and gentle ways would have touched all their hearts, already kindly disposed towards Samuel's bride.

Deborah on arrival in London joined her husband as a member of Gracechurch Street Meeting, a pleasant and interesting one as so many attended from distant places. The vocal ministry there was sincere and offered by those of wide experience and frequently of erudition as well as deep conviction. Here she must have learnt much that helped her later on during her long ministerial journeys.

1777/8

Deborah and Samuel were an attractive young couple and at the beginning of their life together all seemed to promise well, but the latter was evidently not very well in the city where the pollution and pressure of business did not suit him. In those times there was, of course, much smoke and many fumes given off in the Severn Gorge, but the setting there was rural and the dispersal swifter with winds blowing over the area from the hills.

The Knowles who lived at Ingram Court were, of course, kindly and interested, and Mary Knowles kept up her correspondence with her cousin, Susannah Appleby at Sunniside, giving up-to-date news of George Yard particularly when Sarah was staying there. Deborah and Samuel also met James and Deborah Townsend, (she had been a Waring), who kept open house inviting many visiting Friends to their home, as well as others who lived in London.

Deborah had her first child, a boy, on 8th September 1777 at George Yard, the birth being registered in the Parish of St Mary's Somerset, in the City of London, the witnesses being George Hooper and Mary Pryce. The baby was named Abraham, but was unfortunately delicate from birth and soon developed fits. As soon as his grandmother, Abiah Darby, heard about this she prescribed her favourite remedy of Amber Cakes, recommending only a very tiny piece, but she doubted if the doctor would allow even a few crumbs and indeed this would have seemed unwise for a child of such a tender age. The little boy proved generally to be frail and only lived until the following early summer of 1778, to their great sorrow.

Samuel had evidently developed, in boyhood, a taste for literature, probably fostered by his uncle, Isaac Thompson, who had presented him with a copy of his own poems written in his youth. Early on while living in London, Samuel had his own book-plate printed with the simple inscription 'Samuel Darby – London' which he put into his new purchases, which he bought from the bookshops near to George Yard, where he collected with pleasure what volumes he could afford. Two leather bound copies in English of Montaigne's Essays were among these purchases. He enjoyed both prose and poetry, and one practical small volume he added to his modest library was a leather bound pocket-size book of Coach Travel[4] containing all the halts, times and prices of the journeys throughout the United Kingdom.

1779

At the beginning of 1779 Samuel became dangerously ill of a violent fever. As soon as he was better and able to travel, he and Deborah went to Sunniside and stayed there some time so that he could recover his health. As Deborah was expecting her second child they remained there for this event much to Abiah's pleasure. In a letter to her niece, Rachel Maude, in Sunderland dated 29th March, Abiah wrote that Samuel and Deborah 'seem likely to be with us for some time as London does not agree with him'. Also in this same letter she goes so far as to express the wish that they should in future 'live in the country'.

Deborah's baby was born on 30th May at Sunniside and the certificate signed by Benjamin Wright, the surgeon, who was the doctor always called in by the family and the witnesses were Abiah and Sarah who helped her through the ordeal. The baby was called Samuel after his father but unfortunately also had fits like his elder brother had had, though happily recovered from them and grew up to be strong and healthy. Deborah was not very well and unable to feed her child. This information was given in a letter[5] from Jane Harry to Mary Knowles in London as Jane was staying at Sunniside at the time.

On 1st August 1779 Deborah began her diary and in the first entry she described how she attended General Meeting at New Dale 'where Dear Mother Darby and Ann Summerland were engaged', and how they afterwards 'drank tea at the bank'. A day later Abraham Darby and his family dined at Sunniside and on the 3rd they 'drank tea in the summer house' as the weather was fine. These few sentences describe the usual pattern of their days when they were at home and during that summer.

Benjamin Birkbeck, Deborah's first cousin, came to stay and the whole party from The Bank[6] came over to dine. Efforts were being made by them all to save the foundry and business in London which was evidently in difficulties. Benjamin was connected with the Birkbeck business of insurance and banking in the capital, and Wilson, his brother, had been Samuel's partner and helper from the beginning at Southwark and George Yard. The possibility of failure and the worry this caused meant considerable distress was suffered by Samuel – and his family – for his part in the affair.

Beginning of Deborah's Diary

On 14th August, Deborah began to transcribe 'My Dear Mother's Diary' and this activity may have encouraged her to write a Journal for herself, which she had started two weeks earlier and continued until the end of her life. Evidently, in both cases, the daily entries were made in small notebooks and later written out in large volumes such as unused company ledgers.

Deborah wrote in a less colourful manner than her mother-in-law Abiah, whose cryptic sentences and downright descriptions of personalities and picturesque turn of phrase brought to life long passages of religious comment. She was also without the apparent zeal of Abiah's strong personality, though was equally steadfast in her commitment to Ministry, and her soft musical speaking voice, one of her chief attractions, captivated her listeners and was often remarked upon, so perhaps her spoken words were more powerful than her written ones.

On 20th August, Abraham and his family, with Thomas Hills from London, dined at Sunniside. Samuel had gone with others to Ivetsy Bank, a coaching stop on the road from north to south through the county, to meet Warren Maude and his wife Sarah, son Jacob and daughter Jane, who were expected there, but who however, did not come until the following day when Abraham Darby and his family came up again from Dale House to Sunniside for supper in order to meet them.

Deborah still complained of 'painful feelings' which were perhaps increased by Samuel having to explain his difficulties to his relations, as Friends took a very serious view of any business failure. The visit of the Maudes was followed by Thomas Waring coming from Leominster and holding, as was his custom during visits, a Public Meeting. He also cheered Deborah's 'drooping mind' using the language of scripture, 'show thy people their work and their children thy Glory'. He had no doubt of her 'being a Blessing to many', and when he left he expressed the wish that she 'might be strengthened to persevere'.

On 25th August Deborah attained her 25th birthday, and she 'humbly desired that it might be a season of renewing of my acquaintance with that arm of power that had hitherto proved sufficient for my support and preservation my life long'.

On the last day of the month the Abraham Darbys dined at Sunniside and went on to drink tea at William Goodwin's. John Cash also arrived from Coventry to stay: he had come to give a lecture the following day on the subject of 'Air': this was a 'philosophical discourse in which he gave us many instructive examples'. John Cash was a successful manufacturer of cloth in Coventry and had become a minister, but he did not travel more widely than to the counties adjoining his home.

On 4th September, Abraham, Samuel and Richard Reynolds dined at John Smithman's at Little Wenlock to discuss the Coalbrookdale Company's business – John's wife's family having been in part possession of the land and buildings at Coalbrookdale from the beginning, as she had been a Brooke of Madeley, and it was from Sir Basil Brooke, her father, that Abraham Darby I had leased the original furnace and premises adjoining.

Deborah found her mind 'becoming more sensible to divine over-shadowing', but most unfortunately her peace was of a sudden deeply disturbed by 'My dearest friend differing from me in sentiment'. Any lack of understanding between herself and Samuel caused her pain and perhaps this was to occur more frequently because of his nervous temperament, though she did not continue to remark about any further disagreement in her Journal.

On 8th September they all dined at Thomas Addenbrook's, who advised them on legal business. Deborah was finding all these days 'an exercise of faith and a prospect of things being gloomy'. On 13th of the month Uncle Maude and his family left for home accompanied by Samuel and Sarah as far as Ivetsey Bank. Sadly it was to prove the last time that Warren and his sister Abiah were to be together, for he died the following year, so later on these days must have held poignant memories for her. Deborah, still very depressed, wrote 'our feelings still gloomy but we wish to confide in him that can cast up a way where none for a reason appears'. Also she found 'many are the tossings the mind is subject to until fully stayed on God – may I be found to attain that unspeakable blessing'.

'On 17th September, after many discouragements, like the weight of the Mountains', she and Samuel set out for the Western Counties Circular Yearly Meeting which met at Gloucester on the 19th September 'in company with our beloved Mother and lodged at Kidderminster'. On the 18th they reached Worcester for breakfast and passing by Tewkesbury arrived in Gloucester in good time, lodging 'at The Bell where we met several Dr Friends whom we were glad to see'.

The day after they 'called upon several much valued Friends before we went to Meeting, not so large as expected but solid. George Boone, Thomas Rutter and Ann Young appeared in testimony and my mother in supplication. Hannah Plumstead Junior dined with us'. This young woman was related to Abiah by the second marriage of her grandfather William Warren of Scarborough to Frances Plumstead. The afternoon Meetings were much crowded and held in two different places, and at 'The King's Head' in the evening there was a religious opportunity in which Deborah and Timothy Bevington and his sister, Elizabeth from Worcester, were all engaged.

On 20th September, George Boone breakfasted with them and Lydia Hawksworth gave Deborah 'an agreeable opportunity of her company before the Society's select Meeting' in which Martha Pryor and Ruth Fallows took a prominent part. In the afternoon there was a large Meeting opened by George Boone and Abiah Darby. After a very crowded and long Meeting, which lasted until one o'clock on the following day, they rode to Worcester where Benjamin Birkbeck left them for Sheffield. They then went on the 21st to Enville to lodge, a hamlet on the road to Coalbrookdale.

On the 22nd they dined at the village of Norton and reached home to tea, where they had the company of Rebecca Darby and her sister Ann Smith and Catharine Young. Two days later William Chapman and Wilson Birkbeck arrived and these Friends rode over to The Bank on the 25th. She found the Meetings the next day painful to her feelings and confessed that 'as a lately enlisted soldier in the Lamb's warfare perhaps I have not learnt to bear hardiness'. On this day, the 26th, 'one of the furnaces (she does not say which) was on fire but through providential care was soon extinguished'. Wilson left on the 28th and on the 30th Samuel and Thomas Addenbrook went to London. The men of the family had been in increasing consultation together about the London premises all the last weeks, helped by their advisers, but whatever conclusion they had come to had still to be acted upon.

On the evening of 1st October, John Barnard, Deborah's father and her brother Wilson arrived to stay, also Joseph and Mary Rathbone from Liverpool 'and William Rathbone Junior and Samuel Galton'. Of these two young men the first, William Rathbone IV, son of William Rathbone III and Rachel Rutter, was a very intelligent and energetic member of the important family firm of shipowners and importers in Liverpool. The second, Samuel Galton, was a friend of his and worked in his father's gunsmith business in Birmingham; he had married Lucy Barclay, a daughter of David Barclay, a son of the Apologist, and at this time these young people were living at Five Ways near Birmingham. Samuel Galton was a clever man and much interested in the developments of the day being a member of the Lunar Society. Later Deborah was to stay with them and their near relations.

The day after they arrived these two guests went on to The Bank. Deborah continued to be very depressed and anxious. On 3rd October, after attending New Dale Meeting, they dined at The Bank returning to Sunniside for tea, where she thankfully received some comfort in their small evening gathering and spoke a few words, 'where Dear Mother appeared in supplication'. On 4th October they dined at Dale House and she received a letter from Samuel 'who had got well to London and was encouraged in the prospect of things for which cause may we bow in thankfulness'. On the 6th her father and brother left and the next day 'hearing again from my dear S.D. tended to relieve my anxious mind', she called upon Ann Summerland and drank tea at the Abraham Darbys, happily becoming more resigned.

On 9th October, Joseph Rathbone went up to The Bank and found 'a disposition to help with brotherly sympathy'. This was on the part of Richard Reynolds and he and Joseph left a few days later for London and on the 12th Deborah was comforted by another letter from Samuel. Abraham Darby's family dined with them on the 13th bringing John Zachary from London, and afterwards she wrote a few lines to Abraham expressing 'her belief that we shall see the Lord's dealings with us had been marvellous'. It cannot be envisaged that her brother-in-law Abraham was yet to view the situation in quite the same light, as failure was always dreaded and a good deal of financial loss was evidently also involved. Then on 18th October, Abraham himself went to the capital followed by Richard Reynolds and Joseph Rathbone, so all the men of the family had gathered to endeavour to deal with these financial difficulties.

Deborah, on the 20th, rode pillion behind Daniel Rose to Shrewsbury Monthly Meeting beside 'sisters and mother in her chaise'. The Meetings were low but Abiah had an evening Meeting there 'an open time in testimony' [vocal ministry], and Deborah felt strengthened 'to cast in my mite'. The next day they reached home again and Thomas Addenbrook returned from London where he found unfortunately 'our prospects gloomy at present'. This was followed by a letter from Samuel telling her that 'they had concluded to part with our Concerns in London – thus wonders are working in the deeps and a way is making for more freedom to follow the Lord in the way of his leadings though in a manner the Creature would not have chosen'.

These sentences were significant as Deborah had begun to realise that without responsibilities in the capital, and their probable future residence with Abiah, she would be far more at liberty to undertake her ministry, as indeed became the case in the ensuing years, when the children were still too young to leave in the care of others, save near and devoted relations. Indeed her decision on this made a year later was to be providential because of Samuel's recurring illnesses as he grew older, and she was able to leave home for months at a time almost yearly, as well as for frequent shorter periods to attend local Meetings.

Deborah then received a further letter from Samuel on 25th October, saying he intended having their linen, china and plate packed up and sent down to the Dale. She found her mind was in some degree relieved 'to which the prospect of having my Beloved husband's company has not a little contributed'.

On 27th October in another letter from Samuel which came in the evening, he mentioned his 'intention of living with his honoured Mother' and that 'the prospect of it was comfortable to him'. On 2nd November, Rebecca Darby's father, Francis Smith and her sister Elizabeth, came to stay at Dale House and the next day they all dined at Sunniside. On the 4th November Deborah mentioned that her cousin George Braithwaite, the son of her mother's sister and George Braithwaite left Sunniside after only staying a few days. Mary and Joseph Rathbone spent the same day comfortably with Samuel discussing the family happenings as they must have often done in the past in Samuel's youth when he lived for several years with them during his apprenticeship. Perhaps, out of these days spent together, the suggestion came, that Samuel should go and take charge of the family business in Liverpool – but this idea appears to have come to nothing and is not mentioned again.

On 19th November, Richard Reynolds and Joseph Rathbone were in consultation at Sunniside and Deborah said again 'they were still tried not knowing which way the Lord may be pleased to dispose of them'. To divert them a little that week there was a total eclipse of the moon from six to nine o'clock – a matter always noted in their family diaries and letters.

Samuel went to Ketley on 27th November, returning for dinner – 'he keeps steady and sweet under the many things he has had to investigate'. On the 29th they 'had a letter from London telling them of the disposal of the foundry' and Deborah commented she was 'glad our outward concerns are lessening'.

'On 30th November, Michael Cartwright and Thomas Addenbrook with us, no doubt completing some business' and she found her mind 'continuing to extend a state of deep conflict, I see but little that comforts me and yet in the Lord's time my sorrow may be turned into joy'.

Deborah heard on 9th December of 'My Dear Sister Dickinson being safe in bed having a fine boy to be called Joseph', and in this news she found another call for gratitude. Christmas Day she did not 'find one of rejoicing for her' and she was not well for some days afterwards and stayed at home, and later in the month there were 'at times the Company of those not professing with us who tho' moral Characters not feeling the necessity of gathering to the Root some of them – it requires great watchfulness to keep enough center'd – indeed this is the case with too many amongst us, a highly favor'd People'.

On 30th December they attended Quarterly Meeting at Shrewsbury 'in which he that brings healing Virtues with him condescended to arise' and Deborah's 'infant tongue was employ'd amongst those of more experience in speaking well of His Name'. Afterwards she went to stay for a day or so with Richard and Rebecca Reynolds at The Bank at Ketley, stating that these hours proved to be 'to my own instruction' although she also remarked when she remained another day that 'it was one of humiliation, but she trusted not unprofitable spent'. This remark appears to refer to their difficulties in London and the business failure.

1780

When Deborah returned home early in the year she 'heard of the death of my Uncle Maude, brother to my beloved Mother Darby'. Deborah then wrote to her sister, Mary Dickinson, finding that it was a privilege that 'this mode of intercourse may be maintained and far separated of each other'. While the Samuel Darbys had been living in London perhaps they had received more frequent first-hand news. The sisters had missed each other greatly, for they had always been together until Deborah's marriage.

Deborah began to prepare little Samuel for his imminent innoculation against the smallpox. On 15th January the two brothers, Abraham and Samuel, went to Stourport on business, probably about river transport, because from that place the sailing vessels called trows were hired for use by the Coalbrookdale Company. Also on the 15th Hannah Mary Reynolds came to dine and Deborah found her a 'fine young woman'. She was the daughter of Richard Reynolds by his first wife, Hannah Darby, and therefore Samuel's half-niece. Her father was very devoted to her and she was his constant companion listening to his philanthropic ideas and his plans for woodland planting. To her he passed on his love of nature when they were walking together and his general interest in the world around them. He had a delightful cottage constructed for her among the trees, in which she could stay for a day or two, looked after by an elderly couple who lived in part of this house.

Deborah was passing again through 'tedious days and wearisome nights', as she described them and was a good deal indisposed, the reason for this being she had begun another pregnancy as well as still being very anxious over the London situation and little Samuel's impending smallpox innoculation.

On 20th January the child went for immunisation to Buildwas, the same place to where his father, uncles and aunts had been sent a generation earlier, and now 'his kind aunt, Sarah Darby, took charge of him as it was not thought prudent for him to stay at home for fear of spreading the complaint'. He was innoculated a few days later and Deborah wrote 'having done what we apprehend right we commit him to the Lord, desiring resignation as to the choice of his disposal'. Thankfully she was soon able to see the little boy and he appeared 'in a fine way to get over the complaint', and on 29th January she could even go and dine there with Sarah and the child.

Abraham and Samuel rode over to The Bank on 3rd February on business, and that same day there were visitors, Priscilla Foster a cousin of the Lloyds, and Jane Harry arriving to stay. Immediately there were difficulties as Priscilla became poorly 'not having been much accustomed to be separated from her near relations, it appeared to depress her spirits'. She continued to be unwell and it became apparent that she would have to return home to Birmingham. Rachel Thompson and Deborah offered to take her, setting out accordingly on 6th February after morning Meeting first dining at The Bank with the Reynolds, where they found Elizabeth Rathbone who was staying as she frequently did being a great friend of Hannah Mary Reynolds. Sadly because of these frequent visits, Elizabeth Rathbone was later to develop a hopeless love for William Reynolds, Hannah Mary's very attractive and intelligent brother, and this unrequited love finally spoilt her life.

That afternoon the travellers went on and lodged at Dodson on the outskirts of Birmingham, the home of Samuel Galton senior 'where they were very kindly received'. It was a delightful place and their host was still active although he had retired from the family gunsmith business in Tile Street, Birmingham, some years before, leaving all in the hands of his son, the younger Samuel. He had bought the property of Dodson, situated about a mile and a half outside the town, to be able to keep in touch with the business and also to attend Friends' Meetings which he could do without difficulty. He was a clever, kindly man, wise and benevolent, who bestowed the help he gave in an orderly manner; he also understood the new direction industry was taking where a number of Friends, up and down the country, were developing the main sources of skill and wealth of the nation, feeling that certain innovations that were being introduced would improve conditions for mankind.

Lydia Forster, who was his housekeeper, was a Friend 'in appearance as well as conduct'. She had been looking after his house ever since he became a widower and had formerly been governess to his daughter. The staff in and out-of-doors was quite a large one, including a butler and a number of others, and there were several gardeners and other estate employees, as Samuel Galton was very interested in his small property. He kept bee-hives partly made of glass so that the habits of the insects could be studied, and also had many beautiful kinds of pigeons, which were fed near a window so that they could be seen and enjoyed. He also encouraged waterfowl to come on to a pool fed by the River Rea at a little distance from the house.

The day after their arrival the visitors attended Meeting in the old Meeting House in Bull Street, and afterwards drank tea at the Widow Farmer's at Bingley, where they had a religious opportunity at which Mary Lloyd and Catherine Phillips were present. Their hostess, Priscilla, formerly Plumstead, was the widow of James Farmer a very successful businessman who had bought the property and had constructed his country house, a building of red brick with two stories of bow windows reaching to the roof. There were spacious apartments within and the house, later to be the principal home of her son-in-law, Charles Lloyd and his wife Mary and their children and descendants, remained in the Lloyd family for several generations.

Next day, Rachel and Deborah dined with the Charles Lloyds in Edgbaston Street, where Charles and his brother Nehemiah lived in adjoining houses, the latter containing the counting house and offices of the Bank. Edgbaston was, at that time, a long street leading from Dudley Street to St Martin's Church and Lane. At the time of their visit, Charles and Mary, who had married in 1774, had several small sons and were to rear 11 children. Charles became increasingly involved with the banking side of the Lloyd business, finally being known as 'Charles the Banker'. He was a very prominent citizen in Birmingham promoting the establishment of an infirmary (or hospital), acting there as Treasurer for many years; he also had interests in other philanthropic activities.

On 11th February Deborah attended a marriage in which George Boone was 'engaged in testimony and supplication' and they drank tea that day with 'Sampson Lloyd's family at Farm'. This was another property on the outskirts of Birmingham acquired by Sampson Lloyd II at Sparkbrook.

There he built a pleasant three-storied house of brick and planted an elm avenue which, at the time of Deborah's visit, was beginning to provide an agreeable approach to the house.

They left for Dudley on 12th February accompanied by Catharine Lloyd after 'seeing the infirmary and calling on Cousin Binjoice'. Deborah took part in the Meetings, but she felt 'an exercised spirit much tried in this journey' which came to an end when they left their kind Friends James Payton and Catharine Young next day arriving home for tea. Almost immediately Abraham went to London and Rebecca being alone, came to dine and on the same afternoon Deborah went again to Buildwas to see how little Samuel was progressing after his smallpox innoculation.

Monthly Meeting followed at New Dale on 16th February, and at the Women's Meeting a few lines were read from 'our Dear Mother [Abiah] who was not able to attend in person, but felt her mind warmly engaged for the prosperity of Truth'. Sarah and the child Samuel returned from Buildwas: 'we esteem it a great favour he was got so well through so an afflicting complaint'. Deborah continued in 'a tried situation, many temporal concerns wanting adjusting for which purpose our Dear Sister, S.D. [Sarah Darby] kindly accompanied Brother J[oseph] R[athbone] to London' and Deborah 'hoped they may be preserved in their journey as kindness to us in their inducement we ought to crave preservation for them at that hand that can both bless and blast'.

On 26th February came the welcome news of their safe arrival. Sarah returned on 2nd March and Deborah stated 'her company is always consoling to me and being devoted to serve her Heavenly Father her example is animating'. The Reynolds family dined with them after General Meeting three days later and Deborah had Jane Harry to tea, commenting 'she is a sensible young woman that has joined the Society by Convincement, having forsook for Truth's sake wordly greatness'.

Deborah was engaged on 7th March in the laundry as towards the spring there was always an increase in the amount of washing to be undertaken as it was easier to dry out-of-doors, and the whole household usually took an active part.

They were still finding 'their situation required best direction in a peculiar manner', but both she and Samuel were coming to the decision that they would have to make Sunniside their permanent home. There followed 'a painful duty' in that they had to sign some deeds and her feelings fluctuated over the next few days between being 'comfortable among themselves and deeply distressed'. It was a difficult decision for them to make for it meant giving up their own home life and living in another's house. However familiar and welcoming Abiah's home would be, it would mean their independance in the fullest sense would be over, though one consolation for Deborah as has been stated was that this freed her to travel in the Ministry.

The 'concern' of many Quaker women, often with large families, which took them on ministerial journeys of many thousands of miles away from their husbands and children, always seemed to astonish the world at large, but was accepted in their community and fully understood. Deborah found also in Coalbrookdale that as we 'are comfortable amongst ourselves it makes us not much dependent on those not with us for our consolation which is a blessing'.

On 20th March Deborah was once more busy in domestic concerns 'our Dear Little Son a pleasing care, may we be favor'd with wisdom to discharge our Duty to him as his mind expands and wants information'. Sarah and Jane Harry drank tea with them in their rooms and a day later Deborah and Rachel Thompson went to the Hortons close by for the same refreshment. Then Hannah Mary and Elizabeth Rathbone came on the 28th for a visit of four days which gave great pleasure to Abiah who delighted in the presence of the younger generations. Dorothy Owen, their gentle Welsh Friend, was there also with others from Wales to attend Quarterly Meeting.

On 4th April, Mary and Joseph Rathbone arrived to stay for a time at Sunniside bringing a servant with them. They were to remain there for some months until they could move into Dale House which Abraham and Rebecca Darby were leaving in order to take possession of their new home at The Haye which for a long time had been prepared for them. More furniture arrived from London, from George Yard, for the Samuel Darbys and they seemed 'like settling down', but Deborah appeared still somewhat uncertain. Peter Price from Devonshire who had joined Friends by convincement, came again that week; he was in the iron trade and connected with the Fox family in his area.

Deborah spent the day with Elizabeth Rathbone, the sister of the fourth William Rathbone, who she found 'a sensible young woman'. She was well educated and had been brought up in an interesting circle in Liverpool. That week Deborah also walked into the Dale and called upon 'some of my Friends'. The way down the hill was steep and she probably went by the path across the little park and down the side of Dale House garden into Darby Road, and in her condition, for she was pregnant it would have been an effort. She was evidently well because she left with Sarah Darby and Susan Appleby, accompanied by Daniel Rose, on 15th April for Monmouthshire, going by Leominster. They were kindly received the following day at William Young's and breakfasted at Thomas Waring's house where Deborah was engaged in testimony and supplication in the morning, and after Meeting at which only Daniel Rose appeared, they rode on to Hereford reaching Usk the next day in time to dine. They had private lodgings, but ate at 'The King's Head' where they also found Henry Wilkins, John Townsend and others.

They attended Meetings and then left again on 17th April, reaching Mitchell Troy for breakfast, and later at a Friend's house near Monmouth they met John Townsend and Henry Wilkins again, returning to Ledbury where they lodged. They dined with their kind friends Timothy and Hannah Bevington and reached Stourbridge late that night where they attended Meetings, travelling on to Coalbrookdale in the evening of the next day. At the end of the month they were 'busy in settling our things and putting them in their places', but Deborah remarked 'while the cares of Martha are necessary, may Mary's example have due weight'. Her first cousin George Braithwaite came to stay on 5th May, and a day or so later Robert and Sarah Grubb, (daughter of William and Elizabeth Tuke), arrived from Clonmel in Ireland, with Maurice Marks from Limerick who, after dinner the next day, having attended Meeting, went on to Birmingham.

A week or so later on 15th May, 'John Wilkinson and his daughter drank tea with us', having come over from their home at Broseley: John was already a well known Ironmaster, and Deborah found his daughter a 'well accomplished young woman'. Samuel, and Abraham, this time accompanied by Joseph, went to Stourport again on business.

On 25th May Samuel and Deborah heard of their house in London being sold and Deborah's reaction was again 'it is a favour to have care lessened'. She now spent much time in the garden 'which at this season is very beautiful'.

Thomas Marks and Abraham Neale dined with them on their way from Holyhead, and on the 2nd June Hannah Waring, a woman of extensive knowledge and deep religious experience whom she was very glad to see, was met by Samuel and brought to Sunniside. There followed a time of pleasure and of being able to sit in the garden with her friend where they always appeared to drink their tea on fine days. She obviously obtained much comfort from the edifying company of Hannah.

Deborah attended General Meeting at New Dale on 4th June. She was still riding, and on the way home had a fall from her horse, but mercifully she was not seriously hurt; however, this cannot have been good for her in her advanced state of pregnancy. On 8th June they had 'some company to tea that was termed Noblemen, but it is nothing but virtue that truly enobles mankind'.

Next day Hannah Waring had a letter from her sister, Deborah Townsend, giving a distressing account of a riot in London 'occasioned by the Protestant Association'. These were the Gordon Riots which caused much fear in the capital, and later they received further news which was still alarming. However, by the day they drank tea again in the garden on 11th June, the news was much more favourable.

There followed for them more summer days 'spent in free communication, our kind Friend read us some Church History'. Mark Gilpin came and the following day they all drank tea with his brother Robert, and Peter Price from Devonshire was again mentioned.

During these weeks Deborah wrote often of time being spent in the garden, so the fine weather evidently continued although this ultimately culminated in a 'remarkable thunderstorm' on 2nd July.

Deborah felt very depressed when Hannah Waring left her for her visit to The Bank before finally leaving the neighbourhood, and had parted from her with reluctance. On 16th July at the afternoon Meeting, Abiah 'had an open time, people of the Society and other Societies present on account of a burial' – she had always been at her most powerful when her audiences were varied.

On 20th July, Jane Harry got an account from Jamaica of the death of her father. This news coming to her at Sunniside must have been made easier for her because of the sympathetic understanding of her friends Sarah, Abiah and Deborah, for, as had been threatened, she was now cut off from her large fortune and only left a subsistence because of her change of faith.

On 24th July Rebecca Darby gave birth to a daughter whom they named Mary. Because Rebecca had been expecting this child they had postponed moving from Dale House to The Haye, but again the pregnancy had never been mentioned in the accounts written of that year. On the 26th Lydia Hawksworth and Catherine Phillips came to stay, both taking part in the Weekly Meeting and also their small evening sittings.

On 4th August Deborah herself 'after a time of deep trial' had her baby 'being put to bed about 9 o'clock in the evening for which Blessing may suitable returns be made – my life has been given me for a prey contrary to human probability – the child very ill'. Indeed little Hannah died after breathing about 12 hours 'it was a trial for us to part from this sweet babe but was enabled to say the Lord gave and He has taken away, Blessed be His Name. Continue much indisposed yet the Lord graciously sustains'. Deborah continued very ill herself and next day when General Meeting was held at New Dale none of the family left her side to attend 'except servants on account of my indisposition'. Rebecca Reynolds visited her on the 9th August, having evidently come from The Bank that afternoon to attend the burial of little Hannah. Deborah was still 'much indisposed but kindly cared for' and during the following days she began to gain strength.

On 15th August, several of the family were at New Dale Meeting, which George Boone and Sampson Lloyd III also attended, and fortunately Deborah now found herself so much better that she could walk into the next room and write to her parents.

Jane Harry left for London on 1st September and Deborah 'got out among our Friends and was glad to find myself equal to the exertion'. General Meeting took place at The Dale and Richard Reynolds dined with them. Deborah writes 'in a spiritual sense I viewed myself as one learning the spiritual warfare and many things opened which I was preserved from expressing unbidden – I thought my Friends that were publicly engaged were Divinely assisted'. She still, however, found herself 'understandably low', and an added anxiety was when she received a letter from John Barnard, 'our Dear Father who I fear is much loaded with business – may a way be opened for his release'. She spent a good deal of time with the Abraham Darbys at Dale House 'sympathy in the Day of Trial lessens sorrow – I hope ours hath had a tendency to unite'.

On 13th September Abraham and Rebecca left Dale House and came to stay at Sunniside with the three children until their home at The Haye was ready for them. The Rathbones were then able to move into Dale House and Deborah hoped 'that the Blessing of the Everlasting Hills descend on them'. She expressed the feeling that 'the family kept near to one another and willing to aid one another' and said 'this was a sweetner of bitter cups'. She also emphasized how 'Dear Mother Darby was always interceding for a Blessing both secretly and openly' and that Mary Rathbone was 'cheering to her Friends and entered deeply into their feelings', a quality she had had ever since, as a young woman, she had comforted her mother Abiah at the time her father died.

On 1st October, they were at New Dale Meeting and dined at The Bank where Deborah 'appeared in supplication after a silence of near three months'. A day or two later she went up to see Abraham and Rebecca at The Haye, greatly hoping that their new home 'could prove a comfortable habitation' for them. On 12th October, John Whinny came on business 'he was once in America and married a daughter of the late John Hunt'. Deborah was still finding it 'a winter season with me, may the sap only be returned unto the root and not wholly gone', but her mind 'often had to admire at the dispensation of kind Providence in bringing us here' as she considered it 'a Blessing not to be oppressed with domestic cares and that living with an affectionate Mother gives leisure for improvement'.

Sarah Darby and Joseph Rathbone set out for London on 20th November, not returning until the last day of the month, so Deborah spent these days with Mary Rathbone who would otherwise have been alone in Dale House. In early December Deborah decided to accompany Rebecca Darby into Yorkshire 'who is going there on account of Uncle Smith's illness', and so on 3rd December they went to The Haye accompanied by Samuel and Peter Price, travelling on to Lichfield where they lodged. The day after they reached Sheffield and were kindly received by John Barlow, Rebecca going on to Doncaster and Deborah to Upperthorpe where she found 'her Dear Relations well'. The following day, John Barlow and her cousins Samuel and Wilson Birkbeck came to dine at the Barnards.

On 7th December they went to Monthly Meeting at Warmsworth and John Barnard then accompanied his daughter to Leek where they visited Mary Aldam. On returning Deborah went to see Mary Rutherford – they again lodged at John Barlow's. Deborah spent some days 'among the Friends of her youth who were glad to see her and are kind in their attention'.

She was engaged in the early part of the Meeting on 14th December 'after which Mary Proud spoke largely to many states and we spent the day at Cousin Fairbanks'. Her father had, by then, returned from Leek – Mary Proud and other Friends dined. Deborah went to High Flatts Meeting where they met Martha Ridgeway and Jane Watson, but she regretted that she 'deferred my little offering to the end of the Meeting as it ought to have been given up to earlier – which made the work harder for our Friends and prevented my having as much reward'.

She then returned to spend several days with her own family where she was always 'most kindly cared for'. She went on 17th December to the Meeting at Woodhouse which was rather low, but 'as an act of dedication afforded peace'. Samuel, Richard Reynolds and Caleb Birchill then arrived from home, but they did not appear to attend all the same neighbourhood Meetings in which Deborah, Elizabeth Hoyland and C. Tricknett had 'solid opportunity', and on 24th December at Sheffield were 'engaged in the cause of Truth'.

On the 25th December, John Barnard and Charles Tolley went to Uncle Dickinson's funeral at High Flatts. Deborah and others then attended a Select Meeting at Leeds, and after two Women's Meetings she travelled the same afternoon with her sister, Mary Dickinson, who had joined them at Brotherton, to Ackworth School[7] on the 27th. There Samuel joined them and they found it was 'a pleasing sight to see the children dine, 300 of them, in the greatest order'.

Deborah and Samuel dined at 'Uncle Smith's at Doncaster and Brother Reynolds accompanied us to Upperthorpe that evening'. Next day Jane Watson appeared at Preparative Meeeting, where Mary had an encouraging opportunity 'after which I was engaged in supplication. In the afternoon I stood up first, after which the Friends were much favor'd and on the whole it was a season to be thankfully remember'd'.

1781

In the New Year of 1781 Samuel and Richard Reynolds left them for home, and on 3rd January other Friends dined at her father's. Deborah accompanied by Jane Watson and Martha Routh, whom she described as 'being as Mothers to me', left in a chaise for Warmsworth where they were engaged in Meetings. Rebecca Darby then joined her from Doncaster and they lodged with Deborah's Aunt Barnard and travelled on by diligence to Lichfield where their husbands had come to meet them.

Soon after reaching home Deborah developed, by neglecting a cold, 'a putrid sore throat'. The doctor was sent for and was 'arduous in his attention', but she took some time to recover, and during her convalescence she read *John Churchman's Journal* in which she found 'many instructive remarks'. When well enough to venture out-of-doors she was prevented by deep snow, followed by floods, which proved so severe that the water of the River Severn overflowed to such an extent that 'one of the furnaces at Madeley Wood was stopped'.

Towards the end of February the worst of the weather had passed and Deborah, Sarah and Rebecca, were all able to go to The Bank to see the Reynolds where they spent a very agreeable day.

Deborah found herself at this time uneasy over a journey she wished to undertake in her capacity as Minister, and expressed her desire 'to be more perfectly instructed in what is required at my hands that I may never run without being sent'. She may have consulted Richard Reynolds on this occasion as she quite frequently took his advice.

In mid-February they were all upset by the death of Agnes Horton, a woman of great integrity and one whose life had been very closely bound up with the Darbys and their small community.

On 25th February, Ann Summerland told Deborah she found 'her mind drawn to the same parts of the vineyard that I had looked at which was a great encouragement to me'. She and Ann then spent time at Dale House with the Rathbones, and on 16th March while dining there met Cousin William Rathbone III and Sarah Stephenson, who were engaged in visiting families, although rather slowly, as Sarah was not well at the time. On 22nd March, Ann and Deborah laid their concern 'before Monthly Meeting to visit some of the southern and western counties'. This was readily endorsed and they were given their certificates. The next days were spent in preparing for this journey, but Deborah found this time was 'one of secret conflict, viewing [her] own unfitness for the work before me, yet an experience of the Lord's goodness'.

They left home on the last day of March accompanied by Samuel and Robert Horton as far as Stourbridge, and also Samuel Sankey who 'goeth with us on the Journey'. They attended Meetings next day and dined at J. Morris's after which she and Samuel 'took an affecting leave of one another'. Deborah and Ann accompanied by their host went on to Worcester where they attended Quarterly Meeting and 'sat in several families'. They were staying as they usually did, with the Bevingtons. They then journeyed on to Alcester, Evesham and Camden where the orchards would have been beginning to blossom at this time of the year; their way was through the ancient places in this fruit growing and agricultural area of farms and small villages, with the Malvern and Bredon Hills in the far distance. They reached Shipston-on-Stour where Susannah Waring, Thomas and Hannah's sister 'kindly cared for them'.

After Ettington Meeting they had a session of retirement in Jeffery Bevington's family and next day 'sat in S. Lamley's to mutual comfort'. They then went to Warwick and Coventry, and there Ann Summerland heard that her son Isaac had died, but despite this sorrow they attended the Balsall Street Meeting, where they found very few members and went on to Hartshill and to Hinckley next day.

It was there that Deborah also had news of a grievous loss in the death of her dear sister, Mary Dickinson, in child birth; she was much distressed yet she 'desired resignation by being no doubt our loss is her gain'. A frequent expression used for comfort prompted by a strong faith in the future life of the spirit. The child was called Barnard, and when grown up, was destined to spend much of his life in Coalbrookdale, finally marrying Ann Darby and becoming, for a time, head of the Company.

On 16th April they reached Geddington and lodged at William Dodgtion's.[8] His wife, Frances Henshaw, was a lifelong friend of Abiah Darby, but had proved to be a neurotic and difficult woman, who had caused them all disquiet, particularly her own family. They then visited Wellingborough and Olney, and after an 'opportunity in Richard How's family with his young people' they attended Hogstyend Meeting and had an evening Meeting in Leighton, there Mary Brook was kind to them. Mary was a fine and very energetic minister and her letters reveal a very strong character – it was her child who a year later became the bride of John Grant of Leighton Buzzard and their only child, Hannah Grant, was destined to marry Francis Darby, eldest son of Abraham Darby III in 1808, and lived for the rest of her life in Coalbrookdale.

By 23rd April they had reached Luton and had a Meeting which 'was nearly silent'. At [St] Albans they had 'opportunity's in several families' and went on to Tottenham where they had 'a kind reception' holding Meetings in the morning and evening and lodging with Cousin Wilson Birkbeck. He had a very pleasant house at Tottenham and was, at that time, married to his first wife, Hannah Plumstead. On 27th April they were at Gracechurch Street Meeting, Deborah's old Meeting, and the next day she spent with James Townsend.

Meetings followed at Devonshire House, Westminster, Bromley, Peel and Park, and on the last day of April Richard Chester and his wife dined; shortly after they went to stay with them in their house in the country. Ann and Deborah continued attendance at Meetings in and around the capital, and as far out as Kingston 'which was low in the beginning but closed well'. This place on the Thames was large and ancient: an extensive corn trade had grown up with the capital. From there they went on to Guildford on the River Wey, the county town of Surrey, with many fine old buildings, particularly the Town Hall. There they found 'close doctrine but some clearance'.

They visited Godalming situated in a beautiful valley where many people were employed in the manufacture of woven stockings, and blue and mixed kersey, a kind of narrow ribbed cloth made from long strips of wool. Travelling into Hampshire they visited Alton which they found 'wide and modern built', lodging with John Blow. On their return journey they went to Capel and through the hills with the splendid views over the countryside to Dorking and Horsham, called after the Saxon Horsa, where they found trees in almost every street, a most pleasant sight in early summer. On 24th May they reached Ifield where Deborah found 'the state of Society makes it necessary to wade deep to get at the Spring of Life'.

Returning to London through a valley with many mineral springs about the town of Reigate where there were the ruins of a fine palace belonging to the Archbishop of Canterbury, she felt 'peace in our little journey into the country' and indeed these days had been very pleasant ones at that beautiful time of the year.

They then began again attendance at Meetings in and around the capital and on 7th June at the Women's Meeting at Gracechurch Street testimonies were read out for Thomas Gawthorpe and William Cookworthy and several others, and Deborah concluded that 'on the whole I think we might say that the shout of the King is still in Israel's camp'. On 12th June they parted from Friends and reached Staines next day, attending Meetings both there and at Uxbridge.

Finally they reached Jordans [Deborah spelt it Jourdans] which was a 'time of favor'. They were in the heartland of early Friends set in a beautiful wooded valley in Buckinghamshire. The Meeting House they attended was substantially the same as when first built in the late 17th century, a brick and tile building with lattice windows, the whitewashed walls inside partially panelled with an unvarnished wood, and a brick floor on which stood tables and benches: there was also a large stable adjoining which could hold 20 horses, as Friends travelled to attend Meeting from a wide area. William Penn and his family had been buried in the Burial Ground in front of the Meeting House.

On 13th June there was a moving Meeting at Chesham in the morning, and at Amersham in the afternoon – an old town on the River Misbourne. At the foot of Grove Hill there was a farmhouse which was the home of Gulielma Springett, who became the first wife of William Penn. The main street held fine old buildings of many periods, together with a 17th century market hall supported by arches.

At Maidenhead, Ann was engaged in 'Gospel Love'. This place had an important bridge and, for centuries, had been a stopping place on the journey from London to Bath.

At Reading Meeting on 17th June 'First day Friends were exhorted to faithfulness'. Here they only stayed a few hours in this ancient town, going on to attend the afternoon Meeting at Newbury, which proved less satisfactory. Marlborough Meeting was also a disappointment and there was 'little to visit'. The history of this town went back to Anglo-Saxon and Roman times for it was in a strategic position on the way westwards and had eventually grown wealthy in the making of cloth, with the result of the citizens being rich enough to construct many fine buildings of stone in the 17th and 18th centuries.

On 20th June, at Devizes, another place of early origin, they were also able to 'speak remarkably to the state of individuals', and a day later they reached Melksham where they spent a day resting, but Deborah only reported they 'had no Meetings'.

They then went to Calne, Bromham and Pickwick, the last resulting in 'a trying Meeting' and even at Melksham she found 'an occasion painful'. At Hullington on the 25th June 'mixed marriages had opened the way to much desolation'. At Chippenham that same afternoon, she expressed her feelings by saying 'let there be no strife between my Herdsman and thine for we are brethren, for which there proved to be a Cause'. This had been a market town for centuries, where King Alfred had spent much time and hunted in the then nearby forest.

There was a Meeting in Wiltshire at Westbury in the morning and at Salisbury, which Deborah found 'exercising'. They could not have failed to have observed the great spire of the cathedral as they went towards the city, and it must have been pleasant to pass through the well-planned streets on their way to Lavington, but she never mentioned her surroundings. At Bradford-on-Avon they 'entered into the arduous exercise of visiting families' and remained there for several days, Deborah remarking 'our engagement, tho' in itself trying, is made easy by the receivings of best help'. Bradford was a hilly place with streets going down to the river bank, and a bridge over the River Avon, still with the 'old lock-up' on the centre of the crossing arches, the whole place being built of the local honey-coloured Cotswold stone.

On 6th July they finished their engagements and went on to Bath, pausing only to hold a Meeting, and travelling on to Bristol the same day. In the morning they were at Friars – the same Meeting House which earlier Darbys had attended many times in the past. Deborah reports that there was a grave there of a woman Friend – 'her name was Fry' as this family had a connection with Richard Reynolds, who had been apprenticed to William Fry, from whose firm Abraham Darby III regularly bought drinking chocolate. The afternoon and evening Meetings were described as 'laborious sessions', for Deborah, as Abiah before her, found some of the Bristol Meetings difficult. They continued their attendance however and had an opportunity one evening at their lodgings, but she does not say with whom they were staying, and on 10th July they continued to travel once more.

In Bristol they had a large number of acquaintances; Rachel Champion, second wife of Sampson Lloyd II had lived there and Deborah had visited one or two of the Lloyds, her descendants, in Birmingham. The Champions had been trading with the Darbys throughout the century, and there were also the Goldneys of Clifton who had largely financed the Coalbrookdale Company from the beginning until the death of Thomas Goldney III in 1768.

On 10th July after attending morning Meeting they left Bristol for Portishead [spelt Prospect in the diary] 'where there was a small number'. Claverham and Sidcot followed and a day later they had a comfortable Meeting at Bridgwater in the morning, and at Taunton in the evening. The 14th found them at Wellington Meeting in which Deborah was 'silent', and they were 'kindly received at Nicholas Were's, a merchant whose wife Mary of Bristol was a minister.

By the 17th July they reached Minehead which had been an important port in the middle ages. At the western end of the town were a flight of steps, paved with cobbles and tiles, going down between rows of thatched cottages built of stone, some being colour-washed, and with tall chimneys. They were at Chard on 18th, the highest point in Somerset, a place formerly much occupied with tanning and, in the 18th century, with the weaving of cloth. Here there was a Grammar School dated 1671, a prominent building noticed by travellers.

They reached Ilminster by the evening where the Meeting was held in silence. Centuries before the place had been an important Roman military station on the Foss Way. They had 'an opportunity' in the Friends' house where they lodged and then went on to Montacute, a village of some importance with local stone buildings and a very fine country house in the vicinity. From there they continued to Yeovil for an afternoon Meeting, a very busy place indeed with the working of leather as the traditional trade.

They were at a Meeting at Puddimore next day, followed by one at Long Sutton on 21st July, then visited Street and Glastonbury. This last very impressive place is not commented upon in any way, but must have been noticed by them on passing. They stayed for the night at Hallatrow and the following morning went to Batton where Deborah found 'the goodwill of

He that was in the Bush was extended to the people'. They were again at Bristol by the 23rd for a weekday Meeting and appeared to lodge at P. Tuckett's; the day after they were at Frenchay Meeting and had an opportunity at the Work House belonging to Friends. They visited Jane Reynolds, Richard's mother, whose lively and delightful letters about her grandchildren, William and Hannah Mary, who came to stay with her from Coalbrookdale, indicated a person of imagination and sensibility.

By 26th July they had arrived at Tockington and Thornbury, the latter an historically interesting place, going back to the time of King Athelstan, with fine views across the River Severn, and on the edge of a woodland valley. They rode on to Painswick, high up in the Cotswolds, where they found Friend Joseph Davis 'not very well', and travelled on to Cheltenham by 30th July, where there were only a few Friends. On First Day they were at Tewkesbury and reached Bromyard that night. There they had a satisfactory Meeting next day and were met by Samuel and Robert Gilpin who accompanied them home.

The first part of August was spent among the relations and attending local Meetings and Deborah's 'mind was much gathered into stillness which is a Blessing not at our command'. They gave in their Certificates at Monthly Meeting on 15th August, and on the 20th Sarah Beck came, whom Deborah described as 'a laborious and faithful servant' and she gave 'a warning to the disobedient at Meetings encouraging the upright to trust in the Lord'.

Early in September, Deborah found her 'mind led into a deep exercise not feeling too much of Divine regard as in times past, yet remarking that day and night succeed each other and the Lord kept covenant with both'. Dr Thresher of Bilston was with them for some days leaving on 7th September. He probably came because of Samuel's health, but she does not specifically mention this matter which can only be guessed at in view of later happenings. At the time Samuel must have been reasonably well, as some days later he went on business to Bromsgrove.

On 25th September, Deborah mentions George Young as being present. On 5th October she was employed in caring for her little son Samuel who she wished 'maybe fully dedicated to the Lord'. She again had a period of 'indisposition accompanying a time of much desertion, yet desired to wait patiently upon God who is the true Comforter'. On 12th October, Peter Price, J. Tregellis with John Brewster and his sister Hannah, all arrived to stay and they sat together in the evening. Deborah went again to Shrewsbury on the 17th for Monthly Meeting, and in the evening there was a public meeting called by 'my beloved Mother Darby in which she and Ann Summerland were favor'd'. These two elderly ministers continued the work they had carried out so forcibly over the years, and on the 18th Deborah spent the day with Hannah Brewster whose company she found pleasant.

On the 25th October other Friends arrived for dinner, amongst them Ann Wilson from Worcester.

These autumn days passed in quiet religious and family life, the tranquility unbroken for Deborah until the sudden arrival of her father, John Barnard, and her brother Wilson. She also received a letter from her brother Robert Barnard giving an account of 'my dear father's inability to carry on his business'. She felt 'her mind greatly distressed feeling for my dear parents' and her time was spent in much 'Secret sorrow desiring to bear the present afflication in an acceptable manner well knowing that the Lord afflicteth not willingly'.

It is possible that John Barnard had come to discuss his financial difficulties with the Darbys and Richard Reynolds, but they would be unlikely to be able to help him. A Tannery required much capital, but the Coalbrookdale Company needed all available finance at that period for their own work, for although the famous bridge was just finished some of the expenses had fallen on Abraham, and the partners had various other commitments over purchases of land and expansion of manufacture.

John Barnard left on the 18th November, and Deborah continued 'too much depress'd to be sensible of much consolation yet was thankful that others could rejoice in the Lord'. During this time she was sustained as always by Ann Summerland and 'Dear Mother Darby who continued to minister to them'.

On the 30th November she had a letter from her father which 'revived my sympathy with him'. On 13th December 'My beloved Mother Barnard and my Aunt Thompson came – our meeting affecting but glad to have her with us'. She found the 23rd 'to be an exercising day with me tho' measurably thankful that Divine regard was manifested to the flock through my fellow labourers'.

The Select Quarterly Meeting appeared to be held on the evening of 25th December and they had with them Dorothy Owen and George Young. Her last entry for the year was an appreciation of Ann Summerland 'who being near the fountain of life herself she is often favor'd to bring up water from the well of salvation to refresh the heritage'. Deborah had come to have a great admiration for her, which had increased during their journeys together.

1782

By the second week in January, Deborah again complained of 'tedious days and wearisome nights', which was her usual description of unhappiness. She was once more pregnant although, as in 1780, she does not explain that this was part of the reason for her unease, though indeed it was the case, as the baby was due in the spring. However, by 16th January she was feeling well enough to go to Monthly Meeting in Shrewsbury and 'found that they were still favor'd to know that in the World there is Christ Jesus' peace', afterwards she was feeling 'more liberty of spirit than for sometime past'.

On 4th February, Lewellin Jones came from South Wales accompanied by Mary Hunt and they were 'engaged in speaking much to our edification, but they spoke in the Welsh language so we could not understand the subject'. How they came to be edified is obscure, no doubt some enlightenment had been possible, although unexplained. A little later John Barnard, Deborah's father, came in order to reside in the Dale and she said 'I esteem it a favor to have he and my Beloved Mother near me, though the occasion has been trying'. Failure of their own business was always a very difficult situation for Friends, particularly for an older man who had owned his own firm, but tanning required much capital and this may have been the reason for John's difficulties, as he appeared unable to sustain sufficient funds.

The few 'moments of confidence' for Deborah at that time seemed to be the 'strengthening and refreshing opportunities' after supper at Sunniside when her mind was 'often turning to look unto Him who afflicteth not his Children willingly, but in all His dealing with them seeketh their refinement'.

On the 12th March, they received the sad news that 'two of our Collyers was killed in the pits which was deeply affecting to our minds'. Any accidents to their employees was always felt by the family and they did what they could to assist the dependants of the unfortunate men.

At this time Deborah's mind was 'too much sunk' from a variety of reasons but chiefly because Samuel's health was evidently deteriorating, and also her advanced pregnancy did not allow her to go to Meeting. The Welsh Friends had left them and during the following days Quarterly Meeting took place at Shrewsbury which was 'attended by some of our family'. Mary Ford died on 1st April and was buried at Broseley. She was the eldest unmarried daughter of Richard and Mary Ford and had been living in Worcester for some years where she had a number of relations.

Sarah and Susannah Appleby left to go to Brecknock to attend Wales Yearly Meeting although the situation was difficult at Sunniside, but Deborah now had her parents living in Coalbrookdale, who had by then moved into their own home. As her time approached, Deborah hoped that she would be 'supported through the conflicts allotted tho' great'. On 22nd April after 'a day of trial' her son Edmund was born and happily during the next days she was 'favor'd to recover finely'.

Friends returning from Brecknock on 27th April gave an account which, by then, interested her of others who had been attending Wales

Yearly Meeting including Timothy and Hannah Bevington, Samuel
Spavold, Jane Hunt, Ruth Fallows and Esther Marshall. Sarah and Susannah
then returned home and Deborah rejoiced to see them. She continued to
recover 'which is the more to be commemorated my exercise being great',
(this now referred to Samuel). In the middle of these difficulties Peter Price
and his wife, Anna Tregellis and her sister, Sarah, arrived from the west
country; Sarah was to make a long stay with the Darbys and Deborah found
her 'a valuable young woman and a sitting was held on 10th May'. On the
11th Deborah received a sudden shock as Samuel went off to Newport
causing her acute anxiety, which became even greater when she heard he
had gone to London. On account of this she became 'very distressed indeed'
and all the more so as she was still confined to her room.

The Prices set out for the capital on 13th May, having been with them
during 'these unspeakable anxious days' which lasted until early June when
they were partially relieved by the news that Samuel 'had got among his
friends and likely to be placed under Robert Harrison's care at Hoxton'.

Because Deborah had to forgo the happiness of a marriage in the fullest
sense of human love and companionship with a partner able to share with
her the strains and stresses of existence, she was also never free of anxiety
and had to depend entirely on the spiritual strength vouchsafed to her. The
result, though at that time hidden in the future, was her ever increasing
ability to help others in their distress, through her own conquest of this deep
personal sorrow.

Esther Marshall was, by then, with them and was a comfort to Deborah
who had found herself to be well enough to go with Esther for an afternoon
sitting at The Bank, where they both stayed the night, Esther going on to
Nantwich the next day and Deborah returning home. Judging from this
visit Deborah could not have been feeding her baby, and indeed was
probably too troubled to do so, for she continued to have disturbing news of
Samuel's health.

After receiving further accounts of Samuel, Sarah and Deborah on the
24th June 'concluded to go to London' and they 'set out by coach, had
agreeable company' and 'travelled all night' reaching London on the 27th
June.

The weather was hot which made the journey tiring; however once
there, they met with a kind reception at her cousin Wilson Birkbeck's at
Tottenham. His home was where Deborah had stayed on several occasions
and continued to do so in the future. They also found that brother
Dickinson was in London on business. They began to attend Meetings in
the capital and had 'an opportunity at Cousin George Stacey's after tea and
again after dinner with that family on another day'. Mary Stacey, his wife,
whom he had married the year before, was a first cousin of Deborah's, and a
daughter of Isaac and Rachel Wilson of Kendal.

Sadly, Sarah was now to discover that Samuel had become very poorly and while Deborah spent a day at their lodgings, Sarah went to see Samuel which Deborah herself 'was not permitted to do for fear of making him worse' – a tragic situation for her as her life had now begun to be lived in the realisation that she would never probably be able to help fully the man to whom she had given her heart and who was the father of her children.

She attended Gracechurch Street Meeting, to which she and Samuel had belonged in happier times, and on 3rd July 'Sarah Beck, J. Wallis and myself engaged to speak to the People'. She goes on to record that Friends were 'kindly attentive to us, but my feelings such as receive little consolation therefrom'. They dined at Deborah Townsend's and that day were at Peel and Devonshire House Meetings, and continued to spend the days of the next weeks attending weekday Meetings, some of which 'was low – yet we know that it is good to wait upon Him that has the Blessings of time and eternity in His Hand'.

Deborah felt that her 'conflicts are only fully known to my Heavenly Father', but she 'was fearful when comforted spiritually of being deceived, knowing that the enemy can transform himself into an Angel of light'. She was deeply unhappy for she could not have fully recovered her own physical strength after the birth of her baby and the added frustration of not being able to visit Samuel herself was increasingly difficult to bear, although she strove and sought for resignation.

On 11th August, Deborah was again at Gracechurch Meeting in the morning and Devonshire House in the afternoon 'both sessions of some favor. Deborah Townsend was beautifully enlarged to a visited state, to which I made some addition'.

Deborah and Sarah left London on 12th August and 'got to Worcester that night, travelling 112 miles in one day', again by coach, where next day they attended Meeting and 'had an opportunity' at Timothy Bevington's. After tea on 14th they reached Coalbrookdale and found her 'dear children and other relatives well'. The following day, despite the joy of being again with her baby and little Samuel, she found her mind 'much exercised to be so long deprived of the Company of a Beloved connection – requires much of Divine Support to keep perfectly resigned'.

On 1st September there was General Meeting at The Dale and John Cash, who was a frequent visitor to Sunniside, was with them and they had 'acceptable service in the afternoon'. Two weeks later, Deborah had a letter 'from my Dear Husband which I esteem a favor – may I wait patiently for his perfect restoration which in the Lord's time I hope will be granted'. At Monthly Meeting on 18th September 'Cousin William Rathbone III minister'd unto us reviving the Passage of Elijah's being taken up and Elisha's request'. The family returned from Tamworth and the following day James and Deborah Townsend with Hannah Stephenson came to stay at

Sunniside. They visited The Bank and were engaged in the Meetings there, being entertained by the Reynolds. Hannah and Deborah Townsend were great personal friends of Deborah's and had been very kind to her during the weeks in London, where the Townsend house was always a centre for Friends visiting the capital.

They then attended at Quarterly Meeting in Shrewsbury on 25th September, and afterwards Deborah went to supper at John Young's, when she had to advise one of his daughters, Rebecca, that she would have to 'tell unto others what God had done for her'. This young woman was to be Deborah's constant companion in the Ministry on very long and arduous journeys in the future, and to accompany her in 1793 on her American visit.

They then set out for Llanidloes in Wales, where she lodged at William Hunt's, whose wife had travelled with them from Shrewsbury. They were away until 5th October, during which time she received more favourable accounts of Samuel which she found 'reviving', adding that 'prospects were brightening a little'. They were again in Shrewsbury on 24th October to see Ann Byrd, 'who was on her way to Ireland' and found this Friend 'very low but after an encouraging opportunity she seemed revived'. The next day Ann set out by coach and Deborah came home, and although the visit had been brief, Deborah had been 'thankful for having had her company'.

Rebecca Young and Ann Crowley came on 27th October 'whose Company was truly acceptable', and they remained some days at Sunniside. Deborah found them both 'to be promising of much usefulness to the Church'. At this time her mind 'was much exercised in viewing a work which appeared formidable', and the feeling of 'unfitness for the Lord's work' and apprehension continued. Her mind was in a conflicting state – 'deep calleth unto deep – at the sound of thy water spouts all thy Waves and thy billows have gone over me'.

She often told brother Richard Reynolds of some of her exercises for he had always been able to advise and comfort her in her religious doubts; she so wished as she said to be 'found faithful to the trust committed to me tho' it may be under many discouragements'.

Abiah was frequently, despite her age, 'favor'd in supplication and Ann Summerland in Testimony', and Deborah felt that 'they may be justly called Mothers in Israel'. These two elderly women, always present in the background over the years, were an abiding help and support to Deborah and the younger generations of the family.

For Quarterly Meeting at the end of the year Dorothy Owen came with other Friends and Dorothy was 'beautifully enlarged on the subject of sanctify yourselves'. Deborah also had 'the company in the closing days of December of Rebecca Young' whom she described as 'a precious plant' during her visit: while she was there they went to see Rebecca's brother George Young who at that time lived and worked at Horsehay.

1783

· Deborah, with Susannah Appleby, left home on 3rd January and, after having stayed at The Bank, rode on to Leek where Esther Marshall and Robert Barnard joined them. At Leek Meeting on 5th January, Esther had 'to exhort to more diligence in labouring for the arising of Life', and later that day had a solid Meeting with the Widow Chorley's family at Hare Gate.

Susannah then returned to the Dale with George Titterton, the others going on to Uttoxeter where they had a Meeting in the afternoon. They reached Birmingham to stay at Bingley with Priscilla Farmer, attending the weekday Meeting on 7th January, when they showed their certificates, but that evening some objections were raised to their immediate procedure which, 'caused searching of the heart' for them and subsequently they found the next few days a time 'when the exercise of both faith and patience seemed necessary'.

However, on 13th January they were allowed to begin the family visits on which they were accompanied by Richard Dearman, but Deborah ended the description of this time with the comment 'The Justice of the Almighty is not requiring more than He gave ability to perform'. Some of the visits were in the country and all were, as usual, time consuming, but by then they appeared to be staying at Dudson with the Galtons, and there the whole forenoon of the 24th January Deborah spent with Mary Galton, towards whom she felt 'much nearness'. Also after tea at this house 'many Friends were present in which some spirits were united'. They set out on 25th January for Dudley accompanied by Mary Galton, where they attended a weekday Meeting and also had some sittings with families. On returning to Dudson, Esther Marshall unfortunately became ill and Deborah had to leave her for a time to fulfill an appointment made previously in the country accompanied by Richard Dearman. She then returned to Dudson and spent the time 'comfortably, and attended to Esther, who tho' better was still confined', and a few days passed before she fully returned to health, which had taken place by 11th February when she was able to take part in Monthly Meeting.

Travelling to Tamworth on 13th February they were able to visit families, continuing to Polesworth and Hartshill where Esther invited her hearers 'to more diligence in the Lord's work'.

On 17th February they went on to Coventry staying with E. Gulson, with whose family they sat that evening where 'deep dwelling and faithfulness affectionately [was] recommended'. The Gulsons were Rebecca Darby's mother's relations and so well known to the Darbys; Rebecca Reynolds was also one of this family. On 28th February 'had a number collected together', but Deborah found it 'more difficult to divide the word than in more select opportunities'.

The arduous task of visiting families continued and 'their departure was delayed by snow', but they finally left Coventry for Warwick on 4th March. Journeys in winter, although frequently undertaken were inevitably difficult, and Friends' families were not always living near to each other or easy to reach. She said of one 'the testimony of truth went forth this morning at Meeting unto Worldly wise state to whom the cross of Christ still remains foolishness', and that there were 'minds much exercised in some families under a sense of hardness of heart and unbelief'.

Despite the wintry weather and, therefore, the bad state of the roads and lanes, they visited families on their way between towns. They reached Ettington on 9th March and went on to Radway sitting with five families there. Next day they continued to Shipston and Deborah tells of an opportunity with the Friends from Brailes, saying of these visits 'some hope that a Blessing attended'. On 16th March they reached Chipping Norton and by then appeared to be lodging at Charlbury with William and Sarah Squires where they had a 'satisfactory opportunity with the family', attending Charlbury Meeting next day. Their journey continued to Witney, a place well known for the manufacture of bedding, and attended evening Meeting appointed for 'People of other Societies in which many Gospel Truths were convey'd'.

The Meeting in Burford was to 'some satisfaction', and another at Long Compton 'was comfortable'. They lodged at Shipston with Susannah Waring whom she described as a 'Mother in the Truth'. After a Meeting at Ettington they rode on to Birmingham accompanied by Jeffery Bevington on the 22nd March, and attended the Meeting for Ministers and Elders which was 'a favor'd season'.

Quarterly Meeting for Warwickshire was held on 24th March, but Deborah did not say where they lodged, only that on the 25th they 'spent with Friends'. Worcester was reached on 27th March and in the evening she attended a Meeting for Ministers and Elders there at which 'Jeffrey Bevington was acceptedly engaged'. They then continued their visits to families in that place and set out for Quarterly Meeting at Bromsgrove on 2nd April, but 'on the way met a messenger inviting us to Dudson as Mary Galton was poorly'. They, therefore, hurried to see her, leaving again the next day for Bromsgrove in time to return with Friends to Worcester.

The next week was spent in visits to families, and on 21st April George Beetrel accompanied them to Stourbridge. Finally on the 24th they returned to The Dale where Deborah found all well and remarked 'what can I render to the Lord for all his benefits'. Esther Marshall had given Deborah support all through this journey and Deborah was herself feeling happier because Samuel, although still away, was now able to write regularly to her and evidently was making progress towards recovery.

Robert Valentine from America, and Joseph Heath from Coventry were at Coalbrookdale Meeting on 27th April. Robert, almost immediately, became 'very ill' and was nursed at Sunniside for some time. The others, who now included Esther Marshall, joined in the family visiting.

By 2nd May, Robert fortunately, appeared to have recovered sufficiently to go with them into the country and Friends Mary Proud, Martha Routh and E. Holly had, by then, joined them. They spent some time very agreeably out-of-doors in the garden, the little park and woodlands, and also visited Richard and Rebecca Reynolds at Ketley Bank. Deborah herself was not feeling very well, but she does not, as usual, explain why, though she had recovered enough to go to Shrewsbury on 7th May, where they continued family visiting and dined at John Young's house.

On 12th May they all went to Bridgnorth, lower down the Severn, for what appeared to be the Circular Yearly Meeting for Wales. It was probably the first time some of these Friends had visited this ancient town; a port and market of considerable activity on the River Severn – the lowest part of the town being situated on the banks of the river with a bridge connecting this area with the 'High Town' on a red sandstone cliff which had for centuries been a strong fortification.

The whole area had been granted to Roger de Montgomery, the powerful follower of William the Conqueror, who had been connected with the development of the defence of the whole region against the Welsh.

At the Meeting for Ministers and Elders, Catherine Phillips 'beautifully opened with the disciples waiting at Jerusalem' and she was also engaged in the Meeting for Friends as were George Boone and Robert Valentine. There was a Public Meeting on 14th May 'in which many Gospel truths were convey'd by different servants'. The afternoon Meeting was divided, Deborah 'went with several others to the Town Hall, Mary Proud much favor'd, Richard Valentine and Martha Routh also had acceptable service'. In the evening they had a time of retirement at the 'Pig & Whistle' and she also mentioned Lydia Hawksworth as being with them.

Next day Deborah 'parted from her Beloved Companion', (Esther Marshall), who went to Bristol while she returned to the Dale. The following days were spent 'in quietitude' and writing to Friends, and she received a letter from Esther giving a good account of her 'getting to Bristol'. There was also a letter from Samuel who was continuing to improve in health, a fact which cheered her heart. William Bryant then came from Bristol and brought a first-hand account of Yearly Meeting. On the 2nd June in the evening 'Ruth Fallows and Ann Byrd arrived accompanied by Joseph Williams, Richard Shackleton and J. Russell'. The men Friends departed the next day for London Yearly Meeting with Sarah Darby.

Deborah accompanied the others to The Bank on the 4th and they went to Meeting there on 8th June in the morning, and Broseley in the afternoon. Llewellin John from South Wales was by then also with them, and Ruth Fallows had 'an awakening Testament to bear both to Friends and those of other Societys'. They all breakfasted at Dale House with the Rathbones and dined at Sunniside, the proximity of these houses again showing their easy use when they had guests. Deborah was again with Friends in Shrewsbury where Ruth Fallows 'after a long silence express'd an apprehension that a want of faithfulness had withheld good things from us'. Ann Byrd was also engaged and Deborah 'concluded the meeting in prayer'.

There was Monthly Meeting at Coalbrookdale on 19th June, which Elizabeth Jones and Mary Proud attended and they had 'to encourage this wrestling seed and warn an unbelieving state'. Another welcome letter arrived from Samuel for Deborah brought by Sarah Darby when she returned from London.

Deborah went to Shrewsbury on 24th June for Quarterly Meeting, and the next day on to Welshpool, where they had the company of Hannah Bevington, Ann Wilson and Elizabeth Houghton, all from Worcester. They all returned together to Coalbrookdale and Deborah 'accompanied these Friends, that were strangers, to call upon several families'. On 1st July they breakfasted at The Haye, before leaving for a short journey to Dudley and Stourbridge; on returning to the Dale, Deborah found her 'mind exercised under a prospect of being able again to leave my near connections and run the Lord's errands'. So she and Ann Summerland 'laid their concern before Friends at the Shrewsbury Meeting for business on 16th July to visit South Wales and the Western Countys'.

Robert Gilpin, who had long been a faithful and active member of Coalbrookdale Meeting, died on 6th August and was buried on the 12th, where 'the Meeting was large and solemn' and Deborah had to revive the 'Passage of our Saviour miraculously feeding the Multitude'.

She and Ann received their Certificates at New Dale Meeting on the 16th August and left for Leominster where they were kindly received by William Young, with whom they stayed. At Almeley on 18th August there was a Meeting 'attended by some not of the Society', and the following day they rode to Pales, where they had a kind reception. This was always an interesting Meeting situated high upon a hillside amongst beautiful scenery.

They reach Tynnabla on 21st August, riding through 'desolate country' to Landovery where 'they held a satisfactory Meeting . . . People of other Societys flock'd to it and some of them seem'd like the thirsty ground to whom the showers of Gospel rain flow'd freely.' The party then rode 26 miles without stopping to Llanidloes 'for a Meeting at New Inn in which a state which had known better days was called upon to return'. They reached

Haverfordwest on 28th August and 'lodged with Friend John Lewis, an honourable member', and there was an opportunity in which the younger branches of the family were invited to 'enlist under the Banner of Christ'.

Travelling on to St Clairs they reached Swansea with some difficulty, 'our guide losing his way'. It was not always easy to bring a party of travellers through the hilly country of Wales although this was at the height of summer with the long light evenings and they avoided the most difficult mountain roads.

After a refreshing opportunity in Widow Bevan's family and attending a Meeting they rode to Neath where they found 'some people who were called to seriousness'. This was in an area of great activity with Iron Forges and Smelting Works for copper and brass; also many coal-mines, all near a navigable river to Bristol, which encouraged trade with that port and other places in the Kingdom. At Neath there was a ruined castle and an abbey of well-known historical significance, to where Peter Price from Marazion in Cornwall was to move his family business some years later.

On 30th August, accompanied by Elizabeth Reece, they travelled to Cowbridge and were with a 'Valuable Frd Elizabeth Edwards'. They finally met with Richard Reynolds and his daughter Hannah Mary and travelled with them to Bristol where they 'drank tea with Hannah Stephenson and visited Fds in affliction'. On 6th September they rode to Frome where the Circular Yearly Meeting was held at which 'Frd Nicholas Waln from America appeared'.

Frome was situated to the east of the Mendip Hills, and the surrounding countryside was pleasing with valleys and uplands, good farms and woodlands of the country estates. On 10th September they were at Melksham for an evening Meeting in which 'Divine regard was manifested and Edward Jeffries accompanied them to Salisbury to attend a weekday Meeting'. By the 12th they had reached Devizes in the evening for 'a Meeting chiefly of People of other Societys'. This large and prosperous borough had a considerable trade in manufactured wool, and held one of the best markets in the county; also the inhabitants were, for the most part, tenants of the King.

They dined at Glastonbury and had 'a time of waiting upon the Lord', but they would not have had the leisure to look at the ruins of the famous Abbey, as their thoughts and energies were wholly taken up with their ministry, as can be seen in the entire Journal, and the question of any diversion very seldom arose. That night they reached Bridgwater, near Sedgemoor, a considerable port on the River Parrett of about 3,000 inhabitants, and where the tide flowed past in 'an impetuous manner'. Nearby, in this river, was the Isle of Athelney, where long ago King Alfred was reputed to have burnt the cakes. While at Bridgwater, Deborah and Ann had an opportunity at Cousin Ball's, who was a brother-in-law of

Richard Reynolds, and they then travelled to Taunton, visiting families for several days. Taunton was a well built town of considerable trade in serge and other woollen materials set in a fertile area known as Taunton Dean.

They were at Wellington by the 20th of the month and visited families there for a period of three days. This was an active Meeting in a pleasant place of four principal streets. On 22nd September they rode to Milverton where William and Ann Byrd met them and they had an opportunity in Meeting on the subject 'It is better to trust in the Lord than to have confidence in man'. The next day they were in Cullompton on their way to Exeter where they attended morning Meeting, then, in the company of many rode to Kingsbridge, a small place having a good cattle market and a harbour well situated upon an inlet.

On 30th September they were at Beer and had a sitting with Roger Trefny, his wife and children. The next day they rode 39 miles to Parr and on to Redruth a day later. This town was situated in the midst of a tin mining area and they lodged with William and Catherine Phillips 'who received them most kindly'. They spent a few days there attending morning and evening Meetings with their hosts, leaving on 5th October for Penzance to attend Quarterly Meeting, staying there with Grace Dennis. Next day, at a Meeting for Worship, Deborah stood up first and had 'to commemorate the Blessing of living Elders being preserved in the Church, which proved the efficacy of Grace'.

They were at Marazion Meeting on the 7th and spent the next day with their friends Anna and Peter Price. Marazion Meeting was a very early one and the little Meeting House, dated from the 17th century, had been built in local stone with the Burial Ground adjoining. On 9th October they were with the Prices at a weekday Meeting at Penryn and Deborah had to point out 'the work of Redemption as a deep and inward work'. This port had a great trade in catching and curing pilchards for export and also in the manufacture of serge. Several streams ran through the small town so it was particularly well watered.

By 11th October they had reached Falmouth where they soon concluded that 'nothing short of going from house to house would be an acceptable service', and they therefore spent the next few days in carrying out this work. Falmouth was a considerable sea port, a place where the packets sailed to and from America and the West Indies. There was a fine harbour dominated by two castles originally built by Henry VIII, one at St Mawes and the other Pendennis Castle.

They left to ride to Mevagissey on 16th October, where they found the 'Life of Religion seem'd low'. The day after they held a Meeting at [St] Austell and stayed with Thomas Fox, where 'waiting upon the Lord with the family was resorted to'. Going to Wadebridge the next day they called upon a family in a lonely situation and had a satisfactory Meeting, and at

Port Isaac Deborah found that they 'departed under a thankful sense of unwarranted kindness'. Accompanied by Edward and Robert Fox on 22nd October they reached Liscard and in [St] Germans on 21st they 'had a sitting in a family to some relief'.

Ann seemed able to stand up to the tiring journey well, although she was of an older generation. The country they were travelling in during the autumn days, although often very beautiful by the rocky coast, could be windswept from the ocean, and the rides, some after dark, were very difficult on the steep roads as the days shortened. By 24th October they had reached Plymouth where they entered 'the arduous engagement of visiting families'. Plymouth situated at the mouth of the Rivers Tamar and Plym in a bay called Plymouth Sound, was capable of receiving 1,000 sailing ships. It had been a great naval port over the centuries and an active trade was carried on to all parts of the world. The Eddystone Lighthouse off the harbour mole had, nine years before Deborah and Ann's visit, been rebuilt by a Mr Smeaton, and they must have seen the light in the night sky, a beacon of hope and warning which must have been of interest to them. Their task accomplished they left for Newlyn visiting families and then went to dine at Park on the 29th October before going on to Exeter, which they reached on the last day of the month. Here they carried out family visiting with varying success.

In this city, which was a crossing place of main roads from all directions, the newer types of transport were in evidence. There were stage coaches, elegant private carriages; some cabriolets, a type of vehicle fairly recently imported from France; as well as the covered waggons, carrying goods and drawn by six or more horses, the leaders with bells on their harness and the waggoners wearing smocks. There were also many riders and country carts of all types passing in the streets. Away in the rural areas on side roads and lanes, the strings of pack horses were a more usual sight, as the lanes were often far too narrow for the larger wheeled coaches and carts to use, and so the traffic outside the main towns remained much as it had been for most of the century.

In this west country, particularly, the banks bordering the narrower roads and lanes were very high, just as they still are. The earth cleared from the base, continually churned up by the passing of men and animals, was piled on to the banks thus increasing their height and deepening the minor roadways.

By 5th November they were riding to the north of Devon and lodged with Thomas Milward, sitting 'with Friends and some of their Neighbours' to whom 'the Gospel Day in which we live was pointed out'. An evening Meeting followed in the Town Hall at Torrington, situated on a steep hill above the River Torridge – one of the finest sites in Devonshire. Ann first spoke 'in interceding for a Blessing on the People, after which Ann Byrd had to speak on Womens' preaching', and Deborah 'had many Gospel Truths to convey'.

Returning to Exeter on 7th November 'thankful for the Blessing receiv'd' they continued their family visits, Deborah having 'open times in families although silent in Meeting'. They spent a 'forenoon agreeably' at Uffculme with the Byrds and were again at Wellington in Thomas Fox's family having a satisfactory opportunity in which 'seeking the Lord and his strength was affectionately recommended'.

They attended Meeting at Milverton in the morning, followed by a public one in the evening. On 14th November they rode to Bridgewater 'accompanied by several Fnds'. During the next days they visited Cullompton, Sherborne and Bridport, where they lodged with J. Pilnes on the 19th and on to Poole where A. M. Neave kindly received them. On 24th November they 'rode to the House of our Valuable Fds Thomas and Jane Shipley' having an opportunity with their neighbours which proved satisfactory. Poole was a considerable port near the borders of a heath, and traded with such diverse places as Newfoundland and the West Indies. A great quantity of fish and oysters were also pickled and barrelled here for export. On the 26th November they reached Shaftesbury Meeting where Deborah ministered, and rode on to Marnhull arriving at Bristol by 27th November.

They visited Frenchay Meeting and the school; Deborah seldom missing a chance of being with the young. By evening on 4th December they were at Cirencester Meeting in which 'Henry Wilkins, the American Friend, minister'd'. Next day there was a weekday Meeting at Cheltenham and in the evening one at Tewkesbury. They rested at Worcester, receiving 'a kind reception from our Dr Fds the Bevingtons'. The company of these cousins of the Fords always afforded Deborah great pleasure and there are many mentions of them in her Journal.

They held an evening Meeting at Bromsgrove on 8th December and another at Dudley on the 9th, and by the 10th they finally reached home to be 'affectionately received by my relations, which, with every other favor calls for humble walking before the Lord'.

They attended Monthly Meeting at The Dale and gave in their certificates and Deborah speaks of 'feeling a degree of peace in looking back upon my late journey'. The 29th December she spent at The Bank 'reading Brother Richard Reynold's manuscripts', but she does not say of what these consisted. She also records that for some weeks there had been a 'severe frost', which always caused much hardship in the community and must have been exceptionally severe for her to have mentioned this state of the weather in her Journal.

1784

. The first few weeks of 1784 were sad for Deborah as she received the news of the death of Mary Galton – 'She was truly amiable and much beloved by me'. Mary was an unusual and attractive person to young and old, but her life had been rather difficult and she had suffered bad health for some time.

At the end of January little Edmund, not yet two years old, then went up to The Haye in order to be innoculated with his cousins. Young Samuel, his brother, had been sent to Buildwas for this, as was his father before him, but evidently the smallpox innoculation was now thought possible to be carried out safely at home. Abraham and Rebecca Darby had three children, Abraham aged six, Ann five and Mary four, but it is not possible to know how many of them were innoculated with Edmund. Most probably the youngest one as this protection would probably have already been carried out on the older children.

On the 7th February Deborah recorded that 'my dear husband return'd from London', but by the 15th February she was troubled by a cold and was kept from Meeting for some days, but she hoped that her 'mind was turned unto the Great Object of Worship'. She was better by 14th March and at Shrewsbury dined at A. Clarke's and brought Rebecca Young back to Sunniside with her, and from then on can be seen the gradual beginning of Rebecca's ministry, encouraged step by step by Deborah. Little did either of them realise how far this companionship of thought and action would take them in the long years to come, and through what unaccustomed surroundings. Here Deborah expressed thankfulness in being 'favor'd with health'. She had found that silence had been much her lot of late but hoped that she might now have 'discerning times and seasons'.

Deborah and Susannah Appleby went to Bromsgrove on 5th April and 'attended Select Meeting in the evening'. Next day was Quarterly Meeting and George Boone and J. Grey appeared, and Deborah 'in the Womens' Meeting had a share of public service'. She came home on the 7th by Stourbridge, where at Meeting she had to 'minister unto some states'.

On 20th April she was again in Shrewsbury to meet Timothy and Hannah Bevington and Sarah Stephenson who had arranged a Meeting there that evening as the two women were on their way to Ireland. Sarah Darby and Deborah on 29th April set out in order to attend the Welsh Yearly Meeting at Rhayader, and in the company of Martha Routh and other Friends went on to Newtown and Llanidloes in which 'Martha had acceptable service' to which Deborah made some addition.

They reached Rhayader on 3rd May for 'dinner and met many Friends', and she said of these days 'in select Meetings some weighty remarks made, the Meeting of Friends owned by the Wing of Ancient Kindness being spread over us and some living testimonies borne'. In the Women's Meeting Martha Routh was 'very instructively enlarged'. The first Public Meeting was 'solid, the testimony of Truth flow'd freely'. Several English Friends were there and they took part. Dear Dorothy Owen spoke in Welsh and her subject was 'Plough up the fallow ground of your heart and sow not amongst thorns'. In the afternoon two Meetings were held at the same time – Deborah having to open a Meeting at the Barn where Henry Wilkins, Thomas Waring and Martha Routh were also engaged to 'espouse the Cause of Truth'.

At a Public Meeting on 6th May, 'our principles were largely spoken unto by John Townsend and others' and she had 'an opportunity after dinner with some Welsh Friends to good satisfaction'. On the following day they rode to Ludlow, a distance of 45 miles, and were a 'good deal fatigued': fortunately the spring had come and so the weather in that hilly country made travelling easier to support, but the long ride over the very poor roads and tracks of that period, up and down steep gradients, was formidable. No doubt they had sturdy horses used to such work, but the fatigue of this travel must have been considerable even in the month of May.

Soon after their return on 16th May, Mary Rathbone and Sarah Darby left Sunniside to accompany Joseph Fawcett, a Rathbone relative who was consumptive, to the Bristol Hot Wells. Their journey was undertaken to try and help this young man (but he was near the termination of his mortal illness). The waters were, at that time, considered beneficial for that particular malady.

Deborah attended local Meetings and it was after a Meeting at New Dale on 6th June that she went to dinner at John Young's at Horsehay. It was possible that the Young family had a dwelling which they all used when they were in the Severn Gorge as well as their home at Shrewsbury. On 28th June, after dining in Shrewsbury, Deborah went on to Welshpool accompanied by Rebecca Young and other Friends, and then to Llanidloes for the Quarterly Meeting on the 30th, but on the way back, she became unwell and only reached Shrewsbury with difficulty and was 'thankful to get home to dinner on 2nd July'.

She continued sick and confined to the house, but the nature of her illness is not disclosed.

Cousin Joseph Beesley and his wife, accompanied by the wife of Thomas Newman, then came to Sunniside on 14th July and spent one of the days at The Haye with the Abraham Darbys. Deborah was again attending Meeting 'under a deep sense of weakness' It is not clear whether in her mind or body, or both.

Richard Shackleton and his daughter Mary, with Anstice Sparkes came on 26th July on their way back from the south to Holyhead. No proof has yet been found of a relationship between these families, although they called each other 'cousin' and were very close friends. Robert Barnard, Deborah's brother, and Mary Shackleton kept up for a time correspondence on poetry, exchanging verses as Mary wrote well and Robert also appeared to have a good deal of talent. She became a friend of Deborah's and was an interesting person, later to marry William Leadbeater, a young foreign language schoolmaster at Ballitore, her father's school. The Shackletons left on 9th August for Ireland by the usual Holyhead route.

After Monthly Meeting at New Dale, Deborah, with Rebecca Young, dined at Horsehay and on 21st August Deborah, Samuel, Sarah and Susannah Appleby went to Worcester where the following day, in the afternoon, there was the burial of Jane Thresher. 'The Meeting was much crowded as was the opportunity at the house of mourning' later. Deborah's relations then went back to the Dale and on 23rd August she went on to Tewkesbury for the Select Meeting. On the 25th she and Thomas Waring attended Quarterly Meeting before continuing on to Gloucester. There, Thomas called a Public Meeting, as he always arranged such occasions wherever he went.

When Deborah arrived home again on the 28th August she was not well and was laid up 'poor in spirit'; she also found that her mind was depressed from various causes, and hoped 'the eternal God is still my refuge'. However, she was fit enough again on 10th September to leave with Abiah Darby and Susannah Appleby for Yearly Meeting at Shipston, which they reached the next evening and found lodgings with some difficulty. On 12th September, in the morning, George Boone and Thomas Waring had the chief service, and in the afternoon 'Mother and Thomas Colley'. Two days of Meetings followed and they returned home again on 16th September.

Unfortunately on 21st September Deborah became ill once more, this time with a 'nervous fever' which she described as a 'time of much suffering'. There is continued evidence in the diary that she was not feeling as well as usual during the autumn, and there were also fewer entries, indicative of less activity and of ill-health. She was unable to attend Meetings and Samuel went to Quarterly Meeting in Shrewsbury at the end of the month without her, but by 24th October she was able to go there with Sarah, and they sat in with some families during the following two days, returning home 'with sweet evidence of peace'.

Deborah was taking up her normal life again and took part in the burial service of Joseph Fawcett who 'closed an innocent life in much peace'. Thomas Waring had come up from Leominster to be present and was 'acceptingly engaged'. But she was again prevented from attending Monthly Meeting at New Dale on 17th November by continuing ill-health; however, she sent a written request for a certificate to visit Wales, so her illness could not have been considered really lasting or serious.

Another sad occasion occurred on 24th November when 'the remains of Cousin Susannah Ford was brought to Sunniside'. She had been living in Worcester and several Friends from there attended and the next day 'they accompanied the Burial to Salop [Shrewsbury] where, after a solemn Meeting, the corpse was interred'. Evidently she had asked to be buried beside her parents. Timothy Bevington who was a cousin of Susannah's 'had an awakening opportunity at the service'.

On 26th November, Deborah and Rebecca Young set off for Wales, so her illness must have been completely over for her to undertake such a journey. John Young, Rebecca's father, accompanied them from Shrewsbury as far as Welshpool and they went on to Tythynegarrick arriving on 27th November.

1785

In January they visited families in Wales and Herefordshire and were 'favor'd with support and preservation through many difficulties' returning home in peace at the end of the month.

Deborah described this time by saying on the 30th January 'My Dear Companion, Rebecca Young, and myself visited the families of Fds in Wales and Herefordshire in which we was favor'd with support and preservation through many difficulties. Returned home in peace the end of the 1st mo. having been out since the 11th mo. 24th 1784'.

In February she attended local Meetings finding that 'it has been a low time with me of late, but I greatly desire the Lord's Hand may not spare nor his Eyes pitty until he has made me what he would have me be'.

On 3rd April, Deborah attended General Meeting at New Dale then journeyed on the 9th to Dudley to see an old Friend, James Payton, who was ill, attending Meeting there before returning home. However, on 15th April, she, Samuel and Susannah Appleby left for Welshpool – a place always haunted for them by the historic memories of the persecutions of the Thomas family's antecedents, who, with the Lloyds of Dolobran were held in an obnoxious gaol. It was now a welcoming place, built on a pleasant hillside where Friends could come and go in peace. They went on to Machynlleth meeting many Friends and holding two Public Meetings, one in the Market House in which 'our Dear Frds Nicholas Waln and Patience Brayton were favor'd to proclaim the acceptable Day of the Lord'.

They then rode on to Aberystwyth where 'they found pretty good accommodation'. It was a place of trade in lead, ore, wool, fish and oak bark. The walls and castle of the town were in partial ruin, having been the scene of much fighting in the civil war of the previous century. Wales Yearly Meeting began on 19th April and 'was satisfactory', they also had 'soul uniting season' in their Inn. Returning they stopped again at Machynlleth where Patience had appointed a Meeting and then made a long day's journey to Shrewsbury on the 23rd, which they performed with 'tolerable ease'.

After attending Meetings there Deborah returned home only to leave again almost at once, for at the beginning of May she was engaged 'in attending Yearly Meeting in London at which were many Friends from America – Dear Samuel Emlen, R[ebecca] Jones, R[ebecca] Wright, J[ohn] Pemberton, W[illiam] Matthews, besides N[icholas] Waln and P[atience] Brayton and Ann Jessop. It was thought to be a Meeting owned by the Company of the Great Head of his own Church'.

On her return to Sunniside she found, on 5th June, her 'mind, after a season of Trial, enabled to commit all unto the Lord, and in the ability received to improve under every dispensation'. On the 6th of June there was a Meeting at the Dale 'in which we had the company of our Dear Friends Richard Shackleton, his daughter Sarah with James Abel from Cork'. Their visit was made on the way home from Yearly Meeting in London and they spent the best part of a week at Sunniside – a great pleasure for Abiah as she always found the friendship of Richard agreeable and inspiring. They left by the coach from Shrewsbury to Holyhead seen off by some of the Darby family.

After a week's illness Samuel's aunt Rachel Thompson died on 18th June. She had expressed the wish to be buried near her husband at Newcastle-upon-Tyne, so on 24th June Samuel and others accompanied her remains as far as Ivetsy Bank, Samuel returning the same night to Coalbrookdale. Rachel was the last of Abiah's own Maude family and though Rachel in her widowhood spent in Coalbrookdale had proved to be a difficult member of the family, Abiah would always treasure memories of her sister and their youth together in Sunderland, so Rachel's death left a void for Abiah, bringing with it the increasing realisation of mortality.

During the last weeks of June and early July they attended only local Meetings, but on 15th July Deborah accompanied Abiah, Sarah, and attended by Samuel Sankey went to General Meeting at Atherstone in Warwickshire, and two days later also to Bosworth for a Public Meeting which 'had been appointed' for Abiah, returning home the following week.

The last day of the month Deborah found 'we continue living witnesses of the Lord's goodness, who still careth for us every way'. August came and the harvest was being gathered, and on the 14th of that month 'our valuable neighbour, John Fletcher, was removed by Death and made a peaceful close'. He had been of immense influence in his lifetime but latterly had suffered much ill health. He and Abiah had differed on religious matters and had had encounters and arguments over the years, but they had long respected and valued each other and had inaugurated Sunday Schools together in the Severn Gorge. John Fletcher's influence for good had been very great in the area and further afield, as an early and close follower of John Wesley. Now Mary, his widow, was to remain at Madeley and endeavour to carry on some of his work for the rest of her life.

During the remainder of the month and into September, the usual pattern was followed, of attending local Meetings and Samuel was mentioned as accompanying Deborah on her journeys. On 27th September they were at Quarterly Meeting at Welshpool. On 10th October, suddenly 'in the evening we were agreeably surprised to see W[illiam] Rotch and his son Benjamin from Nantucket,[9] America'. The next day 'they had a comfortable opportunity with him [William Rotch] at Ann Summerland's'. They also visited at The Bank, for the Rotches, besides being Friends, were engaged in whaling both in Nantucket and much nearer in Dunkirk, France. They were, in all probability, therefore, doing business with the Coalbrookdale Company, as a product of the whale oil they produced was used for some machinery and over the years Richard Reynolds appeared to be in touch with this particular family.

Rebecca Wright and Martha Routh also came during the Rotch's visit, and these women Friends then made several family visits with them, and by the 18th were still 'engaged in the same good work of breaking bread from family unto family'. On the 19th October they all attended Monthly Meeting in Shrewsbury returning next day. Deborah then accompanied these Friends to Dudley and Stourbridge and on to Birmingham where were also Rebecca Wright, Ann Jessop, Mahetable Jenkins and Martha Routh and they all 'labor'd I trust harmoniously in the spreading of the Truth'. Deborah herself also 'had some public engagement'. They returned to the Dale on 1st November bringing Mahetable Jenkins and Ann Jessop with them to stay. Unfortunately a day or two later Mahetable fell ill and had to be nursed at Sunniside for some days. Deborah went to Shrewsbury with Ann Jessop on 11th November and met there William Matthews, an American, and they each had 'favorable seasons both amongst Friends and in a Public Meeting appointed for them in the evening'. On returning to Sunniside they found Mahetable better; William Matthews had come with them and he appeared in their weekday Meetings. He had a solemn pronouncement to make, which was sometimes voiced, that 'some present would not be long in time'.

On 14th November 'Our Dear Frd left us' and during the remaining days of that month Deborah went to all the local Meetings, finally going up to The Bank on 5th December. Next day Richard Reynolds accompanied her 'in a chaise' to Middlewich in Cheshire, for Quarterly Meeting, returning back to The Bank by way of Nantwich, Deborah finding that 'Brother seems satisfied with his journey'.

Deborah was again at The Bank on the 11th of December with Susannah Appleby on their way to Leeds Quarterly Meeting, going again by Cheshire, to Morley and Stockport Meetings. They attended a funeral in Manchester, followed by 'an agreeable evening with John Routh and his sister S[arah] Taylor'. They then rode on to Huddersfield to John Hustler's where they met with Mahetable Jenkins and Mary Davis and had an 'opportunity after supper'.

On the morning of the 23rd December they were at Bradford and 'attended a Public Meeting in the evening, in both of which ability was afforded to convey many Gospel Truths'. They were later at Benjamin North's house and next day attended Select Quarterly Meetings at Leeds. At Meeting for Worship Deborah 'stood up first, after which Rebecca Jones had a favor'd opportunity – other Friends also engag'd as they were in the Public Meeting and those for Witness'.

The 29th December was spent 'amongst agreeable Frds' and a Meeting was appointed by the Friends from America in the evening. They then went to Ackworth School[10] 'accompanied by Esther Brady and were favor'd together both in the Public Meeting and when the children were collected in the evening'. Deborah closed the year by being with the young in this successful school, undoubtedly to her satisfaction as education was always of interest to her wherever she went, and it was at a period when the instruction of youth was becoming more widespread.

1786

On 8th January, after spending a week at Thomas Doncaster's at Sheffield, they attended Meetings, travelling on to Leek on 9th January, lodging at Monyash – 'the snow rendering the roads almost impassable'. They were, however, able to reach Hare Gate the following day where they were warmly welcomed by the Tofts, finally reaching home on 11th January and, although they found the family well, the weather continued to make travelling to Meetings very difficult.

Deborah spoke a little of being at New Dale on 15th February 'where I had council to hand to a rising generation'. She then went to Dudley on 16th of the month, accompanied by John Young and his daughter Rebecca, attending in the afternoon the burial of James Payton who had died after an illness of several months. 'Timothy Bevington and many other Friends were there' and Deborah held a public testimony in Dudley next day 'on the Purity of our Principles'.

When they returned home she and Mary Rathbone had the pleasure of a long day spent at The Haye. These visits to Abraham and Rebecca Darby and their family were always delightful to her – there was a farm on the doorstep and the children could play there, although she never said whether sometimes she took little Samuel and Edmund to enjoy a few hours with their cousins. The views of the Severn Gorge from the house were very fine, looking over the countryside towards the slender arch of the now famous Iron Bridge spanning the River Severn to the west, which could be seen against the sky.

The Iron Bridge had already become renowned and was visited by many travellers to the north-west and Wales as the coaches now had a stopping place there from London. This meant also that the Darbys were receiving increased numbers of guests to see this wonderful construction.

In spite of happy days like this one at The Haye, Deborah was going through a period when her 'mind was often much sunk', and her feelings fluctuated between 'no more [being able to] speak in the name of the Lord' and being 'unexpectedly raised up and for Zion's sake can no longer hold my Peace'. She expressed that she was again grateful, as she had often been before, 'in having ancient experienced servants continued amongst us', meaning Abiah and Ann Summerland who provided an ever present assurance of stability in the family circle of Friends.

Their Meetings on 12th March were 'measurably owned' and they had 'Thomas Marks and Joseph Harvey from Ireland' at their house. There were a number of Meetings to attend all through that month, including Quarterly Meeting at Shrewsbury 'in which we felt our Heavenly Father's love to the uniting of our spirits'. The same pattern of life continued through early April, as she attended 'our Meetings as they came in course – tho' it was often my lot to sit in silence'. She also 'at times had to speak well of my Heavenly Father who had done so much for me'. Three days later at Shrewsbury they had the acceptable company of Rebecca Jones and Sarah Grubb with them.

By the end of April Deborah felt her 'prospects increasingly turn'd to other parts of the Vineyard, – my ability to labour amongst my Friends at home seem'd at times very small'. James Birch and Phoebe Blakes from Leeds were at Coalbrookdale weekday Meetings at the beginning of May, and 'George Dillwyn from America and Martha Haworth from Lancashire had an Evening Meeting with People of other Societys'. On the 3rd May the next day they were all at the Shrewsbury Meeting.

The Friends then left for Wales reaching Ludlow in the morning and Leominster in the evening. A large company of them travelled on to Monmouth on 6th May, and next day there was 'a Meeting in the Town Hall in which the Love of God was felt to flow freely to the People'. Thomas Waring, Rebecca Young and Deborah also had a Meeting at Troy in which 'we felt the Good Will of Him that was in the Bush'.

Deborah appeared to be travelling with Ann Summerland, but she does not say so until later. They went on to Cardiff where they met Friends from different parts of the country and also North America, including Rebecca

Jones, Sarah Grubb from Ireland, Henry Wilkins, and Thomas Rutter, together with others also gathered there for Wales Yearly Meeting. On 11th May an appointment was made among women Friends 'to pay a visit to the Meeting for Discipline in South Wales', and Deborah found she was 'one of the number separated to this Work'. In the parting Meeting 'Frd Rebecca Jones was largely and livingly engaged to labour with the Members of our own Society'.

On 12th May, 'Friends found an engagement to have a Meeting at Newport', and they reached Bristol that night where Ann Summerland and Deborah lodged at Thomas Rutter's. They spent the next day with Friends, whom 'amongst others was Catherine Phillips'.

The Meetings on 14th May 'were very large and appear'd like a season of renew'd visitation to many, especially the Youth'. Unfortunately, Deborah was indisposed, but next day managed to attend the Meeting for Business in the afternoon.

George Dillwyn and Rebecca Jones had 'eminent service' on the 16th. Ann Summerland and Deborah then 'called on several families and had some refreshing opportunities'. On the 19th, accompanied by 'Dr George Dillwyn and many other Friends had a favor'd Meeting in the evening at Thornbury'. Martha Haworth was also with them. The following day they held a large evening Meeting at the Booth Hall in Gloucester in which 'George Dillwyn was eminently favor'd' and Deborah and Ann Summerland were also 'able to publish the glad tidings of salvation'.

Next day George Dillwyn and Martha Haworth went to Bristol, and Deborah and Ann travelled to Worcester, attending Meetings there on 21st May. After spending the following afternoon with Friends, they rode to Kidderminster where on the 23rd they had a 'Satisfactory Meeting held at The Lion'. Samuel, who had met them at Worcester accompanied them home.

Journey to North of England and Scotland
2nd June 1786 to 30th January 1787

Hardly had they returned to Sunniside when Deborah, accompanied by Ann Summerland, set out towards northern England and Scotland 'in a one horse chaise' on 2nd June. They first went to Nantwich in Cheshire on June 4th, but found that 'the roads being heavy made it tedious'. This was a large and well built town in an area where much salt was found which provided a local industry with wide trade.

The following day they reached Northwich, finding there only a few Friends and went south again to Middlewich near the borders of a forest of that name where 'several not professing with us, gave us their Company'. On 6th June at Macclesfield, they also found 'the Life of Religion seems low'. Here many of the inhabitants were occupied in the silk mills and the manufacture of articles of dress.

When they arrived at Stockport next day on 7th June they became more hopeful for there 'appear'd to be renewals of Youth', and they also spent time with 'Friends to good satisfaction'. Stockport had become a very important place for the manufacture of cotton from the east. The arched stone bridge over the River Mersey had been built here to replace an earlier one, destroyed to impede the march south in 1745 of the army of Prince Charles Stuart from Scotland.

They journeyed on to Low Leighton, Morley and Frandley and attended 'a very small Meeting' at Newton, finally on 14th June, reaching Chester the county town of Cheshire, situated on the River Dee where much trade was carried on with Wales and Ireland. It was a very ancient walled city and important from the time of the Romans, where some streets had been hollowed out of the rock, in places to one storey below ground level and where, from the town walls, there was a fine view of the surrounding countryside. A description written shortly after their visit had the observation that 'the gates, streets and Cathedral here have all a very remarkable appearance, that a stranger, on entering, must be struck with awe and admiration'.

For Deborah, however, 'Chester Meeting afforded occasion for enquiry "By whom must Jacob arise, for he is small"'. On 15th June they were at Sutton finding there 'a small remnant concern'd for the cause of Truth'. They were at Warrington in the morning and Penketh in the afternoon, and travelled on to Bickerstaff on the way to Liverpool. After spending the morning of the 19th June 'amongst our Fnds' they returned to Warrington, and two days later attended Ashton Meeting. Next day at Langtree Meeting they found 'a very valuable Minister near 80 years of age' called Alexander Parkinson, whose company they found 'reviving'.

On 23rd June they reached Edgworth and went on to Bolton that evening. Next day they rode to Manchester, spending the evening with the John Rouths and attending both morning and evening Meetings there next day. They reached Oldham on Monday where many non-Friends were present at Meeting, then on to Haslingden, Crawshay Booth, Marsden and Sawley. By 2nd July they had reached Settle in the North Yorkshire Dales, a region Deborah knew well, having Birkbeck relations there. They visited many Meetings and families in that district – Airton, Bentham, Lancaster, Preston, Wray and Windemere.

General Meeting followed at Grayrigg 'a time of invitation to the Youth', as was an evening Meeting at Kendal. Once there they were accompanied by some of Deborah's relations to Yelland on July 10th where after a Meeting they visited families. She does not give the names of these relations, with some of whom they were no doubt staying. The name Yelland,[11] with the additions of Conyers Redmayne and Storrs, covered these villages set along a hillside with fine views over pastoral countryside towards Ingleborough. The Meeting House was the ancient one in Yelland Conyers, and had had to be restored after a fire in 1737, but substantially remained the same except for the newer 18th century sash windows. There was a gallery and panelling, and the whole had an atmosphere of deep and abiding peace as well as antiquity. A day school was close by across the Friends' Burial Ground, but Deborah does not record that they visited the children. Then followed on July 24th and 25th Meetings at Wray and Wyresdale, but they found that 'Life of Religion was very low in those parts'.

They continued their journey by visiting Friends at Preston and Lancaster and were with seven families in Ashton. William Rathbone III was, by then, travelling with them and they returned to Liverpool and began a very strenuous round of visits, 46 in number 'where support extended and help in the needful'.

At the end of July they were back in Kendal and spent August visiting Meetings in Yorkshire and Cumberland. At Ulverston on 2nd August Deborah reports sadly 'I hope there is still something left worth visiting – there is a want of that zeal which so distinguish'd some that formerly belong'd that Meeting'. Their visits included Crook and Height Meetings, Cockermouth, Pardshaw, Whitehaven and on to Broughton on the 24th August where she remarked without amplification 'Had a sitting in a Fds family where a young man was particularly addressed that Died soon after'.

By the 28th August she reached Keswick, continuing to Maryport, Allenby and Holme, where she hoped the Meetings 'tho' rather low' were 'not unprofitable seasons'.

On 1st September they reached Wigton where an evening Meeting 'was largely attended'.

Visit to Scotland

From here they travelled north into Scotland where Deborah says 'was at all the Meetings of Friends and spent one day in Glasgow in all which we had satisfaction – tho' in many places the Life of Religion is low and we was often brought in the deep searching of heart'. They had entered upon this journey with hope and expectation but evidently the weeks spent in Scotland had turned out to be disappointing and Deborah gives no specialised account of her time there on this particular journey.

However she did write to Sarah Darby from Newcastle, in a letter dated 2nd October, giving a few more details of the Scottish journey than in her Journal. 'Thou will have heard of me getting back to Edinburgh, by a letter I wrote my Dearest Husband from there on 3rd day last, and through the same protecting *care* we got here on 7th day night stopping at a Meeting at

Kelso on our way and lodged at Jane Waldo's, who was well and made very affectionate enquiry after you all, and in a particular manner our Dear Mother Darby from whom she would be very glad to have a letter, but I told her it was rather difficult for her to write. We met a very welcome reception from M[ary] Ormiston and her daughter. We was at both the Meetings yesterday – on the morning Meeting my Dear Companion had an open time. I said a few words but did not throw off my burden – the afternoon was a silent Meeting. Today we are going with M.O. [Mary Ormiston] Junior in the chaise to Durham to Quarter Meeting and on the 4th day intend returning here again when I hope way will be opened – but at present mine is quite closed up as to how we may be disposed on after the Quarter Meeting. We find, by enquiry, the roads [are] bad in Northumberland that we cannot go to all the Meetings in the chaise – that if we go at all it must be on horseback. We hear George Dillwyn is expected at Durham.'

They returned to Newcastle on 30th September.

At the beginning of October Deborah had had a letter from Samuel, before writing to him 'this day week before it [Samuel's letter] reach'd my hands my heart had been truly sorrowful, sympathising most tenderly with Dear S.A. [Susannah Appleby] on hearing of her Brother's failure of the Truth of which there is much certainty – but intend leaving this unfinished 'till I get to Durham in hopes of hearing more particulars'.

She continued the letter on the evening of the 2nd October, saying 'they had found Susannah's Aunt Hannah well and that Susannah's brother Edward was at Liverpool'. She seemed to think 'he had been very ill-used by the Master he put in his ship', and she 'has no doubt of the honesty of his principle, but that endeavouring to gain more he has lost a certainty – I am sorry for him – and wish his affairs may turn out well'.

'At Newcastle I saw none of our Relations except Captain Maude's widow, who seemed well. I shall probably see Cousin Thompson's on our return, but as they were not at Meeting suppose they was out of Town. Since writing the above, George Dillwyn, Sarah Grubb, Elizabeth Hoyland and Margaret Atkinson just called in which we are very glad of – they lodged at an inn – so that there will likely be several Strangers tomorrow.' She sent her love to Samuel and said she intended writing again soon and finished her letter, saying 'Mary Ormiston and daughter desired dear Love to Mother Darby and all our family as doth H[annah] A[ppleby]'.

Deborah also wrote a letter to Susannah Appleby on another page, full of sympathy over her brother's difficulties and news of her family. She also sent her love to Elizabeth Houghton and Rebecca Young and 'the servants'.

They then returned to Newcastle on 12th October 'finding nothing would bring peace – but resignation to sit in their families, we gave up to the prospect', but they found this 'very laborious – many soaring above the precious witness of Truth'. George Dillwyn and Sarah Grubb were at Shields Meeting and they 'continued with their visiting until 15th October'.

After attending Newcastle Meetings, they went on the 15th October to Benfield side 'getting there with difficulty', but she gives no reason. They then went on to Winnows Hill and Coanwood Meetings, and by the 19th were at Allendale finding there 'our Valuable Frd Rachel Wigham'. The travelling was over 'very trying mountains', but whether this was still in the chaise or on horseback she does not reveal. Allendale still is a very remote Northumbrian dale and in the 18th century a journey through it in October could have presented difficulties, beautiful as the Dale is from a scenic point of view.

On the 22nd October they had Meetings at Austle and entered for the next few days on 'a visit to families in North Shields'. They attended Shields Meeting and then went on to Sunderland on the last day of October where again they began family visits. They attended Meetings there on First Day, 5th November, one of which was in the evening. On 7th they returned to Durham and next day to Bishop Auckland. Successive days found them at Staindrop and Lartington where Deborah was 'much indisposed'. They eventually reached Darlington on 12th November where they had the prospect of more family visits, but at Stockton she found her 'feelings depressed'. Deborah was a younger woman than Ann Summerland, but the difficulties of travelling late in the year at that time she found daunting engendering much fatigue.

In December they visited Ayton, Thirsk, Yarm, Guisborough, Whitby, Scarborough, Hornsey and Beverley, where on 17th December she attended 'the Burial of my brother John Dickinson – he married my sister Mary Barnard in the 8th month 1778 and she was suddenly taken away in the 4th month 1781 – leaving him two sons – there is only Barnard Dickinson left – G. Dillwyn and Esther Tuke with Sarah Grubb and my companion had each acceptable service at the Burial'.

After this they went on to Hull, North Cave, Shipton and then to York for four days, where presumably they stayed with the Tukes as she says they were 'kindly received by our Honourable Fds William and Esther Tuke with their family'.

On Christmas Eve she joined the Meeting held at Esther Tuke's school for girls in Trinity Lane (the forerunner of The Mount in Dalton Terrace, York today) and 'also . . . with the children at the school – in the evening – the Heavenly Father's Love was felt to flow sweetly'.

Return to Sunniside
1787

The following day they rode on to Leeds and continued to be engaged for a month in Yorkshire arriving home on 31st January, Samuel meeting them at Dudley. Soon after her return Deborah suffered a bad sore throat, but it only lasted a short time and she and Ann Summerland gave in their certificates at New Dale Monthly Meeting on 22nd February, describing their journey in northern England and Scotland as 'they found themselves favor'd with Peace'.

On 23rd February, in company with Samuel and Rebecca Young, she visited the prison in Shrewsbury in which 'the Love of God flow'd freely to the Poor Prisoners and intercession was made for them'. During the latter days of February and early March she continued to attend Meetings as usual, but on 25th March she 'found a concern to go to the Methodist Meeting', Susannah Appleby going with her. Her procedure was much the same as her mother-in-law, Abiah Darby, had used long ago – 'I waited until they got through their service and then was favor'd with strength to relieve my own mind. I hope to the comfort of those present'. It is possible at this time, there was less surprise as Deborah had a gentler presence than Abiah and would not have sounded so defiant or overwhelming.

At Quarterly Meeting at Shrewsbury on 29th March, there were many Welsh Friends including as so often, 'Dear Dorothy Owen' who evidently came to Sunniside with them as she was at Coalbrookdale Meeting the next day. She is described here 'as precious woman, preaching both in and out of Meetings', and on 3rd April she, accompanied by Deborah and Samuel, Sarah Darby, Rebecca Young and Margaret Atkinson, went to Worcester, 'the Female Friends intending to go by Yearly Meeting appointment to visit Meetings for Discipline in South Wales'. They attended Quarterly Meeting in Worcester and went on to Wales where their visit was carried out 'to good satisfaction', and they also attended the Welsh Yearly Meeting held at Machynlleth returning to Sunniside on 9th April. Deborah left home again on 11th May with Samuel, Margaret Atkinson and Rebecca Young and attended evening Meeting at Dudley.

By the 13th May they had attended several Birmingham Meetings and then she and Rebecca Young left to attend Yearly Meeting in London, going on to Essex for Yearly Meeting at Colchester – 'John Pemberton and Zacharia Dicks there with Ruth Fallows and other Friends – we had some share in public labour' – after this they visited Meetings and families in Essex where 'we had many low baptising seasons – yet some which were favor'd help'd us on and kept us from fainting'. They went on to visit Meetings in Suffolk, Norfolk and Lincolnshire and families in Highflatts in Yorkshire, coming through Cheshire 'home in the 9th Month, the 17th day'.

Monthly Meeting was held at The Dale on 19th September when Deborah and Rebecca Young gave in their Certificates with an account of their visit to the Eastern Counties. A week later at Quarterly Meeting at Shrewsbury they had their 'much valued Friend John Lewis from

Haverfordwest' who came on to Coalbrookdale and attended Meeting there, evidently staying with them at Sunniside 'to our edification and comfort'. At Shrewsbury again on 16th October they found their 'Dear Friends Jane Pearson from Cumberland and Martha Haworth' who were 'much favor'd at Meeting'. These Friends then came back to Sunniside and were at their local Meeting on 28th October also.

Rebecca Young and Ann Summerland were then granted Certificates for a journey to visit Warwickshire and Worcestershire; Rebecca's father, John Young, and Deborah accompanied them as far as Stourbridge at the beginning of the journey on 24th November. Deborah herself visited Bewdley where two days later at Joseph Cotterill's 'good was near'. – She reached home on 27th November and that evening James Birch from Cheshire and James Brandwood from Lancashire arrived to stay and attend their Meetings. At the end of the year Quarterly Meeting was held in the Dale and several Friends from Wales came as they had done before for this occasion, Dorothy Owen among them, as had been her custom.

1788

The usual pattern of their lives at Coalbrookdale continued throughout the early part of January and Friends Hannah Stevenson and Mary Davis, were at Meeting on 2nd January which was held in silence. Later in the month James and John Birch and John Brandwood are mentioned as being at a weekday Meeting and having a Public Meeting that same evening of the 22nd January.

On 24th February Deborah and Rebecca Young undertook a short visit on horseback to Worcester, where they were kindly received by Thomas and Hannah Bevington. During their stay they visited the prison and found that 'some poor prisoners appeared much melted into tenderness', the like of which Deborah had not seen on any similar occasion. These shorter journeys were to be the beginning for Deborah and Rebecca of many months of travelling together for thousands of miles on both sides of the Atlantic Ocean, and they were evidently each other's perfect companion under all circumstances, however difficult.

The next chapter will deal with their concern at this time to visit Ireland, but before they left, they went to New Dale Meeting three weeks after their return from Worcester and by 15th April Friends were arriving on their way to Wales Yearly Meeting, and John Townsend, Alice Baker, Mary Gurney and Sarah Byrd all stayed at Sunniside and travelled on to Leominster where they met others going on to Hay-on-Wye for this occasion held there from 15th to 17th April.

Dale House   Burial Ground

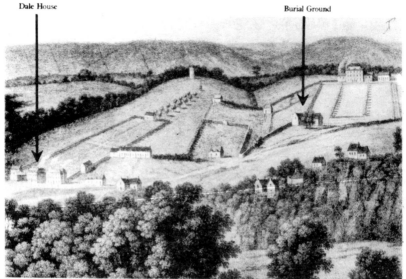

*Friends Burial Ground, Coalbrookdale, right of centre on steeply sloping hill to left of
Sunniside top right. Dale House and Rosehill with smoking chimneys on left.*

NOTES

[1] Sunniside is pictured on the front cover of Rachel Labouchere's book *Abiah
Darby*. See also illustration of Darby Houses of Coalbrookdale on p. 10.

[2] A copy of this book of Isaac's poetry, given to Samuel when young, still exists in
the Ironbridge Gorge Museum.

[3] *Hannah Rose's account* is one of the main sources of information on the early years
in Bristol and Coalbrookdale. Now in the Ironbridge Gorge Museum.

[4] Now in the Ironbridge Gorge Museum.

[5] Now in the Ironbridge Gorge Museum.

[6] Ketley Bank, normally referred to as *The Bank* was the home of Richard
Reynolds.

[7] Ackworth School near Pontefract, Yorkshire, founded 1779 for the education of
Friends' children. Today one of the eight Quaker boarding schools in the country.

[8] As spelt by Deborah in her Diary.

[9] Edward Starbuck and brother Nathaniel migrated to Nantucket Island, off the
coast of Massachusetts in 1659, along with some 20 other families. They
developed a whaling industry, hunting the sperm whale as far as the Falklands.
With the outbreak of the American War of Independence in 1775, the 5,000
Quakers of the island refused to support either side, and their trade suffered
badly. Tariffs were applied by Britain on American goods, which ruined the local
whaling industry. A move to Nova Scotia brought them within a Colony again,
but success was not assured.

[10] Ackworth School – see note 7.

[11] Now spelt Yealand. Still extant.

PART TWO

The First Irish Visit
21st April - 31st July 1788

TOWARDS THE BEGINNING OF 1788, Deborah and Ann Summerland felt the time had arrived to bring their concern before Friends to visit Irish Meetings and families, so on the 21st February they sought their Meeting's permission to carry this out and were encouraged to undertake their journey to Ireland.

They received their certificates for this at New Dale Meeting on the 19th March, and next month set out for Ireland accompanied by Samuel, going on board 'a Packquet' at Holyhead on 23rd April and landing at Dublin two days later where they were 'hospitably received by Joseph Williams and family'. These particular Friends gave a welcome to many visiting Quakers landing in the Irish capital, and Sarah Stephenson in her Journal of a few years before, mentioned their kindness to her when she arrived there much indisposed after a difficult voyage.

Deborah and Ann then attended Meetings for Worship and Discipline, the latter 'proved reviving opportunitys – some minds tendered under a sense of the Love of God'. Many of the Irish Quakers had been soldiers in Cromwell's army in the middle of the 17th century and had settled in Ireland after leaving the forces, and in time joined the Society of Friends.

They had suffered along with the whole country during the Civil War, which existed in Ireland at the end of the 17th century, some even having their property pillaged to the value of thousands of pounds but very few joined the armies of either side. By the 18th century some had been able to settle more peacefully in Ulster, Leinster and Munster, where they prospered as farmers and shopkeepers, and became respected inhabitants of the community. In the 18th century more emotion was shown outwardly than in some later times and tears were not uncommon in public.

Dublin Yearly Meeting ended at the end of April and on 1st May Samuel, accompanied by many Friends left for London Yearly Meeting, sailing in the evening for Holyhead. Ann and Deborah stayed on for Meetings in Dublin on 4th May; attended a burial and also had a sitting at their lodgings. They left for Ulster on 5th May and reached Rathfryland in the evening and found it 'a place which proved rather discouraging'. They were also to find at Ballyhagan three days later that 'many appear to be too little acquainted with the seasoning virtue of Truth'. They went on to attend Meetings at Moyallon, Lurgan, Hillsborough and then to Newtown, where Meeting was held at Thomas Bradshaw's house as it was a 'place of but few under our name'. Thomas had 300 acres of land clear of tythes near Newtown in Co. Down. Several Meetings took place at Lisburn and there 'some Gospel Truths opened to People of other Societys'.

They travelled in a variety of ways, riding on horseback, using a two-wheeled vehicle of the light curricle type pulled by a strong 'chair' horse, or by coach where these ran between places of greater population. They were at Ballynderry by 18th May, which was 'very large and solid but great desolation had crept in by mixed marriages'. They went further north and attended a Meeting at Antrim on the 19th and the day after were at Lower Grange where 'my Companion and our Valuable Frd John Gough had a good opportunity'. John Gough had a school in Limerick with his brother James; they were both able men and had taught in Cork, Mountmellick, Dublin and Lisburn. John's *Practical Arithmatic* published in 1773 was used for over a century: he had also written a *History of Quakerism* and previously the brothers had written a *Practical Grammar* published in 1764, first compiled by James and revised and enlarged by John: a well used book.

By 21st May they reached Ballinacree not far from the north coast: 'a poor little Meeting', but Deborah found it 'not from under the notice of the Holy Head of his own Church'. This was followed by a very satisfactory Meeting at Coleraine. After this they turned south and went on to Toberhead and reached Charlemount by the 25th visiting Castleshane next day, but at Coot Hill on the 28th they found 'but few that profess'd with us'. Crossing the border into Leinster Ann 'had to minister pretty largely to the People' at Old Castle Meeting and at Edenderry, which they reached on 1st June, 'the call went forth loudly unto faithfulness that the places of the Elders already remov'd might be filled up by a worthy succession'.

On 2nd June at Timahoe Meeting they found they had to call upon some 'that appear'd to be in their stronghold of carnal wisdom'. Next day at Rathangan they visited sick Friends and attended Meeting there, where 'after a long time of silence a Door of utterance was opened and some minds tenderly affected'.

They next turned west and from 4th-7th June attended Meetings at Baltiboys, Newtown, Carlow and Kilconner, reaching Ballitore by the 8th June where the 'help of the spirits of our Valued Fds Richard and

Elizabeth Shackleton and some of their children was felt comfortably', and they were to have 'their most precious opportunities amongst Fds at that place'.

There were four Shackleton children: Abraham II; Margaret who married Samuel Grubb in 1776; Mary, a gifted authoress who also wrote poetry, who married William Leadbetter, one of her father's assistant masters, and Sarah who became a minister.

The Shackletons, influential Quakers, were not plain Friends, though the women wore the Quaker bonnets. There was, of course, no music allowed in their home. Water at that time was not safe to drink, and teetotalism was more or less unknown before 1840, so some families, as they did, brewed their own ale. In 1798 they were to be much involved in the uprisings and endeavoured to keep the peace between Protestants and Catholics; and indeed over 100 united Irishmen and their dependents were given shelter by Abraham Shackleton II in his home.

They must have had much to discuss with these Friends and Deborah would wish to bring news of them back to Abiah. Mary Shackleton was in correspondence with Deborah's brother, Robert Barnard, over an exchange of poetry, and the Shackletons had visited Sunniside several times.

Next day they moved on and attended an evening Meeting at Athy which was 'an exercising season'. During the next few days they travelled on to Ballynakill, Knockballimaher in Queen's County and north to Mountrath where the Meeting was 'pretty large and to some instruction'. By the 15th June they reached Mountmellick where a small Quaker school had been established and where the 'honourable Frd Mary Ridgway resided'. Meetings were attended there and then they went on travelling north-west to a small Meeting at Tullamore before going to Moate in Connaught on the 17th where 'renewed visitation was extended to a rising generation', and after a Meeting at Ballymurray, attended the following day the Province General Meeting at Moate which ended on 22nd June where they were 'favor'd with the lifting up of the light of God's Countenance upon us'.

They then turned south again for Birr and Kilkonnil Moor, followed by a 'low Meeting at Roscrea where some appeared to have lost the Dew of Youth'. (Presumably an elderly congregation.)

Moving south-east to Limerick they felt restored and by the weekend arrived on 29th June at Cork for a three-day Province Meeting which 'was one of favour'.

Cork was a large city, where the first Meeting House had been built in 1677 and rebuilt in 1777, just a year before Deborah's visit. Its prosperity of the early 18th century diminished towards the latter decades in spite of an increase in the food trade in the early 1780's. Famine and disease became prevalent at that period and the poor had no reserves to tide them over. Friends, however, being thrifty and careful, gradually assumed positions of financial security: they were trusted by the local authorities, who borrowed money from them and treated them as some of their more important citizens.

Unfortunately, this satisfactory state of affairs amongst Irish Friends did not last, as the larger families who had bought properties to rent found themselves unable to do so, and in consequence lost income on their capital investments. Friends who had been a wealthy and prosperous group earlier were, by the time of Deborah and Rebecca's journey, beginning to be affected by these financial difficulties.

They went on further south to Bandon on 2nd July where they held a good Meeting and then turned back to visit Youghall, where they had a mixed reception 'but doctrine drop'd as dew upon the faithful'.

Returning to Cork on the 6th July for two days where 'some faithful labour was bestow'd', they then travelled on north to Garryroan for 'an opportunity at a Friend's house, [where] my dear Friend E. Pim appeared in a few words much to the satisfaction of her Friends'.

Their journey then led them east, along the River Suir, to reach Waterford on 13th July.

Waterford being a large and very busy port, Friends living there were a wealthy, thriving community during the middle decades of the 18th century, and ships sailing for North America via Bristol were freighted with cattle and corn, and frequently carried young Irish labourers who sailed to work for a season in the New World, some remaining to form migrant groups in America.

There was also trade with Newfoundland, 60-80 ships sailing annually, carrying three to five thousand passengers. Trade also developed with Norway in exporting hay from the rich, fertile area along the banks of the Suir flowing from Clonmel to Waterford. Friends were much involved in all the main activities of the place, cotton mills, ship and timber yards and flour mills built along the banks of the Suir.

In addition there had been a village constructed for the housing of a work-force, ahead by about a century of a later development built by Friends near Birmingham. Penroses, Malcolmsons, Watsons, Jacobs, Gatchells and Ridgways were all prominent in the commercial life of Waterford during the 18th century.

These well-to-day families had as a rule large fine houses, entertaining Friends and their visitors on business, much in the same manner as was carried on in the Darby houses of Coalbrookdale.

Deborah would therefore have known and mixed with Waterford Friends in their heyday, before the dangerous political strife which set in during the 1790's.

They only stayed in Waterford, however, for two days, journeying on further west to Ross, where they 'met with some valuable Friends of whose Company we were glad'. They next went down to nearby Forest and then started their return north by Randles Mills and Cooladine before reaching Ballintore, where they had 'some satisfaction', though further north at Ballinclay on first day, 20th July, they were 'help'd in measure to express our feelings, which on some accounts was painful'. They must have had a similar experience at their next stop at Ballicane 'where the Life of Religion is low'.

On reaching Wicklow they met again 'our dear Friend Sarah Shackleton, [youngest daughter of Richard and Elizabeth Shackleton, retired Schoolmaster of Ballitore School] who met us and appear'd in a few words in a family. This was only the second time of her publickly expounding the cause of truth', although she was to become a minister.

On 27th July they were back in Dublin for Yearly Meeting where before leaving Ireland for home they held a Meeting with Young Friends, after some precious opportunities amongst other Friends.

In Ireland, Monthly, Province, Quarterly and Half-Yearly Meetings were occasions only to be missed for the most serious reasons. Friends gathered in Dublin in May and December, both assemblies being called the National Half-Yearly Meeting until 1797, when it was decided to call the May Meeting 'the Yearly Meeting of Friends in Ireland' and set up a Committee to deal with matters arising between Yearly Meetings. The relationship with London Yearly Meeting was close since Irish Friends sent representatives to attend and answer any queries, which meant accepting the discipline of London Yearly Meeting.

The way into England from Holyhead had resulted in the visits to Coalbrookdale of a number of Irish Friends over the years, and generally a pattern had emerged, as can be seen in Journals of visiting ministers, of certain families who always gave hospitality on their route over several generations, as the amount of travelling was always considerable.

The last week of July was spent in Dublin attending the different Meetings, one of which was 'with the young People', and 'after some precious opportunities amongst our Fds' they started for home.

Return to England 31st July 1788

Deborah and Ann left Ireland accompanied by Samuel Elly in the evening of 31st July on a vessel for Liverpool where they landed on 1st August. They then attended Meetings there in which they felt peace, and still accompanied by Samuel Elly together with William Rathbone III, who had joined their party, they travelled to Chester in time for evening Meeting. Next day they went on to Shrewsbury attending the evening

Meeting at John Young's house, where presumably they stayed. Here Samuel and Sarah joined them, Deborah expressing her feeling that 'they were mutually thankful in being permitted to meet again'.

August

They reached home on 6th August 'where they were affectionately received by their Fds'. Next day they had to part with their 'beloved Frd Samuel Elly who had come with us from Ireland'. Deborah 'greatly desired he may be rewarded for this act of Brotherly kindness' for he had evidently escorted them just to help them with their crossing of the sea. They went to Shrewsbury again on 12th August accompanied by E. Houghton and Deborah 'had some remarks to make respecting Fds shutting up their shops'. This no doubt, refers to those who were (or were not) prepared to close them in order to attend weekday Meeting.

At Monthly Meeting on 20th August, Deborah and Ann Summerland gave in their Certificates 'expressing our thankfulness for the mercys and blessings dispensed to us in our late Journey'.

Once back at home Deborah resumed her usual activities and when Dorothy Owen and Rebecca Young set out to visit Cheshire and Staffordshire, Deborah and John Young accompanied them as far as Stafford where they attended Meeting and also had a Public Meeting in the evening in the Town Hall. Deborah returned for New Dale Meeting on the 27th August and was afterwards at The Bank where she found Mary Davis and Priscilla Gurney, a cousin of Elizabeth (Gurney) Fry, on a visit there. In 1791 Priscilla was to make her home with Richard and Rebecca Reynolds in Dale House to where they had moved in 1789, and she remained there with them until 1804 when Richard returned to Bristol after Rebecca's death.

September

Deborah again attended New Dale Meeting on 3rd September with Ann Summerland, and the day after accompanied the Reynolds and their guests to Shrewsbury to General Meeting where several of them were engaged to speak. She was again in Shrewsbury on 21st September on her way to Wales with Rebecca Young and Dorothy Owen, the intrepid walker who would go as far as 40 miles on foot in the Welsh mountains to attend Meetings. They attended Monthly Meeting at Dolobran and Quarterly Meeting the day after, returning via Wolverhampton which they reached on the 28th to hold a Public Meeting.

October

After a Meeting at Stourbridge, they left to attend Quarterly Meeting followed by a Meeting for Ministers and Elders, leaving for Bewdley and Worcester for weekday Meeting on 5th October. Ruth Fallows and Ann

Byrd were present, and they 'had opportunities in First Day Meeting'. The following day they had a Meeting with the Youth and a 'favor'd Meeting at the School'. On their way home they travelled to Bromyard and Leominster, and by 19th October they had reached Coalbrookdale and 'sat the Meeting in silence'. That evening Sarah Stephenson came to stay and the day after had a 'sweet opportunity with our dear Children' and stayed for several days. Deborah also mentioned that 'Sarah had an encouraging season at Meeting and a memorable occasion at Brother Rathbone's'. This would have been at Dale House to which William and Mary had moved in 1780 and where they were to spend some years.

November

By the middle of November Rebecca Young was with them attending most of the Meetings with Deborah. Susannah Appleby and Ann Summerland were also present.

December

On 4th December, there befell a great family sadness, as young Abraham, 10 years old, the eldest son of Abraham Darby III and Rebecca Smith, died suddenly at Sunniside of 'a putrid fever' after only two days' illness. Deborah said of him 'he was an agreeable thoughtful child, and happily taken from evils to come'. He had been living at Sunniside for several months in order that he could be taught with the other children – some his cousins – as The Haye proved to be rather far off for him to attend the lessons arranged for Friends' children in Coalbrookdale. The little boy was buried on the 9th December and Deborah says 'The Dear Child was Buried this morning – we had a solid Meeting and an opportunity after Dinner'.

Thomas Waring and Rebecca with her father, John Young, were with them that week. Thomas was active as well in local Meetings, and they had a Meeting in Broseley on 8th December.

On the 24th of the month – Deborah's father, John Barnard, having been indisposed for some days – they sent for Dr Darwin, he being the chief doctor in Shrewsbury (son of Erasmus Darwin and the father of the famous Charles Darwin). He was an intelligent and skilled man and was always called in by the Darbys when they needed a second opinion, but on this occasion he gave them 'little hope of John Barnard's recovery'.

1789.

Quarterly Meeting was held on 1st January and that day Ann Rose was buried. As in other years Dorothy Owen, Richard Brown, with others, were present in Coalbrookdale, leaving for their homes in Wales on 2nd January.

Death of John Barnard

Deborah's father John Barnard continued to be very ill during the first days of the new year and died on 10th January. 'My Endeared Father closed a Life (that had been attended with much anxiety) in sweet Peace', Deborah wrote. She had found him an affectionate father and a sincere Friend. Unfortunately she was now confined at home by illness, but in their evening sitting was able to 'encourage the young People'. The funeral took place on 13th January in the Friends Burial Ground on the hillside in Coalbrookdale and Deborah was able to share her own family grief with her mother and brother, and also with her sister Rachel, who had been with them since 4th January. She expressed herself by writing 'It was trying to commit to the silent grave the remains of an Endeared Connection, but the consoling hope that our loss was his gain supported us in a good degree of Resignation'.

At the end of the month Martha Haworth and Martha Routh were with them and attended local Meetings, also going with them further afield to Shifnal and Wolverhampton where, at the latter, a Meeting was held at 'The Swan Inn' on 1st February. On 8th February Deborah was in Birmingham and called on Friends' families; Susanna Boone is mentioned as being 'exceedingly kind and attentive' to them and so it is possible that they lodged with her, although Deborah does not specifically state that this was so. Her companion on this short visit was undoubtedly Rebecca Young, but again there is no mention of her name. Two days later they both returned home and immediately placed 'their concern before Friends at the Monthly Meeting to visit Lancashire'.

Lancashire Visit

February

During February Richard and Rebecca Reynolds made their move to Dale House, leaving William and Hannah Reynolds to live at The Bank and Joseph at Ketley Hill, as Richard had made over much of the running of the Horsehay and Ketley part of the business to his two sons.

Young Samuel sustained an accident on the 23rd when he was thrown from his horse – children rode from an early age when their parents were able to provide for them to do so. This fall must have been a serious one or it would not have been mentioned, for he was described as having 'narrowly escaped with his life'. In the early days of March, however, Deborah was able to be in Shrewsbury staying with the John Youngs, so the effect of this accident cannot have been lasting.

March

On the 10th March Deborah wrote 'Brother Darby ill in a fever which caused much solicitude on his account'. Abraham up at The Haye had developed scarlet fever – also Rebecca his wife had suffered simultaneously an acute ulcerated sore throat which, although not appearing to be from the same cause, prevented her from looking after him herself. The whole situation grew rapidly very distressing and dangerous. Susannah Appleby went up to The Haye to help nurse the invalids, followed by Sarah Darby who was concerned for her brother and wished to care for him. Abiah herself was also unwell at Sunniside, but fortunately Mary Rathbone was able to be with her. It is difficult perhaps to understand how Deborah could be going away at this time, leaving Samuel in these very anxious family circumstances, but the sudden onset of his illness and the fact that Susannah and Sarah were already at The Haye appeared to provide the help required.

On 12th March, Deborah and Rebecca Young received their certificates for their journey, and although the former did acknowledge 'that it was distressing to my feelings to have the prospect of leaving home when my Brother Darby continues so ill', they began their journey on the 14th March, calling 'at The Haye to take solemn leave of my Relations', journeying on to Leek and Macclesfield, where 'in the latter place' they 'found that the life of Religion is low'. This town was known for the making of silk materials and the prosperity showed in the fine buildings in the civic centre; part of their journey would have been through a large adjacent forest area called by the same name.

Death of Abraham Darby III, 20th March 1789

They went on to Stockport and from there to Manchester for the 18th March, where they intended to visit families, and it was here they received 'a distressing account of Sister Darby having caught the fever'. However, they continued with the family visits, in number about 36, and on 29th March the dire news reached them 'of Brother Darby's death' which had occurred on 20th March; understandably they 'sat in silence at Meeting'. Deborah's only comments were that she was 'much depressed on account of the loss and Sister Sarah's illness', but she did not feel 'at Liberty to go and share it personally with them'.

April

Martha Haworth and Martha Routh then came homewards to Manchester 'having been up to The Haye and brought a better account of Sarah' by which Deborah 'was somewhat relieved'. She and Rebecca then left and had two sittings with families belonging to Oldham Meeting, and on to Edgeworth for more family visits. They continued their journey via Crawshawbooth and Marsden to Lawley, where they arrived on the 17th April in the morning, reaching Newton in the afternoon.

A satisfactory week followed with a Meeting at Kendal on the 21st April, and on the 24th 'there was a Meeting for conference which went on for six hours but did not seem tedious by virtue of the great truth circulating amongst us'. They then spent some of the following days visiting Friends' families at Yealand Meeting, where 'Cousin William Rathbone III joined them and accompanied them to Lancaster on 26th April'. The Meetings were particularly favoured in the person of an ancient and valued Friend, Anthony Mason, who 'spoke on the text "I have slain them by the word of my mouth"'.

The 'remains of my Uncle Dilworth was inter'd after the afternoon Meeting and in the evening Sarah Taylor and Martha Routh had a solemn opportunity in the family'. During the last days of the month they visited families at Height Meeting and went to Ulverston where they 'invited a rising Generation to follow the footsteps of the flock of Christ'.

May

During the first week of May they visited eight families at Swarthmore and Colthouse, and by the 5th May they were at General Meeting at Grayrigg which 'was a time of invitation to the youth'. The evening Meeting was held at Kendal. Here Deborah was amongst her mother's relations, but she did not say with whom they stayed, only that several of them accompanied her and Rebecca to Yealand. They then visited seven families at Wray and also held an evening Meeting there.

They continued visiting families during the following days, finally finding at Wyresdale that 'the life of Religion is very low in these parts'. The week of 10th May they visited families in File, Preston and Laughtree (Lancaster), and were at the Ashton Meeting, Cousin William Rathbone being with them. On the 17th they sat in silence at Liverpool Meeting, and in the evening had a family visit there, continuing with attendance at Monthly Meeting, and finally visiting as many as 46 families.

On 24th May they were still in Liverpool and engaged in both Meetings and 'felt some relief of mind and acceptance in late labours'. They went to Ashton next day, attending Meetings and visiting several families; they were later at Warrington and this time E. Jolly accompanied them. They attended Penketh Meeting and from there were at Framley on 5th June which she described as being 'small but regarded by Infinite kindness'.

June

The next day they were met by John Thorpe, returning home by Middlewich and Nantwich, and finally arrived at Sunniside on 10th June, where Deborah was alarmed to find my 'Beloved Husband much indisposed'. This can hardly have been surprising, as the sorrow over Abraham's death must have overwhelmed him in his delicately balanced condition of health; also Sarah would have been unable to give him her support as she was only slowly regaining her own strength after the fever.

The rest of the week after Deborah's return proved for her a 'time of deep conflict', as it was evident that Samuel was again disturbed in his mind.

On the 14th June several Friends from Ireland paid them a visit, but unnamed: they were returning from Yearly Meeting in London. At Monthly Meeting on 17th Dorothy Owen 'had acceptable service' and they gave in their certificates.

During the second half of June they went to Shrewsbury and on to Llanidloes. On 28th June Deborah wrote 'Not withstanding the continuance of trials I get out to Meetings', knowing that 'those who wait upon the Lord shall renew their strength', but the rest of the month and into July continued to be a time of great stress for her. The following weeks were also difficult, and there was also the sad news that on 10th August Cousin William Rathbone who had so recently been travelling with them was 'removed from works to rewards'. Deborah esteemed him a 'pillar of the Church'.

August

Robert Fowler then came to see them from Melksham on the last day of August. He was apparently keeping in close touch with the Darby and Barnard families as he was courting Rachel Barnard, who spent much time at home with her mother who continued to live in Coalbrookdale. Deborah went to Shrewsbury with Priscilla Hannah Gurney, who was staying with the Reynolds at Dale House and who 'Help'd to labour in both Meetings there'. September was taken up with Meetings in the Dale and 10th October saw them at Worcester, where next day they attended a Meeting at Chadwick and were 'favor'd with the sweet cementing influence of Truth which greatly humbled the minds of some young people'.

October

On 12th October the attendance at the burial of Friend, Sarah Newman, was 'very large and solemn' and they also called on some Friends when 'the love of God was shed abroad amongst us'. The following day they were at Stourbridge, returning home that day. A week later they attended Monthly Meeting at Shrewsbury on 21st October 'in which Rebecca Young and myself laid a concern before Friends to visit families in Norwich and Yarmouth' which they received. They also went to the prison where they visited 'a father and son under condemnation'.

Northwich and Yarmouth Visit

On 15th November they began this autumn journey by breakfasting at The Bank, now lived in by William Reynolds, Richard's eldest son, and his wife Hannah Ball. Richard and Rebecca were to accompany Deborah and Rebecca Young as far as Birmingham, and they began the journey by visiting Shifnal Meeting where they found Timothy Bevington. They then called at Bilston to see Samuel as, during this attack of illness, Deborah was apparently allowed to see him herself.

On 20th November at Birmingham they attended a Meeting at which were two marriages and 'had favor'd opportunity in a Fds family'. They then went to Coventry and on to a Meeting at Hartshill where 'the youth were invited to follow the footsteps of the Flock'. At Hinckley on 24th November, they were able to have Meeting with the town's people in the evening, which she described as a 'refreshing season'. They attended a marriage at Atherstone next day in which at 'table after dinner, a rising generation was invited to bind themselves to God by Sacrifice'. On the 26th they were at Grooby Lodge, a Quaker School, and had a 'comfortable sitting with them in the Evening'.

On 29th November, they 'finished our visits to the families at Leicester Meeting and went on to Oakham' They sat through a silent Meeting at Spalding, but had a 'comfortable opportunity with some young people' there and had another Meeting next day. Their journey continued by Gedney and Wisbech where they were 'comforted in the renewed visitations extended both there and in some seasons of retirement'. After visiting Swaffham they arrived at Norwich, on 12th December, but Deborah does not say with whom they stayed. However, she was very satisfied with their visits to the families in that city, and in the Meetings there. At both Meetings on 20th December she sat in silence 'but Edmund Gurney edified us with his labours'.

December

They spent the rest of the year there at other Meetings and Deborah records 'my companion and myself had each some counsel to communicate'. They attended Quarterly Meeting on the 31st December, and Deborah ends her narrative for 1789 with the words 'What can I render for all the benefits received'. The earthly difficulties had been considerable, but she had received spiritual comfort which was precious to her above all things.

1790
January

Deborah's first words in 1790 were of her invariable wish that 'the year begins with desires to be increasingly devoted to run the ways of the Lord's requiring with alacrity'.

They attended Meeting on 2nd January, then parting from their Friends in Norwich they lodged 'in another Friend's house in the country'.

On 10th January, they went to Meetings in Yarmouth, and on to family visits, 28 in number, in which they were engaged for several days.

They attended Meetings at Pakefield, and later, on the 13th to one at Woodbridge in the morning, and one at Ipswich in the evening. At Needham, 'a want of faithfulness seemed to hurt the Meeting'. This appeared strange as this Meeting was the one to which the Alexanders, living in the neighbourhood, belonged.

Next day at Bury (St Edmunds) Dykes and Mary Alexander were with them, and they all had 'a share of the Public Labour'.

On the 19th they were at Sutton in the morning and Chatteris in the evening. Deborah always appeared to make light of difficult travelling; this winter journey in wheeled vehicles was probably more easily undertaken than those of a generation past which were mostly on horseback and frequently extremely difficult as floods and freezing conditions often made the roads very dangerous.

They were next at Earith and Swavesey going on to Ramsey where were old abbey ruins, a church, a large mansion house and pleasant dwelling houses: here they went on with family visiting, with Dykes Alexander guiding them through the low-lying fertile countryside where the villages and small towns stood out as distant silhouettes against the pale winter skies as they travelled from place to place.

They reached (St) Ives on 27th January where they also 'saw three families' and returned again to Earith and Sutton, also Littleport and Ely, where they found 'the truth in a suffering state'. Ely, with the ancient and beautiful cathedral, standing out from a distance across the Fen, on a winter afternoon particularly if snow had fallen, would appear spectacular – and was always a landmark for travellers. They then visited Wisbech on the last days of the month and went back to Chatteris again, reaching Huntingdon on the 31st January for further family visits.

February

They were at (St) Ives again on 1st February, and there next day they parted with Dykes Alexander who had accompanied them from Bury.

On the 5th February they reached Wellingborough where they found Elizabeth Hoyland, and were at an evening Meeting at Banbury the following day, where with William Symonds and John Abbott, they had 'testimony to bear'.

Burford Meeting on 7th February was solid, and they had an opportunity at the School in the evening. Deborah also had a pleasing interview 'with my own Beloved Children for whom I felt much solicitude, as well as for others'. The next day they were at Charlbury Meeting and then went on to Chipping Norton and Long Compton in the evening, after which they 'parted with our Dr Frd John Abbott'.

On 10th February they attended a Meeting at Shipston, and on the following day at Alcester Meeting they were 'afforded renew'd occasions to admire the mercys of God'.

On the 14th they went to Meetings in Birmingham, 'in which, and on some occasions of Retirement in Families, the Heavenly Wing was spread over us', and the next day they were at Dudley Monthly Meeting, accompanied by Mary Lloyd. After visiting Bilston, they returned home, and at Monthly Meeting on the 21st gave in their certificates. Next week at Salop Meeting on the 27th Deborah found 'Heavenly Regard was manifested, to our refreshment'.

March

On 3rd March they attended the burial of Sydney Owen in Wales, 'had a solid opportunity in the graveyard'. She was sister 'unto our Beloved Dorothy Owen, and an innocent well-minded young woman'.

They also attended on 5th March one Meeting at Dr Owen's house at Dolgethly [Dolgellau] 'a season of favor'.

Returning home Deborah 'sat in the New Meeting House for the first time, being General Meeting' on 7th March. This was the last Meeting House[1] to be built in Coalbrookdale, and had been erected largely due to the help of Richard Reynolds on the same original site as the earlier one. On 14th March Deborah and Susannah Appleby were at Stourbridge Meeting, 'in which we felt our minds united to those who are standing for the Cause of Truth'.

Monthly Meeting was satisfactory on 17th March, 'was also sweetly overshadow'd after Dinner'. A Friend of the name of Edward Sipkin was there, who was to be frequently mentioned. In their morning Meeting on 21st March Sarah Tregellis Junior 'said a few words acceptably'.

On the 25th they were at Salop weekday Meeting, in which Sarah Tregellis, Rebecca Young and Deborah 'all had an opportunity of expressing our feelings', she herself 'was also strengthened in an Evening Meeting'.

They visited the Prison on 27th March, where Deborah found 'It is always trying to me to give up to these Services, but hitherto they have always been productive of Peace'. In their Meetings on the 28th, 'My Dr Mother Darby had edifying service'. Quarterly Meeting then took place the following day.

April

General Meeting at New Dale on 1st April 'was laborious', but Deborah added 'My Beloved Husband's company gives me much satisfaction'. On

18th April John Cash of Coventry was with them, and the following day 'John Townsend and Richard Baker were much favor'd in our Meeting, also in one in the evening'.

Monthly Meeting was at Shrewsbury on 21st April 'which was a season to be thankfully remembered'; also to some families of Friends they had 'instructive counsel to convey'.

Meetings at Dolobran and Welshpool followed, in both of which they had the company of John Townsend and Richard Baker, 'and above all the Presence of the Great Head of the Church'.

On 23rd April they attended Llanidloes Meeting in the morning with Friends, and in the evening with the people.

On the 25th the Public Meeting was 'mercifully owned. John Townsend, George Dillwyn, Thomas Waring, Timothy Bevington and myself had each a share in the labour of the Day, as well as the Reward'.

In the Select Meeting on the 26th several of the same Friends 'favor'd to communicate very instructive counsel, and our parting Meeting was crown'd with the life-giving Presence of the Master, that we may acknowledge his Goodness and Esteem, this a Memorable Yearly Meeting'.

May

A Public Meeting was held in Welshpool in the morning of 1st May and at Shrewsbury in the evening.

On the way back to Coalbrookdale, at Newtown 'George Dillwyn was much favor'd in the Meeting', and also again at Welshpool and Shrewsbury. He then came to stay at Sunniside, and accompanied by several Friends, including Deborah, had a large evening Meeting at Broseley, followed by one of similar size at Little Wenlock. He was at New Dale Meeting on 5th May, and Deborah here remarked of him 'he is indeed a well qualified servant'. Then with Deborah and Rebecca Young, they had a Meeting at Stourbridge on their way to Birmingham where there was a large Public Meeting in the evening, in which he particularly 'was largely engaged'.

Then they all went on to Warwick where they lodged, being on their way to Yearly Meeting in London. They attended Meetings, and were also in some families, and were at Eatington by 10th May and in Banbury Meeting next day, continuing by Adderbury and Buckingham. By 11th May they had reached Aylesbury, where they found the Meeting 'was low in the beginning but ended well'. Next they had 'lively Meeting among Friends' at Amersham in the morning, and a Public Meeting there in the evening, followed by 'a laborious Meeting' at Uxbridge, before they reached London about eight o'clock in the evening of 14th May.

They attended Ratcliffe Meeting in the morning of 16th May and Peel in the afternoon, which was 'not so lively', and they also had an opportunity at Sarah Pim's in the evening.

In the Select Meeting on the 17th George Dillwyn 'laid his concern before Fnds to go into Germany'. The Women's Meeting opened that afternoon, and Rebecca and Deborah attended both their Meetings next day, which they found 'instructive seasons'.

At Westminster Meeting on 19th May, Deborah herself remained silent. Later that same day, a Committee was held in the evening which 'was solid but held rather beyond it's strength'.

Select Meeting 'was own'd on 20th May and the same day several weighty subjects were spread' before women Friends.

They found the Women's Meeting lively on 22nd May; this would frequently appear to be so, giving the opportunity for many of those present to share news that was of moment from the many Meetings represented from all over Great Britain.

On 23rd May they went to Tottenham, and were also at Devonshire House and at the Women's Meeting in the evening of 24th May, the last one to be held that year.

In the concluding Select Meeting on 25th May of Yearly Meeting, 'the uniting power of Truth was felt and Friends parted under its influence'.

By the 26th May they had gone on to Leighton Buzzard, and the following day attended a Meeting at Buckingham.

By the 28th they had reached Worcester, attending Meetings and visiting some families on the way.

June

On June 6th they were at New Dale Meeting, and by the 10th were travelling to Leek for Quarterly Meeting, though they had returned to Sunniside in between to greet Richard Shackleton and Elizabeth Pim on their way back to Ireland from Yearly Meeting in London. These Friends, together with Deborah and Rebecca Young, had dined with Richard and Rebecca Reynolds at Dale House, 'and had a satisfactory opportunity after Dinner'. This would have taken place in the family dining room looking east over the Upper Furnace Pool: the works to the south, further down Coalbrookdale, were also within sight from the windows. The position of the house had been carefully chosen by the first Abraham Darby, and all who had lived there since had been closely connected with the day-to-day operations in the valley reaching down to the River Severn.

The next day Mary Fletcher, widow of the well-known Methodist John Fletcher, who had carried on as much of his work as she was able to, dined with them at Sunniside to meet their Irish guests. Deborah described her as 'a solid and truly pious woman', but on this occasion 'rather too full of conversation'. This was probably because, with the Irish Friends present, Deborah felt that at least Richard Shackleton had not had sufficient attention. They accompanied these Friends to Shrewsbury on 16th June where they attended weekday Meeting, after which the Irish Friends took the coach for Holyhead.

Samuel and Deborah accompanied Robert Fowler to Kidderminster on 27th June, and next day at Worcester dined and attended Select Quarterly Meeting at Tewkesbury, where Sarah Stephenson, Mary Powell and Deborah were all engaged.

July

They attended a Select Monthly Meeting at Worcester on the way home, and were at General Meeting on 4th July at Coalbrookdale 'in which a renew'd call was extended to those that might have stood idle all the day long, to go into the Vineyard and work'.

Samuel and Rachel Barnard accompanied Deborah as far as Tamworth on her way to Leicester on 9th July and she reached Grooby Lodge by the evening. On the 11th Deborah attended the burial of her 'Uncle Robert Burgess', where she and John Storer were engaged.

By 15th July they were back again in Shropshire, at Shrewsbury with Richard Reynolds, which she found 'a relieving season to my own mind'.

She attended local Meetings, and on the 22nd at Shrewsbury Monthly Meeting, Robert Fowler and her sister Rachel Barnard 'declared their intention of marriage'.

The following day Rebecca Young was at Coalbrookdale Meeting, and also engaged with Susannah Appleby in family visiting. Deborah accompanied them on two of these occasions, which were continued throughout the week.

August

General Meeting was held on 8th August at New Dale, and a Meeting at Broseley in the afternoon, at which Deborah 'had to bear Testimony'.

They had an evening sitting at Sunniside on 15th August where, as so often 'after a laborious day' Deborah found 'those moments precious, when the end crowns all'.

Concern to Visit Yorkshire

A few days later, Deborah and Rebecca 'acquainted Friends at Meeting on 18th August, of a concern we are under to visit Yorkshire'.

Robert Fowler and Rachel Barnard were married on 19th August. Deborah and her mother Hannah Barnard each had 'a share of Public Labour in the Meeting and an opportunity after Supper was encouraging to us'.

The Fowlers left next day, accompanied by John Matravis, Ann Fowler and Hannah Young. Deborah found 'it was trying to part with dear Rachel'. Robert was a wine merchant, and they were going to live at his home in Melksham, which was often to be visited in the future by Deborah, for she felt he was someone in the family on whom she could fully rely.

September

Local Meetings followed, and at the end of the month she and Rebecca Young left to attend Joseph Rathbone's burial at Chester. The funeral took place on 2nd September. 'Thomas Colley stood near an hour, in which Martha Routh made some additions', Deborah also had 'an opportunity in Prayer'.

They left Liverpool on 3rd September and visited families in Chester on the way home, reaching Shrewsbury on 5th September, where they attended Meeting in the morning, and reached Sunniside by the evenig, where in their evening sitting Mary Lloyd was engaged.

They attended local Meetings during the next days, and were at Stourbridge Monthly Meeting on 19th having been at Bewdley on the way. They 'found their minds engaged to attend the Young People belonging to the Birmingham Meeting' on the 21st. There followed next day a Meeting at Coventry, and they went on to Hinckley on their way to Quarterly Meeting at Leicester on the 24th, reaching Loughborough next day.

They attended a Silent Meeting at Castle Donington on 26th September, lodging later at Nottingham. Mansfield Quarterly Meeting was held the day after, where they also 'had some ability to labour among Women Friends'.

October

At Chesterfield on 1st October they were present at a Meeting which was encouraging, and from this time until the 25th of the month they were engaged in family visits in Sheffield, where Margaret Hoyland accompanied them to many of them.

Deborah was thinking profoundly of her youth during these days, remembering that 'near to this town was the place of my Birth. The Meeting in which I had been mercifully visited with the Day Spring from on High, in which my Spirit had often been contrited [sic] before Him who shone gloriously forth. Oh, how I desire a rising Generation might also be thus visited, that there might be a succession of standard bearers raised up from amongst them'.

Meeting at Woodhouse on 25th October was followed by one at Burton next day, and they were then at Pontefract, lodging at Castleford. Ackworth[2] Meeting was 'trying in the beginning but ended well' on 28th October, Deborah adding 'May the Lord Bless this Institution'.

At Meeting at Doncaster 'Sarah Grubb was present, being just returned from Germany, she seems sweetly enrich'd with peace, the result of dedication'. There they had opportunities in several Friends' families and attended Meeting at Thorne on 31st October.

November

On 1st November they had an evening Meeting at Selby where 'various states were addressed'. By the 3rd November, they were at York Meeting, where Henry and Ann Tuke 'laid a concern before Friends to visit Ireland'. A Meeting at Shipton and North Cave followed, and by 6th November they were at Beverley Meeting.

Returning to the east coast at Hull Meeting on 7th November they sat in silence, and from that time until the 14th they were visiting families there. They then went on to Owstwick and Welwick Meetings, and attended Hornsea Meeting on the 17th, 'which seemed comfortable unto the few there'. At Bridlington on 18th November they found that 'truth [was] once prosperous in this place but now there are few to support its precious testimony'.

On the 19th they had two Meetings in Scarborough 'where there are a few valuable Friends'. This place, from the time of the imprisonment of George Fox in the Castle in the 17th century, had always had a number of active Friends, including Samuel's great grandparents on his mother's side, the Warrens.

There followed two Meetings at Whitby on 21st November. At this time of the year, these places on the north-east coast could be very cold and windy, and Deborah found it 'a trying place', though her remark was only indicative of the state of religion they found there, not the weather.

On 23rd November they moved inland to Pickering, at the foot of the North Yorkshire Moors where they 'found the life of Religion low, tho' a living Remnant are mercifully preserved'. After going on to Malton they turned back to Thornton [le-Dale] on 26th November, where they were met by Henry and Ann Tuke, and 'had a solid Meeting'. They returned to York again for Meeting on 28th November, 'and sat with the children in the evening,[3] which as well as some sittings in families were seasons of favour', going north again to the Moors where they joined Meetings in the evening at Helmsley and Bilsdale on the last day of November.

December

They were again in Pickering on 1st December. The season made travelling difficult and on a very cold day on 2nd December they had a Meeting at Hutton-in-the-Hole, where some Friends had settled as early as the 17th century; the Meeting House here had a stable below it and the

Hutton Beck flowed through the village alongside the road. The next day at Castleton Meeting, despite the weather, they were 'comforted in hope that the Lord is preparing servants for his work'. They must have received this encouragement from the young. The following day, however, they were 'much dipped in suffering, tho' we hope the Good Hand was turn'd on a rising Generation'.

They returned to Thornton [le-Dale] on 6th December, and went on to Thirsk, an important posting station in the 18th century where they joined the Youth.

On 8th December they moved west, where there was a small evening Meeting at Masham, an ancient market town on the River Ure, over which a four-arched bridge had been built in the mid-18th century. On the 9th they were in Wensleydale and had a Meeting in the morning at Leyburn, from where very fine views were obtained in this wild and hilly part of the country. By the afternoon they had arrived at Richmond, a town set at the head of the steep-sided entrance to Swaledale, the most northern of the Yorkshire Dales and had a satisfactory Meeting as they had 'some ability to hand counsel in that for Discipline'. In Newton-in-Bowland Meeting 'there was a school for Friends' sons, which appears to be well conducted'. Bentham Meeting 'began by being laborious but improved towards the end'. They had a far more pleasing one at Settle, a place Deborah had always known well from staying with her Birbeck aunt, uncle and cousins.

They went south to Skipton on 22nd December 'where the language of fear-not-little-flock went forth to a few, but many are too much at ease'.

Farfield and Otley Meetings followed, (the latter in Wharfedale at the foot of the Chevin, a hill of 900 ft), a market town for the surrounding district, with evidence of occupation over many centuries.

They reached Leeds on 26th December where they met their 'Dr Friend Samuel Smith from Philadelphia, and Martha Routh: all four were engaged'. Leeds, the capital of the county and a town of much industrial activity was a place where iron had been forged since the 12th century. They were at Monthly Meeting there on 27th December, where 'Counsel was conveyed through several of us'. Next day they also were engaged in the Select Meeting held in the evening of 28th December, and Quarterly Meeting followed on the 29th and continued through to the 30th.

Deborah ended the year by saying that 'The hope of our Holy Head to his temple evidently approved'.

1791

January

On 1st January they were at a Meeting at Knaresborough which they found 'Low'. This town was on the banks of the River Nidd where the houses were built on a slope going down to the water, with the ruins of a Norman Castle above them. A linen industry which occupied many people of the surrounding countryside was centred on a mill within the walls.

Again in the Dales, a Meeting at Netherdale the next day was slightly more encouraging. However, the 'desolation' of the Society at Keighley 'afforded a gloomy prospect'. They were at Lothersdale Meeting on 4th January, where 'deep wading was allotted'; also at Rawdon Meeting where 'Truth got a degree of Victory which was a full reward'. These places in winter cannot have been always easy to reach, for the travelling was strenuous and the cold disagreeable. No doubt in these months of the year ministers who undertook such journeys required strength of body as well as fortitude of spirit.

Deborah and Rebecca then left the Dales and entered into a family visit at Bradford on 6th January, where Christiana Hustler joined them until the 10th in the city, where many of the inhabitants were engaged in the woollen trade. They were at Meeting at Gildersome on the evening of that day, travelling on to Wakefield next day where they found 'some awakened minds which proved to be some rewards'. High Flatts Meeting followed on the 12th and was 'a season to be thankful for' as Deborah was now in familiar country, her memories went back nearly 20 years to the Meeting when John Woolman had so touched their young hearts.

The Journey Home

They attended Brighouse Meeting on 13th January, moving on to Halifax, where they had some sittings in families, and here Ann and Henry Tuke joined them again. Unfortunately, Deborah became ill and could not attend Todmorden Meeting, but recovered sufficiently to travel to Manchester a day later, where they had an evening Meeting for the inhabitants 'to good satisfaction'. They were now on their way home and next day had a Meeting with 'the People at Nantwich in the evening as well as with Friends'.

Reaching Shrewsbury on 19th January they found Samuel, Sarah, and Rebecca Darby all well. They had an evening sitting in which Henry Tuke, who was visiting, was 'favor'd'; also the Tukes had good service in Monthly Meeting next day at the Dale, and on the 21st at New Dale. After attending more local Meetings the Tukes set out from Shrewsbury for Ireland on the 24th by the usual Holyhead route, Susannah Appleby going with them to accompany them through Wales to the coast.

February

For the first days of February Deborah had to stay indoors because of a bad cough, but by the 6th she was once more able to attend Meetings, going to Stourbridge on the 7th for the burial of Joseph Morris, accompanied by

Samuel, Sarah Darby and Rebecca Young. She then attended a Meeting for Samuel Smith at Dudley. He and Mary Lloyd had become engaged: and Deborah and Rebecca also visited two sick Friends after which they went on to Birmingham where again Samuel Smith was 'much favor'd'.

On 10th February they were at Stourbridge Meeting and also attended a Public Meeting at Bewdley. Evidently Samuel Smith was still with them as they were all at Worcester together on 14th February where they visited the prison, after which they parted from this American Friend and returned home to Sunniside. During the following days there were several burials, and Deborah also visited the prison at Shrewsbury on the 24th when Samuel, Sarah and Priscilla Hannah Gurney all accompanied her as well as Rebecca Young, who 'had to convey counsel'. The first funeral was at Dudley, that of Tobias Knock; the second, about which Deborah was evidently much affected, was of 'that Dr Mother in Israel Hannah Bevington' finding 'an affecting occasion to many of us feeling deeply the Church's loss'.

March/April/May

On 20th March they went from Worcester to the Select Meeting at Birmingham but returned for Quarterly Meeting at Shrewsbury on 30th March, where they 'had the company of our Dr Frd Dorothy Owen'. Robert and Rachel Fowler were with them on 3rd April when all of them dined at The Bank with the William Reynolds. By 17th April Deborah was at Tamworth with Susannah Appleby. They visited families, and travelled on to Yearly Meeting at Newcastle [under-Lyme] which continued until 21st April: Thomas Colley, George Dillwyn, John Townsend and others were 'largely engaged'. After this they returned home to Coalbrookdale together with several Friends.

They attended Builth [Wells] Yearly Meeting on 26th April, which lasted for two days, and on 29th George Dillwyn and other Friends held a Meeting at Brecknock in the morning and at Abergavenny in the evening, followed by a 'comfortable Meeting' at Uske the day after. At Bristol Meeting on 1st May Rebecca Young and other Friends were engaged, and 'George Dillwyn was particularly favor'd in the evening'. Yearly Meeting continued until 3rd May, after which they attended Meeting at Frenchay as well as a Public Meeting at Kingswood, and went on to Bath on the 5th where George Dillwyn was again 'favor'd'.

On the morning of the 6th May they had a Meeting in Devizes and in the evening at Melksham, where they stayed with the Fowlers, but in both Meetings Deborah 'sat in silence'. Monthly Meeting at Bromham the day after 'was own'd', but Marlborough Meeting on the 10th proved 'trying' to them. They had Sarah Stephenson and Hannah Wigham with them at Newbury Meeting on 11th May, after which travelling by Reading and Maidenhead, they attended Select Meeting in London on 14th May.

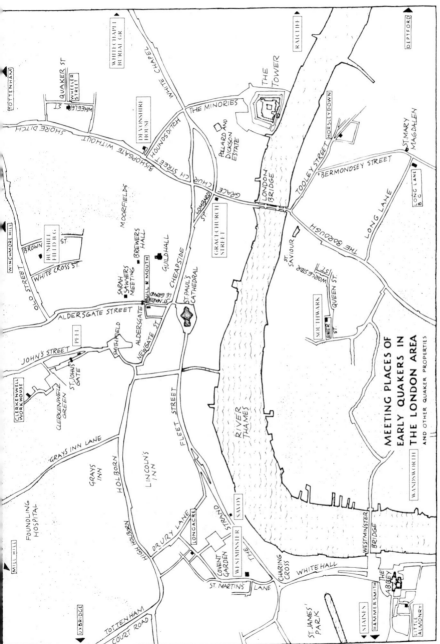

London Meeting Houses

They were at Westminster Meeting on the 15th: the day after was the opening of the Women's Meeting, followed by that for Discipline on 17th May, 'when occasion was afforded to set up our Ebenezers and say, hitherto the Lord helped us'. Weekday Meeting at Gracechurch Street [she called it 'Gracious Street' as did several others] 'was mercifully shadowed by Divine Regard' as was an opportunity in a Friend's family and the Women's Meeting. The rest of the week was spent in attending Meetings 'as they came in course', with Park in the morning of the 22nd and Gracechurch Street in the afternoon. The day after Yearly Meeting concluded Deborah commented in her Journal 'under a thankful sense that the shout of a King had been measurably in Camp'.

May/June

At the conclusion of Select Yearly Meeting on 25th May certificates were signed for 'Dr George Dillwyn and Samuel Smith who had been acceptable labourers in this land'. Deborah and Rebecca attended Meeting at Staines on the 26th and were at Uxbridge Monthly Meeting the day after. The 29th May they spent with Friends at High Wycombe and had a Public Meeting in the evening, going on to Windsor next day. For the remainder of the week they visited families at Reading, in the company of Samuel Smith and had a Public Meeting in the evening of 5th June. At Henley they were met by Hannah Wigham and Louis Majolier who lived at Congénes, near Nimes in the south of France. Later in the spring of 1797 he was to welcome and help William Savery during his visit to France.

They held a Meeting at Warborough on 7th June arriving at Abingdon next day, and reaching Faringdon on the 9th 'where Ann Crowley appeared in supplication which was the first fruit of obedience in a public line'. Here they parted from Samuel Smith, but were to see him again in his own country a few years later. They travelled on to Burford for an evening Meeting, but Deborah did not mention the school on this occasion.

Meeting at Stow on 10th June was largely attended by the townspeople, and an evening Meeting followed the same day at Campden; however 'not feeling that their minds were clear of the People' they arranged for another the following morning 'in a large room in an Inn with the inhabitants of the town'. They went on to Worcester for morning Meeting on the 12th where an 'opportunity at T. Bevington's was encouraging'. He and other Friends then accompanied them to Kidderminster for a Public Meeting in the evening.

June

No sooner had they arrived back home than Rebecca Young and Susannah Appleby 'laid a concern before Friends at Monthly Meeting on

15th June to visit the North of England and Scotland'. Deborah also was soon to be travelling once more, going to Dolobran on 26th June and on to Llanfair, and then Monthly Meeting at Denisbran on the 28th, with Quarterly Meeting next day at Dolgellau, where she dined with Dorothy Owen. During the last day of June Deborah 'sat a poor Meeting at Escergough'. They had a satisfactory Meeting with Friends at Llanidloes, where she, along with Richard Reynolds and Priscilla Hannah Gurney, had gone to 'see after a proper place to establish a school'.

July

On returning home Deborah spent the 3rd July at Shrewsbury where she had a Public Meeting in the evening. On 5th July Sarah Darby went to Melksham to be with Rachel Fowler in her confinement; as often happened to many single women in families at that time, Sarah took on the role of companion and comforter on such family occasions. By 18th July Hannah Wigham was with them and they attended morning Meeting at the Dale, with an evening one at New Dale. Hannah again contributed at Monthly Meeting at Shrewsbury two days later, and Rebecca Young and Susannah Appleby had 'their certificates signed for visiting Scotland'. Samuel and Deborah accompanied these Friends to Leek on 23rd July where they left them to go to Sheffield at the start of their journey north. The Darbys attended Uttoxeter Meeting and had another with the people there before returning home.

August

At the beginning of the month they attended local Meetings and had the company of Martha Haworth at General Meeting at the Dale on 8th August. Deborah, together with Martha Haworth and Priscilla Hannah Gurney, went to Salop 'where all had good service both in the Meeting and with families'. They were at a large Meeting in Redditch on the 14th where both Deborah and Timothy Bevington were engaged, which was followed by Monthly Meeting at Stourbridge next day when Samuel and Richard Dearman were with them.

They were present at Dudley Meeting on 17th August for two marriages. That of William Summerfield and Rachel Lloyd, and also John Biddle and Elizabeth Lloyd, where both Timothy Bevington, who was present, and Deborah bore 'Testimony to the Truth'. For the rest of the month they stayed at home and were engaged locally.

On 25th August Deborah with Priscilla Hannah Gurney had an opportunity with a man in Shrewsbury Prison 'who was to be executed an hour after, and our minds were humbled under a sense of Divine Condescension, manifest at this season'. Next day they were with the prisoners at large and found 'how wonderful [was] the Love of God even as display'd to sinners'. She was again in Shrewsbury on 8th September with Ann Summerland to see Jane Young, Rebecca's mother, 'who lay very ill' – (she was of Ann's generation).

Journey to Wiltshire and Gloucestershire

September

William Cash was at Coalbrookdale Meeting on 11th September and had an opportunity at Richard Reynolds' in the evening, no doubt staying at Dale House.

Jane Ellis was buried on 20th September and Deborah 'had an opportunity at the grave'. Next day she visited families at Stourbridge and mentioned her intention at Meeting of going to Wiltshire Quarterly Meeting. Samuel accompanied her to Melksham on 25th and they attended Select and Quarterly Meetings at Chippenham on the 28th, also weekday Meetings at Melksham, and on the 30th Deborah, Sarah Stephenson and Mary Powell were engaged at Westbury Meeting.

October

1st October found them at Bromham on the way to Cirencester Meeting, and on the 2nd they sat with families there, and Deborah added 'with the scholars of Thomas Huntley's school at Burford, amongst whom we found our dear boys well'.

At Evesham on 3rd October they attended an evening Public Meeting, going on to Stourbridge and the remainder of the week was employed in meeting families of Friends there, also at Bewdley and Bromsgrove in which Richard Reynolds and Mary Lloyd accompanied her. After attending Chadwick Meeting on 9th October they went on to Mary Burton's burial at Stourbridge in the evening, finishing their engagement with attendance at Dudley Meeting and family visits.

They went to Birmingham for the funeral of John Leppington on 12th October and had the 'company of our valuable ancient Friend Sarah Beck, whose lively communications were comfortable'. Next day they were at New Dale Meeting and attended local Meetings until the end of the month.

November

On 10th November Deborah went to meet Rebecca Young and Susannah Appleby in Shrewsbury on their return from Scotland, and by 16th they had the company of Deborah's cousin, Deborah Braithwaite from Kendal, and also Rachel Lloyd from Birmingham. On 20th November Samuel went with Deborah to Shrewsbury attending a Public Meeting in the evening. On 22nd November Samuel Sankey and Susannah Talbot were married at Meeting in the Dale.

After attending the funeral of Isaac Hawkins on 23rd November at Birmingham, Deborah spent the rest of the week there with Mary Lloyd, visiting many families, and attending yet another funeral, that of George Robinson's daughter. There was a third burial, of Thomas Evins, and a fourth at Dudley in the evening of 27th November, a melancholy ending to the month of November.

December

During December the local pattern was followed, and for the last days of the month Dorothy Owen was with them. There were nine Friends from Wales and four from Stourbridge at their Quarterly Meeting on 28th December. Next day Deborah with Dorothy Owen, Rebecca Young and Richard Brown accompanying her, was at Shrewsbury Meeting on her way to Wales.

They held a Public Meeting at Welshpool in the morning, and at Montgomery in the evening of 30th December, and on the 31st, a Meeting with the people at Newtown – the closing event of the year.

1792
Welsh Journey

January

Deborah and Rebecca Young, accompanied by Dorothy Owen, began their journey into Wales leaving early in January to travel in difficult hilly country during the brief winter days. They attended Meetings at Llanidloes, Esgairgoch, Tywyn and Lewendee; also at Dolgellau, Tyddyn-y-Gareg and Barmouth, reaching the small place of Harlech on the coast on 6th January. Here the historic castle on the rocks above dominated the whole area of the shore looking westwards. They held a Meeting there which was 'both solid and still' before riding on 30 miles to Tany Bulch on the 7th, reaching Carnarvon under the walls of Edward I's great fortress, for Meeting there at 11 o'clock on the morning of the 8th January, 'which was open' and another the next day which was 'large and released our minds to leave that place and go to Newburgh where we had a Meeting that Evening'.

A small Meeting was held at Aberdovey on the 10th January and they were 'favor'd with a satisfactory morning Meeting at Holyhead' the following day. This was always a very active port as the packets sailed to and from Ireland on most days of the week. There were a large number of inns along the main street and the whole town's population was chiefly engaged in the receipt and dispersal of people, animals and merchandise across the Irish Sea, in all the unceasing changes of wind, weather and tides. They went on to Beaumaris where they had an evening Meeting in the Town Hall; later they had difficulty in having a Meeting at Llandrust on account of it being Market Day. At Bala they had two Meetings and the last of these gave them 'comfortable liberty to leave the place'. On the 18th January they had an open Meeting in Llangollen and another at Oswestry in the evening. When they reached Shrewsbury next day they 'laid a concern before Fds at the Monthly Meeting to visit Friends in the Western Country, Dunkirk and Guernsey etc, Dear Dorothy Owen whose acceptable company we had in our late journey in Wales was beautifully engaged in this Meeting'.

By the end of January Deborah was again at home attending Meetings at Coalbrookdale; also being in a family sitting at Rebecca Darby's at the White House. She then became unwell and was not able to go out for some days because of a cold, but by 25th January was again able to sit in the family, and on the last day of the month to attend weekday Meeting.

February

She was in Shrewsbury on 2nd February, where she, Rebecca Young and others had an 'opportunity with my Beloved Mother Barnard who is much indisposed', and who the following day Deborah and Samuel accompanied to Bridgnorth on her way to Bath. Susannah Appleby and E. Talbot were going with her 'to care for her'. Deborah found that 'it was hard to my nature to part with her in such a weak state', and indeed in mid-winter this cannot perhaps have been a wise journey, however, it was hoped that the waters would be beneficial, once fatigue from travelling had been overcome.

On the 14th February Deborah attended Meetings and she and Rebecca Young had an opportunity at Richard Reynolds'. The following day at Monthly Meeting at New Dale they received their Certificates for the proposed visit to the West, Dunkirk and Guernsey. This was followed by a satisfactory Public Meeting at Wellington. On the 18th of the month Richard Reynolds accompanied Deborah and Rebecca Young to Stourbridge, and on the morning of the next day Susannah Appleby arrived and they were engaged in the Meeting as well as 'after supper at R. Hudson's'. On 20th February they attended Monthly Meeting at Dudley and had a public one that evening.

Deborah was encouraged on 21st February that 'My Dear Husband accompanied me to Birmingham, where the Meeting was graciously own'd as was some sittings in a family'; she parted with him however the following day and with Rebecca went on to Tamworth to dine. On the 23rd they sat in six families and then J. & S. Fowler accompanied them to Grooby Lodge, 'having an open Meeting at Ashby by the way'. Grooby Lodge was the school where they were to place Edmund later, but she does not give any indication of the purpose of this visit. They had a Meeting with the 'People of other Societys at Cousin Burgess' in the afternoon'.

On the evening of the 25th February they experienced a slight earthquake: the Darby family nearly always recorded unusual natural happenings such as eclipses of the sun and moon. There were several Meetings on the 26th and Robert Fowler who had joined them the day before, went with them 'a few miles on their way to Oakham'. The Meeting there on the 28th was 'open' and they lodged at Ridlington Park; then after a sitting there they rode to Kettering next day.

March

There was a Meeting at Wellingborough on the 1st March, after which they visited two families and went on to Findon, after which they finished the family visits with which they were satisfied, although it had been, as always, laborious. The Meeting at Barton was followed by a 'trying Meeting' at Northampton on 7th March where they lodged at William Simmons'. They continued their journey by Eden and Bybrook Meetings to Olney, arriving on 10th for a Meeting in the morning and visited a few Friends at Newport Pagnel. They were at Hogstyend in the morning of the next day and Leighton that evening, and accompanied by several Friends attended a Meeting at Ampthill on the 12th: next day they left for Luton and by travelling rather quickly had a Meeting at [St] Albans in the evening.

They were again in London by 14th March where they opened their 'concern before Westminster Monthly Meeting to visit the families of Friends'. They attended Ratcliff Meeting on 18th in which they 'had an open time and drank tea at Cousin Smith's'. The 20th was a very sad day for Rebecca as she had 'an account of the Death of her mother, Jane Young, a woman much respected by her Friends and neighbours and who made a sweet end'. Jane was the daughter of George Brawn who had been much in Coalbrookdale and knew well both Abiah and Abraham Darby II when they were first married: it was he who had also greatly encouraged Abiah at the beginning of her ministry.

Deborah was still in Westminster for Meeting on 23rd March, sat with families, and had the 'company of Richard Phillips to our satisfaction'.

April

On 1st April at Westminster Meeting she 'gave counsel as well as at Wilson Birkbeck's with whom we dined'. All the time they were continuing the family visits, and on 4th April 'had a favor'd visit at the Workhouse'. They attended morning Meeting on the 5th April and also went to Park later in the day, and on the 6th Cousin George Stacey and Sparks Moline accompanied them to Epping Monthly Meeting. No method of travel is given, but they probably went by coach; there they drank tea with Sarah Pim.

They continued to visit Meetings in and near London, including Peel on 8th April 'a select Quarter Meeting in which some weighty remarks were made', and at Quarterly Meeting on the 9th they met William Crotch from Suffolk. They attended Horsley Down Meeting on the 10th and were at Tottenham Meeting by the 11th April. After a Meeting at Hertford there was a Public Meeting on the evening of the 13th, followed by one at Hitchin which 'help'd release our own minds as well as in two families – tho' we had been considerably depressed'. Evidently they had to work hard during the family visits to lift and encourage their hearers to make them realise the true conduct for the living of satisfactory lives.

At Baldock and Royston Meetings, they found the latter 'very trying', and next day made a round of visits to places not far from London. By 17th April Buntingford Meeting had been attended, where they were helped by 'People of other Societys'. Here they lodged at Youngsberry, the home of David and Rachel Barclay, and had a sitting in the family. Ware Meeting on the 18th was followed by Ratcliff Monthly Meeting. Richard Phillips joined them in a family visit in that particular Meeting, and on 22nd April 'a renewed visitation was entered into at Devonshire House Meeting especially to the Youth'. They had the company of William Crotch and Dykes Alexander at Plaistow Meeting on the 24th and by the 29th April at Gracechurch Street Meeting 'a door of utterance was mercifully opened, also I hope one of entrance' – this wish Deborah was to express several times during her ministry.

May

Having finished their family visits in Ratcliff Meeting, they attended Plaistow Meeting in the evening of 6th May, and attended morning and afternoon Women's Meeting, in the latter of which Deborah was engaged. They lodged with Mary Crowley and had a sitting with Jane Harris. On the 8th and 9th May they attended Devonshire House and Gracechuch Street Meetings again, and were at Westminster on the 10th for the marriage of William Cooksworthy and E. Haward.

The family visits were finished on 11th May and they had 'a satisfactory Meeting with Young People of the city at Gracechurch Street'. On 13th May they went to Godalming Meeting, George Stacey and Frederick Smith being with them. The town was an ancient one with houses of several centuries lining the rather congested streets. An open Meeting was then held at the county town of Guildford before going on to Esher, which Meeting was 'trying in the beginning but ended well'. on 15th May they attended Meeting at Kingston and Deborah found 'Mercy and Truth followed the few professing with us'. This place was to develop over the next few years and several families coming to live here found it a very pleasant place of residence on the banks of the Thames.

Wandsworth Meeting was on 16th May, with Croydon next day which was 'labor'd', and when they reached London again they found the Gracechurch Street Meeting a large one on the 19th, the next day bringing Meetings for Ministers and Elders. They attended Park Meeting and Horseleydowns in the afternoon in which, and at 'J. Horns where they dined, counsil flow'd freely unto the Youth'. On 21st May there was a Meeting for Ministers and Elders and the opening of the Women's Meeting in the afternoon. Next day in the Women's Meeting 'weighty affairs which came before them' were satisfactorily conducted, after which they attended Gracechurch Meeting and dined at Dykes Alexander's lodgings where they had a Meeting for discipline.

After a Meeting at Peel, in which 'many Gospel truths were conveyed by John Thorp and Deborah Townsend, they were at Devonshire House and Ratcliff at their Women's Meeting on the 27th May. This closed on the 28th and had evidently been highly successful. They were also to find satisfaction at Horseleydowns and went on to attend Gracechurch Street Weekday Meeting, having an opportunity afterwards at supper at 'The Castle & Falcon' where Sarah Darby was lodging. On the 31st May they attended Westminster Meeting in which Elizabeth Tuke had 'good service'. Deborah and Rebecca were also engaged with others and they had an 'opportunity at Frederick Smith's after supper'.

June

On 2nd June Cousin Joseph Smith and Wilson Birkbeck accompanied them to Rochester where they had 'a comfortable opportunity in the Evening with W[illiam] Rickman's family and Schollors'.

Short Visit to Dunkirk and the Channel Isles

On 4th June Richard Reynolds and William Rotch with his daughter Lydia, accompanied them to Dunkirk, going by way of Dover, where they attended the Select Meeting in the evening, and Monthly Meeting next day, sailing on 6th June for Dunkirk where they arrived in about eight hours and 'found Fds well'.

They attended weekday Meeting on the 7th and saw four families the day after. The Meeting on 10th June was in the morning and they sat with nine young men in the afternoon for 'whose preservation we felt deeply engaged'. In the evening they had a 'parting opportunity in Benjamin Rotch's family' – William's son, who evidently lived in Dunkirk and carried on the whaling business which their family had established in France.

They moved on to Calais on the 11th, but could not obtain a passage home and the 'wind being against us we sat down together at the Inn and felt the benefit of Retirement'. They were able to sail, however, on 13th June

The Meeting House Yard, Devonshire House, the old headquarters of the Society of Friends, built in 1791 and demolished in 1925.

reaching Dover in about seven hours where they attended the weekday Meeting in the morning and a Public Meeting in the evening 'to good satisfaction'.

Richard Reynolds, William and Lydia Rotch then left for London, Deborah and Rebecca going on to Folkestone. On 17th June they were at a Meeting for Youth at the Drapers [Almshouses] near Margate,[4] and next day 'sat a silent Meeting at Canterbury to the disappointment of the People, but had a satisfactory Meeting at Ashford and an opportunity in a Fds family'.

By 21st June they reached Lewes for Meeting and visited a Friend in deep affliction, and on the 22nd they attended two 'Meetings in Brighthelmstone finding a few solid Fds'.

July

They went on to Chichester and Arundel for Meetings and visits to Friends at Ifield, Capel, Dorking, Alton and Basingstoke, and by the 3rd July were at Whitchurch and Andover, and after an evening Meeting at Ramsey went on 'board a Vessel at Southampton that evening, landing on the Isle of Portland to hold a Meeting with the Inhabitants to good satisfaction'. On the 9th they set sail again and landed at Guernsey about nine o'clock in the evening where they were kindly received by Nicholas and Mary Naftal, attending weekday Meeting with a public one in the evening on the 12th.

In a Meeting in a 'Fds house five miles distant in the country Gospel Truths flow'd freely, Nicholas Naftal was our interpreter'. They were confined by stormy weather on the 16th, but visited Friends later, sailing on 17th July for Jersey still accompanied by Nicholas and Mary Naftal, and on the 19th walked to [St] Aubin[s] for an open Meeting, returning to Guernsey that evening, leaving for England the next day and arriving at Pool went directly to Meeting.

Visit to Hampshire, Dorset, Devon and Cornwall

They were at Ringwood for Meeting on 23rd July and also had a 'lively Meeting at Fording Bridge which prov'd an encouragement to us'. Salisbury Meeting and an opportunity in a Friend's family 'prov'd the continuance of the Father's Love to his People. On the 26th Priscilla Hannah Gurney and Nathan Haworth was with us at Shaftesbury Meeting and at Marnhull that evening', and after a Meeting at Sherborne they spent 'an agreeable evening with Thomas Thompson'. They were then at Yeovil, Bridport and Spiceland during the last days of the month.

August

On 1st August at Cullompton Meeting 'Mary Naftal had to minister to the People after which we parted, she for Exeter and we to visit our Valued Fds William and Ann Byrd at Uffculm'. They attended Meeting at Exeter on 5th August and Tavistock on the 7th 'a place where Fds reside' and where they felt a 'desire to have a Meeting which prov'd a season to be well remembered'. After a 'trying Meeting' at Liscard they had a poor Meeting at Port Isaac, but a comfortable time in Edward Fox's family after supper.

They reached Falmouth by 12th August and began a family visit in which Sarah Tregelles junior joined them. At Monthly Meeting at Redruth Catherine Phillips was 'lovingly engaged': this town with Camborne was the centre of the largest copper mining area of the time with a considerable population. They continued their family visits in which 'a humbling visitation has been extended into many of the Youth'. Finishing their visits in Redruth and Falmouth they travelled west to Penzance arriving on 18th August and going on to Land's End, that strange historic tip of the country, to have a morning Meeting before returning to Penzance that evening. They paid more family visits en route, and were at Meeting at Marazion on the 21st, returning to the north-west for a Public Meeting next day at Redruth when Catherine Phillips joined them.

They then attended a large Meeting on the south coast of Cornwall at Mevagissy, a fishing port which exported large quantities of pilchards, chiefly to Portugal. On 24th August they went north to St Austell in the morning and on to Looe, another fishing port, in the evening, about 15 to 20 miles further up the south coast.

They went on again to a Meeting at [St] Germans where they had 'to minister unto some who had buried their talents too much in the earth', and at morning Meeting in Plymouth, Deborah was silent, but had some 'openings to labour' in the afternoon. They continued east to Modbury in the morning of the next day and reached Kingsbridge in the evening, a port from the Middle Ages on a huge estuary supported on the landward side by a large fertile area of farmland.

After sitting in two Friend's families they rode north for about 30 miles to Topsham at the mouth of the River Exe and had a satisfactory Public Meeting. This place had been the port for Exeter since Roman times, now sending many ships to catch cod off Newfoundland, and also carrying on trade with Holland. They held Public Meetings there during their visit and were back in Exeter by the 30th August to go on north to Cullompton where they had 'a small poor Meeting' that same evening.

September

After attending 'an open Public Meeting' on the morning of the last day of August at the home of William Byrd at Uffculme and having 'a favor'd season with the family' they parted 'from these Dear Fds' travelling on to Melverton where they had a Meeting and visited Friends, one being made to 'the scholars of a Girls' Boarding School'. On 3rd September Deborah and Rebecca reached Wellington and entered into family visits and by the 6th were in Taunton where Ann Byrd joined them.

They reached the north coast on the 7th September and had a Meeting at Minehead and returning east inland another at Bridgwater next day, and after sitting with Friends on the 9th at Illminster further south in the morning they had a Public Meeting in the evening, a small low one, followed by one at Puddemore in the morning of the 10th and Somerton later in the day. By the 11th September they had reached Glastonbury for a Meeting 'largely attended by People from our Society – a time of favor – Edward Hatton from Cork joined us on his return from the Island of Guernsey'. Martha Haworth and Priscilla Hannah Gurney met them on the 12th and they had a satisfactory Meeting with Friends that morning in the same beautiful place.

Edward Hatton was again with them at Hallatrow Meeting as well as at Robert Bishop's on the 13th where they dined. They were now moving north and reached Sidcot next day where they 'had an opportunity in the family of our Honourable Fd John Thomas'. After visiting sick Friends they were at Claverham Meeting on the 16th followed by an evening one at Portishead by the Severn Estuary.

Deborah and Edward Hatton ministered to the different states at the small morning Meeting at Lawrence Weston's, and then spent the evening with Ann Hunt. Next morning, after an opportunity in the family they attended Oldbury and Thornbury Meetings. They were now in Gloucestershire and found the Meeting at Nailsworth the day after was 'help'd by People of other Societys attending' and at Cirencester they had a Meeting with the Youth followed by a public one on the 20th September.

They then spent a few days with the Fowlers at Melksham, attending Select Quarterly Meeting on the 24th and Quarterly Meeting a day later. Martha Routh and Christiana Hostler were also there and 'had an opportunity at the Fowlers in the evening'. Deborah and Rebecca had a Meeting at Caln on the 26th early in the day, and a public one at Melksham later which was 'to good satisfaction'.

October

Having been delayed in visiting families they did not travel on until 30th September, when they reached Bromham for evening Meeting. On 3rd October they had a Public Meeting at Bradford [on-Avon] which was 'not so large as desirable' and here Deborah explained that on the 5th 'My Dear Boys who had been with me near two weeks returned to Burford, and after a final Meeting at Melksham finish'd our visit'. They went to Westbury and were at Bath next day, and by 7th October were in Bristol for a silent Meeting but Deborah was indisposed later in the day. However, they laid their concern before the Select Meeting to visit the families of Friends in that city, which they began in company with Mercy Ransome of Hitchin and Hannah Stephenson of Bristol and received 'encouragement in the work the prospect of which is weighty'. Deborah found 'much union in the prospect' and they continued with their visits and dined on 14th October at Ann Heath's.

November

In the course of the week that followed they sat with 37 families, but by 28th October Deborah had become ill with a fever and suffered much pain : she found that 'some part of the time my pulse was beating 30 strokes to the minute – medical help so far blest that I am now easier'. By the 31st she had 'gained sufficient strength to go on with our visits', so by 4th November Thomas Colley was engaged in morning and evening Meetings and Deborah helped to 'convey Gospel Truths to many People of other Societys'. They attended Meetings during the ensuing days and finished their family visits in Bristol on 22nd November, and after a Meeting at Frenchay on the 23rd they parted 'from our Dear Companions' and travelled on to hold another Meeting at [Chipping] Sodbury that evening.

Next they travelled to Painswick, Gloucester and Tewkesbury to hold Meetings and to visit sick Friends. Monthly Meeting at Worcester was 'an open time' on the 27th November with a public one in the evening, and then to Deborah's great joy 'My Beloved Husband met us' and they reached home next day finding 'all our near connections in usual health' she feeling that 'all the preservations extended to us in the long journey calls for a tribute of thankfulness'.

Hannah Barnard's last days

December

During the beginning of December Deborah spent much time with her 'Dear Mother Barnard' who was unwell and 'peculiarly claims my attention'. Martha Haworth was with them by the 4th December and went with Deborah and her mother to dine at Dale House with Richard and Rebecca Reynolds, and it 'sadly proved to be the last time Hannah Barnard was to go there'. On 16th December, Deborah and Samuel were at Shrewsbury Meeting and next day Deborah and Rebecca Young dined with the Reynolds and, as Richard was ill, she had 'an opportunity in his chamber'. They gave in their Certificates at Monthly Meeting on the 19th with an account of their journey, Rebecca being 'much favor'd in the Mens' Meeting' and they had an opportunity at Rebecca Darby's at the White House, and also with the family at Sunniside after supper. Winter made the scene of frosty ground in the little deer park unusual with the bright and firey illumination from the furnaces lighting their way fitfully between the houses.

At New Dale Meeting on 23rd December they were 'engaged in Prayer and later dined at John Young's' who had an additional home for convenience near the family workplace. During the last days of the year, Abiah, Ann Summerland, and Deborah with Rebecca Young took part in Meetings, and attended the marriage of Charles Smith and Rebecca Hudson at Stourbridge on the 28th, at which Deborah, William Cash and Rebecca Young ministered and had opportunities with the Company 'both after Dinner at the Inn and after tea at M. Hudson's house'. William Cash accompanied them next day in visiting Friends' families and they were at Wedgbury morning Meeting and later at six o'clock at Birmingham. On the last day of the year they were at a Public Meeting at Bromsgrove where Samuel met them.

1793

January

She attended the Select Quarterly Meeting at Worcester in the evening of 1st January, and also paid a visit to G. & S. Bennet. Quarterly Meeting followed the day after. She and Rebecca were at Bewdley on the 3rd and had a Meeting in Kidderminster in the evening.

They attended the burial of 'an ancient Friend at Stourbridge' on the 4th, where William Cash and Ann Baxter ministered and they had a 'favor'd session with the Relations after'. They reached home on 5th January, John Young having accompanied Deborah and his daughter. The afternoon of 6th January Deborah spent with her 'Endear'd Mother, who was much indisposed'. Hannah's illness was of so alarming a nature by the 9th that they sent for Dr Darwin, who sadly 'gave them no hope of her recovery', but fortunately her mind was 'preserved in much tranquility', and they had a 'sweet season in the evening in which Susannah Appleby was engaged in Prayer'.

Deborah attended morning Meeting on 13th, spending the afternoon with 'my Precious Mother', who continued 'much afflicted'; and she was unable to leave her parent the next day to attend Meeting. The Fowlers came and Hannah Barnard said 'Now I may adopt good old Simeon's language – "Now Lord letteth thy Servant depart in peace"'.

Monthly Meeting took place in Shrewsbury on 16th but Deborah could not attend. 'Mary Rathbone paid my Hon'd Mother a visit, who said how often she admired the resignation she felt'. The rest of the week was 'spent in the Chamber of my Dear Mother', who became very ill in the evening of 20th January. The following day, at about half past one o'clock, Deborah describes how 'it pleased a Tender Father to take unto Himself my much loved Mother without any conflict, and although my affectionate feelings are nearly touched I cannot but esteem it a favor, that the end crown'd all. Her life was a useful one, being truly a sympathiser with the afflicted, and always ready to communicate of what she had to the Poor, in which she has left her near connections good footsteps'.

There was continued sadness as 'A Messenger came to invite to the Burial of Cousin John Burgess, who [had] died on the 21st, as did the King of France, who was beheaded by his subjects, *a cruel thing indeed*'. Her comment thus expressed of the execution on the guillotine of Louis XVI showed how this event had shocked Friends profoundly, as all civilised society. Those who had sympathised with the struggle for freedom were horrified at the bloodshed and terror to which this had led, and there are similar echoes of this reaction in many letters and journals.

On 26th January, Deborah and her relations took 'a farewell of the last Remains of a truly affectionate Parent'. Timothy Bevington, Mary Lloyd and other Friends had 'a calming opportunity after Supper'. On the 27th 'Met our Friends in the house of my Deceased Parent at 9 o'clock, went to Meeting at 10 o'clock', which 'after many loving testimonys', Deborah concluded in Prayer at the graveside. Timothy Bevington repeated there the text of 'Blessed are the Dead who live in the Lord'.

They attended weekday Meeting on the 29th at brother Richard Reynolds' at The Bank, 'Mary Lloyd and myself engaged after dinner'.

They sat with Friends in Shrewsbury, where Mary Lloyd and Susannah Appleby had 'acceptable service', also visiting Ann Clarke who 'that morning lost her husband'; they then travelled to and lodged at Welshpool.

Welsh Visit

On the 31st January, Deborah and Rebecca Young, with Mary Lloyd and Susannah Appleby, were all at Dolobran, after which they went back to Llanfair for a large evening Meeting.

February

After a Meeting at Denis [Dinas Mawdday] on 2nd February they reached Dorothy Owen's the same night, finding her 'indisposed in Body but sweetly tranquil in mind'. They sat with Friends at Denisbran where 'Truth did not rise high but hope it might be an instructive season'.

They then went to Dolgellau which 'promised much to our encouragement', and were also at a Meeting at Llewendee at seven o'clock on 4th, and one at Twyyn next day, with another at Machynlleth. They sat a little at Esgairgoch and were in an evening Meeting at Llanidloes, having another on the 7th with townspeople.

'A small and satisfactory Meeting' was held at Newtown and one at Welshpool on 9th February, but the latter 'proved trying'. They had a Meeting in the Town Hall at Llanberis at nine o'clock in the morning, and on the day following reached Shrewsbury in time for Meeting in the family of John Young in the evening. Here they explained to some 'particular Friends' a concern which 'Rebecca Young and myself had to visit Friends in America'. All Deborah's family had known from childhood of her Aunt Rachel Wilson's journey over 20 years before, the connections with certain Friends families the other side of the ocean remaining strong and affectionate ever since. Many Americans also came over for Yearly Meetings in London that year and each year several stayed at Sunniside.

Samuel and Deborah then accompanied Rachel Fowler, who with her infant son William had been staying at Sunniside, to Worcester on her way home where her husband Robert came to meet them, the others returning to Coalbrookdale after 'visiting the Prison'. They were at the weekday Meeting on 19th February and 'drank tea at John Hotham's'. Deborah and Rebecca Young now definitely 'express'd a concern to visit America' before Friends at New Dale Monthly Meeting on the 20th February 'a degree of solemnity attending'.

Priscilla Hannah Gurney and Richard Reynolds with Deborah attended Shrewsbury weekday Meeting on the 28th, and also visited families and the prison when 'He that declared himself to be the Friend of sinners was near to help'. These special visits were always to be a cause of difficulty for her, however often accomplished, as the conditions for the inmates were nearly always distressing.

March

She felt very low on 5th March 'feeling little preparation for the arduous work before us, but in a spiritual sense the Lord's People have neither Barn House nor Store'. However, she then entered into some strenuous family visits, having as many as six on 6th March. Richard Reynolds, John and Rebecca Young, Edward Sipkin and Priscilla Hannah Gurney were with her and the following day they had a sitting at Cousin Dearman's 'being comforted by the refreshing of best principles'.

After a Meeting on the 10th, Ann Summerland, Deborah and Rebecca had some sittings in families at New Dale, and then lodged at The Bank. They stayed at Newport on the 11th March and on the evening of the next day had a Public Meeting at Nantwich in Cheshire, followed by Meetings in Middlewich which they found trying. Quarterly Meeting took place on 14th March and one was also held in the evening for people of other societies. Two Meetings at Macclesfield on the 15th were 'a season of consolation with Dear Frances Dodshon – we considered a full reward for our ride'. Deborah here described her as 'a tried servant, a woman of account in the World – joined our Society while young and had a Precious Gift in the Ministry bestow'd upon her which she exercised to the edification of her Friends, tho' was at times under a great depression of Spirit'. These are interesting observations as Frances was a life-long friend of Abiah Darby from youth, though Abiah had finally, with Frances' family, found her nervous moods very difficult to deal with at times.

They had a Meeting at Morley of which Deborah wrote in a colourful manner 'renew'd invitation was extended to some – in a peculiar manner – to come higher and see the Bride, the Lamb's wife'. In morning Meeting at Stockport 'Youth were particularly encouraged to press forward towards the mark and the prize of their high calling in Christ Jesus, being reminded that had the Children of Israel sat down by the Palm Trees and Wells of Water on this side of Jordan, they had never inherited the Promised Land'.

Certificates for America signed

A Public Meeting was held in the evening of the 18th March at Newcastle [under-Lyme] and after a sitting in James Dick's family they rode to Newport for an evening Meeting with the people. Then on 20th they attended Monthly Meeting where their Certificates were signed 'expressive of the Unity of Friends with our prospect of visiting America'. In the beginning of April they attended local Meetings and a burial, that of Samuel Thomas 'in which Deborah had many Gospel Truths to convey'.

6.94

From our Quarterly Meeting held at Great Contentney in Wayn County North Carolina the 21st of the 7th mo 1794

To the Monthly Meeting in Shropshire in Old England —

(Dear Friends —

Our Esteemed friends Deborah Darby, & Rebekah Young Ministers from your parts, having visited most of the Meetings within the Verge of our Quarter, produced Certificates from from the Monthly Meeting of Shropshire dated the 20th of the 3d m° 1793. with Endorsments from the Yearly Meeting for Wales; also Certificates from the Yearly Meeting of Ministers & Elders in London dated the 5th 10° 1793 —

Now these may Certifie that there Gospel Labours were sound and Edifying. their Conversation & Deportment Examplary. So we conclude with fervent desires that when there Services are over on this Continent they may be favoured to return to their Native Land with a reward of Peace. —

Signed in and by order of our above said Meeting

By   John Kennedy Clerk

     Mary Newsom Clerk

Acceptance by the Clerks of Quarterly Meeting held at Great Contentney in Wayn County, North Carolina, of certificate for Deborah Darby and Rebecca Young from Shropshire Monthly Meeting, 20th of 3rd month 1793 (endorsed by Wales Yearly Meeting and London Yearly Meeting of Ministers and Elders 5th of 10th month 1793).

April

. Accompanied by Samuel and Rebecca Young, Deborah set out on 6th April for South Wales, having an evening Meeting at Ludlow. They were in Leominster next day and the countryside would now have some early fruit blossom in the many orchards, and the first green haze of the coming leaves was over copse and hedgerow. There was a Public Meeting that evening, and they spent the next day with Thomas Waring, which sadly proved to be their last visit to him; at Meeting they were 'favor'd to feel together the renewings of best fellowship' and in the month of June he died. Thomas had been at Sunniside frequently over the years, always holding Public Meetings in a number of neighbouring places. William Young, Rebecca's uncle 'an extraordinary man for his years' then accompanied them to Hereford where 'The Meeting was very small but preciously quiet', also Monthly Meeting at Ross [on-Wye] followed on 10th April.

There was a Meeting in the Town Hall at Monmouth, and they had a family opportunity at William Dow's after dinner on 11th April. A Public Meeting was held at Abergavenny next day and also a Meeting at James Lewis' in the evening. The Meeting at Pontypool 'was trying for want of more faithful labourers for the arising of Life'; this was followed by a Meeting at Cardiff on the 15th and one in the evening on the same day at Cowbridge. They sat in the Town Hall at Neath on 16th April in the evening, and after Swansea weekday Meeting had a sitting in E. Reece's family.

They went on to visit some Friends recently settled at Milford [Haven] from America, but Deborah was disappointed as she found some of them 'seem to want a nearer acquaintance with the Truth'. Two Meetings followed at Haverford West then, accompanied by several Friends, they 'had a satisfactory Meeting at Narberth'. Wales Yearly Meeting followed at Carmarthen on 23rd April, Timothy Bevington and John Townsend ministering in the Meeting for Friends and Sarah Stephenson in the Women's Meeting, also Sarah Tucknet 'laid a concern before Friends to visit America'.

In the Select Meeting on 24th April, Job Scott from America 'was instructively opened in Council', saying that 'watchfulness was necessary when favor'd of the Lord not to deck ourselves with jewels, but to return them to his treasury'. Then 'finding his mind drawn towards another opportunity with the People, we sat with him in this Meeting, he was enlarged standing an hour and a half, treating with much clearness on many points of Doctrine'. Job Scott was spoken of by his contemporaries as 'a man of strong natural abilities, of singular piety and of exemplary dedication of heart'.

May

Returning on 1st May they reached Shrewsbury for weekday Meeting, and on the 2nd, leaving Rebecca there, Samuel and Deborah went home to Coalbrookdale. General Meeting was held at New Dale on 8th May when Susannah Appleby 'laid a concern before Friends to visit Devonshire and Cornwall, Mary Lloyd her companion'. Deborah and Rebecca Young then had a Meeting at Wolverhampton in the morning of 10th May, going to Dudley in the evening. Deborah had, therefore, only been at home for a week, before she was on her way to Yearly Meeting in London.

They attended Birmingham Meeting on 12th May together with Mary Watson and John Hall, going on to Henley [in-Arden] for a Meeting in the evening, and spending the night in this large Warwickshire village. A morning Meeting at the old market town of Chipping Norton was followed by a Public Meeting that same evening. Reaching Oxford they held two Meetings, a small one in the morning, and a large and more satisfactory larger one in the evening. Mary Watson, Ann Crowley, Rebecca Young and Deborah herself were all 'engaged in labour publicly'. Travelling on to Chillingford they attended weekday Meeting before going on to Henley-on-Thames. 'Job Scott made a few remarks' at the Uxbridge Meeting which he visited on his way to London.

On 18th May Deborah stated 'the Select Yearly Meeting afforded occasion to fear that even the head was sick, however, there is still Balm in Gilead', but what chiefly troubled her she does not explain. They were at Gracechurch Street morning and afternoon Meetings, having there 'a share of the public labour in each'. There was also a 'favor'd opportunity at Cousin Wilson Birkbeck's' where they presumably were staying as usual at Tottenham; Sarah Stephenson, Christiana Hustler with others, were also present.

Concern to Visit America Laid Before Yearly Meeting, 20th May 1793

They then laid their concern 'to visit America before the Meeting of Ministers and Elders on 20th May, with which many Friends express'd Unity, among others Elizabeth Tuke, Martha Routh, Richard Phillips, Mary Watson was engaged in Prayer'. Deborah found she was 'favor'd with Divine Overshadowing' at the Women's Meeting in the afternoon. At the burial of 'Our Friend Joseph Talvin' at Ratcliffe on 22nd May, Rebecca Young and E. Gibson were engaged in supplication – the one opening and the other closing the Meeting. The next day they were present at two Meetings for Discipline.

At Westminster Meeting on 24th May, Deborah's sister Rachel Fowler stood up in 'the early part of the Meeting, after which Samuel Emlen rose and had a favor'd opportunity, and Christiana Hustler concluded'. They dined at Cousin Messer's where they had an opportunity and also later one at D. Moline's and Ann Fothergill's. Deborah was evidently pleased to be seeing many old friends and some of her relations, before she undertook the arduous journey across the seas, an uncertain and strenuous one.

In the Meetings on the 25th May, 'two lively epistles were signed, one for America and one for Ireland'. They were at Westminster Meeting the day after and dined at her Cousin George Stacey's, and there had an opportunity and drank tea at Richard Phillips', where Elizabeth Tuke 'had much excellent counsel to convey'. The last sitting of the Women's Yearly Meeting that year was on 27th May 'in which Divine Regard was manifested'. After attending Devonshire House Meeting on 28th May in which 'the Testimony of Truth went forth with some Authority', they went with Samuel Emlen to visit a Friend's family. Samuel had visited Europe several times and Deborah was to see him frequently during her American journey and was to travel back with him on her return to England. The last sitting of the Meeting of Ministers and Elders took place on 29th May during which 'Job Scott's labours were instructive'.

On 31st May they dined again at her Cousin George Stacey's and 'there had an opportunity in which Sarah Harrison and others were led in an encouraging line'. They afterwards heard that Cousin Mary Stacey 'had that morning been engaged for the first time, to bear testimony to the Truth publicly in a Meeting at Friends' Workhouse'.

June

They had an opportunity at E. Talvin's on 1st June, and then accompanied Cousin Joseph, Rachel Smith, R. Foster and Mary Lloyd to Chelmsford, where although very unwell, Deborah attended a Meeting with Friends in the morning, and people of other societies at four o'clock. Mary Lloyd and Richard Phillips shared their public labour, and they had an opportunity in the evening at Robert Marriage's; these Friends then accompanied them to Coggeshall Monthly Meeting where they also had a Public Meeting in the evening. This village, on the Roman road from Colchester to the west, had many good houses of the Tudor period, some of them with traditional pargeting on their walls. There were also several ancient inns where travellers had halted throughout the centuries, still in existence today.

There was a Public Meeting at Braintree on the River Waveney in the morning of the 5th and at Halstead, a market town on the Suffolk border, in the afternoon. Weekday Meeting was at Colne in the morning of the next day, and a large Public Meeting at Kelvedon, which 'a religious young woman had very carefully arranged was very successful'. They went on then to Mary Alexander's home at Needham to stay. They were to return later, but only had a brief glimpse of the pleasant house and grounds on this first short visit. They were at a weekday Meeting at Kelvedon before going on to a public one at Malden, and on 7th June were at Stebbing Meeting in the evening, staying with Deborah's cousins Joseph and Sarah Smith, before arriving at Colchester for Select Quarterly Meeting at which they found Anna Price.

For the next few days they were at the Meetings which ended on 11th June, when they travelled to Harwich for a Public Meeting that evening. This port, where the rivers Stour and Orwell merge to enter the North Sea, was originally a small medieval town, and later had one of the earliest lighthouses in the country.

They breakfasted at a Friend's house before going on to a Meeting at Manningtree on the estuary of the River Stour, not far away. Needham [Market] weekday Meeting was held on 13th June, where Deborah found 'the young People much tender'd professing something precious among them'. A Public Meeting followed in the evening, also an opportunity after supper at Samuel Alexander's house at Needham where they now spent a longer visit. The house was a comfortable and spacious one with a fine library. Samuel gave much hospitality helped by his two daughters. There was an adjoining farm and a large garden, which also contained a maze with hedge-lined paths leading to a central tree. William Savery who visited Needham some years later described how he and Jasper Capper took a good deal of time to reach the centre and to find their way out again.

Monthly Meeting at Ipswich was on the 14th in the long established Meeting House there, and they also visited families here accompanied by Dykes Alexander, Martha Brewster and Anna Price. Deborah found that the morning Meeting on 16th June 'was hurt for want of faithfulness, however, a large Public Meeting held at 6 o'clock in the evening was more satisfactory'. They then attended Select Yearly Meeting at Woodbridge on the 17th, attending Meetings with families later for worship. After a solemn parting opportunity in Benjamin Ewin's family they went back to Ipswich where after parting with Anne Price they attended a Public Meeting in Stowmarket. Two days later, accompanied by Samuel, Dykes and Mary Alexander together with Martha Brewster, they reached the house of John Holmes. Next, the Meeting they attended at Tivetshall on the 23rd was followed by one at Tasburgh.

The following day they were at the annual Select Meeting, having an opportunity after dinner at Ann Gurney's house. In the evening they were at T. & S. Bland's where they lodged, Deborah remarking that she had always stayed with them on her visits to Norwich. At morning Meeting the following day Deborah and Rebecca were silent at Goat Lane Meeting, after which they went to John Gurney's to dine, presumably at Earlham[5] where they would have met his lively family, which included Elizabeth Gurney then only 13 years old. They were only there a very short time, as a large Public Meeting was held in the afternoon, probably in the large building of Gildencroft Meeting House. During their visit to Norwich they visited several Friends' families and attended the last sitting of Yearly Meeting on 26th June, being in Diss by the evening of that day for a Meeting – this small town being situated on the banks of the River Frere.

After a Meeting at Bury [St Edmunds] and a sitting at Richard Brewster's, they went to Newmarket, the centre for horse racing, and there had a large Meeting sharing the public labour with E. Gibson and William Crotch. They had a small Meeting at Cambridge and another at Huntingdon which was a large assembly, and then rode to Kettering for a Public Meeting at six o'clock in the evening. On 30th June there was a morning Meeting at [Market] Harborough and the next day they travelled to Leicester for a Meeting in which Deborah, J. Abbot and Rebecca Young 'all bore testimony'.

July

A large and satisfactory Meeting was held on 1st July at Ashby [de la Zouch] in the morning and Tamworth in the evening where 'my Dr Husband met me'. They travelled on to a Meeting at Litchfield in the morning of the next day and at Stafford later 'where the People behaved with a solidity – becoming the occasion – wish'd to have an opportunity with the Prisoners which was deny'd us'. On 4th July 'my Dr Companion accompanied by Dykes Alexander and Susannah Appleby went to Salop – I staid [*sic*] with my family and had a little opportunity with my Dear Samuel and Edmund before they went to bed'. Dykes Alexander set out for home on 8th July 'having kindly accompanied us', and Susannah Appleby and Mary Lloyd returned to Birmingham. Thomas Cash had a Public Meeting at New Dale and another 'at the 7th hour at the Dale much to our satisfaction'. On the 11th Deborah and Ann Summerland each had 'a Testimony to bear to the goodness of God at Broseley'. At Oswestry on the 13th Rebecca Young and Deborah had a Meeting in the evening 'to our comfort', and reached Dolgelly on the 16th accompanied by G. Morgan.

On the 17th July they attended the 'Burial of our Dear Fd and Sister Dorothy Owen who finish'd her course on the 13th of this mo[nth]'. They attended Monthly Meeting at Esgairgoch where Deborah 'had to pray for an increase of strength to contend for their faith once delivered unto the Saints'. There followed an evening Meeting with Friends at Llanidloes and at a Meeting at Pool Deborah, Rebecca and her Uncle William Young from Leominster all bore Testimony. Samuel met Deborah on her return to Shrewsbury and they had the largest Meeting held there for many years.

They visited the prison on the morning of 22nd July, riding home later to Sunniside where the boys had been on holiday from school, but they left home again on the 23rd for Burford, Deborah naturally finding it affecting to part with them 'under the prospect of a long separation', which was inevitable with her intention of visiting America, and after 'a comfortable session after dinner' they attended a Meeting at Much Wenlock. 24th July Deborah found 'was a sad day as I took leave of my dear Mother Darby and of the family as I am not likely to see her again. I felt the tie of nature strong and binding, and trust was supported by the evidence, tho' I was leaving my home and dear connections for Christ's sake and the Gospels'. They had a large and satisfactory Public Meeting at Wellington and lodged at The Bank with William and Hannah Reynolds, then on the 25th, accompanied by John Young Junior, Rebecca's brother, and John Ellis they rode to [Market] Drayton where they had 'a comfortable Public Meeting'.

A Meeting at Leek was held in the evening of the 26th July and they reached Sheffield two days later where Deborah saw relations and Friends and acquaintances who would all have been interested to hear about their intended journey. By 29th July they were in Doncaster to dine, having a Public Meeting in the evening in which Deborah and Rebecca with Thomas Colley 'engaged in a rather open time'. This was followed by a large Public Meeting on the 30th in the Town Hall in Pontefract, and next day they were at Ackworth[6] for General Meeting at which 'some of the children were tender and many felt deeply engaged that best wisdom might be sought after, in the conducting of this noble institution'.

August

The next day they sat with women Friends in a committee 'to inspect the state of the institution [Ackworth School][6] in which Divine Regard was evinced, and under which several of us had testimony to bear' and later Deborah and Rebecca had an opportunity 'with the Boys at table when William Crotch and John Abbot ministered to us'. Before leaving Ackworth they attended an evening Meeting at Leeds, lodging that night with Christiana Hustler and riding on to Manchester on 2nd August for an evening Meeting and to Warrington next day. By the morning of 4th August they were in Liverpool for the morning Meeting, where Priscilla Hannah Gurney and Deborah expressed a few words: later they took part in the evening Meeting. After a supper given for them by Richard and Rebecca Reynolds 'who kindly entertained us at Cousin W. Rathbone's Town House', they had a favoured time together.

A Meeting was held at Prescot at four o'clock on 5th August and the day after they went to look at the vessel, called upon Cousin S. Benson and Elizabeth Rathbone 'with whom we had a sweet season, but the latter seemed fast hastening towards an everlasting Rest. She had been a Religious young woman for many years'. As has been explained, Elizabeth had never got over her unrequited love for William Reynolds. Cousin Wilson Birkbeck and Frederick Smith, and Joseph Foster who had accompanied them to Liverpool, although not previously mentioned, then left them.

Ackworth School, founded 1779.

On the 9th August they 'drank tea at Cousin M. and P. Rathbone's' and had counsel to convey in the morning Meeting on the 11th, at which Priscilla Hannah Gurney was engaged in the afternoon but both Deborah and Rebecca were silent.

The journey in prospect could never be taken lightly, whatever the faith in Divine Protection. The sea for the small ships of those days was always dangerous, and added to this at the time were the hazards of the warring privateers and the hostilities with France.

Setting Out For America

Deborah and Rebecca had spent a great deal of time collecting their personal stores which were to be sent to the Liverpool docks ahead of their sailing date for the voyage to America. The Master of the ship in which they were to embark would be responsible for their main food and general needs, but additional items would be required individually, and no doubt they had obtained advice from others who had undertaken this journey before.

Eventually they had two trunks of clothes and some further boxes and baskets; and Deborah took a side saddle and two saddlebags for their long journeys on horseback. For their extra comfort on board they also took two armchairs and a stool or cushion 'for the feet or to kneel upon'. Their list also included '4 quires of Cap paper' and a most important and indispensible item was a medicine chest.

They had two 'glass lanthorns and six pounds of candles to put inside' for their main lighting together with a pound of wax candles and a candlestick, a snuffer and a tinder box, with a box to hold the tinder and packets of rush lights. Also included was a 'tin coffee pot and two tin mugs, common soap and a pound of windsor soap, starch, fuller's earth and blue'.

There was an unusual item of 'two quires of common writing paper, cut into strips and dipped in water in which saltpeter had been disolved to burn in the Cabbin occasionally' presumably to sweeten the air. They took ink, camphor, lavender and cinnamon waters, and camomile flowers.

There was a long list of foods to supplement the ship's supply which included 8 lbs of fresh butter, potted cream, a large box of Rusks, 3 lbs of honey, hung beef, ready boiled, some biscuits, sweet oil and pickles. A quantity of oatmeal, 5 coconuts, small cakes and 2 plum cakes. A bottle of 2 quarts of vinegar, a jar of blackcurrants preserved in honey, cherries, gooseberries, apples, also lemons and limes. They were also to take a hamper of water, a bottle of Brandy and a dozen bottles of Madeira wine with 3 score of eggs, 5 lbs of almonds, tea, coffee, gingerbread and 26 lbs of raisins. They added extra corks to put in bottles when using them and the final item were two loaves of freshly baked bread at 1/-s each.

NOTES

[1] After World War II no longer in use and eventually became a shop.

[2] See note 7, p. 78.

[3] Esther Tuke's School in Trinity Lane, the forerunner of The Mount School, York, extant today.

[4] At the centre of Drapers Almshouses there was a tiny Meeting House. See *The Friends Meeting House* by Hubert Lidbetter, p. 48.

[5] This house now forms part of the University of East Anglia.

[6] See note 7, p. 78.

PART THREE

The American Journey 1793-1796

Historical Background

The American War of Independence had been over for just a decade when Deborah and Rebecca reached the shores of the New United States. The very varied and vast tracts of country, inhabited by different ethnic groups, where they were to travel, were beginning to come together in the different States, a process needing time, patience and resolve.

The tragedies and strains of the late conflict on individual lives had to have time for healing, although they could not be wholly forgotten. The two ministers would experience much of all this during their many miles of journey, but in more detail finally in the State of Pennsylvania, where they were to spend the longest period of time. This State had been founded by William Penn in the 17th century on Quaker principles, and they were there to learn from personal individual Friends the current thinking about the great experiment going on around them in the Union of the States. They themselves had only one object, the saving of souls and the encouragement of all who were to hear them speak to follow the pathway through life which led to the Heavenly Kingdom.

THE FOLLOWING INDENTED PARAGRAPHS HAVE BEEN kindly supplied by Hugh Barbour, who gave his permission to me to add them to my script, as I feel they give an added perspective to the places and people visited by Deborah and Rebecca on their American journey.

Geographic notes on American Quakers and places
by Hugh Barbour:

– *Deborah Darby and Rebecca Young clearly had planned to travel out from Philadelphia using it as their base but were forced by the Yellow*

Fever there to improvise other plans as they were given advice by American Friends, also using the dates of their Yearly Meetings. Yet within each area they managed to visit almost all the local or Monthly Meetings known to have existed then. Many became fully established Monthly Meetings soon after their visit.

– Their first visits were to Meetings on or near the main highway linking the key cities of the new nation from New York to (or around) Philadelphia and on to Baltimore, Richmond, and Charleston, South Carolina. En route they visited the central Quaker area in North Carolina around Contentnea.

– They then stayed many weeks among the small frontier Meetings up-country in South Carolina and Georgia and in the Piedmont close to the Appalachians in North Carolina and between the ridges in Tennessee. Founded by migrants from New England and Pennsylvania after 1750, these were in 1794 the newest southern Quaker settlements, and close to Indian territory.

– To attend North Carolina Yearly Meeting, Deborah and Rebecca then visited the Tidewater Meetings near the sea Sounds of North-eastern Carolina and south-eastern Virginia. These were among the oldest Quaker groups in North America, villages already settled when Fox 'convinced' them in 1672.

– Deborah and Rebecca then went north-west to new Meetings in Virginia's own Piedmont and Shenandoah Valley, and along the Cumberland Road from the Potomac into western Pennsylvania, where Quaker settlers on tributaries of the Ohio were again near hostile Indian territory; these villages would become the springboards for Friends' great westward trek into Ohio and Indiana a decade later. Here Deborah became ill.

– Returning with Deborah still convalescent, they visited solid older Meetings on the upper Potomac and Susquehanna Valleys en route to Philadelphia, where they spent some winter weeks, now the Yellow Fever had passed.

– They travelled down the Delaware/Maryland Peninsula between the Chesapeake and the ocean, concluding with six more months in and around Philadelphia.

– While most of upstate New York west of the Catskills and Adirondacks was still in dispute between the Iroquois Indians and white land speculators, Deborah and Rebecca crossed the New Jersey Highlands to Quaker communities on both sides of the Hudson Valley, going north almost to the Canadian border, into areas where Friends had settled progressively northward during the 18th century.

– They then sailed via Long Island Sound for an all-summer visit to the old Quaker communities in Rhode Island, Nantucket, Martha's Vineyard, Cape Cod, and beyond Boston in Maine. On returning to Long Island Deborah in a famous encounter convinced Stephen Grellet, a French aristocrat refugee from the Revolution, who was to become a world traveller in Quaker ministry. They later met William Savery, having first met him on 12th November in 1793 at Plymouth through whose concern for prisons in England Elizabeth Fry would become a reformer, though it was at Stephen Grellet's instigation she first visited them.

– After five more months in **Philadelphia, New Jersey** *and* **New York** *they sailed home.*

1793
August

Deborah and Rebecca Young left Liverpool on the afternoon of 12th August 1793 'After a solemn and affecting parting with my Dear Husband, Sister S[arah] Darby and other Relations and Friends, Rebecca and myself went on board *The Thomas* – A. George Macey Captain'. The ship was a brig of 169 tonnes net, built in Boston in 1791 and owned in New York, drawing 12 feet of water when loaded, and trading between New York and the United Kingdom.[1]

Deborah's first entry read 'My mind was mercifully sustained in this pinching Time'. They were almost immediately in contrary winds, and most of the passengers were sick, 'Oh it is hard to bear' she was forced to exclaim 'May He that I trust has put us forth enable us to endure all things for his sake'. Their bad seasickness was very disagreeable, and they were thankful that by the 17th 'The Wind came in our favor and we sailed at about 7 miles an hour'.

On First Day, the 18th August, they 'held a Meeting in the Cabbin, which was attended by Thomas Walker and his wife, Susannah Marriot and her Nephew Jonathan Marriot, members of our Society and a young man, a Methodist, refreshing their minds together'. The following day, the wind being contrary again, Deborah found the conditions 'exercising to Faith and Patience, but through favor we are preserved in a good degree of resignation'.

On the 25th August they were 'Much tried [again] with contrary winds'; however they held 'the Meeting in the afternoon which they were unable to do in the morning as the Sea ran so high', but later that same evening, they still found that 'all around look'd awful'. Deborah became 39 on that day but she leaves this birthday unrecorded. By the 29th they spent some time on deck finding 'the company of each other being precious even on this unstable Element', and they had 'Peace in holding our Meeting tho' the motion of the vessel was trying'. By 1st September they were still 'Poorly in

Packages sent on Board the Thomas Captain Macy Master, For Deborah Darby & Rebecca Youngs accommodation on their Voyage to America they embarked 12th 8 mo 1793 —

N.B the Captain finds them with Stores —

Box No 1 Three Score of Eggs & 8 dz and half of Lemons —

Box No 2 26 lb of Raisins —

Box No 3 5 lb of Almonds & 4 lb Coffee & Gingerbread —

Box No 4 Preserved Cream in 5 dozen small ounce bottles — 6 lb of Lanthorn Candles. 1 lb of wax ... 1 lb of Common Soap. 1 lb of ... salt Peter, Fullers earth, Starch blue, Spices, 4 Corks to put in bottles when using, refined and common Liquorish, of each one pound. 6 lb of Rush Lights. 2 Quires of Common writing paper. Cut in small strips & dipped in which salt Peter is dissolved, to burn in the Cabbin in case of ... Sweet Oil. 3 lb wine Biscake —

Box No 5 Potted Beef. Sausages & meat. Pickels. Sweet Oil. 3 lb of Honey. Spirits of Wine and camphor. Ink. Cinamon water. Camomile flowers. Some Biscake. —

Box No 6 Hung Beef ready Boiled and Biscake —

Box No 7. Rusk — — —

Basket No 1 Candle Stick. Snuffers. Tin Coffee Pot, two Tin Cans. Matches, tinder Box. and Box to hold the tinder —

Basket No 2 — 1 Bottle of Brandy. 1 d° of Geneva, 2 plum Cakes, 2 Bottles of Capilline, Liquorish, Small Cakes, 5 Cocoa nuts, Lavender water. Fullers earth —

Basket No 3 Lemons Biscake

A Jar of Black Currants preserved in honey —

A Bottle that holds 2 Quarts of Vinegar —

A Jar of Oatmeal holds one peck —

Large Boxes

Box No 1 DD's Cloathes

trunk No 2 DD's R.Y d°

Box No 3 Side Saddle & Cloathes

trunk No 4 R.Y's Cloathes —

1 pair of Saddle Bags 2 single Bags

4 Arm Chairs —

1 Medicine Chest —

1 Glass Lanthorn —

1 doz of Madeira Wine —

1 hamper of Water —

1 bag for the feet or kneeling upon

A Jar of Tamarins —

Some Limes —

4 Quire of Cap paper

Some Cherries Goosberries and apples —

8 lb fresh butter, 2 loaves of fresh baked Bread at 1/ each

List of packages sent on board the Thomas for Deborah Darby's and Rebecca Young's accommodation on their voyage to America. Embarkation 12th of 8th month 1793.

our health but held our Meeting', and two days later 'the scene was a little brightened by a large number of Porpoises about our Ship. One of them was taken which afforded a fine supply of oil for the Lamp by which the Mariner views the Compass to steer by at night'.

September

On 5th September they 'sat together again', and Deborah made a few remarks on 'the necessity of having the mind stay'd on God and above all things desiring his blessing'. They were finding that they had 'much leisure for meditation', although the physical discomfort of the moving boat and their natural apprehension had to be overcome.

However strong these resolutions were and the depth of their faith in heavenly protection, it was proving very difficult indeed at times to maintain real serenity, particularly during the hours of acute seasickness. By the 8th September, in their morning Meeting 'some ability was afforded to recommend a close dwelling with the spirit of Truth, which would make us preachers of Righteousness – in our conduct'. On 15th September they held their weekday Meeting and during the last week 'had the sea as smooth as Glass and had we been getting forward, [it] would have been very pleasant'.

They 'spoke with a Vessel from New York for Amsterdam; she had been out 15 days. This was a pleasant circumstance to us, as it was the first we had met with'. On 22nd September they again 'sat together tho' in poverty of spirit'. Deborah was finding that 'some of our minds have been deeply abased on this Voyage'. Physically they had been very highly tried by the long periods of sickness, but here she comforted herself by knowing 'that He that strips is abundantly able to cloath'.

Suddenly they had the pleasure of seeing 'many Whales and Birds which is an indication of being near the Banks of Newfoundland', and they were on the Banks themselves by the 23rd, but unfortunately the 'wind was so high could not fish and was mostly in our Cabbin – but getting 100 miles a Day is reviving – after a slow progress'. The fish they should have caught would have been cod and a very welcome addition to their diet. They held their First Day Meeting on the 29th and spoke with a ship from Boston that had been fishing on the Banks, and Deborah was able to say 'We have had fine weather and pleasant Sailing this last week – may we be able to number our blessings'.

October

They passed the island of Nantucket on 5th October and Deborah had 'seldom seen the horizon more beautiful than this evening'. She rarely remarked on the scene around her, but the serene beauty here must have filled her mind, partly because of the loveliness of the reality and also coming after the protracted difficulties of the voyage.

They sat together again on the 6th October and later she read the scriptures remarking 'a treasure too much neglected'. The 7th was a fine day and that evening they had seen land, 'which being 7 weeks without seeing any was a reviving sight to us, but in the evening about 9 o'clock a Pilot came aboard from Sandy Hook and brought an account of the Yellow Fever raging in Philadelphia which turn'd our joy into sorrow'. The epidemic had been at full height in September bringing the number of deaths to over 50 a day, and many who were able to do so had, by then, fled the city; this disaster was to bring some changes to Deborah's and Rebecca's journey, and to turn their thoughts in directions hitherto not anticipated.

On awakening on 8th October they found themselves 'in New York Harbour having a beautiful view of the town'. They had passed between the narrows separating Long Island with the wooded heights of Brooklyn and Staten Island, and the masts of innumeral ships around the New York quays gleamed in the morning light, stretching away into the distance. The city had been built on the southern end of York Island, between the Hudson and the East Rivers, and in the distance the wooded coast of New Jersey could be seen closing the view to the south-west. The scene became very animated as they approached the docks of this great port which was ideal for commerce, as the sheltered approach and safe anchorage made sailing all the year round possible. Trade, by the late 18th century, had become very considerable indeed and had only been badly dislocated by the years of war, but was at the time of their arrival, well revived.

New York was a city of about 30,000 inhabitants, formerly called New Amsterdam by the Dutch, by whom the place was founded. Traces of their architecture could still be seen in some of the earlier houses A wide street, Broadway, traversed the city from north to south, with side streets branching off the main thoroughfare going down to the docks. Brick houses of several stories had been built by the British, though they were still quite frequently interspersed with lower timber dwellings and outhouses. The spires of churches rose into the sky, some of stone, but many of timber with weather-cocks mounted on the steeples painted in bright colours. The Senate House, a large square building, where the Congress of the United States and New York Assembly met, stood out prominently from the other buildings.

Deborah's Journal recorded 'we went to the house of our Fr(ien)d, John Murr(a)y, who, with his Wife, received us affectionately which impress'd our minds with gratitude to the Author of Mercys, both ancient and new, who had brought us safe over the mighty ocean – may he so preserve us to bring us at last into the Port of Haven of Rest, at the end of time, where the morning stars sing together and the Sons of God shout for Joy'. This conviction of Divine Guidance and care for each soul was the true strength of such as Deborah, and gave them the valour and steadfastness of purpose to carry out the work of spreading the message of love and encouragement for all to follow.

There is a description[2] of the home of John Murray, written in 1786 by Ann Warder, just seven years before Deborah and Rebecca's visit, in which their hospitality was described. 'The family [then] consisted of the man, his wife, mother and several children, and a young woman on a visit to Philadelphia.' The Warders were 'very kindly entertained wherein more generosity than taste was displayed'. The Murrays' dress 'was ugly tho' I doubt not, by themselves, reckoned smart, having such . . . as were used with us to be worn half a century ago'. It would appear, therefore, they were untouched by modern fashion and that their way of living was practical and kind, but in no way elegant.

Deborah wrote to Friends in England by a vessel about to sail, hoping that her letters would reach their destination about two months later, if all went well.

Despite Ann Warder's sharp criticism of the John Murrays, they found they belonged to an important Quaker family of successful shipping merchants who had a fine property of orchards and farmland on the outskirts of the city with a comfortable country home situated in an area where now East 37th Street and Park Avenue meet. This estate, part of the fashionable Murray Hill district had been the centre of a considerable drama when in September 1776 those inhabitants of New York who were able to leave had done so, to escape the British Army then beseiging the city. Five British warships had anchored in the harbour and troops had landed to pursue the American forces retreating inland. George Washington, who was commanding the American Army, had 500 men separated from the main force and was endeavouring to bring them to a point where they could be re-united, no easy manoeuvre as the soldiers were spread out trying to make their escape through farms, orchards and woodlands. The British commanders, General Sir William Howe and General George Cornwallis, were acquainted through New York's Governor, William Tryon, with Robert Murray.

It was hot and the Generals halted at the Murray's conveniently situated house, where they partook of Mrs Robert Murray's hospitality in her cool and comfortable rooms. Here they lingered long enough for General Washington's army to escape through the countryside within 'half a mile of the invaders' and leave the city, and by so doing insured that the whole American force would be able to continue the fight: eventually some of them took part in the liberation of New York seven years afterwards. The Murrays had always been an important and influential family, striving to improve the conditions of many, and with other families of Friends remained in the forefront of education and charitable endeavour.

The following day, 9th October, the visitors attended the marriage of Edmund Pryor [Prior] and Mary Haydock, Deborah describing the occasion as a 'time of favor, [and they] dined and drank tea at Henry Haydock's' – the bride's home. The Meeting House in which the wedding took place was a brick building of good proportions with a portico, situated on the east side of Queen Street. Not more than a short distance away was a similar but larger building used as a school, which had been set up by a few interested Friends' families, convinced that a sound education and the teaching of Friends' principles were the best preparation for life. Deborah does not mention visiting the school, but perhaps the strenuous family visits took up most of her attention.

Deborah and Rebecca had 'a concern to visit the families of Fds in this City even while on the mighty Ocean', and now laid it before the Ministers and Elders on 10th October 'who uniting with it, appointed two Fds to accompany us'. They therefore, on the following day sat in six families and 'had cause to believe the work was the Lord's, and if his blessing is upon it no matter how feeble the instruments employed'.

By the time Deborah reached the New World her ministry was at its height, she was still 'comely in person', had a gentle and attractive manner and a musical voice, and it would appear that she held the attention of her listeners as much by her presence and her deep conviction as by her words.

On 13th October they 'attended both the Meetings and sat in 3 families in the morning'. Rebecca Young appeared in testimony and Deborah in prayer; later they drank tea at Ann King's, a Friend from England, and found that 'some of her children appear hopeful'. They were at the weekday Meeting on the 16th and Rebecca was 'enabled to supplicate for a Blessing on the Lord's heritage'. Having visited six families a day 'mostly through the course of the week and have often had to admire the goodness of our Heavenly Father in visiting His church and People', Deborah found that 'some of the Youth appear under visitation', and later, after the afternoon Meeting, it was clearer to her that 'one may plant and another water, it is the Lord that can give increase'.

During the next few days they attended Meetings, visited families and had a Meeting with the people on Staten Island, several Friends accompanying them from New York.

This island had been brought under cultivation by the Dutch many years before, who had established farms, cultivated grain crops and vegetables, also raised cattle and pigs. When Deborah and Rebecca visited the island it was still rural, but there was a growing population, with small towns and large village groupings.

By the time Deborah and Rebecca had completed their family visits in New York they had come to know that city well. Their chief acquaintances, were inevitably among those families connected with the Murrays, who worked with them in education, health and philanthropic innovations.

November

Later, in November, Deborah wrote to a Friend in Ireland, Elizabeth Pim[3] describing their time in New York; 'We spent four weeks in that City, visiting the families of Friends which were 100, and tho' the work was arduous we had cause to hope tended to the encouragement of the honest hearted, and was a time of renewed visitation to the youth of which there were large numbers'.

Leaving on 5th November, Deborah and Rebecca first went to Rahway, New Jersey to lodge, several Friends from New York accompanying them including their kind host John Murray, and next day had a Public Meeting in the evening. They attended Stony Brook Meeting, New Jersey – near Princeton on the 7th and that same evening Trenton, in both places 'the necessity of living in the Lord's fear' was pointed out 'that there might be a preparation to die in His favor'. She had always lived striving to convey this message, and throughout her travels in the New World thought only of conveying to everyone with whom she came in contact; the realisation of the love and presence of God in all things in all places and at all times. She described very little of her surroundings on her many miles of travel, recording only the success or otherwise of the spiritual contact with those she encountered.

They reached Middleton near Falsington by 9th November. There they met 'our Dr Fd and Mother in the Truth, Rebecca Wright'. They went to the house of the Elder, James Thornton, where they found Samuel and Thomas Fisher with their sister Hannah, and 'were affected together in a sense of the awful visitation then prevailing in Philadelphia'. The terrible epidemic of Yellow Fever had broken out in the streets of the water front in July and the climax was reached in September.

Thomas Fisher had stayed at Sunniside for several days in the year 1767 and the family were connected with the Darbys through the Maudes of Yorkshire. Later Deborah was to make great friends with Hannah Fisher during the months she spent in Philadelphia, and Hannah presented her with a book, which still exists today. The Fishers had had to leave their home and business towards the height of the epidemic, although Friends had endeavoured to stay as long as possible in order to give some aid in spite of the danger to themselves, and also to keep up the activities of the place. As the summer progressed the whole situation had become increasingly difficult, so many had taken shelter with friends and relations in places not too far away to enable an early return when possible, and also so that they could retain some contact with their homes and businesses.

John Thornton, before they left, 'very encouragingly expressed his care for us that he had sought the Lord for us and believed we were in the right way'. In the morning of 10th November, a First Day, they were at Byberry only 10 miles from Philadelphia, named originally in the 17th century by three brothers called Walton, Friends who had emigrated from Byeberry near Bristol, England. They had arrived with little more than their tools and had founded this community with others. At first this settlement was known for some time by the former Indian name, where they had lived in hollow caves made in the earth, thatched over with tree boughs.

Deborah and Rebecca attended here 'a solemn Meeting among Fds', many of whom had fled from Philadelphia, and being present in the afternoon had a Public Meeting for those present in the place. Their unfortunate situation provided an opportunity for the travellers to understand rather better the part Friends were taking in helping to bring about unity in this great new country of many States.

Friends, as a whole, had entered less into political life since the middle of the century, but now, as their numbers increased and by their example of order and discipline, coupled with their success in industry and trade, they began to be more involved as valuable leaders of an emerging nation.

Following breakfast next day, on 11th November, 'Dr Fd R[ebecca] Wright convey'd much encouragement which was a reasonable relief to our tried minds' and they attended **Abington** Meeting which was large and solid, and 'here we had the company of Dr John Pemberton and Thomas Scattergood'. Thomas Scattergood, the third of that name, was described as a 'mournful prophet'; he was a member of that particular Meeting and was a few years older than Deborah. He was to go to Europe in the following year, his visit lasting over Deborah's return home.

Abington was built on land purchased by the first American Waln who came over with Penn in 1682.

> **Abington, Plymouth** and **Germantown** *Meetings and their communities lie north-west of Philadelphia, and are now within that urban area. Germantown and its Monthly Meeting at Abington had been the home of Francis Daniel Pastorius and the Rhineland Mennonite communities won to Quakerism by William Penn. This group was the first Quaker Monthly Meeting to propose the abolition of slavery among Friends.*

On 12th November 'our Dr Frd William Savery met us at **Plymouth** where we had a satisfactory Meeting with Fds in the morning and the People in the Evening', they also found some youth 'under affliction'. William Savery, a prominent American Friend of Philadelphia, a tanner by trade and an intelligent and pleasant man of 43, was a minister of some years standing. He had just returned, on 19th September, from an arduous journey to the north-west of the country beyond Detroit with five other Friends – Jacob Lindley; John Parrish; John Ellicott; Joseph Moore and William Hartshorne. These Friends had been asked by the authorities to assist their representatives in talks, to bring about a Treaty with the Iroquois Indian tribes termed the 'Six Nations'. The journeys had been difficult and the talks had proved protracted and unfortunately ended in failure.

William Savery and William Hartshorne had returned by a route entailing travel in a small sailing vessel down the St Lawrence River, through rapids into Lake St Francis, where they nearly suffered total shipwreck. Because of this exposure to the elements, William Savery caught a fever, only just managing to have the strength to accomplish the rest of the journey home. On reaching Saratoga they heard of the epidemic in Philadelphia and acute anxiety was added to their other difficulties. William finally arrived back to find the Yellow Fever at its height, and that his wife, Sarah, had taken refuge with her children at the home in **Germantown** of Caspar Haines at a house called 'Wyck' on the Main Street. Here William joined them until he had fully recovered and to await the time when they could all return home.

At **Valley Meeting** on 13th November, Rebecca 'had a favor'd opportunity', but Deborah was 'silent'; afterwards they held 'a sitting in a Fds family where we took Dinner'. Next day they attended **Goshen** Meeting and had 'to lament over a departure from that zeal which cloathed many of the first settlers in this Country – we had reason to hope, however, there are still a Remnant on the ancient foundation to whom encouragement was handed as well as a rising generation called unto to follow the footsteps of the flock'. They travelled to **Chester** that same evening where they had a 'satisfactory Meeting in the Court House'.

> Deborah and Rebecca seem to have been still too fearful of Yellow Fever to enter central Philadelphia, but went around by **Valley Meeting** near the Schuylkill at Valley Forge to **Goshen,** near West Chester, probably the **Chester** to which Deborah refers.

After sitting in a Friend's family on 15th November they attended **Birmingham Meeting** in which 'notwithstanding the departure of many from the Law and Testimony which caused some close labour to be bestowed, we found some preciously visited minds that called forth our sympathy, and to whom consolation flow'd freely'. That night they lodged at Caspar Wistar's house 'with whose family we found a near acquaintance'. The Wistars had come originally from Germany and the spelling of their name had been Wister, the change coming when vowels in both christian and surnames had been altered. Deborah evidently found herself in sympathy with this family and later received a small Bible with the cover embroidered by M. Wistar which had been given by Samuel Fothergill to that member of the family.[4]

New Garden Meeting House, Chester, P.A., 1743.

East Nottingham Meeting House, Maryland, 1748.

Four Meeting Houses visited by Deborah and Rebecca in Pennsylvania during their American tour.

USED AS A HOSPITAL DURING THE BATTLE OF THE BRANDYWINE, SEPT. 11TH. 1777.   MANY
COLONIAL SOLDIERS ARE BURIED IN UNMARKED GRAVES IN THE OLD CEMETREY.
GENERAL LAFAYETTE WAS WOUNDED DURING THE BATTLE.

Birmingham Meeting House, Birmingham TWP, Chester Co., P.A. Built in 1763 near Chadds Ford, Delaware Co., P.A.

Roaring Creek Meeting House, Pennsylvania, P.A., 1796.

The Quarterly Meeting of Ministers and Elders was held at **London Grove** on 16th November which Deborah and Rebecca attended, travelling on to **New Garden** Meeting the following day where they 'lodged at the house of our much esteem'd Fds, Jacob and Hannah Lindley'. Jacob had just returned from the same expedition as William Savery, but by another route. Deborah found 'our minds were dip'd into sympathy with those that were bearing the Ark of the Testimony on their shoulders'.

On 19th November at a Meeting of more than 1,500 appointed for Youth 'much Counsel was handed'. After a sitting in Joshua Pusey's family they went to lodge with John Jackson, going on to '**West Grove Meeting** and here parted with Samuel and Mary Smith who had been with us some days'.

> **Concord, Birmingham, London Grove** and **West Grove** in Western Quarterly Meeting were rural Meetings progressively west-south-west of Philadelphia near the Baltimore Pike. Their early 18th century Meeting Houses survive. **Nottingham,** farther down the same road, was close to the 'Mason and Dixon line' delimiting Pennsylvania from Maryland; though the town is in Pennsylvania, the Meeting was within Baltimore Yearly Meeting, as were all the Meetings beyond the Susquehanna. The Battle of the Brandywine in 1777 was fought west and north of **Birmingham Meeting House,** when British forces outflanked Washington's army along Brandywine Creek. The Meeting House was used as a hospital.

John Jackson lived at **London Grove**, a man of amiable manner who, with his wife, gave continual hospitality. He was a skilled gardener and botanist, and had begun to make a beautiful garden about 1776. The location was a limestone valley of great beauty and fertility. There was a spring arising in the middle of the area which gave abundance of water for aquatic and moisture loving plants. He had also collected many interesting foreign and indigenous shrubs and trees over the years, and by the 1790's the garden attracted many visitors. It is to be hoped that Deborah and Rebecca were taken to see this garden when visiting the Jackson's home, although the time of the year was the 'fall', when the main beauty would be the dramatic reds and golds of the trees.

In Maryland they attended **East Nottingham Meeting** on 21st November where some 'young People were particularly addressed as well as in a Fd's family'. Next day they travelled on to **West Nottingham**, and it was here that Deborah wrote her letter[5] to Elizabeth Pim in which she gave a short account of why they had undertaken this particular journey. No doubt if the times had been normal they would have gone straight to Philadelphia but the situation had made them look to the south first. In her letter to Elizabeth Pim, Deborah explained their journey rather more clearly: 'we turned our faces towards the Jerseys, and we have since been taking Meetings in a line through Pennsylvania into Maryland, where we are now at the house of George Churchman, son of the late John Churchman. He is an Elder worthy of double honours, and we have had his company for several days past, attending a Quarterly Meeting at **London Grove**, but he is now gone to attend another at Crosswicks, spending the greater part of his time in visiting Yearly, Quarterly and Monthly Meetings. He is an example of Dedication to Elders in this and other lands. In some of the Meetings where we have been with him, he stood up and said a few words *with his hat on*[6] tending to the settling of them in their gathering'.

She also wrote in this letter 'My beloved Companion and myself have been favor'd with good health as common since we came into this land. The weather has been very agreeable, but how we shall bear the extremes of heat and cold to which this climate is subject, time must determine'. She added 'You may have heard before this time of the affliction allotted Philadelphia, nearly 4,000 inhabitants have been removed by Yellow Fever, and some very valuable Ministers and Elders and many Fds, but none of those who have visited our land. S[amuel] Smith and R[ebecca] Jones have both been ill and are recovered tho' R.J. continues weak. The Rod which has hung over for more than two months against that late sumptuous City is now nearly removed and the inhabitants are returning without much fear'.

During the next week they continued to attend Meetings, crossing the Susquehanna River on the 24th November to attend **Fawn** Meeting, and were at **Deer Creek** Meeting next day where they found '50 families of freed Blacks'. They attended **Gunpowder** Meeting on their way to Baltimore which they reached on 29th November, which Deborah hoped would be 'a time of encouragement to some difident minds'. The earth around was of a red colour because of the presence of iron and there was, therefore, much smelting carried out in the area; the adjacent forests providing the necessary charcoal which was the fuel still being used. Baltimore had a larger population than any other town in Maryland, and was situated on a hill near the Patapsco River, beyond which the land was sandy and so easier for travelling. There were woods with black pines and oaks, with here and there a very fine tulip tree.

Deer Creek Meeting *survives though* **Fawn** *did not. Friends'* **Gunpowder Meeting** *was named for the local river.*

December

On 1st December, which was also First Day, in the morning Meeting 'the Youth was particularly visited' and this was followed by 'a solid Meeting with the inhabitants in the Evening'. They found a want of faithfulness at **Elk Ridge** Meeting the next day for 'the professors of Truth measurably obstructed the spreading of the Gospel'. A Meeting was held at Ellicot's Mill on 3rd December when the 'Gospel flow'd freely to some Religious minds differing from us as to Religious profession'. The Ellicott brothers owned a flour mill, and were members of Elk Ridge Preparative

Meeting and of West River Monthly Meeting on the Patapsco, near the present Ellicott City.

At **Sandy Spring** after a weekday Meeting there followed 'an opportunity in a Fds family' which gave them encouragement. On 5th December they also 'had a favor'd season with some Black People' in another family. A number of Friends had, by this time, liberated their slaves in various states, but had often continued to care for them, as this was essential for the well-being of these freed men and women.

> **Sandy Spring**, *west of Baltimore, became the centre for the Yearly Meeting's boarding school from 1815 to 1826, and again after 1958, and since 1968 is the headquarters of the Yearly Meeting, mainly reunited after the long Hicksite split.*

Deborah and Rebecca were in **Georgetown on the 6th December, now part of Washington D.C.**

> **Georgetown** *predated the laying out after 1800 of Washington D.C. as the Federal Capital, within which it is now included. It was never a Quaker centre.*

They travelled next day to **Alexandria**, Virginia, a town of about 300 houses across the Potomac River, where there was a City Hall and several places of worship besides the Friends Meeting House. A number of the buildings were constructed of bricks made from clay found locally, the mortar used being from crushed oyster shells found in abundance on the river banks. Here there were several families of Friends, but 'they had to lament the want of faithfulness to the precious Testimonys of Truth', and left hoping it was 'a Day of renew'd visitation for some'. On 9th December, having finished the visits to Friends' families, they had to part reluctantly with their 'Dr Fd and Brother John Murray', who had been with them ever since they left New York and who had helped them greatly during this part of their journey in the New World.

> **Alexandria**, *Virginia, across the Potomac, dates from the early 18th century. It had a Monthly Meeting and later six small Quaker schools. George Washington belonged to the Anglican Church there. Twenty miles south of Alexandria, the* **Occoquam** *Creek from Manasses enters the Potomac. Most Friends in the* **Virginia Yearly Meeting** *(1689-1845) had migrated down from Pennsylvania and Maryland into the area of small frontier farms near the Blue Ridge and moved later into Ohio, along with many Carolina Friends, to escape communities based upon slavery and hostile to Quaker ideas.*

They went on to Colchester, a village on the **Occoquam**, a stream which emptied into the Potomac River. There they had a Meeting with a small number of people in the morning and at a Mill belonging to a member of the Society in the evening. The next day they reached **Dumfries**, on

11th December, a place where there were some tobacco warehouses. They realised 'that those that might have been light' were somewhat awed and they left hoping that their visit had not been in vain, for there was evidence of much luxury among the inhabitants with a large number of slaves kept to sustain their way of life. The cultivation of tobacco also meant that the land became exhausted after a few seasons, so that fresh acreage was continually taken on, reducing the woodlands and ground for future crops and other types of cultivation, for the practice of rotation was not then understood.

Deborah and Rebecca found their mission depressing here, and reaching **Stafford** on 12th December they were aware that 'the precious Life of Truth was under oppression'. In **Fredericksburg** on 13th December in the Court House and with two young men resident there, they felt 'Divine Regard extended tho' it is a dissipated place'. In this area there were large and small tobacco plantations, where the wealthier planters employed overseers for their slaves and lived themselves in fine houses, keeping households of domestics also in bondage. They bred horses for riding and for driving where the roads were suitable. Those however with more modest incomes oversaw their own workforce and lived less spectacular lives.

In **Caroline** Meeting, matters of faith appeared rather better 'with much Love being felt unto a mixed gathering'. A marriage took place next day at **Cedar Creek** Meeting 'a time of favor especially to the Youth'. When they reached **Richmond**, the capital of Virginia, they had an evening Meeting in the State House which, once again, they found to be 'a trying time'. On 18th December they attended a Meeting at **Curles** and felt much sympathy towards 'Dr Robert Pleasants, a valuable ancient who had liberated his Black People some years before', but many of them surrounded him, not choosing to separate themselves from so good a master.

> **Dumfries** *is down the Potomac and like* **Stafford** *and* **Fredericksburg** *lies on the main road to* **Richmond**, *by then the capital of Virginia. None were Quaker centres and neither* **Cedar Creek** *nor* **Caroline** *Meetings in Caroline County have survived. Probably Deborah, Rebecca and their companions travelled thus far by coach.* **Curles** *is on the north bank of the James River, later the scene of American Civil War battles, as was* **Petersburg**, *south of Richmond on the main road into North Carolina.* **Gravelly Run** *and other communities of small farms eastward and southward to the edge of Dismal Swamp kept Quaker Meetings, of which Corinth at Ivor, Bethel at Franklin, and Somerton at Suffolk survived until the present day. (The oldest Meeting and Quarterly Meeting south of James River, begun by George Fox, were at Chuckatuck from 1673.)*

They crossed the James River, but Deborah does not say in what manner, and visited a Friend at **Petersburg** lately come from England. The evening Meeting there was large 'finding some valuable people in this dissapated place'. (Again Deborah uses that expression.) They rode on to

John Butler's on 21st December, visiting a family on the way, and by the 22nd were at **Gravelly Run** Meeting where their 'minds were particularly exercised on account of the Youth, many of whom call for much sympathy'. They were finding that the needs of the families 'lacked the precious Life of Truth' and that it was no wonder the young 'appear to want the seasoning influence thereof'.

On 23rd December, they 'Dined for the first time in the Woods and found no stable for our horses', but they had a 'Religious opportunity in a Fds family in the evening' where presumably they lodged. Next day there was a Public Meeting, and on the 25th a Meeting was held at 'Widow Ladd's', and they felt 'nearly with some serious people'. A relief which comes through in her writing also shows a thankfulness that their long, and at times arduous, travelling had some encouraging aspects in the help they brought among Friends, not often visited from a distance.

They lodged at the house of a Methodist and sat with the family, the visitors believing their hosts had been awakened but 'wanted more stillness in order to know an establishment in the Truth'.

Two days later they found **Jack Swamp** Meeting 'laborious' to themselves but they 'hoped might prove strengthening to some honest but feeble minds'. They next held a Meeting at **Rich Square** at which there was a large gathering many attended not of the Society, and in the evening they had a sitting at their lodgings where 'the Fd had 10 children'. At **Halifax** on the last day of the month they held a 'Meeting for People of other Societys', where some were encouraged but also there was 'Caution to another class'.

> *Rich Square and Jack Swamp, southward into North Carolina, and Halifax on the Roanoke River were linked to these Virginia swampland Meetings. Rich Square became the centre of North Carolina Yearly Meeting, Conservative, when it split from the more Evangelical Yearly Meeting in 1904. Catherine Payton Phillips from England, travelling, in 1753, also visited the still older Piney Woods Meeting along Albemarle Sound, but it had withered. Deborah Darby and Rebecca Young stayed farther inland, returning to the Sounds later.*

1794
January

On the 2nd January 1794 they 'sat with a few Fds at the house of one in profession with us', but unfortunately they found 'Truth very low'. Afterwards they rode a considerable distance, Deborah finding 'how favourable [it was] to retirement in travelling in the Woods', but discovered even so that a stayed mind was difficult to attain.

The forests they were passing through contained many black pine trees from which pitch and resin were obtained, both profitable products, which were sent down the rivers for export. They rode along the old Indian trails which traversed the great forests and only a few of these were widened and improved here and there for convenience between some of the towns and for the passing of some wheeled traffic. They attended a Meeting for a sick Friend on 3rd January, held in his chamber, and were thankful that on the next day they were able to rest where they lodged. Deborah here became hopeful 'that a good work had been begun in some young minds'. She always mentioned the youth and the importance of reaching the young hearts to inspire them, striving for this, as she knew that the realisation of the Love of God was the most precious secret in life for every living soul.

On 5th January they had a large Meeting in Great Contentnea, North Carolina, which proved 'a season of visitation', which was also the case in their lodging that evening. At this time they had been riding between 20 and 30 miles a day, crossing rivers either by ferry or ford, but Deborah never mentions these difficulties, although other travellers of this period have given dramatic descriptions of similar journeys, when the crossing of swiftly running water, particularly after storms, could be extremely hazardous.

The strength of purpose of these women overcame all dangers and discomforts which were undoubtedly considerable. They were accompanied from Meeting to Meeting by men Friends of each place they visited, to ensure their safety and to guide them through the very sparsely populated countryside, as yet not always fully settled down after the end of the War of Independence, and with the added difficulty in some districts of continuing disputes with the various Indian tribes. At Bear Creek Meeting on 6th January 'their minds were sorrowfully affected with a sense of the low state of Religion amongst Fds and others', although Deborah hoped there were a few who were 'in pursuit of best things'. They reached **Neuse**, situated on the river of that name, and held a Meeting on the 7th: her comment was that 'after a wrestling season a measure of blessing was obtained to the comfort of the weary traveller'.

> *Contentnea, Nahunta* and **Neuse** *were the central Meetings for eastern North Carolina, and often the site of North Carolina Yearly Meeting sessions.*

After two days of travelling they arrived at **Trent**, but this was a silent Meeting 'to the disappointment of the People such as had their views more to the Servants than the Master'. Fortunately for their personal encouragement there was later a satisfactory Meeting at Trenton, a fishing village where the river was crossed by a bridge.

They were at the Monthly Meeting at **Lower Trent** on 11th January, and were also at the same Meeting House the following morning before going on to **Newburn**, then the capital of North Carolina, in the evening of the 12th. This place was situated on the confluence of the Trent and Neuse Rivers. As the ground near the riverside was flooded in places at times there was some indigo and rice grown in the neighbourhood; also as the climate was mild in winter, many trees and shrubs grew well, such as the bourbon laurel, magnolia, willow-leaved oaks, andromedas and smilaxes. Also along the banks of the Trent River the soil was in places very fertile and suitable for the growing of grain, producing a good yield an acre. The great forests came to within about 30 miles of the city and they had been travelling through areas of these from Meeting to Meeting.

In these forests herds of swine were allowed to feed on acorns and other wild food. Their meat was then salted, packed into barrels and sent down river to sell at home and abroad. This meat was universally eaten in the inns and by less well-off families, so Deborah and Rebecca must have been offered this quite frequently during their travels. Also, though less often, the flesh of the wild turkeys was obtainable.

On their arrival at Newburn, Deborah and Rebecca had a 'solid Meeting' which took place that evening. They had a 'favor'd Meeting' at **Core Sound** on 14th January, where they found to their content 'much tenderness was manifested among the People as well as at **Beaufort**, a small fishing town', where they had a Meeting in the evening.

Upper and Lower **Trent** were seaward toward **Newburn** on **Core Sound**, which like **Beaufort** and **Clubfoot Creek** disappeared early from Quaker history.

The following day, after having 'a refreshing opportunity in Benjamin Stanton's family', they went on to **Clubfoot Creek** Meeting that day. They then rode for three days, a total of 128 miles, to complete their journey to Wilmington in North Carolina, finding their way led through 'a poor country in which the inhabitants look sickly'. **Wilmington** was situated on the shores of the **Cape Fear River**, so called as the waters entered the sea from an estuary by the Cape of that name.

Wilmington, though earlier the North Carolina capital, was less important as a Quaker centre than Carver's Creek, 39 miles farther up the **Cape Fear River**.

There were sandy hills surrounding the town, where the houses were built several steps above street level, with front porches, as this type of building was better ventilated and therefore healthier in hot weather. They held another Meeting there on 20th January, and were surprised to find that it was 'twenty years since a Meeting had been held in that place'. Here Deborah made one of her rare remarks upon the weather, exclaiming it was 'very hot' on that particular day. After all it was only the first month of the year which must have surprised her even if they were now so far south. As they travelled she does not say if they noticed any of the 'feathered choir' completely new to them, but they could not have helped seeing on their journey the brilliant Cardinal birds, numerous and unmistakable, not only in plumage but for their distinctive song.

They rode pretty hard for the next two days and on the evening of the 23rd 'had a few of the poor slaves collected at our lodgings to whom the love of the Gospel was felt'. On the 26th, a First Day, they had two Meetings in Georgetown 'to good satisfaction, there appearing to be a hidden precious People even in this dissipated country'. **Georgetown** was situated on a low-lying plain on the confluence of four rivers forming **Winyah Bay**. The city had been built on a regular grid plan with straight streets, the houses distant from one another in their gardens, and damage would still have been apparent after the years of war.

On 27th and 28th January Deborah and Rebecca travelled to Charleston through a country 'in which our minds much in sympathy with the poor Africans, enslaved in great numbers in this Country'.

In Charleston at this time the white inhabitants numbered about 5,000, and the blacks 7,000. Food was plentiful: meat, fish, vegetables and fruit, some of which was imported. At the time of Deborah's visit it was natural that she should have been very perturbed over the treatment of blacks, as their emancipation was only coming very slowly in the south, because of the large numbers of slaves, so that the State, as a whole, had not really begun to encourage their freedom sufficiently.

The road they travelled was a beautiful one, though subject to flooding and very hazardous at times.

> **Georgetown** *is still a major town 60 miles up the coast from* **Charleston**, *South Carolina's oldest centre and capital. Yet though Mary Fisher the pioneer Quaker visitor to New England and to the Sultan of Turkey, had moved with her husband John Cross to Charleston before 1685, and her granddaughter Sophia Hume also led the Meeting there, the Meetings in both cities had died before Deborah's arrival.*

They were at weekday Meeting on 29th January where Rebecca 'was enabled rightly to divide the word' and Deborah was engaged 'in seeking a blessing'. **Charleston** was situated on a point formed by two navigable rivers, the Ashley and the Cooper, which formed a little above the place and emptied into the ocean seven miles below near Sullivan Island. There were wharves above the banks where the ships anchored and the entrance to the port was defended by Fort Moultre on Sullivan Island. The streets cut across each other at right angles dividing the city into various blocks, where the houses situated in them all had gardens. The State House, Law Court, Senate and House of Representatives, Churches, Chapels and Friends Meeting House were the main public buildings.

February

On 1st February they had a Public Meeting in the Exchange, remarking that 'Silence in most places seems irksome to the People, yet on the whole they behaved well'. They also visited families, but found since coming to this place a disappointment that 'the pure Life' was low. The next day morning Meeting was 'trying but one in the Exchange in the afternoon was more open', and they had a further opportunity that evening at their lodgings.

On 3rd and 4th February they were accompanied by John Lloyd from Pennsylvania, and reached **Pope's Swamp** where they attended a Meeting. John Lloyd was a descendant of Thomas Lloyd of Dolobran who had emigrated to Pennsylvania in 1683, later becoming Deputy Governor. John was related to the Lloyds of Birmingham, well known to Deborah, so they had mutual acquaintances and familiar places to talk about during their long hours of riding.

A further three days of travelling followed on the road to **Augusta**, the second largest city in Georgia and the seat of the State Government, situated on the southern shore of the Savannah River which was navigable by boat from there to the coast. Goods such as corn and indigo and local produce were then sent by water to the ports, and there loaded into ships to cross the ocean. These craft returning up river brought European goods for the different destinations inland.

Deborah and Rebecca attended two Meetings the day they arrived on 9th February, but lamented 'the prevalence of a worldly spirit', which was hardly surprising as there had been considerable destruction in Atlanta in the late war, and the citizens were endeavouring to rebuild their homes and restore their normal way of life.

When Deborah and Rebecca left they spent two more days on the road, reaching **Wrightsborough** on the 12th February for weekday Meeting held in silence. A Public Meeting two days later was held in the house of Marmaduke Mendenhall, followed by 'sitting in three families to some satisfaction'. On 16th February they attended a large Meeting where Friends' 'Principles were largely explained'. They also continued their visit to families.

> *Pope's Swamp may correspond to Edisto Meeting north-west of Charleston. In all the Georgia Meetings, even the main centre at **Wrightsborough** west of **Augusta**, Friends found intolerable pressures from slave-owning neighbours. They moved beyond the Ohio River well before the American Civil War. Borden Stanton led the Georgian Friends migration in 1799, and Zechariah Dicks that from Bush River in 1803. Friends from the Meetings at **Bush River** and **Cane Creek**, South Carolina and **Wrightsborough**, Georgia moved through Miami Monthly Meeting, Waynesville, Ohio, to take up new farmland in Indiana, between 1803 and 1807.*

By the 19th of the month, Deborah concluded that their 'desires had been fervent that the youth might be brought under the forming hand of

God, when the Elders were removed there might be such as could stand availingly in the Cause of Truth'. By 26th February they had finished their family visits to Friends in Georgia, so set out for South Carolina, reaching Allwood on 28th February, where they found the Meeting 'exercising, but ended well'. After Meeting at Cambridge on 1st March they went to the house of our 'Valuable Fd Charity Cook'[7] and had a sitting in the family that evening in which our minds were strongly impressed with a belief that she had a prospect of visiting England, this proved to be the case three years later.

Isaac and Charity Cook had lived in the vicinity of **Bush River** Monthly Meeting in South Carolina ever since they married in 1773. This community and other settlements in the area had grown considerably in the last years, additional families having come to join them from Georgia and North Carolina. Charity was the fifth child of John and Rachel Wright, who had moved several times further west in the frontier areas, taking their ever growing family with them, and finally founding the settlement of Cane Creek, South Carolina, which lay to the north of Bush River. They appeared to have been quite undaunted by the proximity of Indian tribes or the strife of the 'French and Indian wars' which had disrupted the frontiers and been so dangerous to the settlers.

They had always led a very active life to ensure survival, and the children all played their part, each having an allotted task in the daily round of work which was essential for existence. There were no schools in the neighbourhood and it is thought that Charity could not read or write until after she was married to Isaac Cook. He was the fifth of the eight children of Thomas Cook who had married Mary Underwood. Thomas, who died in 1752 at the age of 48 was a prominent member of Warrington Meeting in England. Two years later Mary, with her eldest son Abraham and the other children, emigrated from Warrington to Cane Creek Meeting in North Carolina. They attended New Garden Meeting in what was then Rowan County, North Carolina. At that time New Garden was a subordinate Meeting of **Cane Creek** Monthly Meeting.

Charity, at the time of Deborah and Rebecca's visit, had already undertaken one or two missionary journeys to the south for a few weeks at at time each year, and in 1794 she planned to visit Meetings and families in Georgia. When Deborah and Rebecca came to stay with Charity and Isaac Cook and their family, they would in all probability have found their home of the type usually erected by settlers, the main building being of logs, to which additions could be made as the family increased, eventually to 11 children. As a rule these homes began by having one large room with a loft above, and the floor originally puddled of clay found in that particular locality. This was given a good surface by the pounding in of powdered quartz if available. The hearth would have been at one end with a chimney also lined with clay against the risk of fire.

The original settlers always had to ensure that there was a good supply of fresh water nearby their dwelling place before starting to build. The men went ahead the year before the main move, to stake their land claims and to construct a shelter, with a plot for the growing of vegetables to provide for the first few months. The following spring they would move, taking their families, usually in a group together for more security. They took their farm and domestic animals with them and, of course, tools for construction and working the land. Their food would be chiefly what they could find after arrival and what they could grow; the rivers and streams were full of fish and there was plenty of game in the forests where the Indians had formerly hunted for their food. Charity had been brought up to this life and Isaac in part also, so both were naturally resourceful, and Isaac appeared able to take care of their family on his own whenever Charity was away.

March

On the 2nd March, Deborah and Rebecca were at **Rayburn Creek** Monthly Meeting which Deborah said 'was attended with such a measure of holy help as enabled us to convey the language of encouragement to the faithful and to warn the rebellious'. They sat in a Friend's family that evening and were at Mud Lick Meeting next day. The 3rd and 4th March were spent resting, although still undertaking some travelling to give them an opportunity in a Friend's family on their way to Bush River, where they attended weekday Meeting. This was the Meeting to which Charity and Isaac Cook belonged and Deborah remarked of this Meeting 'The Duty we owe to our offspring was strongly enforced and the necessity of waiting for Divine wisdom to aid herein'.

> **Rocky Spring** and **Rayburn's Creek** lay west of Bush River, but never became Monthly Meetings.

In **Rocky Spring** Meeting on 7th March, their 'minds were dip'd unto near sympathy with some diffident minds whom the Lord was calling to show themselves more openly on His side'. There was a Meeting then appointed for Youth at Bush River, where much counsel was handled which eventually they thought 'might prove as Bread cast upon the Waters'. After a precious opportunity in a Friends family they attended Bush River Meeting again, when Deborah and Rebecca were engaged 'to call Fds to faithfulness and C[harity] Cook concluded the Meeting with solemn prayer'. Deborah does not reveal if they had again stayed with Charity and Isaac, although they probably did so while they were visiting this particular group of Meetings.

On 10th March, there was a Public Meeting in a Court House followed by two sittings in Friend's families. Two days later, after 'an opportunity of retirement' at their lodgings 'which it appear'd our duty to promote in passing along', they attended Padget's Creek Meeting 'which was laborious', and they also visited a sick Friend and had 'an opportunity with some Young People'.

Further sittings in Friends' families were made next day and they attended **Cane Creek** Meeting, where Charity's family had created the settlement originally. They were in a County of river inlets and flowing water, which caused them to make a considerable detour of two more days of travelling as they were prevented from getting to Camden by water. There were inevitably long hours in the saddle during these weeks of travelling, but Deborah never mentioned their mounts, except occasionally if their horses' welfare was really in doubt for lack of stabling or fodder.

On 18th March they all attended **Pee Dee** Meeting and were at **Gum Swamp** a day later, both well to the east of Bush River, as well as sitting with several families there. They were then on the road again for two more days to **Holly Spring** (North Carolina) attending Meeting there on 22nd March which fortunately 'ended well'.

Rebecca Young opened Bush River Meeting on 24th March to which they had evidently returned, and next day found them at Tyson Meeting where Rebecca 'was helped to convey a Testimony of Truth' but Deborah was silent. They were at Rocky **Spring** Meeting again on 26th March and there was a sitting in a Friend's family.

Next day, 27th March they 'had a sitting to [their] comfort in David Vestal's family', and found him 'an Elder worthy of double honour', who accompanied them to Sandy **Spring** Meeting where 'Truth appeared to be low – some ability [being] afforded to labour'.

On to **Providence** Meeting, then to **New Garden** for Monthly Meeting where they found 'a remnant bound to the Law & Testimony, the deviation of numbers administer'd much cause for sorrow'. This Meeting was obviously in some difficulty and Deborah goes on to say 'many states [were] spoken to, I trust to the benefit of some tho' it was labouring in the Gospel'.

> **Providence**, *far northward in North Carolina (there were also Providences in Pennsylvania, and Rhode Island),* **Rocky River**, *(Sandy)* **Spring**, *the North Carolina* **Cane Creek**, *and* **New Garden** *(now on the campus of Guilford College in Greensboro) were all in the cluster of new Quaker settlements in the Piedmont, close to the Blue Ridge, along which Friends from Pennsylvania and Maryland had migrated in the 1750's. This area gradually superseded the Contentnea region as the centre of Carolina Quakerism.* **Hopewells** *spring eternally throughout the Quaker maps of Virginia, Ohio, Indiana and Iowa. This one in North Carolina has left few traces.*

By the last day of March they reached **Hopewell** Meeting which exercised them at the beginning, but 'ended to [their] satisfaction'.

April

Dover Meeting proved a refreshing season on 1st April, and on the 2nd they had 'the Company of [their] Valuable Fd David Brooks', and all attended Muddy Creek Meeting which 'prov'd relieving to [their] minds tho' the testimony went close to a libertine spirit'. At **Westfield** Meeting two days later 'where many People of other Societys attended', they found them 'attentive and solid'. By 6th April they were at **Reedy Island** Meeting. The names of some of these places reveal the low-lying land through which they were sometimes travelling.

> **Westfield**, *North Carolina, site of a later Quaker Academy, was north-west of Winston-Salem, and close to the Blue Ridge, by no means 'low lying land'.*

They continued their journey the next day, and by the morning of 10th April they 'had a desire to sit with the family where they lodged'. Unfortunately Deborah seldom gives the name of their hosts or says if they ever had to stay at an inn. Their lodgings were perhaps where opportunity occurred, but local Friends continued to accompany them to ensure the safety of these journeys of very considerable distances in an unfamiliar country. All was of course very strange to these two English women, with the terrain so varied with different fauna and flora. Also in some places the forests and coastal districts were hazardous from fierce animals and poisonous plants. Where they encountered a rattlesnake and how closely is uncertain, but Deborah, brought the stinging tail in a small card box back to England.[8]

After a sitting in a family on 10th April they met a committee of Friends in the woods where 'sitting down together they had a favor'd season'. This occasion must have been long remembered by the two travelling ministers – the quiet group of Friends in their plain dress, the sun of the spring day falling softly through the leaves of the trees on their bent heads and clasped hands, highlighting the white caps and kerchiefs of the woman – it was evidently a time of peace, the unusual event giving them strength.

Deborah and Rebecca then journied back towards **Westfield** and reached the home of Abraham Smith where they lodged. Deborah felt 'glad to get amongst Friends again' and this remark perhaps indicated their lodgings had been lately in the homes of those 'not professing with them'. They were at **Nolichucky** Meeting on 13th April which was large and Deborah hoped profitable. For the next two days their travels took them into the woods where they had to spend one of the nights, which Deborah always recorded. In April this would not have been too chilly and the experience was perhaps rewarding. They were so near to the natural world in these forests which were providing the livelihood for the immigrants who were coming in ever increasing numbers from the Old World to the New.

Deborah's Bible (left) was originally given to Margaret Wistar by Samuel Fothergill (brother of Dr John Fothergill) and their initials are embroidered in red silk in cross stitch under the embroidered cover of cream and green wool. It was presented to her in 1796 by an American Friend, Catherine H. Muire. The bottle was turned from wood from a tree in the garden of Stephen Grellet. On the right is the rattlesnake's tail in its cardboard box still extant and in front is a piece of finely turned bark on pink ground mounting, presented to her by the Indians. COURTESY IRONBRIDGE GORGE MUSEUM TRUST

Three days later they reached **Lost Creek** on 16th April where they held a Meeting and on the next day a further one 'where there were many People of other Societys present to whom the glory of the Gospel Day was pointed out as having brought in a dispensation of *peace* that we as a Religious Society on this ground conscientiously refused joining in war, and Fds were exhorted to bear cheerfully the spoiling of goods', for confiscation had often been the outcome of their refusal to take up arms. They then rode on for 30 miles and in the evening of 18th April had a large Public Meeting where 'no Meeting of the Society had been held before'. In the afternoon of the 19th a Meeting was held at Green's Court House where 'altho' some of the People appeared light, others manifested a becoming seriousness, satisfactory to us'.

> *A visit to **Lost Creek Meeting**, over the Blue Ridge and Smoky Mountains into eastern **Tennessee**, was a formidable challenge to women travellers in that era, though Meeting representatives came to sessions of New Garden Quarterly Meeting. The **Nolichucky** River formed one access into this area; Daniel Boone had blazed a trail on over the Cumberland Gap into Kentucky, the main route for southern Friends moving to Ohio and Indiana.*

On the 20th they attended another Meeting at **Nolichucky** at which 'Friends were exhorted to wait for the Life of Religion to qualify them for every good word and work'. They rode another 21 miles next day and had a Meeting 'in a person's House who had been enquiring after Friends' Principles', and they felt that by Divine help the occasion had been strengthened. Three more days of travel followed, in all about 88 miles, and they had a Meeting on the 25th 'amongst a People that appear'd to be much Strangers unto Friends'. They were at a Meeting at Reedy Island on 26th April and Cheshunt the day after where 'the Meeting House proving too small for the numbers collected we sat out of Doors, when after many Gospel Truths being unfolded, prayer ascended for a Blessing on the People'. They also had a sitting at their lodgings later at which the young people were present.

May

After sitting in a Friend's family they went to **Deep River** Preparative Meeting on 1st May, where they sat in silence except that they made a 'few remarks among woman Friends'. The following day they were at Piney Woods Meeting 'in which encouragement flow'd freely', and had a Public Meeting there in the evening; also a sitting at **Nathan Hunt**'s 'who appears to be walking in his Father's footsteps'. Next day they called upon two Friends on their way to Springfield Monthly Meeting.

On 4th May, they had an open Meeting at **Deep Creek** hoping 'to revive the hope of the humble'. The number of Meetings on creeks, or close to navigable water, reveals how important communication by river was to the earlier settlers, many of whom had come to these places from overseas or neighbouring States. The Indians, who for centuries were the only inhabitants, had followed the forest paths or navigated the waterways by canoe. The travellers had an afternoon Meeting at Sherborn, followed by a sitting at John Talbot's house, who, with his wife Sarah appeared to be 'Valuable Friends'. Sarah was to travel to England two years later with them and other Friends.

At **Deep River** Monthly Meeting on 5th May, 'the excellency of Discipline was much the subject of the Day'. Next day there was a morning Meeting at **Marlborough** and another in the evening in a **Dutch** settlement. They dined with **Zacharia Dicks** and after the usual opportunity in their lodgings they went on to **Uwharrie** Meeting on the 7th. They gave some very serious counsel at **Black Creek** Meeting the following day where their 'attention was much turned to some visited minds', encouraging them to have patience that they might 'none of them prove mar'd Vessels'.

> **Deep River Meeting** *took them back into the New Garden area, where* **Nathan Hunt** *has been regarded as the weightiest of Carolina Friends and helped found the Carolina Quaker schools (see Hinshaw,* Carolina Quaker Experience, *Ch. 6).* **Deep Creek** *was somewhat west of Deep River, and* **Marlborough Meeting** *was a bit south. The* **Dutch** *may have been Friends at* **Uwharrie** *or Moravians from Salem, North Carolina.* **Zachariah Dicks** *was from* **Spring Meeting** *a few miles east, and had buried the dead there after the Battle of Lindley's Mill in 1781;* **Black Creek** *may be* **Back Creek** *near Marlborough, where migrating Friends converged from eastern North Carolina, New York, Pennsylvania and Virginia.* **Uwharrie Meeting,** *established in 1793, was nearby and the building later became the first school for blacks in the county.*

The Meeting at **Centre** on 9th May was 'laborious', after which a time of retirement followed before they attended **Cane Creek** (North Carolina) Select Quarterly Meeting to which they contributed some remarks. The Meeting at **Spring** next day was 'largely attended by those not professing with us to whom our Principles was explained'. Back to **Cane Creek** for a large and solid Meeting after this on the 11th May. After **Eno** Meeting on the 13th, followed by two days of riding for 84 miles, which they found very trying as the weather was extremely hot, they then reached Durham on the 15th where they had a Meeting 'to some satisfaction'.

> **Centre** *and* **Cane Creek Meetings,** *as noted above were in the same New Garden area, and* **Eno** *a little north-eastward.*

They continued their long journey for another 90 miles, during which they visited families on the way, and on 18th May attended **Blackwater Yearly Meeting** which was 'much crowded'. There they had the great pleasure of receiving letters from home 'having been near six months without'. The next day's Meeting for Worship sounded pleasing as she described it as 'lively', and on the same day they had 'an opportunity in the evening which was comfortable'. They were also pleased that the Meetings for Discipline 'afforded cause for hope that there is a renewal of concern for the speeding of the Truth on Earth'.

> **Blackwater Yearly Meeting** *refers to the holding of North Carolina Yearly Meeting sessions in alternate years until 1813 (when not at New Garden), at one of the 17th century Meetings on* **Perquimans River** *near Albemarle Sound, the eastern area Deborah and Rebecca had bypassed going south.*

Yearly Meeting closed on 21st May and the next day they had a sitting at their lodgings with 'some black People who had waited upon Fds with much affection'. They moved on to **Western Branch** Preparative Meeting, which proved 'large and solid' on 23rd May, also attended Monthly Meeting at the same place next day. On 25th May they attended a Meeting in the Court House at **Suffolk**, followed by a Meeting at **Norfolk** on the 26th held in a Riding House which proved 'beyond our expectation solid, the People being attentive to the Gospel of Truth delivered and afterwards manifested much love to us'.

> **Western Branch** *lay north from there in south-east Virginia's Dismal Swamp; the Quarterly Meeting included* **Suffolk, Norfolk,** *Portsmouth and the Chuckatuck area.*

On the 27th May they went to Meeting at Bennet's Creek, followed by 40 miles of travel, reaching **Piney Woods** on 29th May where the Meeting 'ended to satisfaction'. The Select Meeting on 30th May in the evening was followed next day, the last of the month, by Quarterly Meeting at **Symon's Creek**.

> *They probably returned west of the Swamp to* **Piney Woods** *and* **Symon's Creek** *near Albemarle Sound.* **Nickington** *may be the modern Nixonton nearby, at the mouth of* **Little River**, *for which a Meeting upstream was named;* **Newbegun Creek** *on a headland near Weeksville was the farthest east of the Carolina Meetings.*

June

They attended two large Meetings on 1st June 'with those of other Societys' one at **Symon's Creek** and the other at **Nickington**. They visited a sick Friend next day and were at **Newbegun Creek** Meeting followed by one at Three Brooks Creek in the evening. They had a 'religious opportunity' at their lodgings before leaving on 3rd June for **Little River** Meeting where 'the faithful were encouraged to bear the afflictions of the present Day, saying that those who mourn now shall hereafter rejoice'. They were pleased also with the 'opportunity with some invited Young

People where they dined'. The next day they attended Monthly Meeting at **Wells** with two sittings in families.

After **Sutton's Creek** Meeting on 5th June, they travelled to Eakington next day where they had a Meeting in the Court House. These buildings appeared to be hired for a Meeting where no Friends' Meeting House existed, or on an occasion when it was too small to hold Public Meetings when members of other societies were present. On 7th June after a 'solemn parting with our Dr Friends', they had a Meeting at **Gates Court House** where they met 'some solid People', and later sat in a Friend's family 'far removed from Meeting'. They were at Sommerton on the day after where 'an evident want of labour of spirit was felt', but at Johnsons next day they had a refreshing Meeting which appeared to have taken place in a family home, where they later dined.

> *Wells Meeting House 1704, (the first in the area, since they had met in homes), was directly across a ferry on Perquiman's River from the site where George Fox and William Edmondson had held the first Protestant service of worship in North Carolina in 1672.* **Sutton's Creek** *lay south-east, between Wells and Little River or Symon's Creek, and* **Gates** *(County)* **Court House** *north-westward up the Chowan River. From there Deborah and Rachel continued northward into Virginia.*

There was a Meeting at **Black Creek** on the 8th June and they had several opportunities on 10th June, including one with a 'blind Friend'.

By 11th June they reached Vick's Meeting 'to some satisfaction'. At **Stanton's** Meeting the day after and also in a Friend's family the 'Youth were particularly invited to choose the Lord for their enriching inheritance'. After attending **Seacock** Meeting on the 13th they reached **Burley** Meeting on the 14th and sat 'with some hopeful young people in a Fd's house'. The 15th June found them at Wain Oak where 'a renew'd visitation was extended to the Youth, they being invited to faithfulness unto the precious Testimonys of Truth'.

The distressing presence of slave labour, which was present in this State and nationally, continued to disturb them and took up a great deal of their attention. It was in this Blackwater area of Virginia that John Woolman had paid visits to the slave owners to try to dissuade them from this great scourge in society. He and Anthony Benezet[9] had been pioneers in the fight for the emancipation of slaves in North America although they had not been able to achieve more than a beginning towards the ultimate goal of freedom for all. Deborah continued to find the places they were revisiting 'dissapated': an epithet she found always apposite for describing the atmosphere and behaviour of some of the inhabitants; however, she found also there were a 'few precious minds dwelling there', for whom their visits were well worthwhile.

1794

Black Creek, Stanton's, Seacock (*also known as Pagan Creek*) *and* **Burley** (*part of Gravelly Run*) *brought Deborah and Rebecca back again to Virginia's Blackwater Quarterly Meeting in the Dismal Swamp area.* **Wain Oak** *was in Henrico Monthly Meeting which included* **Curles**, *north across the James River.*

There followed a Meeting at **Williamsburg** on the 16th June where there were no resident Friends. This place had been built by the Irish on the banks of the Santes River and with the discovery of indigo in the middle of the 18th century, a crop had been quickly cultivated, which with the growing of rice had given local prosperity. After having a 'favor'd opportunity' at their lodgings and in another family, they attended **Skimino** Meeting on 17th June. Next day they visited the R. Crews family and attended a Meeting at **Wain Oak** 'appointed for those of other Societys'. They had evidently returned especially to attend this. Next day they were at **Black Creek** in the morning and Swamp in the evening.

Williamsburg, *the old aristocratic colonial capital of Virginia, also lies north of the James River. William and Mary College there had been designed early in the century by Christopher Wren. Thus the women seem to have visited a second* **Black Creek** *in Henrico Monthly Meeting before going to* **Curles**, *to* **Richmond** *and on to* **Geneto** (*or Genita*) **Meeting** *40 miles north-west.*

At **Manchester** the Meeting on the 20th was held 'to much satisfaction considering it as the first ever held there'. Deborah and Rebecca then saw the few Friends living in **Richmond** in the evening. On to **Curles** Meeting nearby on 21st June, returning to **Richmond** next day where there was 'a quiet Meeting in the Court House and another in Manchester' which Deborah believed was by some 'gladly attended in the morning' saying 'there are some precious minds even in these very dissipated places'. Deborah found conditions in these out of the way places very little altered from a year ago when she had first visited them and seemed concerned that there had been no improvement in their way of life.

On the way to **Geneto** Meeting on 23rd June they visited two families on their way and three families afterwards, 'there appears to be something worth visiting especially amongst the Youth'. These experiences added continually to their knowledge of how Friends were living in these very different and varied parts of the country. They heard of their work and their human relationship and also their anxieties and fears. The pattern of Government had changed after the Wars of Independence, leaving only small groups belonging to certain religious sects in isolated places, apparently unchanged in their habits and continuing their same ways of life. The forming of independent States, with their own individual Senate and Houses of Representatives federated into one nation, was becoming successful and was to develop ultimately into the very powerful nation of later years.

On the 25th June they attended a Meeting at **Pine Creek** which was held in a Mill in which 'faithfulness to the knowledge received appeared to be the call of the Day'. They sat in two families afterwards. She reports that they 'felt much towards some that kept Slaves greatly desiring they might be strengthened to liberate them'. After a Meeting at **Amelia** on the 27th which was an 'open time especially to those not professing with us', they then took two days to reach South River on 29th, Deborah recording these 'were trying' as they were travelling in difficult country with much swamp and very indifferent roads. The weather was hot and exhausting for man and beast. Deborah and Rebecca had several sittings with families and by the 30th had reached **Lynchburgh** where the Meeting encouraged them 'as some young people were tender'.

> **Amelia** *was south of Geneto in the same Swamp Creek Monthly Meeting, and they evidently rode west through the scrub pine woods to* **Lynchburg** *beyond Appomattox, in the foothills of the Blue Ridge, the first main front of the Appalachians, running north-east to south-west from Pennsylvania to South Carolina.*

July

After riding 30 miles westwards they arrived at **Goose Creek** on 2nd July and after a sitting in families were at **Lower Goose Creek** Meeting on 3rd July and Hills Creek on the 4th, followed a day later by attendance at Seneca Meeting on 5th after which they returned to **Lynchburgh** for a Meeting, 'the first to be held by Friends in that place', which appeared 'more comfortable than we expected'. Travelling for 81 miles in two days they had a quiet Meeting on 9th July at **Columbia**, Virginia although no Friends resided there. Great distances were undertaken by American Friends when visiting ministers came, as the population was much scattered, and an event of strangers attending a Meeting, particularly from across the seas, would cause an extra effort to be made for Friends to come for a considerable number of miles to hear them.

> *The* **Goose Creek** *and* **Upper Goose Creek** *Meetings they next visited would have been the short-lived Meetings westward in the hills of Bedford County, not the more famous one near the Potomac (see Gap and Goose Creek p. 162). All these Meetings would soon be laid down as the members migrated west out of slave territory. The next leg was back through the pines north-east again to Virginia's* **Columbia**, *half-way between Richmond and Charlottesville.*

They travelled on to **Camp Creek** on the 10th and by the morning of 13th July they sat with Friends at Southland and in the evening 'held a Meeting with People of other Societys'. They rode 32 miles on the 14th to attend

Meeting at **Culpeper** which was held the following morning, and afterwards had a trying journey to **Smith's Creek** which they reached by evening on 16th July. In the last two days they had sat in Friends' families and 'travelled pretty hard'. Eunice Allen accompanied them to a Meeting at **Center** in the morning 'which proved laborious' and with two sittings in Friends' families and a Public Meeting in **Winchester** Court House filled their day.

> *Camp Creek Meeting was just beyond Geneto.* **Culpeper,** *later a junction famous in Civil War history, brought them north and to the Blue Ridge again.* **Southland** *was also close to the Rappahannock. Virginia's* **Center** *Meeting was not one of the eight in America so named that became a Monthly Meeting, nor did* **Smith's Creek** *nor this* **Back Creek,** *but these were among the cluster of Meetings which Pennsylvania emigrants had created around* **Winchester** *in the Shenandoah Valley, behind the Blue Ridge which Deborah and Rebecca must have crossed without enjoyment in their 'trying journey'.*

On 21st July after a satisfactory Meeting at **Back Creek** they set out towards the **Allegheny Mountains**, which Deborah recorded 'we crossed in 4 days and a half being tolerably accommodated with Lodgings – found the Roads very bad'. **Westland** was reached in time for Meeting on the 26th where Rebecca Young 'was led remarkably to the state of Things', and they had an opportunity where they dined.

> *They went gallantly over the main plateau of the* **Allegheny Mountains** *to* **Westland,** *on the Monongahela River in western Pennsylvania, the first Monthly Meeting in the Ohio valley (1785), and with* **Redstone** *one of the two through which hundreds of Quaker migrants into Ohio later transmitted their certificates of membership. In Deborah's time this was close to the limit of Quaker settlement. Although there were other settlers and many boats and rafts down the Ohio River, the treaty of Greenville with the native American Indians that made western Ohio secure was only signed in 1795. Northern Indiana was Indian territory until 1819. Martha Routh of Worcestershire also visited* **Pike Run,** *Westland and* **Fallowfield** *in 1795 (see Rufus M. Jones, Later Periods of Quakerism, pp. 390-93). Thomas Scattergood of Philadelphia had visited the area in 1785.*

They travelled on later that day to attend Meeting at **Pike Run**. In **Fallowfield** Meeting on the 29th as well as sitting with families 'The Love of the Life of Truth was felt to the refreshing of the weary traveller'. In Sweetly Meeting on 30th July 'the Gospel message was to press after faithfulness' and they ended the evening with a sitting in their lodgings.

During these days they returned to some of the places they had visited the previous year, but at a different season. Now, being summer, the weather was hot, all nature in flower and some of the fruits ripening. How much of their natural surroundings they noticed as they rode from one

Meeting to another is not known, but inevitably the scenes must have impinged from time to time on their consciousness. It is to be hoped they remembered the beauty of an unusual sight for European travellers but the presence of slave labour everpresent was a continual source of distress to them.

August

On 1st August they attended **Redstone** Meeting, and the next day was at **Old Fort** 'to some satisfaction'. Two Meetings were held on 3rd 'one at Fds Meeting House and another in a Town called Union'. On to **Glades** and by the 7th they had arrived at **Frankfort Meeting** where Deborah 'was much indisposed'. For the next two days she became very ill and a doctor was sent for on 10th August: she found fortunately that she was 'much favor'd in having so truly affectionate a Companion who spares no attention, may the Lord reward her for her tender care over so poor a creature; an emetic was given and 3 Blisters put on'. On the 14th Deborah was put in a carriage on a feather bed, and in three days reached the house of Friend Isaac Brown, who had kindly come 50 miles for her and she was able on the evening of the 16th to sit a little with the family to their 'mutual refreshment'.

Deborah rested for the next three days enabling her to be fit enough to attend **Ridge** weekday Meeting where 'much Counsel [was] handed a rising generation'. They then attended **Hopewell** Meeting in which the word was directed 'to several states'. Rebecca concluded the Meeting with prayer. Afterwards they dined at Abel Walker's and had 'a satisfactory opportunity in his family'. They attended **Middle Creek** Meeting on 22nd August, 'after a time of retirement in their lodgings', and were then at **Martinsburg** where the Meeting was 'chiefly designed for People of other Societys'.

They had two opportunities with Friends' families going on to attend **Bull Skin** Meeting which was 'large and open'. They reached **Hopewell** again for Meeting on 25th which was also a 'large Assembly with some of the Youth tenderly affected', an occurence always pleasing to Deborah. After a sitting in John Pool's family, they attended a Meeting at **Mount Pleasant** but they found it difficult to minister at **Crooked Run** Meeting next day 'as the expectation of the People was much outward'. However, they had a Meeting at the same place with Select Friends 'from whom we parted under a humble sense of the Lord's mercy'. Deborah here stated that she was disinclined to leave a family with whom they had been lodging 'without exampling them in the necessary Duty of silent waiting upon God'. They therefore sat down in their lodgings that morning of the 29th August, and went on later to attend South Fork Meeting.

Mount Pleasant, South Fork and **Crooked Run** *were south of Winchester on the way from the Shenandoah Valley towards the east.*

Goose Creek Meeting was large on the 30th, and afterwards they sat in Israel Janney's family.

Gap Meeting and Goose Creek (a Preparative Meeting since 1757) not to be confused with Goose and Upper Goose Creek p. 159, were just south of the upper Potomac, in what was then Fairfax County, the earliest area of Pennsylvania Friends' migration into Virginia in the 1720's, and near the starting point of the Cumberland Road (later the Old National Road) from the Potomac over the Appalachians into the west. Over this trail Deborah's companions clearly brought her, though they stopped at Meetings they had bypassed on their way south to Richmond and north-west to the Monongahela.

Abiah's Death

On the last day of the month they were at **Gap Meeting** after which Deborah received the news of Abiah's death. 'The account of my Beloved Mother Darby being removed from Works unto rewards, this was a trial to nature, tho' no doubt our loss is her gain. She had been tender over me in all respects and I owe much to her memory.'

Abiah had died on the 26th June and Samuel must have been distressed to lose his mother as it was she who had brought him up entirely after his father's death, and he had always relied on her for help and wise guidance.

Although Samuel's sister, Sarah, had always been of great assistance to him, particularly during his illnesses and was without doubt able to sustain him in their family grief; the foundations of his security would have gone, with Deborah being so far away and unable to be with him during this great sorrow – which was one of the saddest periods of his life.

September

Deborah and Rebecca then continued their journey, attending **Fairfax** Meeting followed by visits to nine families on 1st September, lodging at Sarah Janney's, who years before had accompanied Deborah's Aunt Rachel Wilson when she 'toured into the southern provinces'. They were with Sarah, however, only one day before going on to Leesburg Meeting, where they again visited families as they always did, sometimes giving the numbers, but very seldom names. However, they usually recorded if they had addressed any 'Young People', which was always an important part of their mission, for they hoped that younger generations would be able later to take the places of those who had become too old, or had passed from the scene.

The next two days they attended **Bush Creek** and **Pipe Creek** Meetings.

6.95.

From our Quarterly Meeting held at Wells in Perquimans County No. Carolina the 30th of the 8th Mo 1794

To the Monthly Meeting of Friends held in Shrop=
=shire, Great Britain ——

Dear Friends,

Our beloved Friend Deborah Darby On a Religious Visit in Gospel Love hath Visited Our meetings generally within the limits of this Quarter and produced your Certificate of unity and concurrance dated 20th of the 3rd Month, Endorsed by the year-ly meeting for wales held at Carmarthen the 25th of the 4th Month 1793, Also a certificate from the yearly Meeting of Ministers and Elders in London the 5th Month 1793. and we hereby Inform you that her Exemplary deportment Gospel Ministry and Salutary admonitions have been truely Acceptable and Satisfactory to us and our desires are that She may be through devine aid preserved and Enabled to pursue her further prospects and when the Remaining part of her service is gone through that she may be favoured to Return to her near connections and Friends with that peace and Satisfaction in her mind which is the Reward of the faithfull with the Salutation of the Love we Remain your Friends and bretheren —

Signed on behalf of the aforesaid Quarterly Meeting ——

By Josiah White Clerk
Sarah White Clerk

Acceptance by North Carolina Quarterly Meeting held at Hill's in Perquinmons County, North Carolina, 30th of 8th month 1794 of removal certificate from Deborah's Monthly Meeting in Shropshire.

Bush Creek and Pipe Creek, were at this time Preparative Meetings of
Fairfax Monthly Meeting, which had been transferred from the
jurisdiction of Philadelphia Yearly Meeting to Baltimore Yearly Meeting
in 1790; they were north of the Potomac in Maryland.

Then they travelled all day on the 6th September to attend **Menallen**
Meeting in which the Youth were [again] 'exhorted unto obedience to
Parents and above all to be faithful in following their Heavenly Father that
they might be prepared to stand for the cause of Truth when the present
Standard bearers may be removed'. On the next day they were at
Huntingdon Meeting in which 'things felt low'. Deborah evidently was con-
strained to hand out some good advice here and went on to say 'had an
opportunity in a Fds family which I hope would prove memorable to some'.
By the 8th they reached **Warrington** Meeting, where she found 'we had to
mourn over the Departure of Heart – which has taken place in many'. They
visited two families, and went on to **Newbury** Meeting on 9th September,
attending Monthly Meeting in **Little York** next day, where they also had a
Public Meeting in the evening and saw many families.

Pennsylvania Meetings in **Warrington** *Monthly Meeting, west of the*
Susquehanna, including **Newbury** *and* **Menallen**, *were transferred at the*
same time. In 1790 'Little' **York** *became the County seat and market town*
in this area east of Gettysburg.

They rode on the 11th 'to the Banks of the Susquehanna' near where
they attended the internment of the son of the widow Rebecca Moore and
sat in the family later. Rebecca was the widow of Joseph Moore who had
died of the Yellow Fever the year before, after being on the same expedition
as William Savery when they endeavoured to bring about the Treaty with
the Indian tribes near Detroit.

There followed two Meetings at **Lancaster** and at **Lampeter**, on the
12th and 13th September, after which they had a sitting with A. Gibbins
with whom they dined. On the 14th they had 'two comfortable sittings' and
attended **Ladsbury** Meeting. By the 15th they were at **West Caln** Meeting
described as 'small and low yet not without some evidence of the Master's
care', and the next day attended **East Caln** Meeting where they 'handed out
Counsel to the Youth'.

Lancaster, Lampeter, Ladsbury and Caln are east of the Susquehanna,
on the direct road back to Philadelphia, toward which they had been headed
since Deborah's illness a month before.

Then after sitting in a Friend's family they attended an evening Meeting
at Downings Town.

They reached **Uwchlan** Meeting on 17th September where they felt
help was needed and 'Divine compassion was afresh manifested' and
travelled on to **Nantmill** a day later.

Uwchlan *is a Welsh name; the Meeting lay a bit north of their road; it is still active.*

In all these less frequented Meetings they made a call that 'there should be a return and do their first Works'. It was obvious that their visit was a much needed refreshment to these Quakers and their Meetings so far away from the larger groups of Friends in the towns, but it must have been a very taxing time for Deborah and Rebecca to be continually helping and encouraging these small communities to keep their faith alive. Their experience of this was repeated at Piknel and Willis Town Meetings.

Thomas Fisher, who had been with them for some days, now accompanied them to **Newton** Meeting on the morning of the 21st and **Springfield** in the afternoon 'in which the necessity of bearing the Cross was much enforced'.

This is Pennsylvania's **Springfield Meeting** *which lies on the main Baltimore Pike near Swarthmore. (American Friends can still boast six Springfield Meetings all active in six different States.)*

By the 22nd September they reached **Darby Meeting** (now within Philadelphia) in which they had 'the company of R[ebecca] Jones and N[icholas] Waln to [their] comfort', and next day they travelled to Philadelphia and on the 24th Deborah remarked thankfully 'Attended Pine Street Mo. Meeting in which we had evidence of not being forsaken'. The relief that they had successfully accomplished their late summer journey and finally arrived at the place which was the most important of all to them must have been overwhelming, and they handed in their Certificates with thankfulness. They then dined at Nicholas Waln's who at this time was Clerk of Philadelphia Yearly Meeting.

The site of Philadelphia had, long before the development and administration set up by William Penn a century earlier, been a meeting place for the Indians, accessible from all directions, with the Delaware and Schuylkill tributaries providing convenient waterways for their travel by canoe. These rivers which met at Philadelphia are about 50 miles north-west beyond Reading. There were also tracks through the forests from many directions. The meeting place was on high ground overlooking the Delaware, where the tribes lit their Council fires and met to make treaties with their neighbours. William Penn decreed that this historic piece of ground should be reserved for their use. So, as most fine cities of the world, Philadelphia was founded in a region and upon a site already of importance in religion and traditions of the past. William Penn had received a heavily wooded tract of land, to be called Pennsylvania, as a settlement from the Crown for a debt owed to his father. His handling of the Indians and respect for their rites in his development and occupation of the territory was symptomatic of his deep spiritual faith and his attitude to all men. Thus he

The Great Meeting House, 1695-1800, Second and (High) Market Street. Note the Court House, built 1707, on right hand side.

created and developed a fine State for the future, respected by every class who were prepared to follow him and his guidance.

He had begun by building 80 houses in nine months on the site and arranging for supplies. The houses all had gardens and frequently orchards, and the whole area was planned with wide streets at right angles to each other. The farms, settled further afield, produced much food for the city, and was brought by waggon to the markets. These were very well regulated with the vehicles placed in rows as they arrived and trading was carried on in an orderly manner.

There had been an early link with Coalbrookdale, as Thomas Story, Penn's Master of the Rolls had stayed there in 1735 when he had met Richard Ford and Samuel's father, Abraham Darby II, for a few days. Later, on his return to his native land, Thomas Story's autobiography[10] was published by Samuel's uncle, Isaac Thompson.

> **Thomas Story** *has been referred to as Penn's* Master of the Rolls, *a title which in England was given to the Judge of the Supreme Court and Keeper of the Records. Storey was known, however, to Friends as Penn's secretary, which evidently included these legal obligations.*

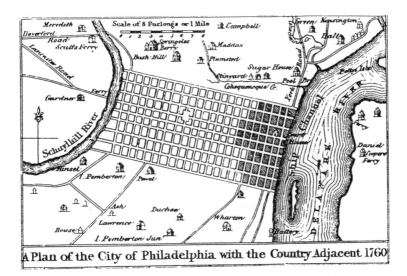

A Plan of the City of Philadelphia with the Country Adjacent 1760

Below: Street plan showing Quaker Meeting Houses grouped to the East on the bank of the Delawre.

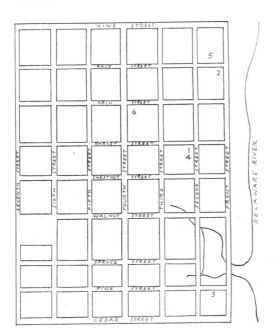

1. The Great Meeting House built 1696

2. Second Bank Meeting House built 1703

3. Pine Street Meeting House built 1753

4. Second Great Meeting House built 1755

5. Key's Alley Meeting House (North Street) built 1790

6. Arch Street Meeting House built 1804

On the 25th they attended Monthly Meeting at Market Street and again ministered, afterwards dining with **Samuel Smith**, and at the same Meeting on the 26th it was recorded that 'our beloved friends Deborah Darby and Rebecca Young, who, having been drawn in Gospel Love to visit Friends on this Continent produced Certificates from their respective Meetings in England and Wales, setting forth their unity and Concurrence with their arduous undertaking, which were read here and afforded comfort and satisfaction'. Later the same day they had an opportunity at the Widow Gilpin's that evening, a family who were connected with the Gilpins of Coalbrookdale.

Market Street Meeting was called The Great Meeting House first built in 1695. It stood on the south-west corner of Second and High Streets. The city had built the Court House opposite it in 1707, with sheds extending down the middle for the local farmers who came in from the country to sell their produce, which was when this thoroughfare was renamed Market Street. The Meeting House was rebuilt and enlarged in 1755 on the same site and remained Friends' principal place of worship. By the 1790's however there was an increase of noise from passing vehicles which became very disturbing during silent prayer. This was not mentioned by Deborah, but in later years it necessitated removal in 1804 of the Meeting to Arch Street. Deborah and Rebecca were to spend a great deal of time at Meetings there and Deborah always referred to this Meeting House as Market Street during the months she spent in Philadelphia.

After Monthly Meeting at Pine Street where they made some remarks in the Women's Meeting in which they had to minister, they later dined at **Nicholas Waln's**. Pine Street Meeting House, built 1753, was situated on the south side of the street of that name, between Front and 2nd Street. The Meeting House, or Hill Meeting as it was called earlier from inclusion in a will of Samuel Powell Junior, was a legacy to Friends. The building was of brick with porticos on the north and east sides over the entrances. The interior had a gallery for youth around three sides with approaching staircases, on the north-west and north-east angles. The men's gallery, over which there was a sounding board, was on the south side of the house; the main body of the Meeting faced south, the women sitting on the east side. A brick wall with two gates surrounded the grounds of the Meeting House dividing the area from the street.

Deborah and Rebecca attended two Meetings of the Select Yearly Meeting and had a sitting in the home of **Miers Fisher** after dinner on the 27th. On the 28th September, First Day, they sat in North Meeting in the morning, where Rebecca Jones 'concluded the Meeting in Prayer'. Then they had a sitting in **Thomas Scattergood's** family where 'encouragement flow'd freely both for those present and the absent head of the family, prayer was put up'. Thomas was away in Europe. The same day they also visited more families and were at Market Street Meeting in the afternoon and Pine Street Meeting in the evening, which meant crossing and re-crossing the city.

Miers Fisher *had been one of the 12 'Virginia exiles' removed from Philadelphia by the 'patriots' during the American Revolution; see Richard Bauman's* For the Reputation of Truth *(1971) p. 164.*

They were soon to know Philadelphia very well, not only by their attendance at Meetings and family visits, but also by the frequent visits to the homes of Friends whom they had met in other places. Deborah found the Meeting for Discipline large and she trusted that the spirit would be 'measurably spread abroad' and that 'the Readings of Epistles edifying'. On 30th September in the reading and answering of the Queries 'a Zeal for the cause of truth was manifested to [their] comfort . . . Some testimonies were read concerning some of the worthies who were swept away amongst the 4,000 dead in the Yellow Fever epidemic of 1793'. The city remained deeply affected by that dreadful time, 'the memory of the righteous continued to be blessed and the Dead they speak'.

October

They attended Select Meeting on 1st October and visited a sick Friend 'to [their] mutual refreshment'. They were at a Meeting for Worship the day after at Market Street 'in which silence was our Lot, others engaged to Minister. In the afternoon, the answers to the Epistles were produced' and 'it was evident best help had been afforded'. They then visited men Friends on 3rd October and afterwards had 'some comfortable opportunities' in families. All the time they were in Philadelphia they continued to visit Friends in the different Meetings.

The city, finely built with many streets of Georgian style houses (still there today), with gardens adjoining was rapidly developing. Trees had been planted, some of them along the wider main thoroughfares and the dislocation and disaster of the worst months of the terrible fever were passed by about a year, so by now the inhabitants had done their best to restore life to normal. There still remained, however, individual memories of the horror of that time, but some reforms against a recurrence had been implemented, although sadly these did not prevent a bad recurrence of Yellow Fever in 1798.

Yearly Meeting closed on the eve of 4th and 5th October, a First Day. There was a Meeting in the morning at Pine Street and at Market Street in the evening; in both Deborah had 'to exhort to a living up to the Glory of the Gospel Day'. They attended the Select Meeting on the 6th, and had opportunities in two Friends' families, the last of which was remarkable, pointing out the necessity of 'being prepared for every event'.

At the house of the second family, the Drinkers, they found Henry's wife Elizabeth was away at this time in England on a religious visit. Sadly she never returned as she died abroad later, and never saw her home again. The Drinkers were an old Philadelphian family from Sweden, their ancestor, Edward Drinker, having come originally in 1668, and had seen William Penn's original house, and had picked berries and shot rabbits in the country where many buildings now stood. This family were to become well known to Deborah and Rebecca while they were in the States.

On the 7th they 'call'd upon some in affliction with whom we felt sympathy'. This conjures up a sad little visit, but well worth paying. They went on to **Chester** to attend a Meeting on 8th October accompanied by Friends from Philadelphia for the day, leaving Deborah and Rebecca to go on to Providence Meeting on 9th October where Lydia Hoskins 'exercised her gift'. This Friend was later to travel with Charity Cook in 1796 into the States of the north-east, as Charity's sister and her other companions were, by then, unable to accompany her.

They attended **Concord Meeting** on 10th October [where an early 18th century Meeting House still survives] and here, as usual, made visits to Friends' families. In **Chichester** Meeting the next day, 'our Fd Samuel Smith gave advice'. They went later to the house of Sarah Talbot with whom they were to travel, amongst others, in the same ship when returning to England in 1796. Sarah and her husband were members of **Wilmington** Meeting, where they attended 'a laborious Meeting', but towards the end happily 'the Door of Utterance was opened to our relief'. Deborah and Rebecca then visited several sick Friends and had a Public Meeting that afternoon in which 'Nicholas Waln joined us in labour'.

> **Chichester** *is now the Marcus Hook oil dockland, between* **Chester** *and* **Wilmington**, *Delaware, now the metropolis of the Dupont industries and many banks.*

Afterwards they 'had an opportunity in the home of **John Dickinson** who was lately Governor of Pennsylvania' in which they 'were called upon to let their Lights shine before Men'. John Dickinson was just over 60 years old and a well known lawyer in Philadelphia who came from a prosperous farming family. He had served in the Delaware and Pennsylvanian Assemblies, and had helped to draft the Constitution of the United States.

By the 13th they were at **Whitely Creek** Meeting in which 'our Fd Samuel Smith and ourselves had some public service'. Next day they took part in a Meeting with a 'poor little company' at Asequinesy.

> **John Dickinson**, *though not formally a Friend like the rest of his family, was a major figure in Pennsylvania during the American Revolution: see* Rufus Jones, *Quakers in the American Colonies, pp. 559-63 and esp.* Arthur J. Mekjeel, *The Relation of the Quakers to the American Revolution,* (1975).

Duck Creek Meeting followed on 15th October where the Meeting was 'attended by many not of our Society' including 'some of them Methodists'.

After a 'confirming season' in a Friend's family next day at **Little Creek** Meeting on the 16th, they had a sitting where they dined and visited 'the Widow and family of a Fd just removed from Works unto Rewards'. At their visits of condolence they were always hopeful of giving some comfort, even though the bereaved were strangers to them.

> **Duck Creek**, *Delaware was a major Monthly Meeting and Meeting House in the 'Eastern Shore' (now called the DelMarVa peninsula) between Chesapeake Bay and the Atlantic; this Southern Quarterly Meeting was transferred from Baltimore to Philadelphia Yearly Meeting at the same time that the Meetings west of the Susquehanna were transferred to Baltimore.* **Little Creek** *near the ocean and* **Dover**, *the state capital, were also in central Delaware, but* **Asequinesy** *and* **Whitely Creek** *are not recorded even in Kenneth Carroll's exhaustive* Quakerism on the Eastern Shore, *(1970).*

Also the same day a Public Meeting was held in the Court House at **Dover** 'to some satisfaction'. This place was described at the time as an old but not very important village situated on a hill above the Cocheco River which flowed into the Assateaque River further towards the sea. There were high banks, cultivated in some places, but mostly covered with pine and spruce trees growing among the rocks. Nearer to the sea the river had shrunk in size and the navigation from below was, therefore, blocked because of a fall in the level of water. A nearby cataract powered a small mill for timber used for building some ships and other construction. The White hills could be seen in the distance to the west, adding their beauty to the scene of the fall with the bright red colouring of the trees.

They were in **Motherkill** Meeting on the 17th October, and later had a sitting with Samuel Mifflin's family and another in the evening 'at His Honourable Brother's and Sister's – Warner and Anne Mifflin – where we lodged – who made a practice of collecting their family every evening'. This quiet gathering must have reminded Deborah of their evening sittings at Sunniside with Abiah and all their relations. Warner Mifflin, who was the earliest Friend to give freedom to his slaves, had a generation before been 'religiously influenced' by Deborah's Aunt Rachel Wilson on her journey to North America.

> **Motherkill** *(kill is Dutch for a creek) was an active Delaware Monthly Meeting;* **Snow Hill** *was a Preparative Meeting near Preston, Maryland on the Chesapeake side of the peninsula.* **Anne Mifflin** *who was Clerk of Philadelphia Yearly Meeting Women's Meeting in 1799 (see Moore, p. 258) may be the same as* **Anna Mifflin** *who travelled to visit Virginia Meetings in 1800; for her and* **Warner Mifflin**, *see Carroll,* Eastern Shore, *p. 139; on* **Daniel Mifflin**, *ibid, p. 97.*

They arrived at **Three Runs** next day in time for Meeting and visited families in the evening. Deborah and Rebecca did not minister in Cold

Springs Meeting, but Hugh Davis and Anne Mifflin 'bore short testimonys to the People'. In the afternoon there was a Meeting at the Court House in **Lewis Town**. They had an opportunity in their lodgings on the 20th with some Methodists and a Public Meeting 'at a person's house of the name of Clayton', where 'the People were attentive to the Truths of the Gospel'. They had an evening Meeting next day in a tavern at **Snow Hill**. The diversity of places in which Meetings were held reveal the distance between Meeting Houses in this particular area, and on the 22nd next day this is illustrated by Deborah saying that they rode to Daniel Mifflin's 'who, with his family, lives 60 miles from Meeting'.

> **Three Runs** *may be Third Haven, near Easton, the oldest Meeting and Meeting House on the peninsula, where Fox had gathered the first Yearly Meeting in 1672.* **Salisbury** *is still farther south, the county seat of Wicomico, where Maryland stretches to the Atlantic south of Delaware.* **Snow Hill** *and* **Accomack County** *were in the southern tip of the peninsula, part of Virginia. From there, Deborah and Rebecca returned northwards.*

They felt 'near sympathy with their hosts' on the 23rd in a sitting with them, and had an evening Meeting at John Teagle's home. There was a Meeting next day in the Court House at **Accomack** where 'a few solid people attended to whom my R[ebecca] Y[oung] and Anne Mifflin ministered, some of them dined with us who manifested much tenderness in a religious opportunity'. Before leaving the house of their Friends John Teagle and his wife, they had a time of retirement together, and Deborah reveals here that this 'family were not Friends, but described them as Solid People'. They then had a Public Meeting at Daniel Mifflin's house.

On the 26th they sat 'with our Dr Fds – few of the White People attended occasion'd by the wetness of the day, but Gospel flow'd freely to a large number of the free Blacks', and they found much encouragement in their sitting in the evening with Daniel Mifflin and his wife, both with a precious gift in the ministry. On 29th October they had a Public Meeting at **Salisbury** in the morning, and another in the evening at a 'Person's house not a Friend'. Next day they attended a Meeting 'amongst the **Nicholites** to whom Ann Mifflin ministered'. They then had to say goodbye to Warner Mifflin, his wife and his brother Daniel, who had been with them for 10 days.

> *The* **Nicholites** *formed three ultra-strict Meetings under the leadership of Joseph Nichols, but reunited with Third Haven Meeting in 1797-98 (Carroll, pp. 118-9).*

November

On 1st November 'many not of our Society attended a Meeting at **Choptank** towards whom they felt Gospel Love'. Deborah, however, found 'the life of Religion is at a low ebb to which the keeping of slaves has greatly contributed'. She was deeply disturbed throughout her American journeys, wherever there was evidence in certain States of this practice. Laws had been passed for the abolition of slavery since the War of Independence but had not been carried out in those States where the crops particularly required the labour of black people, which meant that there still remained large areas of enslaved people, so that the import from Africa had not altogether been halted.

They were at Meeting at **Bayside** and then at **Haven** (TredAvon) on 2nd November 'which was large'. Deborah ministered at the latter, which followed in the morning at the School House. From time to time she mentions the school building and also education generally, later on in her travels, she visited some schools and spoke to the children in the same way she had done at home. They visited an elderly American Friend the day after, (the fact of considerable age nearly always being recorded), on the way to **Tuckahoe** Meeting. Again, 'the spring of the Gospel was low as it has been much the case of late'. Yet Deborah felt their efforts 'bestode in these parts has tended in some measure to the strengthening of things that remain'. They visited a widow and attended 'a poor little Meeting' at **Choptank** Bridge.

Choptank, Bayside, Tuckahoe and especially **Third Haven** *(TredAvon) were old Quaker centres on Maryland's 'Eastern Shore' of the Chesapeake, as were* **Chester River, Chester** *and* **Head of Chester** *(Millington) and* **Sassafras** *Preparative Meetings further north and north-east. All these communities of settlers had migrated away from Virginia's Anglicanism and could claim visits by Fox in 1672.*

By 6th November they were visiting the people at the **Head of Chester** as they were back in that town again. Here they also visited the people at large. Rebecca 'had a solid opportunity with Friends who some of them appeared much at ease'. They also had sittings where they dined, and at their lodgings. When the county had been originally planned, the plots of land had been developed with a good deal of ground around each dwelling, so the smaller places were scattered and unlike the villages in Europe. The general store at a crossroads frequently made a focal point, sometimes with a few other houses and workshops, and the flour mills were not too far distant as a rule from the dwellings, although these, of course, depended on sufficient force of running water. By the end of the 18th century the small places had frequently grown into larger groups of houses worthy of the names of township and village.

On 7th November they were at **Chester River** Meeting, 'where much counsel was handed, especially to the Youth, some of whom [they] feared [were] in danger of selling their Birthrights for a Mess of Pottage'. They also had a Public Meeting in the town where they found 'some of the people were light' but a few amongst them were 'seeking'. They were at **Cecil Meeting** next day and dined at a Friend's house where Rebecca 'bore a living Testimony'. They were then at **Sassafras** Meeting on 9th November 'consisting of but 2 families' – many of other Professions attended and 'some of whom evinced tender minds'. They sat in a Friend's family on the 10th and attended **Hockessin** Meeting, and afterwards went to stay at Caspar Wistar's, with which family they felt such a close accord since meeting them the year before.

> *Unlike those up Chester River,* **Cecil Meeting***, on the next creek northward, lasted until 1900. Deborah and Rebecca had overlooked hardly a Quaker home in all the peninsula. At* **Hockessin** *they were back on the Pennsylvania state-line.*

They were then again at **Concord** for Quarterly Meeting, which began on 11th November. There the 'spring of Ministry was offered and many States spoken unto', but they found 'the Meeting for Discipline [was] low'. The next day they were at a Youth's Meeting which was more satisfactory 'The Lord condescended to be mouth and wisdom', which ended in prayer. On the 13th they were at **Middletown** Meeting, and found encouragement next day at **Bradford** Meeting 'in which a remarkable invitation was extended unto the Youth'. At Robinsons on the 15th 'Fds were encouraged to wrestle for a blessing', and they had a sitting in a family.

> **Concord** *on the Baltimore pike was also familiar to them: the Quarterly Meeting was named for it.* **Bradford***, near Downingtown, was west of West Chester, and* **Reading** *a major county seat well north-west, so this* **Middletown** *would need to be the Meeting at Lima near Media, between Concord and Springfield.*

On 16th November at **Reading** Meeting they were disappointed finding all 'at a low ebb' although they were made hopeful 'by some not professing with us attending'. A 'Door of Utterance was opened' however next day on 17th November, at **Maiden Creek** Meeting, and Deborah adds 'and I hope one of utterance also'. There they had three sittings in families. They were encouraged by **Exeter** Meeting on 18th November, and **Pottstown** Meeting the following day, and also had a time of favour in the family of Dr Thomas Rutter 'who died soon after. His wife and daughter [were] continued valued members of the Society'.

> **Maiden Creek** *was north of Reading, but* **Exeter** *and* **Pottstown** *were on the road south-east into Philadelphia along the north bank of the Schuylkill.*

Ruth Anne Rutter accompanied them to **Providence** Meeting and they sat in two families, where again they found 'religion appears low'. At **North Wales** Meeting, Friends were 'reminded of the Zeal of their ancestors' who in their day nobly espoused the Cause of Truth and the Youth were invited to follow their footsteps and were reminded also of all they had gone through in the way of persecution on both sides of the Atlantic. By the 22nd they were at **Richmond** Meeting and there also had a sitting at their lodgings, and then went on to **Plumstead** Meeting north of Philadelphia. They reached **Buckingham** Meeting next day, 24th November, and 'much counsel was handed to a large number of Young People'. **Wrightstown** Meeting followed the day after, and by 26th they were at Makefield Meeting 'low but not without communication of Gospel Truths'.

Their Select Quarterly Meeting for Bucks County was held at **Middletown**, and Deborah and Rebecca had 'an opportunity in prayer after dinner'. Quarterly Meeting was solid and on the 29th they attended the Youth Quarterly Meeting, also attended a burial at Horsham on the last day of the month.

> *From near Norristown they seem to have cut south to* **Providence** *Meeting in Media, but then they went north again by* **North Wales** *Meeting, (perhaps a local nickname for Gwynedd) to* **Buckingham** *and* **Wrightstown** *(both still strong Meetings in their ancient Meeting Houses) and* **Plumstead** *in the heart of Bucks County, north of Philadelphia, and close to 'Washington's Crossing' on the Delaware, where the Americans had surprised King George's Hessians at Christmas, 1776. So this* **Middletown** *and* **Richmond** *must also have been the ones in Bucks County, the latter long since 'laid down' as rural Friends from this area too moved to midwestern farms in the cloth-covered Conestoga wagons, nicknamed 'prairie schooners', made near Haverford.*

December

On 1st December they visited six families, ensuring and continuing this work during a number of days, finally finishing in **Horsham** on 21st December, having sat with 120 households.

Next day they went on to **Newtown** for a Meeting at the Court House and then on to **Bristol** on the 23rd, where they attended two Meetings, 'the last was with the People'. **Frankford** Meeting on the 24th 'was trying to ourselves but appeared in measure satisfactory to others'.

At **Germantown** on the 25th they also had two Meetings, the last one in a School House, 'affording . . . encouragement'.

In **Merion** Meeting on 26th December they found 'ability was afforded to convey much counsel, both through N[icholas] Waln and ourselves'.

They attended **Haverford** Meeting on the way back to Philadelphia, where they were again in Market Street by the morning of the 28th. Deborah then kept her room for the rest of that day. It was after all midwinter and they had been travelling and visiting for most of the month.

*Newtown, later the site of the Hicksite George School, **Horsham** and **Bristol**, though not in a direct line, were also on Deborah's way back from Bucks County into Philadelphia, within whose northern limits the very early Meetings at **Frankford** and **Germantown** are now included, while **Merion** and **Haverford** (probably the present Havertown), equally venerable, lie in 'the Welsh tract' just across the Schuylkill. Once again Deborah and Rebecca had made a sweep of almost all the Quaker communities, this time in the area north-west and north-east of Philadelphia.*

They attended Pine Street Meeting on the last day of 'the year 1794 spent on the American Continent', and Deborah expressed 'gratitude to Him who has sustained through many conflicts'.

1795
January

On New Year's Day Deborah attended the marriage of Ann Wilson and Reay King at Market Street Meeting House, at which she and Samuel Emlen both spoke. (Samuel Emlen visited England in 1772, travelling there on the same ship as John Woolman.) She was also with the Friends' families the same day. On the 2nd she went to the Children's Meeting, where both Rebecca Young and Rebecca Jones had 'favor'd opportunities' to which Deborah made some additions. The next day they began family visits in Pine Street Meeting, accompanied by Nicholas Waln and Daniel Drinker.

Deborah and Samuel Emlen were engaged in Pine Street Meeting in the morning of 4th January, a First Day, to 'invite the different classes of People to hold up a good light to them all', and in the evening Deborah and Rebecca went to Market Street Meeting where they ministered. Pine Street weekday Meeting 'was a time of some favour – as has been the sitting in Fds families'. How much easier they found it to attend Meetings and visit families in Philadelphia, where life was less difficult. On 11th January there was a Meeting in North House which was silent. They wisely spent these winter weeks in Philadelphia as the cold could be considerable. Deborah does not say where they were lodging, although they partook of many meals in the very pleasant homes of several Friends, and visited many families, intending to accomplish as comprehensive a number of these visits in the different Meetings as time and strength would allow.

For a week, Deborah was unwell and was unable to go out for a few days but had recovered enough by the 13th 'to join in sending an Epistle to Fds at the next Welsh Yearly Meeting which [was] enclosed' in a letter to Richard Reynolds. Rebecca Jones had visited them while Deborah was confined to the house 'to their pleasure'. She got out again to afternoon and evening Meetings by the 18th and was at weekday Meeting at Pine Street on 21st January, but a week later it was Rebecca's turn to be ill, so Deborah was

Pine Street Meeting.
·BUILT·1753·

Between Second at Front Streets on the south side of Pine. First used in 1753. Also called Hill Meeting.

accompanied by Hannah Fisher to North Monthly Meeting. The illness fortunately proved to be brief, and they both attended Quarterly Meeting together on 30th January.

February

At Market Street Meeting on 1st February they had to abjure Friends 'to avoid anxious pursuit after the world', and after a sitting in a Friend's family, attended a Public Meeting appointed for them at North Street Meeting House, which although much crowded was 'held to General Satisfaction'. On 2nd February they attended Quarterly Meeting, at which they and Ruth Anna Rutter 'had to press Fds to keep close to the monitions of the holy spirit'. They also paid a visit to men Friends in which they 'were enabled to magnify the Cause in which they were engaged calling them to the Law and Testimony'. They went on to pay several other visits that day, the last being to 'Esther Lewis [who] tho' near leaving this world, supplicated sweetly on our behalf that the Lord might carry us through *all* to his own Praise'.

On 3rd February, in the Youths' Meeting, Deborah found 'many minds were humbled'. In the afternoon she attended a large Meeting of black people in which 'the truths of the Gospel flow'd freely'. They were at the marriage of Peter Baxter and Abigail Drinker which took place on the 4th of the month, followed by a visit to an afflicted family, and spent the evening at Daniel Drinker's house, the father of the bride. Deborah and Rebecca had come to know this family well, and were to meet one or other of them again during the rest of their stay in the United States.

On the 5th February Ruth Anna Rutter and Samuel Smith accompanied Deborah and Rebecca to Abington Quarterly Meeting, and the next day they attended a Youths' Meeting on which Deborah comments 'much counsel was handed . . . which I hope may prove as bread cast upon the Waters and found after many Days'.

These terse little comments of Deborah's are very much an indication of the spirit in which she undertook so much of her ministry. They returned to Philadelphia on the 7th to attend the burial of Esther Lewis, where Deborah bore 'testimony both at the house and the Ground' and again in the family after. Esther Lewis 'had been remarkably visited, but towards the close of her Day – had to lament the want of faithfulness, saying that she might have moved in a much more exalted sphere – but it is a comfort to believe through the mercys of God the end with her crowned *all*'. This reflection was not unusual in the description of the death of a Friend, as all were much concerned with the closing hours of a pious life.

Pine Street morning Meeting on the 8th February was held in silence but in the evening Meeting at Market Street Deborah, Rebecca and Ruth

Second Bank Meeting House, Front and Arch Street, Philadelphia, built 1702 with materials from the old Centre Meeting House when it was dismantled because its position was too far away from the town. There is little doubt, however, of the whereabouts of the first Bank Meeting, constructed solely as a place for Meetings for Worship. A subscription of £60 had been raised by Friends while others donated materials or labour and the structure was completed in 1684. It was a wooden building which decayed badly within a few years and was eventually removed in 1698. The Second Bank Meeting was renamed North Meeting and used until 1791 when it was closed and Friends transferred their membership to a new Meeting House across the road named Key's Alley, built 1790.

Anna Rutter all 'handed counsel'. They then, accompanied by the latter, renewed their family visits.

An evening Meeting at Pine Street was appointed for them on the 13th with 'People of other Societys' and 'held to satisfaction'. A great deal of their work was carried on in this way in an endeavour to strengthen the Society and to help increase understanding towards both the purpose and practice of members. They were again at Pine Street Meeting on the morning of the 15th February and Market Street that same evening as well as carrying out more sitting in families.

Deborah and Rebecca visited the Prison on 17th February accompanied by Samuel Smith and William Savery 'who each had a share in the labour, – gracious regard was evinced, – showing that the Lord delighteth not in the Death of a Sinner'. Afterwards they visited the Hospital : this building was on the outskirts of the city in pleasant surroundings. Deborah was, no doubt, encouraged to see the well regulated places which Friends had helped to establish and which were better and more humane than many of those in the British Isles of the period. She was able to join William Savery in this work and his presence obviously gave her the required assurance.

Philadelphia Prison – 1778. At Third and Market Streets; one block from The Great Meeting House.

*Both the Pennsylvania Hospital and the Philadelphia Prison were
influential as models for hospitals and prisons throughout Europe, though
superseded after Deborah's time by more sophisticated Quaker projects,
such as the Friends Hospital or Asylum in Frankford for the insane and the
Eastern State Penitentiary which pioneered in solitary cells.* See Sydney
James, A People Among Peoples: Quaker Benevolence in 18th
Century America, *(1963);* Negley Teeters, They Were in Prison: a
History of the Pennsylvania Prison Society, *(1937);* Kim Van Atta,
Account of Friends Hospital, *(1976).*

A weekday Meeting was held on the 18th February, finishing with visits
to families in Pine Street Meeting, where some of the Youth 'evidenced their
joining in there with us to our comfort'.

Next day the Market Street Meeting was large and 'a time of favor', and
they had later had 'several sittings in familys . . . to mutual refreshment'.
The following day, the 20th, they had a 'Season of Retirement' at their
lodgings with Rebecca Jones – all three of them speaking, and then went on
to Burlington (built 1675), which next to Salem was the oldest Quaker
settlement in New Jersey, and for some decades was the meeting place in
alternate years of Philadelphia Yearly Meeting.

At Mount Holly, a few miles to the east, the home of John Woolman,
they attended Meeting on the 21st February. Meeting was held in a brick
built structure newly built in 1785, the original Meeting House of 1685
having been occupied by the militia during the late wars. They also had a
Public Meeting at Burlington. **Bordentown** Meeting was attended on the
24th February followed by Ringwood Meeting two days later 'which the
extreme cold weather rendered less satisfactory than it might have been'.
They were at **Hardwick** by the 28th at a Meeting appointed for them, which
appeared to have been much in need of their visit.

> *They went by **Bordentown**, at the bend in the Delaware River,
> northwards again towards Trenton, by this time the New Jersey capital.
> The small Meeting at **Hardwick** (later called Quakertown, north-west of
> Flemington, NJ) and **Westwood** in the Shewangunk hills in north-
> western New Jersey (**Sussex County**) have left no records. [Dates for
> Quaker communities in New York and northern New Jersey are the formal
> setting up of a Preparative Meeting (or if this is not recorded, of a Monthly
> Meeting).]*

March

On 1st March they attended a Meeting in Sussex Court House and the
same evening held one at **Drowned Lands**, in both of which 'help was
extended'. They visited **Cornwall** Meeting on the 3rd and later had an
opportunity in the family of David Sands, who himself was away on one of
his visits to Europe. Deborah was to meet him quite frequently in future in

the British Isles and to receive him to stay at Sunniside. On their way to
Newburgh they had an evening Meeting in the School House, and on
arriving at Newburgh Valley on the 4th next day attended one there and
another at **Marlboro** on the 5th, followed on the 6th by one at Little Esopus
Meeting and three days later a Meeting in the Court House of
Poughkeepsie. In **Crum Elbow** Meeting on 9th March 'Exercise of
Religious care towards the Youth was recommended and they were invited
to purchase the Truth for themselves'.

> *It was a long journey to* **Cornwall, Esopus, Newburgh** *and* **Marlboro**
> *on the west bank of the Hudson River, 60 miles north of New York City,
> and across to* **Poughkeepsie, Crum Elobow** *(near Hyde Park) and the
> town of* **Hudson** *on the east bank. There the Englishwomen were in the
> heart of the New York Yearly Meeting's Hudson Valley settlements,
> founded by New England Friends in the 1760's to escape restrictions on
> landholding by non-congregationalists.*

By 10th March they had arrived at **Hudson** on the great river of that
name, which had been founded by people from Rhode Island, Connecticut.
It was a chartered city, built with wide streets, and by the time of Deborah's
and Rebecca's visit contained about 200 timber houses. Here there was one
curious difficulty, in that the drinking water had to come by a wooden
aqueduct for four or five miles. At the Meetings, Deborah hoped that 'the
door of Utterance' would be followed 'by one of Entrance'. On the 11th a
Meeting was then held at Kilney Hill in the neighbourhood and next day at
New Britain Meeting (later to become Chatham Meeting) they 'felt [their]
minds united to some lonely travellers towards a better country . . . but the
backsliders were call'd to flee from wrath to come'.

After sitting in with families they rode to **Lenox** on the 14th and had a
Meeting in the Court House. The next day 'some remarkable counsel was
handed' at the **East Hoosack** Meeting and they had a time of retirement in a
family. In the **White Creek** Meeting on 17th March the people were 'invited
to attend unto the teachings of Christ', and next day the Meeting at
Pittstown was held in the 'room of a Young Woman who had kept her bed
for 10 years'. At **Saratoga** they had a sitting with young people on the 19th
'which was a time worthy to be had in grateful remembrance', and next day
attended an appointed Meeting to the 'refreshment of many'.

> **Lenox,** *east of the Hudson, is across the Berkshire Hills in Massachusetts
> and* **East Hoosack** *(1774),* **White Creek** *(1777) and* **Pittstown** *(1796)
> north from there beyond the old Mohawk Indian trail back into New York
> State.* **Saratoga,** *a Meeting from 1776, not yet a spa nor a racetrack, lies
> on the upper Hudson above Albany. Here in 1777, General Burgoyne's
> surrounded British army had surrendered, in the War of Independence. In
> that war, as allies of the British, the Iroquois Indians had destroyed most
> white settlements west of Albany, though they had been turned back 100*

miles west up the Mohawk Valley at Fort Stanwix, and there , after the British withdrew, had made in 1783 a treaty ceding the area between. The Iroquois remained neutral in the war in Ohio between whites and other Indian tribes in 1791-95, but relations were still insecure when Deborah and Rebecca came north.

By 22nd March they had reached **Queensborough** Meeting near the foot of Lake George and on 24th at Skeensburgh, (now Whitehall) 'a Town where no Meeting had been held, had one in a Tavern, which was a satisfactory opportunity'. A weekday Meeting was held in **Ferrisburgh** on 26th and another in a schoolroom at **Vergennes** on the following day. They were at **Monkton** on the 28th and next day back to a Hicksite Meeting at **Ferrisburgh**, which place was attended by 'some sober enquirers' and on the 30th 'a satisfactory Public Meeting was held in an Inn at Middleburgh in which the danger of attending vain amusements was pointed out'.

> **Queensborough** *Meeting (1767) was near the foot of Lake George, 20 miles north of Saratoga.* **Skeensburgh** *may be Schroon beside Schroon Lake on one way north to Lake Champlain, which they would have had to cross to reach* **Monkton, Ferrisburgh** *(1790, laid down 1845) and* **Vergennes** *which were near its eastern shore. These were the northernmost American Quaker settlements at this time, only 75 miles from the Canadian border. The region had only become the State of* **Vermont** *in 1791, but within 20 years Friends and others would push farther north-east.*

April

On 2nd April they reached **Rutland** where they had an instructive Meeting. No Friends lived here. At a Meeting at **Danby** next day Deborah comments 'there appeared to be more of the form than power'. They went on, and by the 5th April were at West Saratoga where at Meetings there they found 'some visited minds' and 'the more distant part of the flock were not forgot . . . nor were some Fds lately married' with whom they dined.

On 6th April they were at Greenfield Meeting, followed next day by one at **Galway** in the morning and **Ballston** in the evening. They then met for evening Meeting in an inn at Lancingburgh on the 8th, the first held there by Friends, and on 9th April held a Meeting in the Court House at **Troy**, which 'was laborious', followed by a 'solid Meeting' next day in the evening also in a Court House at Albany. In **Coeyman's** Patent Meeting on the 12th 'many Gospel Truths [were] convey'd'.

> **Middlebury** *and* **Rutland** *were major Vermont towns west of the Green Mountains. From* **Danby** *they returned to the west bank of the Hudson, to* **Ballston** *and* **Galway** *south-west of Saratoga,* **Troy** *near Albany, and* **Coeymans** *where a Meeting House was built on an old Dutch estate.*

All these small communities either had just formed their own Meetings or were in the process of doing so.

After a time of retirement in their lodgings they went on the 14th to attend **Little Nine Partners** Meeting, and next day were at Monthly Meeting at **Great Nine Partners** where 'that [Meeting for] Worship [was] lively, – that for Discipline low'. At a Meeting on 16th April to which Tiddiman Hull belonged, 'the Lord was pleased to comfort the feeble minded as well as renew his calls unto the rebellious' and after sitting in a Friend's family next day they attended **Creek** Monthly Meeting. Ceaseless travel in the spring weather in a landscape of rivers and forests although of much beauty, was probably fatiguing.

> *Nine Partners (1742) and Creek (1771), 60 miles south, were older, being the central Meetings in the Poughkeepsie area; Little Nine Partners (1800) lies north of the cluster, which also included Crum Elbow.*

During the following days they travelled and held Meetings in West Branch, **Oswego** and **Chestnut Ridge**; **Branch** Meeting following on the 20th April. They sat with Friends in Goshen Meeting on the 21st in the morning and held a Meeting with the inhabitants of **Litchfield** in the evening. On the morning of the 23rd they had a Meeting in the Court House at **East Hartford** and with the people at **West Hartford** in the afternoon, where afterwards they heard that a Meeting had been settled there of 13 members. **New Milford** was reached by the 26th April where they had a 'Public Meeting and a sitting in a Friend's family in the evening', and next day they reached **Valley** Meeting.

> *Oswego Meeting (1758) was another old centre in Dutchess County. New Milford Meeting across the Taconic hills in Connecticut, was also part of New York Yearly Meeting, as were Litchfield and West and East Hartford in central Connecticut, 50 miles east; they needed to ride long distances to visit systematically all Meetings in each quarter. Then they moved southward.*

In **New Milford** Meeting 'things [had] felt low' but they left encouraged by their successful Public Meeting that evening.

Death of John Young, Father of Rebecca

On 28th April Rebecca Young heard of the death of her father, John Young, who had 'in much peace closed a Life of usefulness on 24th January'. Deborah described him as a 'Valuable Friend and Elder in the Church'. He had lived in Shrewsbury, with an interlude when he had been in the Coalbrookdale Company at the time of Richard Reynolds' management.

They attended Select Quarterly Meeting that day and were at Quarterly Meeting at **Oblong** on Quaker Hill on the 29th and where 'some of the Women Fds appeared well qualified for the support of Discipline'.

*Oblong took its name from a strip of land New York State had acquired along its border with Connecticut in return for Greenwich, Conn. There Friends settled near 'Quaker Hill' (**Ridge**) or **Chestunt Ridge**, south of Milbrook. **Oblong** and **Nine Partners** were set off from **Purchase** Meeting in 1744, and the latter became a separate Meeting in 1769. **Peach Pond** (1799), **Bedford** (1792), **Chappaqua** (1750) and **Amawalk** (1774) were close together southward in Westchester County. **Purchase** was also the name of the whole area between Scarsdale and Long Island Sound, where in the 1690's the first Quaker settlement on the mainland in New York State was made by Friends from Long Island.*

The month concluded with a Meeting for Worship on the 30th where they explained their Principles 'to the comfort of some seeking minds'. This Meeting was held in a sitting in a Friend's family where some young people were present.

May

They had a 'low trying Meeting at **Peach Pond** at 4 o'clock' on the first day of May, then after a time of retirement in a Friend's family were at **Bedford** Meeting next day 'where the exhortation went forth to faithfulness unto the light of Truth'. **Amawalk** Meeting on the 3rd was large, and they also had a sitting at their lodgings, and on the 4th they had a comfortable sitting with some young people, and attended **Chappaqua** Meeting 'in which Parents were exhorted to cultivate the plant of Righteousness in the minds of their children'. This was followed by a Meeting in the afternoon at a Friend's house 'largely attended by People of other Societys'.

They were in a Friend's family on the 6th where they 'felt concern'd that the Heads of it might stand dedicated and that the Youth might improve under the Lord's gracious visitations'. In **Purchase** Meeting they 'felt near simpathy [*sic*] with such as were bound to the Law and Testimony and they addressed in the comfortable language that he that had been their morning light was waiting to be an Evening Song . . . much counsel was handed to the Youth'.

On 7th May in **Mamaroneck** Meeting 'the nature of Discipline was set forth, and the uniformity in principles and practice which prevails amongst the faithful in different parts of the World'. They had a sitting in Richard Mott's family before they attended **Westchester** Meeting on 8th May. They crossed in the evening of the 9th to Long Island, and in Cowneck Meeting on the 10th Deborah records the 'State of Society appeared low'. There was a large Meeting with many Youth at **Westbury** on 11th May and next day at **Matinecock**, which proved 'a season of favor; as was a Meeting at **Oyster Bay**'.

*Mamaroneck (1716) and **Westchester** (1716) were on the Sound, both Meetings long gone, but **Westbury** (1671, the site of the first Quarterly and*

Yearly Meetings), **Matinecock** *(1671) and* **Oyster Bay** *(1659) were across on Long Island. These were with* **Flushing** *(1671) and* **Jericho** *the first Quaker communities in New York State. They are still an area of Quaker strength. By Deborah's time, however, New York Yearly Meeting was no longer held at Westbury, but in New York City itself.* **Elias Hicks** *of Jericho and other New York Friends were planning a Quaker boarding school at Nine Partners, to be like Westtown, Pennsylvania and Ackworth in England (est. 1779). Bible and Christ-loyal though the women were, they did not hesitate to stay with Hicks, around whose Spirit-centred Quietism the agonising 'Hicksite' separation later erupted.*

Deborah and Rebecca then attended **Jericho** Meeting on 13th May which Deborah trusted was to be 'the strengthening of some tender minds'. She was most unwell next day, but managed to attend a Meeting in the home of **Elias Hicks** and his wife Jemima, though for two days she was confined to her bed with a fever – always prevalent in the warmer months of the year. She was then removed to **Jericho**; and by the 20th May 'bore to travel to **Flushing**' although much fatigued. Next day she got to New York 'through much Bodily Suffering', but appeared able to attend the Select Yearly Meeting by 23rd May. Meeting on the 24th was large and in the evening she had a 'humbling opportunity' in their lodgings 'in which some Young People were much affected'. Yearly Meeting was to continue until the 1st of the 6th month 'throughout which gracious help was afforded to attend weightily to the state of Society, and a Committee appointed to visit the Meetings constituting this – the subject of establishing a school on a plan similar to Ackworth engaged Fds solid attention'.

On 26th May they 'went on Board a Packet but was drove back by a hard Gale of Wind endangering the Vessel's sinking, but through Providential Care we escaped this imminent danger and returned to New York, having a desire to visit the Prisoners which not being able to effect, we went on board next morning, Peter Yarnall feeling the weight of our concern visited the Prison after our sailing'. Two days later they landed at **Newport** about three o'clock and was 'kindly received by our Friends there, lodging at Thomas Robinson's'. They rested next day and had a religious opportunity in the evening. On 30th May they attended a 'Meeting on the island of **Conanicut** and sat in a Frd's family'.

Deborah and Rebecca went on to **New England** *by boat along Long Island Sound.* **Newport**, *Rhode Island was the usual site of New England Yearly Meeting, and* **Portsmouth**, *close by on the same island in Narragansett Bay; the British fleet based here in 1776 had found many Quaker 'Loyalists'.* **Conanicut** *is another island to the west, and* **Tiverton** *and* **Little Compton** *were on the mainland to the east.* **Swansea** *north within the Bay area has been part of Massachusetts, but like* **Westport**, **Apponegansett** *and* **Aquidneck** *near New Bedford,* *all were very old Quaker settlements most independent of the* **Massachusetts** *government.* **Long Plain** *and* **Acushnet** *are east of New Bedford, the whaling centre.*

June

A week later they were at Newport by the 7th June and had a satisfactory Meeting with the inhabitants in the evening, followed next day by an 'exercising Meeting at **Tiverton**'. On 9th June they were met at **Little Compton** by Samuel Smith and that afternoon were joined by their 'Beloved Sister M[artha] Routh from home', and Deborah and Rebecca felt 'under a solemn sense of our Heavenly Father's Love who had been with us by Sea and Land'. Martha was just beginning a ministerial journey to North America. They reached **Portsmouth** on 10th June and next day several of them were engaged to minister in a Meeting for Worship.

Yearly Meeting was held at **Newport** on the usual site of New England Yearly Meeting, continuing to 16th June, and on '1st day of evening, the 14th [they] had a large Meeting with the Black People'.

The 17th June found them back at **Portsmouth** where they dined with one of the families there and went on to a Public Meeting at Tiverton in the evening. They continued on to **Swansea** Meeting on the 18th and at Meeting there 'a renewed visitation was extended especially to the Youth', followed by a 'sitting in a Fds family [where] a daughter of our late esteemed Fd P[atience] Brayton was present'. By the 19th they were at **Freetown**, 'sitting in a Fds family where was a Friend more than 80 years of age alive in the Truth – also some hopeful Young People'.

They attended **Westport** Monthly Meeting on 20th June 'much crowded by People of other Societys'. Center Meeting next day was 'much the same but rather unsettled in the early part of it yet ended well'. In the evening they were again at Newtown at a Meeting 'which was laborious but some counsel was handed to the Youth invited to come up to the help of the Lord against the mighty and some of the aged to return and do their first works'. By 22nd June they were at Monthly Meeting at **Apponegansett** which again 'was much crowded with People of other Societys to whom counsel was handed'. By the 23rd they had reached New Bedford Meeting and had a sitting with a sick Friend 'to mutual refreshment', and next day they attended **Long Plain** Meeting where their 'line of visiting Fds was set forth' and also their 'Certificates of our approbation'. They were told that 'this might be intended for information' as there was 'a serious Clergyman at Meeting'. This shows how visiting Friends could be challenged by those not of the Society of Friends and that it was very necessary for them to be able to produce their Certificates to visit issued by the relevant Monthly Meeting. They attended a trying Meeting at **Achushnet** on the 25th and a Public Meeting at New Bedford in the evening.

Deborah was 'from this time until the 5th of the 7th month detained at Bedford, some part of the time by illness', but was still able to have several religious opportunities and attended their Meetings.

Visit to Martha's Vineyard

July

By 6th July, Deborah was evidently well enough to sail across to a 'village [*sic*] called **Martha's Vineyard** and had a Meeting in a Fds house that evening'. Next day they were able to ride 19 miles to **Gay Head** for an evening Meeting with about 100 Indians 'who manifested much solidity, . . . evincing that God is no respector of Persons – we lodged with great content in one of their houses'. It is possible that it was here that Deborah was given, as a keepsake, the small circle of finely cut bark crossed by cut patterns which she brought home and which exists today as one of her treasures from North America.[12] (See p. 153)

> *Martha's Vineyard and **Nantucket** are famous in Quaker tradition because of Quaker whalers in Moby Dick. The early Christianisation of the **Gay-Head Indians** was the work of the pre-Quaker Mayhews. These islands were also the seedbed from which many Quaker families, including those of Maria Mitchell and Lucretia Mott, were transplanted to the Hudson Valley and North Carolina. The **Rotches** of New Bedford, however, were a unique family, not only for their travels, but later for their founding in Ohio of the Quaker commune of Kendal, now Massillon.*

The Indians in the neighbourhood told visitors of the Legend of **Gay Head**, a hill of different coloured earths at the eastern end of Martha's Vineyard, on the summit of which was a hollow, like the crater of an ancient volcano. The Indians claimed that before the Europeans came there, a very large deity went down to the sea and caught a whale, roasted it in this hollow, and then asked them to dine with him. In return they gave him their whole tobacco crop of the island, which filled his pipe, the ash then being thrown into the sea, to form **Nantucket** Island, situated to the east of Martha's Vineyard, with a large commerce in whale oil. Many ships sailed annually from there and several Quaker families were profitably engaged in this occupation, including the **Rotches**, whom Deborah had known since she visited them in Dunkirk in France in 1792, where they had set up a whaling station in 1786. William and his wife Elizabeth, and daughter Lydia, met Deborah and Rebecca in some of the other States and William had stayed at Sunniside earlier with his son.

Visit to Nantucket

On 8th July they had a sitting in a family with whom they breakfasted, in which some 'gay[13] Young People were much broken in spirit'. This was followed by a Meeting in the Court House at Newton, and on the 9th, after a sitting with a solitary family of Friends residing on the island, they sailed for Nantucket arriving for dinner and had a Meeting with young people in the evening. A Meeting was held on 10th July with Friends in the North Division 'in which simpathy [*sic*] was felt' for the many perils their husbands were subjected to by a seafaring life. It must have been a dangerous occupation in those times, as it still is today.

This was followed next day by a Public Meeting five miles away in the country. On the 12th she found 'strength to bear testimony unto the Truth' both in a Meeting with Friends 'and another in the evening with the inhabitants at large'. After a religious opportunity on the next day, they left Nantucket and 'reached the place of landing', riding on to **Falmouth** for an evening Meeting. They attended a Meeting next day at **Yarmouth** in the morning and **Barnstaple** in the evening in a Court House. 'Both laborious but hope seasons of profit', Deborah was thankful to find.

> *Falmouth, Yarmouth and Barnstaple are east on the mainland on Cape Cod, which had been part of the Plymouth colony before its merging with Massachusetts about 1650. Thus **Plymouth** was the oldest New England town and more tolerant of Friends than Boston, where Mary Dyer and her companions had been hanged in 1659-61.*

After a season of retirement in a family they attended a Meeting at **Sandwich**, and on the 17th July had a Meeting in a Court House at **Plymouth** 'a considerable town where no Fds reside – it was held I trust to edification tho' very trying to us. The People tho' high in Profession are in general very light in their conduct, which made it hard labouring amongst them'.

The next day they sat with Friends in **Pembroke** Meeting and again during the next two days were with Friends at **Boston**, where Rebecca Young had a trying time at an evening Meeting in a Public Hall. On to **Lynn** next day and by the 21st July they were at **Salem**, the oldest and strongest Meeting on Massachusetts Bay where they ran into difficulties as Deborah reports 'Salem Meeting was hurt by a forward appearance which prevented the work going on as it otherwise might have done. Oh the awfulness of speaking in the Lord's name without being called hereunto by him': however, the Public Meeting in the evening was held 'to good satisfaction'. There was a large Meeting next day in the Court House at **Newbury**, and afterwards they had a select opportunity with Friends. After the **Amesbury** Meeting on the 23rd, 'Thomas Rotch, his Mother and J. Moreton left [them] that afternoon at 5 o'clock', and they had a very small but satisfactory Meeting at **Newton**.

> *· The early **Sandwich** Meeting on the Cape gave its name to the Quarterly Meeting. The old **Pembroke** Meeting House halfway to Boston was in Plymouth County and Sandwich Quarterly Meeting, though it was used by Boston Friends in the summer after 1962. Now they travelled up the coast*

rapidly, stopped only briefly in **Boston**, *and hurried on by way of the* **Lynn** *Meeting to* **Salem**. **Newburyport** *and Whittier's home Meeting,* **Amesbury**, *are on the Merrimack at the New Hampshire border.* **Newton** *may be the township west of Boston, which now includes 13 suburbs.*

'Accompanied by William Rotch Junior, [they] attended **Seabrook** Meeting on the 24th July where the alarm was sounded to the unfaithful. Doctrine drop'd as dew on some tried minds – here [they] met with Comfort Collins who was then an ancient lively minister and had some years before felt a concern to visit England to which being brought into resignation – she sailed from Boston with her Companion Sarah Barney, but after a few days at sea she heard this language "Thy resignation is accepted – now I see – thou loves me more than man". They were soon afterwards drove by a contrary wind into Port and she returned to her family with the sweet evidence of Heavenly approbation.' They enjoyed an opportunity in this family.

Massachusetts

Across the river **Seabrook** *has again become a famous name because of protests about an atomic power station there.*

Boston the capital of Massachusetts was, at this time with New York and Philadelphia, one of the three major cities of America.

The city of Boston was solidly committed to its Puritan parishes, though some were drifting towards Unitarianism. The Anglicans had two churches, and many individuals had defected to the Baptists from the start. There was a Meeting House on Quaker Lane in Boston from 1709 to 1829, and a Meeting there throughout the War of Independence but it ceased after Ebenezer Pope's death in 1808 and was not revived until after 1870.

The waterfront of Boston supported a long wharf with a large number of buildings and shipyards, and behind it Beacon Hill sloped to a spacious meadow called the Common with houses on three sides. The city had been built to no special plan so the streets cobbled with river stones were often irregular. The principal houses were of brick in the English style, their roofs covered with slabs of white cedar, which grew in quantity in the State and withstood the weather. The roof peaks were of terracotta tiles as in Europe, though some houses used slabs of black stone instead, a recent discovery by the city, which was more durable and safer. There were also houses of timber, painted in light colours and with a roof terrace to enable the occupants to enjoy a cool night in summer. The rooms were not large and for the most part, simply furnished, even in the grander houses, but each house had a garden where many fruit trees were grown: apple, peach and pear and other European fruits being planted.

'They attended **Epping** Meeting in the morning [of 25th July], and Lea in the evening', also sat with a sick Friend. Here they were moved to encourage the revival of weekday Meeting which had evidently lapsed, and Deborah comments this had 'an humbling affect on some Young Peoples minds'. During the next two days they attended **Dover** and **Rochester** Meetings, 'to good satisfaction' followed by those at **Tetbury** and **Berwick**. After Portland Meeting on 30th July, they undertook 'a perilous journey [on the 2nd August] in which we were overturned and broke both axle trees', reaching **Vassalboro** soon after Friends had started Meeting. They were however 'well rewarded for the labour we had taken in getting there, by a refreshing Meeting'.

> *Epping, Rochester (Gonic) and **Dover** are a few miles back from New Hampshire's short shoreline, and remain strong Monthly Meetings in Dover Quarter. **Berwick** and **Tetbury** (perhaps Kittery) were just over the State-line in **Maine** though thus in **Falmouth** Quarter, to which the women later returned. **Vassalboro**, however, is in the other area of Quaker strength, in central Maine, 50 miles up the coast and the Kennebec River beyond Augusta, the State capital, with **Winthrop** just westward. This area later produced the Oak Grove Friends boarding school and the family of Rufus Jones.*

August

On 3rd August, after 'a sitting at [their] lodgings' attended **Fairfield** Meeting and on the 5th were back again at **Vassalboro** Meeting 'attended by many not of our Society, but where Gospel Truths and encouragement flow'd freely . . . after parting from many of our Fds in those parts we lodged at an Inn'. The 6th August was extremely hot and they attended **Winthrop** Meeting followed by a Meeting at **Lewiston** on the 8th 'where there are few in number but some tender minds'. After a sitting at their lodgings they were at Durham Meeting on the 9th and went on to visit families in **Portland** Meeting on the 10th and 11th August. At **Falmouth** Meeting which they reached on the 12th they had the company of Joseph Cloud.

They sat with Friends on 13th August at **Windham** Meeting and the two days following were spent in travelling to reach **Pittsfield** where they attended Meeting and had a sitting with local Friends. In the evening where they were 'much exercised on account of the Youth'. A Meeting was held in the Court House at **Concord** next day, 'which was small but in measure own'd'. At Weare next day a Select Monthly Meeting was attended, 'only Fd members present', but next day at a large Monthly Meeting Deborah found things 'low at this place, a dividing spirit having crept in to the hurt of some who have been favor'd of the Lord'.

*Lewiston on the Androscoggin, and **Portland** (Maine's little metropolis) and **Falmouth** on the shore were on their way back from their easternmost visit in the United States. **Windham**, now a pastoral Meeting like most of these older groups, is between Portland and Sebago Lake. **Pittsfield** is 40 miles west in New Hampshire, of which **Concord** is the capital.*

They then rode fast over woodland roads in a circuit of Meetings, north and west of Boston, and had a Meeting at **Bolton** on the 22nd August 'attended by many not of our Society'. The day after they rode to **Leicester** where sadly and disturbingly 'Various passages also opened respecting the Divinity of Christ – we had reason to believe that there were some present unsound in the faith'. The 24th found them at **Northbridge** Meeting where they were able to feel that the 'Spring of the Ministry was opened and various states spoken to'. On the 25th they found that **Douglas** Meeting 'was disturbed by the Company of young children'.

*Bolton and **Leicester**, Massachusetts are 100 miles south near Worcester, so evidently they were riding fast over woodland roads in a circuit of the Meetings north and west of Boston. **Northbridge, Mendon, Uxbridge** and **Douglas** Meetings, no longer extant, were south again, close to each other and to the Rhode Island state-line.*

They attended **Mendon** Meeting on the 26th and during the next few days visited families at **Smithfield** and **Uxbridge** as well as attending Meetings in these places. Deborah remarked that she trusted 'it was an instructive season to some visited minds – amongst the Young People'.

Smithfield near Woonsocket was, like Northbridge and East Greenwich, the centre for a Quarterly Meeting in this heavily Quakerised Rhode Island region, the first in America to welcome Friends.

They were with families at Lower Smithfield on the 29th and on the morning of the 30th August reached Providence Meeting in the state capital which was mainly attended by Friends. In the evening there was a Public Meeting. Deborah and Rebecca were staying with Moses and Mary Brown, which in her Journal, Deborah adds was 'to our comfort'. Indeed this would be so in both a spiritual and material sense. Moses Brown lived at Elmgrove which was a country house overlooking the Seekonk River bought by him in 1772 from the estate of John Merritt. The main part of the house had a portico with grecian type pillars, a gallery along the roof and an adjoining lower building which completed the house. The place had a lovely view of the wide expanse of the river and caught the breezes even in the hottest of summer weather. Moses' first wife, Anne, had died shortly after the purchase of the house, after a long illness. Moses joined Friends in the same year of 1774, though he and his wife had both been interested in the Quaker faith before Anne's death. Moses had partially retired from business devoting most of his time and energy to charitable and educational interests, and was a pioneer in liberating slaves, having freed his own slaves and encouraged others to do so.

*He was the creator of the Portsmouth Friends School 1784-88, the first
Yearly Meeting boarding school in America, and in 1819 of its successor in*
Providence, *called in his honour the Moses Brown School. He was also
involved in starting the Athenaeum Library, the Rhode Island Peace
Society and Bible Society and in the founding of Rhode Island College,
later Brown University.*

In New York he was to enlist the help of Edmund Prior, at whose
marriage Deborah and Rebecca had been present on their first day on
American soil.

Moses married his second wife, Mary Olney, in 1778 and when Deborah
and Rebecca were received at their home they found it most comfortable
with ample though not extravagant hospitality. It was unfortunate that they
could not remain there more than one day, but their host and hostess did
travel on with them, informing them about the countryside and people
living there as they went.

On the 31st they reached Elisha Steer's house where a Meeting was held
'in which people were exhorted to sobriety'.

September

On the 1st September they reached Gloucester Meeting on the western
mainland of Rhode Island and next day were at a Meeting which 'was hurt
by the late gathering of the People and towards the close some remarks were
made on the benefit of silence'. They arrived at **Cranston** Meeting on the
3rd and moved on to **Greenwich** next day, with a Meeting in the Court
House there that evening. Previously they had by-passed these places when
they sailed straight into Newport and headed east. This visit meant that in
all they missed only two of these Quaker communities.

After a sitting with a Friend's family on 5th September they attended
Wickford Meeting; here 'the necessity of exercising our spiritual weapons
was dwelt upon and it ended in prayer for the preservation of those that were
about to leave us, as well as our own that were absent in Body – we might be
present in Spirit, and at seasons know a rejoicing together in Him who is our
only hope'. After this Meeting Moses and Mary Brown left them to return
home.

At **South Kingston** Meeting on 6th September 'many Gospel Truths
were revived and favor extended to the People which tended to the support
of my mind, under trying dispensation, intelligence reaching me of my
Beloved Husband's illness'. Deborah would not have had any further news
of Samuel for some time so her anxiety would therefore continue.

End of Rhode Island Visits

Lower Kingston Meeting on 7th September was followed by one in
Richmond chiefly attended by Friends the next day, and on the 9th, at

Hopkinton Meeting, they had the company of Elizabeth Rotch and Abigail Robinson who met them there. On to **Westerly** Meeting on the seashore the next morning and Potowknett Bridge in the evening; this finished their visit to Rhode Island and at this place 'we parted from our Beloved Fds William and Elizabeth Rotch and Abigail Robinson', on 10th September.

South or *Lower Kingston Meeting, near Point Judith where Narragansett Bay meets the sea, was later the home of John Wilbur and the first centre of the Wilburite Separation of 1843-5.* **Hopkinton** *and* **Richmond,** *Rhode Island were also in the wooded farmland just to the west, and* **Westerly** *on the seashore. The two women were now riding west through Connecticut, Puritan territory where there were few Quakers, even in the cultural centre,* **New Haven,** *which would in 1800 become the starting point of the 'Second Awakening' in American Protestantism, but in 1795 reported no church members at Yale College. At* **Westchester** *they were back in New York state.*

Return to New York State

During the next two days they travelled about 75 miles, having a Meeting at **Newhaven** in the Court House when they arrived on the 13th. Two days later after a religious opportunity in David Titus' house they reached Richard Mott's home where they lodged. They attended weekday Meeting next day at **Westchester** and had 'several sittings in Fds families being disappointed of crossing a Ferry – and on our return were overturned by our carriage wheel coming off, but escaping without much hurt'. Their journeys were not without accidents, which could have proved serious, although Deborah made very little of this one.

They reached **Flushing** Meeting on the 17th across Long Island, and in the evening had a 'Meeting for the Black People and others not of our Society'.

Stephen Grellet

Deborah now came to one of the most important moments of her life. Two of America's greatest Quaker leaders were John Woolman, the mystic and reformer, and Stephen Grellet, the preacher. In her youth Deborah, with her sister Mary, had been deeply impressed by the former when in the last few months of his life, in 1772, he came to Sheffield. Now 20 odd years later she herself was to meet and influence in America, the young Stephen Grellet, who had fled to the United States as an emigré from the French Revolution. The slender chances of such encounters would appear hazardous, but long lasting results were to stem from them affecting many lives.

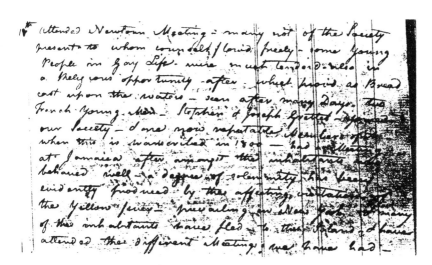

Transcription of Deborah's Diary (above) 1800, originally written 18th September 1795.

18th. Attended Newtown Meeting – many not of the Society to whom councel flow'd freely – some Young People in Gay Life were much tender'd – also in a Religious opportunity – after which prove'd as Bread cast upon the waters – seen after many Days. **Two French Young Men – Stephen and Joseph Grellet** *– joined our Society – and are now reputable Members of it – when this is transcribed in 1800.*

On 18th September, Deborah and Rebecca attended Newtown Meeting not far from Flushing, and the former wrote 'Many not of our Society present to whom counsel flow'd freely. Some young people in the Gay life[14] . . . were much tendered also in a Religious opportunity after which proved as Bread cast upon the Waters – seen after many days'. 'Two French young men, Stephen and Joseph Grellet – joined our Society and are now reputable members of it.' Clearly it was too early a date for her to have realised Stephen Grellet's great potential and the important part he was destined to play amongst Friends, but she evidently felt their first meeting worthy of account.

The Meeting at Newtown was followed by an invitation to them to dine in the home of Colonel Corsa whose wife was a Franklin. He was of Huguenot origin and a former soldier in the British Army, and his family had welcomed and befriended the two young Frenchmen; their daughter Mary also spoke good French which helped the two emigrés during their stay in Long Island, as neither Stephen nor Joseph as yet knew very much English. They were the sons of Gabriel Marc-Antoine de Grellet and Susanne de Seramaud, who were a well-to-do couple and important members of their local nobility. Gabriel owned extensive porcelain factories and ironworks, and for a time had been 'controller of the Mint and as a member of the Household of King Louis XVI' was accustomed to attend in the private chapel. Gabriel's title had been conferred partly on account of his successful manufacture of this porcelain, though as it turned out the factory had been purchased by the King shortly before the Revolution but was never paid for before that storm had broken.

Stephen Grellet had, at first, been educated with his brothers and sisters at home by resident tutors and then later at different schools, finally being sent to the Oratorians at Lyons, founded by Cardinal Bérulle in 1716 whose concepts were that the most important action in life was to 'open oneself to take on, through Grace, Christ's attitude'. This teaching, joined with that of the Jansenists as the two movements from the first were intertwined, prepared Stephen Grellet later to profit by and contribute to, as he did, to Quaker worship, which he adopted.

He and his brother Joseph, at the outbreak of the French Revolution, had joined the opposing army of the Princes and after many adventures and disasters, escaped to Holland. From there they sailed for Demerara where they spent two not very happy years before crossing the ocean to New York in the summer of 1795. After staying there for a short time they went on to Long Island to seek a livelihood in quieter surroundings.

Mary Corsa had helped them throughout these weeks and as she was accustomed sometimes to attend local Friends' Meetings she took the young Frenchmen with her. She also lent Stephen Grellet the book *No Cross, No Crown* by William Penn which he managed to read with the help of a dictionary.

The two Frenchmen had lost everything; their home and their country; their father who was in prison and in danger of his life; and they and their mother, had often not had enough to eat. Their whole livelihood had been taken from them, and Stephen could find no consolation; every 'hand hold' in his life had been removed, and he felt he was in a void without earthly comfort. In this state he was walking in the fields on Long Island one day, when he heard suddenly within the words 'Eternité, Eternité, Eternité' and their true meaning pierced his heart. He explained this happening in these words: 'through adorable mercy the visitations of the Lord was now again extended towards me by the immediate openings of the Divine Light on my soul'. He did not realise then, of course, what the future with all its tremendous consequences was to hold for him, but he knew that the wonder of true life had come and that he must now follow this special path.

He took up again *No Cross, No Crown* and wrote 'I have never met with anything of the kind neither had I felt the Divine Witness in me operating so powerfully'. It was just at this moment that he attended the Meeting at Newtown with Mary Corsa, and although he could understand very little of what was being said, he found that the sight of Deborah and Rebecca brought 'solemn feelings over me' with the effect that he forgot everything around him 'for an inward frame of mind, seeking the Divine Presence I was favoured to find in me what I have so long, and with so many tears sought without me'. Later after the dinner at the Corsa's, where again he could not understand very much of what the speakers said, he discovered that when Deborah began to address him and his brother, 'she seemed like one reading the pages of my heart, with closeness describing how it had been, how it was with me . . . I felt the power of Him who had the key of David. No strength to withstand the Divine visitation was left to me. Oh what sweetness did I then feel! It was a memorable day. I was like one introduced into a new world. The creation and all things around me bore a different aspect – my heart glowed with love to all. The awfulness of that day of God's visitation can never cease to be remembered with peculiar interest, gratitude as long as I have the use of my mental faculties . . . Oh how can the extent of the Lord's love, mercy, pity and tender compassion be followed'.

The French Revolution continued with ferocity, and their parents could not encourage them to return to France because of the risk to their lives, so they had to find work in America. Joseph stayed in New York but Stephen decided to go to Philadelphia, arriving there in December of that same year. Here he received offers from Friends to go into commerce, some from European Friends, particularly the Dutch, but he preferred to teach French.

He was destined to meet Deborah and Rebecca again at Meetings in Philadelphia and when visiting families, some of them French. These two Quaker women were the means of comforting and sustaining him in his faith and he soon made application for membership of the Society of Friends in which he was helped very considerably by William Savery to take the first steps of what was to be an astonishing and inspired life of service.

The day after the dinner at the house of the Corsas they paid a visit to a sick Friend at **Bristol** and went on to a good Meeting at **Frankford**.

On the 19th September, after this first meeting with Stephen and Joseph Grellet, Deborah and Rebecca crossed to Staten Island (now part of New York City) and on to **Rahway** where they met with Friends next morning, and had a Public Meeting in the afternoon followed by a sitting in Hugh David's family.

On to **Elizabeth** town next day and back to **Rahway** to dine with Friends there.

> *Rahway, Elizabeth and Plainfield in eastern New Jersey had been transferred from Philadelphia to New York Yearly Meeting, also **Shrewsbury** and **New Brunswick**.*

They then went on to **Plainfield** Meeting in eastern New Jersey on 22nd September in which 'much close labour was extended to careless professors – the doctrine drop'd as dew upon the humble traveller'. The following day they were in **New Brunswick** Meeting and on to **Princeton** by next day where 'they had the company of many of the Collegians who behaved well and to whom counsel was handed'. These young men belonged to the University which had, from the beginning, had a broad outlook on the different practices of the Christian truth.

It was not therefore, surprising that these two Quaker ministers from England had an attentive audience. The small **Stoneybrook** Meeting House would hardly have been big enough for so many people, so the State House at Trenton was used.

The young men lived at the University, two sharing a room. A Principal and two Vice Presidents taught the main subjects, with additional tutors, so that a comprehensive and valuable education was provided.

> *Princeton was and is a University town, but the small **Stoneybrook** Meeting House on the outskirts is still in use.*

There would have been a good deal of interest in hearing these two women ministers, dressed slightly differently from the American Friends. Deborah no doubt would have made her usual impression, one she had on all the young, of gentleness but also strength of purpose. Rebecca was an able speaker and held her audience, but there is little in Deborah's Journal which describes Rebecca's ministry.

On the 26th September they attended two sittings at Select Yearly Meeting in Philadelphia, one at Pine Street – and the other at Market Street the next day. She says of these few days that 'All last week was engaged in attending to the service of the Yearly Meeting, . . . and some of the Young People manifesting that the care of the Churches was upon them'.

October

On the 4th October at Market Street Meeting, Deborah sat in silence, but this was followed by a Meeting in the North House with 800 Africans 'in which [they] had to rejoice in the renewed evidence that God is no respector of Persons'. Deborah was always particularly delighted when she could help the black people in any way which improved their lot or gave them any happiness. 'After a favor'd season' with Samuel Fisher on the 5th October they went to **Darby** where, in the company of John Wigham, they were at a Public Meeting. After visiting a sick Friend they attended Center Meeting on 6th October and later had a sitting in a Friend's family where they lodged.

The following day in **Kennett** Square Meeting, beyond Concord on the Battimore Pike, they 'feared the spirit of the World had prevented many from coming up to the help of the Lord as they might have done' but they had a 'large and comfortable Public Meeting at Wilmington in the evening', and spent the next two days travelling to **Baltimore** where they attended the Select Yearly Meeting on the 10th. Next day they were at the Friends' Meeting House in the morning and the Court House in the afternoon 'both

Old Kennett Meeting House – built 1710 – on Nottingham Road, now Baltimore Pike.

which was solid favor'd seasons as was one for the Black People in the evening'. Yearly Meeting ended on 16th October where 'an increasing care was felt for the good of the Black People . . . some Fds having felt a concern to visit them in their families'.

They visited the Prison in the morning of 17th October and next day accompanied by 'Fds and Brother Samuel Smith' travelled to attend a Meeting appointed for them in **Annapolis** Court House 'which was a season of instruction'.

> **Baltimore** *itself held the active Homewood and Stony Run Meetings.* **Annapolis**, *an old colonial state capital, holds the St Johns, third oldest college in America, and the Naval Academy.*

At **Indian Spring** Meeting the Preparative Meeting for Sandy Spring, west of Baltimore on the 19th they found 'the life of Religion low', and here Deborah makes an observation on the plight of Friends' slaves after 'sitting with some Black People at our lodgings' finding that although Friends had liberated their slaves 'they scarcely seem to have lost the marks of having once been concern'd in such a practice – yet I hope they are gradually wearing off'.

They were again in Baltimore by the 20th October, entering upon family visits there and continued 'with this employment for the rest of the week'. On the 25th, first day, Deborah sat the Meeting in silence and visited five families, before weekday Meeting on 29th October. After visiting four families they attended a Public Meeting appointed for them on the 30th at the Point which she described as 'an edifying season'.

November

In both Meetings on First Day on 1st November they were engaged and went on to finish their family visits in Baltimore 'under the thankful sense that they had had Heavenly Help' before moving to an evening Meeting at **Little York** the day after. Next day a journey of 27 miles on the 3rd took them to **Harrisburg** on the Susquehanna, the capital of Pennsylvania.

They had made a loop through this country when they returned from the frontier and now came back to visit Friends' Meetings in north central Pennsylvania. Three days of travelling brought them to **Muncy** by 'poor roads and accommodation'. They attended Meeting there on 8th November which required 'deep wrestling of the spirit'. The 9th November brought 'a Meeting with people of other Societys to some satisfaction'.

> *They had returned this way from the frontier, and now went north through it to visit Friends in north central Pennsylvania:* **Muncy** *is on the West Branch of the Susquehanna, just beyond the fork, too far from other Meetings to belong to any Quarter except Philadelphia, 150 miles away.*

Deborah felt at times considerable disappointment at having made the effort to travel to far distant places only to find such little enthusiasm and enlightenment. She had hoped to kindle and encourage faith and trusted that this would be so, but she could not keep, at times, from feeling despondent and apprehensive that, because of the distances and isolation, these small communities might just fade away. They seem to have stayed at **Muncy** until the 13th when they went on to **Fishing Creek** on 14th November where happily their visit was more encouraging. At Cattanipay next day they met a committee of Friends from Philadelphia and had 'an edifying Meeting together', which must, at that time have been a great relief. After a Public Meeting on the 16th they were at Roaring Creek Meeting on the 17th where there was a marriage and afterwards, as was often the case, an opportunity with the young people, which was much welcomed by Deborah. She found 'how sweetly the visitation of Divine Love flows to this class of the family'.

> *Muncy is on the west.* **Fishing Creek,** *near Roaring Creek, between Slabtown and Catawissa on the East Branch of the Susquehanna, built a new log Meeting House in 1796.* **Maiden Creek** *is north of Reading.*

The next two days were spent travelling and she was able to 'commemorate the goodness of Him that can make the wilderness as Eden'. On 20th November they attended **Maiden Creek** Meeting north of Reading and later had a sitting in a Friend's house after dinner, and again in the morning at Thomas Lightfoot's family, where presumably they had lodged before going on that day to Reading where there was an evening Meeting in the Court House. They were at Ports Down Meeting two days later, and spent the remainder of that day at the Widow Rutter's 'who is come into the Vineyard at the 11th hour of the day – and likely to obtain her Penny – her daughter Ruth Anna is a Valuable Minister to whom we are nearly united'.

Return to Philadelphia

They returned to Philadelphia and on 24th November attended North Monthly Meeting. They were at Pine Street Monthly Meeting the day after in which 'our Dr Fd and Father in the Truth, Samuel Emlen, labour'd publicly and we had Counsel to hand in the Meeting for Discipline'. They attended Market Street on the 27th for Monthly Meeting and visited Friends' families, travelling on to Falls Meeting on 29th November and on the 30th attended Chesterfield Quarterly Meeting, after which her final observation was that 'many minds united'.

December

The 1st December found them riding on to Shrewsbury where they lodged with Richard Lawrence's family and attended Meeting next day. Swan Meeting followed on the 3rd 'and they waited for a renewal of strength in a family' – an unusual admission – before attending Squancum Meeting.

A day later they were at Robins Meeting, where Ruth Anna Rutter and Rebecca Young 'were led in an encouraging line to Friends by the Young People and some further advanced in years' to which Deborah made some addition, but had to warn against 'a Diestical Spirit'. They then had 'a comfortable opportunity with our Beloved Fd Rebecca Wright', and went on to William Rogers' house. Hadenfield Quarterly Meeting was large on the 7th and next day they entered upon visiting 'taking eight families a day'. They had returned to Philadelphia by the 13th and were in Pine Street in the morning, continuing after with their family visits.

On the 14th December in morning Meeting 'Our Dear Friends Samuel Emlen and William Savery spread before Friends a concern to visit Europe with whom sympathy and unity was felt'. Unfortunately, by 20th December, Deborah was confined to the house by sickness, 'Rebecca Young alone to Meeting in the morning'. The illness appears to have passed by the 24th, because she was then again visiting families and they were at weekday Meeting at which was also Able Thomas, 'a valuable Minister', who spoke and Deborah made some addition to what he had to say.

On 27th they were at North Meeting having also 'a precious opportunity in young Samuel Emlen's family, also in Joshua Howell's'. They also managed to attend the burial of Samuel Elliot in the Market Street House: 'many young people affected'.

They closed the labour of the day on 28th December 'with a sitting with some young women who have formed an association to visit and relieve the Poor'.

1796

January

On 1st January they attended the Children's Meeting in 'which much concern was handed unto them and their teachers'.

Deborah was at Market Street Meeting on the 3rd January, and in the evening she and Ruth Anna Rutter 'were engaged'.

They then rode to **Westbury** next day and on 5th January reached Upper Greenwich where they met and spoke with some young people. They visited Pine Neck on the 6th, and at Pines Grove Meeting next day they 'felt sympathy with some under peculiar trial', but she does not divulge the nature of the trouble. They had three Religious opportunities in Friends' families and were at **Salem** Meeting on 8th January. Next day they reached **Alloways Creek** Meeting, 'the solemnity of Death and the absolute necessity of preparing for it was much press'd'. What had occurred to cause this sombre mood was not revealed, but it may have been the hazards of the frequent proximity of much water in the creeks fed by the fast flowing rivers; also the swampy ground in places, and the dangers of winter weather to all living creatures.

Greenwich Meeting on 10th January 'afforded an occasion for the exercise of patience, yet in the end was rewarded with a degree of Victory'. How often on these long journeys Deborah must have endured frequent disappointment and frustration, although she gives the impression throughout that dedication and endurance were always worthwhile.

Visits to the Coast and New Jersey

The 12th January found them at **Cape May** on the coast, and this proved satisfactory.

They reached **Great Egg Harbour** Meeting the following day where there were only 'a small number of our Society, but others attending, Divine regard was felt towards them'. At **Upper Egg Harbour** Meeting on the 14th she found 'help was afforded to relieve our minds'. These places were, as their names indicate, ports on the coast, carrying on local trade. They went on to the third of the name Egg, **Little Egg Harbour**, to a Friend's family, and also to Meeting. On the 17th they reached Barnagat Meeting 'large and exercising', and they were relieved to find themselves that evening lodging in a Friend's family, where they 'had a season of retirement'.

> *Salem, **Alloways Creek** and New Jersey's **Greenwich** lay along the eastern shore of the Delaware estuary toward **Cape May**, later to be a resort town and the site of Friends' summer conferences, but at this time a fishing village. **Great Egg** and **Little** and **Upper Egg Harbours** north-east along the Atlantic coast were also neglected Quaker outposts, close to the line which George Keith had surveyed between the non-Quaker East and Quaker West Jersey colonies.*

> *Their next stops were in the heart of New Jersey at **Newark** and across New York City to Long Island at **Westbury** for Quarterly Meeting, then back to **Freehold** (Topanemus Meeting near Shrewsbury) in the corner of New Jersey south of Staten Island; and on south-west by Springfield and Burlington, towards Philadelphia.*

The next two days were spent travelling to Rahway once again. This was probably in a wheeled vehicle, as Deborah does not mention that they rode. There was a Meeting of Ministers and Elders on 20th January, the day they arrived, followed by Monthly Meeting.

The Select Quarterly Meeting was on 22nd January, 'in which much counsel was handed to various states'. They visited the youth and were also encouraged 'to hear the turning of the Divine Hand'.

At First Day morning Meeting on 24th January, 'Friends were invited to walk in the Light which cleaneth the Soul'. Afterwards they 'had the company of many Black People residing in that neighbourhood', and in the evening they 'had a humbling opportunity in Hugh David's family'.

They had a satisfactory Meeting in the Court House at Newark, New York on 25th January.

By the 27th they had travelled across New York City to Long Island for the Select Quarterly Meeting at **Westbury**, and in the evening had a sitting with some young people in their lodgings. Quarterly Meeting was 'large and favor'd' on the 28th and that same evening, they had an Open Meeting with the blacks. Parting Meeting, which was large, followed next day, and they had a Meeting with 'People of other Societys' at Brookland on the 30th before returning to New York.

The last day of the month they sat with Friends in both their Meetings. Deborah hoped they would 'prove memorable seasons' for they were on one of their last visits to the city.

That evening they had a Meeting with many of the inhabitants, but unfortunately she gives no names although they had spent some time with Friends there in the past, and knew a number of families well.

February

On 1st February they visited prisoners and had 'a sitting also with three under condemnation for forgery' and afterwards with 'two young men lately disowned who were confined because of debt'. In the afternoon they 'had a large Meeting with the Black People', 'and they appeared grateful for the opportunity'.

Then they visited a sick Friend from England, Hannah Shipley, who died shortly afterwards. They then spent the next day visiting the sick and had an evening Meeting with young people. Rebecca was largely engaged on 3rd February at Monthly Meeting.

On the 4th they travelled to Elizabeth Town, an 'old and pleasant place'. Deborah hoped that it was to some profit, but was doubtful because she found them 'a high people', by which she inferred that a rather worldly atmosphere prevailed. The well-to-do Friends probably lived in some of the pleasant 18th century houses which had been built in recent architectural style, influenced by those of Philadelphia, and which were comfortable and often well furnished.

They had a Meeting at Upper Freehold on 6th February 'in which things felt low' and were in C. M. Newbold's family the day afterwards, 'the latter a valuable Minister, who had some promising children'. They continued south-west to Springfield where Rebecca Wright was with them at Meeting 'where she was powerfully engaged to ask a Blessing', and the same evening they had a sitting at the home of William Newbold who was their 'kind companion through the States of New York'. Springfield had the most interesting Presbyterian Church in the State with a square tower surmounted by a cupola.

The two days following they attended Mount Meeting ('laborious but ended well') and Old Springfield Meeting which they found supportive.

At Mansfield Neck on the 10th they particularly 'laboured with the Youth', and there followed a Meeting for the black people at Burlington in the afternoon, followed later by an opportunity in the house of John Hoskins who had a connection in trade with the Browns of Providence in the production of cotton materials. Next day at Ancocas Meeting they experienced 'a season of some profit' and had an opportunity in a Friend's family which 'was comfortable and like a Brook by the way'. In the evening they then attended a Public Meeting at Mount Holly, which had been the home of John Woolman, and a place of which Deborah would have frequently heard.

On 12th February at **Vincent Town** Meeting they 'had the company of some not of our Society' and continued to visit families as opportunity arose during their travels, as well as attending the Meetings in the places they passed through. A Meeting at Upper **Evesham** was held on the morning of 13th February and an evening one followed at **Cropwell**, 'both seasons wherein the spring of refreshment opened as well as in a family sitting'. They next visited Lower **Evesham** and reached **Haddonfield** by the evening 'both seasons of favour'. These Meetings were followed by a large Quarterly Meeting at **Woodbury**, which 'afforded cause to hope'.

*Vincent Town, Evesham, Cropwell and especially **Haddonfield** and **Woodbury** were old West Jersey Quaker settlements east of the Delaware opposite Philadelphia, where Deborah and Rebecca spent the winter months among Friends who became personal friends like Moses Brown and Samuel Emlen.*

They were at **Newtown** Meeting on 16th February to which eminent minister Joshua Evans belonged 'who uses no foreign article, uses no dyed garments, nor eats anything that occasion life to be taken'. **Moorstown** Meeting on 17th was 'large and labor'd'. They then returned to **Burlington** for a marriage, and there also they mentioned their wish to visit Friends. Deborah was from the 21st 'confined for two days by my stomach in the house of our Beloved Friends J. & S. Cross', but she was well enough to sit with their family in the evening.

They were carrying on steadily with their family visiting and in one had 'the company of a worthy Elder [Grace Buchanan] who had come over with Jane Hoskins the last time she visited Europe'. The day after they attended weekday Meeting and a Select Quarterly Meeting and continued visiting families. They found the Meeting on 28th February 'Measurably Owned' although Deborah thought 'all did not fully keep their ranks which often prevented the Word of the Lord having free course to run and be glorified'.

As this year of 1796 was Leap Year, Quarterly Meeting was held on 29th February and Deborah records here that 'our Holy Head revealed himself as a Spirit of Judgement to those that sat in Judgement'.

March

After an appointed Meeting for Youth on 1st March, which appeared to go well, they completed their family visits next day 'with a sitting in the family of our Honourable Friend John Hoskins where Divine regard was evidently manifested under a thankful sense after which [they] left Burlington and reached Philadelphia that night', a distance of 15 to 20 miles.

Philadelphia

They were now to spend some five months there, visiting families and attending Meetings, and started immediately visiting Market Street Friends, some under affliction.

News of Death of Wilson Barnard and John Young

On 8th March they visited eight families, 'a laborious day'. They then received the sad intelligence of 'the death of two Beloved Brothers, John Young and Wilson Barnard, the first my dear R.Y.'s and the second my own, which was affecting to our minds'. Wilson was her youngest brother and only 21 years old.

On the 9th after sitting in seven families, they were sent for to visit Sarah Gilpin, related to the Coalbrookdale Gilpins, a young woman who had been ill for about a year. Deborah was engaged with her for nearly an hour before she died 'her removal is a great trial to her affectionate Relations'. They attended the burial on the 12th March, which proved 'a humbling time for many of the youth who were exhorted to faithfulness'.

By the 20th March they had during the week before visited 53 families and Deborah found 'Divine Regard was manifested to the refreshment of our often weary spirits'. Being a Sunday, they attended all three Meetings that day 'in which [their] hope was revived'.

On the 22nd March they were at North Monthly Meeting where they 'spread a concern before our Friends to visit their familys with which much unity was manifested . . . One Friend in the Men's Meeting express'd a desire that [they] might stand resigned to the pointings of Truth. [They] were Soldiers for Life and should meet with trials whether at home or abroad'.

They went on 'diligently with the work before [them]' and also attended the weekday Meeting at Market Street. Monthly Meeting was on 25th March and General Spring Meeting began next day where Martha Routh and Lydia Rotch joined them, 'just returned from a visit to the Southern Provinces'. In this Meeting 'our Dear ancient Friend Samuel Emlen spread his concern to go the 7th time to Europe with which there was much concurrence expressed'. In the afternoon Meeting William Savery and Sarah Talbot spread their concerns to visit Europe 'which was very feelingly united [by] one Friend [who] beautifully remarked "Moses preservation in the Ark of Bulrushes and that when delivered therefrom he refused to be called the son of Pharoh's daughter, setting forth encouragement in times of difficulty, and caution in times of favor".'

They were at three Meetings at Market Street on 27th March, 'all of which were open seasons, many Gospel Truths being conveyed under best authority which was relieving to our deeply exercised minds'.

Next day they informed Friends 'of [their] prospect of release and return to [their] Native Land. Our esteemed Friend P[hoebe] Speakman also spread her concern to visit Europe which met the feeling approbation of Fds'. They then sat Pine Street Meeting in silence, 'others had to bear Testimony to the Truth'.

Their different Certificates were signed by 29th March, and they were beginning to speak as if in farewell. The last day of the month they finished their visits to the families in Market Street Meeting, 300 in number, and started on the ones in the North Meeting the same day.

April

They parted from Martha Routh and Lydia Rotch on 2nd April, Martha 'speaking rather prophetically' to Rebecca and Deborah, before they went on to the 'Eastern Shore of Maryland'.

They had a Meeting with William Savery on the morning of the 3rd at the Prison, 'in which Divine Love flow'd freely to the Sinners, as well as those that had not widely stray'd from the paths of rectitude'. This visit must have been long treasured by Deborah, as William Savery's presence would have made the visit that much easier and lifted her heart in a task which she always found very difficult. Indeed a man of so much experience in this kind of visit must have given her extra courage and insight as to how best to undertake further such visits.

During the following week they visited 54 families and on the 10th they went to Haddonfield 'to attend the burial of Sarah Hoskins', the Friend who had accompanied Deborah's Aunt Rachel Wilson into New England when she visited America in 1768.

That evening they attended Market Street Meeting, and also found themselves 'a little favor'd' in the North Weekly Meeting on 12th April and managed six family visits that day.

After this, they were confined to the house with colds, but were able to have 'a refreshing opportunity with some Young People at their lodgings', on 16th April. On the 19th they attended a wedding at North Meeting and during the following week visited 51 families, Hannah L. Fisher going with them. On the 23rd they went to Derby in the evening, visiting a family on the way. They spent next day with Derby families and after attending Radnor Meeting on the 25th returned to Philadelphia, again re-meeting Martha Routh and Lydia Rotch 'to [their] mutual comfort' and were again at North Meeting next day. They attended Horsham Meeting on 27th April where many Friends seemed 'glad of their unexpected visit'.

May

On the first day of May they attended North Meeting and 'in the evening had an appointed [large and satisfactory] Meeting for People of other Societys'. Quarterly Meeting next day was 'a time of Liberty to speak of the excellence of Zion, many minds were united in a travail of Spirit for Truth's Prosperity'. Then on the 3rd at the Youths' Meeting 'under a feeling of Divine Regard' they took a solemn leave of our Beloved Friends'.

They continued their visits to Friends' families on the 4th and dined with Martha Routh at Samuel Wistar's, after which they 'departed very sensible that there is Strength in Love and Fellowship in the Gospel'.

In the course of that last week they had 'between forty and fifty religious opportunitys in familys'. Having completed their visits to the North Meeting (250 in number) they attended Pine Street Meeting in the morning of 8th May where they were both engaged in Testimony, and where there were many Friends from other Meetings, presumably some of them to say farewell.

After dining in their lodgings in the company 'of a large number of dear Friends under the precious influence of that Love which has often united our Spirits' they left the city where at different times they had spent five months.

Last Months in America

Deborah's entry in her Diary here reveals little of her reactions to the three years spent in America, but she does say 'we parted and left that city [Philadelphia] where we have at different times spent 5 months and visited between 600 and 700 familys, in the course of which we have taken many weary steps and been sensible of singular mercy being display'd towards its inhabitants – some of the precious Youth are emmanently [*sic*] under the forming hand whom we desire the Shepherd of Israel may keep as the Apple of his Eye'.

After an evening Meeting at Chester on the day they left Philadelphia they attended Concord Meeting on the 9th May, and the day after were at the Youths' Meeting 'where many states were spoken to'.

They also had sittings in families on the 10th and 11th including on the 11th 'some of that of R[obert] Valentine', and were in Middletown Meeting on the same day, in which Deborah and C. Albertson 'had counsel to hand'. They dined in Ely Yarnall's family and were afterwards at Westown, 'where Friends have since settled a school, it is a beautiful situation, and they have purchased 500 acres of land'. She adds 'May the Lord prosper the work'. After a time of retirement in a Friend's family they attended Birmingham Meeting on the 12th followed by an opportunity in the family of J. Sharples 'in which there appeared a prospect of the Mantle descending'. They lodged at Caspar Wister's, where sadly 'two of their children had lost the use of their limbs'.

On the 13th they had a Meeting at New Garden in which 'the Love and Life of Truth was felt'. They spent the rest of the day with Jacob and Hannah Lindley, who by now were old personal friends, and had a sitting in the family that evening.

In the Select Meeting in London Grove on the 14th 'had to convey some counsel tending to stir up the Fds to watchful care over the Youth – many Friends came to us from Philadelphia'. They were there in the morning of the 15th and then 10 miles away at Fallowfield by the evening.

Quarterly Meeting was held on the 16th May 'which was a large and solemn opportunity'. In the evening they had a sitting with a number of Friends at Joshua Pusey's in which 'our hearts were afresh united to the willing in Israel and the Young People in particular claimed our sympathy, some of whom promised usefulness in the Church'.

Next day they took leave 'of many Friends', going south again to Newcastle from whence they were to sail. Nowhere was the influence of the Philadelphia style of Georgian architecture more pronounced than in the small town of Newcastle, an important port on the Delaware River where seagoing vessels could dock, and where trans-shipment took place for the further journey to Philadelphia. The Strand, bordering the river, was built in the same style, with the addition of wharves and warehouses and other facilities.

At Newcastle, after a time of retirement at their lodgings, Deborah and Rebecca attended a Public Meeting, an important one, 'in which the work of Religion was described as redeeming the mind of man and producing that holiness that ensured an admittance into the Kingdom of God. The Meeting ended in a solemn prayer for a Blessing on the inhabitants of this Continent. After dining with about 150 Friends [they] had a solemn parting opportunity in which much encouragement was handed and prayer put up for mutual preservation under the influence of humbling goodness that had put us forth and gone before us, and now condescended to be our reward'.

The Friends, although Deborah does not mention this, 'received a signal courtesy from the Court then in Session, it adjourning and devoting the Court Room to the Meeting, Judge Basset and many of the Magistrates and lawyers remaining through the Session'.[15]

The Return Journey

Elizabeth Drinker wrote in her Journal on the 14th May the details of the payment for the passage to Europe paid for by the Yearly Meeting, as Henry Drinker was at that time the Treasurer. 'Philip Atkins, Master of the Ship *Sussex* from Liverpool was here this evening, H.D. paid him £210, equal to 120 guineas, for the passages of Samuel Emlen, William Savery, Deborah Darby, Rebecca Young, Phoebe Speakman and Sarah Talbot.'

The *Sussex*[16] was a ship of 270 tonnes net, built and owned in Philadelphia in 1790 of live oak, cedar and pine, drawing 15 feet of water when loaded, trading between her home port and the United Kingdom.

Deborah and Rebecca went on board the *Sussex* anchored a little off shore, at about five o'clock in the evening. They were to travel with William Savery, Samuel Emlen (on his seventh visit to Europe), Phoebe Speakman, Sarah Talbot and Benjamin Johnson, who were to prove an agreeable and kind company, which was fortunate as the voyage was to be very rough at times. The Captain commented at the close that the gales were the hardest he had ever experienced at that time of the year, 'the sea continually breaking over the main and quarter deck'.

On 20th May Deborah told of how 'The Pilot left us this morning and by him we sent letters back to our Friends in America, of which shore we lost sight this evening and turned our faces, I hope thankfully, towards the land of our Nativity'.

Deborah and Rebecca wrote to Stephen Grellet from the *Sussex*. He had evidently been amongst the Friends in Newcastle who had come to say farewell. It is a letter of encouragement to him on the way he had chosen. They had watched his spiritual evolution in Philadelphia from his first convincement, and had even then realised his potential. They also sympathised deeply with his and Joseph's anxiety over their parents.

They also sent messages to Joseph, who evidently was in correspondence with them.

They wrote further at Liverpool telling him of their safe arrival on 19th June, the day before they set out for home.

They 'sat together on the 22nd at 10 and 5 o'clock; in the latter they had the company of some of the sailors', which pleased the Friends who hoped they had 'benefitted by the Gospel Truths' they had conveyed. The life of these seafaring men was very hard and difficult, living in very cramped quarters and there was also continuously the danger at that time of conflict from pirates and warring vessels of several nations, as well as the hazards always present of the sea. The Atlantic Ocean had at times very great storms and these sailing ships were small for such long voyages. Their courage however was great and had to be sustained over many days, with at times an uncertain outcome.

Deborah's entry on the 25th expressed her pleasure in their having 'such a comfortable harmonious company'.

Their Friends in America had provided them on leaving with an excellent sea store for the journey, though Deborah felt that they would have been 'contented with much less, especially when the poor Blacks are remembered', but she was nevertheless 'thankful to *Him* who is the author of all blessings'.

These Friends had first of all replenished their medicine chest and added two quarts of peppermint water. They had also given them a small cellar as the drinking water was uncertain, and the voyage of unknown duration. This consisted of:

8 dozen Lisbon Wine; 5 dozen Port; 10 dozen Tanton Ale; 12 dozen Cyder; 2 gallons of Brandy; and the same of Spirits; and, thoughtfully, 2 corkscrews. There was also a keg of Rum for the Sailors, which would have been well deserved.

They were provided also with beds, bedding and linen, 6 wash-hand basins, 3 tin saucepans and 3 tin cups, and 6 yellow mugs. The following list made up what they took with them for food. They had 24 lbs of Coffee, 8 lbs of Hysum, and 3 lbs of Susang Tea, also 12 lbs of Chocolate. They had 30 lbs loaf sugar and ¾ cwt of East India sugar. There were spices and seasonings, also an ample supply of oatmeal, pearl barley, rice and sago; biscuits, rusks, and half-a-barrel of rye meal and a barrel of flour, together with much butter and fat.

Fruit and vegetables were included, with 100 lemons, the same of limes, and 50 oranges. Amongst the vegetables were 12 bundles of asparagus, which it is hoped were eaten before the bad weather set in.

They had much salted meat and fish, and 30 dozen eggs, and also live animals and fowls, presumably most to be killed and eaten during the journey; also their fodder was included – hay, corn, buckwheat and bran. Included in this was presumably the food for the gift of deer given to Deborah to bring back for the little Sunniside park. Tradition has always had it so, but there is no mention of the animals in this list, and they must have been very young and few in number to have survived such a voyage.[17]

The date on the list of stores was wrongly given, and Sarah Darby corrected it to 1796. (See illustration, p. 213).

100 lb Beef &c. Dry —
18 Tongues —
6 Pigs about 30 lb
2 Sheep & 1 Goat —
12 Couple Fowls —
some Ducks
Geese & Turkies —
70 lb Butter —
30 doz Eggs —
3 Cheese about 60 lb
50 lb Flour
24 lb Dry Rusk —
6 lb Table Biscuit —
15 lb Ginger Bread —
6 lb do Freely —
half Barrel Rye Meal —
do do Indian do —

14 lb Pearl Barly —
24 lb Coffee —
3 lb Hyson & Souang Tea —
3/4 cwt East India Sugar —
50 Loaf Sugar —
1 lb Ground Pepper —
lb Ginger —
2 Boxes Raisins —
1 lb Mace —
1 lb Nutmegs —
1 lb Cloves —
2 lb Cinnamon —
1/2 lb Allspice —
6 Quarts Oatmeal —
6 lb Rice —
6 lb Pearl Sago —
12 lb Chocolate —
6 Bottles Snuff —
6 Bottle Cayan pepper —

1 Jar Olives —
2 Bottles Capers —
2 do Anchovies —
2 do Sweet Oil —
12 lb Pruens —
20 lb soft Shild Almonds —
100 Lemons —
100 Limes —
50 Oranges —
1 Jar Pickels
Potted Shad
2 Kegs Pickeld Oysters —
Pickeld & Smoked Salmon
4 Gallons Vinegar —
5 do Molasses —
1 do Honey —
2 Quarts pepper Mint Water
1 Bottle Wine bitters —

Dry Peaches
Cramberries
10 Bushel Potatoes —
1 Keg Onions —
Horse Redish —
12 Bundles Asparagus —
Sallad & Sprotes —
50 Loaves Bread —
20 lb Candles —
2 doz Fowls —
Pipes & Tobacco —
3 lb Castile Soap —
Some plug Tobacco for Sailors
8 Quire whited Brown paper
Linen for Bags —
6 Pewter Chamber potts w covers
6 Wash Hand Basons —
3 Tea ... different Sizes

List of stores sent on board the Sussex, 1796, provided by American Friends for Deborah's journey home.

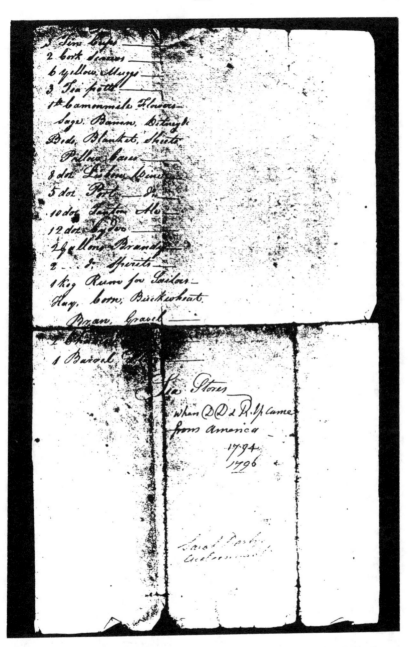

Note this date should have been 1796. It was later corrected by Sarah Darby.

On 25th May when they were gathered together tranquilly, Benjamin Johnson read to them a part of John Pemberton's Journal, which afforded them 'encouragement to follow the Shepherd of Israel wherever He leadeth'.

Benjamin had, with his brother, founded a publishing house in Philadelphia. He was aged 30 when he undertook this voyage, and was to travel with William Savery in the British Isles, including Iceland, France and Germany. His conversation and literary tastes would have helped them through the long hours whenever they were together in their cabin for recreation.

On 28th May they met the *Alliance* from Liverpool 'with 34 passengers on board, and were able, by her, to send [back] letters to America'.

They sat down together on 29th May, First Day, as usual 'to their mutual satisfaction'.

On the 31st of the month they were on the Banks of Newfoundland – 'where it is frequently so misty that the Fishermen carry horns to apprise each other of their approach, it is supposed there are 300 sail of ships now Fishing, we took 7 fine cod'. William Savery wrote of ships carrying a 'Conch Shell' for the same warning, and described how the fishing was done with long leaded lines each with two hooks.

June

They held their weekday Meeting on 1st June in which Samuel Emlen 'handed encouragement, he proved his dwelling to be near the sacred source of Good'. The morning of 2nd June found them 'near a Mountain of Ice which appeared to be in motion southward, and as we passed it at half a mile distance we thought it to be 200 yards long and 40 feet high, supposed to come out of Davis's Straits'. The weather was cold so 'we got a fire lit in our cabin and all settled down to our little employments as if by our own fireside. Oh, how pleasant when all are of one mind – it unites in sweet harmony when the same important things are desired. Samuel Emlen often exclaims "Oh, that thousands were acquainted with this fellowship"'.

By 5th June they experienced 'a very great storm. Samuel Emlen said he had not been in so great a one since crossing the ocean with John Woolman in 1772. We were enabled to confide in *Him* whom the winds and waves obey, but could not sit down together to bear a public testimony'.

They were thankful that by 10th June they were again to be able to hold their weekday Meeting for they had found the last days and nights very trying and their sense of relief for the calm was 'vocally expressed'. During the storm Deborah found 'many of us had comfortably to remember Addisons' Hymn of "How are thy servants blest oh Lord"'.

At their Meeting on First Day, the 12th June 'Samuel Emlen expressed his thankfulness for this and every other mercy'. Soon after their usual weekday Meeting on the 16th, they were 'visited by a French Privateer, her name L'Espèrance (or Hope) from Brest – she enquired where we came from'. When she found their ship was American, she 'wished us a very good voyage. Some of us desired to be thankful for being preserved out of the hands of unreasonable men'. William Savery gave more details about this encounter, saying that the ship had 200 men on board and carried 20 guns; also that they were boarded before being allowed to proceed. However as France at this time was friendly towards America and the *Sussex* was owned by the United States, they were probably in no danger.

They had their first glimpse of land on 17th June which they 'found reviving to many of us to whom the sea is always trying'.

Arrival Back in England, 18th June 1796

They were awakened early on the day following 'by the Pilot coming on board, and after a uniting opportunity in which Gratitude was felt to the Preserver of men, we landed about 9 o'clock in the evening at Liverpool, being kindly received at Cousin R. Benson's', a Rathbone cousin in Liverpool.

NOTES

[1] Surveyed for Lloyds in Liverpool and classed A1.
[2] Written in the form of a Journal/Letter by Ann Warder, wife of John Warder, who had been seeking lodgings after living in New York, and was received by the same John Murrays. It was sent by Ann to her sister, Elizabeth Head Cadbury, wife of Richard Tapper, now in possession of Elizabeth H. Cadbury, widow of John Warder Cadbury III.
[3] This letter, sent 21st November 1793 from East Nottingham, Maryland to Elizabeth Pim c/o Sarah Grubb Annan Mills, in Clonmell, Ireland, arrived on 15th February 1794.
[4] In Ironbridge Gorge Museum.
[5] See note 3.
[6] From *The Quakers, Their Story and Message* by A. Neave Brayshaw, reprint 1982 by Sessions Book Trust. 'In the matter of "hat-honour", as the Quaker called it, this uniformity of which we are speaking soon prevailed. It was not the natural thing for the master in his own house to take off his hat, though he insisted on his sons doing so in his presence; the worshipper, and sometimes even the preacher, wore it in church, taking it off in time of prayer and the singing of psalms. The Quaker also, to the honour of God, took it off in time of prayer (he did not sing psalms), but he refused to give in to the spirit which led judge or magistrate to demand its removal in his presence and led social "superiors" to demand the payment to them of an honour which they would not pay to their "inferiors". Accordingly he wore his hat on almost all the occasions when others took theirs off.'

[7] Charity Cook is the subject of lively biographical details in the biography of her by Algie Newlin, and in Seth Hinshaw's *Carolina Quaker Experience.*

[8] Now in Ironbridge Gorge Museum, in its original box.

[9] Anthony Benezet, a prolific writer, born in France, was apprenticed to a Quaker in London and convinced as a Friend there; he came to Philadelphia with his family at the age of 18 in 1731. For a while he tried business with his well-to-do brothers but gave it up to become a teacher and dedicate 40 years of his life to the service of humanity. He became a leader in the education of women and of poor blacks. He crusaded tirelessly against slavery and cultivated friendship with the Indians. He and Deborah never actually met.

[10] *The Life of Thomas Story* written by himself in two volumes, published by Isaac Thompson of Newcastle. There is a copy in the Ironbridge Gorge Museum.

[11] See note 7, p. 78.

[12] At Ironbridge Gorge Museum.

[13] Apart from the name Gay-Head Indian there was a distinct difference at this period between 'gay' or 'high' Friends and the 'plain Friends' in dress, and these terms were used to denote their difference; the former meaning apparel similar to that currently worn and the latter clothes in material and style of a much simpler fashion reminiscent of the previous century.

[14] See note 13 re use of word 'gay'.

[15] Quoted from *Life of William Savery of Philadelphia 1750-1804*, by Francis R. Taylor, A.M., LL.B., 1925, Macmillan Company, New York.

[16] Surveyed for Lloyds in Liverpool, Vol. 1796 and classed A1.

[17] The front cover of Rachel Labouchere's book *Abiah Darby* shows the deer in the Sunniside park, and they can also be seen in the bottom right hand corner of the front cover of this book (see enlargement below).

PART FOUR

Return Home

June 1796

THE DAY AFTER THEIR LANDING on 19th June they attended morning Meeting and had an opportunity at Isaac Hadwen's after dinner.

The next day they took an affectionate leave of their fellow passengers and travelled to Shrewsbury, staying the night with Rebecca's family where next day Sarah Darby, Mary Rathbone, Richard Reynolds, Richard Dearman and Deborah's son Edmund met them to escort them home. They arrived at Sunniside in time for tea, but there was no mention of Samuel, who was evidently away from home, whether unwell, or travelling, was not disclosed.

The deer that Deborah, according to tradition, had brought from America, were supposedly fetched from the dockside immediately, but there is no record of this . The story of their origin has, however, always prevailed down the generations and their descendants were referred to as 'Deborah's Deer'. The herd was crossed with animals from neighbouring parks, latterly with the herd of Attingham Park, near Shrewsbury, and they were controlled by culling, the venison being eaten by the family, and given away as gifts – all being carefully listed. These animals from America must have been young to withstand such a journey, and the whole episode has always had a slightly 'fairy-tale' element in the telling of it but has always been believed.[1]

Coalbrookdale Meeting on 26th June 'was large, on account of the burial of a workman, George Thomas, who lost his life in the Mill'. Deborah was engaged to give thanks for the many mercies extended: Ann Summerland also spoke. George was one of the Thomas family connected with the Darbys from the days when the first Abraham had, with the help of the young John Thomas, cast the first iron bellied pot in Bristol in 1704. In the evening Deborah's son Samuel came home and she found 'our meeting was affecting'.

July

In spite of her long visit to America, she was off once more in two days' time to Llanidloes in Wales to attend 'the postponed Monthly Meeting', followed by some public service in different Meetings before returning home.

On 3rd July Deborah had an opportunity in their morning Meeting, in which 'Fds were exhorted to faithfulness in their Lot'.

To her great joy Samuel returned home on 4th July. For this she felt much thankfulness, declaring 'whose company I deem a great blessing'. She did not vouchsafe any information as to where he had been or his state of health. The communications of the day could have accounted for the reason that he had not been at home to welcome Deborah on her return, as it was impossible to know far ahead when her ship was going to dock until approaching their destination. She exclaimed how much she 'enjoyed the company of my near connections of which I desire to be enabled to make suitable returns. My dear R. Young came, my endear'd husband and her much affected at meeting after so long an absence'.

After attending Monthly Meeting at Shrewsbury on 20th July, where Deborah and Rebecca gave an account of their late arduous journey in America on which they had 'renew'd occasion to adopt David's language, "Return unto thy rest, oh my Soul, for the Lord thy God has dealt bountifully with thee"', Deborah, Samuel and their two sons were at New Dale Meeting and afterwards dined with Joseph Reynolds on 24th July.

They all had the sudden bad news on 25th July that Elizabeth Dearman, the wife of Richard Dearman, 'was taken away not having time to speak'. She was buried on the last day of the month and at the burial service Deborah 'appeared first in prayer and afterwards in testimony'; also Mary Beasley, (Richard Reynold's sister), Mary Capper, Rebecca Young, Ann Summerland, Susannah Appleby and others were engaged in the afternoon Meeting. Some Friends came to supper with whom they had an opportunity afterwards.

August

In early August Deborah and Samuel took Edmund to Grooby Lodge 'in order to place him a while there'. The boy had been a pupil at Thomas Huntley's school at Burford, as had his brother Samuel before him, but the establishment to which he had now been entered was perhaps of a different kind, as he would shortly be coming up to his apprenticeship. After leaving Edmund there they attended Leicester Meeting, and later had an opportunity at J. Prestman's, at Shannon Lodge. After dinner on 4th August, young Samuel left them for London, and they returned home, reaching Sunniside on the night of 6th August.

At afternoon Meeting next day Deborah had to 'press Friends to faithfulness and all the discoverys of light'. Her sister, Rachel Fowler, was with them on 12th August, and she with Deborah and Susannah Appleby were all engaged in their evening sitting. Robert Fowler, who had come with his wife Rachel, then left with her next day to return home to Melksham 'after an agreeable visit'. The sisters must have been very happy to meet once more after Deborah's long absence in America.

Deborah then went to Shrewsbury with Susannah Appleby for several Meetings, and was at Monthly Meeting at New Dale on 17th August, where she and Ann Summerland ministered, and at which Rebecca Young and Priscilla Hannah Gurney 'got liberty to visit some neighbouring Counties' They returned home to Sunniside in time for dinner as Sarah Grubb and her daughter were with them before returning home to Ireland.

Deterioration of Samuel's Health

Sadly, by the 18th Samuel was 'becoming much indisposed', which caused Deborah to feel 'very uneasy'. Fortunately, Rebecca was with them and able to share her anxiety; she was a great help to them both 'having a sweet season with my S.D.'. On 20th August the Grubbs left to continue their journey home. That same day Deborah found that her 'Precious husband was inclined to go to Bilston with S. Proud, his being so weak made the separation trying beyond expression, and my feelings on this occasion seemed more than I could sustain under, being also myself in a poor state of health, and had not the Eternal God been my refuge, I must have fainted'.

The 21st August proved 'a deeply trying day' to her and during the whole week she was 'in near sympathy with my Precious Husband, sharing his conflicts – surely this is a time never to be forgot, but was enabled to relieve my mind in both Meetings, which afforded a degree of true peace'.

On the 30th they received an account 'of my S.D. being worse, when Sister S(arah) D(arby), E. Haines and myself set out and found him very ill'.

She spent the day after 'attending upon my Dearest S.D. – trying it is to have the prospect of an awful separation – with what anxiety did I view the approach of Death – the Dear Sufferer had no painful apprehension, but appeared to be passing away in the innocency and sweetness of a Little Child – may I, when the like solemn period approaches, be alike mercifully dealt with. He continued all the evening, appearing pleasant and happy, but to me it was a season not easily described, tho' on his account I desired to be thankful'.

Death of Samuel Darby

September

On the morning of 1st September Samuel 'was released from *all* his *conflicts*', Deborah being left to feel the 'pangs of separation', yet she saw that 'mercy and truth had followed us to this day, and desired to be enabled to drink the cup handed to me in an acceptable manner, believing that the weary are at rest towards evening. I was under the necessity of bidding a final adieu to the Remains of him who had been so *Dear* to *me*, and who had throughout our union been affectionately kind to me, and indeed his Life had been distinguished by acts of benevolence – when favor'd to enjoying a sound understanding. It was a close trial to consider I was never to view those fine features – and amiable countenance more'.

About seven o'clock on 3rd September 'accompanied by many near Relations, the Dear Remains of my S.D. were removed from Bilston and we reached Sunniside about 2 o'clock'.

The following day she spent mostly beside the coffin of her late husband; in the evening her sons and she found 'our meeting was affecting'.

On 6th September 'the Remains of my Dearest Husband were taken into the Meeting House – I sat by it'. At the burial service 'Susannah Appleby appeared first after which M[ary] Lloyd was engaged in Prayer, when dear A[nn] S[ummerland] and E. Simpkin had each an opportunity. I was strengthened in the end to call upon the name of the Lord. After this solid and affecting Meeting, his Precious Remains were committed unto the Silent Grave. May the Lord strengthen me so that I finish my Day's Work, that my head also may go down to the grave in Peace.

'I continue conflicting' she wrote on the 9th, 'it is to me a stripping time, may the Lord sanctify the dispensation. This evening in our little Meeting Sister Fowler and A. Summerland ministered unto us.' There was always a tranquility shared in these small evening Meetings at Sunniside, remarked upon year after year.

Young Samuel and Edmund left home on the 15th September, Deborah finding herself 'much concerned for their preservation'. 'May the Lord grant so singular a Blessing, and then I ask on their account *no more.*'

Samuel's Will

Samuel left a Will dated 4th February 1794, so made several months before his mother's death which assigned Mary Rathbone and Sarah Darby all his shares, rights and interest in the mines, works and estates belonging to the partnership or companies called the Coalbrookdale and Ketley Companies in Shropshire in trust for the benefit of his wife Deborah and his children subsequent to the favour and benefit of the children of his late brother Abraham Darby.

He left the messuage or dwelling house called 'The Summer House' then in the occupation of John Whitacre at the top of Dale House garden, and also a statute acre of land to be taken out of a certain piece of land adjoining the said summerhouse called the 'Whales Back' on the new

Coalbrookdale Meeting House *as it looked until 1960, when a shop took its place on the site. It was originally built in the mid 18th century and rebuilt by Richard Reynolds and opened for use in 1790. (Deborah gives an account of this in her Diary for 1790.) It was situated on the Darby Road, which leads from Coalbrookdale to Little Wenlock.*

Sunniside's Park *is just beyond and* **Chesnuts** *stood next door and can just be seen at the foot of steeply wooded hill side on the left.*

Redrawn by Rachel Labouchere from a 1975/80 photograph of the original drawing by Henry Newman.

orchard to Deborah for her life and then to her assigns and also the residue of his real estate not comprised in the above settlement.

He bequeathed his books, plate, china, linen, household furniture and all his wearing apparel to his son Samuel. To Deborah he left the money to be paid out in legacies of £100 each to Susannah Appleby, Rebecca Darby his sister-in-law, Rebecca Young and Mark Gilpin. Then £200 to his executors – William Reynolds, Robert Fowler and Samuel Thompson (son of Rachel and Isaac Thompson, his nephew, who had come from Newcastle to Coalbrookdale). Deborah was to be the guardian until the children reached the age of 21.

Samuel left his ready money and all his personal estate before dispersal to convert into money to pay his debts, legacies and funeral expenses, other than such debts as he might owe on account of the companies. The residue of this money to go in trust for his wife, one third and two thirds, with interest for his children in equal shares, if any child should die before the age of 21 and without issue, then that share to be divided equally, but not paid sooner than the original shares. The interest of these shares was to be paid to Deborah as long as she remained a widow and to be applied to the maintenance, education and benefit of his children, for which she need not keep any account; after her death or if she remarried the same was to be applied by his executors in such manner as they thought proper, giving them the right also to place either or both his sons in trade or business. It was added that the trustees were not to be answerable to each other.

Deborah continued her attendances at local Meetings during the next week, and on 21st September, 'after a time of retirement in William Holtham's family', and having breakfasted there, she and Rachel Fowler set out towards York. It would seem that Rachel was trying to help and comfort her in this way after Samuel's death by taking her north among the relations and Friends they had known in their youth.

They were with James Dick's family on 22nd before riding to Leek, where they had 'an open Public Meeting in the evening' making later 'some remarks in Toft Chorley's family'. They reached Sheffield Meeting by the 25th September 'where different states were ministered to, the Meeting ending in Prayer'. She may have remembered the day, 20 years before, when she and Samuel had been married in the same Meeting House, but she had little time for recollection as by the evening they had travelled to Rotherham for a Public Meeting. Then, after 'a comfortable opportunity with our esteemed Fd, E. Payne' they went to Ackworth[2] and sat with the family that evening 'Gospel Truths flowing freely unto the children and their instructors'.

In the Select Meeting at York on 27th September, Friends 'were exhorted to keep near together in the Love of Truth. The Meeting for Worship was large and the invitation went forth to those who were far off to draw nigh and those that were nigh to acknowledge the Lord's Night, to which Mary Proud made some addition and Deborah concluded the Meeting in Prayer'. The Meeting for Discipline was held on the 28th and 'Parents were advised to begin early with their children and to keep up a steady line of conduct'. In evening Meeting after Henry Tuke had spoken, Deborah had 'a full opportunity of setting forth the nature of Religion and its effect upon the mind'.

They were later to stay at Henry and Mary Maria Tuke's pleasant house 'between King's Staithe and New Walk on the banks of the River Ouse'. Henry was an exceptional person, intelligent, able and kindly, and had made a success of conducting the family grocery business. He had literary tastes and had studied the classics in his spare time. His wife who had been Mary Maria Scott, was intuitive and friendly. They had a growing family of children around them and the house enjoyed a good garden in which they could play.[3]

Deborah and Rachel visited York Prison on 30th September where 'Joseph Brown and other Friends were confined on account of our Testimony against Tyths', and afforded them some encouragement. This seemed late in the century for such a situation and must have been causing a good deal of distress.

The residence of Mr Lindley Murray, Holdgate, near York in the 1780's.

Deborah dined at Lindley Murray's on Holdgate Hill 'where the language of "be of good cheer" was conveyed'. They would have had much to tell the Murrays of his relations and Friends in New York and also about education in North America. He was an American lawyer, the brother of John Murray junior, and son of the intrepid lady, Mary (Lindley) Murray, who had invited the English generals to dinner in 1776 and thus enabled the American General Patnam, under George Washington, to escape from the capital city. His home in Holdgate Village was an attractive house with a garden and summerhouse. He compiled an English Grammar, which had been published in 1795, the year before this visit, and which had become very popular, going into over 100 editions in England and many other countries including America. Deborah and Rachel would, no doubt, have seen the round summerhouse[4] in his garden in which it is reputed much of this famous school book was written. They did not stay very long as by the evening they were going to attend a large Meeting in a schoolroom in Tadcaster, a few miles to the south of York.

October

On 2nd October they were at Bradford Meeting, dined at William Hustler's and had an evening Meeting at Leeds, which was large and laborious. They sat in John Jowitt's family on the 3rd and went to Meeting at Gildersome, followed in the evening by one at Huddersfield. On 4th October they attended Select Meeting at Manchester, followed next day by a large Quarterly Meeting. Deborah was engaged in supplication and Testimony in a Public Meeting in the evening 'which proved relieving to several of our minds'. They attended Monthly Meeting on 6th October in which 'Christiana Hustler and Deborah each bore Testimony', going on for an evening Meeting with Martha Haworth at Stockport where they paid visits to Friends and their families. They continued with visits in Manchester on the 8th and next day attended morning Meeting having had 'a pretty full opportunity in Isaac Cook's family'.

They were staying in Manchester with Deborah's brother, Robert Barnard and his wife, who were at that time living there, but they were there only very briefly, as they went on to Warrington the next day. The Robert Barnards were later to move to Coalbrookdale to make their permanent home in Shropshire.

The travellers reached Liverpool on 13th October, also attending a Meeting at Ashton and returning home to Sunniside by the 15th. Rachel Fowler left for Melksham the following day. Deborah had much enjoyed her companionship during this first journey after her bereavement and it had helped to give her the necessary strength to continue her mission. She attended Shrewsbury Meeting on the 18th where they 'had the Company of Lydia Robinnet' whom they brought to Coalbrookdale on 23rd October, and who expressed the strong desire 'that obedience might keep pace with knowledge'. At an opportunity after dinner Deborah had encouraged R. Harford 'to follow on and to know the Lord'.

In the evening Meeting on 28th October 'Lydia Robinnet and others ministered and it was a comfortable session'. Deborah accompanied Lydia to 'some disown'd members in New Dale' so they must have thought their guest was suitably persuasive in this task. At New Dale Meeting on 30th 'many not of our Society were present' and they also had a Public Meeting at Coalbrookdale in the evening at which both Timothy Bevington and Lydia Robinnet ministered. Lydia continued her visit for most of that week, visiting families; she also had 'an instructive season in our own family' before leaving for Worcester on 5th November.

November

By this time Rebecca Young had arrived to stay; a great consolation to Deborah, as she remained attending Meetings and having opportunities in families including their own on the 13th November. Joseph Gilpin was with them at this time from Philadelphia, having come to visit his brother Mark, so he brought Deborah and Rebecca the latest news of Friends in that city, which they now thought of as their American home. By the 15th of the month they had Cousins Ann and Hannah Burgess with them, also Deborah's son Edmund.

John Rose, the owner of the Coalport China Works died, and was buried on 17th November. Ann Summerland and Edward Simkin 'had the public service', and Deborah and Rebecca Young visited the bereaved family later that day. Ann Burgess was then engaged in their Meetings until the end of the month.

December

On 4th December, Deborah and Rebecca Young were both engaged in morning Meeting and Deborah also had some remarks to make at Richard Reynolds' house that evening. By the 9th they were in Cheshire at Middlewich and were engaged at Monthly Meeting there and were 'strengthened to convey counsel in both the Mens and Womens Meetings for Discipline'. On their way home they were at Meetings in Nantwich.

Ann and Hannah Burgess left Sunniside on 15th December after their long stay which Deborah hoped had been beneficial for them all. At Monthly Meeting on 21st December, Deborah and Rebecca 'laid before their Friends a concern to visit Wales', and for once, she commented on the weather saying 'it being remarkably cold' on 25th December. They dined at Cousin Dearman's on the 27th where she had to address 'different states' afterwards. Quarterly Meeting took place at the end of the year and they then prepared for their journey into Wales.

1797
January

After the death of Samuel, Deborah was to take a more active part in the Coalbrookdale Company because of the family division of shares and assets. Mary Rathbone, Sarah Darby, and Rebecca Darby (the widow of Abraham Darby III) were all partners with Richard Reynolds, who guided the general industrial conduct of the company, having now Richard Dearman to oversee the day-to-day running of the works and mines.

Deborah was to join the others on the board and her name appears in the minutes from time to time, for she with Rebecca also represented the interests of their children.

As can be seen from her Journal, she was to travel a great deal in the ensuing years, but her own and her sons' interests in this family business were never neglected, even in her absence.

The first day of January found Deborah and Rebecca at Wednesbury and by that evening they had reached Birmingham for Meeting, in which they had a share of public service joined by Mary Lloyd, who went on with them to Stourbridge and then to Worcester for Select Meeting. They travelled to Tewkesbury and Gloucester where, at the latter place, a Meeting was held in the Booth Hall, and here also they were at the home of Joseph White, breakfasted with the Bennetts in Cheltenham and were in Oxford by 8th January.

Oxford

They had made so many journeys in North America in much more difficult country, that their winter journeys at home now could not have seemed very hard for them: they appeared to be travelling in a 'chair', a simple horse-drawn vehicle which made the journey easier than on horseback, also in this particular year they were not impeded by snow which would have made the roads over the Cotswolds impassable.

Once in the university city, Friends were collected at their inn, in which 'Youth was particularly encouraged'. Quarterly Meeting was 'favor'd' and a Public Meeting was held on 9th January, and they reached Witney on the 10th and Burford a day later. Deborah mentioned 'Young People', but not the children at the Thomas Huntley School where her boys and her nephews had been, who she had visited in the past.

Gloucestershire

They then travelled to Cirencester, Malmesbury and on to Melksham for a Meeting on the 15th, staying for only one night with the Robert Fowlers and going on to Bath for a Meeting on 16th January. Next day, on their way to Bristol, they were 'in great danger from the horse drawing their Chair, but were Preserved through Providential care'. Once arrived, C. Davies and Deborah were engaged in testimony at the weekday Meeting, and in John Lewis' family in the evening. They were at Frenchay, at the school, before returning to Bristol for a Public Meeting in the evening.

Prison Visit

They visited the Prison in Bristol on 19th January, and Deborah found this as she always had, 'much in the Cross', feeling great compassion for the inmates. At all places to which they went, they fitted in a few family visits, something they were well accustomed to do.

They reached Claverham on 20th January, and there appeared concerned 'for the Poor amongst the People'. They had a Meeting in Joseph Nash's house 'with his neighbours and family' and dined the day after with Ann-Till Adams. E. Davies now appeared to be travelling with them and they reached Shirenewton on 24th January, going on to Chepstow. On the 25th there followed a trying Meeting at Penhow Castle and another at Uske in the evening, before reaching Pontypool on the 26th where they met in the room of an inn.

Wales

On arrival in Cardiff on 27th January they found 'the language of encouragement flow'd freely to some visited minds'; Deborah also remarked that there were many Methodists in these parts. They then returned to Neath for a Public Meeting in the evening. The Price family, having purchased the works at Neath, were there to greet them, but Deborah does not say they lodged with them, but this was probable.

February

Llandeilo Monthly Meeting was held at Job Thomas' house with very few members, and on 5th February there were two Public Meetings held in a Malt House 'to which people came freely', but only 11 members were present at Quarterly Meeting. They travelled on to attend Meetings in Carmarthen and Pembroke where no Meeting had been held for several years. They sat with Friends at Milford on 9th February and had a Public Meeting at Hubberston in the evening, and they all were again at Milford on the 12th but Deborah was very unwell. Rebecca and E. Davies were engaged in Testimony and Deborah 'enabled to be so in Prayer'. Although still poorly she attended Haverford West weekday Meeting on the 15th, and they dined at A. Clibbern's home next day attending a large evening Meeting.

On 18th February they rode to D. and S. Starbuck's and sat in their family. The day following they were again at Haverford West and at two

Public Meetings attended by many 'serious People' whose company Deborah found satisfactory. Later they were in James Lewis' family and there followed in the next two days evening Meetings at Brecknock and Hay [on-Wye]. Susannah Howell came with them to the sittings in the families of William Young and S. Waring at Leominster on the 24th and here they left David Starbuck, who had accompanied them from Wales, reaching home on 28th February.

March

They were about to embark on concerns which would take them hundreds of miles over the British Isles, hardly ceasing to travel since arriving from North America, as Deborah, having now lost Samuel and with her boys away from home, had nothing to keep her at Sunniside.

She attended several local Meetings during the next week and on 13th March the Ketley interests were sold to William and Joseph Reynolds and 'all large things finished'. The Coalbrookdale Company sold these works and mines to Richard Reynolds' two sons who had now taken over his share interests in the Company. That same day Mary Rathbone and Deborah went to Shrewsbury, intending to visit the prison next day, but were not granted admittance.

Concern to Visit Ireland

At Monthly Meeting on 15th March they laid before Friends a concern to go to Ireland by way of Scotland. They spent two days at Birmingham attending Quarterly Meeting, finding 'Dear Ruth Fallows there and we all had to minister to the People'. Deborah then returned home with Sarah and Susannah Appleby on the 21st, where they found Mary Rathbone and Rebecca Young at Sunniside who had stayed at home, both in good health.

April

On 1st April they were in Shrewsbury attending local Meetings and three days later attended the burial of Benjamin Gilpin. On 6th April they held a Meeting with the workmen at Horsehay, where the furnaces and rolling mill were in full production and where, much later, the plates for the ship the SS Great Britain were to be made. They travelled on to the old market town of Newport where they found 'the People attentive'.

Wales

By the 16th April they were again in Shrewsbury, after which Deborah and Rebecca went to Oswestry for evening Meeting, Susannah Appleby being with them until she returned home leaving the others to go into Wales, to Llangollen and Tythinagarrick and Bala, only to find in that place a 'small low Meeting'. At Machynlleth they found that 'People were long in gathering'. They were with Friends in Llanidloes and also had a Public Meeting there, and a Meeting was held in the Town Hall at Newtown on 23rd April, but they were refused the use of the Town Hall at Montgomery by the priests which prevented them from holding a Meeting there. They attended Yearly Meeting at Welshpool, where they found the two Public Meetings on the 27th rather low, neither of them evidently being well attended. Women Friends waited upon the men for 'an Apprehension of Duty proposing to them the Discontinuing of Yearly Meeting', with the intention of recommending Half-Yearly Meetings to be held instead.

May

On 29th April they attended a Meeting at the Windmill appointed for Ann and Mary Alexander (sister of Dykes Alexander), and sat with Friends at Shrewsbury in the morning next day, arriving home to attend the 'Burial of William Holtham at 4 o'clock which was a favor'd season'. On 2nd May Ann and Mary Alexander were at weekday Meeting and also attended a Public Meeting held in a school house at The Bank, lodging with Cousin William Reynolds and visiting families.

On 12th May they were in Shrewsbury again and at Broseley Meeting in the evening. After dinner next day they had a solemn opportunity at Sunniside after which they took leave of our 'Beloved Connections' attending that evening a Meeting at Bridgnorth which was satisfactory, and had 'a comfortable Meeting at Kidderminster', followed by a morning Meeting at Worcester on 15th May, and at Evesham in the evening. At Campden on the 16th, after an open Meeting in the morning they 'parted with our Dr Fds Ann and Mary Alexander', having a Public Meeting at Chipping Norton later which was 'very solid'.

London Yearly Meeting

They arrived at Oxford for an evening Meeting on 17th May 'where Divine Love was felt towards the People'. After a Meeting next day at High Wycombe they went by way of Uxbridge to London where 'we were kindly rec'd by Joseph and Rachel Smith, attending Select Meeting on the 20th when many remarks were made'. On 21st May they attended both Gracechurch Street and Devonshire House Meetings and during the week was 'closely engaged in attending Meetings for Discipline'. William Savery was with us at Wandsworth Meeting on the 28th and on the 31st they were at 'Yearly Meeting closing with a thankful sense that mercy and truth yet follow our poor Society'.

June

They were at Ratcliffe Meeting on 1st June, following with one at Plaistow in the morning and Barking in the evening of 4th June, and after a

Meeting for Worship: Gracechurch Street Meeting in the 1770's.

sitting in a Friend's family they attended a Meeting at Bromley with William Savery when 'we all had opportunities with the People'. They travelled on to go to Meetings at Deptford, Peel and Stoke Newington, and by the 8th were at Tottenham 'breakfasting with many of our Beloved Fds' at Thomas Horn's home and had a solemn parting opportunity, Dr David Sands ministering 'unto us poor pilgrims'. After a Meeting at Hitchin and several sittings with families, they reached Royston by the 13th, and next day 'parted from our Dr Fds Ann and Mary Alexander going on to Huntingdon for an evening Meeting'.

Lincolnshire

By 16th June they reached Wisbech and had two Meetings at Spalding and Waddington, followed on the 20th by Quarterly Meeting at Lincoln which was 'low tho' there are a few Valuable Fds in these parts', but the Public Meeting held later was large 'affording us thankfulness in a place where our Society is little known'.

At the evening Meeting on the 21st at Gainsborough they found 'a seeking People here in this town'. Gainsborough in the 18th century supported much trade. It was situated on the River Trent with many warehouses lining the river banks where in spring there was a considerable bore. It was an old place with a history going back to King Alfred and King Canute, the Dane. Next day they had a Meeting at Brigg and then one at Barton where they found 'some solid People', giving them strength to reprove a number of 'light young Persons'. They reached Hull on the 25th where they had two Meetings, both successful; the evening one was 'attended by the inhabitants who behaved well'.

Yorkshire and the North

In the morning of the 26th June they had a Meeting at Beverley in the Town Hall 'attended by many of the higher class of inhabitants, [by] whom the uncertainty of Life and the awfulness of Death was largely proclaimed'. Deborah here appeared apprehensive for these people who were not sufficiently serious, but the area had produced famous sons, among them William Wilberforce with whom she could identify completely, particularly after her travels in certain states of North America.

They had 'a favor'd time for those called Methodists' at Pocklington the following day and a Select Meeting at York where after being at various Meetings they 'sat with Fds still in Prison for Truths Testimony when sympathy was felt for our suffering Bretheren'. This seemed an imprisonment made rather late in the century, but courts differed in verdicts in different parts of the country. They afterwards 'visited an Asylum established by Fds for the reception of Lunaticks where comfortable accommodations are prepared and I cannot but think it a singular blessing that the Society has made such a provision'[5] and they had a Public Meeting in the city that evening.

July

After a period of retirement in a Friend's family they attended two Meetings at Thirsk on 2nd July, and a Meeting at Northallerton was freely attended by neighbours when 'the solemnity which prevailed was remarkable'. By the evening of the 3rd they had reached Darlington, going on to Bishop Auckland on the 5th July, after which they travelled on for a 'large and solid Meeting' at Barnard Castle.

Meetings were held at Stockton, Yarm, Norton, Shotton, Sunderland and South Shields and they returned to Darlington for morning Meeting on the 9th July where there were 'some serious young People whose encouragement we sought'. At the Sunderland Meeting she found the reception 'very satisfactory' as many of the inhabitants appeared 'like thirsty ground which drinketh in the rain' and although many of the Maude relations of Abiah were still living there she does not mention them on this visit.

By 16th July they were at Newcastle holding 'a Meeting at 6 o'clock in the Circus supposed to contain twelve hundred'. On the 18th 'after a religious opportunity in Cousin Hadwen Bragg's family' (he had married Margaret, daughter of Isaac and Rachel Wilson, a first cousin of Deborah's) they went on to Morpeth and on 19th July to Felton for morning Meeting and Alnwick for the evening one, this was followed by another at Belford and at the garrison town of Berwick, 'the latter trying from the unsettled conduct of the People'.

Scotland

By the 21st July they had reached Dunbar where they held a Meeting and were next day at Haddington where they 'found the people much strangers to Fds'. The evening Meeting on the 23rd was at New Edinburgh 'at which two thousand people were assembled', and on the 25th there was a Meeting at Dalkeith and they reached Edinburgh next day, having travelled through the lowland country when harvest was ripening, where they had visited small towns and villages clustered near several fine 18th century houses, all of which had an air of prosperity. They attended Edinburgh weekday Meeting at six o'clock and the day after had a Meeting in the 'Friends Meeting House for the People'.

They travelled west to Linlithgow on the 27th for a Meeting with the inhabitants which was 'conducted with considerable respect and solidity'. This town, with the ancient palace, which had been placed in the dowry of Mary of Guise, the mother of Mary, Queen of Scots, on her marriage to King James of Scotland had been the scene of much turbulent history.

Deborah found at Falkirk, which they reached on the 28th July and where they had a Meeting, that the 'people were little acquainted with Religion tho' high in Profession'; fortunately a Meeting at Stirling in the morning next day was more satisfactory. They were travelling fast, possibly by coach, across the country and they reached Glasgow in time for a large Meeting on the morning of the 30th, which Deborah found 'was a favor'd time in this place'. John Robinson had joined Friends and appeared 'a solid character', and she added 'he sits down twice a week with his family to wait upon the Lord'. On the last day of the month they had another Public Meeting in the same room which was equally satisfactory so they had 'reason to believe there is a solid People in this place'.

August

On 1st August they were in Paisley and Port Patrick later, followed by a 'very trying Meeting' at Greenock, but afterwards Deborah 'sat in John Robinson's family to our comfort', as his home was outside the City of Glasgow. That evening they had a Meeting at Dumbarton and another at a village called 'Luss', where Henry Tuke from York, who was with them, was 'much favor'd'.

On 6th August they arrived at Inverary on Loch Fyne where Deborah and Rebecca were silent in Meeting: which Deborah 'apprehended [was] to the great disappointment of some who had a curiosity to hear a woman preach'. This was 'a beautifully situated place' and they held their 'Meeting at the Inn and in the Evening under the Shade of some large trees in the Duke of Argyle's Park and which were in some degree relieving'. This small gathering of Friends in their traditional dress in these unusual and romantic surroundings brought a special 'flavour of piety' in this setting of natural beauty, which was reminiscent of the small Meetings held in the forests of North America at which they had been present. The prayers and supplications were enhanced by the beauty of the natural setting on both occasions, and raised the quality of their ministry as those present felt the strength of spiritual love.

They had a small Meeting at Bonawe where Deborah found at this place, as in others, 'the memory of John Pemberton seemed pleasant to the People', but sadly although they were well behaved to her 'the thirst after rightousness [was] much awanting'. By the 8th August they reached Oban on the west coast, a very active port for fishing and trade as well as boat repairs, where they held a Meeting in the schoolhouse. By the 10th August Deborah told how they had travelled for several days through a grand romantic country with fine lakes, but the rain had been troublesome and 'sometimes dangerous from the sudden falls of water running down the hills bringing large stones upon the road'. The fine scenery was, at that time of the year enhanced by the colour of the heather in full bloom, covering the mountain sides in contrast to grey rock and dark fir trees, and the shimmer of the lakes.

They had a Meeting at Dalmally and another at Tyndrum 'the poorest village my eyes ever beheld which occasioned us to feel much with the inhabitants every way'. They then travelled northwards for several days and had poor accommodation, but Deborah found that 'having been in the Woods of North America it was not new to Rebecca Young and myself'. They had two Meetings at Fort William on the 13th August 'where the public appeared much strangers to Friends'.

On the 14th August they travelled 30 miles to Fort Augustus on Loch Ness where they had 'a small low Meeting', and on the 16th had returned to the east coast to a large town called Inverness – the capital of the Highlands – for a Meeting which proved 'a trying opportunity to us and we left the place unrelieved not feeling strength to appoint another Meeting'. Even the lovely situation on the Firth was no attraction seen from some of the streets there. Next day they found little reception also for the 'precious testimonys of Truth in Nairn' further east where they had an evening Meeting.

Continuing east, they went on to Ferris, Elgin, Fochabers and Cullen to hold only small Meetings, but finally on 20th August they had a large and satisfactory Meeting at Portsoy in the morning, and in the evening a 'deeply trying' one at Banff. The one at Turriff the next day was easier and they 'sat with Fds in their Meeting at Old Meldrum in the evening of the 22nd August'. At Kinmuck weekday Meeting 'a marriage was accomplished – S(arah) Talbot and companion S(arah) Shackleton – there and it was pleasant to meet fellow Pilgrims'. They reached Aberdeen on the coast next day, returning north on the 25th for a satisfactory Meeting at Inverurie, followed by a large one where the house was too small so it was held in the open air.

The following days were taken with attending Select Half-Yearly Meetings and Deborah and Rebecca were then again joined further down the coast by S. Talbot and a companion at Stonehaven for a morning Meeting to good satisfaction, also a Meeting in the evening some 10 to 15 miles further south at Lawrencekirk was large.

September

During the first few days of September they continued their journey southwards, holding Meetings at Brechin, Montrose, Inverkeilor and Arbroath, with another at Forfar in the evening which was 'trying due to the unsettled behaviour of the People', but the Meeting on 4th September at Dundee 'gave us cause to believe there was a seeking People in that place'. At Kirkbride next day the Meeting was attended 'by many who are termed Gentle People, but it is more often literally that to the poor the Gospel is preached'. They had an extremely wet ride to Queen's Ferry where the Forth Bridge now stands and on arrival 'were obliged to sleep on the floor', but they 'got some rest'. They held Meetings at Inverkeithing and Queen's Ferry reaching Edinburgh by the 7th September in time for weekday Meeting, 'in which we felt thankful for being brought so far back after a laborious Journey with a measure of that peace which passeth understanding'.

There was a 'trying Meeting at Leith' on the 8th and next day they called on some families in the company of Sarah Talbot and her companion. Two Meetings were held at Edinburgh and Musselborough, both satisfactory, and on the 11th September further south there was a crowded Meeting at Lanark. After travelling for two days across Scotland they held a Meeting at Stranraer where the 'solemnity of the Meeting was interrupted by some light young People who, tho' reproved continued so to the end'. They had a Meeting at Port Patrick at six o'clock that day and on the 17th 'a Fd meeting us from Ireland released our kind George Miller and our fellow labourer Henry Tuke also apprehending himself at liberty to return home to York' – both had been with them for most of the journey in Scotland.

Second Irish Visit

18th September to 26th February

'We sailed about 8 o'clock and arrived at Donaghadee due east of Belfast on the coast below the inlet to that place about 5 o'clock in the evening.' A Meeting was held in a barn belonging to Thomas Bradshaw who had an estate of about 150 acres tythe free, which then and later saved him from persecution. After a 'religious opportunity in the family came to Lisburn for an evening Meeting'. On 21st September they sat with Friends at weekday Meeting and Deborah ministered to Friends at J. Conrain's, and on the 22nd at Hillsborough Meeting where she found that their 'feelings had been deeply trying since coming to this shore, perhaps in sympathy with others, as well as for my own refinement'.

The following day they 'sat a Meeting at Ballinderry and felt the way difficult to obtain relief', and attended a burial at Lurgan Meeting, south of Lough Neagh. There was much poverty among the country people in these places, evident to the traveller and in many accounts remarked upon. By the 26th they were at Moyallon Meeting in which some 'labour was bestow'd' which Deborah hoped 'would strengthen the right minded', and they also had an opportunity with Widow Phelps followed by a 'trying Meeting at Richill'.

October

Going south to Coothill and Monaghan the Meetings were low and small, and by 1st October they had returned north again to Grange on the south side of Lough Neagh, finding the Meeting there was one which was where 'the seed suffered', however, the Public Meeting in the evening was more satisfactory. They had a Meeting at the Sessions House at Dungannon on 2nd October which was large and 'many Gospel Truths were convey'd' and this was followed by two opportunities in Friends' families. They then visited Cookstown where 'the People were attentive to the Testimony of Truth' and next day still moving northwards had a 'comfortable Meeting at Newton Stewart, but a trying one at Straban in the evening'.

By the 6th October well up in the north of Ulster they were at Londonderry with an Open Meeting at Newton 'where no Fds reside'. Two Meetings at Coleraine nearly to the north coast were encouraging and Deborah had a 'comfortable season' at their lodgings, also 'Gospel Truths were convey'd to the People at the Meetings at Ballinacree and Ballimena' on the 9th October. Small Meetings were held at Lower Grange and Castle Dawson, and a Meeting was appointed with a few scattered around Toberhead. On the 14th Monthly Meeting was held at Lurgan and Deborah stated that 'My Dr Companion has been unwell, but better today' and after sitting with Friends in the morning when 'much counsel was handed' there was a large Meeting with the townspeople 'much to the relief of our minds'.

The Meetings at Moyallon and Portadown on 18th October 'afforded cause to believe that Light and Truth is breaking forth'. These were followed by a Public Meeting at Banbridge. On the 21st Deborah was disturbed as they 'got accounts of the Yellow Fever having again awfully visited the inhabitants of Philadelphia which has affected our minds with sympathy for our Dr Fds'. This outbreak, despite all precautions, proved to be a severe epidemic.

They had Meetings at Armagh and Richill, followed by various others as they travelled, but by the 27th October they had moved north again and were at Antrim Meeting with Sarah Harrison and Sarah Birkbeck in which 'favor was extended as well as to the family of our Fd Jarvis Johnson now visiting America'. On 28th October they visited the Provincial School[6] at Lisburn just south of Belfast where about 50 children were being educated and which 'appears to be well regulated and likely to be productive of good to the Society'.

They arrived in Belfast on 29th October for a Meeting 'supposed to be one thousand People who conducted with more solidity than could have been expected'. Next day they had a Meeting at Carrickfergus in the morning and White House in the evening, both satisfactory.

November

On 1st November they 'had a Meeting in J. Christy's barn – thus are we turned about amongst the People very unexpectedly in these parts', followed by a large crowded Meeting at Downpatrick when they 'felt easy to leave the Place'. At Castleshane on the 3rd November the 'inhabitants came freely to Meeting and behaved commendable which we hope will open the way for further service'.

They were at Rathfryland on the evening of the 4th November and next day moving southwards had Meetings at Newry and Dundalk which were satisfactory, but that at Drogheda was 'very trying'.

The entry for 9th November found them in Dublin 'intent on a visit to Fds familys in Dublin, having long had it in prospect'. They were at Meath Street Meeting in the morning of the 12th and during that week they visited 32 families 'in which strength was afforded'; then on the 19th November Deborah sat two Meetings 'in silence to the disappointment of many but I trust in the appointment of Him whose ways are unsearchable'.

December

They continued their family visits and were again at Dublin's Meath Street Meeting on the 26th, but were silent at Sycamore Ally. On 4th December Deborah says they 'had to labour amongst the People but difficult to get much relief notwithstanding there is a precious seed in this City', however, the evening Meeting at Sycamore Ally was 'large and solid'.

On 6th December 'William Savery and myself had to bear testimony in the weekday Meeting' and during the next few days Deborah attended various Meetings in Dublin but missed a business Meeting as she had 'left short on account of my Dr Companion being unwell'.

The rest of the month was spent in attending Meetings in the south, visiting Friends' families and holding Meetings with Youth, and by 23rd December had reached Ballintore and were 'favor'd there'. They reached Waterford on the 29th December. On 31st December Deborah 'appeared in Testimony and my Precious Companion in Prayer, both our minds are often as under the weight of the mountains, but she having bodily indisposition added to it'.

1798
January

The general atmosphere was becoming uneasy throughout the country and this visit was undertaken at a time of unrest. The alarm and fear of a French invasion had much increased and insurrection was threatened and broke out violently in 1798, particularly in Leinster between Catholics and Protestants, and a number of Irish Quakers chiefly in the counties of Carlow, Kildare and Western Province, became separated from the main body of Friends doctrinally. These people, termed 'the New Lights' were accused of underrating the Scriptures and casting doubts on the Divinity of Christ. Partly this was also due on grounds of policy since the dissentients strongly objected to what they regarded as repressive action on the part of Meetings for Church affairs.

The beginning of this movement associated particularly with Abraham Shackleton of Ballitore and can be traced back to the 1770's. Deborah and Rebecca's visit was fortunately in late 1797 and the early months of 1798 so they had left before the main conflicts took place, which affected many of the same Friends they were to meet during the weeks of this journey and brought about some very terrible incidents.

On 1st January 1798 they visited a 'young woman that appears to be sweetly drawing towards the close of time, herself, her Mother and two sisters of the name of Fisher, have lately joined our Society'. This family had built up a successful business in Waterford of export in grain, meat and fish. One of her sisters had died a few weeks before and the youngest seemed 'in a declining state of health'. Deborah and Rebecca had much satisfaction in sitting by the 'Dr Young Woman, nearly gone, who appears perfectly resigned and her Mother greatly supported under these pungent trials'. This family evidently struck Deborah forcibly in their distress.

They attended Monthly Meeting on 3rd January and an adjournment of Select Meeting. They also again visited the Widow Fisher and her family, and after 'a favor'd sitting in the house of J.T. left Waterford on the 4th and lodged in a Fds house'. They travelled west, along the Suir and had a Meeting at Carrick next day where William Savery and Mary Dudley met them, and after dining together they took a 'solemn leave of William [Savery] and other Fds feeling the humbling power of Truth to be near'. Deborah was to see William again that year in London and other places; he was also to come to stay with them in Coalbrookdale.

There were many Friends in this part of Ireland and Deborah and Rebecca took part in morning Meeting at Clonmell on 7th January where they had a large Public Meeting in the evening in which 'important Truths were convey'd'. They dined with Mary Dudley whose husband, Robert, had a comfortable house and property near the town, and was one of the Friends who William Savery found bordering on luxury in their style of living. On 9th January after a 'Religious Opportunity at Mary Dudley's home' they visited the school at Suir Island established by Sarah Grubb:[7] here they sat with the girls for evening Meeting and 'felt an engagement to those concern'd for their welfare' – this school had been established in 1787, and the skeleton of the house still stands today, partly in ruins.

They visited the Prison at Clonmell on the 10th, several Friends accompanying them, and 'felt the Love of the Everlasting Gospel towards the poor objects in our care, some of them discover'd sensibility'. After attending Monthly Meeting in which they assisted, they, accompanied by Elizabeth Pim and Ann Broadhead, went to Richard Spencer's near Clonmell in County Tipperary, where they had 'a favor'd opportunity in the family'. Richard operated mills on the River Suir which were the most modern in Ireland at that time and had a style of living with stables, brewery, coach house and dairy which William Savery likened to that of a nobleman.

On the 12th January they had a Meeting at Garryroan and an evening one at Clogheen and by the 14th had turned south-west for Cork where they attended two Meetings.

They went back to Youghall on the 16th for Meetings and on the 18th January returned the six miles to Cork for two more, one being satisfactory with the young people which was followed by one for 'the Heads of familys where Truth measurably own'd the opportunity'. On the 20th the Select Quarterly Meeting 'was very trying'. The strain in Society can be envisaged from the chance word added to Deborah's account of these times, but she would have not had any premonition of the violence and misery to come upon the community during the next few months. Many terrible things were to come to pass even near the communities they were visiting.

After a week Mary Dudley accompanied them to Glanmire on the 25th January to an evening Meeting where they had 'an opportunity with Fds that had for sometime been at variance', and on the 28th they were at Meetings at Kinsale and Bandon, returning to Cork for weekday Meeting

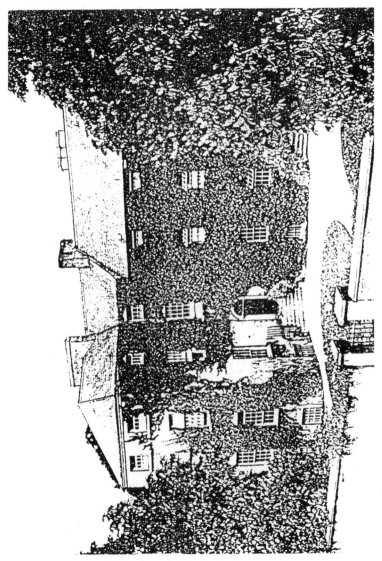

The Friends' Provincial School, Mountmellick, Ireland. Established as the result of deliberations at Six Weeks' Men's Meeting, Leinster Province, 1784.

1798

Suir Island School, Ireland, founded by Sarah (Tuke) Grubb in 1787 after she came to Ireland to marry Robert Grubb in 1782 (see note 7). The remains of the house are still standing, but it is uninhabitable.

where they ministered, and on the 31st attended a Public Meeting at Mallow to which E. Hatton and Mary Dudley accompanied them. This was followed by a weekday Meeting at Limerick 26 miles away where 'strength was afforded to hand council to different states'.

February

They travelled all the next week holding morning and evening Meetings and sitting with families at Birr, Roscrea and Knockballymaher. On the 9th February they were back at Mountmellick where they had a Meeting 'with Young People when some ability was afforded to call to the Law and Testimony at Mountmellick', and on the day after they had 'two religious opportunities in Fds schools, in both of which He that commanded little children to come unto Him was near'.

Mountmellick School had been set up as the result of deliberations at six weeks' Men's Meeting of Leinster Province, held at Moate on the 14th August 1784, when representatives from Carlow, Dublin, Edenderry, Moate, Mountmellick, Wexford and Wicklow 'and other choosing to attend' had formed a committee to decide 'on the most suitable means of supplying the deficiency which appears in some places with respect to the education of Friends in low circumstances'. This committee encouraged the establishment of a Provincial School for the education of these particular children and their report was accepted, and it was agreed to finance the establishment of a school 'for the sum of £500', to provide [or arrange for] a house with proper accommodation for this purpose.

On the 12th February after visiting 'a Fds family under affliction to whom they ministered' they had a Meeting with the 'inhabitants of Tullamore to good satisfaction', and the Meeting at Moate the next day was 'laborious but were comforted in a Fds family afterwards'. Crossing into Connaught they had a satisfactory Meeting on the 14th at Ballimurry and 'came to James Clibborn's to lodge'.

During the following week they travelled back towards Dublin, holding Meetings at Rathangan, Timahoe, Athy, Kilconner, Ballitore, Baltiboys and Carlow, also visiting families including three widows, one of whom had been left with 11 children.

On the 25th February in Dublin they attended Meath Street Meeting where we felt 'the Clouds were gathering and that the trials of the faithful would yet increase'. Unfortunately they had met active opposition here which was described by William Savery, who was holding a Meeting in Sycamore Alley at the same time. The two women ministers had had an unpleasant experience as many at Meath were of 'the lowest class of the people'. It was also suspected that they had been stirred up by the priests, which was an unusual occurence against the Quakers, even in difficult times. Fortunately after these difficulties Deborah and Rebecca had a 'religious opportunity in their lodgings that evening many being present'.

The 26th February was their last day in Ireland after five-and-a-half months of visiting some 80 places and families. They had called upon 'several Fds and amongst the rest David Sands who is confined by indisposition and after dining at our lodgings [at] Dr Joseph Williams', we parted with them under the renewed feeling of best Love and sailed that evening'.

Return to England, 27th February 1798

After an easy passage next day of 17 hours they landed at Holyhead, and on the 28th February 'parted with our kind Fd Jonas Stot who accompanied us from Dublin and John Lury, set out towards home'. At Bangor Ferry they were met by Mark Gilpin Junior and Thomas Witton and eventually reached Shrewsbury on 4th March and found their 'relations in tolerable health' and Deborah says 'they were thankful for Preservation through a journey in which a large portion of suffering of spirit was allotted'. These remarks were made because of the rising tide of violence in Ireland. Next day they attended morning Meeting with a 'favor'd opportunity at John Young's and came home'.

March

Deborah attended local Meetings, going on the 15th March to Shrewsbury with Priscilla Hannah Gurney. Rebecca Young returned with them, and on the 21st they attended Monthly Meeting at the Dale when they 'handed in their Certificates'. On the 23rd March they 'had the company of our Dr Fd and Brother William Savery from America' and on the 26th they had a Public Meeting at New Dale and another at Shrewsbury in the evening 'in which he was emminently qualified to preach the Gospel of Life and Salvation'. An evening Meeting at Ellesmere was held on the 27th and one at Wrexham, and afterwards Rebecca Young and Deborah returned to Shrewsbury, arriving back home on the 29th March.

April

On 8th April Deborah was indisposed 'my endear'd Rebecca Young kindly attending upon me'. However, she managed to get to Shrewsbury on the 11th but was unable to attend Meeting 'yet got to Wrexham to lodge'.

Deborah attended two sittings of Lancashire Quarterly Meeting held at Liverpool on 16th April and next day 'attended the Northern Yearly Meeting in which William Savery, William Jephson, Charity Cook, Martha Routh and myself were engaged' followed by an opportunity at their lodgings. They were present at a 'Meeting for Conference for 6 hours' on the 19th and a Public Meeting was held next day with an opportunity for young people afterwards. William Savery wrote in his account for Liverpool 'A Public Meeting this evening was large, at which were Deborah Darby, Rebecca Young and Charity Cook, the Lord in Great Mercy owned us, and favor'd with a renewed eating and drinking together as in His presence when His Banner was love in which I believe many not professing with us partook and parted in great sweetness'.

'William Savery and us had a Meeting at Chester in the morning of 22nd April and another at Wrexham later', Deborah wrote. She then reported a Meeting was held at Oswestry and that William Savery went on to a public one at Welshpool. Wherever he went his discourse was very welcome and he had a particular appeal to the young, an attraction which both encouraged and also made them face the realities of life.

They attended Wales Half-Yearly Meeting on 25th April when William Savery paid a very acceptable visit to the Women Friends' Meeting, and a large Public Meeting was held in the evening.

The Half-Yearly Meeting on the 26th was concluded by one o'clock when they had a visit from William Rickman and James Haworth, who agreed to visit their Monthly Meeting. Then a large evening Meeting was held at Montgomery, followed by another at Westbury, and by the 28th they had reached Shrewsbury and William Rickman was 'favor'd in our Meeting at The Dale' that evening.

William Savery, Tanner, aged 40
1750-1804
From Francis R. Taylor's The Life of William Savery.

May

Deborah reported 'Sarah Talbot and companion Sarah Shackleton, my Sister Barnard, Martha Routh and other Fds at our Meeting on the 8th May, some being concern'd to minister unto us as they did in a sitting at Brother Reynolds' in the evening at Dale House.' Monthly Meeting was held at New Dale next day with an opportunity at James Jackson's, and on the 11th May 'Rebecca Young, Sarah Talbot and companion and myself held an evening Meeting at Dudley', followed by Meetings at Stourbridge, Alcester and Ettington. By the 14th they 'were favor'd to get safe to Banbury tho' our Fds Sarah Talbot and Sarah Shackleton were overturned; they travelled at times in one-horse carriages, and these accidents were not infrequent. The evening Meeting was laborious but not unprofitable'. They had an Open Meeting next day at Adderbury, but Rebecca was much indisposed 'with a pain in her teeth' and she had the tooth extracted on the 16th which was 'very trying to us both but she was relieved after'.

After an evening Meeting at Amersham on 17th May they attended two sittings of Select Yearly Meeting in London on the 19th. Next day William Savery accompanied them to a Meeting at Wandsworth in the morning and Stockwell in the evening, with visits to families. On 27th May Deborah stated that having 'attended closely to the weighty affairs that came before Women Fds this week' they were at Peel Meeting in the morning and Islington later with William Savery. Next day 'Charity Cook and M. Swett paid a visit to Men Fds and the Yearly Meeting closed in the evening'; these two American Friends were travelling together in Europe having arrived in the summer of 1797.

June

The next week was spent attending various Meetings and they left London on 2nd June after 'a parting opportunity with our many Fds at which William Savery minister'd very encouragingly to us', reaching Brentford later for a Meeting. On 3rd June they sat with Friends in the morning at Uxbridge and attended a large Public Meeting in the evening. They travelled on to hold Meetings at Amersham and Chesham, and reached Aylesbury where they were 'comforted in the Company of some serious people to whom the Gospel message was encouraging'. By 7th June they were at Leighton [Buzzard] weekday Meeting with a public one at Woburn in the evening, and next day visited 'a young man that had left Fds and joined the baptists, also sat with a deeply afflicted woman not professing with us towards whom we felt much sympathy'. An evening Meeting was held at Olney, the small town surrounded by fields and water meadows where the poet Cowper had written the hymns and poems that became part of literary heritage.

The following day, Deborah told how 'we were favor'd together in a full Meeting of Fds and others at Wellingborough with a large one at Northampton next day, John Abbot, his wife and Anna Price with us'. A Meeting was held at Wigston in a barn, and on the morning of the 12th at Leicester, with another in a barn at Grooby Lodge, and on the 14th June 'after a season of retirement in the family of Cousin Burgess we parted with Dr Anna Price and Sarah Abbot and held an evening Meeting at Mountsorrel'. By the 17th June they held Meetings at Atherstone and Coventry, and on the 20th at Stratford-on-Avon and Stourbridge – and by the 22nd they 'got safe home and found our connections well'.

There Deborah attended local Meetings and towards the end of the month she mentioned the burial of Thomas Roberts at Coalbrookdale 'a young man that was drowned by bathing in the Severn'.

July

On 1st July Deborah, Rebecca and Susannah were all at Church Stretton Public Meeting and Select Meeting at Leominster, and next day attended Quarterly Meeting when Deborah and Timothy Bevington ministered, arriving at Ludlow on 5th July. At Dawley Meeting on the 8th there were about 500 people, and in the evening they had 'an opportunity after supper when Susannah Appleby appear'd in prayer and Rebecca and myself in Testimony'.

'My Dr Sister Sarah Darby and Susannah Appleby set out for Bath on the 9th July.' On the 15th Deborah and Rebecca were engaged at Shrewsbury Meeting and another one held under the Town Hall at Wem at four o'clock. On the 17th July Anna Price and Sarah Abbot were present at the Dale Meeting and 'handed counsel after an opportunity at our Table', when Deborah and Rebecca then left for Wolverhampton to attend a Public Meeting. Next day they were at the 'marriage of Samuel Hodgson Junior and a young woman by the name of Southall, it was a time of favor'. After an opportunity at Samuel Galton's they attended evening Meeting at West Bromwich on the 19th, and the following day 'at weekday Meeting M[ary] Capper and myself [were] engaged, after a sitting at Joseph Gibbins, we attended a Meeting in a barn near the Soho'.

They attended a large solid Meeting at Walsall on the 22nd July as was another one at Wedgbury [Wednesbury] in the evening. Anna Price and Sarah Abbot were at weekday Meeting on the 24th 'having called upon many Fds families'. On the 27th July Deborah stated 'our Fds Phoebe Speakman from America and Ann Crowley had a Meeting at New Dale with a public one in the evening to good service'. These Friends attended various local Meetings and on 31st July were in Shrewsbury and attended the internment of George Titterton on 1st August.

Wales

August

By 3rd August they were 'Accompanied by Cousin Joseph Birkbeck and others towards Leominster, and Brother and Sister Reynolds, Cousin Dearman, Sister Rathbone, Rebecca Young and myself towards Wales to visit Monthly Meetings'. They were at Hay [on-Wye] for an evening Meeting on 8th August, and on the 12th arrived at Tenby for a large solid Meeting followed by another at Narbeth in the afternoon. They had the company of 'Dr Sarah Talbot and companion at the Harford [Haverford] West Meeting where things appear sorrowfully low', however, a 'comfortable one' was held next day at Kidwelly. They travelled on to reach Swansea where the Meeting was also 'distressingly low' followed by a public one at Neath.

They sat with 'Friends who are few in number' and had a Public Meeting at Aberavon which was 'small but solid', and by the 19th were at Cardiff and next day had the company again of Phoebe Speakman and Ann Crowley at Pontypool Monthly Meeting with another Meeting in the Town Hall. They attended the Half-Yearly Meeting at Brecon on the 22nd and next day after a morning Meeting and dining together 'participating in the best of refreshments, we parted, Rebecca and myself having an evening Meeting at Creekhowell'. By the 27th they had reached Ledbury and were at Worcester next day for Monthly Meeting, arriving home on the 29th August after 'visiting the Prison and parting from our Friends'.

September

Now for the second time in her life Deborah was to influence very strongly a young person of exceptional character and ability, who was to become of great benefit to thousands of her fellow men and women.

Early in the year William Savery had visited Norwich and there his effect upon Elizabeth Gurney, afterwards to become the famous Elizabeth Fry, is well known. She first heard him speak in the Meeting House in Upper Goat Lane which the young Gurneys called 'Goats', where he, although there was war in Europe and invasion much feared from France, spoke movingly to his hearers, to encourage them to turn their thoughts towards goodness and away from strife.

Elizabeth had been deeply moved by his words and his presence, coming as he had at a moment in her life when she was seeking a path for herself and was torn between what she knew in her heart to be the best and most enlightened way, but tempted to take part in all the amusements of the many young people living in the neighbourhood.

Being very much struck by this meeting with William, whom she also saw at home as well as at her Uncle Joseph Gurney's on several occasions,

Elizabeth Fry (1780-1845), born Gurney.
From a reproduction of a pencil sketch by Amelia Opie

she later went up to London in the hope of seeing him again at Meetings or in the houses of their many relations and Friends. This she succeeded in doing and in consequence found herself in an increasingly volatile state. During the summer, her father, John Gurney, finding her so, decided to try what a little diversion would do to help and took her and some of her sisters on a tour of the western counties and Wales. They reached Coalbrookdale early in September on their way home to Norfolk, where he knew he would find an interesting and closeknit Quaker community of much sense and enterprise, in which his first cousin Priscilla Hannah had lived for so long in Dale House, the home of Richard and Rebecca Reynolds. Deborah in her Journal wrote that on 2nd September 'there were many strangers' at their Meeting in the Dale, adding 'that evening Elizabeth Gurney from Norwich called upon us to whom I minister'd, she appears to be under best notice'.

The Gurneys remained some days visiting the different houses, the works, the famous Iron Bridge and the riverside with many boats sailing up and down the Severn. Elizabeth appeared to be very happy in these surroundings and her father decided to leave her there for a few days on her own with his cousin, Priscilla Hannah Gurney. This proved to be just what Elizabeth most enjoyed; Priscilla had always driven herself about the neighbourhood in her own carriage and would have taken her young cousin everywhere. She was a delightful and interesting person in her plain Quaker dress, and she created an unforgettable atmosphere of both elegance and serenity.

This must have been a most memorable visit for Elizabeth, for out of the windows of Priscilla's rooms she could see the view across the narrow Coalbrookdale valley and below on to the Upper Furnace Pool, and further to the south the Upper Furnace[8] and the works. During these days of Elizabeth's visit, Deborah came to have breakfast at Dale House and afterwards Elizabeth wrote that 'she preached in a deep clear and striking manner'. She spoke particularly to Elizabeth herself, saying to the girl that she 'was sick of this world' and that her future life 'would be dedicated to God'.

These words, spoken in the dining room of Dale House, gave Elizabeth great encouragement. This family home had been built by the first Abraham Darby and finished in the second decade of the 18th century: the dining room had been the scene of many meals in which guests had taken part from all over the British Isles when visiting the Darby and Reynolds' families, as well as Friends from across the Atlantic such as William Savery himself.

In Deborah's Journal mention was also made on the 4th September when she and Rebecca Young had some 'Counsel to hand to a visited state'. The evening of that same day proved to be of great significance, for when Elizabeth called upon the Darbys at Sunniside[9] Deborah foretold how the

4th day In our Week Day meeting dear Rebecca Young
and myself had some counsel to hand to a
visited state – **in the evening Elizabeth
Gurney from Norwich called upon us** – to
whom I ministered – she appears to be under
best notice.

*Extract from Deborah's Diary, 29th August to 19th September 1798, mentioning
Elizabeth Gurney aged 18 years, who visited Priscilla Hannah Gurney when she resided
at Dale House with Richard and Rebecca Reynolds.*

eager girl was to be 'a Light to the Blind, speech to the dumb and feet to the lame': Elizabeth then experienced a mystical sense of the Almighty and wrote in her Journal 'suddenly my mind felt clothed with Light as with a garment and I felt silenced before God and cried out with a heavenly feeling of humility and repentance'. The intensity of this feeling was to fade, but the knowledge that she had had these moments was always to remain with her and gave her strength.

Deborah had spent the rest of the early part of September attending local Meetings including a large public one near the Iron Bridge. In 1798 the Monthly Meeting to which the Darby family belonged was not large. Coalbrookdale (referred to as The Dale) had 29 men and 37 women including the Darbys, Reynolds, Roses, Gilpins, Hortons – also Ann Summerland, Priscilla Hannah Gurney and Susannah Appleby. From the beginning the members of New Dale Meeting had mostly been members of the Reynolds' family, some Youngs and other employees of the Horshay and Ketley areas of the Company's concerns – they were in all seven men and 13 women. The final closure of this Meeting in the 19th century probably came about when the Reynolds family moved from their Ketley homes.

Shrewsbury was the smallest of the three Meetings comprising Shropshire Monthly Meeting – its members being two men and seven women – chiefly Youngs and Philips. However, it was an important Meeting strategically, being on the way to the north and to Wales and Ireland, so it was on the itinerary of many ministers as the Minutes reveal, and was mentioned in the Journals and letters of visiting ministers from early in the 18th century.

At Meeting on 19th September at Coalbrookdale, Deborah and Rebecca requested certificates to visit the Isle of Man and some of the northern counties. After Meeting at Shrewsbury on the 21st, another was held at Whitchurch and in the evening at Nantwich, with others following at Stone and Eccleshall which were 'trying as the People being much strangers to Fds, but the large one at Newcastle [under-Lyme] was relieving our minds'. A Meeting at Burslem was held in the open market place on the 27th September and, after an opportunity in Robert Rhode's family they came to Macclesfield for an evening Meeting where Deborah found 'amongst the Potteries a seeking People, to some of whom I hope the present visit may be blessed'.

By the 29th September they had reached Stockport for a 'comfortable' Meeting, followed by a very large one at Altringham.

October

They got to Preston in time for an evening Meeting and on 2nd October attended Select Quarterly Meeting at Lancaster, and went on to Kendal where they met Henry Tuke who was also to go with them to visit the Isle of

Man. A large Meeting was held in a schoolroom at Sedbergh and an open one in Kendal, and on 9th October they attended the 'marriage of Dilworth Crewdson and Deborah Braithwaite [to whom Deborah was related] which was conducted with solidity and crowned by a Religious opportunity later'.

Visit to the Isle of Man, 10th October

They had an evening Meeting at Keswick on the 10th and sailed from Whitehaven about two o'clock on the 12th October, landing at Douglas after a 'trying passage but it is a great mercy to get safe'. Meetings were held at Castletown, Peel and Ramsey where the 'Bishop forbid our having the schoolroom, but a kindly man fitted up his warehouse which accommodated a great number of people'. They returned to Douglas on 21st October, held two Meetings and sailed for Whitehaven on the 23rd having 'pleasant weather and landed that night, we esteem'd it a favor to cross the sea in safety a Vessel having been wrecked near the island and the crew lost while we were there'.

Cumberland

They had a large Meeting at Workington on the 26th October and another was held at Greysouthern, a morning Meeting at Pardshaw and one later at Cockermouth, at the confluence of the Cocker and the Derwent, a small market town of ancient historical importance since Roman times.

November

They attended Maryport weekday Meeting and a Meeting on 1st November held in a brewery at Workington 'gave us hope'. They were present at a burial and then on the 3rd 'had a comfortable opportunity in the family of our Dr Fds John and Hannah Hall both Valuable Ministers'.

On 5th November 'had a large and solid Meeting at Maryport, the low room of a Thread Mill being fitted up for the occasion and it was supposed 800 people attended who behaved in a becoming manner'. They had an opportunity at their lodgings on the 6th as well as 'in the family of the widow of Captain Harris who lost his life at sea; she appears to be growing in the truth and the children are hopeful'. Other Meetings followed and at one at Scotby they met with Mary Robinson, aged 80, 'weak in Body but lively in Spirit'. Two Meetings were held at Carlisle then they went on to Moorhouse, Eastcot, Moredale and Penrith, but on the 15th November they 'rested at a kind Fds house my Dear Companion being unwell'.

On 18th November they had an 'instructive opportunity with Fds at Penrith with a large Public Meeting in the evening'. They rode on, holding Meetings as they went, and on the 23rd, after a Meeting at Shap reached Kendal again, attending a Meeting at Long Preston next day. After Crook Meeting in the morning they had a large public one in the evening at

Burnside in a cotton mill. By the 29th, after a 'time of retirement in a Fds family' they were at a Public Meeting at Brigflatts and in the evening at Kirkby Lonsdale, both to some satisfaction.

December

On 2nd December they sat with Friends in Settle Meeting and had a public one in the evening 'which my Dr Companion closed with solemn supplication'. 'After a sitting in Cousin Birkbeck's family we rode to Coln[e] for evening Meeting at which there was supposed to be 15 hundred People, I hope it was held to some profit.' On 5th December the evening Meeting held in a cotton mill at Readyford was quiet and satisfactory and was followed the next day by a 'Trying one at Todmorton'.

A small Meeting was held on 9th December at Bury and in the evening at Bolton and they went on to a larger one at Warrington. On the 11th they sat weekday Meeting at Knutsford, also a public one. After Northwich Meeting they went on to Quarterly Meeting at Middlewich and had the 'Company of J. Abbott and S. Rundall with Dear Martha Haworth'. They sat with sick Friends and had an opportunity with some young people, riding on to Ashton and Wigan for evening Meeting on 16th December.

The Meeting at Chorley on the 17th was 'trying to our feelings yet I hope attended with a measure of holy help'. Next day found them at Preston with 'People not of our Society' and they reached Lancaster for family visits, but by the 23rd Deborah's dear companion was 'confined with a soar throat'. Up until the end of the month they visited many families . By the last day of the year Rebecca had fully recovered and Deborah and she appeared in the Meeting for Discipline where 'our minds were dip'd into sympathy with the few'.

1799
January

Deborah and Rebecca Young attended Lancashire Select Quarterly Meeting held at Preston on 2nd January and were at Quarterly Meeting next day, then returning to Lancaster to continue the family visits, in one of which they 'had an opportunity with some that had been disown'd' – an unusual entry for Deborah to make in her Journal.

They finished the family visits and went on to Wharton near Preston, for a Public Meeting in the evening of 8th January, after which they went by Langtree and had another Public Meeting at Ashton 'to some profit', before having an opportunity in Thomas Cropper's family, whose wife had been ill for some years. An evening Meeting was held at Newtown on 12th January, and the day after they attended morning Meeting at Warrington on their way home ; they were now accompanied by E. and J. Bludwick, and went on to William Bradley's in Cheshire where 'they had an evening Meeting with the People'.

Return to Sunniside

On the 14th they reached Whitchurch and were at Shrewsbury next day where they handed in their Certificates and found their 'connections generally well except Constantine Young who appears gradually declining'. They returned to the Dale on 17th January to find 'Mark Gilpin fast approaching the confines of the Grave': when Deborah called on him again on the 19th she had 'an opportunity in his room'. At morning Meeting she had to 'advise Fds to live up to the Glory of the Gospel Day' and she also went again to visit Mark Gilpin with whom she had 'a sweet opportunity'. It would appear that he and Constantine Young were suffering from tuberculosis – a scourge of that period and indeed one which lasted well into the present century, as the knowledge and subsequent treatment at the time was insufficient to render the disease curable.

February

Rebecca Young was still with Deborah taking part in Meetings and family visits; Mary Lloyd was also with them for some days sharing the visits to Mark Gilpin who died early in February and was buried on the 10th 'having been sick for about six months', during which time he became 'gradually weaned from the world expressing that all the comforts he had in this Life were as nothing in comparison to the Joys he had prospect of'.

March

Deborah and Rebecca Young were at Shrewsbury on 17th February and bore Testimony at morning Meeting, later visiting Constantine Young. Deborah with Susannah Appleby attended local Meetings during February and on 10th March Mary Lloyd with Ann and Joseph Burgess came in on their way from Chester when 'a favor'd opportunity was had after dinner previous to their leaving us'. Deborah was silent at New Dale Meeting on the 17th but dined at The Bank and drank tea with William Holtham.

Towards the end of the month while at Shrewsbury they again visited Constantine Young 'who had become increasingly ill'. On 31st March Deborah and Susannah Appleby visited a family in Bewdley, attending later an appointed Meeting at Stourport followed by an evening Meeting at Worcester; at both they were 'favor'd to convey Gospel Truths'.

April

On 2nd April Deborah dined with John Pumphrey and attended Quarterly Meeting – returning home on the 7th where she found her son 'Edmund very ill and they sent for Dr Evins, [however], he was found to have a return of his complaint but was soon relieved', although she did not state what this was or refer to the illness again. They were then present at the burial of Constantine Young and had a 'favor'd season with his Relations after Dinner'.

On 12th April, in the morning, Robert and Rachel Fowler, Mary Jeffrys and Sarah Stephenson came to stay at Sunniside, but they found Deborah 'in a Tried State' although she does not give any explanation as Edmund was much better; however, it is possible that her son Samuel had begun to trouble her seriously by the kind of companionship he was seeking and his increasing desertion of Friends.

A few days later they were again at Shrewsbury for Monthly Meeting when 'Susannah Appleby had a Certificate signed to visit Ireland, and with Robert Fowler, Sarah Stephenson and Mary Lloyd set out for Holyhead that evening'. Next day, again at Meeting, Rachel Fowler, Rebecca Young and Deborah had to bear 'Testimony unto the Truth'. On 28th April Deborah was at Leominster Meeting with Martha Routh and James Haworth and was engaged 'to exhort Fds to attend unto those things that are excellent', also in the evening Meeting she stated 'Fds were engaged and Cousin Ann Burgess and myself concluded in Prayer'.

On the 29th several of them had a Public Meeting at Weobley and a small Meeting for Ministers and Elders took place the next day.

May

On 1st May a Public Meeting was held in a barn when Sarah Lamley ministered acceptably to the people, and in the Meeting for Discipline, in addition to those Friends already mentioned, they had Ann Ashby, Rachel Fowler, Susannah Horne and Lucy Alexander.

Deborah, James Haworth and Rebecca Young had 'a solid Public Meeting at Hay [on-Wye]' in the morning of the 5th May, after which 'other Friends mostly left Town'. At Knighton they found 'among the People some that appeared like thirsty ground receiving with gladness celestrial rain'; and another Meeting was held at Leominster in the evening to which place some of them had returned, and this proved 'an open time and Cousin Ann Burgess joined in public labour'.

The next day, 6th May, William Young and other Friends accompanied them to Ludlow where they held a 'favor'd morning Meeting, many minds appearing thankful for the visit, this was the Meeting which occasion'd a little publication in opposition to Fds principles especially Women preaching, which appears to be a stone of stumbling and Rock of offence to those that wish preaching to continue a Trade'.

They reached Shrewsbury for morning and evening Meetings, both 'rather trying' but no reason was given. They had an evening Meeting at

Hodnet, a village some distance from the county town, where they found that 'the people appear raw yet some ability to labour'. Another Meeting was held the following day in a barn at Watling Street which 'was solid', they then returned to Much Wenlock and Broseley where Rebecca Young had 'solemn counsel to hand mixed with encouragement'.

On 13th May Deborah set out for London, having an evening Meeting at Darlaston and going on to Dudley and Birmingham. They held another evening one at Chipping Norton, also at Stow [on-the-Wold] and Moreton [in-the-Marsh] reaching Henley [on-Thames] by the 19th for two Meetings. They attended two sittings of the Select Yearly Meeting in London followed by one for Discipline, also another on 26th May for 'transacting the weighty affairs of the Church and best help being near was a cause for thankfulness which was the case at Devonshire House this morning and Ratcliffe this evening'.

June

Yearly Meeting closed on 1st June with two Meetings for Ministers and Elders in which 'John Hall was liberated to visit his Bretheren in America'. The following day they were at Gracechurch Street and Westminster Meetings and on 3rd June after 'calling upon several familys and dining with a large Company of our Fds at Cousin Joseph Smith's, among whom was Dr Sarah Harrison about to return to America', they had a Public Meeting at Croydon. Next day Deborah dined with John Townsend at Wandsworth and had a Meeting at Kingston [upon-Thames].

Visit to Isle of Wight

Going outside London they held Meetings at Esher, in a village called Molesey; then another in a barn at Cobham, going on to Staines, Chertsey and Alton. On 13th June they left for Winchester and Southampton, where they held a large Public Meeting in the Assembly Rooms on the 14th, crossing next day 'in a Packet' for the Isle of Wight where some 'serious people called upon us at our Inn at Newport'. The following morning they were with Friends at Meeting in Newport and went on to Cowes for a Meeting in the evening; another was held at Newport next evening which was less satisfactory 'owing to the Crowd'. They were enjoying to the full the summer loveliness and the views of the sea, particularly during an eight mile ride to attend a small Meeting at Newton Bridge when Deborah described the island 'as a beautiful one'.

After breakfasting with James Clarke they had an opportunity with some young people 'who know the Truth' followed by a Meeting on the 19th June in the Assembly Rooms at Newport. Next day they had an evening Meeting at Yarmouth and on the 21st they 'left this sweet island and had a fine sail of about an hour and a half to Lymington' where they held a large

Meeting when they had reason to believe the 'opportunity was comfortable to some enquiring minds'.

Return to the Mainland

They left next day for Salisbury where they had an opportunity after dinner and a Public Meeting in the Assembly Rooms in the evening. On the morning of the 24th June Deborah explained 'my Dr Companion not relieving her mind the evening before had another Meeting in the same place, she being strengthened to convey much instructive counsel, followed by another at Fordingbridge that evening'.

They attended Hampshire Quarterly Meeting held at Ringwood on the 25th June, and had the company of Nathaniel and Mary Capper and 'were comforted not only in unexpectedly meeting each other, but in feeling our Master's Presence near'. Quarterly Meeting for Dorsetshire was held the following day and after calling on Friends they went to Wareham accompanied by Thomas Thompson and others and had a satisfactory Meeting next evening at Dorchester. On the 29th June there was a 'Meeting with some serious People on the Isle of Portland', and after a Meeting at 11 o'clock in Weymouth they rode on to Bridport on the 30th.

July

On 2nd July had a large Meeting at Lyme [Regis] 'where the People were much strangers to the Fds, but I hope we left them under some favourable impressions'. By the 3rd they had reached Exeter and after Meetings at Chudleigh and Ashburton arrived at Plymouth for a favoured one at the Docks. Accompanied by Deborah's cousins Francis and Sarah Fox they departed on 9th July for Madbury and Dartmouth, attending a four o'clock Meeting at Tiverton. They attended Spiceland Meeting on the 15th, also one at Honiton in the evening which was 'much too crowded to be comfortable'. A small one was held at Ilminster and another at Chard next morning and a further one later at Crookham, before going on to Montacute and Yeovil. Deborah spent two nights at the house of 'our kind Fd James Isaac and in the evening was at Ilchester Meeting'. They held Meetings as they travelled at Sherborne, Marnhull, Blandford, Sturminster and Shaftesbury, and after completing family visits they came to Gillingham accompanied by William Byrd for a 'large and satisfactory Meeting in a barn'.

August

On 1st August Deborah and Rebecca attended Wincanton Meeting which was 'not so solid as some of late', with other Meetings in Somerset at Bruton, Castle Cary, Shipton Mallet, Street and Glastonbury. After making family visits they reached Wells by the 6th August but no mention was made of whether they made time to visit the magnificent Cathedral, before they left to attend Monthly Meeting at Long Sutton with a public one in the evening.

By the 8th August they had finished their family visits to Friends in Street and Glastonbury Meetings where they were 'favor'd with support'. They went on to Frome for Meeting which was 'not as large as we would have wished' and another held in the evening at Westbury. The morning of the 11th found them at Warminster Meeting and at Bradford [on Avon] later, arriving next day at Broomhall for Monthly Meeting and on to Melksham in the evening. They had the company of David Sands on the 13th August who was on his way to Bristol, and held a Meeting at Devizes. After a 'satisfactory opportunity at William Powell's they went to a Meeting at Caln at which was a marriage, and in the evening of the 14th at a village called Laycock. Next day they arrived at Bath and were 'comforted in belief that even in that dissapated place the Lord had a People that in sincerity called upon his Name'.

Evening Meeting at Trowbridge on the 16th August was 'rather unsettled by some part of the place giving way, but it afterwards ended well'. Next day they had an 'Evening Meeting in a Fds barn, his name Isaac Serjant which was solid'. Meetings were held during the next two days at Malmsbury, Cirencester and Minchinhampton and on the 20th after an opportunity in a Friend's family they 'parted from Robert and Rachel Fowler who had been accompanying us thus far' and had a Meeting in the morning at Stroud and another later at Nailsworth, reaching Painswick next day for two Meetings, all in the beautiful Cotswold countryside, reaching Gloucester on the 22nd August, which Meeting was 'trying to us both but I left some of my feelings amonst them'.

Another 'trying' Meeting followed at Monmouth which Deborah 'hoped was to some profit' and after an opportunity with some Friends who accompanied them they rode on to Abergavenny. Select Half-Yearly Meeting for Wales began at Brecon, where they had the company of John Wigham from Scotland and Margaret Hoyland from Ireland, and at Meeting on the 29th at Presteigne had the company of William Byrd. Morning Meeting at Knighton was followed by one at Clun; they then went to Shrewsbury.

September

On the 2nd September 'William Byrd, having finished his business at Salop [Shrewsbury] for the present accompanied me home, having made a weighty proposal to my tenderly Beloved Rebecca Young, which I greatly desire she may determine to her own peace and the Glory of God, whatever loss it maybe to me, for our Friendship, I trust increases not only in firmness but disinterestedness. After supper William Byrd had some tender counsel to hand to my children and I was help'd to make some addition also to ask a blessing'.

Deborah, who of course had seen this situation developing for some time, had clearly faced the prospect of losing so much of Rebecca's companionship but being unselfish, was really glad for the sake of the younger woman that she should find love and companionship in such a suitable marriage, for William was a good and intelligent man and also devoted to the same mission in life.

On the 3rd September they all breakfasted at the White House with Rebecca Darby: William Byrd then left them after Meeting. Some days later Margaret Hoyland from Waterford 'enter'd on a family visit to Fds of our Monthly Meeting' and on the 14th September she with Rebecca Young had a 'favor'd opportunity with my Children and myself when excellent counsel was handed and myself permitted to ask a blessing upon the nearest connections in Life'.

Next day Deborah went with Margaret Hoyland and Rebecca Young to see some families 'on the New Dale side and I think I may say that mercy and truth follow'd, also evidenced in a sitting with my Dear Sisters last evening which was a memorable season'. Mary Rathbone was at that time living at Sunniside with Sarah and Deborah, having been a widow for some years.

Various family visits followed during the next few days together with many local Meetings and on 20th September Deborah took Margaret Hoyland and Rebecca Young to Shrewsbury to set them on their way to Cheshire, while she returned home. On 22nd Hannah Jarret from Banbury 'espoused the cause of Truth' in the afternoon Meeting, and they were engaged in weekday Meetings. On the 24th Deborah and Hannah Jarret went to Stafford Meeting and sat with Friends at Rugeley, followed by a Public Meeting. Next day they went on to Uttoxeter and attended a public one at Leek and also had a sitting in Francis West's family.

On the 29th Deborah left Hannah Jarret and attended Macclesfield Meeting which was 'crowded and solid'. In the evening she was joined by Margaret Hoyland and Rebecca Young at a Meeting at Stockport, 'where it was supposed 1,000 people were collected'. On the 30th they had a Meeting at Bullock's Smithy with a comfortable season in George Jones' family.

October

After Meeting at Cheedle Deborah set out for Quarterly Meeting at Manchester on 1st October, and next day 'Thomas Scattergood was much favor'd to which I made some addition and an evening Meeting was held at the request of Susannah Horne in which she was engaged and Rebecca Young concluded the Meeting with solemn supplication'.

An evening Meeting was held on 3rd October at Hardwick Green which 'was a time of Enlargement of Heart towards the People', many attending. Next day they had reached Bolton where Friends had fitted up a barn to accommodate the people. After a 'favor'd season in John Wood's family' they reached Manchester in time to dine in the home of Robert Barnard, Deborah's brother, who was at that time living there, followed by a sitting, which was closed by Thomas Scattergood with supplication. On 6th October a large Meeting was held at Congleton and from there they all travelled home.

The burial of 'our ancient Friend Thomas Wall' took place in the Dale on 13th October, and on the 16th Monthly Meeting was held at Shrewsbury at which both Deborah and Rebecca bore testimony, followed by a Meeting in a large room which was 'a solemn occasion'. Next morning they had a 'moving Meeting at Wem', an old market town, and that same evening a Meeting in a village called Cogshot 'which afforded peace'.

William Byrd's Proposal of Marriage to Rebecca Young

After dining with Mary Young in Shrewsbury, Deborah attended evening Meeting, appointed in a malthouse near the wharf, which was a 'season to be thankfully remembered', returning to Coalbrookdale on 22nd October in time for weekday Meeting. Deborah left Rebecca in Shrewsbury, recording 'it was hard for us to part when she was under deep exercise under a sense of the important subject she has to decide'. William Byrd had proposed marriage to her and she, having always been rather reluctant to contemplate that state, was disturbed and uncertain.

At Sunniside Deborah was engaged in morning Meeting on 27th October, having Joseph and Bulah Sansome staying with them from Philadelphia, also Ann Pryor from Harford. On the 29th Thomas Luccock was buried in the Friends' Graveyard 'many not of the Society attending' – the Luccock family had been in the Dale since the time when Joan Luccock, the second wife of John, father of Abraham Darby I, had lived there and brought that family to the area. The Sansomes left at the end of the month for London.

November

At the beginning of November William Byrd came to stay with them at Sunniside, and on the 6th they had a Meeting in a 'large warehouse near the Welsh Bridge in Shrewsbury in which we partook of the Solemnising Presence of the Master of Ceremonies'. This beautiful bridge was painted at that time by well-known artists, usually from the river bank so that the fine building on the arch could be well depicted.

Deborah was silent at their Meetings in the next few days, but made a few remarks in the evening sitting at Brother Reynolds' at Dale House. By

17th November Rebecca Young was with them again and both were taking part in Meetings. They were again at Shrewsbury Meeting on the 21st and were evidently going frequently between the two places as Deborah wrote that she 'was engaged at our Table after Dinner, also in the afternoon Meeting on the 24th'.

Visit to Yorkshire

December

In early December, Deborah and Rebecca 'set out towards Yorkshire, [through Staffordshire], having a Public Meeting on the 8th at Penkridge in the morning and Ridgeley [Rugeley] in the evening'. They reached Tamworth next day for an evening Meeting in which the 'harmonising power of Truth was pointed out as the means of producing private and public happiness'.

After an opportunity in Joseph Fowler's family on the 10th December they 'rode to Burslem for a Meeting none having been held there for many years'. The next evening the 'Meeting at Derby was trying perhaps in part owing to it being held in an unsuitable place', and by the 12th they had reached Castle Donington. They then had a 'refreshing opportunity with our Honourable Fds G. & R. Fallows' and an evening Meeting at Loughborough. After attending two Meetings at Nottingham on the 15th December they were at the Select Quarterly Meeting next day for the counties of Derby and Nottingham held at Chesterfield, which was 'measurably comfortable'. They rode on to Worksop for a Public Meeting on the 18th and had a weekday Meeting at Broomhouse the following day with another in the evening at Blythe.

After an opportunity in a Friends family they reached Bawtry on the 20th December where they had a Meeting at 11 o'clock with the young people followed by a large one at Tickhill. At Doncaster on the 22nd they sat with Friends and attended a large Meeting with the inhabitants which was a 'time to be remembered with Gratitude'. On the 23rd evening Meeting was at Sherborn and on the 24th they were at Select Quarterly Meeting at York, where they spent a few days attending various Meetings before travelling on the 27th to Leeds, after an opportunity at Lindley Murray's home in York on Holgate Hill, which must have given Deborah much happiness. Later that day in Leeds they entered on family visits to Friends of that Meeting, and on the morning of the 29th John and Elizabeth Hoyland, Henry Tuke and Martha Smith ministered to them.

1800

January

They continued with their family visits during the first week of January, and had a large Public Meeting at Huddersfield, among whom, Deborah had reason to believe, 'there were many enquiring minds'. She 'convey'd counsel to Friends' at Brighouse Monthly Meeting on the 10th, where Rebecca ministered 'to some not of our Society'.

They were at Meetings at Gildersome and Leeds next day; the latter was very large but as it was in the fine Meeting House there, it was big enough to hold everyone.

There was Monthly Meeting at Otley on 13th January, and also a Meeting for the inhabitants of that place. The Public Meeting at Rawdon Meeting House a day later was 'to a seeking people', but to Deborah and Rebecca they appeared 'too much outward'.

They had Meeting in a riding school in Leeds, which could hold 2,000 people – more than the Friends Meeting House there could accommodate, and Deborah added 'considering the number, stillness prevailed'. Their next Meeting was held in a brewery at a village near Leeds, 'which was satisfactory'.

Martha Routh was with them by 17th January at an evening Meeting at Beeston. There followed more family visits in the Leeds area, and a large Public Meeting on the 20th. Next morning they left, after an opportunity with the servants where they had been lodging. This is an entry Deborah occasionally made, evidently giving particular attention to the people who had cared for them in the houses of Friends who had given them hospitality; occasionally a few among them would have taken an active part in the Meetings also.

That same day, 21st January, they reached Wakefield, and went on to Ackworth[10] for a Public Meeting. Next day, they had a 'sitting with this large family', and then continued on to Pontefract for a Public Meeting in the evening; a small one of the same kind having been held at Barnsley and on 24th January they attended a small evening Meeting there and another in a schoolhouse at Penistone, further south, the day after. They attended another, 'remarkable for solidity', on the 25th at Wortley and were at Sheffield by the 26th, for both Meetings that day. They also had one with the young people 'to whom much encouragement was convey'd.

The Heads of Families met them at their request on 28th January, followed by a visit 'to see some Prisoners' before leaving for a Meeting at Attercliff. They had a Public Meeting at Woodhouse next morning, and at Crooks in the evening. These Meetings being close to Sheffield they attended their weekday Meeting and that same evening 'had a Meeting in a Riding School' on the last day of January.

February/March/April

They were in Monyash and Buxton for large Meetings on February 2nd; fortunately the roads were open, for in mid-winter this whole region could become entirely impassable with snow. On 3rd February they reached Leek, and were at New Dale Meeting on the 5th, arriving home in time to dine.

Return to the Dale, 5th February 1800

Deborah was silent in all the Meetings on 16th February, and Rebecca 'was engaged in our evening sitting'. On the 23rd William Byrd and Deborah were engaged in Shrewsbury Meeting in the morning, and Deborah again in the evening.

Mary Lloyd and Susannah Appleby returned from Ireland on 26th February; all their Friends now at Sunniside appeared in their evening sittings. Also, during the last days of the month and into March these Friends attended the local Meetings. On 19th March at Monthly Meeting at the Dale, Deborah felt she must point out 'the care necessary to avert a spiritual famine'.

She and Rebecca then went a little further afield to Stourbridge, Dudley, and Worcester, including Quarterly Meeting at that city during the end of March and the first days of April. In Tewkesbury on 6th April, she had 'to counsel Friends to choose Divine Wisdom', and that evening there was a large Meeting at Upton-on-Severn, where Timothy Bevington joined them.

They were engaged at Worcester on 7th and 8th April, and had a large Public Meeting at Bromyard on the evening of the 8th, and then went to Leominster a day later. On 10th April they spent the day with Friends, and were in John Southall's family. Deborah left Rebecca with her 'valuable Uncle William Young' on 11th April and reached Sunniside that night.

She then attended the local Meetings over the next days, and on 17th April John and Sarah Abbott, with Jane Honeychurch passed through the Dale on their way to Ireland 'but made no stop with us'.

On 20th April in their morning Meeting Deborah 'had to point out the excellence of Religion, as sustaining the mind under trials, and the Meeting concluded with Prayer for support'. She 'sat with M. Jones in company with R[ichard] Dearman and Edward Simkin, and he and Susannah were engaged at our table after Dinner'.

On 27th April, Richard Gilkes from Devizes was with them, and they had a Public Meeting in the evening. At Monthly Meeting in Shrewsbury the same Friend 'ministered', and at this Meeting Susannah Appleby 'spread a concern to accompany Mary Ridgway on a visit to some parts of England'.

On 29th April they were at Welshpool attending Monthly Meeting for North Wales where Half-Yearly Meeting took place on 30th April. Visiting

Friends were William Crotch, Richard Gilkes and Mary Sterry, and this whole Meeting 'ended under a thankful sense of the Lord's tender care over his flock and family'.

May

Friends held a Meeting at Shrewsbury on 2nd May, and came to the Dale Meeting that same evening at six o'clock. Then on the 3rd William Crotch and Mary Sterry left them with John Hull, a Friend she had not previously mentioned, Richard Gilkes staying on with them for morning Meeting. He was also at New Dale in the evening.

Rebecca Young and Susannah Appleby were engaged in their weekday Meeting on 6th May and on the 9th the women set out with Deborah for London, going by way of Coventry and Warwick, and on the 13th had a Meeting at Dunchurch, a village 'where no Fds Meeting had been held of late years and it was to our comfort'. They were travelling in fine agricultural country at a beautiful time of the year, when the hedges were in full leaf and the flowers in an abundance of scent and unfolding beauty.

They sat with Friends in the morning of the 14th May at Northampton and were at Newport Pagnall Meeting in the evening. They reached Bedford next day in time for evening Meeting, travelling on to Hitchin where they dined at Joseph Wheeler's and held a Meeting at Ware with another the day after at Hoddesdon. On the 18th they attended two Meetings at Tottenham, the last with 'some of the inhabitants', and the following day were at two sittings of the Select Yearly Meeting and a further one next day .

A few days later they were at Southwark where they had an opportunity at Thomas Smith's. On the 25th May they were twice at Westminster where Deborah, Rebecca and Mary Ridgeway all ministered, and they had an opportunity after dinner at John Corbyn's. They attended Ratcliffe Meeting on the 29th and the Women's Yearly Meeting closed next day. The last day of the month they called on Ann Fothergill, John and Samuel's sister, who 'tho' in some measure weakened in her faculties appears lively in spirit'.

June

They were at Devonshire House Meetings, morning and evening, on 1st June with an opportunity at Sarah Row's, and attended two Select Meetings on the 2nd 'which were in some respect trying and exercising, yet a degree of strength was afforded to keep the ancient foundation'. This comment could be applied to several of the occasions during the years of her ministerial journeys, but the very rewarding times were, to her, always what she mentally formulated in between.

They attended a Public Meeting at [St] Albans on the evening of 3rd June, were also present at their weekday Meeting there; an evening Meeting at Hemel Hempstead followed and they arrived at Banbury on 6th June in time for weekday Meeting which 'tho' small was refreshing'. The 8th found them at Birmingham where they sat with Friends in the morning having a Public Meeting in the evening, arriving back at Sunniside the next day.

On the 15th June Deborah was engaged in testimony and Rebecca Young in prayer in morning Meeting when Deborah had 'to exhort Fds to mind the Lord's work in preference to their own'; at Monthly Meeting she also 'spread a concern before Fds to visit the Western Countys'. On the 22nd Deborah was at Shrewsbury Meeting and at a public one at Donnington that evening.

Sarah Lynes had a Public Meeting at the Dale on 27th June and also several religious opportunities. 'R[ichard] and Joseph Burlingham came with her and they with Edmund Darby, [all] went to Birmingham in order to meet Mary Stacey with whom she is to visit some Northern Countys.' Deborah and Rebecca Young attended morning Meeting at the Dale on the 29th and had a large public one in the evening in a barn at Buildwas 'when Counsel was convey'd to the People who many of them behaved remarkably well'.

July

Deborah was with Rebecca Young, William Byrd and R. Gregory on the 6th July at New Dale and afterwards had an 'opportunity at James Jackson's after dinner and then attended Public Meeting in a barn at Bran Lees, a season to be thankfully remember'd'.

Deborah recorded that on 8th July 'at an adjourned Monthly Meeting my Fds William Byrd and Rebecca Young acquainted Fds with their intention of entering into a Married State – the Meeting was a season of favor'. On 14th July Deborah stated 'my Beloved Fd took leave of the Dale where we had spent many peaceful days together; we dined at William Holtham's and got to Shrewsbury for tea' and on the 16th Deborah was granted her certificate to visit some of the Western Counties.

Marriage of Rebecca Young and William Byrd
17th July 1800

The 17th July wrote 'This Day my long lov'd Fd Rebecca Young was united in marriage to William Byrd of Marnhull, Dorsetshire, the day was crowned with the consoling Presence of Him who on a similar occasion turned the Water into Wine, and I humbly hope is a presage of the many Days of comfort they may have to enjoy together'. The next day Deborah left Shrewsbury early in the morning 'accompanied by my Rebecca's sisters to [Church] Stretton where we breakfasted and after a comfortable religious opportunity we parted with them and got to Leominster that night'. After several family visits, Deborah accompanied by William and Ann Young and others rode to Hereford for evening Meeting on the 21st.

On the 24th July they visited sick Friends and Deborah spent the day with Robert Gregory who 'had been our kind companion from the Dale', and held a Public Meeting at Yatton. They reached Marnhull on the 26th 'the habitation of my Dr Fds William and Rebecca Byrd where we were kindly received'; on the 28th they drank tea at John Raikes, and Deborah spent the 29th July 'with my Dr Friends enjoying in some degree their peaceful Dwelling – feeling in measure thankful for the blessings dispensed'.

Visit to the Channel Isles

August 1800

She attended weekday Meeting in which she and William Byrd ministered advising 'Fds to look to the Lord for help', and on 1st August held a Meeting in a barn in a village and they sailed next day from Weymouth for Guernsey, landing early on the 4th. After holding several Meetings they sailed on again to Jersey on the 7th holding a Public Meeting at the landing place called Wormes Bay, and the following day were 'bound together in a Meeting held in the house of one professing with us – the place called Owens'. That evening they had another Meeting in 'Mary's Parish and lodged at the Widow Lacouter's who entertained with hospitality'.

They went on to hold two Meetings in a large room at [St] Aubins 'in company of many serious people as well as some not so well acquainted with the harmonising power of truth', and on the 11th August sat with Friends at Hilliers to 'whom Gospel truths flow'd freely', followed by a Public Meeting in the evening, again at the landing place, leaving for Sark to hold two Meetings on the 13th and sailing back to Guernsey on the 15th when Deborah had a remarkable escape as 'having just moved my seat the mast fell which would have endangered my Life had I continued where I was'. She then in thankfulness quoted Addison's words:

> How are Thy Servants, blest the Lord
> How sure is their defence
> Eternal wisdom is their Guide
> Their help Omnipotence

That evening they held a Meeting in Guernsey in which Deborah and Rebecca ministered and William Byrd closed with prayers. In the morning of the 17th August they had the largest and most open Meeting they had had in the island with another in the country later in the day. Next day they visited the French prisoners 'who received them with openness and to them the Love of God flow'd freely – prayer was also put up for them', and later they had a religious opportunity at George Walker's. Two further Meetings were held at different places in the countryside and they attended weekday Meeting on the 20th August where Rebecca was engaged in prayer.

Then they sailed for Alderney at four o'clock to arrive about nine in the evening. Next day evening Meeting was 'not so still as we could have wished', but the afternoon one on the 22nd was 'crowned with solemnity'. Another afternoon one was held at Bray in which 'some stout minds were a Little Humbled'. They sailed back on the 26th but unfortunately had contrary winds to Weymouth where they landed to dine on 27th August.

Return to England

The small group arrived back at Marnhull on the 28th and Deborah 'desired gratefully to commemorate mercys' and they then spent a few days quietly with their Friends.

September

A Public Meeting was held in Shaftesbury on 3rd September and next day at Monthly Meeting they had to 'labour with the Youth in a particular manner that they might bend their necks to the Yoke of Christ'. Deborah and Rebecca had a Public Meeting at Cerne [Abbas] in the morning of the 7th and at Sherborne in the evening, and after sitting in Thomas Thompson's family rode to Bridport for Monthly Meeting where both were engaged in Testimony. This was followed on the 10th September by Quarterly Meeting with a large public one in the evening held in the Town Hall 'about 700 had collected and we had both to minister unto them as well as ask a blessing'.

They went on to Yeovil on the 11th for evening Meeting and next day 'after a sitting in Dear Samuel Isaac's family we parted from our Beloved Fd William Byrd'. They had all three been travelling together ever since Rebecca's marriage to William, but the time was fast approaching when Rebecca would be going to Marnhull for good and would only be with Deborah for some journeys together in their Ministry. The Byrds were to continue active in the Ministry until their death, sometimes visiting on their own, and at other times together. Deborah and Rebecca went on to Somerton for a solid Meeting at 11 o'clock with another at Glastonbury in the evening of the 13th September. Arriving at Bristol next day it appeared they had a more successful time than had sometimes been the case. It was the largest Meeting outside London's Devonshire House, but had not always appeared easy to the Darbys.

On 15th September they were 'favor'd with a large Public Meeting near R. Bishop's' which sounded as if it had been held out-of-doors. After a

Meeting at Chew [Stoke] Select Quarterly Meeting was held in the evening of the 16th in Bristol, when Mary Ridgway and Susannah Appleby were engaged in Testimony and Deborah in prayer. This was followed by Quarterly Meeting and a public one in the evening in the Temple Meeting House.

After family visits they attended a 'Meeting appointed for them in a Riding School at which was near 1,800 persons and tho' accidentally interrupted was a remarkably solid one'. The morning Meeting on the 19th was at Pill, but the evening one at Lawrence Weston's was not so open a time. They rode to Keynsham for evening Meeting on 20th September and went to Friars Meeting House for morning Meeting next day where the first Abraham Darby had worshipped a century before; Deborah and Rebecca were silent there though Mary Ridgway was 'largely engaged much to edification'. After a time of retirement in a Friend's family they attended a Meeting at Kingwood on the 22nd and had an opportunity with 'Fds at the Inn'.

After morning Meeting at Claverham they attended a public one in the evening at Axbridge when Rebecca was engaged in supplication. Weekday Meeting on the 24th September was at Bridgwater, and after a family visit, they were similarly engaged with a Meeting at Taunton. The morning Meeting next day was at Milverton and they had a sitting in a Friend's family in which 'Divine Regard was manifested', and at the public one next evening at Wellington, William Byrd joined them. On the 28th after morning Meeting at Uffculme they went on to another at Cullompton and were able to have an opportunity in a Methodist's family before reaching Exeter for evening Meeting.

They attended Quarterly Meeting on 30th September where 'the Counsel of God laid deep and it was not without much exercise that the well was attained which when it springs up the living can sing unto'. They sat with a sick Friend 'sister to our Dear William Byrd with whom we partook of best refreshment' and from whom we parted along with Richard Gregory next day, riding on to Oakhampton for evening Meeting.

October

Launceston Meeting on the 2nd October was 'sweetly closed in prayer by John Dyamond, who accompanied us', followed by one at Bodmin Meeting and they got to Edward Fox's to dine and for a Meeting at Wadebridge next day.

On 5th October, a First Day, Padstow Meeting was 'still and solid' and they went on to Penryn Wharfe where 'some visited minds were encouraged to follow on to know the Lord'. They then had a 'favor'd sitting in George Fox's family' and attended Select Meeting at Falmouth on the 7th, followed by Quarterly Meeting which was successful as was the public one held in a warehouse in which 'much Love was felt to the People'.

Scilly Isles, 13th October 1800

A Public Meeting was held at Penryn where they also had a sitting with the family of 'our Dear Fds Peter and Anne Price in which we felt much sympathy with them'. They had a 'comfortable time' at Helston Meeting, sat with Friends afterwards, and went on to Marazion for evening Meeting. For morning Meeting on 12th October they were at Land's End, going on to Penzance later, to sail to the Scilly Isles on the 13th returning that evening as the winds were contrary.

Weekday Meeting at Marazion was followed by another at Hale, and in the evening of the 15th October they attended one in a theatre at Penzance in which we had about 'a thousand people to whom Gospel truths were convey'd'. After the Newland Meeting we were 'silent in Penzance weekday Meeting to the disappointment of the People'.

They sailed again for the Scilly Isles on the 18th and had a bad voyage, landing on the morning of the 19th October at St Mary's. They then on 20th went on to St Martin's Isle for a Meeting 'amongst a People who appear'd but little acquainted with Religion'. Next day they reached the island called Tresco 'where they appear'd to be more civilized, some showing much respect'. After two more Meetings at St Mary's they sailed back to Penzance on 24th October and after getting some sleep attended weekday Meeting which was 'measurably owned by Him whose Voice had proved to be stronger than the noise of many Waters, yea than the mighty waves of the sea, and had a large and satisfactory Meeting at a place called St Ives'.

They rode on the 25th to Redruth for a six o'clock Meeting, and on to Truro where the people were 'exhorted to call upon the Lord in a Day of Prosperity that He might hear them in the Day of trouble'. They had an opportunity there with many 'Dr Fds that had met us and from whom we was [sic] about to separate' and went on for evening Meeting at [St] Austle which was crowded. On the 27th October 'much Love was felt to the People in an evening Meeting at Mevagissy' and after Monthly Meeting at St Austell had an evening one with the People at Polperro Mine followed by a large Meeting in a warehouse at Looe on the 29th.

November

On 30th October, after morning Meeting with Friends, a public one was later held at Liskeard 'to some relief'. They reached Callington the next morning and moving south to Salt Ash later, crossed the estuary to Plymouth on 2nd November, when Deborah was engaged in testimony and Rebecca in prayer at Meeting – the evening one being held at Plympton.

After holding a Meeting at Kingsbridge they rode on east to Totnes by the 4th and there parted from Cousins Francis and Sarah Fox, going to to Topsham below Exeter for evening Meeting.

They attended Exeter weekday Meeting on 6th November, and on into Somerset for two Meetings at Chard in which 'we was become a threefold band by our Dr Fd William Byrd having met us at this place'. Here Deborah thought the evening Meeting was a 'relieving season'.

During the next few days they travelled to Axminster, Bridport, Beauminster and Hazelborough in Devon where 'we had to minister to a People much unacquainted with Fds, but who behaved well'. After weekday Meeting at Compton they reached Marnhull on the evening of the 13th November where they spent a week quietly, attending local Meetings and sitting with Friends. On the 18th they had a Meeting at Blandford, and next day at Tarrant Mongton, and Deborah entered into family visits on the 20th November at Poole accompanied by William Byrd. He left them a week later on the 27th and Deborah and Rebecca held a Public Meeting at Longham, and another next day after a sitting with families at Christ Church going on to Lyndhurst for morning Meeting and to Southampton for the evening of the 30th November.

December

On 2nd December a Meeting was held in a Baptist Meeting House at Portsea which 'held 1,500 but proved too small for this occasion – it was an open time'. Next day they attended another one at 11 o'clock in the same Meeting House, at which 'much tenderness was manifested'. There they met with a blind woman 'who appear'd well acquainted with the work of Religion of the Heart: she was asked if it was not a great trial to have lost her sight, to which she replied "Yes" but having turned to the Lord I can bear it with resignation'. They dined at the house of a Methodist minister and drank tea with a Baptist. On 4th December they had a solid Meeting at Gosport and got to Chichester that night, and after a satisfactory Meeting at Arundel sat with Friends at Brighthelmstone [Brighton] and had a sitting with some young people in the evening. Meeting followed at Shoreham [by-the-sea], Steyning, Horsham and Crawley and on 11th December Deborah visited a 'Fd under great affliction'. They rode on to Lewes for a large Public Meeting and next morning held one at Newhaven; back to Lewes for Select and Quarterly Meetings on 15th and 16th, returning to Brighthelmstone for evening Meeting. The Public Meeting at Chichester was held in the Assembly Room supposed to contain 1,000 people, but on 18th December Rebecca Byrd being poorly Deborah attended weekday Meeting and visited Friends on her own. Morning Meeting on the 21st was held in the Town Hall at Wilton, when William Byrd joined them, and a public one in the Assembly Room at Salisbury was 'large and solemn'.

'This morning, the 22nd December', Deborah wrote, 'My long Beloved nearly united Companion Rebecca Byrd and myself separated, I trust for Christ's sake, and tho' it was unspeakably trying to our natures, I trust we were enabled to make in measure a cheerful sacrifice – she went with her husband home and I continued to Salisbury, her mind being drawn to her own Monthly and Quarterly Meetings and mine to see the familys which I began to visit about an hour after I had parted from Dr William and Rebecca Byrd.'

Deborah then continued north and on the 24th December she attended weekday Meeting, finished family visits and sat Select Quarterly Meeting 'in all which a measure of best help was near'. Quarterly Meeting on the 25th was 'a time of favor N. and M. Naftel from Guernsey and Sarah Elgar from Kent were there and we had a satisfactory opportunity and dined with Fds'.

On the 28th Deborah spent the day with her relations, the Fowlers, and sat with Friends at Melksham also had a sitting in her brother-in-law's family. During the next two days she attended Select and Quarterly Meetings at Cirencester at which both 'Sarah Stephenson and myself minister'd'. On 31st December Rachel Fowler and Deborah began a family visit 'in which we had cause to hope the Shepherd of Israel had put us forth and mercifully went before us'.

1801
January

On 1st January Sarah Stephenson, Mary Jeffrys and Deborah were all engaged to minister in their weekday Meeting and Sarah also joined in family visits. For her, Deborah 'felt her spirit had long been bound in near Gospel fellowship'. On 2nd January, in the evening, they had a Public Meeting in an Assembly Room, but next day they parted with these 'Dr Friends' at Cirencester and, accompanied by several men Friends and Sarah Bowley, went on to hold an open Meeting at Stroud.

In Painswick on 4th January they attended morning Meeting and an evening one in the Booth Hall in Gloucester, a place mentioned on several occasions in the Journal. They travelled on north to Tewkesbury for a Meeting in a village called Stoke which was on the road to Worcester where they attended Quarterly Meeting. This lasted several days before they returned home on the 8th, accompanied by Deborah's son Edmund and her brother-in-law, Robert Fowler.

On their arrival home they found Mary Ridgway staying at Sunniside where she had spent some days attending local Meetings. William Rawes from Marnhull went with Deborah on the 17th January to visit the grandson of the late Ann Summerland, who was very ill, and next day 'Priscilla Hannah Gurney appear'd in Prayer and myself in Testimony and we had a favor'd opportunity at Richard Reynolds home at Dale House'. They were at Meeting in Shrewsbury on the 21st of the month and again on 1st February with sittings in several families.

February

On 6th February, Martha Routh, Elizabeth Cogshall and Thomas Cash were at New Dale Meetings and at the 'evening sitting with us when E.C. was favor'd to minister acceptably'. These Friends stayed with them for some days and took an active part in local Meetings, leaving them for Dudley on 9th February. On the 10th John Summerland's son was buried.

March

Mary Ridgway stayed with them into March and on the 4th Deborah accompanied her to evening Meeting at Shrewsbury, followed by visits to families there and dinner at Ann Clark's house. Deborah with Priscilla Hannah Gurney rode to Newcastle [under-Lyme] on 7th March 'which was a fine day' and they attended Meeting at Leek next day. On the 9th after an opportunity at Toft Chorley's they rode into Macclesfield 'to attend an open solid Meeting', and by the 11th were at Select Quarterly Meeting at Stockport in which Deborah and John Thorpe 'had counsel to hand to the Members of our Society', followed by evening Meeting. They visited families on the way to Oldham and on 13th March attended 'a Meeting at William Midgley's near Rochdale' arriving in Manchester next day for a Meeting with some Friends to whom Deborah ministered, and in the large evening Meeting Priscilla Hannah Gurney and Deborah shared the 'public labour'. On 16th March, after riding 'through some difficult roads we reached Nantwich for a Public Meeting', and arrived back at the Dale at 10 o'clock in the evening of the 17th, again 'with some difficulty'.

Concern of Priscilla Hannah Gurney to Visit Eastern Counties

At Monthly Meeting on 18th March, Priscilla Hannah Gurney 'laid a concern before Fds to visit the Eastern Countys'. Mary Ridgway was still at Sunniside; often in winter guests remained for longer visits because of the state of the roads, and she and Susannah Howells who was also there took a frequent part in local Meetings.

They rode to Birmingham on 24th March to attend Select Quarterly Meeting where they also visited Cousin Lloyd's family in the evening and while there Deborah, with Ann Alexander, M. Brewster and Thomas Shillitoe were engaged in family visits. Susannah Howell and Edmund Darby then returned home on 26th March, but on the 31st they with Mary Ridgway rode back to Birmingham, while Deborah and Priscilla Hannah Gurney went to Shifnal to meet with Ann Alexander again and Martha Brewster. Next day after a small morning Meeting these Friends went on to Lichfield and Deborah returned to Coalbrookdale.

April

On 11th April Deborah, Susannah Howell and Edmund attended the marriage of Joseph Burgess and Rebecca Summerland at Uttoxeter and were with the family afterwards. Rachel Lloyd and Dorothy Braithwaite arrived at Sunniside to stay on the 12th and a few days later Deborah 'spread a concern before Fds to visit the Eastern Countys and [received] a certificate'. In Worcester Meeting on the 19th April 'close labour was extended to the wanderers' and that evening a Meeting was held at Bromyard, followed by another at Hay [on-Wye] the next evening. They then attended Select Yearly Meeting at Brecon on the 22nd and the Meeting for Discipline next day was lively where they had the company of Anna Price and Sarah Rudd. On 24th April after two satisfactory opportunities at Hay they parted from Susannah Howells and rode to Leominster for an evening Meeting, reaching home in time for tea on the 26th.

May

During the last days of April Deborah attended local Meetings and on 9th May she went to Stourbridge leaving Mary Darby very ill; she was a daughter of Abraham Darby III and Rebecca Smith who had been at the Tukes' School in York, as had her older sister Ann. There was a Meeting at Bromsgrove next morning and at Alcester in the evening with a Public Meeting at Shipston [on-Stour] on the 11th. Then travelling by Long Compton and Charlbury, and having two opportunities in Friends' families the next day was 'occupied pretty fully'. They reached Witney on the 13th May for morning Meeting with an evening one at Abingdon, and others at Shillingford and Henley [on-Thames] and Uxbridge, arriving in London on the 16th to be met with the sad news that Cousin Mary Darby had died. Deborah here described her as a fine young woman of 21 years 'a striking instance of the uncertainty of time', but she was somewhat consoled by Rebecca Byrd joining her at Cousin Smith's about eight o'clock that evening.

They were at Southwark in the morning and Peel in the evening of the 17th May, lodging outside London at Hampstead for the night of the 20th, but two days later had returned to the city to Meeting at Gracechurch Street followed by 'several religious opportunities in the course of the week'. They attended Westminster Meeting in the morning of the 24th May and Devonshire House in the evening, and the Women's Yearly Meeting ended on the 29th during which 'acceptable visits were paid us by Richard Jordan, Samuel Smith and George Dillwyn'.

Visit to the Eastern Counties
4th June to 26th July 1801

On the last day of the month they attended Southwark and Gracechurch Street Meetings and on 3rd June the 'Select Meeting closed our engagements at this time in this City which we left in the afternoon and lodged with W. Dillwyn'. After Tottenham Meeting and a public one at Waltham Abbey, later on the 4th they rode to Hertford with Meetings at Hitchin, Royston, Erith, Sutton, Chatteris and March by the 12th June, and after a sitting in a Friend's family were on the 14th at Wisbech Meeting which was held in a Wool Room and was 'considered a well conducted assembly': the Meeting at Downham (Market) was held in the evening.

During the next days of travelling Meetings were held at Wareham, [King's] Lynn, with a trying one at Swaffham and weekday Meetings at Fakenham and Wells and on the 18th June in the Town Hall at Walsingham, which had been a place of pilgrimage since the 10th century but had now fallen into disrepair. They reached Norwich by the 20th and sat with Friends' families and had a large Meeting with 'People of other Societys', and on the 22nd June they spent the day with Lawrence Candler and the following day 'E. Wigham, Ann Dymond, Rebecca Byrd and myself all minister'd to a backsliding people'.

July

The small party rode on holding Meetings as they went and arrived at Yarmouth by 29th June, where they visited families, going on to Ipswich for morning Meeting on 5th July and attending a marriage. They were at Needham [Market] Meeting on the 9th with an evening one at Stow Market, followed by visits to Friends' families and a Meeting at Bury [St Edmunds]. Among others attended were those at Long Melford, Sudbury, Cavendish, Clare and Haverhill and on the 14th at Stoke Meeting there were 'a large number of Military Men who behaved well'. They sat weekday Meeting at Saffron Waldon on the 15th July and next day at Thackstead and Dunmow, all being 'seasons to be thankfully remembered'. By the 22nd they had reached Colchester Meeting for a burial which was 'A heart rendering season as was an opportunity at the house amongst the near connections of the Deceased'.

On to Halstead for a Meeting held in a barn which 'was a crowded assembly' and a Meeting in a village in the morning and at Coln[e] later occupied the day well, they rode on the 26th to Malden and Chelmsford Meetings which were large, and next day visited 'the convicts in Chelmsford Jail' with a large Meeting in a barn at Braintree.

Return Home by Marnhull

August

On 29th July they rode 30 miles to Ware for an evening Meeting, with another at Rickmansworth and then on to Reading, with satisfactory Meetings at Basingstoke, Whitchurch and Andover. At Stockbridge on 4th August Deborah met with 'our Dr Fd Wm Byrd' and they were at

Salisbury next day, and by the 6th were at Fordingbridge where a Public Meeting was arranged in the evening at Cranborne, so that by the 7th August Deborah was glad to get to Marnhull and 'be once more under the Roof of my Beloved Fds W(illiam) and R(ebecca) Byrd'.

On the 9th August Deborah sat with Friends in silence at Marnhull and they attended a Public Meeting at Bradford in the evening. Monthly Meeting was at Bridport at which 'Rebecca Byrd gave in her certificate for the Eastern Countys and got one for Staffordshire and we both had public engagement in the Meeting for Worship'. Richard and Rebecca Reynolds dined with them on the 11th August and afterwards went to evening Meeting at Beaumister and on to attend the burial of Jacob Rumsey at Poole. Monthly Meeting was at Ringwood where William Rawes was present and by the 23rd August reached Chepstow, attending Wales Half-Yearly Meeting at Brecknock where they had the company of 'William Byrd and R. Gregory, who with B. Middleton and his wife, William Tuke and his daughter Mabel accompanied us together with other strangers, George Dillwyn from America amongst the number' and by the last day of the month, S. J. Middleton and Rebecca Byrd attended our First Day Meeting at Coalbrookdale.

September

On the morning of 6th September they went to a Public Meeting at Wrexham and at Chester in the evening, and after visiting Friends' families attended a 'large and favor'd Meeting at Northwich', in the evening, followed by Quarterly Meeting at Macclesfield on the 10th. They went to Meeting next day in Francis West's barn at Basford and on the 14th September were at Meeting in Burslem held in a Methodist Meeting House 'supposed to hold 2,000 but not near equal to the number assembled, who behaved with much decorum . . . there are many seeking minds in these parts who we desire may be strengthened to make a full surrender of all that is called for at their hands'.

Another large Meeting was held at Hanley next day 'also to the relief of our own minds which has been generally the case in the Potterys'. In Meeting at Stone on 16th September 'those who had wander'd were united to look upon Zion that their Eyes might behold Jerusalem, a quiet habitation, a Tabernacle that can never be taken down'.

At Thane on the morning of the 17th September they had a small Meeting and another at Uttoxeter in the evening, riding on to Lichfield for a large gathering a day later. They were at Stafford and Cannock by 20th September, 'at the latter place no Friends' Meeting had been held before in any one's memory that we appear'd like signs and wonders unto the People'. The evening of the 21st at Birmingham Meeting was 'hurt for the want of more notice', but by 23rd September they were attending Quarterly

Meeting at Warwick in which 'a sober call was extended to prepare for our final change' and an evening Meeting was held in the Court House.

Meeting next day at Kenilworth was 'a season of deep exercise for lack of stillness amongst the People', and this was followed next day by a large one at Evesham. They reached Droitwich for a morning Meeting on 27th September which was a 'lively opportunity', but the one in the evening at Worcester was 'more exercising'. They rode on to reach Tewkesbury by 29th for a 'large and satisfactory Meeting with the inhabitants that evening'. Newnham Meeting the following day was described as 'exercising', and the evening one at Newport on 1st October was 'satisfactory to themselves and appear'd so to others'. Weekday Meeting at Thornbury was followed by an evening one at Tetbury, but on 3rd October Deborah parted from 'my Endeared companion' as she called Rebecca, whose husband William Byrd had met her at Tewkesbury to accompany her home. That same day Deborah attended Meeting at Nailsworth followed by one at 'The Fleece' at Rodborough where she was pleased to find 'some precious awaken'd minds'.

October

By the 4th October Deborah was in Cheltenham for a large Meeting in the Long Rooms with another at North Leach later. After breakfast at Cheltenham she had an opportunity with Samuel Grubb and his daughter from Ireland, riding on to Tewkesbury to dine where she met with Ann Byrd and Hannah Stephenson returning from visiting the families of Friends at Liverpool. On the 6th October Deborah attended weekday Meeting at Worcester and Select Quarterly Meeting later that day in Bromyard at both of which 'G[eorge] Jones and myself were engaged in public labour'. Morning Meeting was held the following day at Bewdley and they reached Sunniside on the 8th accompanied by 'George Jones who has been our kind companion for four weeks'.

During the middle of October Deborah attended and ministered in their local Meeting: she also attended 'to the harvest and the goodness of Him who had filled our Barns with plenty and again caused the Despoiling Sword to be sheathed' – this probably being a reference to the war in Europe being temporarily halted during that year.

Deborah went to Dale House to have tea with the Richard Reynolds' on 22nd October and had an opportunity afterwards with R. and G. Ball, who as relations of Richard Reynolds were staying there. She visited in two families on the 25th; Arthur Enoch who was lately married was one of them, and this couple along with James Lewis spent the day with them at Sunniside on 30th October.

November

On 4th November Deborah 'dined with my S.D. at Cousin Dearman's but do not find much room to hope for comfort from him at present' – the situation over her son Samuel was evidently one which still caused her much pain.

The climax came at New Dale Meeting on 18th November when Deborah sat in silence 'it being a day of humiliation and deep conflict to my poor mind – a Testimony going forth against the conduct of my poor Son S.D. with which I fully united yet nature felt deeply, and had not the Eternal God been my refuge, I must have sunk under such a great trial'. The situation was indeed insupportable for Deborah – a real agony as Samuel had been disowned by Friends. During these weeks of acute depression Deborah was often silent in Meeting but striving for the 'clear inshinings of Heavenly Light'. On 29th November she had an exercising day and described how she was also 'deprived of the consolation of a letter from her dear Rebecca Byrd by the deep snow that had fallen in the south and west, but wrote a letter to her'.

December

At weekday Meeting on 1st December Deborah felt she had 'to express something on the analogy between nature and grace – winter seasons in both cases being necessary preparations to the fruitfulness of summer'. On 6th December she had to revive the language 'those that will not plough because it is cold, shall beg in Harvest time without being satisfied'. She also had to address the children, admonishing them 'to mind the Eternal monitor' and found that this 'was a Day of Deep exercise to my mind – tho' was strengthened to convey some counsel also in the evening at Brother Reynolds'. Edmund Darby returned during the following week from a visit at Melksham to the Fowlers and also to the Byrds at Marnhull. Monthly Meeting was held on 16th December when Deborah, Edward Simkin and Susannah Appleby took part. Stanley Pumphrey lodged at Sunniside from that date and by the 19th some Welsh Friends were also with them. By the 27th Deborah complains of 'weakness of body' but attended Meeting on the 29th, (a day when Mary Whitaker was buried), but she was entering a period of illness during these winter months.

1802

January/February/March

Deborah became ill at the beginning of the year, and was confined to her bed. She prayed for patience but was still unwell when John Thorpe and her brother Robert Barnard and his wife came to stay and took part in their Meetings in the Dale. They left on 13th January, leaving Deborah very weak in body and low in mind.

She got out on 2nd February for the first time since her illness began and was able to take part in their local Meetings, and to go as far as Shrewsbury on the 11th. However, she then became ill again for a few days, but this time she recovered sufficiently by the 21st, to give a warning, reminding Friends that 'when the Sons of God were met together Satan presented himself also'. She was now engaged in ministry quite frequently again as was Susannah Appleby.

On 8th March they both had an opportunity with Lowry Jones and Ann Pew, who had been staying for a few days.

At Monthly Meeting in the Dale on 17th March, J. Davis and Edward Simkin were engaged in the Meeting for Worship, and Deborah and Susannah 'in that for Discipline'.

John Robinson and Rosannah Emmery were married at The Dale on 18th March; both at Meeting and at the table after dinner they 'thankfully had the favor of the Great Master's Company'.

Cousin Mary Beesley and Mary Capper came the same evening to stay, Mary taking part on the 21st at their morning Meeting; these Friends leaving them on 22nd.

Deborah then reveals the possible cause of her illness by saying that G. Bott had been with them nearly a week, and during that time 'took me out 7 teeth', a considerable ordeal in those days, but she does appear to have been much better in health for the rest of the year, as she was to travel extensively for many months.

Her brother Daniel Barnard was with them for a few days, leaving on 29th March to go to the Fowlers at Melksham.

They had an account of 'the Treaty of Peace being signed' on 30th March. This was the 'Treaty of Amiens' and she called it 'a joyful intelligence'. Unfortunately, this cessation of hostilities only brought about a brief period of peace to Europe.

April

Priscilla Hannah Gurney was now with them at Dale House, after 'an absence of eleven months', to their pleasure, and she, Deborah and Susannah were engaged in a number of Meetings during the following days.

Deborah and Susannah then travelled to Leominster for 'morning Meeting on 19th April through a beautiful countryside, with the fruit blossom out in the many orchards in that neighbourhood: on the 20th they had 'a sweet opportunity at William Young's in the evening'.

Monthly Meeting was at Haye [on-Wye] followed by Select Meeting at Brecknock on 21st April; 'David Sands, Jacob Bell and Sarah Hack had each counsel to hand in the Meeting for Worship', Deborah having 'moved first in supplication'. However, later the 'Women's Meeting proved not so lively as sometimes'.

On 22nd April, their Meeting for Discipline was 'comfortable as was a Public Meeting appointed for David Sands'. They had another Public Meeting on 23rd April, and 'had some precious opportunities at the Inn' for which 'some of their minds were thankful'.

Visit to West of England and on to London

Deborah reached Bristol on the evening of 24th April, accompanied by James and Sarah Hack and Francis Wright, being met there by William and Rebecca Byrd with whom she spent the following day, always to Deborah's content, both among Friends in the morning and at a Public Meeting in the evening.

Bath Monthly Meeting was on 26th April, in which Rebecca was engaged, in Testimony and Supplication, but her companions were silent. Returning to Bristol, for Monthly Meeting there, they went on to weekday Meeting at Claverham the day after and paid a family visit in that particular Meeting.

May

Before leaving Claverham they had a favoured opportunity in Joseph Nash's family, and were at a Public Meeting at Sidcot on the evening of 2nd May.

They spent the next two days 'sitting with Friends in the familys', and then rode to Marnhull on 5th May, to the peaceful habitation of William and Rebecca Byrd. This would be delightful for her, as Rebecca's companionship was of the greatest joy.

Robert Jordan was at Meeting on 9th May, where Deborah was herself silent. On 11th May Monthly Meeting at Sherborne found 'the wing of Heavenly Kindness' spread over them. Then on the 12th they set out for London and attended no Meetings until they arrived at Guildford on 14th May.

They reached Wandsworth in the morning of the 16th May, and had an opportunity at John Townsend's, where they dined. Southwark Meeting was in the evening, in which 'our Dr Fnd Joseph Cloud from America had acceptable service'.

The Meeting for Ministers and Elders was on the 18th and they dined at Cousin Wilson Birkbeck's at Tottenham, where Deborah had an opportunity after the meal.

She had to appear both in Testimony and Prayer in the Select Meeting on 19th and then dined with Mary Sturge; Ann Crowley was also there. At the Women's Meeting for business which opened on 20th May, Deborah hoped they were 'under some sense of that power which first gathered us to be a people'.

On 22nd May weekday Meeting was at Southwark 'in which Holy help was extended – and a sweet visitation renew'd my Dr Fnds William Rebecca Byrd and myself – and had a share in the public labour'.

At Gracechurch Street Meeting in the morning of 23rd May she and Rebecca kept silent, though William Byrd and many others 'had to bear testimony to good authority'. They dined at Frances Eveleigh's and had an opportunity 'afterwards', and at Devonshire House Meeting, she and Rebecca 'were each strengthened with others to minister'. There also followed an opportunity at Cousin Smith's, after supper.

During the week they were 'closely engaged in attending upon affairs relating unto Society'. Robert Jordan paid women Friends a visit, after which Deborah 'was engaged in supplication'. George Dillwyn and David Sands 'had satisfactory opportunities one day in Women's Meeting, and Thomas Shillitoe another'.

June

'The Business of the Meetings' closed on 28th May, and as they 'found themselves at liberty to leave the City'. They travelled by Godalming, reaching Farnham on 31st May for a large Public Meeting in the evening, 'where the people appeared open and kind'. Then, after attending weekday Meeting at Shaftesbury on 2nd June they reached the home of the William Byrds, at Marnhull in the evening. Deborah stayed there for a few days, attending Meeting in the morning of 6th June before going on to Sherborne for a Public Meeting there in the evening, in which both Deborah and Rebecca took part. Later, they visited Thomas Thompson's, a home which had recently lost 'the female head of the family'.

On 7th June they were in Evershot Meeting, and the day after, also late in the day, reached Dorchester.

On 9th June they had a crowded Meeting at six o'clock in the evening on the south coast in the Town Hall at Weymouth, 'in which some visited minds were feelingly visited, as well as some distant wanderers called home'. Weymouth had become a fashionable watering place, where there was much sea bathing.

They crossed to the Isle of Portland on the 10th and had an evening Meeting, where she found 'there had been good work begun amongst this people'.

They rode west to Bridport on 11th June, and had an evening Meeting in the Town Hall. On the 13th they had a Public Meeting at Lyme [Regis] in the morning and Charmouth later that day. Returning to Bridport they visited families on the 14th and in the evening had a Public Meeting at Chidcock 'amongst a people much strangers to Friends, but they treated us with much respect'.

After attending Monthly Meeting in which they had some service they rode north into Somerset to Somerton, and at Glastonbury Quarterly Meeting on 16th June, 'my dear Companion was also engaged in the Women's Meeting'. They were in John Benwell's family on 17th June, and attended a Public Meeting at Claverham 'which was a solemn time'. After sitting 'with some familys' they had a Public Meeting at Portishead on the 18th, which was laborious, 'the life of Religion being low'.

They finished their family visits the next day in that Meeting, and began one in Hollowtree, but in going to that they had an unfortunate accident as the chair in which they were travelling broke. They escaped 'without much hurt', feeling that their Guardian Angel had protected them. Rebecca had 'vocally to return thanks and commemorate the mercy'. This account of the mishap reveals their method of travelling in a 'chair' – a one horse type of light carriage, very suitable for the smaller roads across country and at that time frequently used.

They had a Public Meeting in Hollowtree in the morning and Pensford in the evening of 20th June, and on the 21st another Public Meeting at Keynsham. This was followed on the 22nd by an exercising Meeting at Bathford, from where they returned with Susannah Nash to Bath. There they sat with some families on 25th June and in the evening had 'a precious Meeting' at Radstock.

On the morning of 24th June there was a Public Meeting at Bath, and they then went to Cappel Nap to lodge. They spent the morning of 25th June with the Fowlers, and then Robert accompanied them to Blandford, where unfortunately 'the Meeting was impoverished for want of more general information'. They then attended a Meeting in the evening at Corsham, which was 'a large gathering'.

On the 27th June, the sad news reached them that Sarah Stephenson had died in Philadelphia 'when on a Religious visit'.

After a uniting opportunity at Brother Fowler's, they went to Newstead near Devizes and had an open Meeting in William Powell's barn. They also had a 'comfortable Meeting' in the evening at Witton, where many minds 'were tenderly affected'. Attendance at Hampshire Quarterly Meeting at Fording Bridge on the 29th was small, and at Quarterly Meeting for Dorsetshire held at Poole on 30th June they found 'best help was near both in the Meeting for Worship and that for Discipline'.

Isle of Wight
July

After evening Meeting in Lymington on the Solent on 1st July, they crossed the Passage to Yarmouth on the Isle of Wight and had a solid

Meeting there in the evening, which was held in a malthouse. The Isle was at the height of summer beauty, and their journeys must have been both soothing and uplifting between Meetings, with the scent and sight of flowers, the flight of birds, butterflies, and winged creatures of all kinds crossing their way – and distantly at times the sound of the sea.

They had a Meeting at Ryde in the morning of 4th July, and at Newport in the evening, the latter proving 'very large and solid'. Evening Meeting the day after at Cowes was, however, rather trying, 'yet some young people appeared sensible of the force of Gospel Truths'.

Return to the Mainland

They 'crossed the Passage' back to Southampton and had a Meeting that evening on 6th July, and after an afternoon Meeting at Romsey they rode to Ringwood. They were at the weekday Meeting there on the morning of 8th July, and had an evening Meeting in Canford, 'held in a Barn to our relief'.

They had a large Meeting at six o'clock at Swanage on 9th July, 'attended by many serious people'. After a 'comfortable opportunity where we breakfasted' they rode to Corfe Castle on 10th July, where they had a solid Meeting in the forenoon.

On 11th July after sitting a little in William Neave's family, they rode to Monkton. They met there William Byrd and they had 'a large and open Meeting' at Sturminster, reaching Marnhull that evening. Deborah appeared to be there only one night before going on to a Public Meeting at Stalbridge on the 14th. At a Meeting at Henstridge on 15th July, they found 'the People much strangers to Friends'.

The Meeting next day at Gillingham was a 'season of favor, our Fnd Jane Shipley joined in the Public labour'. They had a Meeting at Shaftesbury in the morning of 18th July and another at Stour in the evening, Deborah felt that 'the Lord had renew'd his visitations to the People'.

They had returned to Marnhull by 20th July as Thomas Cash had a Public Meeting there, in which 'he had good service'. Deborah and Rebecca were engaged in weekday Meeting, and in a Public Meeting that same evening of the 21st at Milborne Port. By the 22nd July they were at Compton Meeting, after which Deborah and Rebecca left their Friends and went to Martock for a Meeting in the evening, and on to Langport, where in the evening Meeting there, they found the people 'much strangers to Friends'.

They lodged with a Friend on 24th July 'who lived in a solitary situation as to Friends', and had an evening Meeting at Montacute, going on to Crookham the next morning, and Ilminster in the evening.

On 26th July they were at an evening Meeting in Sidmouth; 'a bathing place, the room was too small for the company which lessened the solemnity, tho' there appeared no disposition to behave amiss'.

The 27th found them at Meeting in the morning at Exmouth, 'which ended well after having taken time to settle down', and after an opportunity in John Dyamond's family he went with them to Teignmouth, a fashionable seaside place where 'the Meeting was somewhat disturbed'. They rode to Plymouth from there, with a Meeting at Saltash in Cornwall in the morning, and Plymouth Dock in the evening – both occasions being largely attended.

August

They continued their visits to Friends and their families, and returned for another Meeting at Plymouth Dock on 2nd August. 'The warehouse in which this Meeting was held contained about 700 people, who behaved well; there appears to be a visited people in this place, to whom the Love of God flow'd freely.'

On 3rd August they had a Meeting in the Assembly Room at Plymouth, but 'there had been a shortness in spreading the notice, which impoverished the Meeting'. On the 4th, although not well, Deborah managed to attend weekday Meeting in the morning, and also one in the evening in a village near Francis Barkwell's, when she and Rebecca both took part. After sitting with Friends, they were at Tavistock for evening Meeting on 5th August, next day attending Meeting in a small town called Hatherleigh. They had a Meeting at a Friend's house on 7th August at Whitley.

They were travelling quickly now, as on the 8th they were in the morning at Torrington, with an evening Meeting at Barnstaple, and the following day held an evening Meeting at Ilfracombe 'to some satisfaction, but not so still as would be desirable'.

On 10th August they rode to South Moulton for a Meeting after being in Phillip Jones' family. They had a long ride on the 11th to reach Uffculme for tea (where the Thomas Byrds lived) and had 'a favor'd Meeting in a Fnd's malthouse'. The following day they parted with their 'kind attendants', John Abbot, Francis Fox and Grace Dennis in the morning, who had been accompanying them for some days, and rode to Honiton where they had a Meeting and reached Chard to lodge.

On 13th August they dined at Ilminster, and then in the evening 'had a very precious Meeting at South Petherton', going on to Thomas Thompson's, who received them with his usual hospitality.

At Wincanton William Byrd met them on 15th August, and joined in the religious labour in the evening at Meeting at Evercreach. On the 16th Deborah parted from her 'Endeared Friends William and Rebecca, to whom my heart is bound in near Gospel Fellowship, but apprehending the right time come for separation, thus supported, and I went on pretty comfortably to Bristol, and had a Meeting in the Temple Street House, to satisfaction'.

Deborah and Thomas Cash both ministered at weekday Meeting on 17th August, and in the evening she was at Hot Wells, and a day after at Frenchay weekday Meeting followed by a Public Meeting in a barn belonging to Thomas Gregory, also having an opportunity in P. Tricknet's family. There were opportunities in families and a Public Meeting in Oldston in the evening of 19th August. Deborah and Hannah Stephenson ministered to a sick Friend on 20th and had afterwards 'a solid Public Meeting' at Sodbury, dining at R. Lovels, and having a sitting in his family. There was then a Public Meeting in Bristol 'which was disturbed by an alarm of the Room giving way, which was not true. We were favor'd afterwards to part quietly'.

On 21st August, accompanied by E. Hatcher and wife, and young Sturge, Deborah rode to Pontypool, where the Meeting was small in the morning, but there was a large one at Abergavenny later.

The Select Half-Yearly Meeting for Wales was held in the morning of 24th August followed by Meeting for Worship 'in which Sarah Lynes was largely engaged and Mary Naftel and Richard Jordan made some additions, closing with Prayer'.

In the Women's Meeting 'Ann Crowley had acceptable service, also Christiana Hustler'.

On 25th August 'our Women's Meeting was own'd to some encouragement, Mary Bevan and Sarah Hustler joining the other Women Friends, that were Strangers in Public Labour. Our valuable, ancient Friend Hannah Plumstead, made some lively remarks at the close in the line of an Elder'. In the evening Meeting, for people of other societies, Deborah and Richard Jordan had 'the chief of the public service, [and] had many strangers, 9 ministers, and a great many in private stations'. It would seem that these Half-Yearly Meetings in Wales were proving a considerable success.[11]

Accompanied by several Friends, Deborah attended a Meeting at Keynton on 26th August and went on to Leominster for a Meeting in the evening, where she considered 'Christiana Hustler, Richard Jordan and Ann Crowley were well qualified to exalt the Cause of Truth publicly'.

Next day, Deborah and Christiana Hustler attended the burial of 'the long esteem'd Friend Sarah Beetnet', at Worcester, Deborah being later in John Burlingham's family.

In the morning they were with the family of the departed Sarah Beetnet, and then rode on to Birmingham, where they attended morning Meeting on the 29th and dined later at the Charles Lloyds. She does not say if this was at Bingley or in the city. Later, she drank tea with H. Robinson – 'in the latter place', and had a religious opportunity, and again in a large Public Meeting that evening.

She got 'well home' on 30th August accompanied by Christiana and H. Hustler, who stayed for some days nearby, taking part with her in local Meetings during late August and early September.

September

They went together to Birmingham to attend the burial of Charlotte Phelps, a daughter of Sampson Lloyd III 'who had left a husband and one child, the occasion was solemn'.

The roads going to Wolverhampton and Birmingham were some of the best in the Midlands, and it is probable that they went quite swiftly in the chaise or by one of the coaches.

Monthly Meeting on 7th September followed, where Deborah found 'best help was near', and they then all visited Joseph Gibbons' family. This same day the Hustlers 'turned their faces homewards', and Mary Capper and Deborah drank tea at Sampson Lloyd's, and had an opportunity in the family; that evening also in that of S. Baker's.

The day after they visited some sick Friends and dined at George Boone's, and then, accompanied by Sampson and Mary Lloyd, they went to Dudley for evening Meeting.

Deborah went home on 9th September and was set on the road by her sons and Francis Darby. Their Meeting on 14th September was larger than usual because of the burial of Mary Ann Mason: Thomas Speakman was there and made a contribution, and was also at their Meeting on the 15th when Deborah gave in her Certificate for her visit to the West of England, and Friends gave her liberty to appoint Public Meetings 'in my own and neighbouring countys as Truth may open the way'.

Charles Trusted and his wife, and Thomas Speakman, who had been staying at Sunniside, then left on 16th September, Deborah accompanying Thomas to New Dale.

Deborah with her son Edmund was at morning Meeting at Dudley on 26th September where there was a Public Meeting and also one at Wolverhampton 'which was supposed to consist of a thousand persons'; Deborah and Mary Lloyd both ministered to this large gathering.

October

Deborah then got home for weekday Meeting on 28th September, but she and Mary Lloyd left again for Walsall on 2nd October, followed by a large Public Meeting at Wednesbury on the 3rd and an opportunity after dinner at the inn, with another large Meeting for the people at West

Bromwich the same day. These gatherings in the Midlands were important, reaching very many people as the population was increasing with the development of industry, albeit that much of the work was carried out in the home.

On 4th October they were in Stourport. Deborah never said if they ever travelled by water, for the canals which were beginning to link a number of the towns, sending their merchandise by boat throughout the country, offered a far more convenient way of transport in some areas.

Quarterly Meeting took place at Leominster on 6th October, Deborah, Mary Lloyd and Ann Low taking part, with Sarah Howells also in the Women's Meeting. They were at Kidderminster in the evening of 7th October, and reached home next day.

After 10 days at home, Deborah and several Friends had a Public Meeting at Wellington on 17th October, 'which tho' a little interrupted for lack of room in the beginning, ended well', and there was a sitting in Arthur Enoch's family in the evening. On 21st October, Mary Ridgway and Susannah Appleby returned from a journey to the northern counties, and with Sarah Darby, also coming home from Bath on the 29th, 'it felt pleasant to be all together again'.

During the next few days, Mary Ridgway appeared in their Meetings also.

November

On 9th November, J. Burlingham and J. Bradley came and stayed until 12th, Edmund accompanying them to Worcester 'having a prospect of one day being united to John Burlingham's daughter', Lucy. She was one of a large and united family, and Deborah was probably happy at the prospect of this marriage for him; she and Sarah must have together, (probably with Richard Reynolds), entered the necessary negotiations.

December

Deborah was with Richard Dearman and Mary Rathbone at Shrewsbury for morning Meeting on 2nd December, and a large public one in the evening. She was during late November at Meetings in the neighbourhood, and on 1st December had her 'valued cousin M. Sargent with me at a Meeting at New Dale, followed by an opportunity at J. Enoch's and the Youngs (M. & J.)'.

Mary Ridgway appeared to be still with her on 5th December, and next day Priscilla Hannah Gurney returned from Bath in time for the evening sitting, in which Mary and Deborah were engaged. Several other Friends, Lewis Edwards and his son, and Lowry Jones, are mentioned as leaving on the 16th December, having been with them for some days.

Deborah was at Tamworth on 19th for their Meeting, and at John Fowler's after dinner, and the Widow Fowler's next day. There was an evening Meeting also at Polesworth, and a sitting in William Lythal's family.

They were at a Meeting at Hartshill on 21st December, and then a Select Meeting at Coventry, held in silence. Quarterly Meeting there took place on 22nd December, where they also had an evening Meeting with 'people of other Societys'. Evening Meeting at Warwick on the 23rd was followed next day by a visit to the Prison there, where 'one young man sweetly expressed his thankfulness for the opportunity, and said his coming within these walls had been a blessing to him, that he humbly hoped he had made his peace with an offended God. He feared he had brought much unhappiness to his excellent Mother, whom he was afraid his conduct would bring with sorrow to the Grave'.

On 25th December, they had a Meeting at Market Harborough before reaching Northampton the following day for Quarterly Meeting which was to begin on 27th December, after which she left Mary Lloyd, who had been her companion, and travelling all night by the coach, reached the Dale the next afternoon. 'It was a time of great conflict, my son Samuel having been some time very ill.' She mercifully found him better, and after spending two days with him she set out again 'to pursue my prospect'.

1803
January

They rode from Birmingham to Oxford in the coach accompanied by Robert Enoch on 1st January, and had two satisfactory Meetings 'in which Gospel Truths flow'd freely to the People'. They then attended the Select Meeting followed by Quarterly Meeting, which was opened by Thomas Huntley, 'bearing a lively Testimony'. He was the former Master of Samuel and Edmund's school at Burford. Deborah then followed with a 'pretty full opportunity both in Testament and Prayer'. They reached Thame for a Public Meeting in the evening; Sarah Squire, D. Molline and other Friends were with them.

They then rode to Aylesbury for Select Quarterly Meeting. Deborah thought that she 'had seldom of late felt more room for the reception of Gospel Truths amongst the members of our Society than in the Quarterly Meeting' which was held on 5th January. Mary Lloyd joined her at three o'clock and they had a large Public Meeting in the Court House, 'supposed to contain 800 people!'

They reached Amersham for Monthly Meeting on 6th January, 'John Wilkinson appeared sweetly in Prayer, as did Ann Crowley after Dinner'. On the 7th Deborah was ill, but was able to have 'a religious opportunity' with Friends who drank tea with them.

They sat with Friends at Wycombe on the 9th in the morning, and had a Public Meeting at Amersham in the evening. They rode on to Chesham the next day and had a Public Meeting there in the evening 'which was a lively season'. They had an opportunity on 11th January with prisoners confined in Aylesbury Gaol, and had in the evening a Public Meeting at Buckingham, which 'although small, owing to its being a very cold evening, was a season of favor'.

They reached Banbury on the 12th January, where they attended a large and satisfactory Meeting, and the day after had an evening Meeting at Ettington. They sat with Friends in their weekday Meeting, and on the 14th had a Public Meeting at Stratford [on-Avon].

Returning to Birmingham on the 16th January for morning Meeting, 'the Young People were preculiarly exhorted to be obedient to the Lord and their parents as the way to obtain the Blessing'. Mary Lloyd was engaged in Prayer, and that evening they had 'a large and favor'd Meeting at Bilston'. Deborah then came home.

On 18th January, Ann Till Adams came to stay, and on 21st Mary Ridgway; these Friends taking part in their Meetings.

February

This pattern continued into February, Jane Watson joining them on the 13th and leaving two days later, her visit being 'very acceptable'. Monthly Meeting at New Dale was on 16th in which Mary Ridgway, Richard Brown and Edward Simkin were engaged. Susannah Appleby at that Meeting obtained 'a Certificate for going with Mary Ridgway towards Bristol and London'.

Deborah on the evening of 20th February 'sat in the families of Richard Reynolds and Richard Dearman'. She went to Shrewsbury on the 24th for weekday Meeting, Ann Till Adams, Priscilla Hannah Gurney and Mary Ridgway going with her. Mary was still with them the day after, as she was 'much favor'd in our Evening Sitting', and they then went again to Shrewsbury where she had 'good service' on 27th February, before leaving on 3rd March with Susannah Appleby for the West.

March

A day later, Deborah and Priscilla Hannah Gurney rode to Nantwich, presumably in a chaise. On 5th March, they attended Meeting in the morning at Sandbach, 'the first that had been held in anyone's remembrance'.

On the 6th the Meetings at Manchester 'were large and solid, that in the evening for those not of our Society'. They called and dined with William Doewray 'to whom counsel was handed' on 7th March, and later had an evening Meeting at Eccles, and a sitting in William Marriot's family. There was Meeting at Crawshay in the morning, and at Hardshaw in the evening next day. They sat at the Select Meeting at Stockport on 9th March, 'to some satisfaction', but the Quarterly Meeting, although large, 'was rather laborious', followed by a small Public Meeting in the evening.

They were at Meeting at Macclesfield on the morning of the 11th and Leek in the evening, 'both attended by People not of our Society, and seasons of favor'. Deborah was engaged in the morning Meeting on 13th March, and at their evening sitting they were joined by Charles Whittle and his wife and her mother Anna Rawes, 'both these female Fds had something to say in the way of Testimony'.

On 14th March, when Sarah Sweatman came to stay they had returned to Sunniside. At Monthly Meeting in the Dale in which Deborah, Priscilla Hannah Gurney and Edward Simkin were all engaged, and also Priscilla Hannah 'spread a concern to visit Middlesex', Deborah also made some remarks in the Women's Meeting.

They went to Worcester for Meeting on the 20th and Sarah Sweatman opened the way for Deborah 'to labour by bearing a short sweet testimony to the truth'. Meeting in the afternoon was attended by those 'not of our Society, occasioned by the Burial of our valuable, ancient Fd Claudia Burlingham'. Deborah was engaged in Testimony and Prayer, and they had an opportunity in the evening with many of her relations.

Deborah visited the Prison on 21st March, and found that 'the love of God flow'd freely to the poor, wandering sheep, some of whom manifested much tenderness'. They drank tea at J. Pumphrey, Jnr.'s, and had an opportunity afterwards. They attended the Select Quarterly Meeting at Birmingham on the 22nd March, Quarterly Meeting following on the 23rd and next day there was a Public Meeting at a Riding School, in which Deborah and Mary Lloyd häd each to 'bear Testimony to the spirituality of the Gospel Day'.

On the 27th Deborah, Priscilla Hannah Gurney and Sarah Sweatman were all engaged; at this time there appeared to be much sickness and influenza among the relations as Mary Rathbone and Richard and Rebecca Reynolds were all ill. Deborah had that evening 'peculiarly to invite the Servants to fear God and give Glory to His Name'.

Susannah Edwards, the grand-daughter of 'our late worthy Fd Ann Summerland, was buried before our Meeting this morning', on 29th March.

Deborah, Priscilla Hannah Gurney and Sarah Sweatman attended New Dale Meeting the day after, and she and Priscilla Hannah paid a visit to Hannah Thomas. On 31st March Sarah Sweatman left to return home, and Deborah went to attend the burial of Rachel Southall at Dudley, which was large, and she was 'exercised both there and in the evening amongst the family that it might be a sanctified season to survivors'.

April

On 1st April, Deborah went to see Richard and Rebecca Reynolds, 'who both continue very ill'. On 6th April, she accompanied Sarah Hume and Sarah Hack to New Dale Meeting 'in which they had good service'; there was also one in the afternoon in the Dale. Deborah then accompanied these Friends to Shrewsbury, where they were all engaged, and on return she went again to see Richard and Rebecca Reynolds, who were still very ill, indeed 'the latter of whom appears to be sweetly closing a useful life'.

Death of Rebecca Reynolds

Two days later, Rebecca Reynolds 'attained her wish of leaving this mortal tabernacle, and peacefully bidding adieu to time. Her close was as her life had been, an honour to the Christian Religion'. On 12th April, 'the Remains of our Beloved Sister were assigned to the Grave, long will she be remembered and the Dead speak. Priscilla Hannah Gurney, Edward Simkin and myself were engaged in Testimony to the Truth – the Meeting was very large and solid'.

Deborah's Concern to Visit Southern Counties and Wales

On 13th April, there was a Meeting in Shrewsbury in which Deborah spread a concern before Friends to visit some of the southern counties and Wales. On the 14th she went with Mary Rathbone, who had evidently recovered, again to Shrewsbury, on her way to Wales.

William and Ann Young and other Friends went with Deborah to Annelly where they had a large and satisfactory Meeting. Sarah Sweatman met Deborah at Whitney where Deborah had a Meeting in a barn 'to some relief'. She then sat in two families at The Hay [on-Wye]. Select Yearly Meeting followed and there 'were sessions in which the poor of the Flock were remembered'. David Sands, Susannah Horne, Sarah Hack, and S. and L. Alexander 'had each a share in the service of these Meetings'. David Sands held a Public Meeting on 21st April.

By the 24th Deborah was back in Shrewsbury for morning Meeting, and on the 26th David Sands was with them in Coalbrookdale, and was 'largely and livingly engaged in our weekday Meeting, as also in a solemn Public Meeting in the evening'. Deborah found herself permitted 'to ask a blessing at the close of each'. She then on 27th April accompanied David to New Dale where 'he had very satisfactory Meetings, and some opportunities in families', in which Deborah was also engaged.

They breakfasted at Arthur Enoch's, and David Sands 'had two open Meetings at Shrewsbury on 28th April and some opportunities in families'.

May

On 1st May Deborah and Priscilla Hannah Gurney 'were each drawn to give counsel' in Richard Reynolds' family at Dale House, and were afterwards able to ask a blessing, for the loss of Rebecca was very recent and a deep sadness.

Deborah and Priscilla Hannah in the ensuing days were engaged in their Meetings and family opportunities, as also was Richard Brown in a morning Meeting on 8th May. There then followed a very important occasion, for on 10th May they were in Worcester for the Meeting, in which Deborah's son Edmund 'was united to Lucy Burlingham'. He had passed some of his apprenticeship in the business of John Burlingham, who, as well as being a successful glover, had also a small business in nails and iron. He employed 800 people who worked chiefly in their own homes in this manufacture, the chief trade of the city. John Burlingham had made gloves for King George III and Queen Charlotte, and several of the Princesses. The King was always kind to the Quakers, speaking to them individually if he met them personally, as he had done to John Burlingham.

Also in Meeting on the 10th May, James Lewis and Mary Beasley were married. David Sands, (whose signature is on the marriage certificate of Edmund Darby and Lucy Burlingham), and John Abbot were publicly engaged, both there and after dinner. They also had an opportunity later 'at the other Inn with the second couple after tea, and their Fnds'.

Lucy was to prove a very suitable and attractive daughter-in-law. She had beautiful deep blue eyes with long dark lashes, which were inherited down the Darby family to the second Alfred Darby's children. She was to bring up her family well, and was again destined early on to have to do this, like so many of the Darby wives, as a widow. Deborah as Edmund's mother was for her remaining years to find their home a pleasure to visit, and their children a joy.

Leaving Worcester after the wedding, Deborah attended Meeting at Evesham on the 11th May, on her way to Yearly Meeting in London, going by Camden, Chipping Norton and Woodstock, and on to Oxford and High Wycombe, in both of which latter Meetings she and David Sands were engaged.

At Meeting at Devonshire House on 15th May, Deborah and William Byrd were engaged, but in the afternoon she was silent. After the Select Meeting on 16th May, 'Ann Alexander spread concern before Fds to visit America'. The day following, Thomas Shillitoe 'spread his prospect of visiting some places on the Continent of Europe'. In the afternoon of that same day, Deborah and Rebecca Byrd went to visit William Raw, who was sick, at Brentford, Deborah conveying 'some encouragement to him'.

Yearly Meeting continued on 18th May, followed by the usual Meetings and Committees the day after, and these were 'reasonably own'd'. They had a 'Religious opportunity at John Raw's after supper'.

Gracechurch Meeting on the 20th, though interrupted, was a 'time of some favor'. They had an opportunity at Joseph Allin's after supper the following day. In Southwark on the 22nd at morning Meeting, Rebecca Byrd concluded with prayer 'after several Testimonies were borne'. They dined at William Mancer's. Devonshire House Meeting in the afternoon 'was largely attended by People of other Societys', and Deborah and S. Lynes 'had the public labour'; Deborah lodged 'in Cousin Stacey's', having an opportunity there after supper.

On 23rd May, the Meeting 'was completely overshadowed', but they had an 'opportunity at John Pim's lodging'. On the 24th they 'had the opportunity of waiting upon the Lord' in John Smith's family, and after attending the Meeting for Discipline, were at a sitting at Jasper Capper's after dinner.

Yearly Meeting ended on 26th May, after which they had a sitting at John Kersey's. Select Meeting was the next day, 'in which, after a time of instruction, Thomas Shillito was liberated to return to America'. They dined at William Allin's on 28th May.

Deborah bore a Testimony at Gracechurch Street on 29th May, and met Rebecca Byrd there, after which they dined and 'had a time of overshadowing' at Charles Dudley's, 'who was under affliction'. She then next day attended Meeting at Clapham which was appointed for David Sands, going on to an evening Meeting at Rochester, where Deborah 'had some counsel to convey'.

Southern Counties and Wales

June

On 1st June they had a large open Meeting at the Assembly Rooms at Margate. They were travelling along the south-east coast visiting the towns, all popular with visitors in summer, so that their Public Meetings were large. On 2nd June they sat with Friends at Drapers[12] in the morning, and in the evening were at Ramsgate. They reached Deal on the morning of 3rd June, Dover in the evening, and sat with Friends at Folkestone on the morning of the 5th where they had a Public Meeting in the evening.

On the morning of the 6th Henry Tuke, Elizabeth Hoyland and Mary Smith were at Meeting and that evening they attended a Public Meeting at Hythe. They had another the day following at Ashford in Kent, and a small 'but tendering Meeting at Cranbrook', and in the evening a large one at Maidstone, 'in which there was much openness to convey Gospel Truths'.

Drapers Almshouses, Margate, Kent.
The first wing built in 1702, with the Clock House in the centre, containing the Meeting House and the Warden's dwelling.

They sat with a Friend's family on the 9th June 'who was solitarily situated', and had a Meeting at Tunbridge in the evening, 'where there appear more strangers to Fds'. After a 'small and trying' Meeting on 10th June at Tunbridge Wells, they were three days later at a Public Meeting at Gravesend. They then rode to Deptford for an evening Meeting, and on the following day again reached Southwark. By the 16th they had a large Meeting in the evening at Peckham. As they were not able to obtain a proper place for a Meeting in the evening of the 17th at Islington, they went to lodge at Cousin Stacey's, and next day had a small Meeting at Hammersmith. Then, on 19th June, with Cousin Stacey accompanying them, they went to a Meeting at Harrow-on-the-Hill. There, John Hull met them from Uxbridge, and 'expressed a few words by way of encouragement to us poor labourers'. After this they had a full Meeting in Westminster Meeting House, and lodged at her Cousin Messers.

They 'drank tea and had an opportunity at the Widow Pim's', before attending on 20th June a Meeting held in a Riding School at Islington, 'in which about 700 people were collected'. On 21st June, they attended a marriage at Southwark, in which Deborah 'asked a Blessing, and Henry

Tuke concluded the opportunity with Prayer'. Deborah and Rebecca Byrd also had a Public Meeting at Brentford.

On 23rd June, they breakfasted at Elizabeth Llynes and then attended a burial at Uxbridge, which was 'a heart tendering season'. The following day they were at Brentford, and in the evening had a 'satisfactory Meeting in a Barn at Slough'.

July

By 3rd July they reached Winchmoor Hill for Meeting, 'both for those not of the Society and some that were of it', and were also at a Public Meeting at Gracechurch Street in the evening.

Next day, with Elizabeth Hoyland and M. Smith, they attended Select Quarterly Meeting at Reigate. Quarterly Meeting on 5th July was successful, and some young people appeared to feel it 'a precious season'. After the other Friends had left the town, Deborah and Rebecca had a Public Meeting. On 6th July, a Meeting was held at Bletchingley in the morning, and at Dorking in the evening. They then rode to Alton on the 7th for evening Meeting. They were at Islington by the evening of 8th July, and a day later 'had a season of retirement in Walter Heath's family', after which they returned to Alton, where they sat with Friends in the morning of the 10th and went for an evening Meeting at Aylesford.

In Claverham weekday Meeting on 20th July, Deborah and William Byrd 'had something to communicate'. Deborah reports that 'also Dr Hannah Stephenson, and myself and my R. Byrd were each enabled to bear Testimony to the Truth in the evening Meeting held at Joseph Nash's'. On the 21st they were called upon by Richard Gregory and others. William Byrd went towards Marnhull, and Deborah and Rebecca attended a Meeting appointed for them at Nailsey, held out of doors, 'to satisfaction'. The following day they rode to Pontypool, and then on 23rd July were with Robert and J. Gregory 'who had kindly accompanied us, and were setting off towards home'.

On 24th July, they sat with Friends, visited the sick, and had a Public Meeting in the evening. They also had an evening Meeting on the 25th with Richard Harford's workmen at Ebbw Vale. Then after an opportunity with his family, they 'rode over the hills to Merthyr and had a tendering Meeting in a large room at an Inn'.

There was Meeting at Cardiff in the evening of the 27th July, and two days later one at the same time of day at Neath. They spent the 30th with Peter Price's family, renewing old friendships with much pleasure. There followed Meeting at Neath on 31st July in the morning, and another at Swansea in the evening, 'which was supposed to be the largest ever held there by Fds, near 1,500 people being collected in a Granary', – Deborah likened it to the feeding of the five thousand.

August

They spent the 1st August with T. and M. Biggs, having an opportunity with the family and also with the workmen in the evening. They had an evening Meeting on 2nd August at Carmarthen, before a trying ride over the hills to reach Newcastle [Emlyn] where fortunately the Meeting was 'satisfactory'. They reached the Irish Sea at Cardigan in the evening of the 4th which they found exercising, as was the night spent at the inn, 'but meeting with some awakening minds made us willing to suffer'.

Going north up the coast they had a small Meeting at Aberystwyth on 6th August, and rode on to Mahuntley [Machynlleth]. The Meeting at Tythingarrick was laborious, as was the one for the people there also; they had an open Meeting at Conway in the morning of the 10th and at Abbergellis in the evening.

There was a Meeting in the Town Hall at Denby in the afternoon of the 11th 'evincing with readiness the people in these parts accept an invitation to attend Religious Meeting'.

Deborah, in one of her rare exclamations on the beauty of the scenes around her, said that on the 12th they had 'a fine ride afterwards through the Valley of Cluied'. Turning south they had a large Meeting at Ruthin on the morning of the 12th and across to Mold in the evening. They then left Wales and reached Chester where they had two large Meetings on the 14th August, 'Friends having enlarged their Meeting House so that it will now contain about 700 people'.

They then turned back to Wales for an evening Meeting on the 15th at Holywell, where they had 'an opportunity after supper with Isabella Wait and her children who were on their way home to Ireland by Holyhead'.

On the evening of the 16th back in England, they had a large Meeting in the Town Hall at Wrexham, and then had a very warm ride to Llangollen where they attended Meeting, after which they rode south for another at Oswestry before making for Shrewsbury and home. They reached Sunniside the next day, the 19th, and took part in their evening Meeting.

Deborah set off for Shrewsbury again on the 21st August for a Public Meeting, and went on next day with Rebecca Byrd to Llanfyllin for a Public Meeting. After a Meeting at Lanfair on the 23rd they 'had an opportunity with the Landlord of the Inn, who was sick'. They attended Wales Half-Yearly Meeting, 'tho' not all it might have been – that for Discipline rather low'.

They finished their business at Newtown and went on to Welshpool on 25th August, to dine, and went back to Shrewsbury to lodge. Rebecca Byrd was with them, and she and Rebecca spoke at their evening sitting on the 26th. Next day, Brother and Sister Burlingham left them, and they dined with Richard Reynolds, also having an opportunity at the home of Mary Rose.

Rebecca and Deborah were engaged in Testimony on 28th August in morning Meeting. The Meeting in the evening was attended by 'some not of our Society, to whom Thomas Clarge and Rebecca Byrd ministered'; Deborah then 'closed an opportunity in prayer'. She spent the day after with relations and Rebecca, and then left for Shrewsbury where they lodged on 29th August. Next day she had to part from Rebecca, reaching the Dale in time for Meeting, which she sat in silence.

September

At Alcester on 1st September, she attended the marriage of Richard Burlingham and Mary Trusted, describing the occasion as having 'infinite kindness condescended to be near both of them and in an opportunity after dinner'.

Their attendances at local Meetings were as usual during September, and on the 14th of the month, Susannah Appleby and Sarah Darby went to Bath. On the 17th Thomas Cash came in the morning, and also John and Sarah Grubb in the afternoon, and they drank tea at the White House with Rebecca Darby, and had a religious opportunity later. These Friends were at Shrewsbury for morning Meeting on the 18th which they sat in silence, but after dinner had an opportunity. Later, John and Sarah Grubb 'went towards Ireland'. Thomas Cash had a favoured Public Meeting that evening, and they had supper at J. Enoch's, at which Deborah 'convey'd some counsel'.

Meeting at New Dale on the 19th September was 'large and solid'. William Cash then left them after sitting the Meeting for Worship on the morning of the 21st in which he ministered 'in that for Discipline'. Deborah 'gave in her Certificate, and had a minute granted to appoint Meetings in this or any neighbouring county'.

She was then at Meetings at Tewkesbury and Gloucester on the 25th August, describing the latter as 'both large and open, in which Love was commended as the best cement in the Heavenly Building'.

She attended Quarterly Meeting on 27th September, 'wherein a renew'd visitation was extended, [to] its different states', both in the Meeting for Worship and that for Discipline. There was also an evening Public Meeting. Her sister Rachel Fowler was also present, and 'acceptably engaged'.

After an opportunity at T. Brown's on the 28th, Rebecca went to Dursley accompanied by Joseph Yenbury [or Yerbury] and his wife, D. Dent, and some young people. This Meeting proved 'large and solid', D. Dent being 'engaged in supplication at the close'.

They had Meeting in Berkley on the morning of the 29th September, held in a Malt House, 'remarkable for its quietude and solemnity', and also an evening Meeting at Shrewsbury.

After visiting John Player, who was ill, they rode to Wooton-under-Edge and later, with some difficulty, reached Painswick for evening Meeting.

October

On 1st October, they visited some young women and attended an afternoon Meeting at Mitchell Dean. After Ross [on-Wye] Meeting on the morning of 2nd October, they dined with T. Pritchard, and there was a Meeting in the Town Hall on the 3rd October. Then they had a 'large and solemn Meeting' in the Town Hall at Hereford.

After a sitting in Walter Chandler's family on the 4th they rode to Leominster for Select Quarterly Meeting. Quarterly Meeting itself was next day, and in the evening a Meeting was held in a large schoolroom. Cousin M. Lewis and Mary Capper had a share of the service in both morning and evening Meetings.

They then had an evening Meeting at Bewdley on the 6th October, where Mary Lloyd met them and was also engaged, and had another at Solihull, spending the next day among their Friends in Birmingham. On the 9th morning Meeting was held among Friends, and they also had one for the people in the evening at Knowle. Deborah and Mary Lloyd had an evening Meeting at Dudley on 10th October. They were at a burial the next day at the same place, and they then dined and had a sitting in Richard Southall's family; Deborah with Sophia Holdship 'were favor'd to get well home'.

Deborah continued to attend local Meetings, a few in silence. John Burlingham was with them on the 23rd; his daughter Lucy who had married Edmund were both living at Sunniside at the time. Susannah Appleby returned from Bath on the 25th. The burial of an ancient Friend, Mary Storey, took place on the 27th October.

November

On 1st November, John Jilkes was at their Meeting. Richard Burlingham, his wife and sister came to stay for a few days, evidently all of them to see how Lucy was settling down in her husband's family.

Deborah then made this entry on 6th November – 'After a time of deep exercise was helped to caution Friends against taking their flight in the winter season, any more than on the Sabbath Day', and she spoke on the same subject during an opportunity in the evening.

She went on the 9th to Shrewsbury with Susannah Appleby, and they spent the evening with Margaret and John Young, returning home next day.

Monthly Meeting was at New Dale on 16th November, which she found a 'suffering time', but 'felt some satisfaction, as certainly one of our first duties is to attend Meetings both for Worship and Discipline'.

December

She continued to be very active into December, often ministering with Susannah Appleby, and on the 4th she explained that she 'also took part in the afternoon Meeting, which I had not done for some time, having been much indisposed, in consequence in part of some close trials, in part arising from my son's [Samuel Darby] marriage and going into the army, and had not Divine Support been near, I must have sunk, but *He* that is the Hope of Israel and Saviour thereof in time of trouble, graciously sustained, tho' at some seasons so secretly that I was scarcely sensible of it'.

Deborah continued to attend Meetings until the end of December, bearing 'testimony to the truth' and so closing a difficult year.

1804
January

Deborah was rather depressed during the first part of the year, because of the ill health of her son Samuel. Robert Fowler, her brother-in-law, brought the young man to Sunniside on 15th January, as he had been staying with these relations at Melksham, and he was still too unwell for Deborah to leave him to go to Meeting the day after his arrival.

Samuel's wife, Frances, came on 18th January to take him to their home in Berwick near Shrewsbury, but he was evidently still in a very disturbed state, and as the situation generally with this daughter-in-law was an unhappy one for Deborah, she cannot have liked Samuel leaving Sunniside when he was so unwell. Robert Fowler left for home on 19th January: Deborah was always glad to see him as he had been such a support to her during the years of her husband's illnesses and after his death.

Susannah and Margaret Fox drank tea with them on 22nd January, but Deborah does not say where they were staying. There were local Meetings during this time, when Deborah, Priscilla Hannah Gurney and Susannah Appleby were all engaged.

Richard Reynolds Leaves Coalbrookdale
February/March

They dined with Richard Reynolds at Dale House on 8th February as he was about to leave Coalbrookdale after having lived there for over 40 years. This move was to take place on 14th February to a house he owned in James's Square, Bristol, accompanied by his cousin Sarah Allen, who had been housekeeping for him since the death of Rebecca, his wife, the year before. His eldest son, William, had also died, but Joseph his other son was still active in the Severn Gorge, managing the Reynolds' interests in the Company and the mines.

Richard Reynolds also intended to concentrate on various philanthropic initiatives, which he thought to be much needed in the great port of Bristol with its large population. He was soon, therefore, to be engaged in new plans for education, the care of the sick, and the alleviation of poverty, and he continued to be so engaged until the end of his life.

The next weeks passed in attending local Meetings and on 17th February Samuel went to Droitwich and Deborah hoped 'that a blessing may attend the means made use of for his recovery'. Priscilla Hannah Gurney, after having lived for 25 years in Coalbrookdale, at Dale House, also decided to leave and on the morning of 19th March set out for Bristol after saying a fond farewell to all her Friends who 'gave her up with reluctance', for she was a charming and much loved person who had made an unusual contribution to their life in the Severn Gorge, driving round in her little carriage to visit them all, and adding words of wisdom to their discourse as well as being a very special presence at their Meetings.

April

Deborah and Susannah Appleby went to Worcester for Select Quarterly Meeting on 3rd April, when they had an opportunity with Sarah Beesley at Mary Capper's house. Deborah then went on to Droitwich on the 5th to see her son, Samuel, when they dined together and she had the satisfaction of believing 'he had all the comforts he is at present capable of enjoying'. Next day Deborah and Susannah travelled home, Samuel Lloyd being with them, and went on to Shrewsbury for Monthly Meeting on 13th April, at which Deborah 'spread a concern before Friends to go into the Northern Counties'.

By 15th April Deborah was at Leominster, accompanied by Susannah Appleby who engaged in Testimony and on 17th April they 'Sat with Fds at The Haye when Joseph Cloud was present'. Returning to Sunniside Deborah set out for London on 8th May for Yearly Meeting. Susannah accompanied her part of the way going by Birmingham and Warwick to attend the funeral of a Friend after which she returned to the Dale.

May

Hannah Evins accompanied Deborah to Banbury on the 12th May and a day later she and Mary Lloyd 'convey'd Gospel Truths' at Sibford in the morning and Chipping Norton in the evening Meeting. On 15th May they had two Meetings at Burford and then went south to Faringdon on the 17th, travelling east on to Henley [on-Thames] and Staines the day after, reaching London the evening of that day. William and Rebecca Byrd spent that evening with Deborah, to their mutual great pleasure, although Deborah does not record where they were staying.

Deborah was engaged in the Select Yearly Meeting when William Crotch spread a 'concern to visit America and Joseph Cloud requested a Certificate in order to return home having finished his service on the 23rd of that month'. Deborah was unwell on 24th May, but after three days she recovered sufficiently to attend a burial at Gracechurch Street on the 28th followed by an opportunity at Wilson Birkbeck's at Tottenham. She was also engaged in the afternoon Meeting at Devonshire House where Rebecca Byrd, J. Abbot and other Friends were 'fellow labourers'. On 29th May she 'attended the Meetings, to my comfort' and dined at Joseph Savory's – he was a goldsmith in the Strand and the cousin of William Savery with whom he stayed when in London. On the last day of the month they attended Devonshire House Meeting and had supper at William Atkins.

June

They dined with Wilson Birkbeck on 1st June and attended Select Meeting when William Crotch was 'liberated to follow his prospects' and Joseph Cloud 'was furnish'd with a certificate to return home'. At Uxbridge on the 3rd June where 'the evening Meeting was attended by many not of the Society' Deborah was joined by Rachel Fowler and other Friends on their way home from Yearly Meeting.

After two opportunities in Friends' families they rode to Chorley Wood for a 'favor'd evening Meeting', and Deborah joined Rebecca Byrd attending an evening Meeting appointed for them at Beaconsfield, although she was still 'very unwell'. With Joseph Cloud she was at Wycombe Meeting next day followed by a Public Meeting at Great Marlow, and she and J. Cloud were engaged at Amersham Monthly Meeting on 7th June, after which they travelled on to Luton and Dunstable.

Visit to the North

They attended a Meeting with Friends in the morning of the 10th June at Ampthill and one in the evening with the people, both to satisfaction, and a Public Meeting at Hitchin was 'a season of encouragement to enquiring minds'. After an opportunity at E. Wheeler's on the 12th Deborah and Rebecca Byrd rode to Biggleswade for an open Meeting. This was a town on the River Ivel and was an important place in Roman times being on a road crossing the river where it was a centre for the agricultural market-garden neighbourhood. The evening Meeting at Stilton next day was 'more trying to our feelings than some we have had of late'.

Morning Meeting held on 14th June was at Peterborough and was 'trying to begin but ended well', and after a sitting with the family of William Massey at Spalding they rode on the 15th to Market Deeping for a 'comfortable Meeting in a Barn'. The following day found them at Stamford and at Cottesworth on the 17th going on to lodge at Joseph Jollins' at

Newark on 18th June. They held a 'large and favor'd Meeting' at Lincoln in the evening and attended Quarterly Meeting next day.

Thomas Cash joined them on the 21st June for Gainsborough Meeting, followed by another at Bawtry held in an inn, and by the 24th, after a Meeting with Friends in the morning, they held a Public Meeting at Thorne. They rode on to Snaith and continued north for a Public Meeting at Selby in the morning of the 26th and attended Select Meeting later. Arriving at York on the 27th June 'the Quarterly Meeting was a season of enlargement in the Love of the Gospel with M(ary) Watson engaged in prayer and D(avid) Sands, Rebecca Byrd and myself in Testimony'. On the 28th Meeting were 'imminently favor'd and we had an opportunity in Lindley Murray's family', and the next day, after an opportunity at a school,[13] Deborah and Rebecca rode north to Thirsk, 30 miles or so, for an evening Meeting. At Northallerton Meeting, 10 miles further north, they found it 'tho' not large appeared acceptable to the People'.

July

After an opportunity in Jonathan Taylor's family they attended an open Meeting in a barn and on the evening of 1st July had a 'large and solemn one at Darlington'. They had a sitting with E. Pearce, who was sick, and rode on to Durham in time for Select Quarterly Meeting on the 2nd. Turning south they were present at Ferryhill Meeting, a mining village in the Durham coalfield and afterwards held one at Sedgefield on 5th July, a pleasant small market-town set in agricultural country on the edge of the coalfields, going on to Newton and Yarm followed by an evening Meeting at Stockton [on-Tees].

After three sittings in Friends' families they turned north to Hartlepool on the coast to hold a Meeting in the Town Hall where they 'found some serious minds'. This was followed on the 10th July by one at Scotton which afforded 'a fresh proof of the Love of Him' and Deborah had a favoured Meeting next day at Easingwold, but there was 'obliged to leave my Beloved Companion sick at the Inn', Rebecca was, however, recovered sufficiently to go on to Sunderland on the 12th for an evening Meeting where they had an opportunity at Cousin Ogden's after supper. Elizabeth Ogden was the widow of Bernard Ogden and a sister of Abiah Darby's favourite nephew William Maude, so family news would be exchanged.

Shields Meeting on 13th July was followed by two public ones at Newcastle 'held in a Store Room supposed to contain a thousand people' – these could be rather difficult and airless occasions, very exhausting to the speakers. On the 16th they 'met with some Collyers a few miles away' and as Deborah was used to coalminers and their families at Ketley and Dawley she understood their difficulties and the hazards of their work. By the 17th July they were at Gateshead Meeting, held in a timber shed containing 800 people and next day after sitting weekday Meeting they left Newcastle for evening Meeting at Hexham. During the next few days Meetings were held at Haltwistle, Brampton, and Longtown, and they reached Carlisle by the evening of the 22nd where they held two 'large and favor'd Meetings for which praise be given to God'.

Scotland

After visiting Scotby they reached Springfield in Scotland on 24th July and dined with Henry Duncan 'a kind clergyman' and attended a Public Meeting at Dumfries. The Annan Meeting on the 26th was 'much crowded and open'.

Returning to Carlisle they visited the Prison and had a Public Meeting in the evening with another at Moorhouse on the 28th July. After a satisfactory sitting in John Harrison's family they attended Wigton Meeting with an evening one at Allonby where 'some young people appear'd to be a good deal affected with the Testimony of Truth'; then riding on to Maryport they had an evening Meeting in a timber yard.

August

By 31st July they were at Holm and Abbyholm, leaving for Workington on 3rd August, and by the 5th 'convey'd counsel at Whitehaven morning Meeting and attended a Meeting of inhabitants in the evening which, with some religious opportunities, occupied [sic] the day pretty fully'. During the next two days they had several opportunities in the family of Isaac Bragg and on 7th August were at Seaton Meeting followed by one at Brigham. Morning Meeting was at Pardshaw and in Cockermouth in the evening, where they dined with 'our Valuable Fds Elihue Robinson and his wife who appear'd lively in advanced age'. The ride to Keswick on 10th August was 'stormy' and at the two Meetings held at Penrith on the 12th they felt 'best help was near'.

Further up into the Dales Meetings were held at Gamblesby, Alston, Coanwood and Allandale, and on 16th August had an 'encouraging testimony from our Valuable Fd Rachel Wigham and I had to address the family and my Rebecca Byrd in prayer'. They then rode 40 miles to hold a late Meeting at Witton [le-Wear] and by the 21st were travelling south for Darlington Monthly Meeting. There was a Public Meeting in the evening at a nearby village together with a religious opportunity in two Friends' families. Next day, after a family visit, they had a large and open Meeting at Ormsby, concluding the day with a sitting at their lodgings.

Next morning Cotherston Meeting was followed by an evening one at Guisborough which was large and satisfactory. On 24th August after a sitting in William Coning's family they held a Meeting later at Whitby 'to our comfort', travelling on for morning Meeting at Staithes, a large and important fishing village where James, later the famous Captain Cook, was apprenticed. In the evening of the 26th they were at a Meeting 'in a Theater at Whitby containing about a thousand people and if it had been twice as large it would have been filled, such is the desire in this place to attend Fds Meetings, and indeed there is reason to believe they are a very Valuable People amongst the inhabitants of this Sea Port – may the Lord prosper his own work amongst them'.

Further down the coast they held an evening Meeting, largely attended and well conducted, at Robin Hood's Bay on the 27th, and after an opportunity next day with the family of 'our very kind Fds J. & J. Saunders we left Whitby for evening Meeting at Pickering'. Deborah dined with her nephew Barnard Dickinson, on the 30th August who then accompanied them to Scarborough where they had a comfortable evening Meeting. Many Friends went south with them next day to Filey for a satisfactory morning Meeting, after which they parted from these Friends, others accompanying them to Bridlington for evening Meeting.

September

They had two Meetings at Hull on the Humber estuary on 2nd September with an evening one inland at Beverley, and on the 4th after a sitting in Joseph Dickinson's family reached Cottingham for an evening Meeting 'amongst an awakened people'; they subsequently held two Meetings at South and North Cave.

York, between 40 and 50 miles away, was reached by 7th September and Meeting there was 'in some measure relieving to us'. After an opportunity at a school[13] they rode on to Leeds for two Meetings, and by 10th September reached Bradford. 'After a sitting in the family of our much Valued Fd Christiana Hustler we had an evening Meeting at Halifax' and on the 12th were at Brighouse weekday Meeting with a public one in the evening. They went on to a solid one at Flockton and by the 14th were at Barnsley Meeting. Morning Meeting was at High Flatts and they sat with Friends at Sheffield in the morning of the 16th at which 'counsel flow'd freely as it did to the inhabitants in the evening who flock'd to Meeting beyond what the house, calculated to hold 1,500, would contain'.

On 17th September Deborah dined with Catharine Aldam at Wansworth, someone she had always known and with whom she had a religious opportunity; this was followed by evening Meeting at Doncaster which was a 'time of instruction'. On 18th September they called upon some sick Friends 'to whom some Gospel Truths were convey'd' and had a Meeting at Ferrybridge. The next day they sat with Friends in their Meeting at Ackworth 'to whom and the Children counsel was opened; they also had two opportunitys in the family and an evening Meeting at Gildersome'.

A Meeting was held on 20th September at Skipton with a public one at Settle, and on the 22nd Deborah had an opportunity with her relations, some of whom accompanied her to Thornton for a 'favor'd Meeting'. On the 24th they visited Mary Marriott, who had lately lost her husband and who accompanied them to evening Meeting at Barnsley. Next a large open Meeting took place at Blackburn held in a Methodist Meeting House, and on the 26th they sat weekday Meeting at Preston, riding on to Lancaster to lodge at the house of their dear Friends James and Hannah Jackson.

After attending two Meetings at Lancaster Deborah left her beloved companion with her sister and attended Monthly Meeting at Kendal, returning to hold a morning Meeting at Preston and an evening one at Langtree.

October

On 1st October they visited 'a young woman who appear'd to be in a decline to whom encouragement flow'd freely', and next day they were at Liverpool for Quarterly Meeting held on 3rd October. They reached Chester for evening Meeting by the 4th, riding on to Shrewsbury to attend two Meetings on the 7th, going home that evening in a post chaise 'being hastened by an account having been brought of the sudden death of our much Valued Fd R[ichard] Dearman who went to bed in usual health and was found Dead in the morning'.

On 8th October Deborah visited Mark Gilpin's family where they had an opportunity: 'he appears to be advancing towards his everlasting rest'. On the morning of 12th October 'Cousin Dearman's remains were consigned unto the silent grave – his memory is Dear to many – who gave their Company on the occasion. M[ary] Lewis and M[ary] Capper with us – they my R. B[yrd] and myself were all publicly engaged'. Deborah's entry for the 13th October was 'our Valued Fd Mark Gilpin was removed this morning – we visited his family and had a religious opportunity at Cousin Dearman's after which some of our friends went to Birmingham'. Morning Meeting on 14th October was silent, but in the afternoon 'my Dr Rebecca Byrd was engaged in Testimony and in the evening Susannah Appleby, myself and also Dr William Byrd, who came last evening, had an opportunity with Mark Gilpin's family'. On 16th October 'the remains of Mark Gilpin were interred at which my Rebecca Byrd and myself ministered and at Monthly Meeting next day I gave in my Certificate'.

She went to Shrewsbury for a Public Meeting on the 18th and next day 'after a solid and sweetly uniting opportunity we parted from our Endeared Fds William and Rebecca Byrd and came home, they going towards Leominster'.

November

Deborah with Susannah Appleby, went to New Dale Meeting on 29th October, and on 1st November they both attended weekday Meeting at Shrewsbury. She attended the burial of Candia Pumphrey on 4th November, lodging with Cousin Lloyd, and next day Jane Young, with Deborah, arrived at Worcester where they dined with Stanley Pumphrey and took tea with John Pumphrey.

December

During the next few weeks Deborah attended local Meetings and visited sick Friends, but on 12th December she, with Susannah Appleby, attended a Meeting at Nantwich and went to Quarterly Meeting at Middlewich in which David Sands ministered. After morning Meeting at Macclesfield and two opportunities in Friends' families they went to two Meetings at Chesterfield, and 'after sitting in a Fds family rode to Mansfield to attend Select Meeting'. By the 20th they were at weekday Meeting at Nottingham with a satisfactory public one in the evening.

Next day they breakfasted at George Bott's and had a time of favour with his family and later had a Meeting at Loughborough. By the 22nd they were at a Meeting at Castle Donnington, dining with Joseph Fallows whose 'Ancient Mother Ruth Fallows appear'd glad to see us'. Two Meetings were then held at Leicester and on the 24th after a sitting in Cousin Joseph Burgess's family they rode to Hinckley, going on to Select and Quarterly Meetings at Coventry during the next two days.

1805
January

Deborah opened her Journal for 1805 with these sentences – 'A New Year commences, how awfully rapid is the progress of time, how difficult to keep pace with it. On this subject I had to speak at our weekday Meeting and to petition for strength to walk worthy of our *holy vocation.*'

Joseph Huntley of Sibford Gower, Oxon, was at Meeting on 10th January. He was the son of the schoolmaster Thomas Huntley of Burford, whose family, with that of the Palmers, were to found the well-known firm of biscuit manufacturers, Huntley and Palmers in 1822.

Deborah and Susannah were at Shrewsbury morning Meeting on 17th January, and also went there for Monthly Meeting three days later.

Jessy Kersey from Pennsylvania then came to stay at Sunniside and was present at their Meeting and at a Public Meeting on the evening of the 21st January. Deborah accompanied him to New Dale for a further Meeting, where Jessy was 'livingly engaged in counselling the youth, and had in the evening a precious opportunity in our family'. These moments, at this time of the year, were by candle and firelight in the comfortable home over which Sarah Darby presided, making this house a family centre which she ruled from her room, where her desk was littered with papers, and was described as 'not unlike a lawyer's office', as she frequently gave guidance in the conduct of the business as well as in family matters. Deborah had fallen in with this direction, being away so much from home, and Susannah Appleby, so long one of this circle, was in a sense 'in waiting' to Sarah, although she too travelled quite frequently with Deborah and other Friends.

Deborah, during Jessy's visit, went with him to Shrewsbury, at which place 'he had many Gospel Truths to convey in a Public Meeting', which Deborah concluded in prayer.

They went to weekday Meeting on 24th January, later having an opportunity at the Clark's, where presumably they had dined, and coming home in time for tea. On 25th January they had a large and favoured Meeting at Dale Meeting House in the evening, their American Friend leaving them next day for Birmingham.

February

During the rest of January and well into February Deborah attended and ministered at local Meetings, where she mentioned Susannah as taking part with her.

March/April

On 1st March she told of the grave illness of Mary Gilpin, whose death followed on the 9th, and the burial took place three days later, after a 'solid Meeting'. Deborah left on 13th March for Kidderminster, going on to Worcester, the day after weekday Meeting. On 14th March she was at Tewkesbury, and found that 'Divine Goodness was near' in an evening Meeting at Stroud on the 15th. There was a Meeting at the same time of day at Frenchay the day after, and they reached Bourton [on the Water] on the morning of the 17th and had a Public Meeting that evening, and then visited the Prison the following day.

On 21st April, they began a series of family visits at Birmingham, and went on with this work for several days; Deborah 'had something to communicate in each of the Meetings'; and they were joined by Rachel Fowler on 8th May at a Public Meeting.

May

Birmingham was rapidly developing in importance as a place of many trades, with much of the activity carried on in the homes of the artisans in their small workshops. The circle of Friends in the heart of the Midlands influenced the organisation of commerce and finance, as well as the inauguration of charitable institutions for health and education. The Lunar Society was promoting research and innovation, in which were a number of members they knew, such as Josiah Wedgewood and Samuel Galton.

Deborah finished her account of this particular visit by saying that they 'closed their arduous engagement on the morning of 9th May', and went on to Coleshill, where they had a Public Meeting in the evening.

They had a large evening Meeting at Bedworth on 10th May, and reached Warwick on the morning of the 12th moving on to Leamington Spa later that day. They went south to Radway on the morning of the 13th and on to Shipston [on-Stour] that evening. They then visited Sally Lambley's family a day later, and went to Meeting at Brailes.

There was a Meeting at Charlbury on the morning of 15th May, and a small one in Oxford that evening. At Shillingford they attended a Public Meeting, and another at Brentford on 17th May, lodging with Cousin Stacey at Hampstead the day after. Back once more in London they attended Westminster Meeting on the morning of 19th May, and dined at Cousin Messer's, and went to Devonshire House Meeting that evening.

Select Meeting was on 21st May, and Yearly Meeting began a day later, 'under a grateful sense of His Love who is the same today as yesterday unchangeably good'. They were by then lodging at John Smith's, going to Southwark Meeting on the 24th and Devonshire House all that day where 'Gospel Truths flow'd freely'.

Deborah attended the burial of their Honourable Friend William Tomlinson on 25th May and met William and Rebecca Byrd afterwards at John Lloyd's, where they all dined. John was the third son of Sampson Lloyd II and Rachel Champion. He had married Elizabeth, daughter of Thomas Corbyn of Bartholomew Close near the Royal Exchange and was in his father-in-law's firm of Hanbury, Taylor, Lloyd and Bowman. John and Elizabeth lived in a house in Tower Street and he was at that time a man of 54, described as 'full of trust and simplicity' and had become very prominent in the campaign against slavery.

The Women's General Meeting closed on 30th May, in which they had been visited by Jessy Kersey, William Jackson and Joseph Bevan; they dined that day at Thomas Compton's. Select Meeting was held on the evening of 31st May, and on 1st June they left London after visiting several Friends. They attended Tottenham Meeting in the morning and had an opportunity at William Dilwyn's and a Meeting at Epping in the evening, which 'William Foster closed with lively supplication'.

June

They had an evening Meeting on 3rd June at Chelmsford, and reached Thaxstead for Monthly Meeting the day after, followed by one for the people in the evening. They had an evening Meeting at Halstead on 5th June, and after weekday Meeting and visiting a sick Friend there, rode on to Sudbury, where they attended Meeting in the new Meeting House.

They went on to Bury [St Edmunds], visiting families, and had a Public Meeting on the 7th. The next day they spent at Needham with the Alexanders. This would have been very pleasant with the fine garden full of summer flowers. On 9th June they 'found their way opened both publicly and privately' at Ipswich, 'and for the help afforded we desire to return praise where due'.

They had a comfortable Meeting at Manningtree in the morning of the 10th and were at Colchester Select Meeting later. Quarterly Meeting was on 11th June, and they had a Public Meeting on the morning of 12th when Susannah Horne was with them, as well as Mary Round. In the evening they went to Meeting at Kelveden, in which Mary Alexander also joined them, and later were at Joseph Dockwray's, where they lodged.

They then visited William Grover, where they parted from their ancient Friend George Gibbons. Later they had a satisfactory Meeting at [St] Albans in the evening of 14th June, going on to Uxbridge and an evening Meeting at Longford on 15th June.

There followed a large Meeting at Maidenhead in the morning, and later one at Reading on 16th June. The next day they reached Basingstoke and Whitchurch, and on the 18th with Friends and others arrived at Andover.

The 19th June found them attending Monthly Meeting at Salisbury, where next day Quarterly Meeting was 'a favor'd season'. They parted from William and Rebecca Byrd on the 21st, Deborah and Hannah Rake riding on to Sherborne for breakfast, where the former had a religious opportunity afterwards in J. James's family. That evening they had a large and satisfactory Meeting at Chard.

They were with Friends in Exeter in the morning of 23rd June, where they had a Public Meeting in the evening, all being satisfactory, as well as visits to Friends' families.

'Gospel Truths flow'd freely to the People' at Dartmouth the day after, and on the 25th they went to morning Meeting at Modbury, which, with a sitting in William Prideau's family, 'were seasons of favor', as was the Select Meeting at Plymouth. They were disturbed by 'a fire about 7 o'clock in the morning, which was very near some houses of our Friends, which were wonderfully preserved'. Quarterly Meeting, though smaller from this circumstance, was a 'season of favor, as was a Public Meeting in the evening'.

On 27th June, there was an opportunity in a Friend's family and at Plymouth Dock a Public Meeting, which was not so large as they would have hoped, and the following day they had some opportunities in Friends' families, followed by another Public Meeting at Plymouth. An evening Meeting at [St] Germans on the 29th June was followed next day by two Meetings at Liskeard, which were 'large and satisfactory'.

July

They had an evening Meeting at Callington on 1st July, held in a Methodist Meeting House, and an open Meeting at Looe followed next morning. Quarterly Meeting at Liskeard was 'a season in which much counsel was convey'd to the People', and an evening Meeting at Tavistock followed on 3rd July.

On 4th at Moretonhampstead, the other side of Dartmoor, there was a 'large and favor'd' Meeting in the morning, and they reached Cullompton the next day where they met 'our Dear Friends Wm. and R. Byrd, – this Meeting and one in the evening were favourably own'd'. An evening Meeting in a schoolroom at Uffculme 'afforded some comfort to my mind', and a day later, on the 7th they had a 'large and favor'd Meeting' at Ulverton in the morning, followed by one at Wellington in the evening, which 'with two Religious opportunities afforded cause for thankfulness'.

On 8th July they had several religious engagements at Wellington, the last of which was with Mary Were 'who died that day week, after having been an ornament to the Church many years'.

After Meetings at Ilminster and Taunton, there was a Public Meeting at Crookham on the evening of 9th July, after which they went on for a Public Meeting at Yeovil, 'which was small'.

Weekday Meeting followed on the 11th at Compton, and after an evening Meeting on the same day at Sherborne they went on to Sturminster [Newton] and Marnhill and south to Pool – both of the latter 'to some relief of my own mind'. They sat with a 'family in affliction' on the 15th and had a Meeting with Friends 'in which a renew'd invitation was extended to lift up a Standard for the Prince of Peace'. They then went to Meeting at Beer Regis 'amongst a People little acquainted with Fds who conducted themselves agreeably'.

After Meetings at Blandford, Marnhill and Shillington, they attended on 20th July the burial of William Norris at Shaftesbury, and ministered in conjunction with R.B.H. to a 'pretty large assembly'. A Meeting with Friends on the morning of the 21st was followed by a larger one in the evening in a barn at Gillingham. They went to a comfortable Meeting at Bruton in the morning of 22nd July and another at Shepton Mallet in the evening which was 'too much crowded'.

By 24th July they had reached Claverham where they had a 'favor'd' opportunity at R. Gregory's in the morning, also at J. Nash's', and at six o'clock a Meeting in a large barn at Churchill, 'which was solemnized and comfortable'. An evening Meeting in Bristol was followed by weekday Meeting on the 26th and then evening Meeting in Coalpit Heath 'in each of which Divine Regard was evinced unto Different States'.

On the 27th 'after a favor'd opportunity in Brother R.R.'s [Richard Reynolds] family, my dear Fds W. and R. Byrd set out towards home, and P.H. [Priscilla Hannah] Gurney and myself went to drink tea with our ancient Fd John Gayner, who appears green in old age'.

They were 'largely engaged' in a Meeting at Bristol on 28th July, 'supposed to consist of 1,000 persons'. Monthly Meeting at Chew on 29th July was 'a solid opportunity', and they were at a large Meeting at Bath in the evening. On the 30th 'was at a large Meeting at Melksham to my comfort; M. Jeffry's was acceptably engaged in supplication'.

August

On 2nd August they rode to Bromham 'where tenderness appeared among the People', and then an evening Meeting at Calne, with a sitting in a family there; 'here my dear Sister Fowler left us'.

By 5th August they came to Minchinhampton where a large Meeting in the evening was held in a 'Dissenting Meeting House'. They went on to Nailsworth and Painswick and on the 7th had two Meetings at Cheltenham. They sat weekday Meeting at Tewkesbury, reaching Kidderminster by the evening of 9th August, where the Meeting 'was not as satisfactory as it might have been, had more notice been given'.

They returned to The Dale on the 11th and at Meeting there, 'P.H. Gurney was engaged in Prayer, and myself in Testimony'. Deborah and Priscilla Hannah Gurney dined at The Hay on 15th August and Brother Reynolds with William and Hannah Mary Rathbone and Anna Price sat the evening Meeting on 16th August in silence. On the 18th Anna Price and Deborah attended New Dale Meeting 'in which best help was near', and at an opportunity after dinner at Cousin Joseph Reynolds', they attended evening Meeting in which Sarah Charman a Friend from Reigate ministered, as also did Anna Price. On 21st August, 'we had the Company of many Strangers' at Salop Monthly Meeting, and the day after Wales Half-Yearly Meeting was held, in which 'it was supposed there were 50 Strangers – J. & S. Hadwin and George Jones with Sarah Charman and John and E. Bludwick were among the Strangers now acceptably with us'.

On 23rd August Deborah and Susannah Appleby visited Hannah Holtham, 'who appears not likely to continue long in mutability', and at their·evening sitting they had the company of 'many Strangers', amongst their number John Abbot and Hannah Evans; 'with our own family we sat down about 40, to whom John Abbot, P.G. and S.A. ministered and I closed the opportunity with Prayer'.

September

After morning Meeting on 1st September Richard Reynolds and Sarah Atkins left them. The following day Priscilla Hannah Gurney and Deborah paid a visit to Mary Sankey, and afterwards Priscilla Hannah Gurney went towards Wales, to join Sarah Charman at The Hay, they having a prospect of uniting in a visit to South Wales. The burial of Hannah Holtham took place on 3rd September, and the day after Cousins J. and M. Birkbeck and their daughter Hannah came to stay until the 5th when they left together with Brother Fowler and Cousins S. and E. Bradley. Weekday Meeting took place on the 17th and the following day Deborah received her Certificate to visit Worcester and Herefordshire.

On 22nd September Deborah and Rebecca Byrd attended morning Meeting at Evesham, and in the evening nearly a thousand people gathered at the Town Hall there. They left for Alcester the morning after for a Meeting with Friends and an evening Meeting at Alveston.

After a Meeting at Ettington and Select Quarterly Meeting at Warwick, they had a Public Meeting at Barford, and on the 26th sat with John Whitehead and later went to two Meetings at Coventry, the second of which was 'largely attended by People of other Societys'.

On the morning of the 28th William and Rebecca Byrd departed for Worcester, and Deborah and Cousin Sargeant went on to Uttoxeter, where there was 'a large and favor'd Meeting, and an opportunity in two families'.

Meetings at Leek in the morning of 29th September and Macclesfield in the evening 'were occasions own'd'. There was a Meeting at Morley on the morning of the following day, and Select Quarterly Meeting at Manchester in the evening.

October

Monthly Meeting on 1st October 'was large and solid, M. Routh closed it with Prayer'. Deborah went on to dine at Cousin Isaac Crewdson's, where she had a religious opportunity.

Quarterly Meeting was on the 2nd, 'a time of favor', and they dined at David Dockwray's. There was a Public Meeting in the evening at Stockport, 'M. Routh joined in labour, and we had an opportunity after supper'. On the 3rd they attended a 'large and truly comfortable' Meeting at Congleton in the morning, and another one at Tunstall in the evening. Evening Meeting at New Dale was on the 4th where Deborah found Rebecca Byrd. A Meeting with Friends at Salop was held in the morning of 7th October, and with the people that same evening, going on the following day for evening Meeting at Leominster with weekday Meeting at Bromyard on the 9th. After Meetings at Worcester (where they also entered on a family visit), Stourbridge and Dudley, they attended Monthly Meeting at

Bromsgrove. On the 20th they finished their visits to the families at Worcester, and after a large Meeting there in the evening, went on to Tewkesbury and Gloucester.

Monthly Meeting was held on the 22nd October at Cheltenham, 'at which a renew'd invitation appeared to be extended to some Young People', and there was a Public Meeting at Painswick in the evening.

After weekday Meeting at Nailsworth on 24th October and some opportunities in families, William and Rebecca Byrd set off towards [Chipping] Sodbury on their way home, and Deborah attended a large evening Meeting in the Assembly Rooms in Gloucester. There was 'a solid Meeting' at Cobberly on the evening of the 26th held in a Friends house 'in which I had to admire the order that prevailed in seating and accommodating the People, who behaved well'.

On 27th October, they attended Meeting in a 'Meeting House situated about half way to Monmouth, . . . and it was thought there were 1,000 people collected in the evening in the Town Hall in Monmouth, to whom my heart was enlarged in Love'.

They sat with Friends at Ross and went to evening Meeting in Hereford, and by the 29th October were at Ludlow, 'which closes my present engagement, and may I be truly thankful to Him who has been my Helper'.

On the 30th Deborah 'got well home, and finding all my Dear Connections in Health calls for thankfulness'.

November

During the first weeks in November, Deborah was engaged in local Meetings, and on the 20th Monthly Meeting took place at New Dale, 'in which towards the end I was engaged to ask a Blessing'. Morning and evening Meetings took place on the 24th and weekday Meeting was on the 27th.

December

On 1st December, Deborah wrote that 'Our Meetings have been exercising of late, but we were refreshed and edified by the company of John Cash'. On the 8th she attended Salop morning Meeting, and was at evening Meeting at Nantwich on the 11th 'to good satisfaction'. Quarterly Meeting at Middlewich the following day was 'a season of favor', as was a Public Meeting in the evening, and a Meeting at Burslem on the 13th 'met with some tender People'.

There was a Meeting at Stone in the morning of the 15th and Stafford in the evening 'both seasons own'd, tho' the latter was not so still as might have been desired. I lodged with a person that appeared to be piously disposed'.

After Meetings at Rugeley and Lichfield, Monthly Meeting was held at Coalbrookdale on 18th December.

A 'satisfactory' Meeting at Warwick on the 20th was followed by a visit to the Prison 'in which Divine Regard was manifested to its inhabitants'. On the 22nd Deborah, accompanied by several Friends from Warwick, attended a Meeting at Daintry [Daventry] in the morning, after which she attended Select Quarterly Meeting at Northampton. A Public Meeting followed the next day at Wellingborough, and then Meetings at Finedon and Irchester on 24th December. A Meeting in a barn was held at Doddington in the morning of the 25th after which they dined with Mary Barns and attended Meeting in the evening at Northampton.

Deborah dined with her 'valued Fnd William Symonds' on the 26th and after sitting in a family the following day, attended Eydon Meeting, and Banbury Meeting in the evening. Deborah wrote on 28th December that she had 'a trying ride to Witney' for an evening Meeting, and then had two Meetings at Oxford, 'the People behaved very well'.

Quarterly Meeting followed on the 30th December, and after an evening Meeting at Chipping Norton, Deborah closed the year with a Select Meeting at Worcester on 31st.

1806
January

Quarterly Meeting at Worcester was a time to be 'thankfully remembered' on 1st January 1806 and next day, after visiting the prison, they had a Meeting in a village called St Johns and reached home on 3rd January to find everyone well, but unfortunately Deborah herself became ill during the next few days; however, by the 19th she was once more able to attend Meeting.

February

On 12th February she and Susannah Appleby were in Shrewsbury and had a 'precious opportunity with Mary and John Young [Junior]' and dined with Ann Clark. Deborah's son Samuel was with her in Shrewsbury and they returned home together. Deborah had an opportunity on 19th of the month at the home of Edward Simkin, and visited Henry Boxall who 'is very ill but in a sweet frame of mind'.

March

On 16th March she dined with Edmund and Lucy Darby at Dale House; Robert Barnard her brother was also there. At Monthly Meeting at the Dale on 19th March Deborah spread a concern before Friends to visit Friends' families in Devonshire House Monthly Meeting and also parts of Gloucestershire and Somersetshire.

Ann Dickinson gave birth to a son at half-past ten in the morning of the 20th March at The Haye. Deborah attended Warwickshire Select Quarterly Meeting on the 25th March and on 4th April the burial of Henry Boxall.

April

On the 6th April she sat with Edmund's family at Dale House in the evening as he intended to go to London next day on account of 'a Tax proposed to be laid on Iron', and on the 8th Susannah Appleby and Deborah set out for Wales, lodging at Welshpool and attending Meeting at Newtown on the 10th. After sitting with Friends at Lanidloes [Llandudno] they had a Public Meeting on the 13th April and 'got with Difficulty to Meeting on account of snow, but were comforted together – also at Joan Bowen's in the evening'. It was late in the season for snow falls which made travelling in that country much more difficult.

On the evening of the 15th April they attended Select Half-Yearly Meeting and rode to Nailsworth for a Public Meeting on the 17th, and by the 20th were at Melksham with a Meeting in the evening at Devizes. Deborah was very glad, as always, to be able to meet there 'my Dear Fds William and Rebecca Byrd'. After lodging at Uxbridge they reached London on the 22nd to attend the marriage of William Allen and Charlotte Hanbury, and Deborah met with a cordial reception at Devonshire House Meeting when she spread her concern to visit families. By the 27th April she and Rebecca Byrd had visited seven of these each day, finding this a tiring and 'laborious work – [though] the kindness of our Fds is very great'.

May

The first two weeks of May were spent attending various Meetings; they also dined with Joseph Chorley, and Cousin Stacey. On the 24th she visited men Friends with Ann Dyamond, and next day attended Gracechurch Street Meeting where she ministered to the 'People and dined at Jasper Capper's and drank tea with Hannah Stammers'.

June

Deborah was at the burial of Eliza Foster at Ratcliff on 5th June and the following day at Meeting in Guildford and visiting families in Godalming where Meetings were also held.

Visit to the South-West

They travelled on to Basingstoke, Andover and Salisbury and on the 16th June reached Winchester in the evening where they 'had the company of many French Prisoners'. Quarterly Meeting for Ministers and Elders [Select Meeting] was held at Glastonbury on the 17th and on the 19th June Deborah's 'beloved Fds Wm and Rebecca Byrd went home', but other

Friends accompanied her to Wells where they had a 'large and relieving Meeting and an opportunity at table – afterwards I proceeded to French Hay', where Deborah and her 'Dear Sister Fowler entered into family visits', and later they were at Quarterly Meeting for Gloucester and Wiltshire held at Frenchay. After several more Meetings they arrived at Bristol for Monthly Meeting on the 27th June, and on the 29th had an 'open time with Fds there in the morning and with the inhabitants in the evening'. Deborah visited Richard Reynolds on the last day of the month and by the 1st July she was at the home of Rachel Fowler at Melksham ministering at Trowbridge Meeting later that day where Robert and Rachel Fowler joined her, also D. Dent.

July

They rode to Salisbury on the 2nd July to attend Quarterly Meeting followed next day by a Public Meeting at Wilton in which 'Priscilla Hannah Gurney united with my Rebecca Byrd and myself in labour'. During the next few days she stayed with the Byrds at Marnhull. They went to Shaftesbury Meeting on the 10th July and dined at James Isaac's. After attending a Meeting appointed for them at North Petherton she parted from 'my Beloved Fds William and Rebecca Byrd and my sister and self proceeded for Ilminster', attending the Meeting there in the morning of the 13th and Taunton in the evening. An 'open season' was held at the Wellington Meeting next day, and another Meeting at Cullompton in the evening.

On the 15th July they attended two Meetings at Exeter, with a laborious journey to Kingsbridge which ended with a satisfactory Meeting. They travelled on for the next few days into Cornwall holding Meetings, reaching Lew [Looe] to sit with Friends on the 22nd July and in the evening met with the people of Liskeard. They visited Francis Fox at Parr on the 24th July 'who had been long indisposed' and went to [St] Austell, where they had a Meeting with Friends in the morning and with the inhabitants in the evening.

The next day they attended a small Meeting at Germans in the morning and a large one at the Penryn Wharf in the evening, 'both to satisfaction'.

After a sitting with George Fox's family they dined on the 26th at the home of R. Fox. This was followed by an open Meeting at Penryn, also two Meetings were held on the 27th with Friends in the morning and the inhabitants in the evening.

They went to an evening Meeting at Flushing and afterwards on the 29th an agreeable parting opportunity with George Fox's family, followed by an evening Meeting at Penzance.

On the 30th they were at Marazion in the morning and Hale [Hayle] in the evening and on the last day of July had two Meetings at Redruth 'to satisfaction'.

August

The 1st August found them at Portreath in the morning and Truro that evening and they lodged in the family of William Tweedy, who were 'under convincement'. They attended two Meetings at Wadebridge on 3rd August and another two on the following day, 'the last in Launceston'. An evening Meeting at Crediton on the 5th they found 'exercising' and were at Uffculme next day with Friends in the morning, reaching Wellington for Meeting the same evening. After a sitting in Thomas Fox's family they were at a Meeting with Friends at Milverton in the morning and 'in conjunction' with Ann Dyamond went to a Public Meeting in Dunster in the evening.

The 10th August was 'a Day of some favor, both to the Members of our Society and others at Bridgwater'. They reached Bath on 12th August usually having held two Meetings on each day. They sat with Friends at Bristol in the morning of the 15th with a Meeting for the people in Temple Street Meeting House in the evening, and next day called upon the 'Widow James at Newton on our way to Cardiff where we lodged at John Harford's to attend the Select Half-Yearly Meeting at Neath'.

They visited a sick Friend at Swansea on the 20th August followed by an opportunity at Thomas Biggs' family and a Public Meeting at the Copper Works. 'After a uniting opportunity at our Fds Peter and Anna Price we rode to Merther [Merthyr Tydfil] for an evening Meeting', and they breakfasted at Dowlas with an opportunity in Thomas Guest's family. On 24th August they sat with the people at Ebbwr Vale with an open Public Meeting at Pontypool later. After visiting with the family of James and Mary Lewis they parted from 'our Beloved Fds R. & A. Gregory but little expected it was to be a final one with respect to A.G. but so it proved'.

They continued their journey, riding to Ross and Ledbury to hold Meetings and arrived at Worcester on the 28th August to dine at Cousin Bradley's and visit a sick Friend. Deborah 'got home on 29th and desire to be thankful for the many blessings dispensed to me'.

Again in Coalbrookdale

September

On 7th September, after morning Meeting, Sister Sarah Darby and Susannah Appleby went to Bath, and on the 11th Deborah with Priscilla Hannah Gurney and Lucy Darby went to Shrewsbury where 'during the morning Meeting the Meeting House gave an awful crack, but we kept still and mercifully escaped hurt, but it was afterwards taken down'.

Deborah gave in her Certificate on 17th September and requested leave to attend Quarterly Meeting at Liverpool. At the Meeting on the 21st 'Priscilla Hannah Gurney was engaged in supplication after which Edmund Darby read the Yearly Meeting Epistle to the tendering of some of our minds'.

Cousins Wilson and G. Birkbeck came with Mary Hoare on the 22nd, then on the day after Arthur Enoch came to bid us farewell. He is going with his family to settle at Merther. The next weekday Meeting was silent and Deborah dined with the Edmund Darbys at Dale House; she spent the 25th at 'Cousin Joseph Reynolds with our relations. Next day, the 26th, Priscilla Hannah Gurney and myself had an open Public Meeting at Leek'; another at Stockport was followed by two at Manchester, and they were at Quarterly Meeting at Liverpool on the 1st October.

October

After dining with Cousin Benson, and an opportunity at Cousin Hadwen's family, Deborah attended Meetings at Prescot and Penketh, and by the 4th attended Meeting at Frandley accompanied by John and Elizabeth Bludwich. They sat with Friends at Warrington and attended a Public Meeting at three o'clock and 'at the request of some serious people had another at their Meeting House at 7 o'clock which tended to our Peace'.

They rode on to Frodsham and Chester next day and after a sitting with Friends at Shrewsbury got home on 8th October, accompanied by Robert and Hannah Barnard who were 'coming to settle at Coalbrookdale'. This was pleasing to Deborah who had always found her brother an intelligent and pleasant companion. Local Meetings followed during the next week or so and on the 22nd October our 'Beloved Fd Priscilla Hannah Gurney left us'.

November

'My Sister Sarah Darby was taken very ill on the 5th November so as to raise a doubt respecting her recovery', but on the 7th 'Dr Darwin came to give us some hope of her recovery which happily took place.'

On the 23rd November Deborah's Cousins F[rancis] and S[arah] Fox, their daughter and Cousin John Birkbeck Junior were with them for several days as well as Robert Fowler. Cousin Fox, Deborah and Susannah Appleby were all engaged in New Dale Meeting. Hannah Barnard was at evening Meeting on the 28th and Robert Fowler made some addition, Deborah being also engaged. On the 30th in their morning Meeting, Deborah 'had to enlarge on various parts of the Book of Moses' and in the evening they had a large Public Meeting at the Dale.

December

Deborah and Susannah Appleby were in Shrewsbury on 7th December where they had a Public Meeting in a room 'kindly lent us by the Heads of the Manufactory, which was an open season as was the opportunity in their family afterwards'. Deborah attended local Meetings during the rest of the month until the 22nd December when she was with 'Mary Lloyd at Amsley' and at Select Meeting at Coventry. There they dined with Joan Gibbons.

At Quarterly Meeting on 24th December, G. Jones and M. Lewis were engaged in public Labour and there was a Public Meeting at Kenilworth, and on the 25th she sat with Friends at Warwick: then on to Kineton and Ettington. They spent the morning of the 27th with 'our aged Fds J. & B. Bevington who are lively in spirit' and after dining with J. and M. Lowe had a Meeting at Tredington that evening.

After an opportunity at Cousin Lumbly's family, they were at a Public Meeting at Long Compton and another at Chipping Norton, and on the 29th December went to Burford Meeting in the morning and attended Select Quarterly Meeting at Cirencester in the evening. The last day of the year they attended Quarterly Meeting where Priscilla Hannah Gurney opened with Prayers and Deborah was engaged in Testimony.

1807
January

Deborah paid a visit to 'Dear Hannah Bowley who is very ill' on 1st January, dined at Joseph Yerbury's and went to Meeting at Tetbury in the evening. They were at Nailsworth for morning Meeting on 2nd and had 'a large Meeting about 2 miles from Minchinhampton in a Chappel'. On the morning of 3rd January they attended 'Meeting in a large room at "The Fleece" and another in the Methodist Meeting House at Gloucester in the evening, both to good satisfaction'.

They went on to Cheltenham and Tewkesbury where they were 'with Fds in the morning and the People in the evening', reaching Evesham by the 5th where Susannah Horne joined them. After sitting with Friends and dining in William Robert's family, Priscilla Hannah Gurney, who had been with them, returned to Bristol, and Susannah Horne and Deborah attended Worcester Select Quarterly Meeting, where both were engaged.

Death of Deborah's Grandson, Samuel

On the way home on 8th January they went to evening Meeting in Bridgnorth, arriving at Sunniside next day where Deborah found 'our Dr little Samuel very ill' (the son of Edmund and Lucy) and she wrote sadly 'Sat with our sweet Babe who closed his precious Life this evening at about half past 4 o'clock, happy spirit thus to be released from the conflict of time, at about five months old, by convulsion fits'. Deborah and Susannah Appleby endeavoured to give consolation to Edmund and Lucy the following day. These sad little scenes took place at Dale House and on 14th January 'the Dear Babe was consigned to the silent grave and we were afterwards favor'd together in our weekday Meeting'. John Blows, who had accompanied them from Worcester, then returned home with John Burlingham, who had attended his little grandson's funeral.

February

During the next few days Deborah attended local Meetings and on 15th February Ann Dickinson had a daughter, to be called Mary; these family events were almost always entered into the Journal with a degree of real thankfulness.

March

On the 8th March Deborah attended morning Meeting and had a Public Meeting in the schoolroom at The Bank in the evening, which must have been large enough for this purpose. They lodged with Hannah Reynolds who was living at The Bank as a widow with her children. On 10th March Deborah went with Francis Darby, her nephew, to Monthly Meeting at Leek. She attended a Meeting at Congleton in the evening, where there were several Friends from Macclesfield. Next day they breakfasted at John Barlow's followed by Select Quarterly Meeting held at Stockport, in which Deborah 'had to revive the situation of the Prophet when sitting under the Juniper Tree, when he said that Death was better than Life'.

Quarterly Meeting on 12th March was large 'and favor'd'. John Thorpe and Deborah that evening 'had a large Meeting at Macclesfield held in the Methodist Meeting House supposed to contain 2,000 people'. Next day, after sitting in William Paxton's family, they rode to Newport for a Meeting where Edward Simkin also had 'some of the public labour'. After breakfasting with the Bankes family, where they had a 'religious opportunity', they got safely home. They lodged on 17th March with Joseph Reynolds at Ketley Hill for a Meeting at Lilleshall: Joseph had lived at that house since undertaking the direction of part of the Company owned by the Reynolds' family and had married Deborah Dearman, a niece of Richard Dearman.

Concern to Visit Ireland, Scotland and Northern Counties

Deborah then 'spread a concern before Fds to visit Ireland, Scotland and some of the Northern Counties'.

They held Meeting in a large room at Richard Bollus' on the 19th March and after being at morning Meeting she went to a public one at Sheriffhales, a village south of Newport, lodging at The Hay where they had a comfortable opportunity after dinner. They attended a Public Meeting at Coalport on the evening of the 23rd which was held in part of the works. Next day there was a Public Meeting at Horsehay. These Meetings among the employees of the Company were important for the family as well as their workforce.

April

On 1st April Deborah received her Certificate and expressed 'the desire to make a proper use of' [it].

Samuel Simkin and Ann Bradley were married at the Dale on the 2nd April, and Deborah and Susannah Appleby dined with them afterwards, and on 3rd April, Isaac Hadwen and his wife came to stay with them. After morning Meeting there was a public one at Little Wenlock later, and on the 6th a further one at Wellington. On 11th April, they left home for Wales, leaving 'my Dr Sister Rathbone ill', which made them all anxious. They had a Public Meeting on the 12th at Leominster, Mary Young accompanying them. They then joined weekday Meeting at Hay [on-Wye] going on to Brecon for Select Half-Yearly Meeting on 13th April, and next day, after attending Meeting for Worship, where Deborah, William and Rebecca Byrd, Priscilla Hannah Gurney, Mary Lewis and Edward Simkin were engaged in Testimony, and Rebecca Byrd in Prayer, Deborah's Certificate was endorsed at the Meeting for Discipline.

They attended Meetings next day and on 16th April 'parted from Dr William Byrd and other valuable Fds' to have a cold ride to Builth [Wells] where Deborah received the news of the death of Mary Rathbone, saying 'She sweetly closed a useful Life, leaving many to lament her loss', but Deborah did not doubt 'it being her everlasting gain, I desire to be enable to say "the Judge of all the Earth doth right"'. Mary had always been a great comfort to them, and her loss was a very real one. Meetings were attended during the next few days as they travelled through Pales, Rhaydergowey [Rhayder], Llanidloes and Mahuntly [Machynlleth]. On 20th April 'Dr Owen and his wife spent the evening with them' after the Meeting in Dolgelly, and the next two days they were at the Meetings in Caernarvon 'which were not so still as might have been wished'.

Third Visit to Ireland

They reached Bangor for evening Meeting, and sailed on 24th April for Dublin, a passage of 17 hours. There they lodged with Jonas Stot, and two days later were at Monthly Meeting at Sycamore Alley, where Deborah 'had some counsel to hand' at the Meeting for Discipline on the 27th: they dined with Samuel Bewley.

Next she attended weekday Meeting at Meath Street to some satisfaction, where all was now quiet. She dined with Rachel Jackson and had a time of retirement afterwards. On the 29th April, she attended Meeting for Discipline and dined with Thomas Fayle on the 30th. After two more Meetings, she dined with Thomas Pym, whose family they had come to know well.

May

On 1st May she was at Sycamore Alley and dined at Joseph Saunders'. After a 'favor'd sitting with Women Fds paid a visit to the Men's Meeting' on 2nd May, followed by dinner with Joseph Williams, with whom she had stayed during her visit in 1788, nearly 20 years before.

On 4th May 'we parted from Brother Barnard who had kindly accompanied us to this place, and had ourselves a Meeting at the Black Rock, lodged at Elizabeth Dawson's, and had a sitting with her'. Going south they attended Wicklow Meeting on 5th May, in which Mary Watson, Rebecca Byrd and Deborah were publicly engaged. Next day they had a morning Meeting at Ballicane and at Arklow in the evening with a sitting in a Friend's family which 'afforded Peace to our minds'. On 7th May Mary Watson and Ann Stot returned to Dublin while Deborah and Rebecca continued south and had Meetings at Gorey and Ballinclay.

After a sitting with a family they had a Meeting on the 8th May at Ballintore, followed by one at Cooladine when she 'handed some counsel to Fds after dining with them'. Meetings followed at Forest, Wexford and Enniscorthy, and on 12th May Monthly Meeting was held and one with the inhabitants, as well as some visiting. On 13th May evening Meeting was at Ross and she sat with S[amuel] Elly's family; he had kindly escorted them home in 1788 to Sunniside. After attending weekday Meeting, they travelled on south to Waterford for a public one in the evening of the 14th and after Meeting next day, on the 16th May visited the Provincial School.[14]

On 18th May, they held a Meeting at Kilmac Thomas, when several Friends accompanied them from Waterford. The next days were spent in travelling and attending Meetings at Cappoquin, Tallagh, Youghall, Middleton and Glashmore, where they lodged with Ann Church, going on to Cork next day, where they sat with Friends and met the young people: 'also the Inhabitants'. On 26th May, after sitting in Samuel Penrose's family, the owner of the Waterford Glass Works, they rode to Clonmell, and had an evening Meeting in Samuel Grubb's Mill on the Suir, but on the 29th May, Rebecca Byrd was taken ill, so they rested, but on 31st May they 'entered into a family visit'.

June

On 1st June they finished their visit to Garryroan and had a Public Meeting at Caer on the 2nd. Then they began family visits in Clonmell and attended Monthly Meeting there, Deborah being engaged to 'exhort Fds to mind their callings'. The troubles were passing that had so bitterly divided communities in the last decade, but memories of the horrors remained. Deborah and Rebecca were fully occupied with many family visits, and on 8th June, after visiting seven families, held an evening Meeting when many of the military attended, which they found was to their comfort, perhaps hoping from such an occurrence some degree of harmony and understanding would be restored.

By 12th June they had ridden north to Limerick on the Connaught border and were at morning Meeting, with a public gathering in the evening. They held a Meeting in the Court House a little further north at Nenagh, and a large Meeting at Roscrea in the morning, with an evening one at Birr which 'proved trying'.

They continued north and went to Meeting at Athlone on the 15th, were at Ballinmurray in the morning of the 16th and back to Moate, just outside Athlone in the evening. After family visits, they were at weekday Meeting at Moate and held a public one at Tullamore, and another at Mountrath on 18th June.

They were at Meeting in Knockballimaher in the morning of the 19th June 'attended by some serious people', and one at Maryboro in the evening. After sitting with Friends at Mount Mellick in the morning of 21st June, they had a Public Meeting there in the evening, and this with 'opportunitys in familys proved relieving to our exercised minds'. Next day they went on to Portarlington followed by a Meeting at Edenderry on 23rd with a public one at Rathangan the day after.

Here they sat again with Friends and had a small Public Meeting at Munster Even at seven o'clock on the 24th, and the following day went south again to Athy and Carlow, and the morning of the 26th June found them at Kilkenny for Meeting. A day later they were back at Enniscorthy where two Meetings took place, with Quarterly Meeting on the 29th at which Mary Watson and others contributed to a 'season of favor'. On the last day of the month Deborah and Rebecca were at a parting Meeting with a public one in the evening at Newton Barry.

July

On 1st July at Kilconner Meeting they 'had the good old way to point out to a rising generation and another Meeting at Carlow in the evening'. By 3rd July they were back in Dublin at weekday Meeting with a public one at Sycamore Alley later. Next day they visited our 'Beloved Fd Joseph Williams' with whom Deborah had stayed during her first visit to Ireland in 1788. Afterwards they went to the County Prison and later visited the City Prison, and then, after a Meeting in Meath Street where all appeared now to be calm, they had an opportunity at Jonas Stot's. They left Dublin on 8th July after a satisfactory Meeting at Kells 'where no Fds have been for many years'. Going north into Antrim they had the company of the Catholic Priest at the Meeting at Coothill, and the Meeting at Monaghan in the evening of the 10th July was 'largely attended'.

They sat with Friends at Charlemont in the morning of 12th July and held a Public Meeting in the evening, and by the 14th were in the far north at Coleraine with Meetings being held at Ballinacree, Alwghill, and Randalstown 'at the time of the Fair'. They sat with Friends and held a satisfactory Meeting at Lurgan on 18th July, but on the 20th they had a 'providential escape from hurt by an overturn in our Chair', and on the 26th July they attended two Meetings at Lisburn and visited the Provincial School 'which appears to be regularly conducted'.[15]

They had Meetings at Hillsborough and Belfast on 27th July and were at Whitehouse next morning and Milecross in the evening. On the last day of the month they were at Dunaghadee Meeting, sailing from there the same evening to land at Port Patrick in Galloway about six o'clock on the morning of the 1st August, from which place they were to make a considerable journey of several months.

Scotland
August

Morning Meeting on the 2nd at Girvan up the coast was 'large and solid', and the evening one at Ayr in Strathclyde was held 'in a Methodist Meeting House, the Court House, which we would have preferred, being engaged'. Two Meetings on the 6th August were held in Glasgow and Paisley but they could 'get no place at Hamilton but the Play House tho' not desirable, did not prevent it being held to some profit'. Hamilton, south of Glasgow, was at the gates of the Duke's Palace of the same name, a building set in ancient parkland.

Deborah and Rebecca spent several days visiting and attending Meetings in and around Glasgow, and on 10th August 'attempted holding a Meeting in an Inn at Kirkintilloch, but it would not contain the People', so they held it out of doors; this was followed by an evening Meeting further north in Stirling. They had Meetings at Dunblane and Crieff on the 11th, both 'to good satisfaction' which were followed by two at the City of Perth to the west where they were 'kindly accommodated in a Fds house'.

They reached Dundee on the Firth of Tay on 14th August for a 'small not very relieving Meeting', but further along the coast at Arbroath another one fortunately proved 'comfortable' the day after. Moving north they had two Meetings at Montrose and Bervie, followed by a small trying one at Stonehaven on the 17th. Arriving at Aberdeen next day they held a satisfactory Public Meeting in the Friends' Meeting House with a public one at Kilmuck on the 19th August and Monthly Meeting at Old Meldrum on the evening of the 20th: they found 'very few Fds in this place', but were, however, rewarded 'for a difficult journey to Peterhead [back on the coast to the north] by a satisfactory Meeting'. They had a Meeting at Ellon on 22nd but in the public one in Aberdeen in the evening proved 'much too crowded to be comfortable'. A large Meeting was held at Old Aberdeen on 24th August, and there they sat in Select Half-Yearly Meeting later.

The Orkneys

After much conflict Deborah and Rebecca set out on 26th 'towards the Orkney Islands accompanied by Alexander Crookshank' and had a Meeting at Inverarie. Two Meetings followed at Huntley and Keith next day with two satisfactory ones at Tarne, and after a fatiguing journey across the bogland they reached Thurso in safety, holding a comfortable Meeting there on 2nd September.

September

Deborah's entry for the 3rd September states 'came in a Fishing Boat 45 miles in five hours to Kirkwall – wind and tide being in our favor'. On the 4th they had a Meeting on 'an Island called Shapinsay lodging at Captain Balfour's' and went back to attend a crowded Meeting at Kirkwall and on 6th September had two satisfactory Meetings, one in the Court House and one in a Meeting House in the evening, supposed to contain 700, followed by another the next day in the same place, so their hearers were many and these two English Quaker ministers were able to make an impression.

It was a time of less turbulent weather and of great beauty of land and sea, with large numbers of seabirds on the rocks, though no mention is ever made by Deborah of their surroundings. On 9th September they went round the coast to Margaret Stewart's at Burnice for a five o'clock Meeting, and after supper had 'a precious opportunity in the family'. They parted from this kind Friend on the 10th 'who accommodated us with a cart drawn by oxen to Stromness, at which place we had a Meeting in the evening'. At 10 o'clock the following morning another Meeting was held in the same warehouse, both being 'large and satisfactory'.

On 13th September they had a Meeting at 'Margarets Hope in the Island of South Ronaldsay and about 12 o'clock sailed for Leith' on the Firth of Forth, landing about one o'clock on the 15th 'having had a good passage'. On reaching Edinburgh next day they had a Public Meeting in the evening and stayed there for three days visiting families and attending Meetings before travelling the 47 miles south to Hawick for two Public Meetings.

Return to England

By 22nd September they were back in Cumberland at Carlisle for a Meeting with Friends in the morning and the people in the evening, and attended Quarterly Meeting at Cockermouth next day, and on the 25th the 'parting Meeting was sweetly closed by our Fd Jane Pearson being engaged in Prayer'.

A Public Meeting was held on the 27th at Hawkshead and another at Height in the evening. Yealand Meeting was held on the 28th and they travelled to Lancaster the following day, stopping at James Jenkinson's until after dinner and then had an evening Meeting in Charles Parker's works at Bentham on the 30th.

October

Select Meeting took place on 1st October at Kendal before Quarterly Meeting next day. They also made some family visits, several of them probably being Deborah's relations, so she must have enjoyed those occasions.

Crossing south into Durham they were at Staindrop in the morning of 4th October and Bishop Auckland in the evening. After visiting a sick Friend they rode on east to Sunderland to attend Select Quarterly Meeting on the 5th, which Deborah described as an 'open time' in which she, Joseph Metford and Thomas Clark were engaged in Testimony and Rebecca Byrd in Prayer. There was a large Public Meeting at Durham on the 7th October and further south at Darlington in the evening the following day, with another at George Raws' house. They travelled on into North Yorkshire to Leyburn with fine views over Wensleydale and on to Aysgarth with its spectacular waterfalls on the River Ure.

By the 11th they were at Bainbridge, Haws and Settle, Lawley and Marsden, reaching Todmorden further south on the 14th with an evening Meeting at Rochdale in a large Methodist House. The evening Meeting they attended at Stockport on the 15th was held in a 'room supposed to contain 3,000 people', and they went on for Meetings at Macclesfield, Tunstall, Handley Cross, Burslem, Stoke and Lane End on the 19th 'closed our engagement in the Pottery'. Travelling by Stafford they reached home in time to attend Monthly Meeting at Coalbrookdale and to 'give in an account of my journey and the desire to be thankful that mercy and truth hath accompanied this long and laborious undertaking'.

William Byrd had now joined them and they attended several local Meetings together, but on the 24th October Deborah 'parted from my Beloved Companion and her Precious Husband gratefully acknowledging there is strength in Love and fellowship in the Gospel'.

November

On 5th November they attended John Sweatman's burial at Amelly going on to the Hay [on-Wye], but by the 7th Deborah heard that her son, Samuel Darby, had had a violent nose bleeding so she went in haste to his home at Berwick near Shrewsbury, where fortunately she found him much better. She was at Shrewsbury Meeting on the 8th as he was well enough to leave and indeed he dined with his mother at Mary and John Young's (Rebecca Young's brother and sister-in-law), although this was to prove to be his last visit to Shrewsbury.

From the middle of the month Deborah was engaged in their local Meetings, those on 12th November being held in silence. She was in Berwick with Samuel on 17th November as he fell ill again. She spoke of him sadly after spending the day with him 'My Beloved child who appears in a declining state of health'.

December

She arrived back home on the 4th December, but on the 6th 'was sent for to my Dear Son who continues very ill'. She saw him yet again on 23rd December it 'very trying to leave him': however, she went to Quarterly Meeting at Coventry accompanied by her cousin Barnard Dickinson on 24th December.

1808
January

They had a Meeting at Ackworth on the first day of the year, and 'twelve sittings with the family in which renew'd ability was granted to minister'. The day after they spent the morning there and went on to Doncaster in the evening. They were with Friends the following morning and went on for a large Meeting at Carlton, moving on to Worksop on 5th January, and by that evening were at Sutton. They sat with Friends in the morning, and reached Lichfield by the evening of the 6th.

They were at home again on 10th January, and Deborah went later that same day to see Samuel at Berwick, 'my Dear Son who I found declining fast'. She left him again on the 15th 'tho' he still continued much indisposed'. She may have had the intention of returning very early to his sick bed, but the next day she herself unfortunately fell at home and hurt her leg 'which proved of serious consequence'. She managed however to get to Monthly Meeting at Shrewsbury, and went on to see Samuel in Berwick again. There, she sadly 'took a last farewell of my Beloved Son' on 23rd January, before visiting Richard Phillips, who died the next morning.

On 24th January they attended the Shrewsbury Morning Meeting in which she and Susannah 'were both engaged'. Returning home on the 25th, she had her leg 'laid open which was attended by much suffering', and she added on 31st January that she had 'had a time of deep affliction'.

Death of Deborah's Son Samuel, 1st February 1808

On 1st February Samuel – she described him as 'my Endeared Child – sweetly departed this life about 2 o'clock this morning, having been mercifully cared for, so that we may say the Lord's mercys are new every morning'.

A few days later, on 6th January, 'the Dear Remains of my S.D. were brought to his Brother's house'. This was Dale House, the scene of so many family events, since his great-grandfather, Abraham Darby I was brought there in 1717 before burial, to the parlour of the home that he had just finished building, but was never to live in.

The burial of Samuel took place on 7th February 'after a favor'd Meeting' in which amongst others Deborah, his mother, 'ministered to the People'. Samuel had been in some measure, perhaps, accepted back into the fold.

Deborah was at morning Meeting a week later on the 14th but was prevented by sickness from attending Monthly Meeting in New Dale on the 17th and also the marriage of James Newby and Sarah Simpkin the day after. She was however able to take part in the other Meetings until the end of the month and at the beginning of March.

March

On 8th March she attended Select Meeting at Birmingham, followed by Monthly Meeting, and visited Priscilla Dearman after dining with the Charles Lloyds, and having 'an opportunity in both families', also at Rachel Lloyd's. Priscilla was now a widow, having lost her husband since Deborah had last been with her.

On 10th March Deborah breakfasted at Charles Bucker's, and had an opportunity with his sick daughter. She then parted with Mary Capper, and came home by way of Dudley, having an opportunity in Thomas Martin's family: he had lately lost a child. Deborah then attended several local Meetings, and on 27th March Barnard Dickinson accompanied her to Alder Mills. On the 28th they attended the burial of the Widow Fowler 'which appeared to be a time of renewing to her numerous offspring'.

April

At the beginning of April they were at Select and Quarterly Meetings at Worcester, and before leaving visited the Prison on 7th April, in which Deborah found 'the Love of God through his Son Christ Jesus flow'd freely to the Poor Prisoners'.

At weekday Meeting on 13th April Deborah obtained 'a Certificate for visiting the Eastern Counties'. They also attended the burial of Elizabeth Barrett at Worcester on 15th April and went to Ross [on-Wye] for two Meetings on the 17th, also a public one at Trosnant the day after.

On 21st April 'had an exercising Meeting with Friends at Leominster, and a precious opportunity with our Dr Fd William Young, whom I never saw again'. Hannah Evins and Ann Harford of the Bristol family were with them, and they had a large Public Meeting at Shrewsbury that evening.

May

Deborah was at Pooley on 1st May, and on the 2nd she breakfasted with her daughter-in-law Frances Darby at Berwick. She was with child and therefore her baby Mary was to be posthumous, born some months later. Samuel and she had had a first daughter who died at Sunniside when young. Deborah never mentioned this grandchild in her Journal, but it was known through the letter of a cousin that the little girl was beautiful and that Deborah was always anxious as to how she was going to be religiously brought up by her mother, Frances.

Deborah was then at a Meeting at Dudley on 3rd May in the morning; John Kensey from London was there. Weekday Meeting took place on the 4th at Stourbridge, and she reached Alcester that night, the next day having an evening Meeting in the Town Hall. They were then at Ettington and Warwick and sat with Friends at Banbury on 8th May, and with the People in the evening.

On 9th May they went to Adderbury Meeting in the morning, and reached Buckingham on the 9th on their way to London.

On 11th May they went across to Hogsty End for a special Meeting where her Cousin Francis Darby and Hannah Grant declared their intention of marriage. This came about in some measure because Deborah had put her cousin's case so strongly to Hannah's parents to further his suit.

This was followed by a Public Meeting at Leighton [Buzzard] where Hannah's father and mother, John and Hannah Grant, lived, and they then went on for a Public Meeting at Luton on 12th May.

They reached Hemel Hempstead for Monthly Meeting the day after, and had a Public Meeting that evening at Wycombe. Deborah had the great joy of meeting William and Rebecca Byrd again at Uxbridge on 15th May, where they had a Public Meeting, followed by another at Brentford on their way to London.

Select Meeting began on 16th May and continued the following morning, and Yearly Meeting started two days later, where many minds were 'exercised for the Prospect of Truth'.

On the 20th Deborah was at Devonshire House weekday Meeting, in which, with others, she was 'engaged in Public labour'. Yearly Meeting was always very crowded with many Friends from all over the country and some from overseas. She sat with Friends at Gracechurch Street in the morning of the 22nd and was at Westminster for a Public Meeting in the evening.

She then attended the Meetings for Discipline on 25th May 'as they came in course' and also the weekday Meeting at Southwark, dining at John

Smith's, and on 29th was at a Public Meeting at Peel in the evening. They were with some other Friends at a Meeting for Worship and one held with the servants in Gracechurch Street Meeting House; also a public one at Ratcliffe in the evening.

Visit to the South and South-West

June

The Byrds and Deborah then travelled to Maidstone for Meeting the next evening, and on 1st June reached Rochester for a Public Meeting in the evening. They went on to Chatham for Meeting on the evening of 2nd June at the Naval dockyard. The friendly sailors and dock workers with their families who attended were interested but not surprised to see the 'plain dress' worn by Friends, for a number of them had seen various other types of dress on their travels abroad.

They had a Meeting with Friends at Billericay on 3rd June, and lodged with J. Marriage at Chelmsford. Two days later they had another Meeting with Friends and one with the inhabitants in the evening.

A Meeting at Kelveden followed, where Martha Routh joined them. Quarterly Meeting was on 7th June, and they went on to Colchester and Harwich, with a morning Meeting on the 10th at Manningtree. They reached Needham next day, where Deborah was always pleased to be, but as so often the visit appeared to be brief, for they were at a Public Meeting at Ipswich on 12th June.

There was Select Quarterly Meeting on 13th followed by Quarterly Meeting on the 14th. Deborah had visited the old Meeting House several times during her ministry, and from there on this occasion they went on to attend a Public Meeting at Woodbridge.

Further Public Meetings were held at Saxmundham and Wrentham on 16th June. They were at Lowestoft on the morning of the 17th and reached Yarmouth that evening. They then attended a Public Meeting on the 18th at Northwalsham, and sat with Friends on the morning of the 19th at Norwich, followed by a Public Meeting in the evening: here Deborah was on familiar ground.

They dined with John Gurney at Earlham, and there 'had a Religious Opportunity'. Perhaps they would have talked of Elizabeth, then married to Joseph Fry and the mother of children. Later that day they attended Select Quarterly Meeting, and 'visited some sick Friends'. At Quarterly Meeting on the 21st she found a 'time of favor', Samuel Alexander from Needham and George Saunders being their 'fellow labourers'.

After the visit to Richard Gurney's family, they attended Tasburgh Meeting, and 'dined in the family of our late valued Fnd W[illiam] Blakeley', and had an evening Meeting at Tivetshall, lodging with John Holmes 'who had a promising family settled about him'.

They had an open Meeting at Bury [St Edmunds] on 23rd June in the evening, followed next day by a Meeting at Saffron Walden, where they visited George Gibson, 'who was near a happy close'.

On 26th June they attended the funeral of Deborah's cousin John Birkbeck at Winchmore Hill, 'a large and solemn Meeting' and then attended a Public Meeting in London at Plaistow that same evening. Next day they were at Select Meeting, and visited Cousin R. Beaumont. On 28th June, at Quarterly Meeting – 'Counsel and encouragement went forth freely'.

Then on 29th June they went as far as Horsham in West Sussex, about 20 miles from Worthing, for an evening Meeting which was 'held in much quietude, tho' the town was filled with Military People'. The threat from France and Napoleon's forces was ever in mind, particularly not very far from the Channel coast. A large Meeting was held on the 30th further east in the Assembly Rooms at Lewes in the evening.

July

They then had a Meeting at the fashionable watering place of Brightelmstone [Brighton], and on 2nd July visited Friends' families on the way to Arundel for an evening Meeting. They were travelling quite fast as they sat with Friends at Chichester on 3rd July and had an evening Meeting there.

Now they went north for Select Quarterly Meeting at Godalming, meeting with an accident to Deborah's horse. She said 'My poor Fox got kicked in the stables, from which he never recovered. I felt much for the loss of a faithful servant'. It would seem that she had been riding this horse, but perhaps he had pulled a chaise. The kick must have been a bad one to incapacitate him in this way, even regarding the veterinary skill of the time. She went on however, attending Meetings, Quarterly and a public one on 5th July, but evidently lost the use of this good and useful animal.

Select Quarterly Meeting, as well as a public one, followed at Alton, described as 'seasons to be thankfully remembered'. D. Wallis then took Deborah, who was now without transport, in a post chaise to Portsmouth, some 25 miles away, where they had a Public Meeting in the evening, and another at the same time next day at Southampton, a similar distance on, 10 miles further west.

On 10th July, after dining, they went to Ringwood in the New Forest, where they had a Meeting in the evening. They went the day after to Fordingbridge and held a satisfactory evening Meeting there, following which, on the 12th, they had a Meeting in a barn. A weekday and a Public Meeting were held on 13th July at Poole, also an evening Meeting at Swanage, followed by an open Meeting at Weymouth on the 15th held in the

Town Hall. This latter place had become a fashionable seaside resort, partly because King George III frequently stayed there during the years of conflict across the Channel.

They moved north to Sherborne where they sat with Friends in the morning of the 17th July, and attended a Public Meeting in the evening, and on the 19th went on to Stalbridge for an evening Meeting. They reached Marnhull by the 20th in time for weekday Meeting, and in the evening joined a Meeting with the people at Shaftesbury. They would appear to have been centred at Marnhull for a few days, and visited Meetings in other places from there. They had an open Meeting at Warminster on the 25th, after which once more Deborah 'parted from my Beloved Fds William and Rebecca Byrd, and went to Westbury to lodge'.

Leaving Rebecca was and always would be difficult for Deborah, they had been so much in each other's company, and Deborah had no-one else with whom she had so close an accord. She, however, was on this occasion going to Melksham, to the Fowlers, where she sat in weekday Meeting on 26th July. From there she went on to visit some neighbouring Meetings with her sister Rachel in Corsham on the 28th. On the 29th they had a Public Meeting in Melksham, when Rachel took part also in a Public Meeting next day, when Deborah 'had to exhort faithfulness in the discovery of light'.

They sat with Friends in Bath on the morning of the 31st and with the people in the evening 'to a degree of comfort'.

August

On 1st August, at evening Meeting at Caln, Deborah was joined by 'my acceptable companion Mary Jeffreys'. They went to evening Meeting at Marlborough, and one in the morning at Newbury next day, and a further one at Reading that evening. A Meeting at Basingstoke on the evening of 4th August 'was not very large but solid'. She found that she was having 'many satisfactory opportunities in Fds families', and attended a Meeting in a barn at Odiham 'at which were many French Prisoners, with whom we felt sympathy'.

On the 6th August they had a Meeting in William Heath's Mill in the evening 'which was an open season'. They 'felt much sympathy for those under affliction'.

They 'had an opportunity' with the people in Reigate Friends Meeting House in the evening of 8th August and then went on to Dorking before Monthly Meeting at Ifield, which was followed by a public one at Capel on 10th August.

London and East Anglia

They were at Bleachingley on the 11th for an evening Meeting, staying with Thomas Daws, and were by evening next day at Croydon for a Meeting, 'not very large but comfortable'.

They then visited Wandsworth on the morning of the 14th and Kingston in the evening. They had 'a rather suffering day at Esher', but an evening Meeting was easier.

A Public Meeting at Staines was held on the evening of 17th August, before Monthly Meeting and a Public Meeting at Hammersmith, where they stayed with Deborah's cousins, the Messers.

They attended Monthly Meeting at Westminster, and went to a Public Meeting at Tottenham that evening. They then rode to Hertford, where they had 'an open opportunity with the People'.

They sat with Friends at Hitchin next morning, and held a Meeting for the inhabitants later in the day. They also had a Meeting with the inhabitants of Ware on 22nd August, going east to Buntingford and then north to Royston – in both they 'had to minister to the People'.

At Baldock on 24th August they had a Meeting in the evening, and travelled to Ampthill for a Meeting later in the day, before going north to Huntingdon. Again they had a Meeting in the latter part of the day, but the gathering was not large. However, a Meeting in the Town Hall at Cambridge on the 28th in the morning proved to be 'large and open'. The same evening they were at a Meeting to the north of Cambridge at St Ives in the Friends Meeting House, and during the next few days they visited Earith and Sutton, and on 31st August had two Meetings at Chatteris.

September

Going north again on 1st September, they had a satisfactory Meeting at March, the next day one at Downham [Market], and at Wareham for an evening Meeting the following day. Deborah had visited many of these places before, but not in late summer, after the harvest had been gathered on these farmlands of good grain, so it was a new experience.

They sat with Friends at [King's] Lynn in the morning of the 4th September, but had a trying Public Meeting that evening. However, next morning Deborah described a second one as 'large and comfortable' and that evening they reached Wisbech. There followed visits to both Gedney and Spalding on the 6th and they sat with Friends at the latter on the morning of the 7th and went to Meeting at Boston in the evening, 'in both of which counsel was handed'.

Next they went to a Meeting at Wainfleet, 'attended by many not of our Society, and proved comfortable'. A Meeting at Leek was rather small, and they went on for an evening Meeting at Sleaford on the 10th. A day afterwards they were with Friends at [Brant] Broughton in the morning, and a Meeting in the evening at Welsbourne.

. They then spent the 13th September comfortably with Joseph Jollins, 'where, as in many other families, we had a religious opportunity', before attending evening Meeting at Newark.

She found people 'attentive' at Collingham evening Meeting, and on the 15th morning Meeting at Lincoln rather small; also Monthly Meeting at Brigg on the 16th, but evening Meeting there was large. They had a Public Meeting at Gainsborough on the evening of the 17th September, and also one in a large Meeting House the following morning.

They attended Select Meeting at Mansfield and Quarterly Meeting followed the next day, with a Public Meeting in the evening, Deborah describing them as 'seasons of some favor'.

They then went to weekday Meeting at Nottingham, which she found 'a refreshing season'; then on to a Public Meeting at Loughborough.

They sat with Friends at Leicester and had a Meeting at Hinckley in the evening of 22nd September. They dined, and 'had a little of our Friends' company at Coventry, and were comfortable in a Public Meeting at Warwick'. They then spent a few hours at Cousin Lamley's, and had an evening Meeting at Brailes.

They had an 'open Meeting at [Broad] Camden and a pleasant opportunity at Cousin Richard Burlingham's family in the evening at Evesham' on the 25th. In these last days of September they attended Select Quarterly Meeting followed by Quarterly Meeting at Tewkesbury, as well as going to a Meeting for the inhabitants in the evening of 27th September. Martha Routh and John Kirkham attended.

They then went south to evening Meeting at Cricklade, 'a village in which no person could remember one having been held', and sat there with Friends in the morning of 30th September, going on west to Minchinhampton in the afternoon.

Return to the Midlands

October

On 1st October they had a Meeting at Nailsworth, then two at Stroud and Painswick, followed by an evening Meeting further north at Gloucester 'which was solid'. They then went to Wales for Ross Select and Quarterly Meetings, a 'time of encouragement to the honest-hearted', followed by an open Public Meeting in the evening.

They had returned to Worcester by the morning of 7th October, and went to Bewdley for a Public Meeting, and on to Bromsgrove on 8th October, where evidently the Meetings were very successful, and where they also visited families. They were now again in the Midlands, and had a morning Meeting in Halesowen on the 10th. At Dudley the next day they attended weekday Meeting and had another visit with the inhabitants, in which Martha Routh 'was much favor'd'.

At last, on 12th October, they reached home, and found 'the Dr connections well', something for which she always expressed gratitude. Martha Routh was with them for a visit, and was engaged in the local Meetings, including Monthly Meeting in Shrewsbury, and left for home on 20th October.

November

Deborah attended local Meetings in November, sometimes with Susannah Appleby. John Kirkham was engaged in their evening sitting on 18th November, evidently staying with Richard Burlingham at the house of Deborah's brother, Robert Barnard, who had come from Manchester to live in Coalbrookdale. Their Meetings, particularly the evening one at The Dale, were 'very full and solid', perhaps due to the arrival of these visitors.

On 28th November, Deborah visited Mary Talbot's school, and 'called upon several families'. John Kirkham had a large Meeting in the evening at Horsehay. This would have been held in the works' buildings. A day later he had a Meeting in the evening at Coalport, but Deborah was not well enough to attend either of these.

December

However, she recovered sufficiently to go with Susannah to Shrewsbury for morning Meeting on 4th December and during that month made some contributions at Meeting.

On the 21st there was the glad news that Lucy Burlingham had a daughter, 'both mother and child lively'. She was to be called Mary 'in remembrance of their valuable Aunt Mary Rathbone'.

Deborah closed the year with the exhortation for 'Fds to make good use of time'.

1809
January

Deborah hoped, at their first Meeting of 1809 which they held in silence, that the desire of all present was to begin the year well – her usual New Year wish. A few days later she felt also very strongly that her concern was 'to press my Friends to follow on and know the Lord', and during these early days of January she concentrated only on 'encouraging her Dear Friends to wrestle for a Blessing'.

February

In morning Meeting on 5th February, Edward Simkin, Robert Fowler, Susannah Appleby and Deborah each had a testimony to bear. Richard Reynolds was with them at morning Meeting on 11th February during a very sad time for him as his beloved daughter, Hannah Mary Rathbone, had just lost her husband William. He had been as another son to his father-in-law, and this loss in the family was very great indeed. Richard had evidently come to stay with one of his children on his way home from Liverpool to Bristol.

Visit to Bristol and Bath

March

Later, on 5th March, Deborah left for Bristol accompanied by Susannah Appleby and Rebecca Wright. They sat with Nathaniel Hartland's family in sympathy, for Hannah, his daughter, 'a fine young woman [was] then Lying Dead in the house'. These scenes had been familiar to Deborah all her life, as she, as has been seen, visited Friends and strangers in like sorrow. Another visit of condolence followed on 11th March to the family of John Drury 'who had lost a son'. After Meeting on the 12th they then dined at Matthew Wright's.

Select Monthly Meeting was a solid season and afterwards they dined at John Waring's house and drank tea with John Drury's widow. Deborah later 'had some counsel to hand in weekday Meeting and also [attended] Select Quarterly Meeting'. On 16th March they reached Bath for weekday Meeting at which Deborah was silent, and the same day she 'entered a lodgings in order to drink the water'. Robert and Rachel Fowler and Cousin Birkbeck dined with them on 21st March and two days later Priscilla Hannah Gurney, who now lived in Bath 'bore testimony to the truth in weekday Meeting'. Deborah was, no doubt, happy to be with her once more as they had lived near each other for many years, and undertaken a number of journeys together. Now she with Lucy her daughter-in-law, and the dear Darby children were evidently visiting Bath in order to see her. Friends also called upon them and they had an opportunity at Ann Grace's.

April

Deborah took part at Meeting in Bath and on the 27th March attended Select Meeting at Melksham and remarked 'that Quarterly Meeting was a solid opportunity'. On returning to Bath she became very ill, and was taken back to Melksham on 7th April where she could be cared for in her sister's home.

Rebecca and William Byrd came on 14th April to see her, and later her son Edmund Darby who, by that time, found her a little revived. As she was recovering Rebecca Byrd went away and Deborah wrote that she had with her 'some precious seasons of Divine overshadowing during my illness, which have been better than all the cordials administered by my medical attendants'.

May

Deborah was sufficiently well to attend Monthly Meeting at Melksham by 5th May, in which she with Susannah Appleby and J. Abbot were all engaged. They left for home on 8th May, M. Jeffrys accompanying them to Sunniside, which they reached on the 8th, but Deborah became ill again on arrival. Sarah and M. Jeffrys went to London and on 20th some Irish Friends called, as they frequently did, on their way south in early summer, to attend Yearly Meeting in London.

June

Charles Parker was with them on 11th June on business. Later in the month her cousin George Braithwaite came to stay and was there for Monthly Meeting on the 21st. On 8th June Mary Alexander and George Dillwyn and Jeremiah Head all arrived and after supper they were gathered together, as so frequently in the past, and were 'favor'd to read the precious testimony of God's Love to his People in sacred record'. The summer evenings were long and they were in the same rooms where so often before the family and their guests had come together over the years, at Sunniside, where the windows of the house overlooked the small deer park and the ancient woods of the Severn Gorge, against which the smoke from the ironworks rose and drifted away into the background of trees.

Sarah Darby had made a grotto in the garden at Sunniside, embowered in honeysuckle, and over the entrance had written the following sentences – *'Enter in oh! Stranger, undismayed, as no bat or toad here lurks, and if thy breast of blameless thoughts approve thee, not unwelcome shalt thou tread my mansion. Here quietly meditate upon the past, the present and the future; what thou owes the Supreme Creator, and what is due to thy companions through this Vale of Tears! Oh Vale whose gloom is brightened by the Transcendent Crown of Glory held up to view, which those whose life is spent in virtuous deeds clearly behold through Faith, the Christian mirror.'* In fine weather the family would sit here with their guests.

July

They attended Meetings during the following days, and on 25th July Deborah, accompanied Mary Proud and Mary Alexander to The Haye to visit the Dickinsons. A day later these Friends had a Meeting with them again. William Foster and George Jones were also at Dale Monthly Meeting on 30th July before setting out for Wales in order to hold Public Meetings in that province on 1st August.

August

Deborah was well enough by now to attend Meeting locally and on 10th August Hannah Reynolds and her family, with a young woman of the name of Duncan, called upon them and they had 'a Religious opportunity'. Deborah was often silent at Meeting these days, but on the 20th 'was strengthened to speak well of his Name who hath been a God nigh at hand and a present help in the time of trouble'.

September

On 9th September when Joseph and Deborah Prew were with them, she had to 'plead with the People to live near unto the precious principle which brings Life to the Soul'. They were at Shrewsbury on 11th September, where to Deborah's delight William and Rebecca Byrd met her on their way back from a Religious Meeting in Wales. William Foster, George Jones and Ann Burgess and several other strangers were at Monthly Meeting on the 12th at the Dale and 'Half-Yearly Meeting was solid, but there were few Public Testimonys'. Deborah, however, had some concern to minister and Rebecca Byrd was engaged in the Women's Meeting, also William Foster joined them for a visit: this family had a prosperous business in Calico in London.

Weekday Meeting at Shrewsbury followed on the 14th September in which 'strangers minister'd and had a Public Meeting in the evening but we came home'. The Byrds were with them on 15th and both had 'satisfactory opportunitys in the evening sitting at Sunniside'. Deborah was herself again confined by illness on 17th September, but a Public Meeting was held at New Dale followed by one in Shifnal in the evening next day and on the 19th a 'large Meeting was held at Wellington to the relief of the Fds minds who are strangers amongst us'. On the 20th a large Meeting was held in the Rolling Mills at Horsehay, followed next day by one in the warehouse at Coalport. After Meeting at Bridgnorth William and Rebecca Byrd left for Worcester and on the 23rd September 'Mary Capper left us having been at Sunniside for about one week'. William Foster and companions were engaged at morning Meeting on the 24th and Susannah Hadwin went with them to Much Wenlock for a Public Meeting.

October/December

During the last part of October Deborah attended her local Meeting and considered it 'a mercy that she was able to do so' as she was no longer very strong. The last words in her Journal were written by her on 6th December when she heard the evening before, that 'our Beloved Fd Mary Alexander had died at Worcester of the Smallpox, she had been on a religious visit to families there', and she added 'thus the Church is stripped of its Pillars, may the great Lord of the Harvest be pleased to raise up and set forth more faithful labourers'. This had been her lifelong wish.

1810

Deborah's Last Days

As the winter advanced, Deborah became increasingly weak and was soon confined to the house and then from the New Year, to her chamber. Her body had, no doubt, been weakened by the long distances she had travelled in all weathers during her ministry. She had now completed her life's work, as far as was in her power, and she remarked that her 'allotment was often in suffering', but was able to say 'God is good and a strong hold in the day of trouble'.

During these weeks of illness she repeated several times 'it is trying to the Tabernacle but I have no conflict in mind'. She also said 'if I can be of any service to my friends I am willing to stay here, otherwise I had rather go'. The visits of her relations and some Friends gave her comfort, as also those of her grandchildren, although the very young soon tired her. She was fully resigned to leaving for another world, where she felt certain a far greater experience of the spirit awaited. She knew she had completed her work and now only wished for a little ease.

As the days passed into early February she became increasingly ill: her son Edmund staying by her side continuously, often holding her hand. Mercifully the future was hidden from them both, as only a few months later, in the summer of that same year, he also was to die of a sudden food poisoning while staying with the Fowlers in Melksham to attend the wedding of a neighbour.

Deborah's last days of illness leading to her death are best described in Edmund's words in a letter to his brother-in-law, Richard Burlingham, written on the 15th February after her funeral:

> Thou mayst have been aware from the appearance of my beloved mother when thou was last at The Dale, that her health was fast declining; since that period she has fluctuated between sometimes great suffering, and at other times tolerable ease, 'til within this month last since when she has not been able to leave the house and scarcely her lodging room having a considerable inflammation on her lungs; she kept her bed pretty much for ten days and has had much bodily pain, though dear creature she has been favoured with great patience; on third day night last I was with her for a considerable time and I thought her more cheerful and free from pain than I had seen her for days: it was about 8 o'clock when we went to supper, just after we had finished the doctor was called into the room about something, when after having attended to it, he turned to my dear mother to feel her pulse and to see if he could do anything, as was his custom, when he was very much surprised and alarmed to find a very great alteration in her on a sudden, her pulse nearly gone, and a fainting fit

immediately succeeding: he applied directly stimulants which had the effect of reviving her a little, but it was only to struggle with the seizure of death, for about six hours her agony was indescribable, she then became easier and after that got some hours of sleep. I went up with my dear Lucy [his wife] next morning about 11 o'clock and she knew me, which was a very great favor and she spoke to me, but about 1 o'clock a stupour came on, after which I believe she felt nothing. She continued in that state untill about the same hour fourth day evening about 10 o'clock, when her sweet spirit departed to join (I have no doubt) the Church triumphant in heaven, without the least struggle sign or groan, and I believe is now reigning in the presence of her God the reward of her dedication.

Deborah's suffering was inevitable because of the state of medical knowledge of the period, but Edmund's clear description gives a full account of those hours which all wished fervently she could have been spared. She died on 14th February and was buried on the 22nd beside Samuel in the Friends' Burial Ground, which Abraham Darby II had given to Friends, on the hill below Sunniside and the little deer park: in her 56th year.

The family and many Friends gathered on that day, but being mid-winter the travelling of long distances was not possible for the many who had known her so well. Her memory was held dear in many hearts as she had influenced large numbers of people during her long ministry, and within the family the sweetness of her character had a lasting effect, promoting the wish to emulate her example of how best to live a life in gentleness and loving kindness towards others.

The following words[16] were printed in the *Gentleman's Magazine* for February giving an account of Deborah's death:

She was by no means fettered by any Sectarian prejudices, for believing that the Grace of God which brought salvation hath appeared unto all men, it was her earnest labour and desire that all men would attend to this Divine Grace and conform their lives and actions to its pure teaching.

This account also described her as having been a 'very acceptable Minister among the Society of Friends for thirty years'.

A Testimony was given for her by Shropshire Monthly Meeting at Shrewsbury on 11th April and signed by many of her family and other members of that Meeting. In it a brief account was given of her life and work also stressing that 'Being abundantly endowed with the love of the Gospel her life of service was not confined to her own Society'.

Sadly, Stephen Grellet never visited Coalbrookdale until after Deborah's death. He was in the Midlands in 1812-13 during his first visit to the British Isles, and it is to be hoped that he was in the Severn Gorge while Sarah was still alive and that she could have shown him Sunniside as it had been in Deborah's time.

During this same visit in the winter of 1813 he went to Newgate Prison, and upon entering the Women's Quarters he was so horrified by what he beheld there that he straightaway went to Mildred's Court (the Frys' London home) 'to my very much valued Friend, Elizabeth Fry, to whom I described, out of the fulness of my heart, what I had just beheld, stating that something must be done immediately for those poor suffering children'. Elizabeth Fry responded at once, but because of the youth of her own family and another pregnancy, was unable to bring about the full transformation that she was able to do before so very long, and so found her life's work of prison reform. The golden thread of inspiration which linked the four lives of William Savery, Deborah Darby, Stephen Grellet and Elizabeth Fry, was at that moment finally joined and was to engender a great power for good for a multitude of people.

Stephen Grellet came in 1822 to Coalbrookdale, but by that time Sarah had died and Sunniside stood empty, never to be lived in again. He came on the way from Bristol to Birmingham where he had 'two large Meetings' the following day. He then described how 'my beloved Friend William Allen and his daughter met me and we proceeded together to Coalbrookdale where their Half Year's Meeting for the Principality of Wales was held. It was pleasant to meet there several Friends who had come from various parts of England to attend from neighbouring Quarterly Meetings. I appointed a Meeting for them, at which dear William Allen had very good service – my own mind also obtained relief – the Lord's power rose into dominion. I had been under great exercise before that Meeting, and my spirit is bowed again very reverently in gratitude for His continual help and mercy and we proceeded thence to Holyhead'. Thus he followed the same route to Ireland as had many Friends for several generations.

His last visit to Coalbrookdale was to Francis and Hannah Darby at the White House in 1834 on a winter's afternoon in late January. Francis entered in his 'Account Book Journal' a note saying 'Stephen Grellet and John Holmes took tea with us'. They would have found a household of some luxury, as Francis was making a very fine collection of pictures and well-bound books; he was artistic, and was largely responsible for the production of the very fine wrought ornamental ironwork made by the Coalbrookdale Company. His pictures were chiefly Dutch flower pieces and still life, also some good modern landscapes of the day, among which were two of Hampstead Heath by John Constable, as Francis found 'Mr Constable a talented young man'.

Out of the windows of the White House across a small terraced garden, Sunniside could be seen in the park to the south-west. Deer grazed in between in the fading light and beyond in the Severn Valley, smoke rose from the Ironworks. This was the same scene to which Deborah had returned thankfully from her many journeys to find peace and tranquility and a renewal of strength.

It would seem appropriate to close Deborah's story with the words of Stephen Grellet's great prayer:

> I expect to pass through this world but once. Any good therefore that I can do, or any kindness that I can show to any fellow creature, let me do it now. Let me not delay it nor neglect it, for I shall not pass this way again.

NOTES

[1] Regretfully, the little herd was brought to an end in 1940 during the 1939-1945 War, as it was considered that the park grazing was necessary for farm animals.

[2] Ackworth School (see note 7, p. 78).

[3] *The Tukes of York*, p. 21, by William K. and E. Margaret Sessions.

[4] Now in the grounds of The Mount School, York since 1901 when it was presented to them by William Wilberforce Morrell.

[5] The Retreat, just established by William Tuke, 1796.

[6] Ulster Provincial School. John Gough, author of *A Practical Grammar of the English Tongue*, 1764, had been head of this school 1774-1791.

[7] Sarah Tuke, daughter of William Tuke and his first wife Elizabeth Hoyland, married Robert Grubb in 1782 and when her step-mother Esther Tuke started her school for daughters of Quaker families in Trinity Lane, York in 1784, she helped her as one of the staff of some teachers. The school on Suir Island was modelled on the one in York. Sarah died in 1790, but not long before had been on a strenuous ministerial journey in Germany and on her return home had met Deborah in York.

[8] Upper Furnace: the original one where iron was first smelted with coke in 1709 by Abraham Darby I.

[9] Sunniside was pulled down in 1856 and the little Deer Park was lost in the 1939-45 war (see note 1), but part of the area is soon to be within an arboretum area of the Ironbridge Gorge Museum above Dale House and Rosehill.

[10] Ackworth School (see note 7, p. 78).

[11] Wales started Half-Yearly Meetings in 1796 as an experiment.

[12] Drapers Almhouses built 1702 contained the Meeting House under the Clock Tower in the centre. *The Friends Meeting House* by Hubert Lidbetter, 2nd ed., 1979.

[13] Presumably the Girls School in Tower Street, which moved there in 1796 from Trinity Lane where it was established by Esther Tuke in 1784.

[14] Newtown School, Waterford, for boys and girls, founded in 1798 by Friends, is still in the same premises, continuing to promote a sound liberal education for the scholars.

[15] Ulster Provincial School, now called Friends School, Lisburn (see note 6).

[16] Printed in booklet form at the office of William Smith, Ironbridge.

Deborah's 2nd Irish Visit
Sept-Feb 1797/8

Date 1797	Destination	Monthly Meeting	Mileage
1797			
September			
18th	Donaghadee	—	—
20th	Lisburn	Lisburn	18½
22nd	Hillsborough	Lisburn	4
24th	Ballinderry	Lisburn	8
25th	Lurgan		11
26th	Moyallon		6
27th	Richill	Richill	7
28th	Coothill	Coothill	35
29th	Monagham	—	19
October			
1st	Grange	Charlemont	18½
2nd	Dungannon	—	8½
3rd	Omagh	—	—
4th	Cookstown		14
5th	Newton Stewart	—	20
6th	Londonderry	—	27
7th	Newtown Ilmovady		13
8th	Coleraine	Antrim	10
9th	Ballinacree	Antrim	5
9th	Ballimena	Antrim	16
10th	Lower Grange	Antrim	6
11th	Toberhead	Antrim	7
11th·	Moneymore	—	7
14th	Lurgan	Lurgan	23
16th	Portadown		3
17th	Moyallon	Lurgan	3

Date 1797/8	Destination	Monthly Meeting	Mileage
18th	Portadown	—	3
19th	Moyallon	Lurgan	3
20th	Banbridge	—	—
21st	Armagh	—	11
21st	Richill	Richill	4
22nd	Grange	Antrim	7
24th	Cookstown	—	—
25th	Moneymore	—	13
26th	Randlestown	—	17
27th	Antrim	Antrim	4
28th	Lisburn	Lisburn	16
29th	Belfast	—	7
30th	Carrickfergus		10
30th	Whitehouse		—
November			
2nd	Downpatrick		20
3rd	Castleshane	—	—
4th	Rathfryland	Lurgan	16
5th	Newry	—	7
5th	Dundalk	—	10
6th	Drogheda		17
9th	Dublin	Dublin	24
December			
17th	Ballycane	Wicklow	30
18th	Wicklow	Wicklow	6
21st	Gorey	—	21
22nd	Ballinclay	Co. Wexford	4
23rd	Ballintore	Co. Wexford	4
24th	Cooladine	Co. Wexford	5
26th	Forest	Co. Wexford	15
28th	Ross	Co. Wexford	7
29th	Waterford	Waterford	10½
1798			
January			
5th	Carrick	Waterford	25
7th	Clonmell	Co. Tipperary	10½
12th	Garryroan	Co. Tipperary	8½
12th	Clogheen	Co. Tipperary	16
14th	Cork	Cork	30
16th	Youghall	Youghall	24
18th	Cork	Cork	24
25th	Glanmire	—	—

Date 1798	Destination	Monthly Meeting	Mileage
28th	Kinsale	—	26
30th	Cork	Cork	26
February			
2nd	Limerick	Limerick	45
6th	Birr	Mt Mellick	36
7th	Roscrea	Mt Mellick	10
8th	Knockballymaher	Mt Mellick	5
9th	Mount Mellick	Mt Mellick	15
12th	Tullamore	Mt Mellick	12
13th	Moate	Moate	6
14th	Ballimurry		15
16th	Rathangan	Edenderry	40
17th	Timahoe	Dublin	4
19th	Rathangan	Edenderry	4
20th	Athy	Carlow	17
21st	Carlow	Carlow	9
21st	Kilconner	Carlow	8
23rd	Ballitore		14
24th	Battiboys	Dublin	12
25th	Dublin		20
27th	Holyhead – Wales	Total	1030

Places and Meetings visited by Deborah Darby and Rebecca Young during their visit to America 1793-1796

Date 1793	Meeting House (in italics) City and/or State	Yearly Meeting Affiliation 1793-96
1793		
October		
8th	New York, New York State	New York
mid Oct	Staten Island, New York State	New England
November		
5th	*Rahway*, East New Jersey	Philadelphia
5th	*Stony Brook*, near	
	Princeton, New Jersey	Philadelphia
5th	Trenton, near Princeton,	
	New Jersey	Philadelphia
9th	*Middletown*, near Falsington, PA	Philadelphia
11th	*Abington*, PA	Philadelphia
12th	*Plymouth*, PA	Philadelphia
13th	*Valley*, near the	
	Schuylkill, PA	Philadelphia
14th	*Goshen*, near West Chester, PA	Philadelphia
14th	*Chester*, PA	Philadelphia
15th	*Birmingham*, PA	Philadelphia
16th	*London Grove* QM, PA	Philadelphia
17th	*New Garden*, PA	Philadelphia
19th	*West Grove*, PA	Philadelphia
21st	*East Nottingham*, PA	Philadelphia
22nd	*West Nottingham*, Maryland	Philadelphia
24th	*Fawn*, Maryland	Baltimore
25th	*Deer Creek*, Maryland	Baltimore

Date 1793/4	Meeting House (in italics) City and/or State	Yearly Meeting Affiliation 1793-96
25th	*Gunpowder*	Baltimore
29th	Baltimore, Maryland	Baltimore
December		
2nd	*Elk Ridge*, Maryland	Baltimore
2nd	*Sandy Spring*, Maryland	Baltimore
6th	Georgetown, Columbia	Baltimore
7th	Alexandria, Virginia	Virginia
10th	Colchester, Virginia	Virginia
11th	Dumfries, Virginia	Virginia
12th	Stafford, Virginia	Virginia
13th	Fredericksburg	Virginia
13th	*Caroline*	Virginia
13th	*Cedar Creek*	Virginia
13th	Richmond, capital of Virginia	Virginia
18th	*Curles*	Virginia
18th	*Petersburg*	Virginia
22nd	Gravelly Run	Virginia
24th	Jack Swamp, North Carolina	North Carolina
24th	Rich Square, North Carolina	North Carolina
31st	Halifax, North Carolina	North Carolina
1794		
January		
2nd to 4th	Travels in 'the woods' on old Indian trails	North Carolina
5th	*Great Contentnea*	North Carolina
6th	*Bear Creek*	North Carolina
7th	*Neuse*	North Carolina
9th	*Trent*	North Carolina
11th	*Lower Trent*	North Carolina
12th	New Bern, capital of N. Carolina	North Carolina
14th	Core Sound, North Carolina	North Carolina
14th	Beaufort, North Carolina	North Carolina
15th	*Clubfoot Creek*	North Carolina
16th to 18th	Riding 128 miles to Wilmington	
19th	*Wilmington*, North Carolina	North Carolina
20th	Wilmington	North Carolina
21st to 22nd	Continued their journey, riding hard	
26th	Georgetown, South Carolina	North Carolina
27th to 29th	*Charleston*, South Carolina	South Carolina
February		
1st	Charleston	South Carolina

Date 1794	Meeting House (in italics) City and/or State	Yearly Meeting Affiliation 1793-96
3rd to 4th	*Pope's Swamp*, South Carolina	South Carolina
5th to 8th	3 days travelling	
9th	Augusta, Georgia	
10th to 11th	Journeying on the road	
12th	*Wrightsborough*	
26th	Left Georgia for South Carolina	
28th	*Allwood*	North Carolina
March		
1st	*Cambridge*, South Carolina	North Carolina
1st	Bush River, South Carolina	North Carolina
2nd	*Rayburn Creek*, South Carolina	North Carolina
3rd	*Mud Lick*, South Carolina	North Carolina
4th	*Bush River*, South Carolina	North Carolina
7th	*Rocky Spring*, South Carolina	North Carolina
7th	*Bush River*, South Carolina	North Carolina
12th	*Padget's Creek*, South Carolina	North Carolina
13th	*Cane Creek*, South Carolina	North Carolina
18th	*Pee Dee*, South Carolina	North Carolina
19th	Gum Swamp, South Carolina	North Carolina
21st	*Holly Spring*, North Carolina	North Carolina
24th	*Bush River*, South Carolina	North Carolina
25th	*Tyson*, South Carolina	North Carolina
26th	*Rocky Spring*, South Carolina	North Carolina
27th	*Sandy Spring*, North Carolina	North Carolina
28th	*Providence*, North Carolina	North Carolina
29th	*New Garden*, North Carolina	North Carolina
31st	*Hopewell*, North Carolina	North Carolina
April		
1st	*Dover*, North Carolina	North Carolina
2nd	*Muddy Creek*, North Carolina	North Carolina
4th	*Westfield*, North Carolina	North Carolina
6th	*Reedy Island*, North Carolina	North Carolina
6th	Westfield, North Carolina	North Carolina
13th	Nolichuky, Tennessee	North Carolina
16th	Lost Creek, Tennessee	North Carolina
20th	Nolichuky, Tennessee	North Carolina
26th	Reedy Island, North Carolina	North Carolina
27th	Cheshunt, North Carolina	North Carolina
May		
1st	*Deep River*, North Carolina	North Carolina
2nd	*Piney Woods*, North Carolina	North Carolina
3rd	*Springfield*, North Carolina	North Carolina

Date 1794	Meeting House (in italics) City and/or State	Yearly Meeting Affiliation 1793-96
4th	*Deep Creek*, North Carolina	North Carolina
5th	*Deep River*, North Carolina	North Carolina
6th	Marlborough	North Carolina
7th	*Uwharrie*, North Carolina	North Carolina
8th	*Black Creek* (or Back Creek), North Carolina	North Carolina
9th	*Centre*, North Carolina	North Carolina
9th	*Cane Creek*, North Carolina	North Carolina
10th	*Spring*, North Carolina	North Carolina
11th	*Cane Creek*, North Carolina	North Carolina
13th	*Eno*, North Carolina	North Carolina
13th to 15th	Two days hard riding – 84 miles	
15th	Durham	North Carolina
18th	*Blackwater*	North Carolina
23rd	*Western Branch*, Virginia	Virginia
25th	Suffolk, Virginia	
26th	Norfolk, Virginia	
27th	Bennet's Creek, Virginia	
29th	*Piney Woods*, North Carolina	North Carolina
30th	Symon's Creek, North Carolina	North Carolina
June		
1st	Nickington, North Carolina	North Carolina
2nd	*Newbegun Creek*, North Carolina	North Carolina
2nd	Three Brooks Creek, N. Carolina	North Carolina
3rd	*Little River*, North Carolina	North Carolina
4th	Wells, North Carolina	North Carolina
5th	*Sutton's Creek*, North Carolina	North Carolina
5th	Eakington, North Carolina	North Carolina
7th	Gates Court House, N. Carolina	North Carolina
8th	Sommerton, North Carolina	North Carolina
8th	Black Creek, Virginia	Virginia
9th	*Stanton's*, Virginia	Virginia
13th	*Seacock*, Virginia	Virginia
14th	*Burley*, Virginia	Virginia
15th	Wain Oak, Virginia	Virginia
16th	*Williamsburg*, Virginia	Virginia
17th	*Skimino*, Virginia	Virginia
18th	Wain Oak, Virginia	Virginia
19th	Black Creek, Virginia	Virginia
19th	Swamp, Virginia	Virginia
20th	Manchester, Virginia	Virginia
20th	Richmond, Virginia	Virginia

Date 1794	Meeting House (in italics) City and/or State	Yearly Meeting Affiliation 1793-96
21st	*Curles*, Virginia	Virginia
22nd	Richmond, Virginia	Virginia
22nd	Manchester, Virginia	Virginia
23rd	*Geneto*, Virginia	Virginia
25th	Pine Creek, Virginia	Virginia
27th	Amelia, Virginia	Virginia
29th	South River, Virginia	Virginia
30th	*Lynchburg*, Virginia	Virginia
July		
2nd	Goose Creek, Virginia	Virginia
3rd	*Lower Goose Creek*, Virginia	Virginia
4th	Hills Creek, Virginia	Virginia
5th	Seneca, Virginia	Virginia
6th	*Lynchburg*, Virginia	Virginia
9th	Columbia, Virginia	Virginia
10th	Camp Creek, Virginia	Virginia
13th	Southland, Virginia	Virginia
14th	Culpepper, Virginia	Virginia
16th	Smith's Creek, Virginia	Virginia
18th	Centre, Baltimore	Baltimore
18th	Winchester, Virginia	Virginia
21st	Black Creek, Virginia	Virginia
21st	Allegheny Mountain, Pennsylvania	Virginia
26th	*Westland*, Pennsylvania	Virginia
26th	*Pike Run*, Pennsylvania	Virginia
29th	*Fallowfield*, Pennsylvania	Virginia
August		
1st	*Redstone*, Pennsylvania	Virginia
2nd	*Old Fort*, Pennsylvania	Virginia
3rd	*Union*	Virginia
3rd	Glades	Virginia
7th	*Frankfort*	Virginia
19th	*Ridge*	Virginia
19th	*Hopewell*, Virginia	Virginia
22nd	*Middlecreek*	Virginia
22nd	Martinsburg, Virginia	Virginia
22nd	*Bull Skin*	Virginia
25th	*Hopewell*, Virginia	Virginia
25th	Mount Pleasant, Virginia	Virginia
29th	*Crooked Run*, Virginia	Virginia

Date 1794	Meeting House (in italics) City and/or State	Yearly Meeting Affiliation 1793-96
29th	*South Fork*, Virginia	Virginia
30th	*Goose Creek*, Virginia	Virginia
31st	*Gap*, Virginia	Virginia
September		
1st	*Fairfax*, Virginia	Baltimore
1st	*Leesburg*, Virginia	Baltimore
1st	*Bush Creek*, Maryland	Baltimore
1st	*Pipe Creek*, Maryland	Baltimore
6th	*Menallen*, Maryland	Baltimore
7th	*Huntingdon*, Maryland	Baltimore
8th	*Warrington*, Maryland	
9th	Newbury, Pennsylvania	Philadelphia
10th	Little York, Pennsylvania	Philadelphia
12th	Lancaster, Pennsylvania	Philadelphia
13th	Lampeter, Pennsylvania	Philadelphia
14th	*Ladsbury*, Pennsylvania	Philadelphia
15th	*West Caln*, Pennsylvania	Philadelphia
16th	*East Caln*, Pennsylvania	Philadelphia
16th	Downings Town, Pennsylvania	Philadelphia
17th	Uwchlan, Pennsylvania	Philadelphia
18th	Nanthill, Pennsylvania	Philadelphia
21st	*Newton*, Pennsylvania	Philadelphia
21st	Springfield, Pennsylvania	Philadelphia
22nd	*Darby*, Pennsylvania	Philadelphia
23rd	Philadelphia, Pennsylvania	Philadelphia
October		
8th	*Chester*, Pennsylvania	Philadelphia
9th	*Providence*, Pennsylvania	Philadelphia
10th	*Concord*, Pennsylvania	Philadelphia
11th	*Chichester*, Pennsylvania	Philadelphia
13th	Whitely Creek, Delaware	Philadelphia
14th	Asequinesy, Delaware	Philadelphia
15th	Duck Creek, Delaware	Philadelphia
16th	Little Creek, Delaware	Philadelphia
16th	Dover, Delaware	Philadelphia
17th	*Motherkill*, Delaware	Philadelphia
18th	*Three Runs*	Philadelphia
20th	Lewis Town	Philadelphia
21st	Snow Hill, Virginia	Philadelphia
24th	Accomack, Virginia	Philadelphia
29th	Salisbury, Maryland	Philadelphia

Date 1794/5	Meeting House (in italics) City and/or State	Yearly Meeting Affiliation 1793-96
November		
1st	Choptank, Maryland	Philadelphia
2nd	*Bayside*, Maryland	Philadelphia
2nd	*Third Haven* (Tred Avon), Maryland	Philadelphia
3rd	*Tuckahoe*, Maryland	Philadelphia
6th	Head of Chester, Maryland	Philadelphia
7th	*Chester River*, Maryland	Philadelphia
8th	*Cecil*, Maryland	Philadelphia
9th	*Sassafras*, Delaware	Philadelphia
10th	*Hockessin*, Pennsylvania	Philadelphia
11th	*Concord*, Pennsylvania	Philadelphia
13th	*Middletown*, Pennsylvania	Philadelphia
14th	*Bradford*, Pennsylvania	Philadelphia
16th	*Reading*, Pennsylvania	Philadelphia
17th	*Maiden Creek*, Pennsylvania	Philadelphia
18th	*Exeter*, Pennsylvania	Philadelphia
19th	*Pottstown*, Pennsylvania	Philadelphia
20th	*Providence*, Pennsylvania	Philadelphia
21st	*North Wales*, Pennsylvania	Philadelphia
22nd	*Richmond*, Bucks County, Pennsylvania	Philadelphia
23rd	*Plumstead*, Bucks County, Pennsylvania	Philadelphia
24th	*Buckingham*, Pennsylvania	Philadelphia
25th	*Wrightstown*, Pennsylvania	Philadelphia
26th	Makefield, Pennsylvania	Philadelphia
28th	Middletown, Bucks County, Pennsylvania	Philadelphia
December		
21st	Horsham, Pennsylvania	Philadelphia
22nd	Newtown, Pennsylvania	Philadelphia
23rd	Bristol, Pennsylvania	Philadelphia
24th	*Frankford*, Pennsylvania	Philadelphia
25th	Germantown, Pennsylvania	Philadelphia
26th	*Merion*, Pennsylvania	Philadelphia
27th	*Haverford*, Pennsylvania	Philadelphia
28th	Philadelphia, Pennsylvania	Philadelphia
1795		
January	Philadelphia, Pennsylvania	Philadelphia
February		
21st	Mount Holly, New Jersey	Philadelphia

Date 1795	Meeting House (in italics) City and/or State	Yearly Meeting Affiliation 1793-96
21st	*Burlington*, New Jersey	Philadelphia
24th	*Bordertown*, New Jersey	Philadelphia
26th	*Ringwood*, New Jersey	Philadelphia
28th	Hardwick, New Jersey	New York
March		
1st	Drowned Lands, New York	New York
2nd	Cornwall, New York	New York
4th	Newburgh, New York	New York
5th	Marlboro, New York State	New York
6th	Little Esopus, New York State	New York
8th	Poughkeepsie, New York State	New York
9th	Crum Elbow, New York State	New York
10th	Hudson, New York State	New York
11th	Kidney Hill, New York State	New York
12th	*New Britain*, New York State	New York
14th	Lennox, New York State	New York
15th	*East Hoosack*, Massachusetts	New York
17th	*White Creek*, Massachusetts	New York
18th	Pittstown, New York State	New York
19th	Saratoga, New York State	New York
22nd	*Queensborough*, New York State	New York
24th	Sheensburgh, New York State	New York
26th	Ferrisburgh, Vermont	New York
27th	Vergennes, Vermont	New York
28th	Monkton, Vermont	New York
29th	Ferrisburgh, Vermont	New York
30th	Middleburgh, Vermont	New York
April		
2nd	Rutland, Vermont	New York
3rd	Danby, Vermont	New York
3rd	West Saratoga, New York State	New York
6th	*Greenfield*, New York State	New York
7th	Galway, New York State	New York
7th	Ballston, New York State	New York
8th	Lancingburgh, New York State	New York
9th	Troy, New York State	New York
12th	Coeyman's Patent, New York State	New York
14th	*Little Nine Partners*, New York State	New York
15th	*Great Nine Partners*, New York State	New York

Date 1795	Meeting House (in italics) City and/or State	Yearly Meeting Affiliation 1793-96
16th	*Creek*, New York State	New York
16th	Oswego, New York State	New York
16th	Chestnut Ridge, New York State	New York
20th	*Branch*, New York State	New York
21st	*Goshen*, New York State	New York
21st	Litchfield, Connecticut	New York
23rd	*East Hartford*, Connecticut	New York
23rd	*West Hartford*, Connecticut	New York
26th	*New Milford*, Connecticut	New York
27th	Valley, New York State	New York
27th	*Oblong*, New York State	New York
May		
1st	Peach Pond, New York State	New York
2nd	*Bedford*, New York State	New York
3rd	*Amawalk*, New York State	New York
4th	*Chappaqua*, New York State	New York
6th	*Purchase*, New York State	New York
7th	*Mamaroneck*, New York State	New York
8th	*Westchester*, New York State	New York
9th	Long Island, New York State	New York
10th	Cowneck, New York State	New York
11th	Westbury, New York State	New York
12th	Martinecock, New York State	New York
12th	Oyster Bay, New York State	New York
13th	*Jericho*, New York State	New York
20th	*Flushing*, New York State	New York
21st	New York, New York State	New York
28th	*Newport*, Rhode Island	New England
30th	Conanicut, Rhode Island	New England
June		
7th	*Newport*, Rhode Island	New England
8th	Tiverton, Rhode Island	New England
9th	Little Compton, Rhode Island	New England
10th to 17th	Portsmouth, Rhode Island	New England
18th	*Swansea*, Massachusetts	New England
19th	Freetown, Massachusetts	New England
20th	*Westport*, Massachusetts	New England
21st	*Center*, Massachusetts	New England
22nd	*Apponegansett*, Massachusetts	New England
23rd	*New Bedford*, Massachusetts	New England
24th	*Long Plain*, Massachusetts	New England

Date 1795	Meeting House (in italics) City and/or State	Yearly Meeting Affiliation 1793-96
25th	Achushnet, Massachusetts	New England
25th	*New Bedford*, Massachusetts	New England
July		
6th	Martha's Vineyard, Massachusetts	New England
7th	Gay Head, Massachusetts	New England
8th	Newton, Massachusetts	New England
9th	Nantucket, Massachusetts	New England
13th	*Falmouth*	New England
14th	Yarmouth	New England
14th	Barnstaple	New England
16th	*Sandwich*, Massachusetts	New England
17th	Plymouth, Massachusetts	New England
18th	*Pembroke*, Massachusetts	New England
19th	Boston, Massachusetts	
20th	*Lynn*, Massachusetts	New England
21st	*Salem*, Massachusetts,	New England
22nd	Newbury, Massachusetts	New England
23rd	*Amesbury*, Massachusetts	New England
23rd	Newton, Massachusetts	
24th	*Seabrook*, New Hampshire	
25th	*Epping*, New Hampshire	New England
26th	*Dover*, New Hampshire	New England
27th	*Rochester*	New England
28th	Tetbury, Maine	New England
29th	Berwick, Maine	New England
30th	Portland, Maine	New England
August		
2nd	*Vassalboro*, Central Maine	New England
3rd	Fairfield, Maine	New England
5th	*Vassalboro*, Central Maine	New England
6th	*Winthrop*, Maine	New England
8th	Lewiston, Maine	New England
9th	*Durham*, Maine	New England
10th	*Portland*, Maine	New England
12th	*Falmouth*, Maine	New England
13th	*Windham*, Maine	New England
15th	Pittsfield, New Hampshire	New England
16th	Concord, New Hampshire	New England
17th	Weare, New Hampshire	New England
22nd	Bolton, Massachusetts	New England
23rd	Leicester, Massachusetts	New England

Date 1795	Meeting House (in italics) City and/or State	Yearly Meeting Affiliation 1793-96
24th	*Northbridge*, Rhode Island State Line	New England
25th	*Douglas*, Rhode Island State Line	New England
26th	Mendon, Rhode Island State Line	New England
27th	*Smithfield*, Rhode Island State Line	New England
28th	*Uxbridge*, Rhode Island State Line	New England
29th	Lower Smithfield, Rhode Island State Line	New England
30th	*Providence*, Rhode Island State Line	New England
September		
1st	*Gloucester*	New England
3rd	*Cranston*	New England
4th	Greenwich	New England
5th	Wickford	New England
6th	*South Kingston*	New England
7th	Lower Kingston	New England
8th	Richmond, Rhode Island	New England
9th	Hopkinton, Rhode Island	New England
10th	*Westerly*, Rhode Island	New England
10th	Potowknett Bridge	New England
13th	Newhaven, Connecticut	New England
14th	*Westchester*, New York State	New England
17th	Flushing, New York State	New England
18th	*Newtown*, New York State	New England
19th	Staten Island, New York State	New England
20th	*Rahway*, East New Jersey	New England
21st	*Elizabeth town*, East New Jersey	New England
21st	*Rahway*, East New Jersey	Philadelphia
22nd	*Plainfield*, East New Jersey	Philadelphia
23rd	New Brunswick, New Jersey	Philadelphia
24th	Princeton, New Jersey	Philadelphia
24th	Trenton and Stoneybrook, New Jersey	Philadelphia
26th	Philadelphia, Pennsylvania	Philadelphia
October		
5th	Danby, Pennsylvania	Philadelphia
6th	Philadelphia, Pennsylvania	Philadelphia
7th	*Kennet Square*, Pennsylvania	Philadelphia
7th	Wilmington, Delaware	Philadelphia
10th	*Baltimore*, Maryland	Baltimore
18th	Annapolis, Virginia	Baltimore

Date 1795/6	Meeting House (in italics) City and/or State	Yearly Meeting Affiliation 1793-96
19th	*Indian Spring*, Virginia	Baltimore
20th	Baltimore, Maryland	Baltimore
November		
1st	Little York, Pennsylvania	Baltimore
2nd	Harrisburg, Pennsylvania	Philadelphia
8th	*Muncy*, Pennsylvania	Philadelphia
13th	Fishing Creek, Pennsylvania	Philadelphia
14th	Cattanipay, Pennsylvania	Philadelphia
17th	*Roaring Creek*, Pennsylvania	Philadelphia
20th	Maiden Creek, Pennsylvania	Philadelphia
22nd	*Reading*, Pennsylvania	Philadelphia
23rd	*Portsdown*, Pennsylvania	Philadelphia
24th	Philadelphia, Pennsylvania	Philadelphia
December		
1st	Shrewsbury, Pennsylvania	Philadelphia
2nd	*Swan*, Pennsylvania	Philadelphia
3rd	*Squancum*, Pennsylvania	Philadelphia
4th	*Robins*, Pennsylvania	Philadelphia
7th	*Hadenfield*, Pennsylvania	Philadelphia
13th	Philadelphia, Pennsylvania	Philadelphia
1796		
January		
1st	Philadelphia, Pennsylvania	Philadelphia
4th	Westbury, New Jersey	New Jersey
4th	Upper Greenwich, New Jersey	New Jersey
6th	Pine Neck	Philadelphia
7th	*Pine Grove*	Philadelphia
8th	*Salem*, New Jersey	Philadelphia
9th	*Alloways Creek*, New Jersey	Philadelphia
10th	*Greenwich*, New Jersey	Philadelphia
12th	Cape May, New Jersey	Philadelphia
13th	*Great Egg Harbor, New Jersey*	*Philadelphia*
14th	*Upper Egg Harbor*, New Jersey	Philadelphia
15th	*Little Egg Harbor*, New Jersey	Philadelphia
17th	*Barnagat*, New Jersey	Philadelphia
19th	*Rahway*, East New Jersey	Philadelphia
25th	Newark, New Jersey	Philadelphia
27th	*Long Island, Westbury*	New York
30th	Brookland, New York State	New York
30th	New York	New York

Date 1796	Meeting House (in italics) City and/or State	Yearly Meeting Affiliation 1793-96
February		
6th	Upper Freehold, New Jersey	New Jersey
7th	Springfield, New Jersey	Philadelphia
9th	*Old Springfield*, New Jersey	Philadelphia
10th	Mansfield Neck, New Jersey	Philadelphia
10th	Burlington, New Jersey	Philadelphia
11th	*Ancocas*, New Jersey	Philadelphia
11th	Mount Holly, New Jersey	Philadelphia
12th	Vincent Town, West New Jersey	Philadelphia
13th	Upper Evesham, West New Jersey	Philadelphia
13th	Cropwell, West New Jersey	Philadelphia
14th	Lower Evesham, West New Jersey	Philadelphia
15th	Haddonfield, West New Jersey	Philadelphia
16th	Woodbury, West New Jersey	Philadelphia
16th	*Newtown*, West New Jersey	Philadelphia
17th	*Moorstown*, West New Jersey	Philadelphia
17th	Burlington, West New Jersey	Philadelphia
March	Philadelphia for 5 months Pennsylvania	Philadelphia
May		
9th	*Chester*, Pennsylvania	Philadelphia
11th	*Middletown*, Pennsylvania	Philadelphia
11th	Westown, Pennsylvania	Philadelphia
12th	*Birmingham*, near Chads Ford, Pennsylvania	Philadelphia
13th	*New Garden*, Pennsylvania	Philadelphia
14th	London Grove, Pennsylvania	Philadelphia
14th	Fallowfield, Pennsylvania	Philadelphia
15th	Newcastle, Delaware	Philadelphia
16th	Embarked on the *Sussex* 5.00 pm	

SELECTED LIST OF PERSONALITIES MENTIONED

Much of the information is gratefully taken from the typescript Dictionary of Quaker Biography *maintained in the Library of the Society of Friends, London, and in the Quaker Collection, Haverford College, Pennsylvania.*

Every endeavour has been made to check names and dates but further or alternative information will be welcomed if sent to the publishers at the Ebor Press, York.

Abbott, John, 1752-1813. Son of Samuel and Hannah Abbott of St Ives, Hunts. Recorded a minister 1783. Married (1) 1784 Ann King (1762-1791); (2) 1794 Sarah Tregelles (1764-1802); (3) 1806 Sarah Wilson (1759-1843).

Abbott, Sarah, 1759-1843. Daughter of Isaac (1715-1785) and Rachel (Wilson, 1720-1775) Wilson of Kendal. Acknowledged a minister 1794. First cousin of Deborah Darby, Rachel Wilson's sister Hannah having married John Barnard. Married 1806, as third wife, John Abbott (1752-1813).

Abell, James, 1751-1818. Son of Joseph and Mary (Taylor) Abell of Cork, Ireland. Became an Elder 1784: a 'tender friend to the young'. Relinquished trade early. Very moderate in expenses and contributed liberally to good causes. Died at Black Rock, Co. Dublin.

Addenbrook, Thomas. Adviser to the Darby family on business matters.

Alcock, Ruth, 1717-1808, after *c*1740 Follows, *qv* (*quod vide*).

Aldam, Catherine May. Member of the Aldam family of Sheffield.

Alexander, Ann, 1767-1849. Daughter of William (1732/3-1822) and Esther (Maud, 1727-1794) Tuke of Bingley, Bradford. Inclined to religion early in life and at about 19 years was engaged in the ministry. Made several journeys with her step-brother Henry (1755-1814) – Scotland in 1788 and Ireland in 1790 where they visited the Suir Island school which her step-sister Sarah (1756-1790, after 1782 Grubb) had helped to establish on the model of York's Trinity Lane School for Girls, run by her mother. Ann had helped her mother with the York school (opened 1785) and, after her mother's death, helped her father to keep it going. She married 1796 William Alexander (1768-1841), going to Suffolk with him but returning 1808 to York once more to supervise the Friends' School for Girls. She visited America in 1803 and was an active minister all her life. Two sons: William (1799-1864) and Joseph (1801-1810).

Alexander, Dykes II, 1763-1849. Son of Dykes I (1724-1786) and Martha (Biddle) Alexander: brother of Samuel and Mary, *qqv*. Married 1786 Hannah Brewster. Travelled widely in the ministry: lived in Ipswich.

357

Alexander, Mary, 1760-1809. Daughter of Dykes I (1724-1786) and Martha (Biddle) Alexander. Travelled in the ministry; friend of Deborah Darby. Died of smallpox in Worcester.

Alexander, Samuel, 1749-1824. Eldest son of Dykes I (1724-1786) and Martha (Biddle) Alexander. Married 1771 Elizabeth Gurney. In corn business and banker at Needham Market, where he gave much hospitality to Friends.

Allen, Sarah, 1773-1850. A cousin of Richard Reynolds (1735-1816) on the death of whose wife Rebecca in 1803, went to housekeep for him, first at Dale House and then at Bristol when he moved there in 1804.

Appleby, Hannah. Of Durham: aunt of Susannah.

Appleby, Susannah, 1754-1827. Born in Co. Durham, daughter of Joshua and Ann Appleby. Moved to Shropshire in the 1780s and lived at Sunniside, Coalbrookdale, until the death in 1821 of her friend Sarah Darby. Afterwards went to live at The Chesnuts, a house nearby built for her by Sarah. It is owing to her correspondence that the death of Abraham III from scarlet fever, and other family happenings, are known in detail. Recorded as a minister c.1791.

Atkins, Philip. Master of the *Sussex*, in which ship Deborah Darby and Rebecca Young returned from America to England in 1796.

Bacon, Hannah, 1765-1829, after 1786 Evans, *qv.*

Ball, R. and G. Relations of Richard Reynolds (1735-1816), whose sister Mary married George Ball of Bridgwater, Somerset.

Barlow, Elizabeth, 1757-1839, after 1781 Hoyland, *qv.*

Barnard, Daniel, 1774-1853. Youngest son of John (1723-1789) and Hannah (Wilson) Barnard of Upperthorpe; brother of Deborah Darby.

Barnard, John, 1723-1789. Of Upperthorpe, near Sheffield, son of John and Deborah (Fisher) Barnard. Tanner. Married 1751 Hannah, daughter of John and Deborah (Wilson, 1687-1754) Wilson of Kendal: 15 children, of whom 4 sons and 3 daughters survived infancy, the daughters being Mary Dickinson, Deborah Darby and Rachel Fowler.

Barnard, Mary, 1752-1781, after 1778 Dickinson, *qv.*

Barnard, Rachel, 1767-1833, after 1790 Fowler, *qv.*

Barnard, Robert, 1762-1830. Son of John (1723-1789) and Hannah (Wilson) Barnard; brother of Deborah Darby. Married 1796 Hannah (d. 1825), daughter of Andrew and Susannah Gaylard of Bristol and sister of Isaac Hadwen's wife, Susannah. Lived first at Manchester; then came to Coalbrookdale. Clerk of London Yearly Meeting 1803.

Barnard, Wilson, 1766-1795. Son of John (1723-1789) and Hannah (Wilson) Barnard; brother of Deborah Darby.

Baxter, Peter. American Quaker. Married Abigail Drinker, daughter of Daniel Drinker.

Beck, Sarah, 1715/6-1799. Daughter of Henry Sims of Canterbury. Married c1736 Thomas Beck (1707-1788) of London. In 1768 visited Ireland with Hannah Brown, and also Scotland and Wales. In 1766 she and her husband had settled in Dunmow, Essex, moving about 1779 to live with their son's family at Dover, where Thomas died. In 1789-91, despite advancing age, she again visited the north of England.

Beesley, Mary, b. 1743. Daughter of Richard (1709-1789) and Jane (Donne) Reynolds. Sister of Richard, *qv* of Coalbrookdale. Married (1) 1764 William Cowles Jr (1727-1778) a Bristol merchant; (2) 1786 Thomas Beesley, *qv* of Worcester, as his second wife.

Beesley, Thomas, 1724-1797. Son of John and Mary (Moore) Beesley of Alcester. Became glover in Worcester. Married (1) 1754 Hannah Ford (1722/3-1783), daughter of Thomas and niece of Richard Ford I, *qv* who had married Mary, daughter of Abraham Darby I; (2) 1786 Mary Cowles, widow of William Cowles and sister of Richard Reynolds, *qv*. Was executor and trustee of the will of Abraham Darby II.

Benezet, Anthony, 1712-1784. Born at St Quentin, Picardy, France. His family were Calvinists and fled to England, where he was apprenticed to a Quaker and joined Friends. Went to Philadelphia in 1731 where he tried to join his brothers in commerce, but left to teach and dedicate his life to the service of humanity. He gained a place in the Academy of Friends for public instruction, relief of the poor, and defence of universal philanthropy, not common at the time. He early condemned slavery and founded a school in Philadelphia for liberated slaves. On his death he left a trust fund for the education of blacks.

Benson, Sarah, 1751-1827. Daughter of William III (1726-1789) and Rachel (Rutter) Rathbone. Married 1781 Robert Benson (1749-1802) of Liverpool.

Bevington, Elizabeth, 1738-1813. Daughter of Henry (1703?-1780) and Rachel (Applegarth) Portsmouth of Basingstoke, Hants. Married 1761, as his second wife, Samuel Bevington (1733?-1800) of London, brother to Timothy Bevington (1726-1802), the Worcester glover. Recorded a minister by Gracechurch Street MM in 1771 and travelled extensively in Britain. After her husband's death moved to Reading, Berks.

Bevington, Hannah, 1727-1791. Daughter of Joseph (1689-1742) and Ann (born Enock) Freeth of Coventry. Married 1750 Timothy Bevington (1726-1802) of Worcester. Became a minister about 1757 and travelled widely. In 1779 visited Friends' families in Bristol with Sarah Stephenson (1738-1802) and was with her in Ireland in 1784.

Bevington, Timothy, 1726-1802. Son of John and Sarah Bevington of Ettington, Warwickshire. Related to the Fords. Settled at Worcester as a glover. Married 1750 Hannah Freeth (1727-1791) of Coventry. A ministering Friend from the 1760s.

Birkbeck, Benjamin, 1757-1819. Second son of John and Sarah (Wilson) Birkbeck. His mother's sister Hannah married John Barnard and he was therefore first cousin to Deborah Darby. Married 1784 Jane (1758-1793), daughter of Nathaniel and Jane English: three sons and one daughter. A miller who later assisted his brother Wilson in the business he had started with the Darbys in London.

Birkbeck, John, 1749-1810. Son of John (1722/3-1761) and Sarah (Wilson, 1726/7-1773) Birkbeck. First cousin of Deborah Darby. Of Settle, Yorks. Married 1779 Mary Dillworth (1753-1830) of Lancaster.

Birkbeck, Joseph, 1752-1820. Son of John (1722/3-1761) and Sarah (Wilson, 1726/7-1773) Birkbeck. First cousin of Deborah Darby. Unmarried.

Birkbeck, Mary, 1753-1830. Daughter of William (1716-1788) and Esther (Shiers) Dillworth of Lancaster. Married 1779 John Birkbeck (1749-1810) of Settle, Yorks. Recorded a minister 1792.

Birckbeck, Sarah, 1761-1833, after 1799 Fox, *qv*.

Birkbeck, Wilson, 1754-1812. Son of John (1722/3-1761) and Sarah (Wilson, 1726/7-1773) Birkbeck of Settle. First cousin of Deborah Darby. Married (1) 1782 Hannah (1758-1791), daughter of Robert and Hannah Plumstead; (2) Grizell, daughter of Samuel and Grizell Hoare. In the 1770s he was in London and a partner in the Coalbrookdale Company. He had a house at Tottenham and gave much hospitality to Friends: 'He gave liberally and often awakened with action the generosity of others'. After his death, Grizell, his widow, married 1827 William Allen (1770-1843) of Plough Court, pharmacist.

Bland, Thomas, 1739/40-1818. Norwich merchant. Married 1775 Sarah Gurney (1732-1800, born Lawrence, widow of Samuel Gurney). It was at their house that Deborah stayed when in Norwich.

Boone, George, 1730-1785. Son of Thomas and Mary Boone of Kettering. About 1757 moved to Birmingham, where he entered the iron trade. Became a minister at about 20 years of age. Married (1) 1762 Hannah Bullock; (2) 1783 Susanna Waring (formerly Cowles), widow of William Waring of Shipston-on-Stour, Worcs.

Bradley, Ann, after 1807 Simkin, *qv*.

Bragg, Hadwen, 1763-1820. Born at Whitehaven, son of John and Margaret (Hadwen) Bragg. Became a draper at Newcastle upon Tyne. Married 1790 Margaret (1761-1840), daughter of Isaac (1714/5-1785) and Rachel (Wilson, 1720-1775) Wilson: three sons and three daughters.

Bragg, Isaac, 1750-1819. Born at Whitehaven, son of John and Margaret (Hadwen) Bragg. Married 1778 Margaret (1750-1826), daughter of George and Hannah (Blamire) Wilson: four sons and five daughters.

Bragg, Margaret, 1750-1826. Daughter of George and Hannah (Blamire) Wilson of High Wray, Windermere. Her father was brother to Isaac Wilson (1714/5-1785) and she was thus first cousin to Deborah Darby. Married 1778 Isaac Bragg (1756-1819).

Bragg, Margaret, 1761-1840. Youngest daughter of Isaac (1714/5-1785) and Rachel (Wilson, 1720-1775) Wilson of Kendal. Her mother's sister Hannah married John Barnard and she was thus first cousin of Deborah Darby. Married 1790 Hadwen Bragg (1763-1820) of Newcastle upon Tyne. Described as 'endowed with a very superior share of natural abilities'.

Braithwaite, Deborah, 1775-1844, after 1798 Crewdson, *qv.*

Braithwaite, George, 1746-1812. Son of George and Alice (Forster) Braithwaite. Married 1767 Deborah (1743-1821), daughter of Isaac (1714/5-1785) and Rachel (Wilson, 1720-1775) Wilson.

Braithwaite, George, 1777-1853. Son of George (1746-1812) and Deborah (Wilson, 1743-1821) Braithwaite. Married 1806 Mary (1784-1822), daughter of Charles (1748-1828) and Mary (Farmer, 1751-1821) Lloyd of Bingley, Birmingham: six sons and three daughters.

Brayton, Patience, 1733/4-1794 of Massachusetts. Daughter of David and Mary Green, Rhode Island. Married 1758 Preserved Brayton. Set free their slaves. Minister by 1754. Visited Great Britain 1783-6.

Brown, Isaac. Was host to Deborah Darby when she was taken ill at Frankfurt, conveying her 50 miles as an invalid.

Brown, Moses, 1738-1836. Married (1) Anne; (2) 1778 Mary Olney. Member of a distinguished Rhode Island family. Manumitted his slaves and provided for their future care 1773. Became a Friend 1774, having long been moving in that direction. Ardent abolitionist and active in promotion of legislation 1783-4 ending slavery in Rhode Island. Active in promoting education and in philanthropic works generally.

Buchanan, Grace. Went to America with Jane Hopkins.

Burgess, Ann, 1774-1846, after 1815 Jones, *qv.*

Burgess, Joseph, b. 1776. Son of Joseph (1735-1807) and Sarah (Airey) Burgess of Grooby Lodge, near Leicester. Farmer and grazier. Married 1801 Rebecca Summerland, daughter of John and Sarah Summerland of Uttoxeter.

Burlingham, Ann, 1804-1891, after 1839 Southall, *qv.*

Burlingham, John, 1753-1828. Son of John (1717-1782) and Candia (Corbyn 1715-1801) Burlingham. Married 1777 Hannah Bradley (1751-1825). A glover by trade, like his father and grandfather, and one of the leading master glovers of Worcester. Partly invented and introduced a slitting machine; devised ornamentation on gloves; and patented a frame to hold the seam, thus ensuring more regular stitching. Gave considerable employment in neighbourhood. When George III came to Worcester John Burlingham was deputed on behalf of the glovers to present the king with some gloves. There were numerous subsequent occasions when he was received by George III.

Burlingham, Joseph, 1778-1842. Son of John (1753-1828) and Hannah (Bradley, 1751-1825) Burlingham of Worcester. Married 1804 Elizabeth Whitehead (1779-1820). After being unsuccessful in business went to North America, and what became of him is not known. He wrote letters to his family asking for help at one period: some letters are preserved and one to Lucy Darby describes a visit he made to the New York Senate. Several books of his are in the Ironbridge Gorge Museum with his bookplate.

Burlingham, Lucy, 1782-1870, after 1803 Darby, *qv.*

Burlingham, Richard, 1779-1840. Son of John (1753-1828) and Hannah (Bradley, 1751-1825) Burlingham of Worcester. Married (1) 1803 Mary Trusted (1778-1806); (2) 1810 Ann Gregory (1756-1850). Began as a glover, later becoming an ironmonger in association with his brother-in-law Edmund Darby.

Byrd, Ann, 1769-1806, after 1790 Fry, after 1798 Gregory, *qv.*

Byrd, Rebecca, 1758-1834. Daughter of John (1720-1795) and Jane (Brawn, 1722-1792) Young of Shrewsbury. Married 1800 William Byrd (1757-1835). Travelled extensively with Deborah Darby in British Isles and North America.

Byrd, William, 1757-1835. Son of Thomas and Hannah Byrd of Uffculme, Devonshire. Assistant to a Friend at Longworth, Dorset, in 1781. Settled at Marnhull, Dorset, as a small shopkeeper. Married 1800 Rebecca Young (1758-1834) of Shrewsbury. Stephen Grellet described them as 'Zacharias and Elisabeth, so blameless appear their work'. William would deal in no slave-tainted goods. Became a minister in 1792.

Capper, Mary, 1755-1845. Daughter of William and Rebecca Capper of Rugeley, Staffs, members of the Church of England. Went to France in 1776 for her health and to learn the language. In 1784 stayed in London with her brother and became a regular Attender at Meetings, joining Friends in 1788. Became a minister. Moved to Leominster in 1811 but returned in 1816 to Birmingham for the rest of her life.

Cash, John, 1742-1811. Son of John and Sarah Cash of Wilmslow, Cheshire. Moved to Coventry about 1761 and became a cloth manufacturer. Appeared in the ministry at 25 and was a 'faithful labourer'. Married (1) 1765 Margaret Hopkins (or Hopkinson); (2) 1769 Mary Wills (one child); (3) 1778 Elizabeth Newman (11 children). Stayed frequently at Sunniside and was at Dale House in 1779 with Abraham Darby III when the bridge was nearly finished; gave a philosophical lecture on 'Air' with 'Instructive experiments'. Attended Coalbrookdale Meeting when in neighbourhood.

Cash, Thomas, 1739/40-1809. Son of Thomas and Alice (Wright) Cash of Alderley, Cheshire. Appeared in the ministry aged 31; travelled in England, Scotland and Ireland and to many parts of North America. Regularly attended London Yearly Meeting. Married 1801, at Frandley, Hannah Bradley, when he was described as a yeoman, living at Morley, Cheshire.

Champion, Rachel, 1712-1756, after 1731 Lloyd, *qv*.

Churchman, George, 1730-1814. Son of John and Margaret (Brown) Churchman of Nottingham, Pennsylvania. Married 1752 Hannah James. A pioneer in promoting schools for Friends, including Westtown School. He extended hospitality to many travelling ministers.

Clark, Esther, 1738/9-1822. Daughter of John and Sarah Marshall of Calverley, Yorks. A minister at 26 years of age; visited Meetings in Ireland, Scotland and Wales. Married (1) 1784, as second wife, Thomas Brady (1733-1793) of Thorne, and after his death moved to Doncaster where she married (2) 1796 Timothy Clark.

Clarke, Ann. A member of Shrewsbury Meeting who gave much hospitality to Friends.

Colesworthy, Mary, 1741-1805, after 1771 Were, *qv*.

Colley, Thomas, 1742-1812. Brought up in the Church of England; joined Friends in 1768. His wife, Jane, also became a Friend. Was a cutler in Sheffield. Visited the West Indies with Philip Madin in 1779. Described as 'a provokingly slow speaker'.

Cook, Charity, 1745-1822. Daughter of John and Rachel (Wells) Wright. Born near Monorcasy Creek, near present town of Limerick, Maryland. Brought up in Cane Creek Meeting. Married 1773 Isaac Cook (1743-1820): 13 children. Became a minister and travelled both in America and Europe, her husband managing the home effectively during her long journeys. Mary Swett and Phoebe Speakman were her companions on different journeys, both being mentioned by William Savery as travelling together with Deborah Darby and Rebecca Young in Scotland. Charity stayed at Sunniside during her travels in England and also met Deborah at London Yearly Meeting.

Cook, Isaac, 1743-1820. Son of Thomas (1704?-1752) and Mary (Underwood) Cook. His father was a prominent member of Warrington Meeting, Lancashire. Two years after his death Mary Cook emigrated to North America with her children, joining Cane Creek Monthly Meeting, North Carolina, and attending New Garden Meeting, at that time subordinate to Cane Creek. Married 1773 Charity Wright (1745-1822): 13 children.

Cook, James, 1728-1779, born at Marton, Cleveland. Apprenticed to shipbuilders in Staithes, Yorks. Explored and mapped Newfoundland and the St Lawrence river. Charted New Zealand and claimed New South Wales, Australia for England. Introduced limes and fresh vegetables and sound food for his ship's company at sea to prevent scurvy. Married 1762 Elizabeth Batts of Barking: six children. Died in Hawaii 1779 in a fray with natives.

Corbyn, Candia, 1715-1803, after 1743 Burlingham, *qv.*

Corbyn, Elizabeth, 1752-1839, after 1779 Lloyd, *qv.*

Crewdson, Deborah, 1775-1844. Daughter of George (1746-1812) and Deborah (Wilson, 1743/4-1821) Braithwaite of Kendal. Married 1798 William Dillworth Crewdson (1774-1851).

Crewdson, William Dillworth, 1774-1851. Eldest son of Thomas (1737-1795) and Cicely (Dillworth, 1748-1814) Crewdson of Kendal. Married 1798 Deborah Braithwaite (1775-1844): five sons and five daughters.

Crotch, William, 1733-1805. Brought up as a 'waiting boy' at a great inn in Norwich; later became a footman to John Gurney (1749-1809) at Earlham. Eminent minister and noted for readings of character. Died in America. Visited 1799 William Cowper, the poet.

Crowley, Ann, 1769-1826. One of eight sisters. Travelled widely in the ministry, as companion to Phoebe Speakman of Philadelphia in 1797. Covered over 4,000 miles and attended over 4,000 Meetings. She lived at Uxbridge, Middlesex.

Darby, Abiah, 1716-1794. Daughter of Samuel and Rachel (Warren) Maude. Married 1745/6 Abraham Darby II (1711-1763) as his second wife. For fuller information see Rachel Labouchere, *Abiah Darby*, York, Sessions, 1988.

Darby, Abraham I, 1678-1717. Son of John and Ann (Bayliss) Darby. Apprenticed to Jonathan Freeth, a Maltmill maker of Birmingham; moved to Bristol 1698. Married 1699 Mary Sergeant of Fulford Heath, Warwickshire. Set up business in Bristol as a Maltmill maker and founded 1702 the Bristol Brass Wire Company at Baptist Mills. Ironmaster. Cast an iron bellied pot in sand 1704 with the help of John Thomas. Moved to Coalbrookdale in 1708 where he discovered how to smelt iron with coke in 1709; increased partnerships and business until his illness in 1716.

Darby, Abraham II, 1711-1763. Eldest son of Abraham I (1678-1717) and Mary (Sergeant) Darby. Married (1) 1734 Margaret Smith (d. 1740) of Shifnal (one daughter, Hannah, 1735-1762, m. 1757 Richard Reynolds, 1735-1816); (2) 1745/6 Abiah Maude (1716-1794), widow of John Sinclair (d. 1736/7): seven children (three died young) including Mary (1748-1807, m. Joseph Rathbone); Abraham III (1750-1789); Sarah (1752-1821); Samuel (1755-1796, m. Deborah Barnard). He perfected the use of smelting iron with coke for the forges and so brought in the full use of this material. Lived at Dale House; designed and lived at Sunniside 1750 onwards.

Darby, Abraham III, 1750-1789. Eldest son of Abraham II (1711-1763) and Abiah (Maude, 1716-1794) Darby. Married 1776 Rebecca Smith (1752- 1834), daughter of Francis and Ruth (Gulton) Smith of Doncaster: four sons and three daughters. Built the Iron Bridge over the Severn. Lived at Dale House until 1780 and then at The Haye where he died of scarlet fever in 1789. The *Dictionary of National Biography* gives his year of death as 1791, in error.

Darby, Ann, 1779-1840, after 1805 Dickinson, *qv.*

Darby, Edmund, 1782-1810. Youngest son of Samuel (1755-1796) and Deborah (Barnard) Darby. Married 1803 Lucy (1782-1870), daughter of John and Hannah Burlingham of Worcester: two sons and two daughters. Conducted the Coalbrookdale Company from 1804 until his sudden death in 1810. Lived at both Sunniside and Dale House.

Darby, Francis, 1783-1850. Second son of Abraham III (1750-1789) and Rebecca (Smith, 1752-1834) Darby. Married 1808 Hannah (1783-1860), daughter of John and Hannah Grant of Leighton Buzzard: two daughters, viz. Matilda Frances (1809-1903) and Adelaide Anne (b. 1816).

Darby, Hannah, 1735-1762, after 1757 Reynolds, *qv.*

Darby, Hannah, 1783-1860. Daughter of John and Hannah Grant of Leighton Buzzard. Married 1808 Francis Darby (1783-1850): two daughters.

Darby, Lucy, 1782-1870. Daughter of John (1753-1828) and Hannah (Bradley, 1751-1825) Burlingham of Worcester. Married 1803 Edmund (1782-1810), son of Samuel and Deborah Darby: four sons and two daughters. Lived all her married life, and as a widow from 1810, in Coalbrookdale: first and last in Dale House and 1810-1839 at The Chesnuts.

Darby, Mary, 1748-1807, after 1768 Rathbone, *qv.*

Darby, Rebecca, 1752-1835 (born Smith). Daughter of Francis and Ruth (Gulton) Smith of Doncaster. Married 1776 Abraham Darby III (1750-1789): four sons and three daughters (one son and one daughter d. young). Lived at Dale House, The Haye, The White House and Sunniside.

Darby, Samuel, 1755-1796. Ironmaster. Younger son of Abraham II (1711-1763) and Abiah (Maude, 1716-1794) Darby. Married 1776 Deborah (1754-1810), daughter of John and Hannah (Wilson) Barnard of Upperthorpe, Sheffield. After a few years in charge of Coalbrookdale's London foundry he returned with his family to live with Abiah, his widowed mother, at Sunniside. He continued to work in the intervals between attacks of an illness. Of Samuel and Deborah's four children only Samuel (1779-1808) and Edmund (1782-1810) survived infancy.

Darby, Samuel, 1779-1808. Son of Samuel (1755-1796) and Deborah (Barnard) Darby. Married Frances Williams of Welshpool: two daughters, the first of whom died in infancy and Mary, the second, married out.

Darby, Sarah, 1752-1821. Second daughter of Abraham II (1711-1763) and Abiah (Maude, 1716-1794) Darby. Born and lived at Sunniside all her life. Partner and shareholder in the Coalbrookdale Company. Able and authoritative figure who conducted much family and other business. Received many visitors at Coalbrookdale all her life and became head of that household after the death in 1794 of her mother, Abiah.

Darwin, Charles Robert, 1809-1882. Fifth son of Robert Waring Darwin and his wife Susannah, born at The Mount, Shrewsbury. His life and work became famous throughout the world.

Darwin, Erasmus, 1731-1802. Son of Robert Darwin, of a Lincolnshire family; went to school in Chesterfield and to St John's College, Cambridge. Studied medicine in Edinburgh; became a physician in Nottingham and then moved to Lichfield. Married (1) 1759 Mary Howard (d. 1770) and (2) the widow of Colonel Alexander Pool of Rathbone Hall. Children of both marriages. Erasmus Darwin was a friend of Bolton T. Watts, Josiah Wedgewood, Samuel Galton and the Sewards, and founded with them the Lunar Society, the membership of which met monthly in each others houses.

Darwin, Robert Waring, 1766-1848. Son of Erasmus Darwin and Mary Howard. Married Susannah, daughter of Josiah Wedgewood (d. 1817). A successful physician of strong character. Chief Consultant in Shrewsbury who had a particular intuitive knowledge of human nature which helped diagnosis. He was called in as a consultant by both the Darby and Reynolds families.

Dearman, Richard, 1732-1804. Came as agent/manager of Coalbrookdale Company in September 1791, being given power to deal with the business and to recover debts. His second wife was Elizabeth Freeth of Birmingham. Richard had succeeded to the Eagle Foundry and carried on a successful business as Dearman & Freeth, which his son conducted after he moved to Coalbrookdale. His son, John, married Priscilla Fox of Plymouth, whose family were linked by marriage to the Lloyds, the Braithwaites, etc. Later, his niece, Deborah, married Joseph Reynolds.

Dickinson, Ann, 1779-1840. Eldest daughter of Abraham III (1750-1789) and Rebecca (Smith, 1752-1834) Darby. Married 1805 Barnard Dickinson (1781-1852).

Dickinson, Barnard, 1781-1852. Younger son of John and Mary (Barnard) Dickinson. Trained as a farmer; moved to The Haye in 1804. Married 1805 Ann (1779-1840), eldest daughter of Abraham Darby III (1750-1789): seven sons and four daughters. After several years at The Haye they moved to Dale House in 1810 after the sudden death of Edmund Darby, when Barnard took over the superintendence of the Coalbrookdale works until 1828, when Abraham Darby IV and his brother Alfred (1807-1852) became partners with Francis Darby (1783-1850). In 1824 Barnard first spoke in Meeting and from then on he travelled increasingly to Meetings and visited families. He and Ann left Dale House in 1838, as he had built Eastfield up the Dale not far from the Meeting House. Barnard went to America in 1845 and travelled 2,700 miles. He also went to the Shetland Isles, a strenuous journey by sea and land of 2,500 miles. He continued to travel in his later years, but more locally except once to Ireland and to the Orkney Islands.

Dickinson, Henry, 1812-1886. Third son of Barnard (1781-1852) and Ann (Darby, 1779-1840) Dickinson. Married (1) 1841 Deborah (1810-1855), younger daughter of Edmund and Lucy Darby (no issue); (2) 1858 Susanna (b. 1831), daughter of Isaac and Tabitha (Ashworth) Hadwen of Liverpool (three sons and one daughter). Lived at Eastfield, the house built by his father next to The Chesnuts in Coalbrookdale.

Dickinson, John, 1732-1808. Born in Talbot, Maryland. American statesman; served in Delaware and Pennsylvania Assemblies, the Stamp Act Congress and the Continental Congress. Favoured conciliation with England; expressed his calm political views in his *Letters from a Farmer in Pennsylvania to the Inhabitants of the British Colonies*. As a delegate of Delaware he helped draft the US constitution. He was not, however, present at the signing, but asked another delegate to add his name. Dickinson College at Carlisle, Pennsylvania, which had begun as a Methodist College, is named after him.

Dickinson, John, 1744-1786. Son of Samuel and Margaret (Lapage) Dickinson of Beverley, Yorks. Married 1778 Mary (1752-1781), eldest daughter of John and Hannah (Wilson) Barnard of Upperthorpe: two sons, Joseph (1779-1783) and Barnard (1781-1852). By his marriage he was brother-in-law to Deborah Darby.

Dickinson, Mary, 1752-1781. Daughter of John and Hannah (Wilson) Barnard. Known as Polly. Author of the verses *To the Memory of the late Samuel Fothergill, William Hunt and John Woolman* (1772). Married 1778 John Dickinson (1744-1786): two sons, one dying in childhood.

Dillworth, Mary, 1753-1830, after 1779 Birkbeck, *qv.*

Dillwyn, George, 1738-1820. Born in Philadelphia. When young liked fine dress and played the flute. He was engaged in business but was influenced by Anthony Benezet and became serious minded. Married 1759 Sarah Hill of Philadelphia; they went to England in 1784. In 1788 he travelled in Europe with Sarah (Tuke) and Robert Grubb and Mary Dudley, returning to America in 1791. In 1793 he again visited Europe with his wife Sarah, where they remained for nine years. He visited the southern states of America with Samuel Emlen and Thomas Scattergood. At 59 years of age he is described as corpulent, rosy in complexion and dressed in drab.

Dodshon, Frances, 1714-1793 (neé Henshaw). Born at Caldon Hall, near Leek, Staffs. Left an orphan and brought up by her uncle. She became 'convinced of the truth' against much opposition and later became a minister. Married (1) 1745 William Paxton (d. 1753) of Durham (four sons); (2) 1758 William Dodshon.

Dodshon, William. Married 1758 Frances Paxton (born Henshaw, 1714-1793).

Drinker, Elizabeth. Daughter of Henry (1734-1809) and Elizabeth (Sandwith, 1734/5-1807) Drinker. Her journal and letters give a vivid account of the period of the War of Independence.

Drinker, Henry, 1734-1809. Son of Henry and Mary Drinker. Married (1) 1757 Ann Swett (d. 1758); (2) 1761 Elizabeth Sandwith (1734/5-1807): nine children. Member of shipping and importing tea firm, Philadelphia. Also in the grain business, dealing with England and Portugal at a time when high prices were made for American goods, due to the War of Independence. He paid the fares for all in the group on the *Sussex* who returned to England with Deborah. Lived at Clearfield, near Logan, Pennsylvania.

Dudley, Mary, 1750-1823. Born of Anglican parents, Joseph and Mary Stokes of Bristol. Joined the Methodists but about 1773 became a Friend. Married 1777 Robert Dudley of Clonmel, Co. Tipperary, being recorded a minister about this time. After her husband's death in 1807 she settled in England.

Emlen, Samuel, 1729/30-1799. Born in Philadelphia, the only child of Joshua and Deborah Emlen (his second wife). He had an excellent education and trained in the counting house of James Pemberton, but his frail health and poor eyesight, coupled with an ample fortune, led him to give up business. He travelled in the southern states with the ministering Friend Michael Lightfoot and in 1756 went with Abraham Farrington to England and Ireland. Married (1) 1761 Elizabeth Moode (d. 1767); (2) 1770 Sarah Mott (two sons and two daughters).

English, Margaret, 1765-1833, after 1787 Hoyland, *qv.*

Evans, Hannah, 1765-1829. Daughter of David and Mary (Trotter) Bacon; her sister Elizabeth married Thomas Scattergood. Married 1786 Jonathan Evans II (1759-1839): seven children. Hannah visited New York Yearly Meeting in 1816 with her son William.

Evans, Jonathan II, 1759-1839. Married 1786 Hannah Bacon (1765-1829): seven children.

Fallows. *See* Follows.

Farmer, Mary, 1750-1821, after 1774 Lloyd, *qv.*

Fawcett, Elizabeth, born 1740. Daughter of William (1696-1750) and his second wife Elizabeth (Shepherd) Rathbone. Married 1763 Peter Fawcett, son of Joseph Fawcett of Liverpool. This was the connection with the Fawcett family.

Fell, James, 1707?-1788. A schoolmaster who came to Worcester from Glastonbury, Somerset. All the children of Abraham Darby II went to his school. His type of teaching can be seen in the exercise books of Abraham Darby III, now in the Ironbridge Gorge Museum. His wife, Grace, died in 1768 and he later settled at Charlbury, Oxon.

Fisher, Hannah, 1764-1819. Daughter of Thomas and Mary Rodman of Newport, Rhode Island. Married 1793 Samuel Rowland Fisher (1745-1834) of Philadelphia. Recorded a minister 1800. Visited families and Meetings with Deborah. Gave Deborah a book (now in the Ironbridge Gorge Museum).

Fisher, James. He and his brother Thomas were Philadelphia merchants of cotton goods; they traded with the Cashes of Coventry. Thomas stayed at Sunniside in Abiah Darby's time.

Fisher, William. Of Limerick, Ireland. Conducted a large grain and salt processing trade for export of salmon from the River Shannon, and beef and pork from the farms in the countryside. Deborah and Rebecca visited his widow on their 1797/8 journey to Ireland.

Fletcher, John William, 1729-1785. Born in Nyon, Switzerland, son of an army officer (as de la Flechere). Married 1781 Mary Bosanquet. Distinguished scholar, especially in classical literature. After being for some time tutor to the sons of Thomas Mill of Tern Hall, Shropshire, he took Holy Orders in 1752: he was deeply impressed by the teachings of John Wesley and finally became Vicar of Madeley, Shropshire.

Follows, Ruth, 1717-1808. Daughter of Richard and Ruth Alcock of Weston, Notts. Married about 1740 George Follows of Castle Donington, Leicestershire. A recorded minister.

Ford, Hannah, 1724-1784. Daughter of Richard I (1689-1745) and Mary (Darby, 1700-1751) Ford. Lived with her two sisters at Dale House and Rosehill, but after their mother's death went to live at Worcester with cousins. They were the owners of Tony, the bullfinch, and wrote the epitaph poem to him. Hannah went to Clifton, Bristol, becoming housekeeper to Thomas Goldney III.

Ford, Mary, 1719-1782. Daughter of Richard I (1689-1745) and Mary (Darby, 1700-1751) Ford. Lived with her two sisters at Dale House and Rosehill, but after their mother's death went to live at Worcester with cousins. They were the owners of Tony, the bullfinch, and wrote the epitaph poem to him.

Ford, Richard I, 1689-1745. Eldest son of Edmund and Mary (Carter) Ford of Stourbridge. His father was a tallow chandler. Richard came to the Coalbrookdale Company in 1714 as clerk. When Abraham Darby I became ill in 1716 he took increasing responsibility. Abraham died in 1717 and Richard, with the help of Thomas Goldney II (the largest shareholder) had considerable difficulty in taking possession of the company: they finally succeeded. Married 1718 Mary Darby (1700-1751), Abraham I's eldest daughter: three daughters and four sons. They also brought up Mary's orphaned brothers and sister at Dale House. In 1734, when Abraham Darby II married Margaret Smith of Shifnal, the Fords moved to Rosehill, leaving Dale House to the young couple. Thomas Goldney III was sent by his father, Thomas Goldney II, from Bristol to learn the business with Richard Ford, and the Ford/Goldney letterbook gives an account of the transactions between them from 1732.

Ford, Richard II, 1721-1792. Son of Richard I (1689-1745) and Mary (Darby, 1700-1751) Ford. Became clerk to the Coalbrookdale Company on his father's death in 1745 and remained till 1748. Later became a partner in Caynton, Sambrook & Tibberton with William Hallow as his manager, but still retained close connections with Coalbrookdale.

Ford, Susannah, 1726-1785. Daughter of Richard I (1689-1745) and Mary (Darby, 1700-1751) Ford. Lived with her two sisters at Dale House and Rosehill, but after their mother's death went to live at Worcester with cousins. They were the owners of Tony, the bullfinch, and wrote the epitaph poem to him.

Foster, William. He was in the calico trade in London. Married Elizabeth —.

Fothergill, Ann, 1718-1802. Daughter of John (1675/6-1744/5) and Margaret (Hough) Fothergill, sister of Dr John Fothergill (1712-1780) and Samuel Fothergill (1715-1772). Lived in London and entertained Friends, particularly at the time of Yearly Meetings.

Fothergill, John, 1712-1780. Son of John (1675/6-1744/5) and Margaret (Hough) Fothergill: brother of Samuel (1715-1772). Apprenticed to Benjamin Bartlett of Bradford for two years 1734, then graduated at Edinburgh 1736. Entered St Thomas Hospital, London, and studied under Edward Wilmot. 1744 Licentiate of Royal College of Physicians, giving much attention to epidemic disease. He had wide interests in education and philanthropy; also had botanical knowledge and a collection of trees at his property at Upton, Essex.

Fothergill, Samuel, 1715-1772. Born at Carr End, Wensleydale, Yorks. Son of John (1675/6-1744/5) and Margaret (Hough) Fothergill, brother of Dr John Fothergill. Went to Gilbert Thompson's school at Penketh; apprenticed to a shopkeeper in Stockport. Lifelong friend of Abraham Darby II. Married 1738 Susannah Crewdson (1698-1773) of Warrington, Lancs. Settled as an American merchant, also tea merchant, in Warrington. Made successful efforts to revive the declining membership and discipline in the Society of Friends 1753-60. Travelled widely in England, Scotland and Ireland; also made important journeys to North America.

Fowler, Rachel, 1767-1833. Daughter of John (1723-1788) and Hannah (Wilson, 1730-1793) Barnard. Sister to Deborah Darby. Married 1790 Robert Fowler (1755-1825) of Melksham. Appeared as a minister when aged 25 but did not travel much in the ministry, though on various occasions visited Meetings in the British Isles.

Fowler, Robert, 1755-1825. Son of Thomas (1729?-1783) and Catherine (Rutty, 1727-1762) Fowler of Melksham. Wine and spirit merchant but, the trade making him uneasy, relinquished the more prosperous part when the business became his own and became a grocer. Married 1790 Rachel Barnard (1767-1833): their daughter Mary became the second wife of Joseph John Gurney (1788-1847), younger brother of Elizabeth Fry (1780-1845).

Fox, Edward, 1749-1817. Son of Edward (b. 1719) and Anna (Were) Fox of north Cornwall. Became a merchant in Wadebridge. Married 1792 Mary Brown (1768-1841) of Landrake, Cornwall.

Fox, Francis, 1765-1812. Son of Francis (1736-1769) and Sarah (Cookworthy, 1738-1814) Fox of Plymouth. Became chemist and druggist in the town. Married 1799 Sarah Birkbeck (1761-1833) of Settle: one son (d. in infancy) and one daughter. Felt called to the ministry about 1797. One of the founders of the Lancastrian School in Plymouth.

Fox, George, 1624-1691. Born in Fenny Drayton, Leicestershire. Son of Christopher and Mary (Lago) Fox. His father was a weaver, his mother 'of the stock of the martyrs'. Travelled extensively, preaching that there is 'that of God in every one'. Imprisoned many times for his faith. Married 1669 Margaret Fell (1614-1702), widow of Judge Thomas Fell of Swarthmoor Hall, Ulverston, Lancs. He convinced a number of 'seekers' and was the founder of the Society of Friends. He established area Monthly Meetings for church affairs, grouped into county Quarterly Meetings and a national Yearly Meeting.

Fox, Richard, 1764-1841. Son of Joseph (1729/30-1785) and Elizabeth (Hingston, 1733-1802) Fox of Falmouth. Became, like his father, a surgeon in the town. Married 1786 Hannah Forster (1757-1833).

Fox, Sarah, 1761-1833. Daughter of John (1722/3-1761) and Sarah (Wilson, 1726/7-1773) Birkbeck of Settle. First cousin of Deborah Darby. Minister in 1797 and a mistress at Ackworth School, Yorkshire. After leaving Ackworth she travelled for five years in Great Britain with Sarah Harrison, an American. Married 1799 Francis Fox (1765-1812) of Plymouth.

Fox, Thomas, 1747/8-1821. Son of Edward (b. 1719) and Anna (Were) Fox of north Cornwall. Joined the woollen manufacturing business of his grandfather Thomas Were at Wellington, Somerset. Married 1783 Sarah Smith (1759-1833) of London. In the 1780s began country banking concern. Was both elder and minister.

Freeth, Hannah, 1727-1791, after 1749/50 Bevington, *qv.*

Fry, Ann, 1752-1817, after 1777 Till Adams, *qv.*

Fry, Elizabeth, 1780-1845. Third daughter of John (1749-1809) and Catherine (Bell, 1755-1794) Gurney of Earlham Hall, Norwich. Guided by Catherine, the eldest sister, the young Gurneys were taught by governesses and tutors. They were lively and energetic and mixed with their neighbours and a large number of cousins. As has often been recounted, William Savery came to Norwich in February 1798, when his preaching and conversation had a deep religious effect on Elizabeth, later to be confirmed that year by Deborah Darby in September, when Elizabeth was staying with her cousin Priscilla Hannah Gurney at Dale House, Coalbrookdale, as a guest of Richard Reynolds. Married 1800 Joseph Fry (1777-1861): six daughters and five sons. He helped her considerably in her public work and travelled abroad with her once or twice, as more frequently did her brother Joseph John Gurney (1788-1847). Her immense work for reform is well known and much written about, particularly in relation to prisons. It was Stephen Grellet who first suggested to her that she should look into the condition of women prisoners. Her influence produced changes far beyond these shores.

Fry, Joseph, 1777-1861. Son of William Storrs (1736-1808) and Elizabeth (Lambert) Fry of Bristol. Married 1800 Elizabeth Gurney (1780-1845): six daughters and five sons. A banker: lived at Mildred's Court, London, in a house next to the counting house and warehouse. The business got into difficulties with bankruptcy in 1828 and had to be supported by relations. Later he inherited the estate of Plashet where he and Elizabeth made their headquarters. He supported her in her public work all her life and was with her at her death in 1845.

Galton, Mary, 1755-1783. Daughter of Samuel (1719-1799) and Mary Galton of Birmingham. Lived with her father and became a friend of Deborah Darby.

Galton, Samuel, 1753-1832. Son of Samuel (1719-1799) and Mary Galton of Birmingham. Married 1777 Lucy Barclay (1753-1844). Gunsmith, a trade resulting in remonstrations from local Quakers terminating in his disownment. He and his wife continued to attend Meeting and in 1802-3 he gave up the gun business and established a bank. Member of the Lunar Society and close friend of Joseph Priestley.

Gaylard, Susannah, 1756-1827, after 1791 Hadwen, *qv.*

Gilkes, Richard, 1746-1822. Son of Thomas (1703/4-1772) and Mary (Barrett, 1709/10-1768) Gilkes of Sibford, Oxon. Settled at Devizes. Minister at age of 25. Travelled in many English counties and in Wales. Frequent in attendance at London Yearly Meeting.

Gilpin, Mark, 1744/5-1804. Son of James and Jane (Holme) Gilpin of Kendal. Settled at Coalbrookdale, where his brother Robert (1753-1783) had moved by 1759. Married 1770 Mary, daughter of John and Ann Thomas of Coalbrookdale: 12 children. Closely connected with the Darby family in two generations.

Gough, John, 1720-1791. Son of John and Mary Gough of Kendal; father a business man, his mother was interested in education of their sons. John educated at local Friends' school and when aged 15 became assistant at Thomas Barnet's school at Pickwick, Wilts, where Richard Reynolds was educated. John then went to Ireland and succeeded his brother James as master of the Cork school. When James became master at Mountmellick he worked with him there, taking complete charge when James became involved with the linen business in the neighbourhood. In 1750 he became master of one of the earlier Dublin schools where he remained for 23 years. In 1774 he took charge of the Ulster Provincial School at Lisburn and at about this time, appeared as a minister visiting Meetings in England in this capacity in 1785.

Grant, Hannah, 1783-1860, after 1808 Darby, *qv.*

Green, Patience, 1733/4-1794, after 1758 Brayton, *qv.*

Gregory, Ann, 1769-1806. Daughter of William (1708?-1796) and Ann (Hitchcock, 1731-1825) Byrd of Uffculme, Devonshire. Married (1) 1790 Robert Fry (1767-1790) of Culmstock; (2) 1798 Robert Gregory (1755-1817) of Yatton, Somerset. First appeared in the ministry when aged 34.

Gregory, Robert, 1755-1817. Son of Edward (1713-1768) and Ann (Cary, 1720?-1797) Gregory, it being his father's second marriage. A grazier of Yatton, Somerset. Married (1) 1782 Ann Isaac (1754-1794) of Frampton Cotterell, Glos (six children); (2) 1798 Ann Fry (born Byrd, 1769-1806), widow of Robert Fry (five children); (3) 1811 Lydia Lury (1768-1831) of Olveston, Glos. They took over the headmaster and mistress-ship of Sidcot Friends' School, Somerset, from 1812 to 1817, successfully.

Grellet, Stephen, 1773-1855 (Étienne de Grellet du Mabillier). Married 1804 Rebecca Collins of New York (1772-1861). Third son of Gabriel Marc-Antoine and Susanne (de Senamaud) de Grellet, a well-to-do Catholic family, who owned ironworks and one of the famous porcelain factories at Limoges. Gabriel de Grellet was also a director of the Mint. Stephen received a good education and attended the College of Oratorians in Lyon founded by Cardinal Berulle. The French Revolution broke out in his seventeenth year and the family estates were confiscated. His parents were imprisoned in 1793, but saved from execution by the fall of Robespierre two years later. Stephen, with his brothers Joseph and Pierre had joined the Royalist forces of the Princes, but when these were disbanded they escaped to Holland, where there were family business connections and where Pierre remained. Stephen and Joseph went to Demerara in Dutch Guiana for two years, but as there was no possibility of rejoining their parents they decided to go to South America, but eventually left there for New York in 1795 and then on to Long Island to stay with Colonel Corsa, whose daughter spoke good French. She lent Penn's *No Cross No Crown* to Stephen and took him to Meeting, which was where he first met and heard Deborah Darby speak. Subsequently at a gathering at the Corsas' house Deborah spoke directly to the two brothers, her words having a profound effect upon Stephen for he had just previously received a spiritual revelation in the form of hearing the word Éternitie being expressed thrice as he walked in the fields. Deborah's encouragement coming on top of this experience set him upon a life of wonderful achievement in the uplifting of souls to God. On leaving for Philadelphia shortly afterwards, while Joseph returned to New York; he earned his living teaching French. William Savery, Samuel Emlen and Rebecca Young welcomed him to their Meeting and he joined Friends in 1796, being recorded as a minister in 1798. His first missionary journey was to the southern states with John Hall, an English minister. In 1804 he visited Canada and in 1807 went to France to visit his mother and relations, his father having died in 1803. He was in England in 1812 and early in 1813 met and influenced Elizabeth Fry to undertake her great work in Newgate Prison, culminating in far-reaching prison reforms. Over the next few years he paid a further three visits to Europe including the countries of Turkey, Scandinavia, Greece and Russia. His most renowned audiences were with Alexander I, Tzar of Russia in 1818 who was interested in Quakerism, and in 1819 with Pope Pius VII. He also had audiences with several other crowned heads. On these extraordinary and unique travels over immense distances he met innumerable people upon whom he was to have much influence for good because of his gifts of attraction and dedication. He met many heads of states and people in powerful positions, as well as those who flocked to hear him preach and those who were to be moved by chance encounters with him. Some time after Deborah's death he visited Coalbrookdale and stayed with her relations, worshipping with them at the Meeting House in the Dale. In 1834 he visited the Dale for the last time, calling upon Deborah's nephew, Francis, at The White House. He returned to his family in America in 1835 and spent his last 20 years in Burlington, New Jersey. His daughter Rachel, born 1810, lived until 1901. His life story shows how he used his talents to the full potential.

Grover, William, 1752-1825. Son of William (1704-1768) and Elizabeth (Ellis) Grover. Became a grocer and draper at Stansted, Essex. Married 1786 Isabel Weatherald. Prominent Friend and clerk of London Yearly Meeting 1790.

Grubb, Margaret, 1751-1829. Eldest daughter of Richard and Elizabeth Shackleton of Ballitore, Ireland. Married 1776 Samuel Grubb (1750-1815) of Clonmel, Co. Tipperary.

Grubb, Robert, 1743-1797. Of Clonmel, Co. Tipperary, Ireland. Married 1782 Sarah (1756-1790), daughter of William and Elizabeth (Hoyland) Tuke.

Grubb, Samuel, 1750-1815. Corn merchant and miller of Clonmel, Co. Tipperary, Ireland, son of Joseph and Sarah Grubb. Married 1776 Margaret Shackleton (1751-1829), eldest daughter of Richard and Elizabeth Shackleton of Ballitore School where he had been a pupil: 11 children, of whom eight grew up. He was an active minister and they entertained many Friends.

Grubb, Sarah, 1756-1790. Daughter of William (1732-1822) and Elizabeth (Hoyland) Tuke of York. Her mother died in her childhood and her stepmother, Esther, and father brought her up; she had a good education. At the age of 16 she helped to nurse John Woolman in his last illness. When 23 she appeared in the ministry and travelled in neighbouring counties before her marriage in 1782 to Robert Grubb (1743-1797) of Clonmel, Co. Tipperary. Founded a school on Suir Island modelled on that of Trinity Lane, York, set up by Esther Tuke, her step-mother, in 1784.

Gulson, Rebecca, 1731-1803, after 1763 Reynolds, *qv.*

Gurney, Elizabeth, 1780-1845, after 1800 Fry, *qv.*

Gurney, John, 1749-1809. Second son of John (1716-1770) and Elizabeth (Kett, d. 1788) Gurney. Married 1773 Catherine Bell (1755-1794). Leased Earlham Hall 1786 from the Bacon family and this became the family home. Among their children were Elizabeth (1780-1845, after 1800 Fry) and Joseph John (1788-1847).

Gurney, Joseph John, 1788-1847. Son of John (1749-1809) and Catherine (Bell, 1755-1794) Gurney. Norwich banker. Married (1) 1817 Jane Birkbeck (1789-1822); (2) 1827 Mary Fowler (1802-1835); (3) 1841 Eliza Paul Kirkbride (1801-1881). Mary Fowler was the niece of Deborah Darby and daughter of Robert and Rachel (Barnard) Fowler of Melksham. Joseph John was a younger brother of Elizabeth Fry, and he and Mary visited Sunniside in the early 19th century.

Gurney, Priscilla Hannah, 1757-1828. Daughter of Joseph and Christiana (Barclay) Gurney. Brought up a Friend but at 19 joined the Church of England; returned to Friends after a few years. Came to live in Coalbrookdale 1790 as the guest of Rebecca and Richard Reynolds at Dale House and remained until 1804, and it was due to her that Elizabeth Gurney (later Fry) came as a girl to stay in 1798, and became influenced for life by Deborah Darby's words on her future destiny. From Coalbrookdale Priscilla Hannah went to live in Bath. During the years in Coalbrookdale she travelled in the ministry for several months at a time. Catherine Fry described her as 'small in person, beautiful in countenance, elegant in manner, dressed in the old-fashioned black silk hood retained by the Friends, delicate in health and notwithstanding her having become a plain Quaker and a minister, almost fastidiously refined in habit, like a fine portrait by Cornelius Jansen'.

Hadwen, Isaac, 1753-1842. Born at Liverpool, son of Isaac and Hannah Hadwen. Married 1791 Susannah Gaylard (1756-1827), daughter of Andrew and Susanna Gaylard of Bristol. On several occasions accompanied American ministers and became a minister himself in 1813.

Hadwen, Susanna, 1756-1827. Daughter of Andrew and Susanna Gaylard of Bristol. Went to live at Warwick when about 18 and appeared in the ministry when aged 26, being recorded in 1785. Married 1791 Isaac Hadwen (1753-1842) of Liverpool. Her sister Hannah had married Robert Barnard.

Harford, John Scandrett, 1754-1815. Son of Edward (1720-1806) and Sarah (Scandrett) Harford. Partner in Harford Bank, Bristol.

Harford, Richard Summers, 1763-1837. Son of James (1734-1817) and Ann (Summers) Harford. Cousin of John. Wealthy Bristol merchant. Connected with Richard Reynolds and Lloyds' metal trade.

Harrison, Sarah, 1746-1812. Daughter of Roland Richards of Chester County, Pennsylvania. Married Thomas Harrison (1741-1815) of Philadelphia: large family. A minister in 1781. In 1787 attended London Yearly Meeting where it was said she preached in a voice like 'the deep majestic solemn organ blow'. She also visited the southern states of America with Mary England and laboured with much success with Friends holding slaves, and saw over 200 freed. In 1792 visited Liverpool with Sarah Benson and also went to Ireland. In 1793 she travelled to Scotland and in 1798 landed at Hamburg with George Stacey, Charity Cook and Mary Sewell for visits to Germany, returning to America in 1799. Her *Map of meetings of the northern counties*, signed by her, is in the Ironbridge Gorge Museum, evidently left with the Darbys.

Harry, Jane, 1756?-1784, after 1782 Thresher, *qv*.

Hawksworth, Lydia, 1733/4-1788. Daughter of Samuel (1690/1-1775) and Deborah (Hawkins, 1697-1776) Waring of Alton, Hampshire. Married 1768 Abraham Richard Hawksworth (1729-1768) of Bristol: her first appearance in the ministry was at his graveside the same year. Her ministerial journeys took her to most counties of England and Wales and also to Ireland.

Haworth, Martha, 1750-1799. Daughter of George and Martha Haworth of Shuttleworth Hall, Lancashire. Minister at 21 years. Travelled in British Isles and once to Channel Islands. In the United States at the same time as Deborah Darby and Rebecca Young. In later years much engaged in appointing Meetings amongst those of other Societies. Thomas Wilkinson wrote of her as a 'young heroine'.

Haydock, Henry, 1724-1798, of New York. Married (1) 1746 Mary Bowne of Flushing, Long Island; (2) 1759 Catherine Rodman (1731-1760); (3) 1763 Hannah Moode (1738?-1791). Emigrated from Lancashire to America in 1743 with his parents and five brothers and sisters. A prominent New York Quaker merchant.

Haydock, Henry, 1768-1827. Son of Henry (1724-1798) and Hannah (Moode, 1738?-1791) Haydock of New York. Henry's sister Mary (1765-1836) married in New York, 9th October 1793, Edmund Prior, Deborah Darby being present.

Henshaw, Frances, 1714-1793, after 1745 Paxton, after 1758 Dodshon, *qv*.

Hicks, Elias, 1748-1830. Son of John and Martha (Smith) Hicks of Long Island, New York. Married 1771 Jemima Seaman. Acknowledged as a minister 1778. Deborah Darby and Rebecca Young met the family when they were in America. Vigorous campaigner against slavery. By the early 19th century his theological position was being remarked upon by Stephen Grellet as unorthodox. Opposition to his views steadily grew, notably within Philadelphia YM, and his name is used to describe the non-evangelical party after the separations in various American YMs in 1827-8.

Hird, Christiana, 1732-1811, after 1763 Hustler, *qv*.

Holmes, John. Visited Coalbrookdale with Stephen Grellet in 1834.

Holtham, Hannah and William. This family is mentioned several times; members of the local Meeting.

Hopkins, John. In the American cotton trade.

Horton, Robert. Bailiff to Abraham Darby I and later ran the farm at Sunniside for Abiah. His wife, Agnes (Watson, 1722?-1781), accompanied Abiah to the eastern counties in 1762 and on other journeys.

Hoskins, John, 1728?-1814. A faithful attender of Philadelphia Yearly Meeting. He was always punctual and was called 'the Regulator'. His life was a pattern of gentleness and affection.

Hoyland, John, 1752-1831. Son of John and Sarah Hoyland of Sheffield. Married 1781 Elizabeth Barlow (1758-1839) who became a well-known ministering Friend. In 1818 they moved from Sheffield to Northampton.

Hoyland, Joseph. Son of John and Sarah Hoyland of Sheffield. Married 1787 Margaret English (1765-1833). Moved to Waterford, Ireland, in 1791.

Hoyland, Margaret, 1765-1833. Daughter of Nathaniel and Jane English of Sheepscar, near Leeds. Her father was an oil drawer. Married 1787 Joseph Hoyland. At 21 years became a minister. Moved in 1791 to Waterford, Ireland, whence she made visits to Great Britain.

Huntley, Thomas, 1733-1813. Son of Joseph (1706/7-1756) and Mary (Potter) Huntley. He was a former Master of Hillside Academy, Burford, which Samuel and Edmund Darby attended, as also did their cousins, the sons of Abraham and Rebecca Darby. He was a competent scholar in languages and compiled French, Latin and English Grammars. Married (1) 1770 Mary Coles of Henley; (2) 1778 Hannah Cowdry. His son Joseph (1775-1849) established the biscuit bakery in Reading 1822. His grandson Thomas (1803-1857), biscuit baker, became partner with George Palmer in 1841 – the start of Huntley & Palmers of Reading, the biscuit firm.

Hustler, Christiana, 1731-1811. Daughter of William (1694-1762) and Sarah Hird of Rawdon, Yorks. First appeared as a minister when aged 20; travelled extensively; visited 1792 Nantucket Friends who had settled at Dunkirk. Married 1763 John Hustler (1715-1790) of Bradford.

Hustler, John, 1715-1790. Son of William (d. 1759) and Jane (Jowett) Hustler of Calverley, Yorks. Became a Bradford woolstapler and built Undercliffe House. Promoted Leeds and Liverpool Canal. Married 1763 Christiana Hird (1731-1811).

Jackson, John, 1748-1821. Lived with his wife at London Grove, Virginia. A very skilled gardener and botanist, who had begun to create a fine garden about 1776, located in a limestone valley of natural beauty and fertility. There was a spring arising which gave an abundant water supply for aquatic plants. He had collected many indigenous and foreign species over the years, which made by the 1790s a place of considerable interest. It is to be hoped that Deborah and Rebecca were taken to this garden of exceptional beauty when they visited the Jacksons' home where, in the fall of the year, there would still have been much colour of leaf and berry. John Jackson kept a very careful receipt book of all of his payments, in which it is recorded that he bought a horse in 1796 for £25 and in 1797 a cow for £7-1s-0d.

Janney, Israel, 1752-1823. From Loudon County, Virginia. Deborah met him in Goose Creek Meeting. He was sufficiently a chemist to introduce the use of gypsum and red cloves.

Janney, Sarah, 1735?-1815. Fairfax Meeting, Virginia. Travelled with Deborah's aunt Rachel Wilson who wrote on 4.2.1769 that she had been 'exceedingly serviceable to me in Meeting and out of Meeting, her testimony sweet and lively, though not very long. We have travelled together in great unity'.

Johnson, Benjamin, 1766-1822. Son of Caleb and Martha (Davis) Johnson; born in Lancaster, Pennsylvania. He founded a publishing house in Pennsylvania with his brother Jacob. In 1796-7 he travelled with William Savery in Great Britain, Ireland, France and Germany, and was one of the Friends who sailed back on the *Sussex* with Deborah Darby.

Jones, Ann, 1774-1846. Daughter of Joseph and Sarah Burgess of Grooby Lodge, Leicester. First appeared in ministry at Coalbrookdale when 22 years old; visited in British Isles. Married 1815, as his third wife, George Jones (1765-1841) of Stockport, Cheshire. They visited America together.

Jones, George, 1765-1841. Born at Horsehay, Shropshire, son of William and Elizabeth Jones. Became a draper at Stockport, Cheshire. Married (1) 1787 Mary Taylor (d. 1788); (2) 1793 Sarah Hargrave (d. 1811); (3) 1815 Ann Burgess (1744-1846) of Leicester. They were strong conservative elements in British Quakerism.

Jones, Rebecca, 1739-1812. Lived at Brookcourt, Philadelphia. A much-travelled minister and a keen observer of events around her. She had the yellow fever in 1793 but recovered well. She wrote to Esther Tuke saying that 'our dear Friends Deborah Darby and Rebecca Young are in this City engaged in visiting families in the Pine Street Meeting'. She was a minister for many years.

Leadbeater, Mary, 1758-1826. Daughter of Richard (1726-1792) and Elizabeth (Carton) Shackleton of Ballitore, Co. Kildare. She was a gifted writer, poetess and historian. She married 1791 William Leadbeater (1763?-1827).

Leadbeater, William, 1763?-1827. Married 1791 Mary Shackleton (1758-1826), daughter of Richard Shackleton, head of the school at Ballitore, Co. Kildare, where William was a master of languages, a skilled teacher of French who interested his pupils in that country.

Lindley, Jacob, 1744-1814. Son of Jonathan and Deborah (Halliday) Lindley. Married (1) Hannah Miller (1755-1798) of New Garden Meeting, Chester County, Pennsylvania, who died of yellow fever after attending Philadelphia

Yearly Meeting; (2) 1800 Ruth Anna Rutter (1768-1810). Jacob was a worthy and celebrated public minister, by nature outspoken and excitable, and had a voice of great compass. He spoke against war and stood up to General Howe and General Washington. He went on a missionary expedition to the Indians near Detroit, Michigan, where he met William Savery. He was active in the founding of Westtown School. He was killed by being thrown from his chaise going from Meeting and broke his neck. Deborah and Rebecca met the Lindleys at New Garden Meeting in 1793.

Lindley, Ruth Anna, 1768-1810. Daughter of Thomas and Martha (Potts) Rutter, Pennsylvania episcopalians of considerable wealth. She became a Friend in 1787, influenced in part by the ministry of William Savery and Job Scott. In 1790 she became a minister. Deborah met her at Providence Meeting on 20th November 1794 and at Philadelphia Quarterly Meeting on 2nd February 1795. Ruth Anna finally convinced her mother of the value of Friends. Married 1800, as his second wife, Jacob Lindley (1744-1814). She was not strong in old age.

Lloyd, Charles, 1748-1828. Son of Sampson II (1699-1779) and Rachel (Champion, 1712-1756) Lloyd of Birmingham. Known as 'Charles the Banker'. Married 1774 Mary Farmer (1750-1821): 15 children. She inherited Bingley Hall, a country house near Birmingham.

Lloyd, John, 1750/1-1811. Third son of Sampson II (1699-1779) and Rachel (Champion, 1712-1756) Lloyd. Married 1779 Elizabeth (1752-1839), daughter of Thomas Corbyn of Bartholomew Close, near the Royal Exchange, London: 10 children. In 1772 Osgood Hanbury took John into the tobacco business of Hanbury, Taylor, Lloyd & Bowman at Tower Street. John and Elizabeth lived at Tower Street from 1794 and entertained there. In 1794 John began to work at Hanbury, Taylor & Co. in Lombard Street. He worked indefatigably for the abolition of slavery.

Lloyd, Mary, 1750-1821. Daughter of Priscilla (Plumstead, 1725-1796) and James Farmer. Married 1774 Charles Lloyd (1748-1828), 'Charles the Banker'.

Lloyd, Mary, 1763-1816. Daughter of Sampson III (1728-1807) and Rachel (Barnes, 1746-1814) Lloyd of Birmingham. A Quaker minister from about 1788.

Lloyd, Rachel, 1712-1756. Daughter of Nehemiah II (1678-1747) and Susanna (Truman, b. 1675) Champion of Bristol. Married 1731, as his second wife, Sampson Lloyd II (1699-1779) of Birmingham: four sons and two daughters.

Lloyd, Sampson II, 1699-1779. Son of Sampson I (1664-1724/5) and Mary (Crowley) Lloyd. His mother was daughter of Ambrose Crowley, an ironmaster of Stourbridge. Married (1) 1727 Sarah Parkes (1699-1729) (one son, Sampson Lloyd III); (2) 1731 Rachel Champion (1712-1756) (four sons and two daughters, one son dying in infancy). On Rachel's death Sampson's widowed sister Olive Kirton came to help him bring up his young children. Much business expansion came during the Seven Years War (1756-1763) when supplies from the continent were cut off. The Lloyds acquired a charcoal furnace at Melbourne, near Derby, to supply some of their bar iron, and a forge at Powick, near Worcester. In 1765 Sampson set up a Bank with John Taylor, a very successful button maker, with his son Sampson III and young Taylor as equal partners – followed in 1770 by the opening of a Bank in London with his son-in-law Osgood Hanbury, to be known as Hanbury, Lloyd, Taylor & Bowman. The main conduct of the business now passed to the younger generation but Sampson continued to be active until his death. He had paid regular visits to the Darbys over the years, staying with them at both Dale House and Sunniside. The era of canals had arrived, which greatly enhanced all trade in the Midlands.

Lloyd, Sampson III, 1728-1807. Son of Sampson II (1699-1779) and Sarah (Parkes) Lloyd. Married 1762 Rachel (1746-1814), daughter of Samuel Barnes of Clapton, an eminent silk dyer: 17 children, 13 of whom grew up, five sons becoming bankers. Sampson was described as remarkably handsome, with a fine tall figure. When young he was inclined to dress in the fashion and move in worldly society, but about the 1750s he changed and became a serious businessman and a devout Quaker. He helped his father in all the iron trade and was his partner in the Bank in both Birmingham and London with the Taylors. In 1753 Sampson II made over to his son his mother Parkes' inheritance. Rachel and Sampson III when newly married lived at 18 Park Street, and after 10 years moved to 13 The Square, Birmingham. He visited Sunniside on business, first with his father and then alone, once or twice a year, but also attended Meetings (some further afield) going on with Friends to Quarterly and Yearly Meetings in Wales.

Luccock, Thomas, 1692-1754. Thomas's father came to Coalbrookdale about 1714. Thomas' deed of apprenticeship being dated 13th June of that year. Joan Luccock of the same family became the second wife of John, father of Abraham Darby I.

Majolier, Louis, 1764-1842. Lived and kept the school at Congénies, near Nimes, in the south of France. He received William Savery and Benjamin Johnson into his home early in 1797 when they were on their travels in France and Holland. The visitors spent some days visiting Friends there and in neighbouring places, finally making some suggestions, which were accepted, for more formal arrangements of Meetings. There were peasant communities here in which hard work in the vineyards and olive groves were the main occupations. Friends who had visited previously included Robert and Sarah Grubb, George and Sarah Dillwyn and Mary Dudley. Louis Majolier had stayed in the south of England one summer some years before and there Deborah had met him on her return from London Yearly Meeting.

Marshall, Esther, 1738/9-1822, after 1784 Brady, after 1796 Clark, *qv*.

Maude, Rachel, 1714-1786, after 1734 Thompson, *qv*.

Maude, Warren, 1710-1779. Son of Samuel (1665-1730) and Rachel (Warren, 1667-1734) Maude and brother of Abiah Darby. Married (1) Mary (b. 1710), daughter of Thomas Forster; (2) Sarah, daughter of Thomas Holme of Kendal: five children. He and Sarah visited Sunniside.

Maude, William, 1731-1765. Son of William (1700-1730) and Hannah (Freeman, b. 1701) Maude. Nephew of Abiah Darby. Lived at Holmside Cottage, Sunderland, with his widowed mother, his brother and sisters. A coal fitter; at time of his death had begun to appear as a minister.

Messer, Elizabeth, 1753-1821. Daughter of Isaac (1714/5-1785) and Rachel (Wilson, 1720-1775) Wilson of Kendal. First cousin of Deborah Darby. Married 1786 John Messer (1753-1821): seven children.

Messer, John, 1753-1821. Son of Joseph and Hannah Messer of Alton, Hampshire. Married 1786 Elizabeth (1753-1821), daughter of Isaac and Rachel Wilson of Kendal: seven children.

Mifflin, Charles, 1753-1783. A first cousin of Thomas Mifflin, later Major General in War of Independence and first Governor of Pennsylvania under Federal Government. Married 1777 Mary Waln (d. 1777).

Mifflin, Daniel, 1722-1795. Son of Edward (1685-1743) and Mary (Eyre) Mifflin. Married (1) 1744 Mary Warner; (2) 1757 Ann Walker; (3) c.1788 Mary Pasey Husband (1742-1823).

Mifflin, Daniel, 1754-1812. Son of Daniel (1722-1795) and Mary (Warner) Mifflin. Married 1778 Deborah Howell.

Mifflin, Warner, 1745-1798. Son of Daniel (1722-1795) and Mary (Warner) Mifflin. Awakened religiously by Rachel Wilson, aunt to Deborah Darby, in 1768. In 1770 made Justice of the Peace, his only office. Worked against slavery. In 1774/5 freed all his slaves and those he had received from his father's estate. In 1777 with other Friends visited Howe and Washington. Married (1) Elizabeth Johns (d. 1786); (2) 1788 Anne Emlen. Moved to Kent County, Delaware and died near Camden, Delaware, of yellow fever which he had caught in Philadelphia.

Murray, John, 1737-1808. Brother of Robert Murray. Host to Deborah and Rebecca in 1793 in New York and travelled with them that same year.

Murray, John, 1758-1819. Son of Robert (1721-1786) and Mary (Lindley) Murray. Married 1783 Catherine Bowne.

Murray, Lindley, 1745-1826. Eldest son of Robert (1721-1786) and Mary (Lindley) Murray. Born near Swetara, Lancaster County, Pennsylvania. Married 1767 Hannah Dobson (1748-1834). His father built up a considerable mercantile trade in the middle period of his life and moved to New York in 1753. Lindley went to school and was well thought of at an early age. He went into his father's counting house and also to a Philadelphia merchant, but his training did not satisfy him and after various vicissitudes he settled in New York with his family and had a private tutor to instruct him in classics and liberal studies. He then studied for the Bar. His father went to England for a few years, his health being poor, returning to New York in 1775. His mother (a celebrated Quaker belle) was an attractive and amiable woman and it was she who in 1776 entertained the British commander Lord Howe at her home and thus saved the American army by diverting Howe's attention from the retreating troops. Lindley was a successful lawyer and after Independence bought a property named Bellvue, but before he and Hannah moved there he had a bad illness and finally decided to go to England and live in an easier climate. He and Hannah settled at Holdgate House, near York, where they were happy and received many visiting Friends. He was not at all strong for the rest of his life, but wrote the famous *English Grammar* which went into many editions on both sides of the Atlantic and was widely used in schools. He gave support to Esther Tuke's school in Trinity Lane, York, and to the founding of The Retreat, and encouraged Friends to give their votes for the election of William Wilberforce to Parliament. He continued to revise his *Grammar* and remained able to see and hear well and, though an invalid confined to his chair, his brain remained active throughout his later years. He also wrote on religion including *The Power of Religion on the Mind*. His summerhouse is now in the garden of The Mount School, York, and is a delightful reminder of the many hours he spent in it at Holdgate House writing his valuable books there.

Naftel, Nicholas, 1762-1842. Son of Thomas (d. 1764) and Elizabeth (Blondel, 1731?-1809) Naftel of Guernsey. Became a Friend in 1787. Married 1789 Mary Higman (1756-1820) of a family formerly of St Austell, Cornwall. They travelled together in the ministry and were hosts to Deborah and Rebecca when they visited Guernsey in 1792. In 1804 the Naftels moved to Colchester, moving briefly to London and then to Chelmsford. He returned to Guernsey after his wife's death.

Ogden, Bernard, 1734?-1779. Married Elizabeth (1729?-1805), daughter of William and Hannah (Freeman) Maude: one daughter and three sons.

Ormiston, Mary. Of Kelso, relation of the Maudes of Sunderland. Visited by both Abiah and Deborah Darby on their way to and from Scotland.

Owen, Dorothy (Dorti), 1751?-1793. Daughter of Rowland and Lowry Owen of the neighbourhood of Dolgellau, Merioneth, Wales. Appeared as a minister at 22. Her testimony was lively and edifying. She would go as far as 40 miles on foot in the mountains, in all weathers, to attend Monthly Meeting. It was due to her efforts that the Meeting House at Tyddyn-y-garreg was built in 1792.

Paxton, William, d. 1753. Married 1745 Frances Henshaw (1714-1793) of Leek, Staffs, who later married William Dodshon.

Payton, Catherine, 1726-1794, after 1772 Phillips, *qv*.

Pemberton, John, 1727-1795. Son of Israel (1684-1754) and Rachel (Read) Pemberton of Philadelphia. Visited England 1750-1, accompanying his compatriot John Churchman on some of his ministerial journeys. Married 1766

Hannah Zane. Made an extended ministerial journey to Europe 1782-9, including all parts of the British Isles. On his third visit to Europe, beginning 1794, died while visiting Friends at Pyrmont, Germany.

Penrose, Samuel. Started to make Waterford glass in Ireland in 1783.

Phillips, Catherine, 1726/7-1794. Daughter of Henry (1671-1746) and Ann (Fowler) Payton of Dudley, Worcs. Her father was a minister. She was educated at home and then under Rachel Trafford. Began her ministry at 22 years, visiting Friends in British Isles, Holland and America. Lucy Bradley accompanied her to Wales and Mary Peisley (afterwards Neale) to America where they travelled over 8,700 miles. Married 1772 William Phillips (d. 1785) of Redruth, Cornwall, where she was concerned with the establishment of Women's Meetings.

Phillips, William, d. 1785. Son of Richard (d. 1753) and Esther (1681?-1778) Phillips of Swansea. Settled near Redruth, Cornwall, as agent to a copper company. His first wife, Frances, died in 1745 and he married (2) 1772 Catherine Payton (1726/7-1794). His son James (1743-1799) took over in 1777 the printing and publishing firm in George Yard, Lombard Street, which had long been responsible for official Quaker publications.

Pim, Elizabeth, 1749/50-1802. Daughter of John (1718-1797) and Sarah (Clibborn, 1724-1812) Pim of Dublin. The family moved to London in 1773 but about 1786 Elizabeth settled at Anner Mills, Co. Tipperary, being soon afterwards called to the ministry. Deborah wrote to her from America on 21st November 1793 and also mentioned her in later years in her Journal.

Plumstead, Hannah, 1729-1807. Daughter of William and Mary Lunn of London and related to Abiah Darby through the second marriage of her grandfather, William Warren of Scarborough. Married 1748 Robert Plumstead (1724-1760): mother of Mary Bevan and Hannah Birkbeck. An excellent woman of great piety and benevolence, being blessed with ample means for charitable deeds for many. She became an Elder.

Price, Peter, 1739-1821. Brought up a Roman Catholic but became a Friend and settled in Falmouth, Cornwall, as a corn factor. In 1800 moved to Neath Abbey Works, South Wales, becoming a noted ironmaster. Frequently visited Coalbrookdale. Married 1781 Anna Tregelles (1759-1846).

Prior, Edmund. From New York. Married 1793 Mary Haydock (1765-1836). Later became active in the anti-slavery campaign influenced by Moses Brown.

Pusey, Joshua, 1739?-1804. A miller of London Grove Meeting, Chester County, Philadelphia. Son of William and Elizabeth (Liddon) Pusey and grandson of Caleb Pusey, Collector of West Fallowfull Township. A noted minister among Friends.

Rathbone, Elizabeth, 1740-   , after 1763 Fawcett, *qv.*

Rathbone, Elizabeth, 1756-1793. Daughter of William III (1726-1789) and Rachel (Rutter) Rathbone of Liverpool and sister of William IV (1757-1809) who married 1786 Harriet Mary Reynolds. Elizabeth died unmarried.

Rathbone, Hannah Mary, 1761-1839. Daughter of Richard (1735-1816) and Hannah (Darby, 1735-1762) Reynolds of Coalbrookdale. Married 1786 William Rathbone IV (1757-1809) of Liverpool.

Rathbone, Joseph, 1746-1790. Son of William II (1696-1746) and Elizabeth (Johnson) Rathbone, being the only son by the second marriage. Married 1768 Mary (1748-1807), eldest daughter of Abraham Darby II: one son, William, who died as an infant. Managed Coalbrookdale business in Liverpool.

Rathbone, Mary, 1748-1807. Eldest daughter of Abraham II (1711-1763) and Abiah (Maude, 1716-1794) Darby. Married 1768 Joseph Rathbone (1746-1790) of Liverpool.

Rathbone, William III, 1726-1789. Son of William II (1696-1746) and Sarah (Hyde) Rathbone. Married (1) 1750 Rachel Rutter; (2) 1762 Margaret Fletcher. He was a minister and travelled extensively in his later years, being a frequent companion to Deborah Darby. His mother died when he was about two years old and his father became a Friend about 1730.

Rathbone, William IV, 1757-1809. Son of William III (1726-1789) and Rachel (Rutter) Rathbone of Liverpool. Married 1786 Hannah Mary Reynolds (1761-1839): eight children. He was the first importer of American cotton. Published 1804 *A Narrative of Events that have recently taken place in Ireland*, in which he sided with the 'New Lights' who were disowned by Irish Friends: the publication led to his own disownment and his descendants become well-known Unitarians.

Rawes, William, 1755-1803. Son of William (1726?-1803) and Hannah (Clothier, 1726-1803) Rawes of Sherborne, Dorset. Married (1) 1778 Eleanor Beaven; (2) 1792 Anna Fox, (after 1808 Thompson, 1755-1823), daughter of Joseph and Elizabeth Fox of Falmouth, Cornwall. Both he and his father represented Dorset Quarterly Meeting at London Yearly Meeting over a long period and he was its clerk in 1801. He was in business in Marnhull, Dorset. First appeared in the ministry when aged about 37.

Reynolds, Hannah, 1735-1762. Daughter of Abraham II (1711-1763) and Margaret (Smith, d. 1740) Darby. Married 1757 Richard Reynolds (1735-1816).

Reynolds, Hannah Mary, 1761-1839, after 1786 Rathbone, *qv.*

Reynolds, Joseph, 1768-1859. Son of Richard (1735-1816) and Rebecca (Gulson, 1731-1803) Reynolds. Married 1793 Deborah Dearman (1770-1803).

Reynolds, Mary, b. 1743/4, after 1764 Cowles, after 1786 Beesley, *qv.*

Reynolds, Rebecca, 1731-1803. Daughter of William (1695-1775) and Ann (d. 1734) Gulton of Coventry. Married 1763 Richard Reynolds (1735-1816) as his second wife.

Reynolds, Richard, 1735-1816. Son of Richard (1709-1769) and Jane (Donne) Reynolds of Bristol. His father was an ironmaster; his great-grandfather Michael Reynolds had been a convinced Friend and suffered persecution. Richard was educated at a Quaker school in Pickwick, Wilts, from age 5 to 14. Apprenticed 1750 to William Fry, grocer, of Bristol and in 1757 finished his apprenticeship and became a Freeman. Thomas Goldney sent him to Abraham Darby II at Coalbrookdale in 1756. Married (1) 1757 Hannah (1735-1762), eldest daughter of Abraham Darby II and his first wife, Margaret (Smith): two children, William (1758-1803) and Hannah Mary (1761-1839); (2) 1763 Rebecca (1731-1803), daughter of William Gulson of Coventry (three sons). Became a partner in the ironworks and lived at Ketley Bank. On the death of Abraham Darby II in 1763 moved to Dale House to take charge of the whole of the Coalbrookdale Company. When Abraham Darby III was 18 Richard returned to Ketley Bank but again had to help with the general conduct of the business when Abraham III died in 1789. Richard had moved again, by that time, to Dale House. In 1804 he left Coalbrookdale for Bristol after his wife's death in 1803. He achieved as an ironmaster much innovation and expansion; and carried on charitable work all his life. His relationship with his work people continued the policy of the Darbys – complete friendliness and care for their well-being.

Reynolds, Susannah, b. 1736. Eldest daughter of Richard (1709-1769) and Jane (Donne) Reynolds of Bristol. Married Joseph Ball.

Reynolds, William, 1758-1803. Son of Richard (1735-1816) and Hannah (Darby, 1735-1762) Reynolds. Married 1789 Hannah (d. 1844), daughter of Joseph and Susannah Ball, his first cousin: five children. A skilled ironmaster and man of much talent, magnetism and erudition. One of the most gifted of the family, who promoted new innovations, including the Coalport China Company and the Inclined Plane. Died at The Tuckies, Broseley, at the early age of 45.

Ridgway, Mary, 1728-1804. Daughter of Joseph (1700-1776) and Mary (Truslade, 1702/3-1746) Sparkes of Exeter. Became a minister in 1749 and visited Ireland with Sarah Splatt. Married 1754 Joshua Ridgway of Ballycarrol, Queen's Co., Ireland, and settled in Mountmellick. After her husband's death made extensive visits in Ireland, visited England and went once to America.

Rodman, Hannah, 1764-1819, after 1793 Fisher, *qv.*

Rotch, Benjamin. Son of William (1734-1828) and Elizabeth (Barney) Rotch of Nantucket. Spent some years in Dunkirk whence the Rotches had moved some of their whaling from America because of the War of Independence.

Rotch, Lydia. Daughter of William (1734-1828) and Elizabeth (Barney) Rotch of Nantucket. She travelled in 1792 to Dunkirk with Deborah Darby and Richard Reynolds, evidently to see her brother Benjamin there.

Rotch, William, 1734-1828. Head of Nantucket family conducting whale fishing. Married 1754 Elizabeth Barney. Lost financially during the War of Independence. Left to live in France at Dunkirk until 1790, when he returned to America. Richard Reynolds and Deborah Darby travelled to Dunkirk with him and his daughter Lydia in 1792. Deborah and Rebecca met the Rotches at different places in the United States, including their main place of business and home in Nantucket. William and his son also came to Sunniside.

Routh, Martha, 1743-1817. Daughter of Henry and Jane Winter of Stourbridge. In 1760 became a teacher in a Friends' boarding school in Nottingham, succeeding to the post of principal when aged 24. Acknowledged a minister in 1773. Married 1776 Richard Routh of Manchester and relinquished her school. In addition to frequent ministerial travels in the British Isles, she made an extensive visit to America in 1794-7 and a second one in 1804-5.

Rutter, Ruth Anna, 1768-1810, after 1800 Lindley, *qv.*

Rutter, Thomas, 1741-1800. Son of Benjamin and Jane Rutter of Bristol, where he became a bellows-maker. Married (1) 1768 Ruth Waring (1736-1778); (2) 1780 Hester Farley (1750-1806). First appeared in the ministry when aged 18; made several journeys to various parts of England, and visited Ireland in 1766 and 1793. Clerk of London Yearly Meeting 1776.

Sands, David, 1745-1818. Born at Cowneck, Long Island, son of Nathaniel and Mercy Sands, Presbyterians. Married 1771 Clementine, daughter of Edward and Phoebe Hallock. Moved to Cornwall, Orange County, State of New York at age 14: learned farming in new and untilled land. Did not receive a proper education, but by his own efforts learned Latin and with his father's help entered a mercantile business. Convinced through the ministry of Samuel Nottingham: accepted into membership in Nine Partners Monthly Meeting, New York, and recorded as a minister in 1772 and stayed with Moses Brown in Providence on his first ministerial journey. Retired from business to give more of his attention to religion and became a schoolmaster. Went to live with Edward Hallock, a Friend of New Marlborough who attended Nine Partners Meeting. Shortly afterwards returned to his former business involving visits to New York. Travelled extensively in the British Isles and was with William Savery in Holland, France and Germany in 1796. Visited many places in the British Isles, including Coalbrookdale where he witnessed the wedding of Edmund Darby and Lucy Burlingham in 1803. Deborah stayed with his family in New Cornwall Meeting along the Hudson River in 1795, although he was away in Europe at the time. She met him frequently after her return.

Savery, William, 1721/2-1787. Married Mary Peters (1722-1804). He was a fine cabinet-maker of Philadelphia whose work can be seen today in New York's

Metropolitan Museum. Mary (Peters) Savery was of Welsh extraction. The Savery family, who were Huguenots, left Montpelier, France at the revocation of the Edict of Nantes, 1685, one branch of the family going to England under the name of Savory. The American Saverys, it is believed, came to Maryland and eventually reached Pennsylvania. William's and Mary's address was 'The Sign of the Chair a little below the Market in Second Street'.

Savery, William, 1750-1804. Son of William and Mary (Peters) Savery. Married 1778 Sarah Evans of Bradford Township. He received a good schooling and was apprenticed c1764 to a tanner of Goshen Monthly Meeting in Chester County. When first grown-up he and his young companions were high spirited, but were much affected by the revolutionary war leading to Independence. This was followed for him by experiences of a spiritual nature that changed him for life. In 1778 he became a Master Tanner remaining in the trade all his life and the same year he also began to appear in Meetings as a minister. He had a concern for a better understanding of the Indians and later for all people who suffered in the countries of Europe, during and after revolution and war. He made a strong endeavour against slavery which was continually reinforced by first-hand experience of much cruelty personally witnessed by him. He volunteered to attend the first abortive Indian Treaty in 1793 and the second in 1794. He was a lively and appealing preacher and had a deep effect on the young and those of other denominations to whom he spoke frequently throughout his life. He left for Europe in 1796 on the *Sussex*, this same ship that took Deborah and Rebecca home. By then they had met and worked together since they first met in 1793 when he and his wife Sarah were away from home unable to return to Philadelphia, on account of the yellow fever raging. From then on they had met and worked in America at intervals and got to know each other well. He was also to see Deborah and Rebecca during his stay in England and his 1797 journey to Ireland and Scotland; as well as when he stayed at Sunnisïde and again at London Yearly Meeting. In the latter part of 1796 he, along with George and Sarah Dillwyn, William Farrer, David Sands and Benjamin Johnson visited Germany. Fortunately he could speak the language and left a vivid description of their difficult journey which lasted from August to December. It was a time of much upheaval and distress. At this time he was 46 years old, five feet nine or ten in height and inclined to slight corpulence, but with a good figure. His expression was placid but would brighten with an attractive and kindly smile. With David Sands and Benjamin Johnson he then travelled in Holland and France from December until May 1797. France was by then in the period of the Directory which had followed the 1792 Revolution in 1795. They were in Paris and other big towns and also visited Louis Majolier at Congénies near Nîmes before returning to England. Late in the year of 1797 he went to Ireland before the very difficult violent period which followed in 1798. In February of that year he was in Norwich and it was then that his meeting with Elizabeth Gurney produced the profound effect on her which eventually lead to the splendid reforms she brought about in the prisons which she first visited at the suggestion of Stephen Grellet. This awakening was reinforced that same summer when Elizabeth visited Coalbrookdale and met Deborah Darby who, sensing her potential, spoke to her in a manner which emphasised what William had said. William returned home that summer falling a victim to dropsy but continued his valuable work in his own country for the rest of his life, dying in 1804, six years before Deborah Darby.

Scattergood, Thomas, 1748-1814. American Friend, son of Joseph and Rebecca Scattergood of Burlington, New Jersey. Described as 'a powerful profit'. Married Elizabeth, daughter of David and Mary Bacon. Deborah and Rebecca met him at Abington Meeting in 1793 and were with his family in 1794 though Thomas was away in Europe where he remained from 1794 to 1800.

Shackleton, Margaret, 1751-1829, after 1776 Grubb, *qv.*

Shackleton, Mary, 1758-1826, after   Leadbeater, *qv.*

Shackleton, Richard, 1726-1792. Son of Abraham (1696-1771) and Margaret (Wilkinson) Shackleton. Abraham in 1726 started a noted boarding school at Ballitore, Co. Kildare and Richard succeeded him as Head, having been a pupil there with Edmund Burke, with whom he continued friendship. Married (1) 1749 Elizabeth Fuller (d. 1752); (2) 1755 Elizabeth Carton. Richard visited Sunniside and corresponded with Abiah Darby and later sent her a poem in Latin (with translation) on Coalbrookdale.

Sharpless, Joshua, 1746/7-1826. Born in Middletown, Pennsylvania, son of Benjamin and Martha (Mendenhall) Sharpless. Married (1) Edith Yarnall (d. 1787): five sons, three daughters; (2) 1789 Anne Trimble (d. 1837): one son, one daughter. Moved 1769 to New Garden, Pennsylvania; overseer 1775; active worker for abolition of slave-holding among Friends. In 1779 moved to Concord Monthly Meeting and became an overseer there in 1784 and that year bought 200-acre farm in East Bradford and Westtown townships and moved to Birmingham Monthly Meeting. In 1795 was founder of Birmingham Library; wrote about the ravages of yellow fever in Philadelphia, which he had witnessed in 1795. Also paid a visit to the Cornplanter Indians at Tunesassa, Western Pennsylvania. He and his wife Anne became first superintendents of Westtown School 1800-1811.

Shaw, Joseph. Became a Friend in mid-18th century and ran a boarding school of about 50 pupils at High Flatts, near Penistone, Yorkshire.

Simkin, Ann. Daughter of Edward and Margaret Bradley of Shrewsbury. Married 1807 Samuel Simkin, a carpenter of New Dale. He was the son of Edward (1750-1826) and Sarah (Coles) Simkin.

Simkin, Edward, 1750-1826. Married Sarah Coles. Came from London to settle in New Dale 1790.

Simkin, Samuel. Son of Edward (1750-1826) and Sarah (Coles) Simkin. Married 1807 Ann Bradley.

Smith, Samuel, 1737-1817. He and Mary Smith travelled in America with Deborah and Rebecca in 1794. They met with Abraham Smith in Westfield the same year.

Smithman, John. Lived and owned land in Little Wenlock, Shropshire, and was Sheriff in 1762. Partner in Madeley Wood furnace. Married Catherine Brooke, co-heiress of Comberford Brooke and so proprietor of the Lease of the Coalbrookdale Company with her sister, Rose Giffard.

Southall, Ann, 1804-1891. Daughter of Richard (1779-1840) and Mary (Trusted, 1778-1806) Burlingham of Worcester. Married 1839, as his second wife, Samuel Southall (1793-1853) of Leominster. Her portrait is in the Ironbridge Gorge Museum.

Sparkes, Mary, 1728-1804, after 1754 Ridgway, *qv.*

Sparrow, Richard. Of Clonmel, Co. Tipperary. Operated mills on the River Suir with machines from America of the most modern kind. He had a fine house with stables, coach house, brewery and dairy, and lived in considerable style.

Spavold, Samuel, 1708-1795. Son of Josiah and Elizabeth Spavold of Bawtry, Yorkshire. Educated by Friends; apprenticed to a carpenter; moved to London, working at Deptford and Chatham as a ship's joiner. Married (1) 1732/3 Sarah (Piggott, d. 1764), widow of Robert Tucker; (2) 1766 Phoebe, widow of William Lucas. No children of either marriage. Noted minister; went to America in 1757 and was present at the Indian Treaty at Easton, Pennsylvania, 1759.

Speakman, Phoebe, 1739-1828. Daughter of John and Ann Schofield of Bucks County, Pennsylvania, moving to Chester County in 1761. Married (1) Nathan Yarnall; (2) 1781 Micajah Speakman of Concord, Pennsylvania. Recorded a minister 1775; visited Long Island, New York and New England. Sailed from America with Deborah in 1796 and visited Great Britain and Ireland; remained for three years, travelling to attend 297 Meetings, covering in all about 4,000 miles. Returned to America and died at West Nantmeal, Pennsylvania. Sarah Talbot accompanied her on some of these journeys: she belonged to Owchlan Meeting, Downing Town, Pennsylvania.

Stacey, George, 1749-1816. Son of William and Rebecca (Browne) Stacey of Alton, Hants. Settled in Tottenham. Married 1781 Mary Wilson (1755-1836): two sons and four daughters.

Stacey, Mary, 1755-1836. Daughter of Isaac (1714/5-1785) and Rachel (Wilson, 1720-1775) Wilson of Kendal. First cousin of Deborah Darby. Married 1781 George Stacey (1749-1816) of Tottenham: two sons and four daughters.

Stephenson, Hannah, 1745-1804. Born in Whitehaven, Cumberland, daughter of David and Sarah Stephenson. About 1755 family moved to Isle of Man. Became a minister at 21 when in Essex and in 1782 moved to Bristol. Visited Meetings in many counties; particularly gifted in family visits.

Stephenson, Sarah, 1738-1802. Born in Whitehaven, Cumberland, daughter of David and Sarah Stephenson. A ministering Friend who travelled with Mary Jeffreys. Sarah, who then lived in Melksham, visited many places in the British Isles and crossed the Atlantic to travel in America, dying in Philadelphia.

Storer, John, 1725/6-1795. Son of Jonathan and Rebecca Storer of Nottingham, where he entered the wool stapling trade. A minister; travelled in America on various occasions between 1759 and 1786. Married (1) 1762 Sarah (Lindoe) Northen; (2) 1764 Hannah Sparrow.

Story, Thomas, 1662-1742. Brother of Dean of Limerick. Married 1706 Anne Shippen. Joined Friends in 1691. Friend of William Penn; went to Pennsylvania and became Recorder 1701, treasurer of Land Company, and Master of the Rolls. Returned to London 1714 and travelled as a minister. In his *Journal* (published by Isaac Thompson in Newcastle 1747) a reference is made to his visit to Coalbrookdale in 1735 and to Richard Ford, who would have been at Rosehill.

Summerland, Ann, 1709-1798. Daughter of Joshua and Rebecca Waterhouse of Dronfield, Derbyshire. Married 1737 John Summerland (d. 1767) and lived at Coalbrookdale. Had been in the household of Joseph Freeth of Coventry before her marriage. Made many ministerial journeys in the British Isles over the years and accompanied Abiah Darby on several occasions, including her journey to Berwick-on-Tweed in 1759. Also made several journeys with Deborah Darby.

Swett, Mary, 1739?-1821. Daughter of Jacob Howell. Married 1762 Benjamin Swett (1738?-1819). Both were ministers. From 1775 they were of Haddonfield, New Jersey. She travelled with Charity Cook on her visit to Europe 1797-1801, during which they visited many parts of the British Isles.

Talbot, Sarah. Wife of John Talbot. A member of Chichester Meeting, near Philadelphia. Travelled to British Isles with Deborah Darby in 1796 and also travelled thousands of miles with Phoebe Speakman.

Taylor, Sarah, 1717-1791. Daughter of John and Margaret Routh of Wensleydale, Yorkshire. Her mother, a minister, died when she was four years old. Sarah became a minister at 19. Married 1749 William Taylor, who died shortly after. She had a lovely wit and sound judgement; visited most English counties and also Wales and Ireland. Buried at Manchester.

Thompson, Isaac, 1701?-1776. Printer and publisher of Newcastle upon Tyne. Married 1734 Rachel (1714-1786), daughter of Samuel and Rachel Maude: three children (Jonathan who married Hannah Miller of Whitby; Samuel who married Elizabeth Pitt; Rachel who died young). He gave public lectures on natural and experimental philosophy and in 1720 was joined by Robert Harrison the mathematician. Published a book of poems in 1730 and in 1739 published the *Newcastle Journal* with William Cuthbert at their office 'on the head of the side'. The establishment was afterwards removed to Burnt House Entry where it continued until Isaac's death. By 1745 he was a person of 'considerable literary attainments' whose compositions were very numerous and appeared in many periodical publications. He published several volumes of literary works such as *A Journal of the Life of Thomas Story* (1747). His widow moved to Coalbrookdale after his death; his son Samuel also moved there, where he died in 1809.

Thresher, Jane, 1756?-1784, born Harry. Jamaican heiress who joined Friends; protégé of Dr Samuel Johnson. Mary Knowles befriended her when Dr Johnson violently opposed her becoming a member of the Society of Friends. She stayed at Sunniside 1779-1781 and relinquished her fortune in Jamaica to become a Friend. Her letters about her visit to Sunniside have been preserved. Married 1782 Joseph Thresher.

Till Adams, Ann, 1752-1817. Daughter of William (1723-1776) and Hannah (Plant) Fry of Bristol. Married 1777 John Till-Adams (1748-1786).

Till Adams, John, 1748-1786. The Tills were an old Staffordshire family. John was a doctor of medicine. Married 1777 Ann Fry (1752-1817). He was described as 'truly admired and pious'.

Townsend, Deborah, 1728-1794. Eldest daughter of Samuel (1690/1-1775) and Deborah (Hawkins, 1697-1776) Waring of Alton, Hants. Brought up as a Friend. Married 1751 James Townsend (1726/7-1798) of London: nine children. After some years she felt called to the ministry, visiting many parts of the country and in 1792 travelling to Dunkirk with Mercy Ransom. In 1794, again with Mercy, she travelled to Scotland. Wrote an epistle to Aberdeen Monthly Meeting. Died in Edinburgh.

Townsend, James, 1726/7-1798. Son of William (1686-1740) and Mary (Planner, 1686-1751) Townsend of Reading, Berks. Became a grocer in London. Married 1751 Deborah Waring (1728-1794): nine children.

Townsend, John, 1725-1801. Son of John and Mary (Townsend) Townsend of Longcot, near Uffington, Berks. Settled in London. Married 1752 Sarah Hogge (1722-1789): seven children, six dying in infancy. A ministering Friend, visiting Ireland 1765, Scotland 1767 and North America 1785, as well as travelling in various parts of England. His visit to America was at the same time as that of Thomas Colley of Sheffield.

Tuke, Henry, 1755-1814. Eldest son of William (1732/3-1822) and Elizabeth (Hoyland, 1729-1760) Tuke of York. Married 1781 Mary Maria Scott (1748-1815) of Norwich. Very well educated in the classics. Helped his father to run the family business leaving William more freedom to carry out his concerns. His son Samuel (1784-1857) wrote his *Description of the Retreat* in 1813 as the result of his involvement with his grandfather William Tuke's establishment of The Retreat, still in existence.

Tuke, Sarah, 1756-1790, after 1782 Grubb, *qv*.

Tuke, William, 1732/3-1822. Son of Samuel (1703-1748) and Ann (Ward) Tuke of York. Inherited a grocery business 1752. Married (1) 1754 Elizabeth Hoyland of Sheffield: five children, including Henry (1755-1814), and Sarah (1756-1790); (2) 1765 Esther Maud of Bingley: three children, including Ann (1767-1849). William developed his business well with the help of his son Henry and became a leading tea, coffee and cocoa merchant. He was an active Quaker and initiated and carried through many concerns, including the founding of The Retreat, the Quaker hospital for 'persons afflicted with disorders of the mind'; Ackworth School; the Quaker girls' school in York, which he helped his wife Esther to establish.

Waln, Nicholas II, 1742-1813. Son of Nicholas and Mary Waln of Fair Hill, near Philadelphia. Educated at William Penn School, where he learned to speak German and studied Latin. He studied law under Joseph Galloway and practised before he was 21, but after winning a case which defrauded an honest man he never afterwards pleaded in court. Spent time in England in 1763, studying at Temple Inns of Court. Married 1771 Sarah, only daughter of Joseph Richardson, a silversmith: two sons. Began to travel in the ministry 1774. In 1785 he again visited England and attended many Meetings throughout the country. Ten years later, with David Bacon, returned and visited Friends in England and Ireland until he went back to America where he continued to minister at Youth Meetings. Deborah met him at Pine Street Meeting and he stayed at Sunniside.

Waring, Deborah, 1728-1794, after 1751 Townsend, *qv.*

Waring, Lydia, 1733/4-1788, after 1768 Hawksworth, *qv.*

Were, Mary, 1741-1805. Daughter of Sarah and George Colesworthy of St Nicholas Street, Bristol, where she lived when young, afterwards moving to Haverfordwest, Pembrokeshire. Travelled in the ministry 1764-1770. Married 1772 Nicholas Were, a woollen merchant of Wellington, Somerset, where she settled.

Wilkinson, John, 1728-1808. Son of Isaac Wilkinson, a small farmer in Cumberland. Went to Academy of Dr Caleb Rotgerman at Kendal. Left for the Midlands where he erected the first blast furnace (Badsley Furnace) at Bilston: there he and his father succeeded in improving plant for boring cylinders accurately. He set up a forge at Broseley on a larger scale to make wrought iron and built iron barges to carry castings down the Severn. Married (1) 1755 Anne Maudsley (d. 1756); (2) 1763 Miss Lee of Wroxeter (who left an ample fortune). He was a controversial figure and carried on much litigation which used up his fortune.

Wilson, Elizabeth, 1753-1821, after 1786 Messer, *qv.*

Wilson, Margaret, 1761-1840, after 1790 Bragg, *qv.*

Wilson, Mary, 1755-1836, after 1781 Stacey, *qv.*

Wilson, Rachel, 1720-1775. Daughter of John and Deborah (Wilson, 1687-1754) Wilson of Kendal. Married 1740 Isaac Wilson (1714/5-1785), son of Anthony and Dorothy (Benson) Wilson of Windermere: 10 children. Rachel became a minister from 1739 and travelled widely in England. In 1765 she visited North America, travelling many miles on horseback and attending Philadelphia Yearly Meeting 1769. Her sister Hannah married John Barnard: Deborah Darby, who was thus her niece, travelled many of the same areas on her journey in 1793-6, meeting some of the same Friends.

Wilson, Sarah, 1759-1843, after 1806 Abbott, *qv.*

Winter, Martha, 1743-1817, after 1776 Routh, *qv.*

Wistar, Caspar Jr, 1761-1818. Son of Hans Caspar Wistar who came from Jilsbeck, Germany. Arrived 1784 in Chester County, Pennsylvania, and settled on a farm on Brandywine Creek. Caspar's brother, who followed him to the New World, kept the original spelling Wister: from this branch of the family comes the name of the flowering vine Wisteria. Hans Caspar Wistar built a glassworks in 1739 in Salem County, New Jersey, which became the centre of production for small glassworks up to the middle of the 19th century. Called Wistarberg, the glass was green or amber in colouring and of the type used in bottles.

Woolman, John, 1720-1772. Born in New Jersey, fourth of 13 children of a Quaker farmer and fruit grower. Lawyer, tailor, writer and gifted minister. Married 1748 Sarah Ellis: two children. Great protagonist of anti-slavery so, because dye for clothing derived from West Indies slave plantations, he replaced his garments with clothes of undyed wool, giving a strange light appearance to his dress. Visited England 1772. Attended London Yearly Meeting and travelled in Midland and Northern counties. Died from smallpox in York at the home of Thomas and Esther Priestman, being nursed by Esther and Sarah Tuke. Buried in Bishophill Burial Ground, York. Mary and Deborah Barnard heard him at Sheffield and High Flatts in late summer 1772 and after his death Mary wrote a poem in memory of him, Samuel Fothergill and William Hunt, who had all three died since Yearly Meeting that year.

Wright, Benjamin. Surgeon in Severn Gorge. Attended the births of the three children of Samuel (1755-1796) and Deborah Barnard (1754-1810) Darby and signed their birth certificates. He finally emigrated to Philadelphia, Deborah recommending him to the Fishers by letter – his family were to follow him later.

Wright, Charity, 1745-1822, after 1773 Cook, *qv.*

Young, John, 1720-1795. Draper of Shrewsbury. Married Jane (1722-1792), daughter of George Brawn: their daughter Rebecca (1758-1834, after 1800 Byrd) travelled with Deborah Darby. John worked in the Coalbrookdale Company, overseeing the mines at Ketley and Dawley, which caused difficulties after the death of Abraham Darby II. Father of Constantine and John Young Jr.

Young, Rebecca, 1758-1834, after 1800 Byrd, *qv.*

Young, William, 1718/9-1808. Son of William and Mary Young of Leominster; uncle of Rebecca Young (1758-1834, after 1800 Byrd). Married *c*1747 Hannah Payton, sister of Catherine Payton (1726/7-1794, after 1772 Phillips).

Bibliography

Allott, Stephen, *Lindley Murray, 1745-1821, Quaker Grammarian*, York, Sessions Book Trust, 1991.

Brayshaw, A. Neave, *The Quakers, their story and message*, London, Allen & Unwin, 1921; 3rd ed. revised, 1938; reprinted York, Sessions Book Trust, 1982.

Bronner, Edwin B., *Quaker landmarks in early Philadelphia*, reprinted from *Trans. Amer. Philosop. Soc.*, ns vol. 43, pt 1, 1953.

Burlingham, Richard, *Once a Quaker: story of a Worcester family through four generations*, Evesham, Mint Press.

Comfort, William Wistar, *Stephen Grellet, a biography, 1773-1855*, New York, Macmillan Co., 1942.

Corley, T. A. B., *Quaker enterprise in biscuits: Huntley & Palmers of Reading, 1822-1972*, London, Hutchinson, 1972.

Cox, John, *Catalogue of New York City Archives: Religious Society of Friends*, New York, Works Program Administration, 1940.

Forbush, Bliss, *History of Baltimore Yearly Meeting of Friends*, Sandy Spring, Md, Baltimore YM, 1972.

Forrest, H. E., *The old houses of Wenlock and Wenlock Edge, their history and associations*, Shrewsbury, Wilding & Son, 1914.

Gibbs, Nancy Reid, *Children of light: Friends Seminary, 1786-1986*, New York, Friends Seminary, [1986].

Greenwood, J. Ormerod, *The Quaker tapestry*, London, Impact Books, 1990.

Grellet, Stephen, *Memoirs*, ed. Benjamin Seebohm, 2 vol., London, A. W. Bennett, 1862.

Greg, Mrs Eustace (ed.), *Reynolds and Rathbone diaries and letters, 1753-1839*, privately printed, 1905.

Grubb, Geoffrey Watkins, *The Grubbs of Tipperary*, Cork, Marmer Press, 1972.

Grubb, Isabel, *Quakers in Ireland, 1654-1900*, London, Swarthmore Press, 1927.

Gurney, Priscilla Hannah, *Memoir*, 1843.

Hack, Mary Pryor, *Richard Reynolds*, London, Headley Brothers, 1896.

Hill, Thomas C., *Monthly Meetings in North America: an index*, Taft Stettinus & Hollister, computer printout.

Hinshaw, Seth B., *The Carolina Quaker experience*, North Carolina Friends Historical Association, 1984.

Hodgett, Gerald A. J., *Shackletons of Ballitore: some aspects of 18th century Irish history*, in *J. Friends hist. soc.*, vol. 54, no. 5, 1980.

Ironbridge Gorge Museum Trust, *The Darby houses of Coalbrookdale*, IGMT, 1976.

Jones, Rufus M., *The later periods of Quakerism*, 2 vols, London, Macmillan & Co., 1921.

Jones, Rufus M., *et al.*, *Quakers in the American colonies*, London, Macmillan & Co., 1923.

Lloyd, Humphrey, *The Quaker Lloyds in the industrial revolution*, London, Hutchinson, 1971.

Milligan, Edward H. and Thomas, Malcolm J., *My ancestors were Quakers: how do I find out more about them?*, London, Society of Genealogists, 1983.

Moore, John B., *Friends in the Delaware valley: Philadelphia Yearly Meeting, 1681-1981*, Haverford, Pa, Friends Historical Association, 1981.

Mount School, York, *List of teachers and scholars, 1784-1814, 1831-1906*, York, William Sessions, 1906.

Newlin, Algie I, *Charity Cook: a liberated woman*, Richmond, Ind., Friends United Press, 1981.

Penn, William, *No cross, no crown*, [London], 1669; 2nd ed., corrected and much enlarged, London, for Mark Swaner, 1682; reprinted York, William Sessions, 1981.

Philadelphia YM, *Philadelphia Quakers, 1681-1981: tercentenary family album*, Philadelphia, PYM, 1981.

Raistrick, Arthur, *Dynasty of ironfounders: the Darbys and Coalbrookdale*, [London, etc], Longmans, Green & Co., 1953; 2nd ed., revised, York, Sessions Book Trust, 1989.

Raistrick, Arthur, *Quakers in science and industry*, London, Bannisdale Press, 1950; reprinted York, Sessions Book Trust, 1992.

Rose, June, *Elizabeth Fry*, London, Macmillan, 1980.

Schimmelpennick, Mary Anne, *Life*, edited by her relation Christiana C. Hankin, 2 vol., London, Longmans, Brown, Green, Longmans & Roberts, 1858.

Selleck, George A., *Quakers in Boston, 1656-1964*, Cambridge, Mass., Friends Meeting, 1976.

Selleck, Ronald E., T. Wistar Brown Lecture at Haverford College, March 20th, 1986.

Stembridge, P. K., *Goldney, a house and a family*, Bristol, Burleigh Press, 1969.

Taylor, Francis R., *Life of William Savery, 1750-1804*, New York, Macmillan Co., 1925.

Thompson, Mack, *Moses Brown, reluctant pioneer*, Chapel Hill, NC, University of North Carolina Press for Institute of Early American History & Culture, 1962.

Trevelyan, G. M., *English social history*, London, Longmans, Green & Co., 1942.

Trinder, Barrie, *The industrial revolution in Shropshire*, Chichester, Phillimore & Co.,
1973.

Viaggo, *Travels in the United States of North America, 1735-1787*, by Lingi Castiglionis, translated by Antonis Pace, New York, Syracuse University Press, 1983.

Whitney, Janet, *Elizabeth Fry, Quaker heroine*, London, Harrap, 1937.

Wilson, Robert H., *Freedom of worship*, Philadelphia, Old Philadelphia Churches Historical Association, 1976.

Wood, Jack V., *Some rural Quakers: a history of Quakers and Quakerism at the corners of the four counties of Oxford, Warwick, Worcester and Gloucester*, York, William Sessions, 1991.

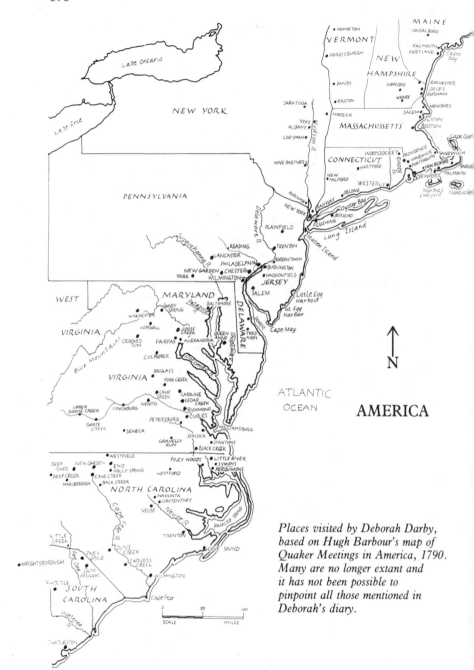

Places visited by Deborah Darby, based on Hugh Barbour's map of Quaker Meetings in America, 1790. Many are no longer extant and it has not been possible to pinpoint all those mentioned in Deborah's diary.

A MAP OF FRIENDS MEETINGS IN IRELAND 1794

ULSTER		MUNSTER		LEINSTER	
Monthly Meetings	*Particular Meetings*	*Monthly Meetings*	*Particular Meeting*	*Monthly Meetings*	*Particular Meeting*
LURGAN	Lurgan	YOUGHALL	Youghall	COUNTY WEXFORD	Enniscorthy
	Moyallon				Rofs
	Rathfryland	CORK	Cork		Forest
			Bandon		Randles Mills
ANTRIM	Antrim				Cooladine
	Ballimena	LIMERICK	Limerick		Ballintore
	Lower Grange				Ballinclay
	Ballinacree	WATERFORD	Waterford		
	Toberhead			MOATE	Moate
	Coleraine	COUNTY TIPPERARY	Clonmell		Ballimurry
			Carryroan		
LISBURN	Lisburn			CARLOW	Carlow
	Hillsborough				Castledermot
	Ballinderry				Athy
	Newtown				Ballitore
					Killconner
CHARLE-MOUNT	Grange near Charlemount			DUBLIN	Dublin
	Cabragh				Timahoe
	Castleshane				Baltiboys
RICHILL	Richill			EDENDERRY	Edenderry
					Rathangan
COOTHILL	Coothill			WICKLOW	Wicklow
	Oldcastle				Ballicane
				MT. MELLICK	Mt. Mellick
					Tullamore
					Mountrath
					Birr
					Roscrea
					Knockballinaher
					Ballinakill

NORTH EA
IRELAND

N

SOUTH EAST
IRELAND

N

ENGLAND, SCOTLAND
AND WALES

N

*Places visited by
Deborah Darby in England,
Scotland and Wales.*

Index

420

Index of Places in America

America, pages 127-216, 344-356, *including Meeting Houses in italics*

Index of Places in England, Scotland and Wales

including Meeting Houses in italics

Index of Places in Ireland

First Visit, pages 79-83; Second Visit, pages 235-292, 341-343;
Third Visit, pages 319-322, *including Meeting Houses in italics*